1-19-sc (set)

The Greenwood Encyclopedia of
Global Medieval
Life and Culture

The Greenwood Encyclopedia of
Global Medieval
Life and Culture

Volume I
EUROPE AND THE AMERICAS

Joyce E. Salisbury, General Editor

Joyce E. Salisbury, Europe
James L. Fitzsimmons, The Americas

GREENWOOD PRESS
Westport, Connecticut · London

Library of Congress Cataloging-in-Publication Data

The Greenwood encyclopedia of global Medieval life and culture / Joyce E. Salisbury, general editor.

    p. cm.

  Includes bibliographical references and index.

    ISBN 978–0–313–33801–4 ((set) : alk. paper) — ISBN 978–0–313–33802–1 ((vol. 1) : alk. paper) — ISBN 978–0–313–33803–8 ((vol. 2) : alk. paper) — ISBN 978–0–313–33804–5 ((vol. 3) : alk. paper)

    1. Civilization, Medieval.   I. Salisbury, Joyce E.

CB351.G743   2009

940.1 — dc22   2008036709

British Library Cataloguing in Publication Data is available.

Library of Congress Catalog Card Number: 2008036709

ISBN: 978–0–313–33801–4 (set)
      978–0–313–33802–1 (vol. 1)
      978–0–313–33803–8 (vol. 2)
      978–0–313–33804–5 (vol. 3)

First published in 2009

Greenwood Press, 88 Post Road West, Westport, CT 06881
An imprint of Greenwood Publishing Group, Inc.
www.greenwood.com

Printed in the United States of America

The paper used in this book complies with the Permanent Paper Standard issued by the National Information Standards Organization (Z39.48–1984).

10 9 8 7 6 5 4 3 2 1

The publisher has done its best to make sure the instructions and/or recipes in this book are correct. However, users should apply judgment and experience when preparing recipes, especially parents and teachers working with young people. The publisher accepts no responsibility for the outcome of any recipe included in this volume.

Contents

Preface for Users of Global Medieval Life and Culture

Two concepts have dominated the twenty-first century: globalization and the information explosion facilitated by the Internet. When we decided to present a new history of the medieval world—also called the Middle Ages—we knew these modern principles could help guide us to new insights into the past. In these volumes, globalization shapes the content that we have chosen to cover, and the electronic age has guided our organization. In addition, the features are carefully considered to make these volumes engaging and pedagogically useful.

Global Content

The medieval age was a European concept. From about the fourteenth century, Europeans defined the 1,000 years from the fall of the Roman Empire to the Renaissance as the "middle," separating the classical world from the "modern" one. Practically from the time of this designation, scholars have argued about whether this periodization makes sense, but scholarly arguments have not substantially changed the designation. Textbooks and curricula have kept the period as a separate entity, and we study the medieval world that extends from about 400 to 1400 C.E. with undiminished fascination.

Scholars of medieval Europe have shown that, during this formative period, many of the ideas and institutions developed that shape our modern world. The rise of democratic institutions, a prosperous middle class, and a vibrant Christianity are just a few of the developments that marked medieval Europe. These are some of the reasons that have kept the field of study vibrant. But what of the world?

Scholarship has disproved the Eurocentric analysis that defined the period of the Middle Ages. Exciting innovations took place all over the world during this pivotal millennium. Religious movements such as the rise of Islam and the spread of Buddhism irrevocably shaped much of the world, innovations in transportation allowed people to settle islands throughout the Pacific, and agricultural improvements stimulated empires in South America.

Furthermore, these societies did not develop in isolation. Most people remember Marco Polo's visit to the China of the Yuan Dynasty, but his voyage was not an exception. People, goods, and ideas spread all across the Eurasian land mass and down into Africa. This encyclopedia traces the global connections that fueled the worldwide developments of the Middle Ages.

To emphasize the global quality of this reference work, we have organized the volumes by regions. Volume 1 covers Europe and the Americas. We begin with Europe because this was the region that first defined the medieval world. At first glance, linking Europe with the Americas (which were not colonized until after the Middle Ages) might seem to join the most disparate of regions. However, we do so to remind us that Vikings crossed the North Atlantic in the Middle Ages to discover this rich new land, which was already inhabited by prosperous indigenous peoples. The organization of this first volume demonstrates that Europe never developed in isolation!

Volume 2 considers the Middle East and Africa. These regions saw the growth of Islam and the vibrant interactions that took place in the diverse continent of Africa. Volume 3 takes on the enormous task of focusing on South Asia, East Asia, and Oceania.

This organization forces us to compromise on some content. Because we are not taking a chronological approach, we must collapse 1,000 years of history in regions that had many diverse developments. We partially address this issue in the Historical Overviews at the beginning of each section. These essays will point readers to the varied historical events of the regions.

However, we gain modern insights through our on Global Ties essays within each section. These essays offer a great contrast with other medieval works because they show the significance of global connections throughout this millennium. Readers will learn that globalization was not invented in the twenty-first century. Indeed, the great developments of the past flourished because people from diverse cultures communicated with each other. Perhaps this was the greatest contribution of the Middle Ages, and this encyclopedia highlights it.

Organization for the Internet Age

The Internet brings an astonishing amount of information to us with a quick search. If we Google Marco Polo, castles, or windmills, we are given an immediate array of information more quickly than we could have imagined a mere decade ago. However, as teachers too readily realize when reading the results of such searches, this is not enough. The very volume of information sometimes makes it hard to see how these disparate elements of the past fit together and how they compare with other elements. We have organized this encyclopedia to address these issues.

Each volume contains two or three regions of the world, and each region includes seven in-depth essays that cover the following topics:

1. Historical Overview
2. Religion
3. Economy
4. The Arts
5. Society
6. Science and Technology
7. Global Ties

These essays provide coherent descriptions of each part of the world. They allow readers readily to compare developments in different regions, so one can really understand how the economy in Africa differed from mercantile patterns in China. In-depth essays like this not only provide clear information but model historical writing. But there is more.

Like other good encyclopedias, we have A–Z entries offering in-depth information on many topics—from the general (food, money, law) to the specific (people, events, and places). All the essays indicate the A–Z entries in bold, much as an online essay might have hyperlinks to more detailed information, so readers can immediately see what topics offer more in-depth information and how each fits in with the larger narrative. In the same way, readers who begin with the A–Z entries know that they can see how their topic fits in a larger picture by consulting the in-depth essays. Finally, this integration of essays with A–Z entries provides an easy way to do crosscultural comparisons. Readers can compare roles of women in Islam and Asia, then see how women fit in the larger context of society by consulting the two larger essays.

This is a reference work that builds on the rapid information accessible online while doing what books do best: offer a thoughtful integration of knowledge. We have enhanced what we hope is a useful organization by adding a number of special features designed to help the readers learn as much as possible about the medieval millennium.

Features

- *Primary Documents.* In this information age it is easy to forget that historians find out about the past primarily by reading the written voices left by the ancients. To keep this recognition of the interpretive nature of the past, we have included primary documents for all regions of the world. These short works are designed to engage readers by bringing the past to life, and all have head notes and cross-references to help readers put the documents in context.
- *Chronologies.* The chronologies will help readers quickly identify key events in a particular region during the medieval period.
- *Maps.* History and geography are inextricably linked, and no more so than in a global encyclopedia. The maps throughout the text will help readers locate the medieval world in space as well as time.
- *Illustrations.* All the illustrations are chosen to be historical evidence not ornamentation. All are drawn from medieval sources to show the Middle Ages as the people at the time saw themselves. The captions encourage readers to analyze the content of the images.
- *Complete Index.* The key to gathering information in the twenty-first century is the ability to rapidly locate topics of interest. We have recognized this with the A–Z entries linked to the essays and the extensive cross-referencing. However, nothing can replace a good index, so we have made sure there is a complete and cumulative index that links the information among the volumes.
- *Bibliographies.* Each of the long essays contains a list of recommended readings. These readings will not only offer more information to those interested in following up on the topic but also will serve as further information for the A–Z entries highlighted within the essays. This approach furthers our desire to integrate the information we are presenting.
- *Appendixes.* The appendixes provide basic factual information, such as important regional dynasties or time period designations.

The Greenwood Encyclopedia of Global Medieval Life and Culture has been a satisfying project to present. In over 30 years of research and study of the Middle Ages, we have never lost the thrill of exploring a culture that's so different from our own, yet was formative in creating who we have become. Furthermore, we are delighted to present this age in its global context, because then as now (indeed throughout history) globalization has shaped the growth of culture. In this information age, it is good to remember that we have always lived linked together on spaceship earth. We all hope readers will share our enthusiasm for this millennium.

EUROPE

Joyce E. Salisbury

Chronology

476	Overthrow of Romulus Augustus, last Roman emperor in the West; this is the traditional date for the fall of the western Roman Empire
485–511	Clovis, king of the Franks, converts to Christianity, thereby establishing a long-standing alliance between the Frankish kings and the popes
527–565	Justinian and Theodora rule the Byzantine Empire
711	Muslims conquer most of the Iberian Peninsula
732	Battle of Tours is fought in what is today southwestern France—the Frankish leader Charles Martel halts the expansion of Islam into western Europe
768–814	Charlemagne, the king of the Franks and (after 800) emperor of the Romans, politically unites western Europe for the first time since the fall of the western Roman Empire
c. 790	Viking raiders from Scandinavia begin raids on northern and western Europe
800	Frankish king Charlemagne is crowned emperor of the Romans by Pope Leo III in Rome
c. 830	Vikings found settlements in Kiev, which will later become the state of Russia
843	Treaty of Verdun divides Charlemagne's kingdom among his grandsons and roughly establishes the early divisions of Europe into France, Germany, and Italy
c. 858–867	Cyril and Methodius make missionary journeys northward from Byzantium to convert the Slavs of eastern Europe; their efforts result in creation of the Cyrillic alphabet
886	Viking seize control of portions of northern and eastern England, establishing there the "Danelaw"
988	Kievan Rus, descendents of Vikings, convert to Christianity
1016	Canute, king of Norway, Denmark, and England, converts to Christianity
1054	Schism (split) in the Christian Church establishes the Roman Catholic Church in the West and the Greek Orthodox Church in the East
1066	William, duke of Normandy, conquers England, thereby establishing a French/Norman dynasty in England; this is the last time England is conquered by foreign invaders
1071	Byzantine emperor calls for help from the rulers of western Europe following the disastrous defeat of a Byzantine army by the Turks at Manzikert

1081–1115	Reign of Byzantine Emperor Alexius I Comnenus
1095	Pope Urban II calls First Crusade to recover Jerusalem from the Turks
1099	Crusaders capture Jerusalem and establish the Latin Kingdom of Jerusalem
1145–1149	Second Crusade, led by Louis VII of France and Conrad III of Germany, is unsuccessful, leading eventually to the fall of Jerusalem
1171	Muslim ruler Saladin conquers Egypt, thus threatening the Latin Kingdom of Jerusalem and leading to calls in Europe for a new Crusade
1187	Saladin defeats the Franks at the Battle of Hattin and reconquers Jerusalem for Islam
1189–1192	Third Crusade, know as the Kings' Crusade because it was led by Richard I of England and Philip II of France, tries unsuccessfully to wrest Jerusalem from Saladin
1204	City of Constantinople is sacked by Crusaders
1215	King John is forced by his barons to sign Magna Carta, the document that establishes that kings of England are not above the law
1237–1241	Mongols conquer Russia
1254–1324	Venetian traders Marco Polo and his family visit the Mongol court in China to trade
1261	Constantinople is retaken from Crusaders by Byzantines
1304–1374	Life of Petrarch, the first great thinker of the Italian Renaissance
1337–1453	Hundred Years'' War is fought between France and England; the intermittent warfare draws in other European states and helps to bring about the eventual end of the medieval feudal order
1348–1350	Outbreak of the bubonic plague, known as the Black Death, claims one-third to one-half of the population of Europe
1360	Treaty of Bretigny temporarily halts the Hundred Years' War by granting Edward III the French province of Gascony in full sovereignty in return for his renunciation of the French Crown
1367	Plague erupts again in Europe though is less violent than outbreak of 1348–1350
1369	Hundred Years' War resumes with the French regaining most of the territory lost earlier in the war by 1380
1389–1415	Although no formal peace is made, a series of truces temporarily ends the Hundred Years' War
1399	Henry IV overthrows his cousin Richard II as king of England
1415	Henry V of England revives the Hundred Years' War by invading France and winning a major victory at the Battle of Agincourt
1417	Council of Constance ends a papal schism that had existed since 1378 and had seen as many as three popes in existence at one time; the papacy now moves back to Rome
1420	Treaty of Troyes technically ends the war between France and England by recognizing Henry V as heir to Charles VI of France; because Charles's son, the future Charles VII, continues to press his claim to the French throne, the war

continues; Henry V seals the treaty by marrying Catherine of Valois, daughter of Charles VI

1422   Death of Henry V passes the throne of England and France on to his infant son, Henry VI

1429   Emergence of Joan of Arc, a 19-year-old girl who rallies the French forces to break the English siege of Orleans and thus make possible the coronation of Charles VII as king of France, achievements that turn the tide of the Hundred Years' War and lead to an eventual French victory

1430   Joan of Arc is captured by the Burgundians and sold to the English

1431   Joan of Arc is burned to death by the English in Rouen, France, for witchcraft and heresy; Charles VII of France makes no attempt to free her

1453   Ottoman conquest of Constantinople ends the Byzantine Empire and making possible future Muslim penetration into southeastern Europe; like his French grandfather Charles VI, Henry VI of England suffers periods of insanity

1455   Wars of the Roses, a dispute over the Crown between two branches of the English royal family, begins with the Battle of St. Albans

1461   Edward IV of York supplants Henry VI of Lancaster on the English throne

1470–1471   Henry VI is restored to the English throne

1470   Ferdinand of Aragon and his wife Isabella of Castile become joint rulers of Spain

1471   Edward IV resumes the English throne; Henry VI is murdered in the Tower of London

1483   Richard III deposes his nephew Edward V and assumes the English throne; Edward and his younger brother are presumed murdered by their uncle

1485   Henry Tudor, Earl of Richmond, defeats and kills Richard III at the Battle of Bosworth Field; Richmond becomes Henry VII, first king of the House of Tudor

1492   Ferdinand and Isabella conquer Granada, the last Muslim kingdom in Spain; Christopher Columbus sets sail from Spain; Ferdinand and Isabella expel the Jews from Spain

Europe and the Mediterranean, c. 1200

The Crusades, 1096–1204 (borders shown c. 1200)

Map of The Crusades, 1096–1204 (borders shown c. 1200)

The Crusades, 1218–1270 (borders shown c. 1200)

Vikings in the North, A.D. 985–c. 1020

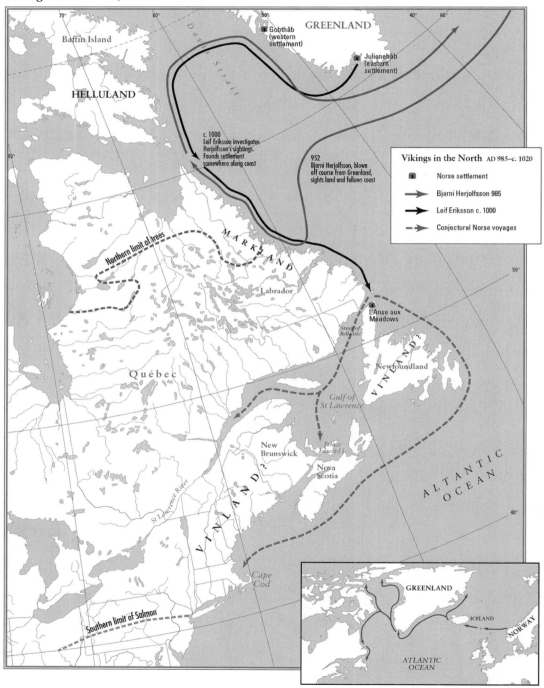

Baffin Island

Gobthåb
(western
settlement)

GREENLAND

Davis Strait

Julienehåb
(eastern
settlement)

HELLULAND

c. 1000
Leif Eriksson investigates
Herjolfsson's sightings.
Founds settlement
somewhere along coast

952
Bjarni Herjolfsson, blown
off course from Greenland,
sights land and follows coast

Vikings in the North AD 985–c. 1020

🏠   Norse settlement

→   Bjarni Herjolfsson 985

→   Leif Eriksson c. 1000

– →   Conjectural Norse voyages

Northern limit of trees

MARKLAND

Labrador

L'Anse aux
Meadows

Strait of
Belle Isle

Newfoundland

Québec

VINLAND ?

Gulf of
St Lawrence

New
Brunswick

Prince
Edward I.

Nova
Scotia

ALTANTIC
OCEAN

St Lawrence River

VINLAND ?

Cape
Cod

Southern limit of Salmon

GREENLAND

ICELAND

NORWAY

ATLANTIC
OCEAN

Spread of the Bubonic Plague, 1346–53

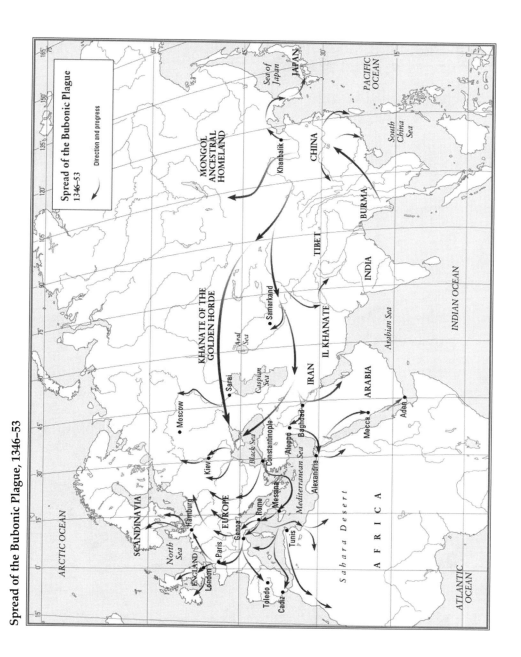

Europe, c. 1300

France during the Hundred Years War, c. 1429

Overview and Topical Essays

1. HISTORICAL OVERVIEW

Once there was a time when philosophers actually did debate how many angels could dance on a head of a pin or whether the bodies of cannibals would arise on judgment day. Once biology "texts"—bestiaries—included fabulous creatures such as manticores and unicorns. During this period, called the "Middle Ages," people looked at the world very differently from today, yet during this age people planted the seeds of many of our modern institutions and ideas.

The "Middle Ages" or "medieval period" extends 1,000 years from about 400 to about 1400 C.E. This long period was first identified by thinkers in Renaissance Italy in about 1300, who believed they had developed an approach to study that would recreate the accomplishments of ancient Greece and Rome. *Renaissance* means "rebirth," and these "humanists" were sure their approach was significantly different from that which had gone before. Therefore, they dismissed the years intervening between the Greco/Roman civilization and their own "reborn" culture as a wasted dead end in the "middle" of these two great civilizations. It was this same dismissive attitude that caused many to discount the medieval period as the "Dark Ages," in which knowledge and accomplishments were overshadowed by violence and ignorance.

Since the Renaissance, historians have reconsidered this analysis and found it wrong. The 1,000 years between the fall of the Roman Empire and the Renaissance were stunningly vibrant in all fields: Artists and architects created beautiful and complex cathedrals, technological advances transformed ancient methods of work, innovative social institutions were developed, and sophisticated religious ideas and institutions spread. The appellation *Dark Ages* began to recede from usage—first to apply only to the few centuries right after the fall of Rome then not to be relevant at all. Even more recently, historians have recognized that western Europe—the geographical location that first gained the designation "Middle Ages"—was never that isolated from the rest of the world. This global view shapes current understandings (and the structure of this encyclopedia).

This essay will give the historical overview of the events that dominated Europe during this millennium and will serve as a background for the other essays and entries of this volume. Before I begin, however, I should say a few words about the rather arbitrary dates that frame the medieval period. The starting point is the fall of the Roman Empire in the West, but there is no consensus on what date that is because there was no definitive fall, only a slow transformation revealed only by historical hindsight. During the fourth century, the empire was split into East and West, and converted to Christianity, yielding one set of changes. During the seventh century, Islam divided the Mediterranean world marking another dramatic turning point. In fact, many historians prefer to set out these few centuries—from about the fourth through the seventh—by the designation "late antique," emphasizing the continuity from the ancient world. Most historians continue to take 476 C.E. as a date to mark the beginning of the Middle Ages—on this date the last Roman emperor in the West died. This makes a convenient beginning point for our discussion.

The end point of the Middle Ages is even more difficult to identify. The earliest Renaissance thinkers emerged in Florence in early 1300, when most of Europe continued to be dominated by medieval culture. It took centuries for Renaissance ideas to spread northward and change European ideas. A convenient turning date for historians is 1453. This was the year when two pivotal things happened. Constantinople fell to the Turks, ending the Christian empire in the east and definitively launching the age of gunpowder that could demolish the great protective walls that had dominated medieval cities. Second, the **Hundred Years' War** between France and England ended, ending the last war between feudal nobles and beginning an era dominated by national armies.

With these rough designations in mind, let us review the main historical events that dominated this medieval millennium. I have divided the essay into the three eras that traditionally mark this period: The early Middle Ages from the fall of the Roman Empire to the year 1000, the expansionist high point from 1000 to 1300, and the late medieval decline from about 1300 to about 1450.

The Early Middle Ages

"The harsh nature of war! The malevolent fate of all things! How proud kingdoms fall, suddenly in ruins! Blissful housetops that held up for long ages now lie torched, consumed beneath a huge devastation" (Radegund, 95). This poem by a sixth-century German nun named Radegund poignantly captures the violence of the early Middle Ages. Here she describes the invasion of her homeland by another Germanic leader who killed her family and forced her to marry him. Violence marked the birth of this new culture we know as medieval.

The Middle Ages began as Germanic tribes in the north and east of Europe invaded the western part of the Roman Empire and established kingdoms in the transformed empire. The main kingdoms included the Anglo-Saxon ones in Britain, the Visigothic in Spain, the Ostrogothic (and later Lombard) in Italy, and the Franks in Gaul (France and southern Germany.) All the kingdoms struggled with similar problems: How would they blend the Christian, Roman, and Germanic cultures of their territories? How would they bring order and law to the violent clans that inhabited their lands? How would they establish centralized monarchies with people who were used to decentralized control? The experience of Radegund reveals the **warfare** and general violence that accompanied all these struggles.

During the turbulent period between about 400 and 800, Germanic tribes settled in regions already inhabited by Christian Romans. For example, the Visigoths in Spain took over about one-third of the estates of the Romans leaving the others intact. The Germans also tended to stay away from cities, leaving them to be run by Christian Roman leaders. Nevertheless, such distribution left many problems unresolved. The first was differing religions: Most of the Germanic tribes—such as the Vandals, Visigoths, and Ostrogoths—were Arian Christians, who held on to their own versions of scripture as they established their own churches and worship. The Ostrogothic king Theodoric established a tolerant coexistence between Arians and Catholics, while the Vandals on the other extreme persecuted Catholics fiercely. The resolution of religious differences only came about as Arian Germans slowly converted to Catholic Christianity.

German rulers also faced problems governing peoples with differing traditions of law. Romans were used to written law codes with a long tradition of jurisprudence, while tribes had their own traditions of **Germanic law** based on oral traditions of the clans. In the early Middle Ages, German kings began to record their own law codes and medieval law arose as a combination of Roman and Germanic.

The first truly successful synthesis between Roman, German, and Christian cultures came about in Gaul, in the kingdom of the Franks. The first important Frankish king was Clovis of the Merovingian family. Clovis ruthlessly united many of the clans and recognized the importance of the Catholic Church as a unifying force. He converted to Christianity and began a long-standing alliance between Franks and the popes in Italy. Clovis's ruthless son Clothar had caused the destruction that Radegund had so lamented. The Merovingian dynasty lasted 200 years, but during that time real power lay in the hands of the "mayor of the palace"—a sort of prime minister who ran the kingdom in the name of the king. By the beginning of the eighth century, one family—the Carolingians—dominated the office of Mayor of the Palace. A new dynasty was in the making.

The most famous of the early Carolingians was Charles Martel (called "the Hammer" for his military exploits). Charles Martel led the victorious force against the Muslims who had crossed the Pyrenees into the Frankish kingdom in 732. After this great victory, the Carolingians were well placed to expand their influence. Charles Martel's son, Pepin the Short, received the endorsement of the pope to take the title of king of the Franks, and the Carolingian dynasty began.

The greatest of the Carolingians was **Charlemagne** (Charles the Great). Charlemagne represented the high point of the early Middle Ages. He conquered neighboring tribes and united all of northern Europe into an empire. He was crowned emperor of the Franks in Rome, which once again established an emperor in the West and created a precedent of a Holy Roman Emperor that would last until World War I. He fostered learning to such a degree that his reign has been called the "Carolingian Renaissance." It appeared that all the problems created by the early Germanic invasions had been resolved and that Europe was unified.

In England, a comparable king arose who was able to unify the kingdoms of that island. **Alfred the Great** (r. 871–901) is the only English king who has been called "The Great" in memory of his military victories and his support of learning and culture in his realm. However, these victories of relative peace and scholarship were not to last.

Charlemagne's grandsons engaged in civil war and ended up dividing the great empire into three kingdoms: roughly, France, Germany, and Italy. Furthermore, the kingdoms confronted pressure from new invaders: Muslims from the south attacked coastal areas, Magyars (Hungarians) from the East swept into the European plains, and most serious, Scandinavian **Vikings** from the north raided and established their own kingdoms in England, Normandy in France, Sicily, and Russia. Decentralization and violence once again descended on northern Europe. Only the structures of manorialism kept the farmlands producing, and **feudal law** linked fighting men in bonds of loyalty.

During the early Middle Ages, the eastern part of the old Roman empire, called the "Byzantine Empire," escaped much of the destruction. The great wall that surrounded the city of Byzantium kept invaders at bay, and in the fifth century, inhabitants of the city watched from the safety of their wall as smoke rose from villages set aflame by the Germanic tribes and Huns surging westward.

The rulers of the Byzantine Empire considered themselves the heirs to the Roman Empire, so they continued to rule by Roman law, and indeed, the Emperor **Justinian** in the sixth century ordered a famous codification of Roman law — the *Corpus Iuris Civilis* (The Body of Civil Law) — compiled. In this form, Roman law survived and was revived in western Europe. The rulers were Christian, and the emperors took an active role in leading the church through controversies concerning doctrine and policies.

At the same time, the Byzantine Empire took a different direction from the western kingdoms. The emperors and administration began to use Greek as the official language (instead of Latin as in the West), and this served to split the two sides of the Mediterranean into two cultural entities. The two branches of the Christian church also began to separate: The emperors continued to exert leadership over the Greek-speaking Eastern Church, while popes in the West claimed religious sovereignty. These religious separations led to controversy that finally caused the two branches to split in 1054 — from then on the Christian world was split into the Catholic West and the Greek Orthodox East.

In spite of pressure from the Islamic lands that surrounded it, the ninth-century Byzantine Empire entered into its "Golden Age." The imperial government was centralized and ordered, trade enriched the courtly coffers and the Orthodox Church expanded. On its northern borders, the Byzantine Empire faced tribes of Slavs — Serbs, Coats, Avars, Bulgars, and so on — who had settled there. The Orthodox Church sent missionaries — Cyril and Methodius — north to convert the Slavs, and they were profoundly successful. As part of their missionary work, they created an alphabet based on Greek letters to record the Slavic languages, and this "Cyrilic alphabet" (named after the missionary) remains the alphabet in Russia and many of the other Slavic lands. The cultural influence of the Byzantine Empire had a lasting impact on the modern nations in these lands north of the great city.

By the year 1000, the Byzantine Empire in the east and the western kingdoms had completed their transformations into medieval territories. Now, both were poised for the expansion and new challenges that we have come to call the High Middle Ages.

The High Middle Ages

After the year 1000, medieval society began to expand in all respects. Agricultural advances spurred population growth, and commerce quickened in thriving cities. Western Europeans expanded eastward establishing new settlements in the northeast. Intellectual life also flourished with the new prosperity of the age, and philosophers, poets, and artists created works that still inspire us today (*see* "Economy," "The Arts," and "Science and Technology" sections).

The church, too, grew more centralized, and popes frequently began to exert their authority over secular matters. Church leaders called for **crusades** against Islam, luring many western Europeans far from their homelands. The church's growing role in secular life ignited criticism from some people who felt that it had forgotten its true purpose. In the face of such criticism, religious leaders responded by both reforming some church policies and repressing those who complained (*see* "Religion" section).

While all these expansions took place in economic, religious, intellectual, and social life, kings and nobles struggled to establish political structures that would keep pace with the dynamic changes that were afoot. In Europe, men and women were bound to their superiors in contractual ties that we have come to call a feudal system. As a law issued by a ninth-century French king ruled: "We will that each free man in our kingdom shall choose a lord. . . . We command moreover that no man shall leave his lord" (Cheyney, 18). Such laws bound members of the ruling classes to one another, and other laws bound peasants to their land to serve their lords. These personal ties were intended to bring order to the warlike ruling classes of society, but the system had built-in instabilities because it evolved locally in response to local situations and varied enormously from place to place.

The heart of the feudal system was military service in exchange for land and the peasants to work it. This unit of land was called a "fief," and noble families, called "vassals," jealously guarded and tried to expand their fiefs over time, building great defensive castles to maintain their power. By the eleventh century, kings were in a position to try to reestablish control over provinces that had drifted away during the turbulent tenth century, even while nobles tried to maintain and even increase their own power. The conflicts between monarch and aristocrats transformed the political map of Europe.

In England, the establishment of royal control was facilitated in 1066, when William I the Conqueror became king after the Norman Conquest of that land. By conquering the Anglo-Saxon kingdoms, William was able to redistribute the land to his vassals and introduce a tight feudal system with a good deal of centralized control. William introduced the Norman dynasty that lasted from 1066 to 1154. Henry I (r. 1100–1135), grandson of William the Conqueror, was an able administrator who further expanded royal control. In 1154, a separate branch of the family introduced the Plantagenet dynasty into England.

Henry II (r. 1154–1189) was the first of the Plantagenets to rule and was a stunningly able administrator, although he was less able to control his unruly family. He further centralized control by careful financial and legal management, and Henry II's marriage to **Eleanor of Aquitaine** brought many lands in France under the control of the English kings. John's (Henry's son) high-handed treatment of the nobles ended when the nobles forced him to sign the Magna Carta in 1215, which is considered one of the precedents of constitutional law, and reestablished the principle that the kings were not above the law.

Another central institution that arose in medieval England (and to a lesser degree on the continent) was **Parliament**. The English king Edward I (r. 1272–1307) brought wealthy merchants to his parliamentary council, and this body with its expanded representation was called the "Model Parliament." Its participants arranged themselves in two houses—commoners and lords—which would become the basis of the two houses of the modern parliament.

Spanish kings faced a different set of challenges as they slowly sought to establish control over their lands. The central issue for medieval Spain was to reconquer the land from the Muslims who in the early eighth century had taken all but the northwest corner of the Iberian Peninsula. Three kingdoms emerged that slowly led the southward push: Aragon, Castille-Leon, and Navarre. These kingdoms sometimes presented a united front to the Muslims and other times fought each other. In the twelfth century, Portugal emerged as a separate kingdom. In 1085, King Alfonso VI retook the important city in the central plateau, which formed the central capital for the continued Reconquest that dominated the medieval centuries.

The French kings also had a long struggle to establish centralized control over their land. The Carolingian dynasty had died out in France, and in 987, French nobles selected a new, very weak, king to head the land. Hugh Capet, lord of the land surrounding Paris, began the Capetian dynasty that lasted throughout the Middle Ages. Hugh and his descendants slowly worked within the feudal system to reestablish their control over one province at a time. The most famous of the Capetians was Louis IX (r. 1226–1270), the only French king to be named a saint.

By the end of the thirteenth century, the French monarchy was the best governed and wealthiest in Europe. It was a power to be reckoned with, but there were clouds on the horizon. England continued to hold and contest lands in France, and the popes seemed to exert a great deal of power in France. These difficulties would explode in the next century.

The eastern lands of the old Carolingian empire spread from Germany eastward into the Slavic lands. Early in the tenth century, the last direct descendant of Charlemagne died. The German dukes (like their French counterparts) in 919 elected one of their number—Henry of Saxony—to be king. The most powerful of this Saxon dynasty was Otto I (r. 936–973). Otto restored the title of emperor, and from this time forward, an emperor would be proclaimed in German lands. Later this unit would be called the "Holy Roman Empire." However, it is one thing to claim a far-flung empire and quite another to exert consistent control over it. The Saxon dynasty (sometimes called the "Ottonian dynasty") and its successors, the Salian dynasty (r. 1024–1125) and the Hohenstaufen dynasty (r. 1138–1268), faced three main challenges: powerful German princes who resisted centralized control, a strong Papacy that wanted sovereignty (*see* "Religion" section), and the difficulties in ruling Italy and Germany.

Italian city-states had maintained a tradition of sovereignty and urban life from the ancient world. Nobles in the cities successfully pitted emperors and popes against each other as they worked to maintain a level of urban independence that was greater than anywhere else in western Europe. Merchants in these cities grew rich in trade and would come into their own during the Renaissance. In the Middle Ages, however, they ensured that German emperors would not be able to unify their empires.

The rule of the Hohenstaufen emperor Frederick II (r. 1215–1250) effectively ended any chance of a unified German monarchy. Frederick was a brilliant ruler and patron of the arts, who had been raised in Sicily and had come to love the diverse Muslim and Christian cultures that existed in that sunny land.

His policy was to confer upon the German princes and nobility virtual sovereignty within their own territories while he lived and ruled the Kingdom of the Two Sicilies in the south.

After Frederick died, the German princes wanted to preserve the freedoms they had acquired under Frederick and elected a man they considered a weak prince—Rudolph of Habsburg—as emperor. This long-lived dynasty would come into its own during the Renaissance and beyond as it survived as the only medieval dynasty to fall after World War I in the twentieth century. Through the Middle Ages, however, the illusion of the Holy Roman Empire as a political unit persisted more in the minds of people than in an effective unit.

While the West grew and expanded after the beginning of the eleventh century, Byzantium struggled. In the eleventh century, Islam had strengthened and the Byzantine emperors looked to the West for help. Emperor Alexis I Comnenus sent a call for mercenary soldiers, but he got more than he bargained for. This appeal led to the series of crusades that established Western crusader states in the Holy Land and lasted sporadically for 200 years until the Muslims retook the crusader outposts (see "Religion" section). The Fourth Crusade in 1204 took the city of Constantinople itself, and Western Christians raided and killed their Eastern counterparts. Western crusaders held the city until 1261, when the Byzantine rulers reestablished their reign.

However, the Byzantine rulers never really recovered from the looting of Constantinople in 1204. Its territory was continually shrinking, and internal disorders regularly interfered with trade and centralized control. Yet Byzantium's great walls and the prestige and intellectual achievements of the Byzantine scholars continued to hold disasters at bay until the fifteenth century.

The Fourteenth Century: Disasters in Christendom

By 1300, the expansion of Europe had reached its limit. People had begun to cultivate marginal, less fertile lands, and the agricultural prosperity that had supported the flowering of medieval culture had begun to seem fragile. In 1315, the weather deteriorated, and years of cold, wet summers introduced famine to the land (see "Economy" section). Some years later, in 1348, a plague raged through the land ravishing the weakened population. This plague, that was called the "Black Death," was probably bubonic plague, but historians suggest that other diseases might have also combined to cause widespread death—up to one-half of the population may have succumbed. The deaths from famine and disease served as the backdrop to political changes that served to bring down the medieval order.

One of the first casualties of the early fourteenth-century disasters was the manorial system, in which serfs worked on the land, owing their labor to lords. The disabling shortage of labor that accompanied the population decline caused desperate lords to increase their customary—and already excessive—labor requirements in an effort to farm their lands. Peasants reacted against these demands and revolted in most areas of Europe. Urban residents also experienced their own struggles as declining population led to a reduced demand for goods and falling prices (see "Economy" section). All these revolts were eventually suppressed, but never again would western European nobles be able to exert medieval rights of serfdom in which owners owned people's labors. Serfdom would remain in eastern Europe and Russia for centuries more.

Another hallmark of the medieval order in western Europe was a unified Christendom, in which one pope was able to rule over religious and even at times secular policy (*see* "Religion" section). In the beginning of the fourteenth century, in a dispute over taxation, the French kings challenged papal power. The French king Philip IV (r. 1285–1314) ordered his troops to arrest Pope Boniface VIII (r. 1294–1303). Although the pope was quickly freed by his supporters, the elderly pope died soon afterward as a result of the rough treatment he had received. Philip IV was able to capitalize on the violence against the churchman; he brought pressure on the college of cardinals—which had elected popes since 1059—and they elected a French cardinal as pope.

The king persuaded this new pope—Clement V (r. 1304–1314)—to rule from Avignon, on the east bank of the Rhône River, where the French influence was strong. For 72 years after the election of Clement V, the popes ruled from Avignon. Many Christians objected to this "Babylonian captivity" as the Italian Petrarch (1304–1374) called it. Some people believed this shocking breach of tradition contributed to the subsequent plague, famine, and violence that accompanied the pope's residence in Avignon, and they urged the popes to resume ruling from Rome. The Avignon popes also expanded their administration and increased their collection of ecclesiastical taxes.

An influential mystic, Catherine of Siena (1347–1380) wrote a series of letters to Pope Gregory XI (r. 1370–1378) urging him to return to Rome, and in 1376 she traveled to Avignon to urge him in person. He was persuaded and returned to Rome, where he died shortly thereafter. The problems in church leadership only escalated: The college of cardinals was pressured by the Roman people to choose an Italian pope (instead of a French one), and the fearful cardinals elected Pope Urban VI (r. 1378–1389). Urban immediately began to take steps to reduce the French influence, so the French cardinals declared his election void (because of the coercion by the Romans) and returned to Avignon. There they elected a Frenchman: Pope Clement VII (r. 1378–1394). Now there were two popes, initiating what has been called the "Great Schism" of the church.

Most people chose to follow one pope over the other based on political rather than religious motivations, and each pope denounced the other as the anti-Christ. As each pope died, their supporting cardinals elected another pope, so the Great Schism lasted from 1378 to 1417. As the Black Death and famine brought destruction through Europe, many lost faith in the papacy to bring a moral authority to the troubled times. Many wondered how unity could be restored?

Some church theorists suggested that a general council of bishops might be able to restore the order and reform the abuses of the church. These men—called "conciliarists"—wanted to convert the church to a kind of constitutional monarchy in which the power of the popes would be limited. The first test of the Conciliar movement came at the Council of Pisa, convened in 1409. This Council asserted its supremacy by deposing the two reigning popes and electing a new one. However, the two previous popes did not step down, so now three popes reigned. Finally, a second Council was called. Some four-hundred churchmen assembled at the Council of Constance, which met from 1414 to 1418. This august body deposed all three popes and elected a Roman cardinal, Martin V (r. 1417–1431). The Great Schism was finally over, and the Western church was once more united under a single head. However, never again did the popes have the power that the medieval popes had, and church councils gathered periodically to address changes in the church.

As if famine, plague, revolts, and religious controversy weren't enough, England and France entered into the Hundred Years' War—a century-long conflict that became the closing chapter in an age in which long-standing traditions and social contracts crumbled. The issue that triggered the conflict was the succession to the throne of France—the Capetians' good luck in producing male heirs finally ran out in 1328, when the last Capetian died. The nearest male relative was King Edward III of England, son of a Capetian king's daughter. The French court claimed that a king could not inherit a crown from a woman, so Philip VI of Valois, a first cousin of the previous ruler, became king. Edward at first did not dispute this decision but soon found cause to do so.

There were two other reasons for the monarchs to clash: The French king sought an excuse to interfere in the lucrative wool trade between England and Flanders, and the French king wanted to claim sovereignty over the lands in France that England had held for so long. The war was long, and as it took place on French soil, it was devastating to the French countryside. The English had striking successes with new weapons and tactics that showed the old medieval knights moving toward obsolescence. Foot soldiers with long bows had stunning successes against mounted knights, and toward the end of the conflict, gunpowder was introduced on the battlefield, definitively signaling the direction of future warfare.

Nationalism also appeared as a new force. No longer did soldiers fight for the personal tie between them and their lord, which was the basis of the feudal ties. Now, increasingly, soldiers fought for France or England. This nascent spirit of nationalism perhaps explains the success of Joan of Arc, who was able to rally the French forces and finally push the English out of France. The Inquisition turned Joan over to the English to be executed before she saw the final victory of France. The war ended in 1453—a date often used to mark the end of the Middle Ages. Future armies would consist more of foot soldiers and mercenaries rather than mounted knights, and kings would use money, not personal agreements, to field armies.

In the fifteenth century, the Byzantine Empire proved to be another casualty of changing technology of warfare. The Byzantine Empire was threatened by the Ottoman Turks, a group of Asiatic nomads who had converted to Islam and who brought a new vigor to Muslim expansion. By 1355, the Ottomans had effectively surrounded the Byzantine Empire that had stood for so long as a powerful state and buffer for the West. Finally, a power sultan—Mehmed II (r. 1451–1481)—committed his government to a policy of conquest. He brought his cannons to the walls of Byzantium and attacked the ancient city. After a heroic struggle, Byzantium fell in 1453, offering another reason to use this date to mark the end of the Middle Ages. The last emperor of the East—Constantine XI Palaeologus—died in the battle. Mehmed made Byzantium his capital under the name of Istanbul, by which it is known today. (The name was only formally changed in 1930.)

The medieval order had ended. The culture of Europe and Byzantium that had developed through a dynamic 1,000 years was transformed by the disasters of the fourteenth century. The way was paved for new ideas to emerge—the Renaissance—that would bring about a resurgence of individualism and a creative spirit that we find familiar. However, the Middle Ages contributed much to modern society: parliamentary democracy, the structures of urban life, deep Christian ideas and religious institutions, artistic creations, and many other features that we take for granted. The Middle Ages also has left us with a fascination for this time long ago when knights in shining armor roamed the land and people believed magical creatures like unicorns.

Further Reading

Cavallo, G. *The Byzantines*. Chicago: University of Chicago Press, 1996.

Cheyney, E.P., trans. *University of Pennsylvania Translations and Reprints*. Philadelphia: University of Pennsylvania Press, 1898.

Curry, Anne. *The Hundred Years' War*. New York: St. Martin's Press, 1993.

Fletcher, Richard. *Moorish Spain*. New York: H. Holt, 1992.

Furman, Horst. *Germany in the High Middle Ages, ca. 1050–1200*. Translated by T. Reuter. New York: Cambridge University Press, 1986.

Hallam, Elizabeth M. *Capetian France, 987–1328*. New York: Longman, 1980.

Radegund. "The Fall of Thuringia," in *The Writings of Medieval Women: An Anthology*. Translated by Marcelle Thiebaux. New York: Garland, 1994, pp. 95–106.

2. RELIGION

The Middle Ages in Europe is often called the "Age of Faith" for good reason. By 400, Christianity was the only official religion in Europe, and the next millennium saw continued progress in creating a uniform religious practice under a tight religious hierarchy. Religious ideas that continue to influence modern Christianity were developed by men who have come to be called "**Fathers of the Church**" in recognition of their influence. However, in spite of a superficial appearance of uniformity, diversity of belief and practice continued to distress church leaders. In 1054, the church split between East and West, separating Roman Catholic from Eastern (or Greek) Orthodox. By the thirteenth century, various heresies seemed so threatening that the church established the **Inquisition** to combat errors in belief. All these developments only served to reinforce the idea that religion was at the heart of medieval culture and society.

Religious Life

The Catholic Church took over the broad Roman administrative organization, which divided the Empire into dioceses with a bishop in charge. The major cities had an archbishop, who was responsible for the other bishops in his region. Each diocese was, in turn, subdivided into parishes, each presided over by a priest, who was responsible for the spiritual well-being of his parishioners. The bishops were theoretically responsible for making sure that all priests were appropriately educated so they could read, write, and be responsible for conveying accurate religious information. However, throughout the early Middle Ages, local priests often did not meet the high standards demanded by bishops but instead were chosen for their ability to comfort and appeal to their parishioners. For example, in the seventh century, Spanish priests were criticized for being chosen for their good humor and skill in music and dance instead of for their religious knowledge. Ensuring the presence of an educated priesthood remained a concern throughout the Middle Ages.

Priests were to perform the essential function of serving as mediators between God and humans, and in doing this they were charged with delivering the sacraments that the Catholic Church believed contained grace and helped bring salvation. Priests perform baptisms, which by the early Middle Ages were increasingly granted to infants to bring them into the Christian community. They also performed the Mass, or the mysterious re-creation of Jesus' last supper, and marriages, which became more and more of a religious, rather than a secular matter throughout the Middle Ages. Priests also took confessions and granted the last rites to comfort the dying.

Priests were assisted by deacons, who helped distribute communion, read the gospel in church, and care for the church's material possessions. If a church were large, a bishop might appoint subdeacons to assist the deacons, and finally, young boys could serve as acolytes, bearing candles and assisting in the church services. Exorcists, readers, and official doorkeepers rounded out the list of medieval church offices. As an example of church personnel in the Roman church of the third century, a letter of Pope Cornelius, preserved in Eusebius' *Ecclesiastical History* claims that in Rome there was 1 bishop, 46 priests, 7 deacons, 7 subdeacons, 42 acolytes, 52 exorcists, readers, and doorkeepers (Eusebius, book 6, ch. 43). By 245, the Roman province on North Africa had 95 bishops. These figures from the third century suggest how quickly church organization became complex.

In the earliest centuries of Christianity, women served in all these capacities. However, from the fifth century onward, women were slowly excluded until by about the tenth century all these roles were restricted to men.

During the violent early centuries of the Middle Ages, the careful regulation of the parishes and dioceses broke down. In many churches, religious discipline was at best lax and, at worst, criminal. Repeatedly, letters from churchmen complained of sexual debauchery, illiteracy, drunkenness, and many other sins being committed by deacons, priests, and even bishops. Beginning in the eighth century, the Carolingians in the Frankish kingdom began to reform the church. Charles Martel's son Pippin was the first to require that everyone pay 1/10th of their income to the church, and this first universal tax in European history put the church on a sound economic footing. The stage was set for the first large-scale religious reform under Pippin's son **Charlemagne** (768–814).

Charlemagne was convinced that his empire needed a cultural and religious revival. His biographers (Einhard and especially Notker) related many accounts of abuses in the church that upset the emperor: illiterate priests, bishops who could not preach, and monks who could not chant the divine office. He issued lots of edicts to correct the abuses, established schools in which promising boys of all classes could learn to read, and insisted that all his churches have a consistent and regularized service. Charlemagne brought some of the greatest scholars to his court, and the most influential was Alcuin of York (c. 740–804). Alcuin had come from England and was instrumental in spreading the British custom of confession and penance throughout the churches of western Europe. The Carolingian renaissance brought an increased awareness of sin and ethical responsibility to the people as well as newly invigorated church services. Carolingian scholars also introduced the study of **canon law**, which was a body of religious law that became very influential in subsequent centuries.

In 1215, Pope Innocent III presided over the Fourth Lateran Council, which was to issue a number of decrees that shaped the religious lives of the Catholics.

It decreed that there were seven sacraments, and all were necessary for salvation. The seven are Baptism, Confirmation, Eucharist, Penance, Extreme Unction, Marriage, and Holy Orders. The rules established for these sacraments were felt in each parish throughout Europe. For example, the council decreed that every Christian had to go to confession at least once a year as part of the sacrament of penance, so this placed priests even more at the center of social life of villages and cities. Furthermore, the council decreed the doctrine of transubstantiation of the Eucharist. This doctrine declared that the bread and wine were actually transformed into the body and blood of Christ. (This doctrine would be later attacked during the sixteenth-century Reformation.)

Throughout this age of faith then, the daily life of the people was centered on a regular cycle of church services that were held either at small, local parish churches or (by the twelfth century) at Gothic cathedrals in the growing cities. The **religious architecture** of these buildings is one of the important remnants in Europe of medieval religious life. These cathedrals, presided over by bishops, might hold up to ten-thousand people at a time. The faithful gathered at the churches once a week (or more, depending on festival days) and took communion, listened to sacred music (like the Gregorian chant or more complex polyphonic music), spoke prayers together, and listened to a short sermon, the average length of which was about 2 minutes.

The range of people's religious expression did not end with attending church services presided over by a strong religious hierarchy. There were a series of practices that have come to be called "popular religion," that is, that were driven by the impulses of the laity (those who held no church office). Many faithful longed for a more immediate experience of the divine that was available in church services, and the most visible expression of this longing was people's attachments to the relics of saints and martyrs. These remains of the holy dead were prominently displayed in churches and shrines, and people came from many miles in pilgrimages to visit the relics looking for miraculous help. Some of the greatest pilgrimage sites throughout the Middle Ages were Santiago de Compostella in Spain, St. Marks Cathedral in Venice, and Rome, Italy, and Jerusalem. But many local churches as well proudly displayed their relics and drew faithful from afar.

In the Eastern and Western churches, popular religion found another expression in the popularity of icons: images or statues of Jesus, the Virgin Mary, and saints. Like relics, these icons were seen to be vehicles through which divine power became accessible to the faithful. People lit candles and offered prayers to these icons, and on feast days, statutes were paraded through the streets in celebration of the power of God working among the people. The veneration of icons led to a controversy in the eighth century called "**iconoclasm**" which contributed to a split between East and West.

Another deep expression of a popular religious impulse was the important force of **mysticism**, which means the feeling of becoming one with God. In the Eastern Orthodox church a mystical contemplation of God permeated the prayer and liturgy within the church. In the West, ordinary Christians often experienced direct visions of God. Many of the greatest church writers—such as Francis of Assisi (1182–1226), and **Bernard of Clairvaux** (1090–1153)—were mystics, but some less well-known also experienced the gift of direct vision of God. Meister Eckhart (1260–1327) was a Dominican friar who wrote of the importance of cultivating an interior life to develop a soul that was identified with God. The Franciscan friar Bonaventure (1217–1274) wrote that the mind is drawn to God by divine love, and people needed to meditate and pray to move the mind to God. A number of women became well known for their mystic writings: Julian of Norwich (1342–1416), Catherine of Siena (1347–1380), and Margery Kempe (1373–1438) showed the range of mysticism, which drew from those with high education to people of lower classes.

By the late Middle Ages, the growing numbers of mystics began to challenge the very need for the hierarchy that had been the backbone of the medieval church. Flemish mystics, such as Ruysbroeck (1293–1381) and Gerhard Groote (1340–1384), became the founders of a movement called the "*devotio moderna*" (modern devotion), which concentrated on concentrating on the life of Christ. They established a group called the "Brethren of the Common Life," who tried to follow Christ. This group was made up of pious laypeople, not monks, who stressed study and piety. The most well-known mystic from the *devotio moderna* was Thomas à Kempis (1380–1471) who wrote *The Imitation of Christ*, which is considered one of the greatest works on spirituality in the history of Western Christianity.

These movements of popular religion grew from the deep faith of medieval people. However, these very movements would undermine the strong hierarchical church that was the hallmark of medieval Christianity. If a person could have direct access to God, what was the need for the church and its sacraments? However, those challenges would only come to fruition during the Reformation in the sixteenth century—after the medieval Age of Faith had closed.

Monasticism—Religious Specialists

From the second century, Christianity embodied a tension between those who sought God in community and those who wanted to do so in solitude. The former made up the Christian congregations, while the latter became monks and nuns. The word, *monasticism* comes from the Greek word *monos* (alone) and points to the idea of religious specialists separating themselves from society to seek spiritual perfection.

Monasticism began in the eastern part of the old Roman Empire when men and women left society to live in solitary contemplation in the deserts of Egypt and Syria. These solitaries were called "hermits." Monasticism proper—that is, a group of religious men or women living together in a community under a formal rule—is credited to Pachomius (290–346) who established monasteries in Egypt. His model was so popular that by his death he was in charge of nearly three-thousand monks in nine monasteries and two convents of nuns. Basil of Caesarea (330–379) in Asia Minor wrote another popular rule for monks that became the model for Greek and Russian monasticism. In the Eastern Orthodox Church, monks were more dedicated to the contemplative life, dedicating themselves to prayer and devotion than in the West. In the East, also, monks gained a virtual monopoly on making icons, and monasteries grew rich on this trade.

News of Eastern monasticism spread to the West and influenced the life of the famous church father, Augustine (354–430), who lived in a monastic community in North Africa even while he served as bishop of Hippo. Augustine's experience is reflective of monastic life in the West, where there was a great deal of monastic influence on society as a whole. Other influential monastic founders in the West were John Cassian, who founded two monasteries in France in about 415. His communities used a rule based on Pachomius. Irish monasticism was particularly rigorous and influential, where it was governed by a rule written by Columbanus (543–615).

However, the most influential monastic founder in the early medieval west was Benedict of Nursia (480–550), and his *Rule* became the foundation of western monasticism. Under the Benedictine *Rule*, the daily lives of monks were divided into three kinds of activities: work, communal worship, and private reading and meditation. All Benedictine monks and nuns had to take vows of poverty, chastity, and obedience to the abbot or abbess, who led the monastery and in turn owed obedience to the local bishops. Monks and nuns in these monasteries of the early Middle Ages copied and preserved ancient manuscripts, and it is thanks to them that we have so many ancient texts available to us.

Throughout the Middle Ages, monastic movements underwent a series of reform movements, and these newly invigorated monasteries became, in turn, agents of reform of the church in general. One of the first groups to reform Benedictine monasticism were the Cluniacs. By the tenth century, many monasteries had fallen under the control of local secular lords. To address this, Duke William the Pious of Aquitaine (in southern France) in 909 made a gift of land to a group of twelve monks at Cluny in central France. According to the charter, the new monastery was to be self-governing and answerable only to the pope. By 1100, Cluny had more than one-thousand "daughter" houses championing the cause of reform. The influence of the Cluniacs spread beyond the monasteries when a Cluniac monk, Hildebrand, became Pope Gregory VII, who introduced a number of reforms in a controversy that is called the "**Investiture Controversy**." Included in these reforms was the enforcement of clerical celibacy on members of the church. The investiture controversy was influential in helping popes exert authority over western European secular as well as religious life.

The Cluniacs focused their attention on prayer and performing the liturgy, but they came under criticism for their acquisition of land and extravagant Romanesque churches. Hoping to revive a more austere monastic ideal, Robert of Molesmes established a new monastery at Cîteaux in Burgundy in 1098. This laid the foundations for a new monastic order, the Cistercians, called "White Monks" dedicated to more austerities and focusing on humility and manual labor. The Carthusians were another order founded in 1084, which intended to be even more ascetic, seeking out rugged and isolated sites for their communities.

The **Crusades** brought about a need for new kinds of religious orders — those who would be soldiers of Christ. These **Military Orders** lived under similar rules as other monastic orders, but their duties included fighting. The first were the Templars, who were founded in Jerusalem in 1120. Subsequent orders were the knights of the Hospital of St. John, or the Hospitalers, and later, the Teutonic Order of knights that flourished in Germany. At their height, the Hospitalers could supply five hundred knights for service in the field, and the Templars, three hundred, and these orders served as the backbone of defense of the Holy Land. Members of these orders helped protect pilgrims and also served as bankers to pilgrims traveling to the religious sites.

The growth of cities and universities in the twelfth century led to new religious impulses that, in turn, spawned new religious orders. Many people in the late twelfth century began to criticize the visible opulence of the church and once again a religious order was established to address this longing. **Francis of Assisi** (1182–1226) gave up all he owned to live in extreme poverty, spirituality, and charity. He founded an order called "Franciscans," and his sister Clare of Assisi founded a comparable order for women called the "Poor Clares." The members of these orders did not live in communities, but wandered about, and thus were called "mendicant orders" to distinguish them from other monks, and they were called "friars," and the Franciscans were called "Grey Friars" because of their clothing.

A second mendicant order was founded by St. Dominic (1170–1221). Dominic was an intellectual with a gift for administration. He decided the best way to combat heresy (that is, incorrect views of religion) was to preach and teach. Dominic went to the Fourth Lateran Council in 1215 to ask the pope's permission to organize an order of friars dedicated to preaching. The Dominicans were thus born and became known as the "Black Friars" in contrast to the Franciscans. The Dominicans emphasized education and thus had a large presence in the universities. Their battles against heresies led them to take an influential role in the religious courts of the Inquisition. A similar mendicant order was founded in 1274: The Carmelites, called "White Friars," lived in towns, where they could beg, preach, and hear confessions.

Just as there were always avenues for popular religious impulses that ran parallel to the official religious outlets, the same was true for the desire to live a monastic life. In the thirteenth century—especially in the Low Countries—groups of women chose to live together in informal religious communities. They were called "Beguines," and they spawned similar communities of men, called "Beghards." During the plague years of the fourteenth century, some groups gathered to wander and whip themselves to try to expiate God's wrath. These Flagellants offered visible and dramatic evidence of some people's belief that the church did not satisfy their religious needs. The official church was never comfortable with these informal religious communities and repeatedly suppressed them.

Leading the Churches: Popes and Patriarchs

Organizing the church by parishes and dioceses left open the question of who is on top of this structure. The Eastern Orthodox and churches in the West separated on this (and other) issues, and the continuing struggle about church leadership not only kept East apart from West but caused centuries of struggle in the West.

After its fall in the West, the Roman Empire continued in Constantinople. Emperors continued to rule there (with a short break in the thirteenth century) until the empire fell to the Turks in 1453. The continuing presence of a strong emperor allowed him to exert a good deal of control over the church; indeed, many have called this form of church leadership "caesaropapism," which means that one person leads church and state.

The Eastern Orthodox Church believed that under the guidance of the emperor the church should be led by five bishops—called the "patriarchs"—who presided in five major cities: Rome, Constantinople, Jerusalem, Alexandria, and Antioch. Each of the patriarchs (which together are called the "Pentarchs") exerted jurisdiction in his own area and met with the other patriarchs in council to regulate matters of dogma and church discipline. Over time, they rejected decisions made outside these councils solely by western bishops. Because the East was outside the influence of western reformers, they never adopted the idea of clerical celibacy, so priests and patriarchs in the East could marry.

With the absence of strong secular leadership in the West, the struggle over who should lead the church was longer and more turbulent. Theoretically, all bishops were believed to be the successors of the original apostles. However, as early as the fourth century, the bishops of Rome began to assert their supremacy over all the other bishops and began to claim the exclusive title *pope*, or "father." Their early claims for supremacy were based on the Petrine Doctrine, which looked to Biblical precedent in which Jesus was to have said to Peter, "upon this rock I will build my church (Matt. 16:18–19). The early popes had claimed that Peter had been the first bishop of Rome, so each subsequent pope said he was the spiritual descendant of Peter.

Claiming supremacy over other bishops did not resolve the issue of who should be on top of an earthly hierarchy — pope or emperor. Pope Gelasius (r. 492–496) tried to resolve this issue by describing authority on Earth as two swords: one wielded by kings and the other by the church, and in Gelasius's view the church's sword was the greater because it was spiritual. This theoretical position was forwarded in a practical way by Pope Gregory the Great (r. 590–604) who was able to exert a good deal of actual authority.

However, the real struggle for supremacy in the West began in the eleventh century in what was called the "Investiture Controversy." What began as a struggle about who could choose bishops and give them their signs of office — king or pope — ended being about who is on top of a divinely ordained hierarchy for ruling western Europe. The controversy began when the Cluniac pope Gregory VII (r. 1073–1085) challenged the German Emperor Henry IV (r. 1056–1106). The struggle moved on to the battlefield as Gregory was supported by the powerful Matilda of Tuscany, and the struggle continued in England as Thomas Becket was martyred in a struggle with his king, Henry II (r. 1154–1189).

As popes began to emerge victorious in this battle with kings, they were able to call on Christian armies from all over Europe to go on Crusade to reclaim the Holy Land from the Muslims. The struggle took time, but by the beginning of the thirteenth century, popes could with some accuracy claim they presided over a universal Christendom. Innocent III (r. 1198–1216) insisted that kings from all over Europe obey him in matters large and small, from waging war to sleeping with their wives.

In the fourteenth century, papal leadership of a universal western Christendom broke down. The French king Philip IV (r. 1285–1314) challenged the authority of Pope Boniface VIII (r. 1294–1303) over the issue of taxing French clergy. Boniface died during the controversy (with a little help from Philip's men), and the French king was able to obtain the election of a French cardinal as the next pope, Clement V (r. 1304–1314). Although named Bishop of Rome, Clement never went to that city but instead set up the papal court in Avignon, under the influence of the French king. For 72 years beginning with the election of Clement V, popes ruled from Avignon. Many Christians objected to critics called the "Babylonian captivity" of the papacy. The Avignon papacy expanded their administration and streamlined the collection of ecclesiastical taxes, both leading to more criticism.

The mystic Catherine of Siena (1347–1380) was influential in persuading Pope Gregory XI (r. 1370–1378) to return to Rome and reestablish the credibility of the papacy, but things quickly grew worse. When Gregory XI died shortly after his arrival in Rome in 1378, the situation was volatile. The cardinals elected an Italian, Pope Urban VI (r. 1378–1389), but then some dissenting cardinals—claiming an irregularity in the election—named a rival Frenchman to be Pope Clement VII (r. 1378–1394). Urban stayed in Rome while Clement returned to Avignon. The faithful in Europe divided their loyalties between the two popes in a split that was called the "Great Schism." From 1378 until 1417, two and three competing popes reigned at the same time, destroying the illusion of a united Christendom.

The Great Schism was finally resolved by the **Conciliar Movement**, which claimed that the authority of the Western church lay not in the person of the pope, but in the bishops meeting in council. The first test of the conciliar movement came at the Council of Pisa, convened in 1409 convened by cardinals of Rome and Avignon. This council asserted its supremacy by deposing the two reigning popes and electing a third. This only exacerbated the problem because the two previous popes refused to step down, leaving three popes reigning. Finally, a second council was called. Some four-hundred churchmen assembled at the Council of Constance, which met between 1414 and 1418. This council was finally able to depose all three popes and elect a Roman cardinal—Martin V (r. 1417–1431). Thus at the end of the Middle Ages, the Great Schism was ended, but this conciliar movement ended the universal power that medieval popes had claimed.

Critique, Heresy, and Response

The history of medieval Catholicism was one of consistently struggling to get a uniformity of belief in the face of constant questioning. Once Christianity became linked with the Roman power structure, differences of opinion about religious matters became "**heresies**," equivalent to treason. In the early centuries, differences were resolved in church councils that established correct belief, and later in the West, popes in consultation with bishops determined what was orthodox and what was heretical. Nevertheless, throughout this age of faith church leaders had to wrestle with confronting and suppressing heresies.

Before the twelfth century, heresies grew from a variety of opinions—many left over from earlier deep discussions about the nature of Christ, humanity, and the clergy. The Eastern Church had always had a tradition of actively discussing theological issues, and three important heresies arose there in the early Middle Ages. In the fifth century, discussions about the nature of Christ led to two different opinions: The Nestorians emphasized the split between Jesus's humanity and divinity, claiming that Mary was the bearer of the human person, but not of God. In response, others emphasized Jesus's divinity, claiming that the divine portion of God obliterated the human at the Incarnation much like the sea would overwhelm a drop of honey. These were called "Monophysites" ("one nature"). The Council of Chalcedon in 451 condemned both positions arguing that Christ was fully human and fully divine. However, Nestorians and Monophysites continued to flourish in Egypt, Armenia, and even as far away as China.

In the eighth century another serious conflict arose in the Eastern Church that further emphasized the differences between East and West. The Byzantine emperor Leo III (r. 717–741) ordered all icons destroyed to avoid idolatry, and in an autocratic style, he intended for this decree to apply to all Christendom,

East and West. This introduced iconoclasm, which raged in the East for a century, during which many mosaics in Constantinople and Asia Minor were destroyed. Ultimately, the iconoclasts were discredited, and icons remained a part of Christian worship.

In the West, the church father, Augustine, spent much of his career battling three heresies. The Manichaeans believed that a good God could not have created evil, so they posited the existence of two gods, one good and one evil engaged in a timeless battle for the soul of humanity. This dualist belief reappeared in the Albigensian heresy that flourished in southern France in the twelfth century.

Augustine also battled against Donatism, which split the North African church for centuries. The Donatists argued that priests who had turned over sacred books during the Roman persecutions should lose their offices. Augustine and the orthodox position was that sins of a priest did not affect the efficacy of the sacraments they perform. The violent proponents of both these positions did not end until North Africa was conquered first by the Vandals then the Muslims.

Augustine's last struggle against heresy took a more intellectual turn when he penned his arguments against the Pelagians. Pelagius was a British monk who argued that free will was possible, that people could choose not to sin. Augustine, drawing from his own struggles against lust and sin, denied this possibility and claimed that people were burdened by original sin. Augustine's position became the orthodox one, and Pelagianism was condemned.

By the twelfth century in the West the greatest critique of the church came from those who believed that the church had become corrupted by wealth. There were many groups who advocated following what they called the "apostolic life," a simple existence embracing poverty, reading the Bible, and preaching God's word. The most famous of these groups was the Waldensians, who were centered in southern France. Their leader, Valdes of Lyons (also known as Peter Waldo) was condemned as a heretic in 1181, but the movement continued in spite of repression. There are even some Waldensian churches today.

Late in the Middle Ages, other critics challenged the hierarchy in ways that foreshadowed the sixteenth-century Reformation. John Wycliffe in England and John Hus, in what is now the Czech Republic, were influential at universities and questioned papal supremacy and other church doctrines.

In the thirteenth century, the established church felt sufficiently threatened by these various heresies to establish a new court to discover and root out heretical ideas. This court was the Inquisition, and it was different from the many criminal courts in the lands because it was concerned with ideas instead of actions. Consequently, it had to resort to torture to find out what the accused was thinking, instead of other evidence to determine what he or she had done. The progress of the Inquisition contributed to the breakdown of the medieval religious structure. *See also* Document 16.

Further Reading

Brook, Rosalind, and Christopher Brook. *Popular Religion in the Middle Ages*. London: Thames and Hudson, 1984.

Eusebius. *The History of the Church from Christ to Constantine*. Translated by G.A. Williamson. Harmondsworth, UK: Penguin, 1984.

Evans, Austin P. *Heresies of the High Middle Ages*. New York: Columbia University Press, 1991.

Lynch, Joseph H. *The Medieval Church: A Brief History*. New York: Longman, 1992.
Morris, Colin. *The Papal Monarchy: The Western Church from 1050–1250*. New York: Oxford University Press, 1991.

3. ECONOMY

Throughout the 1,000 years of the Middle Ages, most people worked on the land, so agrarian life represented the prevailing economic structure. However, throughout human history people have loved to shop, enjoying the novelty of new products. Therefore, although trade dramatically decreased in the violence that accompanied the decline of the Roman Empire, it never completely disappeared, and trade and related urban life would flourish again beginning in the prosperity of the twelfth century and beyond. To understand the economy of the Middle Ages, we shall first look at the agrarian life that shaped most people's lives then study the growing cities and the short- and long-distance trade that flowed on the contours of Europe. It was in these peasant villages and small towns that many of the structures of modern life were formed. Finally, we shall see how the disasters of the fourteenth century disrupted the medieval economy.

Agrarian Economy

With medieval farming methods, most people had to work the land to produce enough **food**. Throughout Europe, there were two kinds of settlement patterns that organized the rural landscape: dispersed pattern and clustered villages. Each developed depending on the kind of land available.

The dispersed pattern of **agriculture** involved peasants who lived in tiny hamlets or isolated farms. This pattern was widely established in regions of poor soils on the fringes of Europe: Scotland, Wales, Cornwall, Spanish Galicia, western Normandy, and most areas of the Scandinavian countries. In these areas of dispersed settlement, each household had a small plot of land close to the house, called the "in-field," which would be cultivated continuously. In addition, a section of land—the "out-field"—was cultivated for a year or two exhausting the soil, then abandoned for another out-field. The land left fallow was left for grazing of animals.

In areas of more fertile land, the economic pattern was of clustered villages that were often further organized into larger manors. This form of agriculture is called "manorialism" and is the defining form of medieval agrarian organization. In these clustered villages, the land is surrounded by large open fields that during the early Middle Ages were divided into two parts. One lay fallow (uncultivated) one year while the other was sown with grains. By reversing the fallow fields, farmers tried to avoid the problem of reduced fertility by overcultivation.

The open fields were divided into long strips, and individual peasants owned different strips. This arrangement allowed the whole village to share large plows pulled by six to eight oxen to plow the large open fields. These large plows could turn over the heavy clay soils that dominated most of northern Europe.

A critical problem for medieval farmers was lack of fertilizer. The only fertilizer available was manure, which was never enough to keep all the fields fertilized.

Farming areas near towns often collected human waste—called "night soil"—to fertilize the fields, which led to increased spreading of diseases. Collecting animal manure required people to keep animals, which in the north had to be fed with hay that was grown on the scarce fields. Therefore, keeping large numbers of animals to produce manure was not economically feasible. People in seaside communities—like Scandinavia, Scotland, and Ireland—collected seaweed to fertilize their beds, but this was a highly labor-intensive activity. In dispersed pattern communities, only the in-field was fertilized with manure, so during the early Middle Ages leaving the land fallow was the main technique of rejuvenating soil depleted by repeated plantings.

A second problem that plagued medieval agriculture was how to sow seeds. Peasants used "broadcast" method which meant walking in the plowed fields casting the seed out by hand. This led to loss of a lot of seeds to birds and other hazards. Yields (the amount harvested versus the amount planted) remained very low.

The most important part of the peasant economy was the cultivation of cereal crops. The main crops were wheat, rye, barley, and oats. In mountainous areas or regions with poor soil, peasants planted spelt. Grains were important not only to make bread, the staple of the diet, but to brew ale, which formed a large proportion of the caloric intake.

Women were usually in charge of the gardens that were grown near the peasant households. Here, families grew turnips, cabbages, leeks, and other vegetables, along with some herbs like dill. In some areas (where the weather permitted), peasants produced grapes for wine.

Animal husbandry supplemented the crops that formed the basis of medieval diet. Only the rich could afford to eat much meat; most people had to be content with using their animals (especially goats and sheep) for milk and cheese. Some texts indicate that sometimes even deer were kept and milked! They kept chickens and other domestic fowl for eggs, and an occasional stew. Pigs were very important because they could fend for themselves browsing in the woods for food. Although they were thin and tough, they formed an important part of the medieval diet.

The most important animals were the large animals that supplemented human labor. Great oxen pulled plows and carts, as did horses and mules. These animals had to be fed through the winter, and there was always a struggle between raising an animal to work and slaughtering it to save on food. When oxen grew too old to work, they were fattened and slaughtered to make a tough, but substantial meal. The church forbad the eating of horseflesh (because it seemed too associated with pagan ritual), so old horses were good only for their skin and to provide food for domestic dogs. (People in the northern parts of Scandinavia and Iceland never adhered to the prohibition against eating horseflesh and continued to do so into the modern era.)

In the tenth and eleventh centuries, medieval Europe saw a number of agricultural innovations that greatly increased food production and fueled a population expansion. (*see* "Science and Technology" section for more technological advances.) By the eleventh century, a new padded horse collar that had been developed in China appeared in western Europe. This harness rested on the animal's shoulders (instead of on his neck like a yoke for oxen) and allowed horsed to be used for heavy plowing and pulling. Because horses can work 50 percent faster and 2 hours a day longer than oxen, the advantages were huge.

Peasants discovered that even placing horses with oxen in front of the large, wheeled plows would spur the oxen to work harder.

The increased use of animal power required peasants to cultivate more land for fodder and hay, and clustered villages slowly adopted a three-field system, over the previous two-field system. In this system, plots of land were divided into thirds: One-third was planted in the spring, another in the fall, and the remaining third was left fallow. This three-field system also stimulated the growth of new crops that boosted production of the all-important grain. Villagers began to plant legumes, such as peas and beans, which add nitrogen to the soil, thus fertilizing the subsequent grain crop. Legumes also provided an excellent source of protein, which improved the villagers' diets.

In the twelfth century, more iron became available in Europe. This allowed horses to be shod and plows to be equipped with iron plowshares, both of which improved agricultural production. However, iron had other less-obvious advantages: Iron cooking pots became more prevalent, and when people cook in iron some leeches into the food, offering an advantageous supplement to people whose diets where often iron deficient. This particularly helped menstruating women, and women's health improved noticeably, so much so that by the thirteenth century, contemporary observers were noticing that there were more women than men in the population. This is the first time in history that we notice such a gender distribution.

This agricultural revolution spurred a population growth, which had further economic ramifications. Between the eleventh and the thirteenth centuries, the population of Europe approximately doubled—from about 37 million to 74 million people. Settlement was expanded as lords and kings established new villages to accommodate the growing population. The increased population and rural efficiencies permitted more specialized labor, which fueled the growth of commerce and the rise of urban areas (Table 1).

Table 1. European Population Growth: 1000–1300

Year	Millions of People	Percent Increase
1000	42	—
1050	46	9.5
1100	48	4.3
1150	50	4.2
1200	61	22.0
1250	69	13.1
1300	73	5.8

Source: Jean Gimpel. *The Medieval Machine.* Harmondsworth, UK: Penguin, 1976, p. 57.

Growth of Trade

The disruptions of the early Middle Ages broke down the trade networks that had fueled the prosperity of the Roman Empire. The invasions of the Germanic tribes in the fifth century led to a decline in trade in the northern parts of Europe. The seventh-century rise of Islam split the lucrative Mediterranean trade, and the Viking invasions of the ninth and tenth centuries further disrupted commerce. However, the new agricultural prosperity beginning in the eleventh century paved the way for a new economic change in the West.

Now economic wealth became increasing based on a vigorous exchange of goods and a growth of **money** in circulation.

The commercial revival began in Italy, whose cities had escaped the devastating decline of the north. By the tenth century, Venice was shipping grain, wine, and lumber to Constantinople and importing silk cloth. Merchants of Genoa and Pisa began to sail along the coast toward France on trading ventures, risking the ever-present threat of Muslim pirates. In 1016, the fleets of Genoa and Pisa conquered Corsica and Sardinia and raided Muslim ports in Africa. When Norman conquerors occupied Sicily in 1091, the Western Mediterranean was opened for western commerce.

The **Crusades** that began in the eleventh century also increased commerce. The kings of Jerusalem and their barons opened trade routes to Baghdad, and goods from the Far East flowed to the Italian merchants in the ports of Syria and Palestine. Silks, sugar, and spices began to move into western courts and created appetites for more. Thus, by the twelfth century, and southern, Mediterranean zone of commerce was reestablished that moved goods from as far away as China to the ports of Spain.

Meanwhile, a northern zone of trade was beginning to flourish around the Baltic Sea. Flanders first took the lead in its production of woolen cloth, and when Scandinavian merchants came down from the north to trade furs and hunting hawks, Flanders was ready to serve as the hub of that trade. Soon, the demand for Flemish cloth exceeded the supply of wool, so Flemish merchants looked abroad for raw wool. They found an abundant supply in England, and English farmers began to raise more and more sheep to supply the seemingly inexhaustible demand for wool cloth. In the late thirteenth century, many cities in northern Germany created the Hanseatic League, an association of cities that united to capitalize on the prosperous northern trade. At its height, the Hanseatic League included 70 to 80 cities.

Although Flanders and northern Italy were active centers of commerce by the end of the eleventh century, trade between the northern and southern zones was comparatively slight. Transportation was difficult between the two zones: Muslim pirates still controlled the Straits of Gibraltar, so shipping from the Mediterranean north was unsafe. Overland trade was dangerous and costly because every local lord along the route wanted to charge tolls to merchants passing through his lands. Early in the twelfth century, a powerful dynasty saw in this situation a chance to reap profits. The Counts of the region of Champagne created a vast marketplace in their lands. At a number of their chief towns, they founded fairs, which came to be called the "**Champagne Fairs**." For about 200 years, these fairs were the most important markets in western Europe and served to link the lucrative trade between north and south.

The Champagne Fairs were by no means the only fairs in Europe, for the model was so lucrative that lords in various areas sponsored fairs. By the fourteenth century, the Hanseatic League offered their own fairs that competed with the popular French ones. These brought not only goods from near and far but also entertainers and new ideas as people mingled in excitement at the bustle that brought novelty to otherwise rather dull days.

The revival of commerce increased the need for coined money. Western Europe had no gold mines, so gold was not widely available for coinage until the fourteenth century. Italy had gold earlier from its trade with Muslims. Genoa and Florence struck gold coins in 1252, but most coins of western Europe through the Middle Ages were of silver. The basic coin was the silver *denarius*, or penny. Twelve of them made a *solidus*, or shilling. Twenty solidi made a *libra* or pound. There was also a *mark*, worth thirteen shillings and four pence. However, these amounts represented accounting numbers, not actual coins. Each lord who coined money set his own standards of weight and purity and changed those standards whenever he needed to. Therefore, important men of commerce were always the moneychangers, who made money by making sense of the different coinage (Table 2).

Table 2. Value of Money in the Thirteenth Century (figures are approximate)

Currency	Purchasing Value	Modern U.S. Equivalent $
1 English pound	1 good cart horse	$2,500
1 Eng. shilling	1 day's wages — knight	$100
English penny	1 day's cheap labor	$10
1 French livre	1 month's rent — Pairs	$1,000
1 French sou	1 Day's wages — craftsman	$50
1 French denier	1 (1 lb) loaf of bread	$3

Source: Jeffrey L. Singman. *Daily Life in Medieval Europe.* Westport, CT: Greenwood Press, 1999, p. 59.

In the twelfth and early thirteenth centuries, the main institutions that dealt in foreign exchange were the two great **Military Orders**, the Templars and the Hospitalers. Because they had far-flung resources and military power, they were well placed to serve as bankers for merchants and pilgrims. They would accept money in one country and pay it out in another, which would save merchants the hazard of traveling with large sums of money.

The continued growth of commerce depended upon the development of banking principles, and Christians were hampered in this activity because of the prohibition on charging interest. Christian prohibition derived from the belief that it was sinful to make money from time, which belongs to God, and charging interest is exactly that — profit made from using money over a period of time. Neither **Jews** nor Muslims believed in this prohibition, so they developed banking and lending money; and by the twelfth century, Jews became the predominant moneylenders and coin changers in western Europe. Although many Christians blamed Jews for engaging in banking, others valued their contribution. For example, in the late eleventh century, the Bishop of the German town of Speyer gave Jews a special charter to urge them to settle in Speyer and freely change coins and stimulate the local economy.

By the thirteenth century, many Christians developed creative ways to avoid the prohibition against making a profit on lending money. For example, an Italian merchant might lend money to an English baron engaging in wool trade. The agreement provided for the baron to repay the Italian in wool priced below market value, thus giving the Italian banker a profit without formally charging interest. Other informal banking mechanisms might include offering a lender a generous gift in "thanks" for a loan. Such techniques led more and more Christians into banking — particularly in Italy and Germany — making Christians believe that Jews were an unnecessary source of competition. By the end of the thirteenth century, Jews were banished from England and France. At the end of the Middle Ages, this anti-Semitism would spread to Spain and Germany.

Throughout the Middle Ages, most European trade was quite local. Most food and other staples were traded within a radius of one day's travel—about 20 to 25 miles, and most people might live their whole lives not traveling more than 5 miles from home. However, the real engine of the economy came from merchants who were willing to travel great distances, with equally great risks, to bring scarce luxury items to the courts of Europe. Most of the long-distance trade brought goods from the fabled East by Muslim merchants who then traded with merchants in the Byzantine Empire or Italian traders. Not surprisingly, some enterprising Italians decided to try to avoid the middlemen and seek the riches of the East on their own. The most famous of these travelers were the Polo family of Venice, accompanied by the young **Marco Polo.**

The Polos left Venice in the late thirteenth century and traveled across Asia to Khanbalik, the capital of the Mongol empire in China, to the court of Kublai Khan. The Mongols knew the value of long-distance trade and encouraged it across their vast lands, and the European merchants found a welcome in the court. Even with the relative peace established within the Mongol lands, the journey was arduous. It took the Polos three-and-a-half years of travel by horseback to get to the Chinese capital. The Polos stayed 17 ½ years in China before returning home to Venice.

During their 17-year absence, their relatives in Venice were certain they had died. When the travelers returned, wearing rough traveling clothes, they pounded on the door of their family home. It took some time for them to convince their relatives that they, indeed, had returned from the Far East. Soon a great feast was arranged to which old friends and the famous of Venice were invited to hear of the travels. The travelers wore crimson robes of silk and told tales of China. However, the most impressive moment took place at the end of the meal, when the Polos left the room and once again donned their rough travel cloaks. When they returned, they took sharp knives and slit open the seams and linings of the cloaks and a king's ransom of precious jewels fell to the table to astound the visitors. Now all of Venice was convinced not only that the Polos had returned rich, but also that trading in the East was a lucrative commercial venture. More merchants went to the East, and by 1300 there was even a community of Italians living in China. The stories of Marco Polo and the wealth of the East would remain a lure for merchants and explorers well after the Middle Ages, when explorers like Christopher Columbus would look for easier ways to the fabled East.

Growing Urban Life

There are two reasons for cities to exist: (1) to serve administrative functions governing local regions and (2) to serve economic functions as artisans and merchants gathered together to make and sell products. The few remaining urban areas in northern Europe during the early Middle Ages served primarily the first function, as churches of bishops drew supporting populations. The growth of commerce in the eleventh century, however, served as a catalyst for the growth of new commercial cities that slowly grew all over the continent.

The first trading cities grew as lay and ecclesiastical lords encouraged craftsmen and merchants to settle in their administrative cities. At first, these lords sponsored artisans who had special skills that they needed, for example, blacksmiths and armorers, but soon other craftsmen—from goldsmiths to shoemakers—gathered in the towns to sell their wares. Other small cities were founded by colonies of merchants who settled along important trade routes. The cities outside the boundaries of the old Roman Empire were usually founded in this way.

All medieval cities were small in comparison with the great cities of the ancient world or of China. A substantial commercial city with a permanent settlement of merchants might have only about five-thousand inhabitants. In northern Europe only the largest commercial centers—like London, Bruges, and Ghent—had as many as forty-thousand inhabitants. The great cities of Italy—Venice, Florence, Genoa, Milan, and Naples—maintained some continuity from the ancient Roman times and boasted populations as large as one-hundred thousand.

At the heart of city life is a division of labor. In rural villages, peasants did everything from grow their food to making what they needed for their households. In cities, by contrast, artisans and merchants could focus on their particular skills and make enough money to buy their necessities including food. While city dwellers were often disdainful of country folk who seemed so backward, they nevertheless depended on the countryside to feed the urban population. Rural people also needed the cities as an outlet for their excess food, but peasants always remained suspicious of "city slickers" who might cheat their rural neighbors. This uneasy symbiotic relationship between city and countryside is as old as city life itself. For example, one estimate suggests that a town of three-thousand inhabitants in the eleventh century required the land of some ten villages to support it (Braudel, 486). Consider how many villagers toiled in the fields to support larger cities of one hundred thousand or more!

There was no urban planning, and the structure of cities reflected their dynamic economic functions. First, towns struggled for safety, and as soon as townspeople could raise the money they built a sturdy wall around the town. Walls were expensive, however, so every bit of the space they enclosed was used. Narrow, winding streets were crowded with two-story houses, and the second story often extended over the street below. Houses were built of wood, so fire was an ever-present danger. The crowded cities had no provision for sanitation, so sewage was either dumped into local rivers or left to run off in the mud during rains. The most enterprising towns gathered the "night soil" to cart to the nearby fields as fertilizer.

Because the business of medieval towns was commerce, all had some kind of public marketplace—whether an indoor hall, an open square, or just a wide city street. Small towns held their markets one day each week, while large cities had multiple marketplaces more often. Beyond the markets, trades were clustered in neighborhoods, often dictated by local conditions or opportunities. Inns and horse dealers were often clustered by the gates of the town to serve travelers. Taverns were often clustered near markets. Artisans that created much waste, like butchers, often set up shop near a river that flowed through town so the flowing water could remove the waste. This practice led to rivers flowing through cities being sadly polluted. This arrangement of trades made it easier for shoppers to compare products: All the goldsmiths would be in one area, shoemakers in another.

The craftsmen and laborers who worked in the cities were normally drawn from skilled peasants from the countryside. This raised a question of the status of urban residents because in the country villages, most residents were semi-free. That is, they were serfs who were not able to move off the land without permission from the lord (*see* "Society" section). However, lords knew the financial advantage to be gained by having a town in their lands, so they granted charters granting towns the privileges they needed to conduct business. These charters usually provided that everyone who lived in the town for a year and a day would be free. Thus, if a runaway serf evaded capture for this time he or she was free. This provision served to draw the most talented and enterprising people from the countryside.

Charters also allowed townspeople, called "burgers," to hold their lands for money rents. In an age when most people owed their labor to their lord, this was also a strong advantage for the towns. Finally, all charters protected townspeople from arbitrary seizure of property. In fact, this last provision usually set limits on the amounts of rents a lord could charge and the amount of fines he could charge for crimes. These basic freedoms were available in most towns and stimulated the growing commercial ventures. Some towns gained even more generous rights, such as the right to try crimes committed within the town or an exemption on tolls on bridges or sales taxes.

If lords did not want to relinquish their authority, inhabitants of some towns—first in Italy they elsewhere—gathered together to for what was called a "commune." This was a sworn alliance of townspeople who agreed to fight to preserve their freedoms from external authorities. The communes in the Italian towns led to their having a great deal of political autonomy.

The charters from lords and the communes determined the relationship between the town and the surrounding estates but did not address the governance within the town itself. In spite of the freedoms granted townspeople, there was a social structure within the towns based largely on money. Rich merchants—often drawn from younger sons of nobility—had status, money, and prestige and generally led the governing of towns. Craftsmen and artisans often felt themselves oppressed by the merchants, so they wanted ways to assert their own rights. Within towns, **guilds** developed as the institutions to regulate trade and protect workers.

Merchant guilds did everything from insuring merchants against losses in long distance trade to burying them when they died. Guilds secured monopolies for merchants, forbidding foreign merchants from selling goods in the town. Guilds for craftsmen served similar functions, caring for widows and orphans of members and regulating the trade. Guilds also regulated prices and quality of goods as well as the skill of the membership.

During the Middle Ages, towns were small and seemed to be peripheral to the great events guided by kings and lords. However, the economic resources generated in these small towns established structures that paved the way for the modern world. In the fourteenth century when medieval Europe was buffeted by large-scale disasters, it was the towns that generated the new spirit that was to be called the "Renaissance."

Economic Disasters

Just as the economic boom of the Middle Ages was built on agricultural innovations that allowed a healthy population boom, the fourteenth century decline of medieval society began with agricultural disaster. By 1300, the burgeoning population began to put a strain on existing technology. With the expansion of population, people cultivated poorer lands and crop yields dwindled. For example, on some marginal lands, farmers harvested only three bushels for every one planted. After setting aside one bushel to plant the following year, the remainder was hardly enough to feed the populace.

As people tried to bring more and more acreage into cultivation to feed humans, there was less open land to feed livestock. Thus, as they slaughtered animals, there was less manure to fertilize fields and yields fell further. Many people were living on the edge of starvation, but then things got worse. Beginning in 1310, the weather worsened. Chroniclers tell of drenching rains all over Europe that flooded fields and washed away the scattered seed. Summers were dark and wet, and already sparse crops failed. This cooling trend helped destroy the Scandinavian settlement in Greenland that had flourished for centuries. But, even the heartland of Europe suffered.

Famine began in 1315, and in some parts of Europe lasted until 1322. Aching hunger drove peasants from their lands in search of food. The food scarcities affected towns as well. For example, in 1322 artisans in the town of Douai in Flanders rioted because of rumors that rich merchants were hoarding grain. As workers stormed the warehouses, soldiers brutally repressed the uprising. This was repeated in towns all over Europe.

People weakened by hunger suffered from respiratory illness and intestinal ailments, but a greater illness soon added to the misery. In about 1348, the **bubonic plague**—known as the "Black Death"—began to sweep through Europe, rapidly killing huge numbers of people. Estimates vary, but historians reckon that between one-third and one-half the population died during this terrible scourge that moved through Europe throughout the century.

The dramatic population drop had significant economic consequences. Many marginal lands were abandoned as villagers moved to better areas. When the deaths ended, there was more food available for those remaining, but labor shortages caused peasants to radically reconsider their lot. Landlords who felt a double pinch of falling grain prices along with rising labor costs tried repressive measures to maintain their old standard of living. This led to **peasant revolts** throughout Europe, including the Jacquerie in France and the rebellion in England led by John Ball. None of these rebellions was immediately successful, but in the end the shortage of agricultural labor brought about changes that transformed the medieval economy. In western Europe, serfdom ended. Peasants owned their own labor and could work for wages and hope to improve their lot. By and large, the landed nobility would never again have the prosperity they enjoyed during the height of the Middle Ages.

The cities, too, were transformed by the population decline. There was an immediate oversupply of goods and a drop in overall demand. The wealthy merchants tried to hang on to their declining fortunes by enacting restrictive guild regulations and city ordinances to prevent more competition. Laborers who saw little hope in improving their lot revolted against city governments. Eventually, like in the countryside, urban workers began to get more freedoms to trade and better their positions.

The changes in the fourteenth century served to transform long-distance commercial transactions as well. The Champagne Fairs declined, and the Hanseatic League in the north became a formidable power that established alternate routes to Venice. Through this, more wealth flowed to the north.

The difficulties of doing business profitably in a shrinking market stimulated merchants to develop new techniques of business management. Records of Italian merchants in the fourteenth century show the development of meticulous double-entry bookkeeping and a growth of capital. Some enterprising families began to be involved in banking, taking that lucrative business away from Jewish families. The most successful were the Medici in Florence, who began as cloth merchants and ended up growing rich in banking. The Fuggers of Augsburg built up a similar financial empire in Germany.

By the end of the fourteenth century, the European economy was transformed. The population decline provided opportunities for enterprising people to conduct business in new ways unhampered by the traditions of the past. Europe was poised for the next dramatic leap forward that we have come to call the Renaissance.

Further Reading

Braudel, F. *The Structures of Everyday Life*. New York: Harper and Row, 1979.

Jordan, William Chester. *The Great Famine*. Princeton, NJ: Princeton University Press, 1996.

Lopez, Robert S. *The Commercial Revolution of the Middle Ages, 950–1350*. New York: Cambridge University Press, 1976.

Sweeny, Del, ed. *Agriculture in the Middle Ages: Technology, Practice and Representation*. Philadelphia: University of Pennsylvania Press, 1995.

Wallerstein, I.M. *Historical Capitalism*. London: Verso, 1983.

4. THE ARTS

Like other aspects of early medieval civilization, the arts emerged from a synthesis of classical, Germanic, and Christian elements. During the early Middle Ages—from about 400 to 800—artistic struggles to form this synthesis were readily apparent. For example, Irish manuscript illuminators in the **Book of Kells** struck an uneasy balance between trying to portray a realistic human figure in the classic style while surrounding it with intricate patterning which represented the Germanic aesthetic.

By the Carolingian age, this synthesis had been achieved, and a glorious new art aesthetic was created that embodied several values. Medieval artists (and critics) believed that art was simply one part of the mystic web that joined creation and God, and that artistic creations could help reveal the transcendent. As part of this quest, artists identified some aesthetic principles that shaped their creations. The first principle was one of mathematical proportion; beauty was symmetrical and proportional, whether it appeared in poetry, music, or the visual arts. Additionally, artists valued bright primary colors (rather than nuanced blends) and bright illuminating light. Finally, medieval artists valued allegory and metaphor in ways that seem extreme and confusing to modern sensibilities. For example, a unicorn could refer to a human lover, Christ, and a fierce prey at the same time without contradiction. Furthermore, because the reality of the message of the unicorn was central to the depiction, it did not matter whether there were real unicorns or not—a metaphor could be more "real" than the observed world.

Literature

The early medieval world had inherited a rich tradition of Latin literature that was preserved in monasteries and venerated by the educated. Some medieval scholars, such as Isidore of Seville and **Bede the Venerable**, made a point to preserve classical knowledge and transmit it to the future. This tradition of Latin prose literature also included the great Christian writings that had shaped and defined Christian belief. These influential writings included works by Augustine, Jerome, Ambrose, and many others who are called "**Fathers of the Church**."

The tradition of classical theater was preserved in monasteries in a changed, Christian form. The most famous monastic playwright was Hrotswitha of Gandersheim, a tenth-century nun who wrote entertaining plays that combined classical traditions with saints' tales. By the twelfth century, **dramatic performances** became part of church services and spread to cities to be performed outdoors to the pleasure of many.

The Germanic tribes had a long tradition of oral poetry, much of which was heroic poetry designed to remember the great deeds of their ancestors. Most of this poetry was lost, but fortunately some was preserved in northern monasteries by monks who had grown up appreciating oral tales. The most famous Germanic epic is *Beowulf*, which was probably composed about 680 and written down in about 1000. Other Germanic epics that have survived include *The Song of Hildebrand* and the *Niebelungenlied*. These works preserved a time when the deeds of heroes were preserved by poets in the dark halls of northern folk.

The prosperity of the twelfth century saw a flourishing of literature in Europe, and more and more of this work was written in vernacular languages instead of in Latin that could be understood only by the educated. One new type of literature is called *chanson de geste*, or song of brave deeds. These poems honored the heroic adventures of warriors who lived under the complex rules of **feudal law** and **chivalry**. The most famous *chanson de geste* is the *Song of Roland*, a heroic version of a minor battle fought by **Charlemagne** in northern Spain, in which his vassal Roland was killed. This was written down in about 1100 and portrayed the struggle as one between Christians and Muslims. A second, more realistic, *chanson de geste* is the Spanish *Poem of the Cid*, which tells of this hero's struggles against the Spanish Muslims.

Although these stories of battles reflected the values of the warrior nobility, a new kind of literature arose that praised **courtly love**, a new value that appealed to noble wives who waited at home for their warrior husbands. This new value of love was first praised by troubadours, poets in southern France, or Provence. The ideal of this romantic love was that the lover would be made better (stronger and more noble) as a result of his love—even though in most cases the love was an adulterous one with a married woman. Perhaps the culmination of this tradition was the thirteenth-century long French poem, the *Romance of the Rose*, which carefully detailed how men might seduce the object of their desire.

As the influence of troubadour poetry spread, the status of women in Western literature was revolutionized as noblemen were to do great deeds in return for the love of noble women. At the same time, the cult of the Virgin Mary flourished throughout Europe. Many critics see a relationship between these movements that praised the feminine in religious and secular realms.

After 1150, courtly romances quickly replaced the feudal *chansons de geste* in popularity. These romances were verse stories that combined miraculous adventures of knights with romantic entanglements with their ladies. One of the romance poets, Chrétien de Troyes, wrote romances centered at the court of

King Arthur of Britain. Another romantic tale that remains influential today is the story of the tragic love affair between Tristan and Isolde. Some critics argue that this praise of romantic love that began in the Middle Ages established a new direction in the emotional life of people in the West, which set it dramatically apart from the rest of the world.

Another literary genre that flourished in the twelfth century was the *lay*, a short lyric or narrative poem meant to be sung to the accompaniment of an instrument such as a harp. The oldest surviving lays were those written by Marie de France, who also wrote fables. Marie's works were profoundly influential in making the classic form of beast fables relevant to the medieval courtly audience.

The growing importance (and wealth) of townspeople stimulated the growth of literature aimed at the more cynical middle class instead of the romantic nobility. French *fabliaux* were short poetic compositions that portrayed hilarious, and often bawdy, stories about medieval life. Many were misogynist in their portrayal of women, but all were hugely influential as writers in the late Middle Ages looked to these amusing tales as models. Fourteenth-century writers like Geoffrey **Chaucer** in England and Giovanni **Boccaccio** in Italy drew from these humorous tales as they wrote works that used humor to confront the disasters they faced in the decline of the Middle Ages.

Perhaps the highest development of medieval literature came in the fourteenth century Italian work, *The Divine Comedy*, by **Dante Alighieri**. In this work, the poet imagines a tour through Hell, Purgatory, and Heaven, and the resulting allegory—that is full of historical figures—marks a brilliant synthesis of medieval thought, while pointing to the Renaissance that was to come.

Music

During the Middle Ages, the greatest composers turned their talents to create religious music that was composed to draw the faithful to a more spiritual experience during church services. The roots of this sacred music lay in ancient Hebrew, Greco-Roman, and Byzantine styles, and we have no records to study these ancient forms. However, theorists of ancient classical music give us some hints about its nature, and one of the important music analysts was the Italian Boethius, who was a significant thinker at the court of Theodoric the Ostrogoth in Italy. Boethius reinforced the aesthetic principle of proportion when it came to music. He echoed the classic view that the heart of music was mathematics, and that beauty in music lay in presenting sounds that were proportional to each other. In this, Boethius was following Pythagoras, who argued that a divine "music of the spheres" existed, which was a harmony produced by the seven known planets orbiting around a motionless earth. He believed each planet generated a note of the scale, and the pitch heightened according to the planet's velocity. From Boethius on, medieval religious musicians sought to come close to reproducing this divine music through appropriate proportional notes.

All musicians may not have considered the abstract mathematical principles articulated by Pythagoras and others, but there was a clear recognition that spiritual experience was enhanced by sacred music. By the early Middle Ages, we know there were a number of important traditions of sacred music. The influential bishop, Ambrose of Milan, wrote hymns for services as did the Spanish poet Prudentius. However, we know laypeople as well wrote hymns because church councils ruled that it was permissible to sing such compositions in church.

By the sixth century, there were hymns to invoke God's aid, celebrate happy occasions, and for funerals. In spite of the proliferation of church songs, the most influential sponsor of sacred music was Pope Gregory the Great (540–604), who was reputed to have codified the existing church music. In the eleventh century, church music was named "Gregorian chant" in honor of Pope Gregory.

The Gregorian chant (which continues to be performed today) was "monophonic," that is, one or many voices sang a single melodic line, and more often than not the performance lacked musical accompaniment. Most of the music consisted of simple chants for the recitation of psalms and the mass at the services. This Gregorian chant was also called "plainsong." In its elementary form, the chant consisted of a single note for each syllable of a word. Gregorian chants lent a hypnotic beauty to church services.

Most of the compositions from the Middle Ages were anonymous, but an exception is the hymns by **Hildegard of Bingen**, a German nun of the twelfth century. Hildegard's works are preserved and performed today, and they show the wide range of creativity that composers could bring to the plainsong of the medieval church.

By the twelfth century, skilled composers like Hildegard began to add complexity to the plainsong, which led to dramatic innovations in sacred music. The first innovation was called a "trope," which were new texts and melodies inserted into the existing Gregorian chants. These musical embellishments slowly changed the plainsong into more elaborate songs and led to the creation of "liturgical drama," musical plays that were held in the middle of church services. In time, liturgical dramas became so popular that they began to be sung in the vernacular (instead of Latin) and performed in front of the church. These spurred the eventual revival of secular theater in the West.

A second modification of Gregorian chant lay in the organization of the notes themselves (instead of simple insertions like the tropes), called "polyphony." In polyphony, two or more lines of melody are sung or played at the same time. In the early eleventh century, polyphony was very simple and known as "organum." It consisted of a main melody accompanied by an identical melody sung four or five tones higher or lower. By about 1150, composers made the second line have its own separate melody, increasing the complexity of the composition. By the thirteenth century, the two-voiced organum gave way to multivoiced songs, called "motets." The various parts of the piece could be performed by either voices or instruments.

The increasing complexity—and beauty—of the sacred music gave concern to some thinkers, who probably quite rightly believed that some listeners would just appreciate the music itself, instead of using it as a vehicle to bring the soul closer to God. Thomas Aquinas, for example, in the thirteenth century said that sacred music should only be sung, because instruments "move the soul rather to delight than to a good interior disposition" (Eco, 9). Aesthetic delight in music was to be left to a second form of medieval music, secular songs.

Secular songs were performed in the courts of the nobility and the squares of the towns. The poetry of the troubadours was designed to be sung, and the earliest musical notation for secular songs came from this music. These songs were mostly about love, but some sang of warfare, and even some everyday work songs, like spinning songs. We have some poetry written by women as well. Some 1,650 troubadour melodies have been preserved. The notation does not indicate rhythm, but it is likely that they had a clearly delineated beat, which sets secular songs dramatically apart from Gregorian chants.

One famous collection of secular songs is the *Carmina Burana*, which are named after the Bavarian monastery in which the lyrics were discovered in the nineteenth century. These songs may have been written by wandering scholars and show a lively range of emotions and humor. The songs include a praise of love (and sex), an exuberance of youth, drinking and gambling songs, and humorous parodies of religion. In about 1935, a German composer, Carl Orff, set a number of these poems to music in a way that was intended to recapture medieval music by blending heavy percussion with choral voices. In this form, the *Carmina Burana* remains popularly performed today.

The earliest surviving form of instrumental secular music is the *estampie*, a medieval dance. The estampie has a strong fast beat and would have been performed by a combination of medieval instruments. The beat would have been maintained by hand drums while the melody might have been played on a *rebec*, a bowed string instrument, a *psaltery*, a plucked or struck string instrument, or on various pipes. The Celtic lands used the ancient bagpipes to accompany lively secular songs and dances.

That we can re-create many of these songs is thanks to the innovations of an Italian monk, Guido of Arezzo, who in the early eleventh century modernized musical notation. He invented the musical staff—the set of five horizontal lines and four intermediate spaces on which notes may be drawn. This allowed a consistent way to indicate the pitch of notes, and we have many beautiful manuscripts that show this system. Guido also began the practice of naming the musical tones by the syllable *ut* (for *do*) *re, mi, fa, sol, la,* that makes it easier to teach music and that survives until today. Although there were significant changes in musical theory and notation after the Renaissance, the roots of all our modern music began in the Middle Ages.

Architecture

In medieval Europe, religion was central to people's lives, so it is not surprising that church buildings were the focus of some of the most remarkable developments in architectural history. At the local level from the earliest years of Christianity, villages were clustered around parish churches. A parish was often considered to extend to the area where parishioners could hear the church bell and gather to services. The buildings themselves were small and plain compared to the great monastic and urban churches that were to follow it, but nevertheless, the structure was large compared to any other building in the village. (The average parish church was probably about four times larger than any peasant cottage.)

These churches were usually built of stone, with thick walls that were whitewashed with lime on the inside. Sometimes these dark interiors were decorated with frescoes with religious imagery. As the candlelight flickered on these images, parishioners were to be reminded of the spiritual life. As in music, the decorative arts in the churches were designed to serve the religious purpose of the building. Churches were built with entries facing west, from where they expected Christ to return on the second coming, and the altars were at the east end.

By the eleventh century, church builders began to strive to make buildings larger. These were mostly in service of growing cities or—more often—monasteries. These larger churches were built in a style that came to be called "Romanesque," which meant developed from Roman models. Romanesque churches—like parish churches—were built of thick stone with solid walls. Architects designed these churches in the shape of a cross, with a long central aisles (called the "nave"), side aisles, and a "transept" crossing the nave toward the front of the church. The altar was in the "apse" at the front.

Architects also tried to make Romanesque churches with high ceilings to help the faithful think of heaven. To achieve this height (without the roof collapsing), architects had to make the walls thick and added support by thickened portions of the walls called "buttresses." The interior of the Romanesque churches were supported with round arches all along the nave and aisles. The feel of Romanesque buildings was one of solidity—fortresses of God that were sanctuaries in a violent world. One of the most famous Romanesque churches was that of the monastery of Cluny, which served as a model for similar churches all over Europe.

In the twelfth century, the growth of cities led churchmen to recognize they needed a new form of architecture to serve the increased populations and the many pilgrims (and tourists) who visited the growing, exciting cities. Two problems with the Romanesque architecture stood in the way of the need for larger churches: The roof was so heavy that the nearly windowless walls had to be very thick to support it, and the rounded arches limited the buildings height to fewer than 100 feet. Eventually, through the creative imagination of Abbot Suger of the Abbey Church at St. Denis, near Paris, a new architectural style was created, that has come to be called "Gothic."

The first brilliant innovation developed by Suger and his architects was to change the vaulting in the churches. Instead of the round arches that had been used in the Romanesque churches, they used pointed arches that had been developed by Muslims. They combined this with a ribbed vault in which the weight of the roof was carried down huge stone pillars. This meant that the weight was not carried by the walls, so builders could incorporate beautiful stained-glass windows into the walls. The exteriors were given further support by the addition of "flying buttresses," great pillars set away from the building and connected by bridges to the heights that further distributed the great weight of stone roofs.

These innovations allowed Gothic cathedrals to grow huge. For example, the interior vaults of Notre-Dame in Paris rose to a height of 110 feet, and the towers to 210 feet. Notre-Dame could easily accommodate nine thousand people, so these urban churches now could satisfy the needs of growing cities. They also became centers of urban pride, as pilgrims traveled throughout Europe admiring the brilliant architecture. By the fourteenth century, late Gothic buildings became ever more ornate as builders elaborated on the basic engineering principles that had stood the test of time.

In the East, the Byzantine Empire had created a different kind of style for church architecture. Throughout the Byzantine Empire churches were designed by local builders, which led to variation among churches. Some had the long nave of Western churches (designed from Roman basilicas), but others were designed in the shape of a Greek cross, with the transept the same size as the nave. The most stunning example of the Byzantine style, however, is the magnificent church—Hagia Sophia—built in Constantinople by the emperor **Justinian** in the sixth century.

Covering an area of almost 58,000 square feet, Hagia Sophia was one of the largest interior spaces of the medieval world. Even more striking than its size, however, was the enormous dome that spanned the interior space. Byzantine architects invented "pendentives" to support the dome. These were supports in the shape of inverted concave triangles that allowed the dome to be suspended over a square base. As a result of such innovations, domed buildings soon became synonymous with the Byzantine style.

The Byzantine style of churches influenced the West a bit. Charlemagne in the ninth century had his chapel at Aachen designed in the Byzantine style with a dome, which was the last domed building in the West until the Renaissance. In the fifth century, rulers from Byzantium built churches in Ravenna, Italy, and used many of the features that marked the Byzantine style—particularly the use of mosaics.

The most visible and remarkable examples of medieval secular architecture are **castles**. Medieval **warfare** was largely defensive, basing victory on armor to protect soldiers and on great walls to protect fortified positions. The height of this defensive posture was castles that dotted the landscapes all over Europe. Walled defenses were not new; the Romans demonstrated their use by circling their great cities with thick walls. For example, the walls of the great eastern city of Constantinople successfully held off the waves of Germanic invaders and ensured the survival of the eastern empire. Castles, however, introduced something new. These fortifications tended to be rural and expressed the reality that defense was a matter for nobility and their retainers. This was the feudal system in action.

In the tenth century, castles were private fortresses made of timber and earth that were built on mounds. By the thirteenth century, they had become large, defensive structures of wood and stone and were virtually impregnable. Many castles consisted of a large exterior wall surrounded by a moat filled with water, and an interior fortified structure, called the "keep," that served as the noble family's home and an extra line of defense should invaders breach the outer wall. The interior fortress had to include a deep well for water and plenty of capacity for food storage, for the castle's ability to withstand a siege depended largely on supplies within.

The real advances in castle architecture came about as a result of the **Crusades**. Because the newly captured lands in the East had to be held by a few thousand knights, defensive fortifications were essential. **Military Orders**, such as the Templars and Hospitalers, lined the frontiers of Syria and Palestine with castles that were the engineering marvels of the age. Architects of these castles drew from Byzantine and Muslim models and rounded the corners of the square keep to fortify the vulnerable corners. The design of these eastern castles quickly spread through western Europe.

Entrance to a castle was through a gatehouse, whose "portcullis," or heavy door, was oak plated and covered with iron. This was raised vertically by a pulley operated from an upper chamber in the gatehouse. Spanning the moat was a bridge. The most famous of all the twelfth-century castles was the "Krak des Chevaliers" (Citadel of the Knights) built by the Hospitalers in the Holy Land. This castle withstood every siege, until in the thirteenth century it was captured by a trick. A Muslim general tricked the garrison with a forged order to open the gates.

Defensive castles dotted the countryside and formed the basis of warfare until the fourteenth-century development of gunpowder. When cannons could breach the thick walls, people could no longer rely on defense to protect them. At that point, the medieval culture yielded to the modern world, in which offensive weapons marked warfare.

Visual Arts

All the medieval visual arts adhered to the same aesthetic principles: a love of proportion, bright color and light, and a heavy use of symbolism. In addition, visual arts in the Middle Ages were virtually always created in service to some other art form and were predominately religious. That is, sculptures and visual representations (frescoes and mosaics) were usually always attached to church buildings, and the best tradition of painting was manuscript illumination, where the painting was subordinate to the book. Painted or sculpted church icons in the Byzantine Empire were used in religious rituals.

The secular arts were also attached to some other purpose. For example, everyday items, such as belt buckles or jewelry, were artistically decorated. Magnificent woven or embroidered tapestries decorated practical wall hangings or clothing. Only late in the Middle Ages did sculpture become free-standing and oil painting developed. One of the characteristics of the Renaissance that saw the end of medieval culture was when the visual arts became valued on their own.

The arts in the early Middle Ages were influenced by a blending of Germanic sensibilities with Roman forms. The Germanic love of intricate patterns appeared on everything from jewelry, to religious objects (chalices, reliquaries, and church buildings), to manuscript illuminations. Vikings also brought this love of patterning into medieval sensibilities during the invasions of the tenth century.

The dark parish churches of the early Middle Ages were frequently decorated with frescoes that showed biblical scenes, religious figures, or even scenes of everyday life. These often included rather crude portrayals of the human figure while elaborate animals, plants, and patterns that were beloved of the early medieval artists dominated the artwork.

The churches in the Byzantine Empire, on the other hand, were brilliantly decorated with mosaics. Mosaic making had been a vibrant art form in the late Roman empire, and so it is not surprising that mosaic artists would have been welcomed in Constantinople that saw itself as the continuation of the glory of Rome. However, Byzantine mosaics differed from the Roman predecessors in significant ways: Roman mosaics were usually of stone and laid in the floor, but Byzantine mosaics were usually of glass and set into the walls. The glass in bright colors with a particular emphasis in gold gives the mosaics—and the churches that contain them—an otherworldly brilliance.

Because Constantinople experienced the conflict of **iconoclasm**—which argued that Christians should not make images—many of the early mosaics in Constantinople were destroyed. Thus, perhaps ironically, the best location to see mosaics in the Byzantine style is in Italy: in Ravenna, where the last emperors in the West established their court, and in Venice, where the magnificent Cathedral of St. Mark was built to glorify the relics of that saint.

The monasteries of the eleventh century, especially Cluny, were instrumental in bringing a new style of art into the new Romanesque churches. Romanesque churches were carved with fantastic creatures, symbolizing all the deadly sins that might ensnare the faithful. Gargoyles that grace the roofs of many churches (Romanesque as well as Gothic) are a good example of how function was infused with symbolism. Gargoyles served a practical purpose of funneling rainwater off the roof but were also symbols of evil fleeing the sacred premises of the church.

At the same time, religious topics were carved into the churches. Christ was portrayed in majesty on Judgment Day in many of the churches. Monastic churches became so decorated that some churchmen wondered whether all this beauty was appropriate. **Bernard of Clairveaux**, for example, wrote, "one could spend the whole day marveling at one such representation rather than in meditating on the law of God. In the name of God! If we are not ashamed at its foolishness, why at least are we not angry at the expense?" (Eco, 8). But Bernard was in the minority; most saw the Romanesque art as drawing the mind upward to God. This belief was continued in the Gothic style.

When Abbot Suger began the artistic revolution that has come to be called "Gothic," he began with new architecture that allowed for huge churches to dominate the medieval urban landscapes. Intimately tied to the new architecture, however, were the visual arts that decorated almost every space of the cathedrals. Gothic designers decorated every external pillar with a sculpture of figures from the Hebrew Scriptures, New Testament, or secular kings. These figures were depicted in an idealized way and served in a literal as well as metaphoric sense to be "pillars of the church."

More revolutionary were the stained-glass windows that filled the walls that were no longer necessary to support the roof. Abbot Suger wrote about his views of the symbolic importance of light; he argued that every living thing has some bit of divinity—that he described as "light"—and the mind and soul long to move ever higher to the perfect and pure light that is God. Gothic builders believed that stained-glass windows created with bright primary colors brought divine light into the church building.

The glass was rolled into long colored strips which were broken into shape by placing hot lead along the design lines, then broken when buckets of cold water were poured on to the heated lead. Skillful artisans learned to create stunning, complex images that retold Biblical tales, sermons, and folk wisdom as sunlight entered the windows.

The whole Gothic cathedral represented a synthesis of medieval life and thought. In these engineering marvels, theologians, artists, and artisans reflected the full panorama of medieval life in which the community of the faithful expressed their longings for the divine and their expectations of heaven. The cathedrals represented a visual expression of the medieval philosophy of **scholasticism**, which argued that everything was linked in a divine order.

In the fourteenth century, scholasticism was attacked by a new philosophy that was less certain that universal principles were accessible to the human mind. This philosophy of nominalism called into question much that had been taken for granted before, including principles of aesthetics that had unified medieval art. Slowly, great art became that which was created by the genius of individuals. This idea began to be expressed in the great paintings of the late Middle Ages, especially in Flanders and Italy. Painters like Giotto in Italy or

Jan Van Eyck began to portray individuals in artwork that was separated from buildings and books. The Renaissance view of art was being born.

Further Reading

Calkins, Robert. *Illuminated Books of the Middle Ages*. Ithaca, NY: Cornell University Press, 1983.

Duby, Georges. *The Art of the Cathedrals: Art and Society, 980–1420*. Translated by Eleanor Levieux and Barbara Thompson. Chicago: University of Chicago Press, 1981.

Eco, Umberto. *Art and Beauty in the Middle Ages*. New Haven, CT: Yale University Press, 1986.

Macauley, David. *Cathedral: The Story of Its Construction*. Boston: Houghton, Mifflin, 1973.

Manog, C. *Byzantine Architecture*. New York: Harry N. Abrams, 1976.

Seay, Albert. *Music in the Medieval World*. Long Grove, IL: Waveland Press, 1991.

Wilson, Christopher. *The Gothic Cathedral*. New York: Thames and Hudson, 1993.

5. SOCIETY

Medieval society was organized very differently from our own. The principal theoretical goal of twenty-first century society is freedom and democracy, in which every individual has the right to pursue his or her dreams and aspirations. In the Middle Ages, on the other hand, the goal was to have each individual linked in obligation to another. In other words, the goal was not freedom, but connection. The wealthy placed themselves under the permanent protection of those more powerful; peasants were tied to their land and their masters, and churchmen and women owed obedience to their superiors. All believed that only when everyone was linked in obligation and place was the social order secured.

Medieval society was also different from modern societies because it was arranged by "orders" instead of class, gender, wealth, or other ways we might understand social divisions. For medieval people, "order" meant one's function, or how the individual contributes to society. By the eleventh century, medieval thinkers saw three orders that made up society: those who pray, those who fight, and those who work. Each of these orders included people of varying wealth. For example, those who pray included everyone from wealthy bishops drawn from the highest nobility to poor parish priests drawn from the peasantry. Those who fought included the wealthiest king to a poor knight. **Women**, too, were arranged within these orders, whether they were nuns praying, noble women producing heirs to fight, or peasant wives working the land.

This essay will explore the social structure of medieval times from the lowest peasant order—those who work—through the warrior class—those who fight—to the highest church official—those who pray. This essay will also look at the growing body of laws that developed to secure the social order. Ironically, the laws formed institutions such as Parliament and created an idea that law was more important than the social ties that bound people to one another—an idea that would ultimately destroy a medieval society based on personal ties. The reliance on law and governing bodies formed the basis for the freedoms that we enjoy today.

Manorialism: Those Who Work the Land

Peasants throughout most of Europe lived clustered together in villages and worked together in **agriculture**, farming strips of land that surrounded the villages (*see* "Economy" section). Beyond this basic structure, the rural inhabitants had varying degrees of freedom, but no one was completely free. All owed some rents and some labor to their landlords. These landlords might be nobility, who did the fighting, or churchmen, who did the praying. *Peasant* is the general name for rural agricultural workers of the Middle Ages and refers to workers who live in villages. Farmers, on the other hand, are those agricultural workers who lived isolated and surrounded by their fields. Scandinavia and a few other regions on the fringes of Europe were inhabited by farmers more than peasants. Farmers tended to be more free than peasants. However, most medieval agricultural workers were peasants clustered in small villages.

Most of the peasants in Europe were serfs (known in England as *villeins*). Serfs were personally free, that is, they were not slaves, but unlike the general term *peasants*, serfs could not choose to leave their land without permission from the lord. In addition, serfs owed a certain amount of their labor in addition to rents. A few lucky peasants had "freeholds," that is they owed no labor obligations to the landlord, only rents and a portion of their produce. Whether a peasant was a serf or a freeholder, he or she worked to support the ruling orders; the only difference was how much they owed. When a lord received a land grant from the king, he also gained the service of the peasants who worked the land, who had to support his noble household.

Serfs' obligations were of two kinds: goods and labor. They had to give the lord a percentage of their crops or whatever livestock they raised, and the percentage depended upon the initial contract that bound the serf to the land. Typically, families might owe the lord one-tenth of their grain, a piglet from a litter, a number of eggs from their hens, and some of the cheese made from the milk of their goats. Rural women might also owe a portion of the cloth they wove, the yarn they spun, or the vegetables they grew.

Serfs found the labor they owed the lord even more onerous than the goods they paid. On some manors, serfs had to work as many as three days a week on the lord's personal lands (called the *demesne lands*). Serfs had to plant his crops, build roads, erect walls or buildings, dig ditches, and do anything else the lord needed. Remember, this work was in addition to tilling their own lands and growing their own food from which they would pay a portion. Women, too, owed work, going to the lord's household to help spin, weave, and do domestic work.

Serfs were supposed to receive some benefits in exchange for this labor and rent. Lords were to provide protection to serfs in times of war, and justice in times of peace. In addition, lords provided things that required a large investment of capital: mills, barns, ovens, large draft animals, and the like. However, most serfs found this a bad bargain. In times of war, too often their crops were burned and their warehouses looted by invading armies, and the justice obtained in the lord's court often was just one more form of exploitation. Even the mills and other equipment became a way for greedy lords to extort more fees.

Throughout the Middle Ages, there was sporadic evidence of peasant dissatisfaction with this arrangement. For example, law cases record peasants who tried to prove they were freeholders instead of serfs so they would at least own their own labor. Some chronicles describe an early form of strike, in which peasants refused to use the lord's mill, preferring to grind their grain on hand mills to avoid the ever-increasing fees. Some peasants even resisted plowing with more efficient horses to avoid doing extra work themselves as they had to walk more quickly behind horses instead of oxen (*see* "Economy" section).

The agricultural expansion in the eleventh century helped some peasants gain some freedoms as lords were forced to negotiate more reasonable terms to encourage peasants to settle new lands. For example, one charter permitted serfs to be free from tax on the wine and food they produced for their own consumption. In the fourteenth century, peasant revolts arose throughout western Europe as peasants resisted the manorial system that bound them to their lords and struggled to gain a better life.

The examples of peasant resistance to lords' demands reveal the importance of **law** and legal contracts in the manorial system. Villagers had always created laws to govern local affairs, and the earliest medieval law codes incorporated what had clearly been previous village legislation. For example, peasants had penalties for people who kept dangerous dogs or who set wolf traps without warning their neighbors. These villagers were participating in an ancient custom of self-governance at the most local level. The contractual basis of the serfs' relationship to the lords was also written down and bound by law, so the importance of the legal system was established throughout medieval society.

The Feudal Contract Binds Those Who Fight

Medieval manors were large rural entities that included one or more peasant villages, agricultural land, pastures, forests, and a large house (or **castle**) for the noble landlord. These entities were designed to serve as the economic base to support the fighting forces that by the ninth century were highly specialized. It took about ten peasant families to support one mounted soldier, so an efficient manorial organization was essential to produce an army.

The next problem was how to organize the nobility who lived spread out in the manors of the land. The French dynasty of the Carolingians first developed a complex way to organize the fighting men so that, like peasants, they were bound in ties of mutual obligations. Elements of this system spread all over Europe, and in the most general sense, this system of mutual obligation formed the political structure of the elites in medieval society. Historians in the sixteenth century called this political system "feudalism," but historians today prefer to avoid this term because it suggests a highly organize system. Instead, **feudal law** governed a loose structure of ties between people that varied from place to place. Whatever we call this political structure, medieval nobility saw themselves linked in a chain of mutual obligation, even if the forms of the obligations varied.

The basis of the feudal tie was that lords (or kings) granted a "fief," usually land but it might be something else (like a monopoly) that would generate enough income to support the nobleman. The nobleman then became the lord's "vassal," bound to the lord in loyalty and service for life. In return for this fief, the vassal owed the lord certain obligations, known as "aid and counsel." The greatest "aid" was to fight, the main function of the nobility. Other aids included monetary support when lord's incurred specific expenses, such as a wedding of his eldest daughter or the knighting of his son. The requirement of "counsel" meant that when a lord required advice, his vassals had to assemble to give it. This requirement of counsel contributed to the growth of democratic institutions, such as **Parliament**. Both parties owed each other fealty—that is, good faith to do the other no harm, and this vow was sealed with a solemn kiss that confirmed the ties between them.

There was a great variation in wealth, power, and status among the vassals, all of whom were aristocrats. Over time, vassals acquired various titles to distinguish their ranks. All were often called "barons," with dukes were the highest, counts guarded borders, and the lowest of the aristocrats, the knights, often owned no more than their fighting ability and their weapons. Whatever their titles, they all shared the same social order: those who fight and who are supported by those who work. All were supposed to be loyal to their "liege lord," the king who commanded loyalty of everyone in their lands, but this was a tenuous tie, and medieval life was marked by violence among those whose purpose in life was warfare.

The fact that these feudal ties were based on mutually binding contracts defensible in law led to precedents that contributed to modern notions of law and democracy. For the United States, the most important such precedent is Magna Carta. This "Great Charter" grew from a dispute between King John of England and his barons. The barons believed (quite rightly) that John was not showing "good faith" in his dealings with them. He was charging new taxes and generally violating the traditional feudal relationships. In 1215, he barons forced John to sign the Magna Carta, which asserted that even the king is not above the law. This document is treasured as one of the precedents of constitutional law.

The feudal system tied the elites of Europe together in mutual obligations that were bound by law. These obligations held society together when other more modern forces—like nationalism—were nonexistent. The ties were sometimes tenuous and sometimes hard to enforce, but they served to forge some sense of order in a violent age.

The ties among the nobility also included **marriage** ties. At all levels, marriage involved a serious economic commitment that created alliances between families. Thus, marriage was too important to let couples choose their partners for love; instead, families carefully negotiated matches and drew up elaborate agreements stipulating the property that would be brought by each party.

The church also had a stake in marriages, forbidding unions that it deemed too close. Today, first cousins are forbidden to marry in most places, but in the thirteenth century the prohibition extended to four degrees. That is, a couple who shared a great-great-grandfather could not marry. Such prohibitions also extended to godparents, making the determination of kinship very complex.

Once a marriage took place, the couple was joined for life and were required to live together. Divorce was forbidden, but the church sometimes allowed marriages to be "annulled" if the marriage had been illegal in the first place. One of the main reasons for annulling a marriage was the discovery that the couple had relatives in common so it was forbidden by the consanguinity rules. A marriage could also be dissolved if it had never been consummated by sexual intercourse.

The main purpose of marriage was to produce children to ensure the continuity of the noble family lines. Children were born at home with the help of a midwife and the other women living in the household and remained in the care of women until they were about 6 years old. After that, the boys were entrusted to men to learn the arts of war, and girls learned the domestic arts surrounded by the women of the household. Even while they were young, their parents began to plan their future, looking for suitable mates or deciding that children would be dedicated to the church to enter monasteries. Like everyone in the Middle Ages, children were to fulfill the obligations that came with the ties that joined them to family and community. No one thought to ask their opinion of their future!

The daily life of the nobility revealed the sense of community engendered by the feudal system. The lords with their wives and children lived together with crowds of their own vassals and their servants. All ate together on long tables in the common hall of the manor house and played games together in the evenings. The nobility also developed an idealized version of their rugged, violent lives in an elaborate code of values and symbolic rituals called "**chivalry**." In this idealized world, knights were strong and disciplined, who used their power to defend the church, the poor, and women in need. They fought mock combats called "jousts" or tournaments, and gloried in the pageantry as they honed their battle skills. In reality, knights probably violated their own ethics as often as they adhered to them; the code of chivalry provided only a veneer of symbols and ceremonies that overlay the violence at the heart of "those who fight."

Marriages were arranged with no regard for the emotions of the couple, so it is perhaps not surprising that nobles often found love outside of marriage. In noble households beginning in the twelfth century, some poets praised new ideals of love called "**courtly love**." In this romantic love, noble men promised to do anything to win the affection of a noble woman. Even though the church frowned on this new praise of adulterous love, some historians suggest that the praise of romantic love is one of the most influential ideas that emerged in the Middle Ages that set the stage for love matches and separated the West from the rest of the world.

Medieval life was violent, and to protect themselves nobles usually lived in fortified houses and castles, which by the thirteenth century had become marvels of engineering. The best castles had concentric rings of walls that guarded an interior fortress that sheltered the noble family and its retainers. These castles showed the importance of defensive **warfare** that marked the Middle Ages. It was only the fourteenth-century development of gunpowder that could breach the walls that made these fortresses obsolete.

The new weaponry developed in the fourteenth century also led to the decline of the feudal ties that had marked medieval society. Lords increasingly wanted money (called "scutage") instead of military service in return for fiefs. Lords then used this cash to hire professional armies—called "free companies" because they had no feudal ties and sold their services to the highest bidder. The feudal system deteriorated into what is sometimes called "bastard feudalism" in which the old ties of loyalty were replaced with cash payments.

Ordering Those Who Pray

From the beginning of the Middle Ages, church organization stressed bringing all religious people into a tight hierarchical organization (*see* "Religion" section). However, just as medieval secular society increasingly relied on laws to regulate the ties that bound people to each other, the church, too, began to look to contract law to confirm its order.

The turning point in church law — called "**canon law**" — came in about 1140, when the church lawyer, Gratian, issued his "Decretum," a collection of canon law that showed that church canons could form as complete a structure of jurisprudence as secular law. This collection argued that the pope was the supreme judge and had jurisdiction over any religious matter. Of course, the question of what constituted a "religious matter" quickly became contentious. For example, since the church was charged with protecting widows and orphans, they could claim jurisdiction over wills and inheritance. Again, since crimes like murder and theft were also sins, did this mean the pope was the supreme judge over these matters?

Table 3. Relationship between Wheat Prices and Crime

Date	Price of Wheat in Shillings	Numbers of Crimes Reported
1302	6	10
1314	18	45
1315	18	350
1318	3	100
1320	12	55
1321	8	200
1350	8	10

Note: These approximate figures from Norfolk, England, in the fourteenth century show a clear relationship between the rise of wheat prices and crime, although there is a short delay for crime to rise. Notice that after the population drop after the Black Death in 1348, crime fell even though prices rose a bit. Notice also how widely the prices fluctuated.
Source: Drawn from Dennis Sherman, et al. World Civilizations: Sources, Images, and Interpretations. 4th ed. Boston: McGraw-Hill, 2006, p. 155.

The eleventh century struggle for power between popes and emperors called the "**Investiture Controversy**" was in large part a question of who had legal authority at the top of medieval society. With the help of a growing number of skilled canon lawyers, thirteenth-century popes like Innocent III were able to exert authority over the secular arm of government to a remarkable degree. It appeared that the right order of medieval society placed the pope at the top of a strong hierarchy of connections that tied each person to another.

In the disasters of the fourteenth century, this situation changed. The French king Philip IV directly challenged papal authority over the issue of taxation and was able to ensure the election of a French cardinal as pope in 1304. This pope, Clement V, did not even go to Rome. Instead, he established a new papal court in Avignon, in the shadow of the French king. For the next 72 years, popes ruled from Avignon, and many Christians objected to what the Italian Petrarch called the "Babylonian captivity" of the papacy.

The Avignon papacy built up its administration, its cadre of lawyers, and its tax collectors and ruled as any effective modern state might. However, there were many who criticized this direction, arguing that the church had become all too secular while disregarding its spiritual charge. The pressure mounted on the Avignon papacy to return to Rome, and an influential mystic, Catherine of Siena was a last straw in persuading Pope Gregory XI to return to Rome.

Pope Gregory died in 1378 almost as soon as he had arrived in Rome, and the situation of the administration of the church quickly grew worse. A disputed papal election ended up with two popes. From 1378 to 1417, the church suffered from the Great Schism in which there were two and at times three popes claiming jurisdiction over Christendom.

The schism (split in the church) was resolved in the fifteenth century by church councils. This **Conciliar Movement** argued that the collective group of bishops, not the pope, held ultimate authority over church matters. This essentially argued that Christendom was more of a constitutional monarchy rather than an absolute one. The conciliarists prevailed, and in 1417 they deposed reigning popes and elected a Roman cardinal, Martin V, as the only pope. The Great Schism was over, but it had transformed the medieval papacy and the social order that it had established. No longer would "those who pray" be able to govern the society as a whole.

As fourteenth-century kings took over control from religious authorities, they also took over legal authority that had been claimed by church leaders. Canon law became incorporated into secular law with the unforseen consequence that many issues of morality—like sexual practices—became matters of secular law. It would take into the twentieth century before secular states began to sort out what was properly religious law and what was secular. This is another long-standing heritage of the medieval struggle to order society.

City Social Structure

Medieval rulers—secular and religious—did not give much thought to how the growing urban life fit into their view of the social order of the world. Indeed, they thought of cities as islands separate from the feudal and manorial ties that shaped their society. Urban residents, however, took matters into their own hands and created influential and enduring social structures of their own.

Once towns had received a charter from a local lord (*see* "Economy" section), they established ways to govern themselves. Town government was likely to take the form of a mayor (or provost) and a council. Sometimes the mayor was appointed by the lord and sometimes he was elected by his fellow townsmen. These offices were almost always held by the wealthy merchants who were recognized as town leaders. However, artisans and craftsmen quite rightly recognized that wealthy merchants were not always looking out for their interests. They formed their own groups to handle their needs; these organizations were called "**guilds**."

Guilds probably began as social, or even drinking, clubs, but they quickly became organizations to look out for the common interests of their members. Guilds maintained schools to train members' sons and helped guild widows and orphans. Guilds also acted as religious fraternities to sponsor religious festivals and help the local churches. For example, some of the marvelous stained-glass windows of cathedrals were contributed by local guilds.

In an age of much lawlessness, guilds also protected the business interests of its members. If a man in a neighboring town refused to settle his debts, guildsmen might capture the next person from that town who entered their town and hold him hostage until the debt was paid. In the freewheeling marketplace of this early capitalism, unorthodox methods were sometimes called for!

Over time, more and more specialized guilds were formed. There were guilds of spinners, weaver, fullers, and dyers, all within the cloth industry. There were also guilds of goldsmiths, bakers, and every other kind of production. Guilds regulated the quality of their production as well as their membership. An artisan began his career in a guild as an apprentice, working for a master until he learned his trade. When he was able to produce a quality product—judged a "masterpiece" by guild members—he could qualify as either a "master" with full membership in the guild, or a "journeyman," who could work in the trade for wages until an opening in the guild came available.

In time, guilds came to be the major power brokers in city government. In some cities single guilds dominated. Often the merchants' guild, which had the wealthiest members, prevailed and virtually ruled the towns. In other cities, like London, many guilds joined together to govern jointly. All in all, however, working people joining together in guilds became a force to be reckoned with.

Throughout the Middle Ages, women participated in all aspects of urban life. Women actually dominated some trades as we can see by the words we use to identify some work: The ending "ster" is a feminine ending, so trades like "brewster" (beer brewing) and "webster" (weaving) were originally dominated by women. Women through their family alliances could be guild members and inherit shops and workshops. By the fourteenth century, however, women began to be excluded from guilds and restricted to supporting family roles. In women's work, the early modern world inherited more from the restrictive Renaissance than from the more open Middle Ages.

The urban groups became significantly influential in England in the thirteenth century when the English King Edward I (r. 1272–1307) desperately needed new taxes to finance his wars. Instead of just calling his nobles and church leaders to Parliament to fulfill their obligation to give him counsel, Edward sent agents throughout the land calling two knights from every county and two townsmen (burgesses) from every city. Edward ordered that the burgesses be elected by the populace. This expanded gathering has come to be called the "Model Parliament" and shaped the future of English representative government.

As the representatives gathered they had to decide how to arrange themselves. In France, the equivalent parliament sat by order: one house for the clergy, one for the nobility, and one for the commoners ("those who work"). In England, however, a different precedent was set. The clergy sat with the upper nobility, but the lower nobility (the knights) sat with the burgesses to act together for their mutual benefit. In time, the nobles would become the House of Lords and the burgesses would become the House of Commons. This medieval institution shaped the democratic structures of the modern world.

The Byzantine Empire

The Byzantine Empire centered on the magnificent city of Constantinople and was the heir of the Roman Empire, and as such its society represented some differences from the decentralized states in the West. The court of the emperor offered a centralized authority over church and state and controlled huge amounts of wealth. Money poured in not only from the lucrative trade with Far Eastern lands, but also from royal monopolies on production of silk and purple dye, both much in demand in the West.

Even outside the royal monopolies, craftsmen in the cities of the East belonged to guilds or corporations that were strictly controlled by the state. The state regulated purchasing raw materials, marketing of finished products, manufacturing methods, prices, and profits. Government inspectors watched all aspects of production. This system led to a good deal of stability and quality control, but little technological innovation.

The emperor himself was viewed as a sacred person appointed by God to rule. He lived in a magnificent, and isolated palace complex overlooking the sea in Constantinople, and his subjects came into the royal presence prostrating themselves on the floor. Not surprisingly, this centralized empire was governed by a complex bureaucracy, which was expensive to maintain, yet quite efficient. These government employees prevented the decentralization that was so marked in the West.

The Byzantine Empire was surrounded by enemies. The Persian Empire in the East, the Muslims in the South, and the Slavs in the North always represented a threat. Therefore, the empire built and maintained a strong military to guard its borders. The backbone of the army was its heavy cavalry, which accounted for about half its force. The army was well supplied with servants who did all their work, and the generals were professional soldiers who tried to keep the old Roman tradition of rigorous discipline. During the **Crusades**, when this disciplined force met the individualistic knights from the West there was a shocking culture clash representing the two different types of armies.

The Byzantine generals used peasants in their armies in a way that the West did not, because free peasants served as infantry supporting the all-important cavalry. By the sixth and seventh centuries, the Byzantine Empire was organized by themes. The theme system made land available to free peasants who performed military service. The emperor tried to encourage this free peasantry by trying to restrict the power of great landholders, but over time wealthy landholders were able to bring a feudal system into the centralized theme structure. As nobles accumulated large estates, free peasants were reduced, and became serfs, who as in the West were bound to the soil and owed their lords rents and labor.

The Byzantine Empire was different from the West in that there always remained a large centralized state that could employ larger resources. Therefore, the Byzantine imperial household continued the ancient practice of owning large numbers of slaves. The emperor's household and lands were served by slaves that were drawn from warfare or slave traders. As slavery virtually disappeared in western Europe, it continued throughout the Middle Ages in the East.

The Byzantine Empire preserved the legal legacy of the Roman Empire. The early sixth-century emperor **Justinian** ordered the codification of Roman law that had been growing and changing for a millennium. Emperors and senators had passed decrees, judges had made precedent-setting decisions, and jurists had written complicated legal interpretations. By Justinian's time, the collections were full of obscure rites and internal contradictions, which the emperor knew needed clarifying for the law to be useful. The results of this formidable project were published in 50 books called the *Corpus Juris Civilis* (the *Body of Civil Law*) published in about A.D. 533. In this form, Roman law was revived in western Europe in about the thirteenth century and influenced canon law and modern law codes.

Although Justinian saw himself as preserving the old Roman Empire, in fact by his reign, Byzantine society was very different from the West. Justinian was the last emperor to use Latin as the language of government; subsequent emperors shifted to Greek, a language largely forgotten in the West. Church services were conducted in Greek, and the differing languages and alphabets separated the two halves of Europe.

The disruptions that fragmented the old Roman Empire in the beginning of the fifth century introduced a new society into Europe. This social order emerged in response to a new, decentralized reality in the West, and an increasingly autocratic empire in the East. Throughout, however, personal ties were important as nobility and peasantry alike found themselves bound to a hierarchy that demanded personal loyalty and contractual obligations. Also throughout Europe, these ties were increasingly legal obligations, and the rule of law slowly rose to be a significant feature of medieval society. In the fourteenth century, when disasters broke down traditional social ties, the rule of law remained as a significant heritage of medieval social order. *See also* Documents 11 and 17.

Further Reading

Arnott, Peter. *The Byzantines and Their World*. New York: St. Martin's Press, 1973.

Hanawalt, B. *The Ties That Bind: Peasant Families in Medieval England*. New York: Oxford University Press, 1986.

Herlihy, David. *Opera Muliebria: Women and Work in Medieval Europe*. New York: McGraw-Hill, 1990.

Lopez, Robert S. *The Commercial Revolution of the Middle Ages, 950–1350*. New York: Cambridge University Press, 1976.

Reynolds, Susan. *Fiefs and Vassals: The Medieval Evidence Reinterpreted*. New York: Oxford University Press, 1994.

Sayers, Jane. *Innocent III: Leader of Europe, 1198–1216*. New York: Longman, 1994.

6. SCIENCE AND TECHNOLOGY

Science refers to a systemized understanding of how the universe operates, and *technology* refers to inventions or practical applications of things to make our lives easier. In the twenty-first century, we usually assume that the former informs the latter and that the science and technology progress together. However, in the Middle Ages, that was not the case. Until the late Middle Ages, scientific discoveries were slow to come though throughout this millennium technology improved rapidly. This essay will look at both these movements.

Science

Progress in medieval science was impeded by two forces: a veneration of ancient science (with all its inaccuracies) that was carefully preserved in the **education** of the Middle Ages, and second was the desire to incorporate religion into a unified theory. In fact, the "science" of the Middle Ages included the desire to study God's laws as well as nature's laws, and to understand the "mind" of God as well as human understandings. Thus, the greatest minds of the medieval world first learned the science of the Greeks and Romans then formulated ways to include that into theology.

Medieval **medicine** remained theoretically bound to the ancient Greek physician Galen's (131–201 C.E.) views. He had claimed that all illness came from an imbalance of the four "humors" or fluids of the body: blood, bile, urine, and phlegm. He argued that each of these humors had its own properties — warm, cold, dry, and moist — and when a person was out of balance, the cure was to restore an appropriate equilibrium. For example, if a person were feverish and flushed, he or she was considered to have an excess of blood, which would be resolved by bleeding the patient. This theoretical understanding of the functions of the body persisted well into the modern age. Medieval medicine also included more practical wisdom about healthy herbs or other cures, which were included in a number of the medieval medical tracts that were preserved and studied especially at the medical school in Salerno. The famous mystic **Hildegard of Bingen** wrote a medical tract — *Causes and Cures* — that combined Galen's system with some popular cures and included a particular consideration of women's health that was absent from Galen's analysis.

The educated man or woman of the high Middle Ages also held the same view of the physical universe as had the ancient Greeks: a motionless world made of four elements: earth, water, air, and fire. Of course, medieval people observed motion in the world — flames rose upward, rocks sank in the water — but they believed all such motion was due to the fact that this world was imperfect, so the four elements were mixed. Motion came about as each element tried to find its "rightful" place. That is, fire moved upward and rocks descended.

The physics of the heavens was also drawn from the Greek Aristotle's view. The four elements of the fallen world were surrounded by circles made up of a fifth element — the "quintessence" — in which were embedded the planets and stars. They believed these circles rotated around the still earth creating beautiful music as they did so (*see* "The Arts" section). Aristotle was so revered that no one in the Middle Ages challenged this view of the universe. Or, if they did, it was not taken seriously enough to be recorded for posterity.

Medieval thinkers were acute observers of the heavens, and as such, they understood that the earth was round, and that's why they could see the motion of constellations circling the sky, and ships disappearing over the horizon. Early Vikings apparently imagined the earth to be round and flattened (like a saucer) surrounded by water.

Observations of the heavens allowed medieval thinkers to recognize that the old Julian calendar inherited from the Romans was inaccurate. Because the year is not exactly 365 days long (which is why we add leap year every 4 years), the calendar had drifted considerably. For example, by the mid-thirteenth century, the winter solstice, which should be about December 21, was occurring on December 15, and the vernal equinox occurred on March 12 instead of March 21. As Roger Bacon in 1267 claimed: "This fact cannot only the astronomer certify, but any layman with the eye can perceive it" (Gimpel, 190).

Heavenly observations included recognition of comets, eclipses, and other events. However, observing and even predicting such heavenly occurrences did not mean that observers used modern scientific techniques to interpret the events. Comets and other unusual things continued to be seen as messages from God, which needed interpretation. For example, when Halley's Comet streaked across the sky just before the Norman Invasion of England in 1066, many saw it as an omen of disaster for the realm. Such interpretations show the great difference between accurate observation of a comet and a modern scientific method — the Middle Ages were accurately called the "Age of Faith," not science.

In the fourteenth century, at the twilight of the Middle Ages, some thinkers began to question Aristotelian physics that had formed the core of medieval understandings of the universe. Two Parisian philosophers, Jean Buridan (c. 1300–1370) and Nicole Oresme (c. 1330–1382) questioned Aristotle's law of motion that lay at the core of ancient physics. They argued that a moving body acquired "impetus" that kept it going until a counterforce (such as friction) stopped it. Oresme further suggested that the idea of heavenly spheres was inaccurate because the heavenly observations could be explained by a spinning earth. When movement, not stillness, was acknowledged to be the main force of the universe, the stage was set for the modern scientific revolution, when people relied on observation, rather than on classical authorities.

In the twelfth century, many Europeans became fascinated by the ancient pseudoscience, alchemy, which is the desire to turn base metals into gold by using a "philosopher's stone." These early chemists believed that gold is the only pure metal, and that all others are impure versions of it. Therefore, if they could only figure out how to distill the pure gold from the mixed metals, they would be rich. Of course, the theory was false, but alchemists in their laboratories became the ancestors of modern chemists in learning how to melt and separate elements. One practical result of alchemists' efforts was the development of effective stills that allowed for the production of brandy and other alcoholic beverages.

The one area of significant scientific innovation in medieval Europe was in the field of mathematics. Like other sciences, Europeans inherited Roman mathematics. However, the Romans (like the Greeks before them) were handicapped by the fact that they did not use a zero. (This is why the B.C.E–C.E. system of dating begins with the year "1" instead of more logically with a zero.) The cumbersome Roman numerals made all but the simplest arithmetic calculations possible only for experts. For example: To multiply VI x VI (6 x 6) might take several steps. You would have to do simple doubling, then add the results:

II x VI (2 x 6) = XII
II x VI = XII
II x VI = XII
VI x VI = XXXVI

Imagine how complicated more difficult problems would be!

Medieval thinkers knew the importance of mathematics. In the mid-twelfth century, for example, Thierry of Chartres argued "on mathematics all rational explanation of the universe depended" (Gimpel, 179). Thierry died in 1155 before the real revolution in mathematics came about that brought the numerical tools that ultimately allowed the calculations that form the underpinning of our modern science. These tools came from India via the Muslim world.

Around 1180, a Pisan merchant sent his son, Leonardo Fibonacci, to study with Muslims in North Africa. Fibonacci discovered the usefulness of the Hindu-Arabic numerals that contained the all-important zero. Leonardo published a widely diffused book called *The Book of the Abacus*, in which he claimed the "nine Indian figures are 9 8 7 6 5 4 3 2 1. With these nine figures and the sign 0, any number may be written" (Gies, 226). Fibonacci's book dealt with practical business applications, such as calculating interest, profit, and percentages. However, he also made great strides in theoretical mathematics. He is best known for originating the "Fibonacci sequence," which describes the relationship between two or more successive terms by a formula. But his greatest achievement was in developing algebra (the word itself is a Muslim term).

The use of what we call "Arabic numerals" (and what the medieval world called "Hindu numerals") spread slowly. However, its impact was great on the early medieval scientists who immediately saw its use. Trigonometry in the West was established in the thirteenth century at Oxford University, and the precise measurements of optics were facilitated by the use of the new numbering system. Truly, Western science began with the spread of Hindu numerals.

We can look back at the new mathematics as a singular turning point in the history of science, but for medieval thinkers, this was only a sideline. They believed the high point of their scientific discoveries lay in the philosophical school of **scholasticism**. Scholasticism was the attempt to reconcile faith with reason—that is, to understand with one's mind what one believed with one's heart. This involved a noble attempt to understand the natural and the divine worlds in one unifying system. The twelfth-century rediscovery of the advanced logic by Aristotle seemed to give thinkers the tools to understand even the mind of God.

The greatest of the scholastics was Thomas Aquinas, whose huge work, the *Summa Theologiae*, represents his summary of all knowledge through which the believer is led to God. Through this long tract full of questions and discussions, he adapted Aristotle's ethics and politics to serve a Christian society. His famous "Five Proofs of God" demonstrate how the scholastics believed that observations of the natural world combined with faith can help us understand God. For instance, he showed that we can observe motion on earth, and all earthly motion is caused by some other motion. When we trace back all the motion that is caused, our logical mind leads us to understand that there must be some first mover that originated all other motion. This "unmoved mover" is God. Thus, our understanding of the physical world of motion leads us to an understanding of one of the elements of God.

For all of Aquinas's emphasis on using the natural world as a path to truth, he did not study the natural world much. Instead, he read Aristotle's views on the natural world. In this way, scholasticism did not lead directly to our modern scientific methods. However, medieval reaction against the shortcomings of scholasticism did. Some thinkers believed that the scholastics were fundamentally wrong to try to approach God through logic. Many felt that the proper way to approach God was through faith alone, because God should not be limited by the rules of logic. These people believe in **mysticism**, or the ability to feel a union with God: a union of feeling rather than thought.

The most devastating intellectual critique of scholasticism came from Franciscan thinkers, and the most important of these was the brilliant philosopher, William of Ockham (c. 1285–1349). Ockham argued that philosophical speculations were interesting logical exercises, but not a path to certain truth. Instead, through his philosophy of New Nominalism, he argued that it was impossible to know God or prove his existence through reason because God was all-powerful, so he did not have to act logically. Therefore, any attempt to know God through logic was a waste of time. Ockham's findings led to a decline in abstract logic, but a rise in scientific observation. Instead of studying God's mind, human intellect should focus on observing and studying the world—this is the beginning of modern science.

The heart of modern science lies in a method of observation and experiment. This scientific method began in the late Middle Ages at Oxford, where philosophers of the New Nominalism had begun to turn their attention to studying the world. One of the important forerunners of this movement was Robert Grosseteste (c. 1175–1253), who was the first chancellor of Oxford University. He emphasized that natural philosophy had to be based on mathematics and experimentation and further believed that the study of optics was the key to understanding the physical world. He suggested that lenses could be used to magnify small objects, and the development of eyeglasses in the thirteenth century may well have been influenced by Grosseteste's studies of lenses.

Grosseteste's fame has been eclipsed by the accomplishments of his successor and student, Roger Bacon (c. 1214–1292). Bacon, too, was a Franciscan at Oxford, and though he had never met Grosseteste, he greatly admired the master's work. Bacon refined Grosseteste's studies of optics, and his description of animal eyes and optics nerves were pathbreaking. Bacon also claimed that mathematics was key to scientific knowledge and was embarrassed by the inaccuracies that had crept into the Julian calendar. Bacon appealed to Pope Clement IV to reform the calendar, but his calls went unheeded during his lifetime. However, papal reform of the calendar would lead Copernicus to offer his heliocentric view of the universe in the sixteenth century—the starting point of the modern scientific revolution. Bacon's most-remembered contribution to science was his demonstration that experimentation was more important than logic. He was a man of the future of science, not one of the medieval past.

Technology

Science may explore the truth and mysteries that lay behind the visible world, but technology makes everything work and our lives easier. In spite of this practical advantage, people through most of the past have seen technology as a poor cousin to the favored science. Aristotle favored a life of the mind in which people contemplated abstract truths—essentially science—over those who practiced what he called "banausic arts," manual labor in creating things. As medieval thinkers venerated everything Aristotelian, they transmitted the devaluation of banausic arts. However, the situation in the Middle Ages was different from that in the classical world in some ways that contributed to the growth of technology. Most significant was the end of slave labor. No longer was there an abundance of labor to produce all that was necessary. Instead, medieval people were remarkably quick to adopt labor-saving devices, which led to a technological revolution that changed the face of European society.

By the ninth century, some medieval thinkers saw the need to dignify technology above the disparaging position it held with Aristotle. John Scotus Erigena in the ninth century invented the term *artes mechanicae* (mechanical arts) to supplement the liberal arts in a well-rounded education. In the twelfth century, another scholar—Honorius of Autun—developed this idea further by adding mechanics to the liberal arts curriculum He wrote: "Concerning mechanics . . . it teaches . . . every work in metals, wood, or marble, in addition to painting, sculpture, and all arts which are done with the hands" (Gies, 11). Thus, from the twelfth century onward, thinkers—and scientists—had recognized the importance of technology in the spectacular growth of European medieval society.

To study the history of medieval technology is to review the many inventions that changed society rather than to consider individual inventors. This is largely because virtually all the great innovations that changed the West were invented in the East. Chinese inventions spread slowly to India, the Muslim world, and then into the West. Sometimes we can trace direct and sudden transmissions—silk worms, for example—but other times we just know that items that had been used in China for centuries slowly appeared in the West. The success of the medieval West was in its ability to adapt the inventions that came from older societies of the East. The easiest way to consider these technological innovations is to look at various industries that benefitted from new technology.

At the heart of most of the change was a revolution in power. Early medieval Europe suffered from a shortage of labor. This caused people to rely more on animal power and, more importantly for the history of technology, on new sources of power: water and wind. Waterwheels in particular offered reliable sources of energy all along rivers and even in the tidal areas of northern Europe where the difference between low and high tide was extreme.

For water mills to work, builders had to solve a specific problem: converting the rotary, horizontal, motion (of a wheel being turned by running water) to vertical motion. This was accomplished by using a cam, projecting from the axle of the waterwheel. Once this technological problem was resolved, builders could harness waterpower to accomplish many tasks. The most common watermills were used to grind grain, freeing people from the essential, but labor-intensive task of converting hard grain into useable flour to make bread. The watermill would power two large horizontal grindstones that made short work of the grain. But this was just the beginning.

Watermills were adapted to power triphammers to stimulate the constant food kneading that was necessary to break down fibers in other occupations. Waterwheel-powered triphammers greatly facilitated the difficult process of making thickened (also called "fulled") wool fabrics, like felt. This had previously involved hard and disagreeable work as people had to pound the wet wool that was soaking in various solvents. Triphammer mills also pounded hemp stalks to make linen and broke oak bark into small pieces for tanning. Other agricultural products needed milling as well: Mustard and poppy seeds were turned into paste, and vegetable products were made into dyes and pigments.

The numbers of watermills that proliferated in the early Middle Ages were astonishing. The Domesday Book, a survey prepared in England in 1086, records 5,624 mills in England: This is a remarkable three mills for every mile of river. Comparable figures exist for other areas of Europe, including the Byzantine Empire in the East. One analysis suggests that there was a mill for every forty-six peasant households (Gies, 113). This meant that peasants ate more baked bread instead of boiled, unground porridge, which allowed for a more portable food supply. Bread travels better than oatmeal.

Once builders had the concept of watermills, they applied it to all kinds of conditions. There were floating mills that could be moved so they wouldn't obstruct river traffic, and mills that were permanently attached to bridges. Some mills harnessed water flowing over the top, but others were undershot mills, harnessing waterpower from a low river flowing beneath. Modern calculations reveal the impressive advantages in power that constantly improved waterwheels offered medieval peasants: The Roman donkey or slave-powered grinding stone produced about one-half horsepower. The undershot (water flowing beneath) medieval wheel produced about three horsepower, and the medieval overshot wheel could generate as much as 40 to 60 horsepower (Gies, 115).

Waterwheels depended upon access to rapidly flowing rivers, so all regions could not be served by this technological wonder. Medieval engineers, however, took the principles of water-driven power and applied it to other sources of energy. Tidal mills were recorded in Ireland as early as the seventh century and in the Venetian lagoon before 1050. However, by the end of the twelfth century, windmills began to appear in the English Channel and the North Sea. Windmills were probably developed in Persia and spread through Muslim lands, but the Europeans modified the design to make it extremely useful. They reversed the waterwheel's design by placing the horizontal axle at the top of the mill to be turned by sails. The power would then be geared to stones below. Wind now joined water a power that was available to medieval people.

I should note that this technological revolution in harnessing power was not universally praised. It required a substantial investment to build these mills, and lords of the land recouped the investment by charging peasants fees to use the mills. Local peasants were required to grind their grain (or press their oil and wine) at the local mill, and pay the required costs. This led to some boycotts in the fourteenth century, but the future lay with technology. In the long run, people will pay for labor-saving devices, and the mills of medieval Europe represented the first major innovation in labor saving in the West.

Beyond power, the basis of medieval technology all over the world was iron. From the beginnings of the Iron Age in about 1200 B.C.E., metallurgists heated iron repeatedly in a hot charcoal furnace to combine carbon molecules with iron. Then the iron had to be pounded to become strong. Smiths were valued craftsmen who could work the metal. Throughout the Middle Ages more and more iron came into circulation, allowing for use of horse shoes, metal plowshares, and cast iron cooking pots. However, in the fourteenth century European engineers (probably inspired by Chinese models) applied the technology of the waterwheel to forging iron and created the water-powered blast furnace.

A waterwheel could pump pairs of bellows continuously into a furnace, substantially raising the temperature. The higher heat increased the carbon uptake rapidly, producing an alloy that had a higher carbon content. Thus, iron was improved. Not only that, but the blast furnaces could run continuously for weeks or months at a time producing more iron than ever before. The molten metal flowed into several large, shallow depressions that reminded smiths of a sow with suckling pigs, so they called this "pig iron," a term that remained long after ironsmiths forgot their rural roots (Gies, 202). The new mechanized forges produced much more iron cheaply, so Europe entered a newly invigorated iron age.

Although iron was useful in tools and cooking, it is best remembered for its application in **warfare**. In the late eighth century, French forces under Charles Martel, fielded horsemen on saddles equipped with stirrups, an innovation that had spread from India. Stirrups gave horsemen enough balance that a mounted soldier could directly engage an enemy (instead of riding by shooting arrows or throwing spears). The mounted knight was born and became the basis of medieval armies under **feudal law**. These knights, often called "men of iron," depended upon defensive armor of increasing thickness and complexity—chain mail, developed by Vikings, was worn over thick padding, and in the fourteenth century, plate mail was placed on top of the chain.

In the fourteenth century, changes in the technology of warfare appeared in the West that transformed feudal society. In the **Hundred Years' War**, the English made use of the Welsh longbow, which offered substantial advantage in range and firepower over the crossbow. Furthermore, in Switzerland, foot soldiers armed with long pikes successfully held off mounted knights. The final transformation in warfare, however, came when gunpowder, developed in China, began to spread. The first European mention of gunpowder occurs in 1268, but by the late fourteenth century, the use of guns and cannons began to change the defensive posture of knights in armor in favor of foot soldiers armed with the new weapons. The future lay with large armies of foot soldiers with guns rather than mounted knights with iron swords.

Through most of the Middle Ages, the Byzantine Empire held the lead in the technology of warfare. Their most dreaded weapon was "Greek fire," believed to be an incendiary mixture of crude oil, bitumen, resin, and sulfur. The secret of this recipe was carefully guarded, and Byzantine forces could pour or pump the deadly mixture on wooden ships in the harbor or on armored knights in the battlefield. The other military technological advance enjoyed by the Byzantines was systems of torches and mirrors for rapid communication. However, the coming of gunpowder leveled the advantage of Byzantine technology: The great walls of Constantinople that had withstood invading armies fell to the cannons of the Turks in 1453, a date that signals the end of the Middle Ages.

In **agriculture**, too, medieval technology created a small agricultural revolution. By the eleventh century, a new padded horse collar that had been developed in China appeared in western Europe, allowing more rapid horses to plow alongside (or in place of) slower oxen. A new, heavy wheeled plow came into service that efficiently turned the heavy clay soils of northern Europe bringing more land into cultivation.

By the twelfth century, many manors moved to a three-field system of cultivation in which one-third of the land was planted in the spring, another in the fall, and the remaining third was left fallow to improve its fertility. This replaced an old Roman system of two-field cultivation in which half the land was left fallow each year and immediately brought more land into cultivation. In addition, the three-field system stimulated the growth of new crops that boosted production. Villagers began to plant legumes, such as peas and beans, which add nitrogen to the soil, thus fertilizing the subsequent grain crop. Legumes also provided an excellent source of protein, which vastly improved the villagers' diets.

These major agricultural innovations were further aided by other labor-saving devices that spread from the East. For example, wheelbarrows appeared in Europe speeding peasant labor. In western Europe, peasants also began to harvest using a sickle, instead of bending over with a scythe. Of course, the increased availability of iron helped produce all these tools. The agricultural revolution in the West allowed the population to double between the eleventh and the fourteenth centuries.

The Byzantine Empire, which always boasted a larger population of workers, was not as quick to adopt these labor-saving tools. Instead, through most of the Middle Ages, the Eastern empire continued agricultural techniques that had served the Roman Empire.

The most labor-intensive occupation for women of the ancient and medieval worlds was making cloth. There was a constant desire to improve ways to prepare the raw materials—mostly wool, but later cotton—to make clothing. It is perhaps not surprising that the nineteenth-century industrial revolution first mechanized the fabric industry. The Middle Ages saw its own improvements in the production of fabric and in acquiring new fabrics. We have seen that watermills were put to use to make felt, but that was only one innovation.

The Byzantine Empire achieved a great advance in fabrics in the sixth century, for at that time, some monks smuggled silk worms and white mulberries to feed them back to Byzantium. This began a silk industry in the Byzantine Empire that finally broke the age-old monopoly held by China. In the thirteenth century, after the Fourth **Crusade**, the secret of silk was brought to Italy.

In most of Europe, however, the main fabric was wool, which had to be washed, combed, then spun into thread. The traditional instrument for spinning was the drop spindle, a stick with a weighted disk at the bottom. The spinner spun the spindle, which twisted the attached fibers into threads. Women spun wool like this constantly, even while doing other tasks. In the thirteenth century, Europeans acquired spinning wheels that had probably originated in the Near East, making the process much more rapid. Once thread was spun, it could be woven into cloth on a loom. The earliest medieval looms were vertical, but by the late Middle Ages, these were replaced by horizontal looms, further speeding a weaver's work. Knitting was introduced into Europe some time in the twelfth century.

A final major revolution in medieval technology came in navigation, which culminated in the explorations of the Renaissance that marked the end of the medieval age. The greatest ships of the early Middle Ages were the Viking longships, astonishingly seaworthy oak vessels propelled by a square sail and banks of oars. Vikings navigated by the position of the sun and of the North Star at night, but their ability to navigate the treacherous waters of the stormy north remains a wonder to modern sailors.

Improvements in sails stimulated shipping so much that by the thirteenth century shipping in the Mediterranean doubled in volume. The first improvement was the development of the "lanteen" sail, a triangular sail that allowed ships to sail closer to the wind, which means they can sail almost into a head wind, instead of waiting for a tailwind. In addition, more masts were rigged allowing ships with two and three masts to capture even more wind.

There remained the problem of how to know where you are going when out of sight of land. In the twelfth century, Christian Europe had acquired the astrolabe from Muslim Spain. The astrolabe essentially projected a map of the heavens on a plate that the navigator could rotate to show the local coordinates. The twelfth-century philosopher Abelard and his wife Heloise were so enamored of this new instrument that they named their son "Astrolabe," which shows the enthusiasm that these new technological wonders stimulated in Europe. The astrolabe allowed ships to sail at night using the stars.

A magnetic compass had been invented in China and improved by the eighth century C.E. This was created by rubbing an iron needle with a magnet, then floating the needle on water on a bit of wood. The needle would then point roughly north (varying with the meridian where the reading is taken). The compass was improved by mountings that allowed it to float independent of the ship's motion. By the thirteenth century, medieval European navigators had access to the improved compass and had begun to make sophisticated use of it in conjunction with navigational charts to find their way when moving out of the sight of land. The technological improvements were in place to allow Europeans to begin to explore outside the Mediterranean, a marker of the end of the Middle Ages.

Further Reading

Crombie, A.C. *Medieval and Early Modern Science*. 2 vols. New York: Anchor Books, 1959.

DeVries, Kelly. *Medieval Military Technology*. Peterborough, Canada: Broadview Press, 1992.

Gies, Frances, and Joseph Gies. *Cathedral, Forge, and Waterwheel: Technology and Invention in the Middle Ages*. New York: Harper Perennial, 1994.

Gimpel, Jean. *The Medieval Machine: The Industrial Revolution of the Middle Ages*. New York: Penguin, 1976.

Long, Pamela O., ed. *Science and Technology in Medieval Society*. New York: New York Academy of Sciences, 1985.

Pacey, Arnold. *Technology in World Civilization*. Cambridge, MA: Harvard University Press, 1991.

Reynolds, Terry S. *Stronger Than a Hundred Men: A History of the Vertical Water Wheel*. Baltimore: Johns Hopkins University Press, 1983.

White, Lynn, Jr. *Medieval Technology and Social Change*. Oxford, UK: Oxford University Press, 1962.

7. GLOBAL TIES

People move around. This truth has characterized humanity as long as there have been humans. From our origins in Africa about seven million years ago, humans have moved in waves from that continent to populate the earth. Movement over long spaces in the ancient world took so much time we can hardly comprehend it. For example, people moving across a land bridge from Asia to Alaska might have taken about 2,000 years to move down to the tip of South America, but move they did. Why do people move? The answers in the ancient world match today's motivations: People want a better life, more goods, novelty, or to escape situations or people they don't like.

Given this reality of human movement, it should not be surprising that during the 1,000 years of the Middle Ages, some Europeans moved to far ends of the earth. Although it is true that most people did not travel more than 20 miles in their lifetimes, a few people traveled very far. However, individuals did not need to travel very far for ideas, goods, and inventions to move great distances (*see* "Science and Technology" section). For example, archaeologists studying the Stone Age have discovered weapons made from bloodstone from islands off Scotland all the way in central Europe. No individual needed to travel that far to bring the weapons; the artifacts themselves could have traveled from neighbor to neighbor across vast expanses of land. This kind of technological diffusion was also present in the Middle Ages. Although we can ascertain that things like wheelbarrows or gunpowder came from China to Europe by a certain date, we do not suggest that one person traveled those distances to bring the artifact. Therefore, when we study global ties in the Middle Ages, we are really looking at the movement of peoples and the diffusion of goods and ideas.

In his Pulitzer Prize-winning book, *Guns, Germs, and Steel,* Jared Diamond demonstrates that Europe was favorably placed for things to move to it. Because Eurasia is on an east–west axis, plants and animals can spread more easily than if it were oriented on a north–south direction. This allowed neolithic farmers and herdsmen to acquire domesticated plants native to the Middle East and animals—such as pigs and horses—from as far away as China (Diamond, 176–191). This whole land mass was set up to take advantage of the best developments from a huge span of territory. At first, China was in the forefront of invention, but with cultural diffusion, the whole Eurasian landmass benefitted.

In spite of the obvious benefits of trade and travel, movement remained very slow throughout the Middle Ages. Overland travel was hampered by bad roads and dangers from weather and bandits, and a speed of 3 miles an hour was considered good. A four-wheeled wagon with a pair of horses (the best the Middle Ages had to offer) might travel about 25 miles a day hauling as much as 1,300 pounds. However, large trains with many wagons and guards usually moved only 10 to 12 miles a day. A boat was more efficient, covering perhaps 80 miles in a day traveling downstream (Singman, 214–217), so it is easy to see why cities grew along the great rivers of Europe.

Seagoing vessels were also slow by modern standards. The crossing from England to the West Coast of France might take 4 days, which today is a day excursion. The Mediterranean Sea that today seems a small barrier was formidable. The trip from Venice to Jaffa (the port that served Jerusalem) lasted a month. Marco Polo and his family took 3½ years by horseback to get to the capital of China in the thirteenth century, and by the fourteenth century, this journey would have taken even longer.

In spite of the pace and hazards of medieval travel, people and ideas did move, and European society benefitted from the dynamic exchange. In this essay, I will tour the world with medieval travelers, showing the most famous global interactions. However, these heroic ventures always took place against a quiet, but steady, drumbeat of slower cultural diffusion that transformed the West.

Middle East, North Africa, and the Muslim World

The earliest "interactions" between Christendom and the Muslim world came through the conquests that split the Mediterranean basin in the seventh and eighth centuries. Muslim armies swept out of Arabia capturing North Africa and Palestine from the Byzantine Empire, then crossed into Spain conquering most of the Visigothic kingdom. It was only the military skill of Charles Martel that stopped the Muslim incursion into northern Europe. By the beginning of the ninth century, the initial momentum of Muslim invasion had ended. From then on, Christians and Muslims had to interact with each other. Sometimes this took the form of trade and negotiation, more often interactions were on the battlefield.

The ninth-century emperor **Charlemagne** was the first medieval ruler who exerted enough centralized power to catch the notice of monarchs outside Europe. Charlemagne and the Muslim ruler of the 'Abbasid Caliphate, Harun al-Raschid (r. 786–809) shared a common suspicion of the Byzantine Empire that bordered both their lands. Consequently, they engaged in friendly negotiations, even exchanging valuable gifts. Harun al-Raschid gave Charlemagne a great elephant named Abulabbas, that caused a stir through Charlemagne's lands as it traveled in the company of the emperor.

Chroniclers of Charlemagne's reign also claimed he received envoys from the "King of the Africans," who brought lions, bears, and precious dyes. Charlemagne in turn subsidized the Africans, who the chronicler claimed were "constantly oppressed by poverty" (Notker, 147). These hints of interactions between Europe and Sub-Saharan Africa are tantalizing demonstrations of the continued global ties that marked European society even in the early Middle Ages.

The most famous contact between Western Europe and the Muslim world came through the **crusades**, in which Europeans fought Muslim armies over occupation of Jerusalem and its surrounding lands, what Europeans called the "Holy Land." In the eleventh century, a tenuous balance of power between the Byzantine Empire and the Muslims who controlled the Holy Land shifted. The Seljuk Turks, a fierce central Asian tribe who had converted to Islam reinforced the Muslim armies threatening Byzantium. The Turks imposed new taxes on Christian pilgrims, offending many. In 1071, Byzantine forces had suffered a crushing defeat by the Turks at the Battle of Manzikert, losing control of Asia Minor. Now the Turks seemed to threaten Europe itself.

The Byzantine Emperor Alexius I Comnenus (r. 1081–1118) appealed to Pope Urban II for military help to hold off the threatening Turks. The pope responded by calling for a Crusade, promising soldiers that God would support them fighting in this holy cause. He told departing soldiers to wear the sign of the cross on their breasts as they left Europe and to wear it victoriously on their backs upon their return. This symbol caused these soldiers to be called "crusaders," and the movement this launched lasted about 200 years as waves of Christian knights left Europe to confront Muslims on the battlefields.

The first crusaders were vividly described by the Byzantine emperor's daughter Anna Comnena. She articulated the Byzantine position that the crusaders were simply devious soldiers of fortune, who wanted to carve land for themselves instead of serving under the command of the Byzantine emperor. She was not far wrong, for many of the crusaders were younger sons looking for land of their own to rule.

The first crusade (observed by Anna Comnena) in 1099 was successful for the Christian armies. After a bloody capture of Jerusalem, crusaders established kingdoms in the Holy Land along the coast of the Mediterranean from south of Jerusalem up to modern Syria and the edge of Modern Turkey in the city of Edessa. The crusader principalities served as outposts of western European culture in the East, facilitating the travel of pilgrims from Europe. However, these crusaders were also transformed by the surrounding Muslim society. Generations in these crusader states learned to eat different foods, bathe more regularly, and acquired a taste for urban life. Even local Muslims commented on how much more "civilized" were the resident Christians than their cruder European relations.

Needless to say, the relations between Muslims and crusaders were not completely friendly, and Muslims slowly began to take back these lands. In 1144, Edessa fell, and in 1187, the Muslim Saladin retook Jerusalem. From 1147 until 1270, there were eight major crusades sent from Europe to try to reclaim the Holy Land. Although many of these crusades were led by some of the greatest leaders of the West—Richard the Lion-Hearted, Frederick Barbarossa, Phillip II, and Louis IX—they were unsuccessful in holding back the tide of Muslim reconquest.

Some of the crusades went spectacularly awry. The Fourth Crusade never reached the Holy Land because crusaders ended up capturing and sacking

Constantinople—the Christian capital of the Eastern empire. The seventh and eighth crusades, led by the saintly French King Louis IX tried to approach the Holy Land by attacking North Africa. Louis even died in Tunis. Perhaps the height of misplaced religious zeal took place during the Children's Crusade (1212–1213) when some preachers argued that crusaders had lost God's help through their misdeeds, and only the innocent might save the Holy Land. Although some historians question whether this appalling incident occurred, contemporary sources say thousands of innocent children died or were sold into slavery as they tried to go on crusade.

The crusades spurred the emergence of new **Military Orders** of knights who followed a monastic rule and who served as a crucial part of the permanent garrison guarding the Holy Land. The Knights Templars were the most famous of these orders, but they also included the Knights of St. John. These Military Orders became very wealthy and powerful for they served as the bankers of the pilgrims.

Finally, in 1291, the Muslims seized the last crusader outpost on the Asian mainland when the fortified city of Acre fell. This was a terrible military disaster for the West, and the last frightened Christians in the Holy Land paid shipmasters great fortunes to take them out of the doomed city. Knights Templars died courageously while guarding the evacuation of Christians from the burning city. The medieval crusades were over, but they left a legacy of mistrust between Christian and Muslim that continues into the twenty-first century.

The Christian reconquest of Spain that was conducted slowly throughout the Middle Ages provided other opportunities for Christian and Muslim interaction. By the eleventh century, Christian Spain was made up of several independent kingdoms: Leon, Castile, Navarre, Aragon and Barcelona. Rulers of these kingdoms slowly reconquered territories previously held by Muslims. However, as areas were conquered, and Christians settled, they interacted with the Muslim residents and cultural mingling took place. Christians learned about irrigation techniques, acquired a taste for some eastern foods (like peaches), and adopted some Muslim building techniques. By the thirteenth centuries, Spanish kings had recovered the Balearic islands of Minorca and Majorca from Muslims, and by 1252, Muslims only held the southern province of Granada, which they held until the fifteenth century.

In the twelfth century, as part of their conquests, Spaniards recovered precious manuscripts of Aristotle—complete with commentaries by Muslim and Jewish scholars. These texts quickly spread through the universities in the West, stimulating an intellectual movement called "**scholasticism**," that came to be the defining philosophy of the Middle Ages.

Outside Spain, western Europeans had the most direct contact with Muslims in southern Italy and Sicily. In the ninth century, Muslims had conquered Sicily and raided southern Italy, where there was considerable political confusion. Byzantine officials ruled some districts and Germanic chieftains ruled others, and there was almost continual warfare among these groups. In the eleventh century, a band of Norman knights returning from pilgrimage in Jerusalem stopped in southern Italy and saw opportunity. Two brothers Robert Guiscard and Roger successfully conquered Sicily and the Byzantine possessions in southern Italy. This introduced a strong dynasty in Sicily. Robert's successors built a strong state with a highly centralized government.

Significant for the cultural mixing that took place in Sicily, the rulers tried to give equal treatment to the various peoples under their rule. Government documents were issued in Latin, Greek, and Arabic, and Muslim laws were enforced in the Muslim community by traveling judges. This acceptance of the diverse traditions of the peoples of Sicily allowed for considerable sharing of knowledge and traditions among them.

Perhaps the height of the interaction between Muslim and Christian in Sicily came in the person of Frederick II (1215–1250), the Holy Roman Emperor. Frederick was half Sicilian by birth and was not interested in his German lands. He virtually ignored those territories and lived in Sicily. He was highly educated and had been deeply influenced by Muslim culture. He was even rumored to have a harem filled with Muslim women, and he happily entered into friendly relations with Muslim princes. In response to papal pressure, Frederick went on crusade to the Holy Land, but inciting the anger of the pope, he peacefully negotiated a peace that promised freedom of religion to Christians and Muslims in Jerusalem. However, this kind of balanced interaction between Muslims and Christians was exceptional in the Middle Ages and was viewed with deep suspicion by the other leaders of Christendom.

Throughout the Middle Ages, Europeans had little knowledge of Sub-Saharan Africa. Europeans knew there was gold in West Africa and seem to have had knowledge of the islands on the eastern coast of the continent. Beyond that, Muslim monopoly of the caravan routes across the Sahara kept Europeans away. Only in the fourteenth century, with Portuguese and Genoese explorations beginning along the West Coast of Africa did the situation change somewhat. The Portuguese conquest of the Canary Islands in the fourteenth century gave Europeans a foothold on the edge of the continent that would be increased in the centuries of the Renaissance.

Asia

Western Europeans were drawn to East Asia for two main reasons: to forward Christendom to find allies against Islam, and for trade with the valuable spices, silks, and luxury goods. These two motives remained intertwined throughout the medieval period and into the explorations of the early modern world.

How Expensive Were Spices?

8 bushels of grain (called a "quarter") can feed one person for a year.
1 quarter of grain cost about 6 shillings.
Spices available in Europe ranged from 1 to 3 shillings a pound.
Saffron cost 12 to 16 shillings per pound.

Source: Paul B. Newman. *Daily Life in the Middle Ages.* London: Macfarland & Co., 2001.

From the earliest years of the Middle Ages there had been a tradition that the apostle Thomas had gone to India to preach and had been martyred there. By the twelfth century, a man claiming to be an Indian bishop named John visited Pope Calixtus II in Rome and gave further details of the church Thomas allegedly founded in India. These stories, along with some crusader encounters with Syrian Christians, spurred European interest in finding Christian allies in the Far East. Travellers began to seek a mythical "Prester John," a Christian king of a great nation—first located in Asia, then in Africa—who would help in crusades against Muslims.

In the thirteenth century, the Mongol invasions changed the circumstances for western travelers. By 1300, the Mongols had established an empire that extended from China to Russia. This empire encompassed an extraordinary diversity of peoples and religions — from Muslims to Christians to Buddhists — and it accommodated them seemingly without conflict. This unified empire also crated a huge trade area through which goods and ideas traveled easily.

The great Kublai Khan, who was the first leader in the Yuan dynasty of China, encouraged non-Chinese people to serve in his administration and expressed an interest in various religions. One of the great Khan's favorite wives was Chabi, a Nestorian Christian. The popes saw a wonderful opportunity to try to convert the Mongols to Christianity and sent a series of embassies to visit the Great Khan himself. One envoy was the Franciscan Giovanni di Piano Carpini who left Europe in 1245 and wrote a *History of the Mongols*, which fascinated his contemporaries. When another Franciscan William of Rubruck arrived in Karakorum, Mongolia, in 1254, he found many foreigners at the court, including Parisian goldsmiths, envoys from Greece, and many others. Neither envoy made much headway converting the Mongols to Christianity, but they did leave a body of information about the Far East that encouraged other Europeans to make the journey.

The missions to the east reached their high point in the fourteenth century with the work of the Franciscan John of Monte Corvino. He described the hostility of the Nestorian Christians, who had been in China for a long time, but also described some positive achievements. For example, he built a church in Beijing with a tower and three bells where he baptized six-thousand people.

Trade missions to the East are probably even more well known than the religious missions. In the middle of the thirteenth century, Italian city-states led the way in international trade as Venetian and Genoese vessels appeared on the Caspian Sea and the Indian Ocean. Of course, any long-distance trade required a stable currency, and in the thirteenth century, Genoa, Florence, and Venice introduced gold coins that were to become international standards of value. Perhaps not surprising given the distances involved, the volume of eastern trade was small: In the fourteenth century the volume of Venetian long-distance trade was only about 1,000 to 2,000 tons (Phillips, 97), but it was very valuable, so the profits were great.

Table 4. Percent of a City's Trade that Is International

Date	Genoa	Marseilles	London
1270	22%	90%	Not available
1293	100%	82%	Not available
1340	42%	100%	Not available
1350	42%	70%	Not available
1400	65%	30%	10%
1450	30%	45%	50%

Note: These approximate figures show the shifting nature of international trade as events like the Black Death affected people's abilities to engage in the lucrative trade. Notice the shifting of trade from Italy to the north at the end of the Middle Ages.
Source: Drawn from R.S. Lopez and H.A. Miskimin. "The Economic Depression of the Renaissance." *The Economic History Review*, 2nd Ser., 14 (1962): 421.

The most famous western Europeans who took advantage of the Venetian experience in trade were Marco **Polo** and his father and uncle, who traveled to the far reaches of the Mongolian empire in the thirteenth century. The journey took them 3½ years by horseback, which testifies to the hardships of overland travel even through the relatively peaceful Mongol empire. The Polos stayed at the khan's court for 17 years, and Marco apparently served as an emissary of the khan himself. When the Polos returned home to Venice, they brought back a wealth of spices, silks, and other luxuries. The extravagant items were so impressive that other anonymous merchants followed; by 1300 there was even a community of Italians living in China.

Perhaps Marco Polo's most important contribution was a book about his voyages. Few believed the exotic tales of the traveler, but the book did excite the imagination of adventurers. It fueled the great age of exploration that followed—Christopher Columbus carried a well-marked copy of the book through his voyages.

By the fifteenth century, however, there had been much that split Europe's connection with East Asia. The **bubonic plague** that caused such damage in western Europe had begun in Asia and contributed to the fall of the Yuan dynasty that had welcomed westerners. The growth of the Muslim Ottoman Empire that took Constantinople in the mid-fifteenth century further disrupted the overland trade routes with the East. At the end of the Middle Ages, Europeans would look for new routes to Asia—across the Atlantic and around the coast of Africa.

North America

In the tenth century, Viking explorers sailed their longships far and wide. They traveled down rivers as they settled in Slavic lands, they sailed around Spain into the Mediterranean as they captured Sicily, and they struck out across the sea to the west and settled Iceland and Greenland. In the course of their westward travels, some Viking explorers landed in North America.

Apparently, a young merchant named Bjarni Herjolfsson was blown off course as he sailed to Greenland and sighted lands to the south and west. Upon his return, he told his story, and about 15 years later Leif Erikson, called "the Lucky" successfully arrived at the land Bjarni had seen. Leif with his crew of thirty-five men landed on several places to the west of Greenland, probably Baffin Island, Labrador, and then "Vinland," somewhere between the Gulf of St. Lawrence and New Jersey (Magnusson, 55–56). They wintered in this land that offered abundant fish, game, and fodder. Leif named the land "Vinland" for the wild grapes that grew there.

In the spring, Leif loaded a towboat with timber and grape vines and returned to his home in Greenland. There was much talk about the rich land Leif had found and Leif's brother Thorvald wanted to return to explore further. This time the explorers encountered and fought some Native Americans. In the battles, Thorvald died and was buried in North America. The remaining Vikings returned back to Greenland with more tales of the new lands.

A captain named Karlsefni decided to go to Vinland to establish a permanent settlement. He took sixty men, five women, and livestock and sailed to the houses that Leif had originally built the first winter in the new world. This is testimony to the skill of Viking navigators, who could return to the same location found by Leif. At first, this settlement traded peacefully with the Native Americans, but then they began to fight. Karlsefni abandoned the settlement and returned to Greenland, deciding they could not settle in peace in the new lands because of the Native Americans. Colonizing efforts were abandoned.

There is no doubt that the Vikings made explorations of North America. Archaeologists have found Viking houses dating from about 1000 in Newfoundland. Unfortunately, these are probably not those of Leif the Lucky, because Newfoundland is too far north for wild grapes to grow (Magnusson, 8–9). This may mean that there were other explorations that were not preserved by saga writers. It is clear, however, that medieval Vikings knew of the existence of North America long before Christopher Columbus made his voyages.

Global Misunderstandings

In spite of the many connections between people in Europe and those in the rest of the world, Europeans retained many misunderstandings about the world right through to the end of the Middle Ages. These errors grew from three main sources: (1) Medieval respect for classical antiquity caused geographers and travelers to respect past views more than the evidence of their own observations, (2) people (even today) recast what they see in terms that are consistent with their expectations, and (3) Europeans fell in love with some travel accounts that were plainly false, but that perpetuated myths instead of realities.

The most popular travel book—the *Travels of Sir John Mandeville*—appeared in about 1356 and immediately became astonishingly popular. This was the only travel book that Leonardo da Vinci possessed, and Christopher Columbus consulted it as he took his voyages. Scholars doubt whether there even was anyone named Mandeville, nor whether the author of this account ever traveled further than his local library. His work is fanciful and entertaining and preserved many global misconceptions from the ancient world. When real travelers came back from abroad, if their experiences did not match those of the fictional Mandeville, they did not trust their own eyes. Thus, global misunderstandings persisted throughout the Middle Ages in spite of a good deal of global interaction.

Medieval travelers were also hampered by the maps they used. They had two main kinds of maps, and both preserved significant mistakes. The first was one drawn by the Greek Ptolemy, and it was fairly accurate in its portrayal of the major continents, but Ptolemy's map did not show North and South America and identified only three continents: Asia, Africa, and Europe. The geographer further believed that land covered three-fourths of the earth's surface, making the oceans too small. Finally, Ptolemy misjudged the circumference of the earth, making it one-sixth smaller than its true size. Nevertheless, this was considered to be the most accurate map, and travelers used it to plan their voyages.

Even more popular—and more mistaken—were the T-O maps, which take their name from the basic outline: a circle with an inscribed diameter and, at a right angle to it, a single radius. This design, that resembled the letter *T* within a letter *O*, gave Asia one-half of the Earth's land mass, with Africa and Europe splitting the other half between them. East was often shown at the top and Jerusalem at the center. T-O maps satisfied Christian understandings of the world that placed the Holy Land centrally and spiritually prominent and relegated the far reaches of the world to Asia. Viking navigators, who saw the world as the North Sea surrounded by land, could have corrected T-O maps with their understanding of the existence of North America. However, there was little communication between the Scandinavians and the mapmakers of the south.

None of these portrayals of the world envisioned a flat space. Those who thought of the world at all envisioned a round earth. Travelers did observe the changing night sky as they moved south, and people living even around the Mediterranean saw ships disappear over the horizon and return, confirming the existence of a round earth. As the popular travel work purportedly by John Mandeville wrote, "It can be proved thus, if a man had adequate shipping and good company, and had moreover his health, and wanted to go and see the world, he could traverse the whole world above and below" (Moseley, 128). Christopher Columbus had read the popular *Mandeville's Travels*, and his view of what was possible was shaped by this medieval text.

Thinkers did quarrel about whether there could be people living at the "bottom" of the earth, some arguing that it was impossible because they might fall off, while others, like Mandeville, believed that people could populate everywhere. His "proof" of this, however, remained medieval not scientific: He argued not for gravity, but that the Bible promised that God would not let people fall off the earth (Moseley, 130).

Travelers also had great misunderstandings about what kind of people they might meet in their travels. Since the time of the Roman scholar Pliny the Elder (23–79), Europeans had heard of unusual races of people who purportedly lived in parts of the world outside the Mediterranean basin, and all travelers who went to India, Africa, and Asia expected to find what they called "monstrous races" described by Pliny. Travelers expected to find beings as bizarre as dog-headed humans, headless people, and one-legged "sciopods" who lay on the ground shading themselves with their one huge foot. The popular pseudo-traveler John Mandeville claimed to have visited islands populated by each of these fantastic creatures (Moseley, 137).

Oddly, the quite accurate account by Marco Polo generated much skepticism. Readers who believed in monstrous creatures refused to believe in such marvels as money made of paper or rocks (coal) that could burn. It is only after the medieval period, when people were more willing to question their assumptions by looking at evidence that many of these global misunderstandings would recede. *See also* Documents 12 and 25.

Further Reading

Diamond, Jared. *Guns, Germs, and Steel: The Fates of Human Societies*. New York: W.W. Norton & Co., 1997.

Magnusson, Magnus, and Hermann Palsson. *The Vinland Sagas: The Norse Discovery of America*. New York: Penguin, 1965.

Moseley, C.W.R.D., trans. *The Travels of Sir John Mandeville*. New York: Penguin, 1983.

Notker the Stammerer. "Charlemagne," in *Two Lives of Charlemagne*. Translated by Lewis Thorpe. New York: Penguin, 1969.

Phillips, J.R.S. *The Medieval Expansion of Europe*. Oxford, UK: Clarendon Press, 1998.

Polo, Marco. *The Travels*. Translated by Ronald Latham. New York: Penguin, 1958.

Singman, J.L. *Daily Life in Medieval Europe*. Westport, CT: Greenwood Press, 1999.

Short Entries: People, Ideas, Events, and Terms

Agriculture

Most of the agriculture in medieval Europe was centered in villages, where peasant families lived in close proximity to each other, and all went away from the villages to work their fields. (There were some places—such as Iceland—that had isolated farmhouses, but this was not the usual settlement pattern.) Villages were frequently clustered into "manors" that were presided over by a lord of the land, to whom peasants owed labor and a portion of their produce.

The manors included various kinds of land: There was pastureland to feed grazing animals; woodlands that provided game for the lords and browsing for pigs, deer, and other animals; and the all-important cultivated fields that produced cereals and legumes. Before the eleventh century, most cultivated fields were divided into two parts: one to plant and one to lay fallow to restore its fertility for the subsequent year's planting. After the eleventh century, most manors changed to a three-field system. In this innovation, only one-third of the field was left fallow, and one-third was planted in the spring in rye or wheat. The final third was planted in early fall in oats or barley.

By the twelfth century, many manors included legumes in the rotational planting. Legumes offered stunning advantages over grains. These plants are "nitrogen fixing," that is they add nitrogen to the soil that becomes fertilizer for the grains that would be rotated onto these fields the following year. In addition, legumes brought a good source of protein to medieval diets, particularly for the poor who never could afford to eat much meat. Finally, the green tops of the legumes provided needed fodder for animals.

The fields on the medieval manors were organized in strips, so that each peasant would own long strips within the large fields. Richer peasants might own many strips and poorer ones might own only one. This organization of land may seem complicated to modern people who are used to thinking of farmland as being made up on large squares of land, however, it was practical because of the technology of plowing. The heavy clay soils of northern Europe were most effectively plowed by means of a large four-wheeled plow that was pulled by six or eight oxen. This large apparatus needed a good deal of space for turning, so long strips of cultivated land allowed for long furrows, minimizing the number of turns that the plow would make. In addition, few peasants could own the large plow along with enough animals to pull it, so it made sense for the community to own the plow. Such technology required villagers to work together, plowing, sowing, and harvesting together. And of course, all the peasants were responsible for working the strips that belonged to the lord.

Some regions were suitable for producing larger-scale cash crops, which allowed lords to make a profit on products for a market beyond the local. The most important of such crops were grapes, which could be made into wine. Wine was produced near major rivers, like the Rhône and the Loire. Locating wine production along rivers allowed for the wine to be transported readily, thus solving the problem of producing for only local consumption. Of course, manors could also produce nonfood items for market. Sheep were raised for wool and hemp planted for linen cloth.

Each peasant household also cultivated a garden for vegetables. These gardens were typically fenced to keep out stray animals and were cultivated with intensive care by all members of the household. Families grew turnips, peas, cabbages, leeks, spinach, and other vegetables and herbs. Peasants owed a portion of their produce from these gardens to the lord, but records indicate that they were often able to grow enough to sell the excess in good years.

Fertilizer for the fields and gardens was always scarce. The main source was the animal waste, which was usually deposited as animals grazed on the stubble left in the fields after harvest. Manors that were near towns had peasants collect "night soil," the human waste that accumulated near the centers of population density. Using human waste, however, made it easier for diseases and parasites to spread, compounding health problems late in the Middle Ages as population grew. In Ireland and Scandinavian lands, people used seaweed for fertilizer, which was labor intensive but significantly improved the soil.

The technology of agriculture in medieval Europe benefitted from global exchanges. We can see evidence of innovations that were developed in China spreading to the rural manors in Europe and improving the agricultural production. For examples, Chinese developed improved horse collars that rested on horses' shoulders to replace the ox yoke that rested on the neck. This allowed horses to be hitched to plows, and because horses work faster than oxen, more land could come into cultivation. Chinese also developed wheelbarrows, a popular labor-saving device for medieval peasants.

The agricultural production through the thirteenth century was impressive, and European population grew. However, as population increased, more and more land came into cultivation for grain and legumes. This led to two developments. First, land that was less productive was cultivated leading to ever lower yields. Second, pastureland began to be plowed which meant there was less feed available for animals, so more had to be slaughtered. Fewer animals meant less fertilizer and yields fell again. By the beginning of the fourteenth century, population had expanded enough that when weather turned cool, famine struck and many died. The fourteenth century saw the failure of medieval agriculture to keep pace with changing conditions. *See also* Documents 11 and 22.

Further Reading
Fossier, R. *Peasant Life in the Medieval West*. New York: Blackwell, 1988.
Rösener, W. *Peasants in the Middle Ages*. Chicago: University of Illinois Press, 1992.

Alfred the Great (849–899)

As the eighth century opened, Anglo-Saxon England consisted of several kingdoms. The pagan Anglo-Saxon tribes had converted to Christianity in the seventh century, and monasteries in that land were vibrant centers of learning. In the ninth century, Scandinavian Danes and other Vikings repeatedly invaded the eastern edge of England, and the struggle against the Danes in the ninth and tenth centuries forged England into a unified kingdom. The founder of the English national monarchy was Alfred (r. 871–899), the only English monarch to be called "the Great." Alfred is remembered for his success in war and his fostering of learning.

Alfred was the younger brother of King Aethelred of Wessex (one of the several Anglo-Saxon kingdoms in England). In his youth, Alfred had been sent to Rome and learned how the Church was the repository and guardian of knowledge, and he passionately wanted to make this Latin learning available to the English-speaking audience. But first, he had to fight alongside his brother against the invading Danes. When his brother died, the nobles chose Alfred to be king (over Aethelred's young sons). Alfred's resolution carried his people through years when the Danes held almost all England, and through his tenacity, the king of Wessex became accepted as the king of all England.

Alfred had reorganized the military to confront the invaders and built the first English navy to patrol the coast against the Danish raiders. Finally, the English and Danes signed a treaty in 886. Under its terms, Alfred and the Danish king Guthrum agreed to divide England between them. The northern lands later became known as the "Danelaw" to recognize that they were governed by laws different from those in the southern parts of the land. As part of this settlement, Guthrum agreed to convert to Christianity, which would make it easier for the two peoples to share the land. Then Alfred could turn his full attention to fostering learning in his lands.

Alfred wrote to all his bishops complaining of the loss of learning in England that was due to the destruction of long warfare. He remembered the old days fondly: "It has very often come to my mind what wise men there once were throughout England, men both of holy and of worldly wisdom, and how happy the times were then throughout England" (Marsh, 133). Alfred further complained that the old books were in Latin, so inaccessible to most people. The king himself translated, or helped to translate, some of the great books of literature into Old English so his people could read them. Furthermore, he initiated the writing of the *Anglo-Saxon Chronicle*, a history of England that continued the work of the Venerable **Bede**.

The rule of Alfred the Great marked the high point of the accomplishments of Anglo-Saxon England. Not only did he leave a legacy of a unified land that valued religion and learning, but his translations shaped the English language itself. *See also* Document 10.

Alfred the Great. Engraving by Vertue. Courtesy of photos.com.

Further Reading
Marsh, Henry. *Dark Age Britain: Sources of History.* New York: Dorset Press, 1970.
Smyth, Alfred P. *King Alfred the Great.* Oxford, UK: Oxford University Press, 1995.

Architecture

The most visible remnants of medieval Europe are the architectural wonders that were built during these years. Travelers today look with wonder at the religious and military structures that dominated the human-made landscape.

In western Europe, the finest churches from the early Middle Ages were in Ravenna, where the imperial court had its capital from the fifth century. Here visitors today can see the beautiful mosaics in churches that were built in a basilica fashion of a long rectangle flanked by colonnaded aisles. These churches like St. Apollinare in Classe and San Vitale can give an idea of the excitement of Christians as they celebrated the acceptance of Christianity by the power of the empire.

The Byzantine Empire maintained the continuity of architectural skill from the late Roman Empire, and this can be most clearly seen in the great church of Hagia Sophia, built between 532 and 537 by the emperor Justinian. Reportedly, when the emperor saw the completed Hagia Sophia, he claimed he had exceeded King Solomon in building a structure that glorified God, and the church remains one of the great buildings of the world. In plan it is a basilica (based on Roman buildings) with a dome above the central space. It has two semidomes along the longitudinal axis. The central dome is 107 feet in diameter and rises 180 feet above the floor. The golden dome seemed to be suspended by heaven itself and remains a visible testimony to the skill of the architects who designed it. Aisles with galleries above ranged on either side, where the faithful gathered — men on one side, women on the other — to participate in the services.

The violence that accompanied the fall of the Roman Empire in the West disrupted the tradition of this kind of spectacular building. Charlemagne, who in the late eighth century once again united western Europe aspired to a renaissance of Roman architecture. He built a chapel at Aachen (792–805) that was modeled after San Vitale in Ravenna and had a dome over the center. However, Charlemagne's unifying work did not long survive him, and memorable religious architecture moved to the great monasteries that served as the sanctuaries of a Christianity that was again besieged by pagan Vikings from the north.

Monastery churches that flourished from around 1000 to 1250 are built in a style called "Romanesque," which indicates that the structures imitated old Roman buildings. These churches were characterized by semicircular arches leading down to great pillars. Even these stones were not sufficient to bear the weight of heavy stone roofs, so the walls were very thick with only small windows. These churches were dark and often decorated with painted frescoes on the walls. Many of these massive churches survive today, like the Speyer Cathedral or the Pisa Cathedral (next to the famous "leaning tower.")

By the twelfth century, new circumstances demonstrated a need for new kinds of churches. Cities had grown so large churches were needed to accommodate the growing urban populations and the many pilgrims who traveled to cities that had famous relics of saints. The brilliant leader of the monastery of St. Denis, Abbott Suger, developed a new architectural style that would come to dominate the late Middle Ages. St. Denis was located about 6 miles north of Paris and was the French royal monastery. Suger wanted to rebuild the old church that was small and somewhat decayed. Suger spoke to travelers from Constantinople for descriptions of Hagia Sophia, and the Abbott wanted to exceed this glorious church. Suger also was fascinated by mystical ideas of light and visual manifestations of spirituality, so when he approved designs for his new structure, they encompassed his ideas.

The new church of St. Denis began what has come to be called "Gothic" architecture, which departed dramatically from the old Romanesque. Gothic architects used pointed arches instead of semicircular ones, which allowed them to build the roofs even higher without thickening the walls because the weight of the roof was brought down along the pointed ribs of the arches to massive columns. This weight-bearing structure freed the walls allowing stained-glass windows to fill the churches with magically colored light.

Architects still had to deal with the problem of wind moving these towering structures, for any movement would create cracks in the stone and weaken the supports. To solve this problem, engineers created "flying buttresses" which were stone towers set away from the walls with stone bridges leading from the tower to the high walls of the church.

Gothic architectural principles created churches that appeared to be miracles of light and space. They were immediately popular, and for the next centuries Gothic cathedrals were built all over Europe. Some of the more famous early Gothic cathedrals are those at Chartres, Paris, and Canterbury, England. However, travelers can admire such buildings all over Europe from Spain to Germany to Scandinavia to England.

Just as frescoes were intimately part of Romanesque churches, the architecture of Gothic cathedrals cannot be separated from the art that is an integral part of the building. Stained-glass windows skillfully told biblical stories and portrayed images of members of the community who contributed money to build the magnificent building. Sculptures surrounded every side of the church, and art historians trace tendencies of sculpture to slowly separate from the columns that supported the building itself.

These magnificent buildings rose in the center of all the major cities of the Middle Ages. All members of the community gathered to celebrate church service in these spectacular structures that embodied the faith and the communities of the medieval world. *See also* Document 16.

Further Reading

Kunstler, Gustav, ed. *Romanesque Art in Europe*. New York: W.W. Norton, 1968.
Panofsky, Erwin. *Abbot Suger on the Abbey Church of St. Denis and Its Art Treasures*. 2nd ed. Princeton, NJ: Princeton University Press, 1979.
Von Simson, Otto. *The Gothic Cathedral*. Princeton, NJ: Princeton University Press, 1974.

Bede the Venerable (c. 672–735)

In the seventh century, Anglo-Saxon England was a fragmented, violent land, recently converted to Christianity. However, Christian scholarship was forwarded by great scholars who came to the northern lands with Theodore of Tarsus, who was appointed to be Archbishop of Canterbury in 669. Theodore brought with him two scholars: Hadrian, an African, and Benedict Biscop, an Anglo-Saxon nobleman who had become a monk after studying in Rome.

Benedict Biscop founded two Benedictine monasteries in the north of England at Wearmouth and Jarrow. He also journeyed several times to Rome and brought back valuable manuscripts to these monastic libraries. Wearmouth and Jarrow soon became the greatest centers of learning west of Italy. Biscop's pupil, Bede, called the "Venerable," was one of the greatest scholars in western Europe between the decline of Roman civilization and the age of Charlemagne. Bede's writings were original and served to transmit classical learning into the Middle Ages.

Bede was born on the church lands at Wearmouth; his father was a tenant farmer of the monastery. When the boy was 7 years old, his parents sent him as a pupil to the monastery. Shortly afterwards, Bede was moved to Jarrow, which had been recently founded and continued his education there. Bede was able to learn from the brilliant scholar Biscop and take advantage of the books that he had brought from Rome.

When Bede was about 13 years old, an epidemic swept through the monastery at Jarrow, and an account reported that it killed everyone except the Abbot himself and one boy, who is assumed to be Bede himself. Bede remained at Jarrow as a monk for the rest of his life. When he was age 30, he was ordained priest, and lived until he was just over age 60. Bede wrote some forty works, including translations, biographies, commentaries on the Bible and history works.

As a product of the monasteries, Bede wrote in Latin, and his writings were essential to generations of subsequent Latin scholars. He was primarily a teacher who wrote a number of works intended as educational tracts. For example in an influential text of science — *The Nature of Things* — Bede incorporated much from the Roman encyclopedist Pliny and the Visigothic scholar Isidore of Seville, but he added his own interpretations. For example, in this work he described the earth as a globe and discussed its geography. This tract was counted among the most important scientific texts of the early Middle Ages.

Bede's most famous work, however, is the *Ecclesiastical History of the English People*, in which he tells the history of early Anglo-Saxon England to 731. Bede's vision not only described England but helped his readers see themselves as a cohesive group instead of a number of different tribes. This was all the more remarkable from a man who probably never went farther than 7 miles from the place he was born.

Perhaps the most influential aspect of Bede's history was that he adopted Dionysius Exiguus's dating system. Dionysius had been a monk and skilled mathematician in sixth-century Italy, and it was he who first suggested that calendars be dated from his estimation of when the Incarnation of Chris occurred. This turned into our B.C./A.D. system, which is now named B.C.E./C.E. Not many people had read Dionysius's tract, but Bede's was read and translated for centuries. Our adoption of Dionysius's historical dating system can be largely attributed to Bede.

Bede died peacefully in the monastery where he had spent his days. Perhaps his best obituary was his own words: "But my greatest pleasure always has been in studying, in teaching and in writin" (Marsh, 107). Indeed, generations ever since have had much to be thankful for his lifetime of scholarship. *See also* Document 5.

Further Reading
Marsh, Henry. *Dark Age Britain: Some Sources of History*. New York: Dorset Press, 1970.

Bernard of Clairvaux (1090–1153)

For more than 30 years during the twelfth century, the monk Bernard of Clairvaux was the major spokesman for western Christendom. He was an adviser to kings, popes, bishops, and abbots and a major proponent of the mystical life through monastic contemplation. He left his mark on many aspects of medieval religious life.

Bernard was born in 1090 in Burgundy. His father was a knight, but he was more influenced by his religious mother, Aleth. He was enrolled in a church school and soon impressed everyone with his love of learning. More than a call to learning, Bernard felt a vocation to serve God as a monk. In around 1113, Bernard and about thirty companions entered the Cistercian monastery of Citeaux, which was renowned for its strict life.

When he was only 24 years old, Bernard's reputation for holiness was established, and he was chosen to found a new Cistercian monastery. During the rigors of building a new monastery, known as Clairvaux, Bernard maintained his asceticism of long fasts and prayers. His austerities made him ill, and he had to take a year to recover his health, but his reputation for holiness only increased. Once he returned to lead Clairvaux, he wrote many sermons and letters addressed to all the great leaders in Europe.

His preaching was so eloquent that many were persuaded to become monks, and the Cistercian monasteries founded on the model of Clairvaux expanded rapidly. When he and his monks first settled at Clairvaux, there were only five Cistercian houses. By the time of his death in 1153, there were 343 abbeys, sixty-eight of which had been founded directly from Clairvaux. His charismatic personality was the single most important factor in the rapid growth of the order.

Not all of Bernard's causes were successful. He vigorously attacked Abbot Suger for his decorating of the church at St. Denis that was to become the model for subsequent Gothic cathedrals (*see* **Architecture**). He believed that elaborate decorations were frivolous distractions from prayer. However, the Gothic cathedrals proved so popular that his reprimands went unheeded.

Bernard was an important mystic, and in his writings, the monk described four stages of love by which a soul could attain to ecstatic, mystical union with the Divinity (*see* **Mysticism**). Bernard also had an important impact on the growing cult of the Virgin Mary because he described her as a tender lady who was accessible to the

St. Bernard of Clairvaux defeating the Devil. Illustration from *The Golden Legend* by Jacobus de Voragine, French manuscript, 15th century. The Art Archive/Bibliothèque de l'Arsenal Paris/Marc Charmet.

faithful. As a mystic, Bernard opposed the growing scholastic movement that was emerging from the study of logic at the new universities. He emerged from his monastery to confront Peter Abelard at the Council of Sens in 1140. Bernard achieved the condemnation of Abelard and the repudiation of the intellectual approach to God that Abelard and the scholastics espoused. Although many continued to pursue scholasticism, Bernard's attack kept alive the mystic path of faith as a legitimate approach to God.

Bernard was also heavily involved in the Crusades—those military expeditions to the Holy Land that consumed many resources during the Middle Ages. In 1128, Bernard drew up a charter for the Knights Templars, establishing critical **Military Orders** that played an important role in the defense of the Holy Land. In 1145, when the crusader state of Edessa fell to the Muslims, Bernard preached the Second Crusade that sent powerful kings to fight. Bernard's popularity waned when the Second Crusade failed. Nevertheless, he remained active until his death at Clairvaux on August 20, 1153. His reputation for holiness and his impact on the religious life of Europe was so important that he was declared a saint in 1174, fewer than 25 years after his death. *See also* Document 21.

Further Reading
Daniel-Rops, Henri. *Bernard of Clairvaux*. New York: Hawthorn Books, 1964.
Evans, G.R. *The Mind of St. Bernard of Clairvaux*. Oxford, UK: Clarendon Press, 1983.

Black Death. *See* **Bubonic Plague**

Boccaccio, Giovanni (1313–1375)

In Italy in the fourteenth century, new ideas that would signal the new age of the Renaissance were beginning to flourish. The new spirit particularly appeared in the city of Florence, fostered by writers, artists, and civic leaders. Giovanni Boccaccio, considered the father of Italian narrative was one of the literary giants along with **Chaucer** and **Dante** who lived on the border between the medieval and modern worlds.

Boccaccio was born in 1313 in Florence an illegitimate son of a merchant. His father legitimized him in about 1320 and sent him to study at the best school of the age. In 1327, Boccaccio's father was sent to Naples to head a bank there, and he took his son with him, clearly intending to prepare him for a career in banking. Naples was a center of learning, and young Boccaccio, who had no aptitude for banking, made the most of Naples' royal libraries and the companionship of bright young poets. During this period Boccaccio began to write, composing poems and tales that would serve as models for Geoffrey **Chaucer** in England.

Boccaccio returned to Florence at the end of 1340 and found a city in crisis. The **bubonic plague** had entered the city and would continue to devastate it through the disastrous year of 1348. The plague took Boccaccio's father and stepmother, but this disaster stimulated Boccaccio's masterpiece, *The Decameron*.

The beginning of the *Decameron* gives the most vivid first-hand witness to the plague in literature. He described how the many deaths transformed traditional medieval life: "In the face of so much affliction and misery, all respect for the laws of God and man had virtually broken down and been extinguished in our city" (Boccaccio, 52–53). This setting of disaster formed the backdrop for the remainder of the work, in which ten young people escape to a villa outside Florence and decide to amuse themselves by telling stories. *The Decameron* is the collection of the stories they tell, and most are highly entertaining.

The stories reflect a new, permissive attitude that arose in the wake of the plague, for the stories talk frankly of sex, lies, and ordinary people. The heroes are not knights or philosophers, but clever men and women who live by their wits, and their stories were intended more to amuse than to teach moral lessons. In fact, some of the stories are so bawdy, that they were eliminated from the earliest English translations of the work. Later in his life, even Boccaccio himself became uneasy with his lighthearted works and tried to urge women not to read them. However, there was no returning to a more modest age—the future lay with witty, clever individuals who forged their own path.

Boccaccio spent his later years in service to his city, actively engaging in diplomatic activities. He too led delegations to the papal court in Avignon (*see* **Conciliar Movement**). He died in 1375, but his influence on the future course of literature has never waned. *See also* Document 26.

Further Reading

Bergin, Thomas Goddard. *Boccaccio*. New York: Viking Press, 1981.
Boccaccio, Giovanni. *The Decameron*. Translated by G.H. McWilliam. New York: Penguin, 1981.

Bubonic Plague (Black Death)

In the fourteenth century a horrible pandemic swept from the East and devastated Europe. The disease spread over vast areas, helped by increased trade from ships moving through the Mediterranean and by the expansion of the Mongol Empire. There is general agreement that the plague arrived in Europe in about 1348 on ships of Genoese merchants who traveled between Sicily and the Middle East, but the historical consensus about this pandemic ends here. What was this terrifying disease, that people in the Middle Ages called the "Black Death?"

Medieval descriptions of the disease were vivid: Giovanni **Boccaccio**, a fourteenth-century observer, described the symptoms that included swellings in the armpits and groins that turned black. Once skin darkened in spots, death was virtually certain. This description causes most historians to identify the disease with bubonic plague, caused by a virulent bacillus (*Yersinia pesta*) that infected rodents in Manchuria then spread to black rats. Some of the most devastating diseases throughout history have been those that move from animals to humans, and this rodent disease was no exception; it passed to humans from the bites of infected fleas. Bubonic plague can also reach a person's lungs, becoming "pneumonic" plague, which spreads rapidly through sneezing and coughing. Estimates are that between 30 percent to 70 percent of people who catch bubonic plague die, but almost 100 percent of those with pneumonic plague die.

Allegory of Demon of the Plague. Engraved illustration from *Feldtbuch der Wundarzney* (Fieldbook of Wound Surgery), by Hans Gersdorff, Strasburg 1540. Dover Pictorial Archives.

In modern times, bubonic plague does not spread quickly, which causes some historians to question whether this disease indeed was the Black Death that brought such destruction. Some argue that this virulent form spread quickly to the lungs, becoming the deadly pneumonic form. Others suggest that several diseases—like smallpox—might have joined bubonic plague in sweeping through a population already weakened from famine. Others surmise that there might be another disease, as yet unidentified that wreaked the havoc.

Whatever the exact disease, the pandemic raced through Europe. It spread quickly in the summer and declined in the winter months—the cold, wet summers helped the plague spread. The pandemic killed a shocking one-third to one-half of the population, but historians are uncertain of the exact numbers of the dead. Modern estimates that agree that one-third of the population died, disagree on what that fraction means in actual numbers—estimates range from twenty million to thirty-five million dead. Disease hit the crowded cities hardest: Paris may have lost half its population and Florence as much as four-fifths. These staggering numbers mean that everyone—especially in the cities where death rates were highest—saw neighbors, friends and family members die.

The psychological impact of so great a plague was perhaps even more important than the actual loss of life. Law and tradition broke down, and many survivors saw no point in trying to preserve medieval customs.

Medicine failed to offer solace for this horrifying disease, for doctors had no idea where the disease came from. Some attributed the cause to "bad air," while others applied leeches to reduce fevers. Some people turned to God to relieve the suffering, leading to the sad practice of "flagellants." These men and women beat themselves three times a day with leather thongs tipped in lead as they marched in procession from town to town. This movement reflected the desperation of people searching for ways to appease a seemingly angry God; instead the disease simply spread more rapidly in the blood that was shed by the pious.

The plague continued to ravage Europe in waves into the seventeenth and even early eighteenth centuries. The plague finally abated when the larger, meaner Norwegian brown rat (today's urban rat) replaced the European black rats that had served as the host pool for the bacillus. Even though the disease eventually disappeared, it left a legacy of fear and despair and helped to break down medieval society. *See also* Document 26.

Further Reading
Herlihy, D. *The Black Death and the Transformation of the West*. Cambridge, MA: Harvard
   University Press, 1997.

Castles

Warfare in the Middle Ages was largely defensive; armies were only as good as the defensive walls that protected their positions, or as effective as the siege machinery with which they attacked fortified locations. Throughout the Middle Ages, the architecture of castle building grew increasingly sophisticated, and the European landscape remains dotted with these masterpieces made of stone that once guarded strategic roads, rivers, or coastlines.

Before the eleventh century, most of the defensive castles were wooden "motte and bailey" structures. *Motte* means "mound" and *bailey* means "yard." To construct these castles, builders selected a small hill (or motte), which would give a good view of the surrounding countryside. They then dig a ditch around the base of the hill, using the fill to enlarge the existing mound. Between the ditch and the hill (the motte) was an open area—the bailey—which served as a temporary accommodation for soldiers, servants, and others who served the castle. Around the bailey, builders erected wooden walls to serve as the first line of defense. Soon, the mounds became further fortified by building a tower of stone on the top, and stones soon replaced wood in the walls surrounding the structure. The central portion of the "White Tower" of the Tower of London, which was built by William the Conqueror in 1078 is a perfect example of this early stone castle construction.

The earliest surrounding stonewalls were made by building two parallel walls of stone and filling the space between them with dirt, stones and rubble. The resulting wall looked formidable, but attackers quickly learned that once the outer stone was pierced, the rubble was quickly penetrated. By the thirteenth century, builders had learned to make thick walls of solid stone.

Castle-building technology was greatly forwarded during the Crusades when Europeans first glimpsed the concentric walls that protected the formidable city of Constantinople and the Syrian castles of the Muslims. Crusading armies desperately needed impenetrable defensive positions to guard the Holy Lands, so castle building came into its own. Sophisticated castle designs spread into Europe from the Middle East and transformed warfare as well as the landscapes. For example, the English king Edward I (r. 1272–1307) built ten castles in Wales as part of his campaign to subdue that region.

These thirteenth-century castles were wonders of fortification. They no longer relied on one surrounding wall, but instead concentric circles of stonewalls confronted invaders who managed to breach the exterior wall. Many castles also had water-filled moats surrounding them that served as effective as a wall in preventing concentrated attacks. Towers were built into the walls at intervals of about 200 feet or fewer, roughly the range of a bow-shot, and the towers rose higher than the walls themselves to provide strong high ground for defenders withstanding attackers.

The flourishing trade in castle building brought an environmental cost. Many great forests were cleared for timber to shore up the stones and build scaffolds as laborers came from miles around to work on the stone. Defenders also wanted surrounding forests clear-cut so they could see any approaching foes. The Castle of Windsor near London, for example, required the wood of more than four-thousand oak trees in its construction. The slow-growing oak forests of Europe would not be the same again.

The main way castles were taken was through siege. If attackers could surround a castle and wait for months sometimes, the defenders might run out of food or water and give up. More often, however, a siege might be lifted when armies friendly to the castle came and attacked the besiegers. All this required time, and it is often hard for modern people used to the rapid pace of warfare to remember that in the medieval world, warfare was often a matter of patience and dogged determination in the face of formidable stone walls.

Although castles came into existence because of warfare, they also served as home to noble families charged with protecting the land. In the early years of castle construction, the nobleman and his family lived in conditions hardly better than those of a peasant family, with cold, sparse rooms and few amenities. By the thirteenth century, the new, larger castles offered finer homes to the nobility.

The main room of a castle was the main hall where the noble family, guests, and retainers gathered to eat, play games, and be entertained by musicians, jugglers, or story-tellers. In the twelfth century the center of the hall was dominated by an open hearth filled with a great fire to offer warmth, light, but filled the hall with smoke. By the thirteenth century, the hearth was moved to the wall as a fireplace to reduce the smoke in the room.

There were also smaller, private rooms where the lord and lady slept, children were born and raised, and the women of the household did the weaving and sewing. The private rooms also served as a bank for the lord: He kept his money and valuables in a strongbox. If someone were able to take the castle, he would be assured of capturing a good deal of wealth as well!

Castle designers working for wealthy patrons placed the living quarters in high towers, out of the reach of arrows. This placement allowed them to put glass in the windows to bring light in without sacrificing too much warmth. Latrines were built into the walls of rooms that were adjacent to the living quarters, but the waste only fell down into a pit that periodically had to be dug out and emptied by an unfortunate servant. More comforts for the nobility were slowly added to medieval living quarter as engineers included pipes to bring water to upper floors.

These impressive structures marked medieval society. However, just as the technology of defensive warfare brought castles into being, new military technology rendered them obsolete. In the fifteenth century, gunpowder came into its own. No longer would stonewalls and the patience of defenders ensure the safety of the nobility. Instead, cannons could rapidly break down even the strongest defensive wall; the great walls of Constantinople were breached by the Turkish guns in 1453. The end of the Middle Ages can be marked by cannon fire that destroyed castles and the life they spawned. *See also* Document 20.

Further Reading
Gies, J., and F. Gies. *Life in a Medieval Castle*. New York: Harper & Row, 1974.

Champagne Fairs

Amid the violence that accompanied the collapse of the Roman Empire in the West, the vibrant trade that had supported Rome's prosperity also declined. By the end of the tenth century, however, long-distance trade began to be reestablished, stimulating an economic prosperity that was to transform medieval Europe.

By the end of the eleventh century, there were two clear arenas of trade: The Mediterranean region was dominated by Italian city-states that sent their merchant ships all the way from the Crusader states and Constantinople in the east to North Africa and Spain. Many luxury goods found their way from the Far East into this trade. Meanwhile, a northern zone of trade began to flourish around the Baltic Sea, which specialized in woolen cloth, furs and hunting hawks. For Europe to really enjoy the fruits of a vigorous trade, these two zones had to find a way to come together.

Not only was travel difficult on land and sea, pirates and bandits threatened merchants if they traveled alone. Furthermore, each feudal lord along the way claimed the right to charge tolls to merchants passing through his land. Nor did these tolls guarantee safety, for armed nobles often did not hesitate simply to claim the goods passing through their lands.

Early in the twelfth century, a powerful feudal family saw a chance to remedy this situation and earn a good income. A key region—between the Seine and Rhine Rivers—was dominated by the Counts of Champagne, and they worked to turn their lands into a vast marketplace. At a number of their towns, they founded fairs, where merchants from both the northern and southern regions could bring their goods. The counts set aside a place for the fair, erected booths for the merchants, and set up moneychangers to handle the varied coins that were brought from many lands. The counts also provided safety, employing some of their soldiers to serve as police, and paying judges to settle disputes.

The fairs were well organized. They were spaced so that there was always a fair somewhere in Champagne. Furthermore, each day was set aside for trade in a different product or group of products. For example, a day for wine, cheeses, cloth, leather goods, and so on. To increase the safety of the merchants, no money changed hands during the days of trade; instead, merchants kept careful account of the orders. Then, on the last day, all the merchants took their money to the exchange, converted all the needed currency into the official currency of the fair—the pound of Troyes—and paid their bills.

The counts made a good profit as well. They collected a sales tax on all the goods sold at the fair, rented the booths, and collected fines from anyone who disturbed the peace during the fair. To ensure the safety of the merchants traveling to the fairs, the counts paid the barons who lived along the trade routes to guarantee their safe passage.

The great fairs were basically wholesale markets. Foreign merchants brought their goods and sold to local merchants, who then distributed them more locally. For about 200 years, the Champagne fairs were the most important markets in western Europe, but they were not the only fairs. Other nobles saw the prosperity that came with commerce and also encouraged fairs on their lands. During the twelfth century, a network of fairs appeared throughout Europe. Many were hardly more than cattle markets, but others drew more goods.

The fairs all over Europe facilitated and stimulated economic development, but they also provided exciting entertainment for all those who gathered there. Musicians, jugglers, and others gathered to take advantage of money that was changing hands. Today, those who attend the popular "Renaissance Fairs" that are put on in various cities can sample the excitement of the medieval fairs, and the Champagne Fairs began them all and remained the greatest of them. *See also* Document 9.

Further Reading

Gies, Joseph and Frances Gies. *Life in a Medieval City* (2nd ed) . New York: Harper, 1981.

Lopez, Robert S. *The Commercial Revolution of the Middle Ages, 950–1350.* New York: Cambridge University Press, 1976.

Charlemagne (742–814)

In the eighth century, northern Europe was slowly overcoming the effects of the invasions of the Germanic tribes into the old Roman Empire and establishing the kingdoms that formed medieval civilization. The most important figure in making this transition was Charles the Great—better know as Charlemagne—king of the Franks. The Franks had been ruled by the Merovingian dynasty from the earliest times of their settlement in France and parts of Germany, but the Merovingians had grown weak. The land was effectively governed by another family, the Carolingians, from the time of Charles Martel, the great general who had defeated the Muslim invasion of France at the Battle of Tours in 733. Charles Martel's son Pepin the Short (r. 747–768) further forwarded the family fortunes. Pepin was not content to simply wield power on behalf of the Merovingians, he wanted to have the title of king. Pepin received the support of Pope Zachary, and the Carolingian dynasty was established in France. The greatest of the Carolingians was Pepin's illegitimate son, Charles the Great—remembered as Charlemagne.

Emperor Charlemagne conveys the status of knight upon a soldier, 14th century manuscript. The Art Archive / Biblioteca Nazionale Marciana Venice/ Alfredo Dagli Orti.

Charlemagne was born in 742 and lived until 814. In his long life, he transformed medieval European society. His main accomplishments were in warfare, church and educational reforms, and in establishing a new empire in northern Europe. Charlemagne was above all else a warrior, conducting about fifty-three campaigns throughout his reign. The warrior king marched with his armies conquering fierce pagan Saxons in the north to Slavs in the East. He also marched into Italy to put down rebellions. By 800, Charlemagne controlled all of western and central Europe, except for southern Italy that was still in the hands of the Byzantine Emperor, and in that year, he accepted (or took, the sources are inconsistent) the crown of Roman emperor. Once more there was and emperor in the West.

Charlemagne was such a powerful force in the West that the other neighboring empires could not ignore him. The Byzantine emperor objected to his taking the title of emperor, but there was little to be done. Charlemagne had more promising relations with the Islamic caliph in Baghdad, Harun Al Raschid, which is also not surprising, because the caliph was always looking to cultivate allies against the Byzantine Empire. Harun sent Charlemagne a white elephant as a gift in 802, and the great beast traveled throughout western Europe with the emperor, shocking his subjects who had never seen such an impressive animal. Charlemagne's connections stimulated trade in his lands, and once again goods flowed into Europe from far reaches of the globe.

As memorable as Charlemagne's political and diplomatic victories were, his most enduring impact came in the area of intellectual achievement. Charlemagne fostered learning for his own interests and to forward the religious health of his kingdom. He wanted priests well trained in reading and writing, so he set up schools all over his lands and improve **education**. He sent representatives around his lands to check on churches to be sure the services were being conducted competently.

Any educational reform in the eighth century (or later for that matter) depended on reliable texts. In the Middle Ages, all books had to be copied by hand, so in the centuries before Charlemagne many errors had crept into texts copied by semiliterate monks and nuns. Charlemagne gathered the best scholars of Europe to his court to consider the problem of incorrect texts. They attacked the problem in two ways: First, they compared many versions of the same text to prepare a correct rendition. Second, they developed a standardized handwriting so that future copyists could accurately preserve the corrected text. This reformed handwriting—called the "Carolingian minuscule"—reduced errors to preserve wisdom accurately for future generations. Moreover, the Carolingian handwriting style formed the basis for our own lowercase letters and the printing-press letters invented 600 years later.

Charlemagne's great achievement hardly outlasted his own long reign. His only surviving son, Louis the Pious (r. 814–840) struggled with new invaders—Vikings, Muslims, and Magyars (Hungarians)—who threatened the integrity of his empire. He divided up his besieged empire among his three sons, Charles the Bald, Louis the German, and Lothair I. This division established the rough nationalities of France, Germany, and Italy, although it would be a long time before those emerged as actual national entities. Yet Europe remembered the idea of Charlemagne, an emperor who united all of Europe in the Middle Ages. In modern times, men like Napoleon and Adolf Hitler would try to re-create his accomplishment. *See also* Document 7.

Further Reading

Butt, John J. *Daily Life in the Age of Charlemagne*. Westport, CT: Greenwood Press, 2002.

Einhard and Notker the Stammerer. *Two Lives of Charlemagne*. Translated by Lewis Thorpe. New York: Penguin Books, 1969.

Chaucer, Geoffrey (c. 1342–1400)

The fourteenth century was a time of disasters and turbulence from plague, famine, and warfare. In this century, new sensibilities appeared that marked the end of the medieval world and the movement toward the modern one. In England, the great author Geoffrey Chaucer exemplified the movement from old to new.

Chaucer was born about the year 1342. His father was associated with the wine trade, and the family lived in London. Young Chaucer was sent to be a page in the household of the Duchess of Clarence, wife of the third son of King Edward III (r. 1327–1377). This was a coveted position, and the young man learned courtly manners and met some of the greatest men in the land. When he was about 17, he went to fight in France as part of the **Hundred Years' War**; he was captured, ransomed, and returned to his career as a courtier. He became a favored valet to the king and married Philippa de Roet, a lady in waiting to the queen.

The king used his valet on international missions, probably dealing with matters of trade. In time he rose through the king's ranks until by 1385 he was the justice of the peace for the county of Kent. He had become quite wealthy in the process. In the end of 1386, however, he lost all his positions because his patron John of Gaunt had lost his influence in the court of the new King Richard II (r. 1377–1399). He was restored to work a few years later, but the interval allowed him to concentrate on writing the poetry that has made him famous.

Throughout his work life, Chaucer loved books. He was a prodigious reader in Latin, French, English, and Italian and studied contemporary sciences, including medicine, physics, and astronomy. His travels to Italy introduced him to the works of **Dante Alighieri** and Giovanni **Boccaccio**, two other men who were on the cusp of the new age, and their works influenced him tremendously.

His works are varied, including a translation of Boethius' *Consolation of Philosophy*, and the Romance, *Troilus and Criseyde*. The work that marked him as the Father of English Poetry is *The Canterbury Tales*. This book, which remains unfinished, consists of the Prologue that described some thirty pilgrims who are going to the shrine of Thomas Becket in Canterbury (*see*

Geoffrey Chaucer, from *Canterbury Tales* by Geoffrey Chaucer, facsimile of Ellesmere manuscript, 1400–1410. Courtesy of photos.com

Investiture Controversy). These travelers agreed to tell two tales each on the way to Canterbury and two on the way back. The tales these pilgrims tell come from all over Europe, some drawn from Boccaccio and other contemporary writers, and almost every tale ends with a moral or idea.

As delightful as the tales are, the Prologue is the real masterpiece of four-teenth century literature. The characters are drawn from all segments of society from a noble knight to a bawdy miller, a gentle nun to a scandalous wife of Bath. Through these realistic portrayals, Chaucer commented on society in a percep-tive way. He criticized corruption in the church by commenting on monks who would rather hunt than pray, or Friars who were not interested in the poor.

He was a medieval man at heart, however. He looked back to what he imag-ined was a golden age when knights were virtuous crusaders, priests cared nothing for money, and scholars loved only knowledge. If that golden age ever existed, it was gone by the fourteenth century. Money was rapidly be-coming the measure of success, and the future belonged to bright individuals with as much character as all of Chaucer's pilgrims.

Chaucer died on October 25, 1400, and was buried in Westminster Abbey. In the fifteenth century a fine tomb was erected over his grave by an admirer, and the site of his tomb became known as the Poets' Corner of Westminster Abbey. The Father of English Poetry became surrounded by other literary giants and continues to draw visitors from all over the world.

Further Reading

Chaucer. *The Canterbury Tales*. Translated by Nevill Coghill. New York: Penguin Books, 1951.

Chivalry

The Middle Ages in Europe were a violent time; men ruled through the power of armed knights at their command, and might often made right. In the twelfth century, a new idea appeared that was intended to civilize this society based on a Military Order, and this idea has been loosely called "chivalry," a word derived from *chevalier*, French for "knight."

Under this code of chivalry, knights were not only to be strong, but also to be disciplined, religious, and ready to use their power to defend the poor, women, and others in need. Such knightly ethics also were to extend to war-fare itself. For example, when one knight captured another, he no longer put him in chains and threw him in a dungeon until his family and vassals ran-somed him. Instead, the captive was treated as an honored guest. In fact, it soon became the custom to let him go free to seek his ransom on his promise to return if he could not raise the money. Nor was it considered honorable to attack a foe unless he had time to arm and prepare himself.

There were several books written on chivalry, and these provide good sources of information on the details of knightly ideals as they emerged through the Middle Ages. An anonymous French poem, called the "Order of Chivalry" from about the thirteenth century describes a hypothetical story in which a knight, called "Hugh," was persuaded by the Muslim Saladin to teach him the rituals of chivalry. Hugh described how a would-be knight was first bathed to cleanse him of sin and remind him of his newly dedicated life. Then he was dressed in a white robe, signifying the cleanness of the body; over that he threw a scarlet cloak, to remind him of the knight's duty to shed his blood. He gave him a belt of white, signifying virginity, to show he must control his lust, and gold spurs to remind him to follow God's commandments. Last, he girded him with the sword, whose two sharp edges were to remind the knight that justice and loyalty should go together (Keen, 7).

As part of the development of the code of knightly conduct was the development of mock battles, called "tournaments." In these tournaments, knights were to show their prowess as well as their noble heritage as they wore their coats of arms on their fighting attire. There were two kinds of tournaments: Melées involved a mass attack of two teams of knights, and jousts were more controlled single combats. Although these events were only mock battles, many came away with debilitating and sometimes fatal injuries. The church repeatedly tried to ban tournaments, but the code of chivalry that required knights to show off proved too strong for such prohibitions, and tournaments continued to be popular until the end of the Middle Ages.

The code of chivalry also appeared in literature, particularly in *chansons de geste*, or "songs of deed," that praised the activities of brave and loyal knights. The most famous of these literary works are the French *Song of Roland* and the Spanish *Poem of the Cid*. Both poems extol the virtues of feudal heroes — Roland, a perfect vassal of Charlemagne, and Rodrigo Díaz de Vivar, known as El Cit ("my lord"), the perfect vassal of King Alfonso VI (r. 1065–1109) of Aragon. In both accounts, the knights embody the values of prowess and loyalty to a fault, and both stories feature specific details of battle and bloody victories designed to delight an audience of warriors.

Although the code of chivalry was praised in the courts all over Europe and in the pulpits of preachers, the reality was never that simple. Knights probably violated these ethics as often as they adhered to them; the code provided only a veneer of symbols and ceremonies that overlay the violence at the heart of "those who fight" — the ruling classes of the medieval world. Yet it was this code that causes people in the modern age to look back with longing to a time dominated by "knights in shining armor."

Further Reading
Keen, Maurice. *Chivalry*. New Haven, CT: Yale University Press, 1984.

Conciliar Movement

At the height of the Middle Ages, popes could claim to rule a united Christendom (*see* **Investiture Controversy**). However, in the fourteenth century, the situation changed, leading to the belief that the authority of the church rested with bishops gathered in council instead of solely in the person of the pope. This idea is called the "Conciliar Movement." It represented a dramatic change from the medieval order, and it did not come easily.

At the beginning of the fourteenth century, the French king Philip IV (r. 1285–1314) attacked the principle of church freedom from royal control. In a struggle over taxation of church lands, the French king arrested Pope Boniface VIII (r. 1294–1303). The pope was freed, but the elderly pope died soon afterward as a result of the rough treatment. Philip IV was able to capitalize on the violence against the church, and he brought pressure on the college of cardinals to elect his favored French cardinal as pope.

Philip persuaded the pope to rule from Avignon (near French lands) instead of going to Rome. The new pope, Clement V (r. 1304–1314) complied, and for 72 years after the election of Clement V, the popes ruled from Avignon—in the shadow of the French king. Many Christians objected to this "Babylonian captivity," as the Italian Petrarch (1304–1374) called it. The Avignon popes expanded their administration and streamlined their collection of taxes, and many believed that the church had become too worldly.

An influential mystic, Catherine of Siena (1347–1380) was influential in persuading Pope Gregory XI (r. 1370–1378) to return to Rome. He did so, but things quickly became worse for the papacy. Gregory died shortly after his arrival in Rome, and the subsequent election was disputed. The cardinals ended up electing two popes: An Italian, Pope Urban VI (r. 1378–1389) and a Frenchman, Clement VII (r. 1378–1394). Clement went back to Avignon, and there were now two popes presiding over Europe. This has been called the "Great Schism" of the church. People chose to follow one pope over the other based on political rather than religious motivations, and the papacy lost its moral authority as the ruler of a united Christendom.

These were the circumstances that allowed the Conciliar Movement to arise. There was ample precedent for church councils to meet to resolve controversies, but these new "conciliarists" wanted to change the church organization into a kind of constitutional monarchy in which the power of the popes would be limited.

The first test of the Conciliar movement came at the Council of Pisa, convened in 1409 by cardinals of both Rome and Avignon. This council asserted its supremacy by deposing the two reigning popes and electing a new pope. Although this should have solved the problem, it only exacerbated it—the two previous popes would not step down, so now three popes reigned.

Finally, a second council was called. Some four-hundred churchmen assembled at the Council of Constance (1414–1418). This body deposed all three popes and elected a Roman cardinal—Martin V (r. 1417–1431). The Great Schism was finally over, and the Western church was once more united under a single head. However, never again did the popes have the power that the medieval popes had. Church councils have gathered periodically ever since to address changes in the church; the medieval church had become the modern one. *See also* Document 28.

Further Reading
Renouard, Yves. *The Avignon Papacy (1305–1403)*. Hamden, CT: Archon, 1970.

Courtly Love

During the medieval period in the West, poets writing in the courts of the nobility developed a new approach to love that has come to be called "courtly love" or even "romantic love." The ideals of this new romantic relationship between men and women have shaped our modern world and have separated the West from most of the cultures in the world. Where did this new sensibility develop?

In the early twelfth century, a new kind of poetry appeared in southern France that changed the social code between men and women. This was the poetry of the troubadours, or court poets. Historians are divided on why these new ideas emerged at this time; some argue for an influence of Arabic love poetry from Spain, others emphasize the patronage of wealthy noble women, while still others see the popularity of the Virgin Mary as influencing how earthly women were viewed. Whatever its origin, this poetry was extremely popular in the courts and highly influential. In these works, the poets praised love between men and women as an ennobling idea worthy of being cultivated.

Although there is a great deal of diversity within the writings, it is still possible to distill some characteristics of courtly love, best summarized in *The Art of Courtly Love* written by Andrew the Chaplain in the twelfth century. Andrew described how lovers must always turn pale in the presence of their beloved and stressed that secrecy and jealousy were essential for intensifying feelings of love. Andrew also stressed that this kind of romantic love was only for the nobility, for the lack of money and leisure interfered with the ability to "love." A final emphasis of this love was that it existed outside marriage. Marriages were about alliances, not love, so the courtly love poets mostly praised adultery, not marriage.

Within these general conventions, there is a range of troubadour poetry. Some poets, like Duke William IX of Aquitaine, grandfather of the famous **Eleanor of Aquitaine**, wrote frankly of enjoying sex with women. Others, like Jaufre Rudel are more mystical, writing of a longing for an absent love in ways that remind readers of religious pilgrimages. Perhaps the greatest troubadour from southern France was Bernart de Ventadorn who was able to combine the earthly with the ethereal in his descriptions and longing for his beloved.

We also have some poems from women troubadours, called "trobaritz"; we can identify about twenty women poets compared to some four-hundred known men, who wrote in southern France. Like the men, these women also write of the game of love, but many express the power differential between men and women, and how even noble women were constrained in their pursuit of passion.

Troubadour poetry spread beyond France to other areas of Europe, leading to even more diversity in the genre. German poets were even more earthy than the French, and the Italians were more metaphysical—leading to the powerful vision of Dante. These poets also influenced a new genre of literature that would be even more long-remembered than the poems: romances.

The most famous romances were those surrounding the fictional court of King Arthur, and the first-known writer to put this king into the long romance form was Chrétien de Troyes, who wrote between 1160 and 1190. He probably wrote under the patronage of the Countess Marie of Champagne, daughter of Eleanor of Aquitaine and Louis VII. He most famous romances included *Yvain, or the Knight with the Lion*, and *Lancelot*. The Arthurian romances were copied and developed well into the fifteenth century.

Perhaps the culmination of the courtly love tradition in the Middle Ages was the long poem *Romance of the Rose*, written in the thirteenth century. The poem was began by Guillaume de Lorris and addresses the quandary of love: How can the Narrator-Lover consummate his sensual love for the rose (woman) without defiling his idealized image of her? This, of course, is at the heart of a romantic love tradition in a society that idealized the Virgin Mary. Lorris left his part unfinished, and some recent critics suggest that the problem was unresolvable. The work was completed by Jean de Meun, whose addition was simply a narration on seduction—a handbook of adultery.

The medieval woman writer, Christine de Pizan (1365–c.1430) attacked the *Romance of the Rose*, claiming that this kind of romantic love leading to adultery was at its heart misogynistic. Men would always believe that women were sex objects and that the masculine behavior implicit in courtly love endangered female honor.

Christine's work gave a preview of historical controversy ever since: Was the ideal of courtly romantic love good for women, or not? Without a doubt, some noble women in the courts of Europe gained some power over their knights by using the conventions of courtly love. Whether romantic love in general — our heritage from the Middle Ages — is good for society remains up for debate. *See also* Document 20.

Further Reading

Andreas Capellanus. *The Art of Courtly Love*. Translated by John Jay Perry. New York: Columbia University Press, 1941.

Bogin, Meg. *The Women Troubadours*. New York: W.W. Norton, 1980.

Wilhelm, James J. *Lyrics of the Middle Ages: An Anthology*. New York: Garland Publishing, Inc., 1990.

Crusades

In the eleventh century, the tenuous balance of power in the Middle East between the Byzantine Empire and the Muslim world changed. The Byzantine Empire had grown weak during the beginning of the eleventh century, and when a new, vigorous dynasty came to power in the person of Alexius Comnenus (r. 1081–1118) the situation of the empire had grown desperate. Late in the tenth century, Islam had been strengthened by the Seljuk Turks, an aggressive new band from Central Asia. In 1071, these Turks defeated the Byzantine armies in a dramatic battle at Manzikert (in Armenia) and even captured the emperor himself. The new emperor Alexius was faced with a strong Turkish presence in Asia Minor and weakened armies. Searching for allies, Alexius sent a plea to the pope in Rome for soldiers to help against Islam. Alexius got much more than he bargained for.

In November 1095, Pope Urban II (r. 1088–1099) establishing a strengthened papacy after the **Investiture Controversy** took up the challenge and preached a Crusade. Urban urged Christians to stop fighting each other and set off on a holy task to retake the Holy Land of Jerusalem. He told departing soldiers to wear the sign of the cross on their breasts and encouraged them to wear the symbol on their back when they returned victorious. He promised them salvation and the opportunity for landless nobles to claim some land of their own. This launched a series of military engagements against the Muslims that continued for 200 years that are called the "Crusades" after the cross under which the Christians fought. This series of invasions remain a source of grievance to Muslims even today.

The First Crusade, that left in 1096, was spectacularly successful for the western Europeans — whom the Byzantines called the "Franks." Emperor Alexius' daughter Anna Comnena wrote a history of this time called *The Alexiad* tells of the growing hostility between East and West as the Crusader armies ignored Byzantine leadership and sought their own fortunes. However, the armies of the First Crusade swept through the Muslim forces and took Jerusalem — with so much

Crusader and Moor in combat, mosaic, 12th century Romanesque. The Art Archive/ Museo Camillo Leone Vercelli/Gianni Dagli Orti.

violence that the streets were ankle deep in blood that had been shed. When the violence subsided, the crusaders had taken the Holy Land and established crusader kingdoms along the coast of the Mediterranean Sea from the Sinai Peninsula up to Edessa on the border of the Seljuk Kingdom in Asia Minor.

Not surprisingly, Muslim armies quickly rallied to attack these outposts of western Christendom. Edessa fell in 1144, and this Muslim victory moved the pope to preach a second crusade to recover the lost territory. The Second Crusade was launched in 1147 and was led by two of the powerful kings in Europe, Louis VII of France and Conrad III of Germany. Louis's wife, the famous Eleanor of Aquitaine, accompanied him and purportedly distracted the crusades by her flirtation with her uncle, Raymond, prince of Antioch. This crusade failed miserably when the armies decided to attack heavily fortified Damascus, and the armies gave up the impossible task and went home.

Things quickly got worse for the crusader states. The Muslims of Syria produced a vigorous leader named Saladin (1137–1193), who controlled Syria and Egypt. This allowed him to coordinate an attack that retook Jerusalem in 1187. This event shocked western Europeans, who quickly called for a new crusade that was launched in 1189. This Third Crusade brought the greatest leaders of Christendom to the field: Frederick Barbarossa of Germany, Richard the Lion-Hearted of England, and Philip II of France. Everyone thought these pillars of chivalry could retake the Holy City, but they had problems coordinating their efforts. After some stunning successes, Frederick drowned while swimming, so his army went home. The French king, too, left after experiencing some losses, leaving Richard and Saladin to negotiate a settlement whereby Christian pilgrims could have free access to Jerusalem. However, these concessions seemed humiliating to Christians in the West who unrealistically hoped for a decisive victory.

The Fourth Crusade launched in 1202 went seriously awry. Christian armies failed to negotiate effective transport with Venetian ships and were lured into attacking the Christian city of Zara to pay their fare. They then were sidetracked into attacking Constantinople itself, defeating that city in 1204. Crusaders sacked the city, raping women (even some nuns), and defiling altars. They held the city for 57 years until the Byzantines managed to retake it.

This Fourth Crusade in which Christians brutally killed Christians caused much criticism in Europe. Many people said no wonder God wasn't giving them victory in the Holy Land because their soldiers were so impure. This line of thinking led to one of the worst examples of crusader zeal—the Children's Crusade, launched in 1212. Preachers argued that only the innocent could march against the infidel, and thousands of children were recruited. They were lost or sold into slavery during this fiasco. (Some modern historians question whether this appalling incident really occurred, but the medieval sources recount it.)

The Fifth Crusade was an odd venture because it was conducted by Emperor Frederick II (r. 1215–1250) who had been excommunicated by Pope Honorius III (r. 1216–1227). When Frederick arrived in Jerusalem, he was denounced by the patriarch as an excommunicate. Ignoring such details, Frederick marched his army around Palestine while negotiating with the sultan of Egypt who held Jerusalem. Finally, Frederick negotiated an amazing treaty that gave him Jerusalem, Bethlehem, Nazareth, and a few other towns. It was an astonishing accomplishment, but it was condemned by the papacy because Frederick was a sinner who did not have the support of the church. Frederick's accomplishment was overturned in 1244 when an army of Turks recaptured Jerusalem and related lands and returned them to the sultan of Egypt.

The final crusades were conducted by the only French king who has been declared a saint—Louis XI. By all accounts, Louis was brave, generous, deeply pious, and universally respected. In 1249 Louis took the cross and collected a great army. His plan was to strike at Egypt as the center of Muslim power. Louis was captured as his army floundered in the Delta of the Nile. The king obtained his freedom at a cost of a king's ransom. Louis IX launched another crusade in 1270, landing in Tunis in North Africa, where he died.

Finally, in 1291, the Muslims seized the last crusader outpost on the Asian mainland when the fortified city of Acre fell. **Military Orders** of knights died courageously on the walls of the besieged city while guarding the evacuation of Christians. Two centuries of Christian expansion into the eastern Mediterranean ended with few concrete results, except a long tradition of anger on the part of Muslims at Christians who came as invaders. One of the high points of medieval Christianity had ended. *See also* Documents 14, 15, and 23.

Further Reading

Lyons, Malcolm C. *Saladin: The Politics of Holy War.* New York: Cambridge University Press, 1985.

Riley-Smith, Jonathan. *The Oxford Illustrated History of the Crusades.* Oxford, UK: Oxford University Press, 1997.

Dante Alighieri (1265–1321)

The most famous of Italian poets from the late Middle Ages was Dante Alighieri, one of the literary giants who wrote at the turning point between the Middle Ages and the Renaissance. Dante was born in Florence in 1265 to a family that had a heritage of nobility, but who was not especially prominent. Dante went to an elementary school run by the Dominicans and came to love French and Italian poets.

As a youth, Dante cultivated a significant friendship with the poet Guido Cavalcanti, who although he was older than Dante, served as his best friend and mentor. Cavalcanti was in the forefront of a new sensibility in poetry called the "sweet new style" (*dolce stil nuovo*) that explored love—and the love of a woman—as symbols of the highest metaphysical longing. In his poem "The New Life" (*Vita Nuova*) Dante acknowledges his debt to Cavalcanti, as he writes of his love of Beatrice, a woman the poet had loved from childhood. Although her identity is uncertain, most assume she was the wife of a Florentine banker who died young and tragically. Dante writes passionately of Beatrice, even going so far as to join his love for her with his love of God.

In spite of his love for Beatrice, Dante had an arranged marriage with a Florentine woman, and they had three, perhaps four, children: two sons, and one or two daughters. However, late in the thirteenth century, Dante found himself embroiled in Florentine politics, which were divided between two parties: the Guelfs (primarily the old military aristocracy) and the Ghibellines (the emerging middle class). In 1302, the intervention of Pope Boniface VIII in the

Dante's guide rebuffs Malacoda and his fiends in Inferno Canto 21 between ditches five and six in the eight circle. Courtesy of Dover Pictorial Archives.

internal political struggles forced many Ghibellines, including Dante, to leave Florence. Dante's wife and children stayed in Florence, and the poet began years of wandering in exile. Dante would never return to his beloved Florence again.

By 1316, Dante found permanent sanctuary in Ravenna. This was a particularly happy place for exile for Dante because two of his children lived there: his son Pietro and his daughter Antonia. Antonia had become a nun in Ravenna and had taken "Beatrice" as her religious name. Dante found respect and peace in Ravenna and completed his famous work *The Divine Comedy*. Dante died peacefully in Ravenna in September 1321.

The Divine Comedy is a magnificent allegory of a soul's journey through despair to salvation. The lengthy work is divided into three sections—Hell (the Inferno), Purgatory, and Paradise—and the poet journeys through them all. He is first led through Hell by Virgil, the Roman poet whose works formed the basis of an education in the thirteenth century. Virgil shows Dante all the damned describing gruesome details of their punishments. Readers can see Dante's opinions of contemporary Italian politics in the condemned souls: For example, Pope Boniface who was instrumental in effecting Dante's exile from Florence was placed by the poet in Hell.

Virgil then leads Dante up the mountain of Purgatory, where sinners who would ultimately be saved were doing penance for their sins. Finally, Dante was led into Paradise by Beatrice, who represents Divine Love. In this, Dante claims that the mind—represented by Virgil—can guide a longing soul only so far; love has to complete the journey to salvation.

Some scholars consider *The Divine Comedy* a perfect medieval work: It incorporates scholastic theology with Aristotelian science in structure as complex as a Gothic cathedral. Other scholars see in the work something new; a departure from the medieval world. Dante with a critical vision criticizes the role of the popes and wrote his epic work in Italian, not in medieval Latin. Either way, Dante assured he would be remembered by this work that reveals the search of an individual for truth through the dangers and temptations of this world.

Further Reading

Dante. *The Portable Dante*. Translated by Paolo Milano. New York: Viking Press, 1969.
Holmes, George. *Dante*. New York: Oxford University Press, 1983.

Dramatic Performance

The Romans had a strong tradition of plays, as had the Greeks before them. It would take medieval playwrights a long time to reestablish the dramatic tradition and pass it on to Renaissance geniuses such as William Shakespeare (1564–1616). The first step in this process was to bring pagan traditions of dramatic performance into a Christian context. A German nun was the first who seems to have accomplished this task.

Hrotsvitha of Gandersheim was a tenth-century nun who came from a noble German family. She was fortunate to have entered the abbey at Gandersheim, which was an important cultural center in northern Saxony. She seems to have been familiar with many of the Latin classics from Virgil's *Aeneid* to Ovid's *Metamorphoses*. Perhaps most influential, she had read the comedies of Terence (written in the second-century B.C.E.). Hrotsvitha used Terence as a model when she composed six plays—*Gallicanus, Dulcitius, Calimachus, Abraham, Paphnutius,* and *Sapientia*—based on Terence, but using Christian themes of martyrdom, piety, and chastity. These plays have earned her the reputation of being the first dramatists (male or female) of the Middle Ages. This creative nun rediscovered classical drama and wrote in rhymed prose, creating a new genre that was suited to medieval sensibilities.

By the twelfth century, dramatic performances began to appear in churches as part of the liturgical services. At times groups would perform scenes from Biblical traditions—like the Christmas story, or the Book of Daniel—within the service. At first these were in Latin but then increasingly were performed in the vernacular languages and became popular.

Religious dramatic performances left the churches and moved into the towns, where players gathered a crowd to the town square. The plays sometimes were performed by craft guilds or by touring actors. By the thirteenth century, plays were performed on roofed wagon stages that were rolled from town to town. In time, people identified three types of drama (although the distinctions in theme were never rigid). Mystery plays dramatized aspects of biblical history, like Adam's fall and the Last Judgment. Miracle plays enacted stories from the life of Christ, the Virgin Mary, or the saints. Third were morality plays in which characters were allegories of virtue or vice.

The most famous morality play comes from the late fifteenth century, at the close of the Middle Ages. It is called *Everyman* and tells how only Good Deeds accompanied the lonely Everyman to his grave, once he had been abandoned by Knowledge, Wit, and everyone else. This play, like the other medieval dramatic performances, was a source of religious edification as well as amusement. It would take the Renaissance before drama once again separated from religion.

Further Reading

Gassner, John, ed. *Medieval and Tudor Drama.* New York: Bantam, 1963.
Woolf, Rosemary. *The English Mystery Plays.* London: Routledge, 1972.

Education

During the Roman Empire, education was very important; it was designed to produce involved citizens who could serve the state. The Germanic tribes who invaded the western Empire valued a different kind of education—designed to produce warriors and others who could contribute to the tribe's needs. Education in the Middle Ages represented a combination of these traditions.

In recollection of their Germanic roots, medieval boys engaged in long apprenticeships learning to fight, plant, or grow skilled in a trade. Girls learned sewing, gardening, cooking, healing, and other arts from their mothers and other women in the household. However, Christian worship required different skills, and the church drew from the Roman past to educated men and women to serve God and the state.

Roman education consisted of the liberal arts and included nine subjects, which would come to be called the *trivium* and *quadrivium*. Students began with the trivium: grammar (particularly Latin grammar, which was the official language of church and state), rhetoric (for skillful speaking and writing), and dialectic (a branch of logic, which was seen to be the principal tool for further studies). Grammar also included literature and its interpretation. Armed with these basics, students added studies of arithmetic, geometry, astronomy, and music (which was valued both as an applied form of mathematics and a key to effective liturgical worship).

During the early Middle Ages, students could get an education in two places: at home or in a monastery. Wealthy families hired tutors to teach their children (often boys and girls) basic literacy. We have tantalizing references that testify to the difficulties of getting a suitable tutor. Some were incompetent, others cruel, and in one case the tutor, Abelard, seduced his student Heloise. Monastery schools prepared their curriculum to train new monks and nuns, but their schoolrooms were open to others. Monastery schools suffered from equally mixed abilities of teachers.

When Charlemagne came to the throne in the late eighth century, he was very interested in education, seeing it as a major way to reform abuses in the church. In a remarkably, forward-looking piece of legislation, Charlemagne ordered that education be provided at churches and monasteries for all boys throughout his kingdom. Although this was too difficult to actually implement (and was repealed by his son), it nevertheless demonstrated the emperor's recognition that education was the key to building an effective church and state.

Charlemagne's reforms brought about a number of real changes for the future. By his support of the best scholars in Europe, Charlemagne's court produced standardized texts, accurate manuscripts, and a solid method of education. When learning was forced back behind monastery walls by the violence of the ninth and tenth centuries, monks and nuns had a clear body of work to use as they conducted their schools that served a much smaller student body.

By the twelfth century, education was ready to take another leap forward. There were enough educated, literate boys who wanted to strive for advanced education. Universities would be born to satisfy these longings. Universities grew up at cathedral schools where students gathered to hear lectures from acclaimed masters and hoped to forward their own careers in the church or in courts. Paris hosted the first institution of higher learning, but soon Oxford in England followed. By the thirteenth century, there were centers of learning in all the major cities of Europe.

Students arriving to study were boys of about 14 years old; girls were forbidden to attend. Groups of students would often seek accommodations together, and townspeople often criticized the rowdy boys who enjoyed their free time. Accounts write of students fighting, drinking, gambling, and generally disrupting the towns that nevertheless enjoyed the income these students brought. Dormitories were later developed to try to alleviate some of these problems that arose between students and townspeople.

Once boys were settled into accommodations, they had to choose a master with whom to study. The master was also young—probably in his twenties and pursuing a higher degree—but was very important to the new student. He would be the source of the lectures and be responsible for making sure the student fulfilled the requirements for his degree. On their part, the masters depended on payments from students for their livelihood, so if a master was particularly unpopular, or viewed as incompetent, he would quickly lose his livelihood.

The heart of the curriculum was the master's lectures. In an age when books were expensive, and thus rare, students did most of their learning by listening. Lecture rooms were small, and only a few students would attend at a time. Morning lectures typically began about 6 A.M. These lasted until 10, when students enjoyed a meal. Then afternoon lectures continued until 5, at which time students would have a second meal. In the evening, students studied their notes, talked about the material, read if they were lucky enough to have access to books, and went to the pubs to drink, talk, and enjoy the companionship of their peers.

The basic curriculum remained the quadrivium, but this framework offered a good deal of flexibility depending on the skill of the master. For example, a study of a work of literature—Virgil's *Aeneid* for example—allowed a skilled master to discuss geography, mythology, religion, and music. By the thirteenth century, students were required to take oral examinations to prove their competencies. They would then receive a "bachelor's" degree. After about two more years of study the bachelors could test for a "master's" degree, which would allow them to teach. After that, if they wanted to go on to higher education, they picked specialized schools to study to become "doctors." Those studying medicine often went to Salerno, for law they attended Bologna, and for theology— called the "queen of the sciences"—they went to Paris.

We can readily identify our debt to the educational system of the Middle Ages. Although the curriculum has been expanded, modern students still strive to achieve the same degrees. The commencement gowns are modeled after the medieval clerical gowns that marked the close relationship between education and the church in the Middle Ages. Finally, then as now new ideas blossomed in the lecture halls and the informal gathering places of students. *See also* Documents 7, 10, and 19.

Further Reading

Ridder-Symoens, Hilde de. *A History of the University in Europe: Universities in the Middle Ages*. New York: Cambridge University Press, 1991.

Sullivan, Richard E., ed. *"The Gentle Voices of Teachers": Aspects of Learning in the Carolingian Age*. Columbus: Ohio State University Press, 1995.

Eleanor of Aquitaine (c. 1122–1204)

The twelfth century was a high point of the Middle Ages. There were powerful kings who consolidated their kingdoms, popes exerted their influence over a Christian Europe (*see* **Investiture Controversy**), and Christian armies went crusading in the Holy Land. The age also saw a reinvigoration of culture and learning with the growth of Gothic cathedrals, universities, and the rise of secular literature. One woman—Eleanor of Aquitaine—exerted an influence on all these developments and is remembered as one of the most remarkable women of the Middle Ages.

Eleanor was born in about 1122 in Aquitaine, a province in southern France, and she was raised under the influence of her father William X, who was a great patron of artists and troubadour poets. William died in 1137, leaving Eleanor as heiress to the wealthy duchy under the protection of King Louis VI (the Fat) of France. Louis immediately arranged for her to marry his son and heir, Louis Capet. Louis was only 16 years old and a boy more suited to be a monk than a king. Shortly after the marriage, Louis the Fat died leaving the youthful Louis VII as king with his equally young wife Eleanor as queen.

While queen of France, Eleanor served as the patron for the building of the first Gothic church at Saint-Denis near Paris (*see* **Architecture**). The couple failed to produce a son and heir, only a daughter, Marie, was born in 1145.

When Louis agreed to go on the Second **Crusade**, Eleanor eagerly accompanied him, actually joining him in taking the cross in 1146. The couple stayed with her uncle, Raymond de Toulouse in Antioch, giving rise to unsavory rumors about the relationship between Eleanor and Raymond. After the Crusade failed, the unhappy couple returned home. After Eleanor gave birth to another daughter, Alix, King Louis had the marriage annulled on the basis of consanguinity.

Eleanor seized on this legal opportunity to escape a miserable marriage and soon contracted a second marriage with Henry Plantagenet, who became King Henry II of England in 1154. Through this marriage, Eleanor's extensive holdings in southern France became joined to England and would remain regions contested between the two royal families until the issue was finally resolved by the **Hundred Years' War** that ended in 1453.

Henry was 11 years younger than Eleanor, and a forceful monarch. Within 14 years, Eleanor bore Henry five sons and three daughters. As queen of England, Eleanor continued her important cultural patronage, bringing troubadour poetry to England, and encouraging the writing of Romances in English. It is likely that the famous Arthurian Romances took shape in England under her patronage.

The marriage remained stormy, however. Henry was repeatedly unfaithful, and his long-term liaison with Rosamond Clifford angered Eleanor. Furthermore, Eleanor was determined to rule her own lands in France, so the couple separated in 1168, each establishing a court. Eleanor established a fine court in Poitiers, the capital of her family's lands, and involved herself in the politics of Europe encouraging her sons to take up arms against their father. The uprising failed in 1173, and Henry marched into Poitiers with his soldiers and took his queen captive.

Eleanor remained in her husband's custody for the next 16 years. When Henry II died in 1189, Eleanor's favorite son, Richard the Lion-Hearted became king. Richard relied heavily on his mother to serve as advisor, and indeed she virtually governed the land when he led the Third Crusade in 1191. When Richard was captured and held for ransom, Eleanor went to Germany personally to negotiate his release. After this in 1194, she retired from public life to live at the monastery of Fontevrault in northwestern France. She had King Henry buried there.

Eleanor died on April 1, 1204, at the venerable age of eighty-two. She was buried beside Henry. Her influence over medieval life and culture continued through her children, who ruled many territories in England, France, Germany, and Spain.

Further Reading

Owen, D.D.R. *Eleanor of Aquitaine: Queen and Legend*. Oxford, UK: Blackwell, 1993.

Weir, Alison. *Eleanor of Aquitaine: By the Wrath of God, Queen of England*. London: Jonathan Cape, 1999.

Fathers of the Church

One of the most significant contributions of medieval Europe was the establishment of the Roman Catholic and Eastern Orthodox (or Greek Orthodox) churches. Both of these churches developed a tradition of theology that has shaped the future course of Christianity. The men (and these early theologians were all men) have come to be called "Fathers of the Church," and the studies of their writings is called "patristics."

The term *Fathers of the Church* generally refers to the theological writers of the first six centuries of Christianity who were instrumental in shaping orthodox religious thought and action. (*See* **Heresies** for thinkers who were suggesting alternative Christian patterns of belief.) There is a further distinction between the Fathers of the West, who shaped the Latin Roman Catholic Church, and the Fathers of the East, most influential in the Eastern Orthodox Church, although there was never a full distinction between the two churches, and the Fathers of both influenced each other. By tradition, the last Father in the West was Gregory the Great, who died in 604, and in the East, John of Damascus, who died in 749.

Within this general designation of which writers are deemed Fathers of the Church, there was a further designation of certain of the fathers as "doctors" of the church, which means their writings were particularly valued to instruct the faithful. In the East, the doctors were Basil the Great, Gregory of Nazianzus, and John Chrysostom. These doctors were most noteworthy in developing a theology of the Trinity and an orthodox Christology that says Jesus was fully human and divine. Their theological influence on the West was profound as these ideas became accepted as orthodoxy.

In the West, Ambrose, Augustine, Jerome, and Gregory the Great are singled out as particularly worthy doctors. Their writings dealt less with theological disputes and more with details of a Christian life, although such reflections did have an impact on the growing body of theology. Jerome is best known for his translations and revisions of the biblical books. His version, called the "Vulgate," became the accepted text in the Latin West. Ambrose is remembered for his many writings on practical pastoral matters, to his Christian hymns, and his rigid championship of the defeat of Arianism and paganism in Italy. Ambrose also strongly articulated the idea that emperors were subject to the church.

Augustine was the most prolific and influential of the Latin doctors. His writings shaped such important ideas as original sin, the nature of sexuality, and the relationship between the church and the state. Gregory the Great's contribution lay mostly in his transmission of the ideas of the earlier Fathers, and his description of how a life of prayer can fit with an active life. His life marked what was considered the perfect life of a bishop.

The writings of the Church Fathers formed the background for all the medieval writers. Their vision shaped the medieval church and people's daily lives. It is impossible to overstate the importance of these pivotal thinkers. Late in the Middle Ages, with the rise of **mysticism,** two women were admitted to the ranks of "Doctor of the Church," whose writings were deemed worthy of study: Catherine of Siena (died 1380) and Teresa of Avila (died 1582). The writings of these women point to a more personal Christian quest that belongs more properly in the modern world, when the teachings of the early Fathers no longer seemed sufficient. *See also* Document 1.

Further Reading
Campenhausen, Hans von. *The Fathers of the Greek Church.* New York: Pantheon, 1959.

Campenhausen, Hans von. *Men Who Shaped the Western Church.* New York: Harper and Row, 1964.

Salisbury, Joyce E. *Church Fathers, Independent Virgins.* London: Verso, 1991.

Food

The overriding characteristic of cuisine in medieval Europe was that the food was produced locally. Transportation over long distances was time-consuming and expensive, so unsuitable for moving perishable food items. Therefore, people had to eat what they could produce locally—within a range of 20 miles or so, which was about one day's journey. The need for consuming locally produced food led to varied diets across Europe. For example, in the south near the Mediterranean, people could rely on olive oil, while in the north out of the range of olive production all but the wealthy had to depend on lard or animal fat for cooking.

Regardless of the location, however, medieval diets—like today's—consisted of various food groups. Everywhere peasants planted grains to form the basis of the medieval diet. Cereal crops included wheat, barley, rye, spelt, and oats. (Maize and potatoes that are so ubiquitous today were only imported into Europe after the discovery of North and South America in the late fifteenth century.) The more northern lands had to rely on the hardy barley, rye, and oats, while the lands in the south could plant the more-popular wheat.

Grains were consumed in three ways: bread, ale, and pottage. Most grains were ground into flour, which would allow them to be stored for relatively long periods as long as they were kept dry. Flour was then most commonly baked into bread. Medieval bread was generally hearty, full of bran and roughage, for only the very wealthy could afford bread made of refined white flour. Food was often served on slabs of thick bread, which would soak up the liquids. An average aristocrat or prosperous peasant consumed about two to three pounds of bread in a day.

Table 5. Changing Peasant Diets

	1250	1350	1390	1430
Ale	8%	20%	20%	40%
Dairy	28%	20%	10%	8%
Fish	10%	15%	20%	5%
Meat	2%	5%	30%	30%
Bread	52%	40%	20%	17%

Note: These approximate percentages of total diets drawn from accounts of harvest workers' diets in Norfolk, England, show the changing diets through the late Middle Ages. In the more prosperous times after the Black Death, peasants came to eat more meat and ale.
Source: Figures drawn from Christopher Dyer. *Standards of Living in the Later Middle Ages.* Cambridge, UK: Cambridge University Press, 1989, p. 158.

Ale—unhopped beer—was brewed all over Europe. Wives in small households brewed enough for their own consumption and perhaps to sell a little of the surplus, and brewers in "public houses" (pubs) made the popular beverage to sell to locals and travelers alike. In northern Europe, where grapes would not grow, ale was the primary beverage. Ale made up a significant part of the medieval diet and provided a means by which grains could be preserved, because the alcohol content served as a preservative. A typical aristocrat would drink up to a gallon of ale a day, and a prosperous peasant might drink two to three pints. This may seem like a lot, but the alcohol content of the ale was less than that of modern beers that rely on hops and more sophisticated brewing techniques to increase the alcohol content.

The cheapest way to consume grains was preparing pottage, also known as porridge. To produce this, grains were boiled in water or stock causing them to plump and become more digestible. Cooks added many ingredients to pottage, from beans to meat or fish or vegetables, and they were served as a side dish or a thick main dish.

Grains may have been a staple of medieval households, but like today, people had to find sources of protein. Meats of all types were relatively expensive, so only the aristocracy or wealthy merchants and peasants could regularly eat it. More regular protein sources came from milk products from cows, sheep, goats, and even sometimes deer. To preserve milk products, much was made into cheeses, yogurt or salty butter. The wealthy could eat roasted or boiled meats of all kinds—cattle, goats, sheep, pigs, and game of all sorts. Chickens and geese were also regularly raised for meat and eggs. Fish, too, was central to the medieval diet, particularly because there were many holy days when Christians were forbidden to eat meat except fish.

Another significant difference between modern and medieval food production is in the processing. Medieval peasants had to find ways to preserve and process the foods they produced, and this was particularly important with meat. Animals were regularly slaughtered in great numbers in the fall of the year so their owners would not have to feed them through the winter. That raised the problem of preserving the meat. In the far north, people could simply freeze meats outdoors. Some medieval travelers describe sales of completely frozen carcasses displayed on frozen northern rivers. However, most people had to rely on other means of preserving the valuable meat. The most popular means of preservation were smoking, drying, and salting animal flesh, all methods of drying or curing flesh by removing watery tissue that fostered the growth of bacteria. Smoking was achieved by hanging meat or fish over a smoking fire that speeded up the evaporation of fluids so the meat was thoroughly dried before the oils could go rancid. In addition, the smoke imparted a pleasant taste to the smoked flesh, like hickory smoked bacon or ham that we enjoy today.

Drying was particularly suited to fish, which could be spread on rocks in the sun. This was less reliable, because it depended on several days of sunny weather and low humidity. The most common and secure way of preserving meat and fish was salting. Partially dried meat was packed in salt, which drew the moisture out of the meat, leaving none for bacteria. The importance of salt in curing meats led to a valuable trade in salt that either came from evaporated sea water or deep salt mines. When these dried meats were prepared, they had to be well cooked to reconstitute the flesh and remove much of the salt.

The most common source of protein for most people was various legumes — beans, peas, lentils, and so on. From the eleventh century onward, these were planted all over Europe and caused a dramatic improvement in the health of the lower classes who could not afford to eat much meat. Legumes were also easily dried for long-term storage and boiled alone or with grains and vegetables to make a healthful dish.

Fruits and vegetables made up the final component of a healthful medieval diet, and the constraints of local eating were most apparent when it came to these perishable items. Most vegetables, except legumes and herbs, were unsuited to preserving by drying. Root vegetables, like carrots, turnips, and parsnips, can be stored for several weeks in cool conditions, and some vegetables can be pickled in salt brine and vinegar. Fruits can be dried, and through the long winters many people made do with dried apples and pears. The wealthy could obtain candied fruits — dried and coated in expensive sugar — such as Syrian figs. Beyond these preserved items, people celebrated the coming of spring as they looked forward to lettuce, spinach, cabbages, mushrooms, and many local berries and cherries. The best-preserved fruits were, of course, grapes that were converted to wine and saved in barrels for years.

The skill of medieval people in making the most of the foods available to them must not obscure the fact that when people depended on a local food supply, hunger was an ever-present threat. In years when weather was bad, as in the great famine of 1315, or in the declining settlement of Greenland in the fourteenth century, people died. In the following passage from the *Divine Comedy*, **Dante Alighieri** describes starvation in a way that captures the vulnerability of medieval people:

> The disease of the starving, I mean hunger, is a pitiable affliction. Of human calamities hunger is certainly supreme. It brings about the cruellest end of all deaths. Hunger is a disease that torments with slowness, a pain that endures, a sickness that lasts, and is hidden in the bowels, a death that is always present and everlingering. (Camporesi, 27)

Further Reading

Camporesi, Piero. *Bread of Dreams.* Chicago: University of Chicago Press, 1989.

Dyer, Christopher. *Standards of Living in the Later Middle Ages, Social Change in England, c. 1270–1520.* Cambridge, UK: Cambridge University Press, 1990.

Newman, Paul B. *Daily Life in the Middle Ages.* London: McFarland and Company, 2001.

Francis of Assisi (c. 1182–1226)

In the thirteenth century, the medieval church was under attack by many for its wealth and power. Some **heresies** called for religious people to follow the "apostolic life" of preaching, wandering, and poverty. One such critic, Francis of Assisi, was able to found a religious order that allowed those who valued voluntary poverty to remain orthodox members of the medieval church.

Francesco di Pietro di Bernardone, better known as Francis of Assisi, was born around 1181 in Assisi, Italy. He was the son of a prosperous merchant and received a good education and grew to enjoy the luxuries of life. In about 1202, Francis participated in a war between two warring city-states (Perugia and Assisi); he was captured and imprisoned for a year. When he returned, he was in poor health and had a long period of recuperation. In about 1205, he tried to take up his military career again but had a mystical experience in which he was told to return to Assisi to await more information on his life's work.

According to Francis's own accounts, he received several spiritual experiences directing him to rejuvenate the church. He renounced his father's wealth and began to renovate churches in need of repair. He began to preach and followers gathered around him. In 1209, Pope Innocent III approved of his band's simple rule of life and the establishment of the Franciscan Order.

At the heart of the Franciscan rule lay the idea that Franciscans—called "friars"—should not confine themselves to monasteries but instead should help others by working in the world. They should preach the Gospel, care for the sick and dying, and lead lives of simple poverty and chastity. Francis also developed a new theology of nature, arguing that all God's creations were interconnected. His famous hymn "Canticle of the Sun" articulated this worldview of human integration into the natural order.

The Franciscan Order grew rapidly, extending throughout Italy and beyond. By 1215, there were more than five-thousand men in the Order. In 1212, Francis had established an order for women, named the Poor Clares after its first member, Clare of Assisi.

Francis spent the last years of his life in Assisi. He had another mystical experience in 1224 during a prolonged fast. In a vision, an angel appeared to him to help him share the experience of the crucified Christ. As a physical manifestation of this vision, Francis was reputed to bleed from his hands, feet, and head in imitation of Christ's wounds. This bleeding is called the "stigmata." His health declined steadily after this, and he died on October 3, 1226, in Assisi.

After Francis's death, the Franciscan Order continued its growth. Its very success led to a crisis within the Order. In his will, Francis left strict orders prohibiting ownership of any property to try to preserve the poverty that was at the heart of his theology. By as early as 1230, the pope said Franciscans could "use" property and acquired numerous buildings to accommodate the growing Order. However, this practice also generated critics who argued that the ideals of Francis were being compromised. These critics, who came to be called "Spiritual Franciscans," caused so much disruption that in 1318 four Spiritual friars were burned as heretics on the grounds that they refused to obey a papal order that called for them to stop cricizing the practice of owning property. Pope John XXII's condemnation of the Spirituals was later criticized, but the force of his opposition drove many Spirituals underground and out of the church. Thus for all of Francis's reform, the issue of poverty would remain unsolved until the early modern period, when the Reformation rendered the dispute moot.

Further Reading

Iriarte, Lazaro. *History of the Franciscan Order*. Chicago: Franciscan Herald Press, 1983.
House, Adrian, and Karen Armstrong. *Francis of Assisi: A Revolutionary Life*. London: Random House, 2000.

Guilds

The growth of commerce and a European-wide population increase led to the growth of towns in the late eleventh century. By the end of this century, townspeople, including artisans, merchants, and laborers had obtained charters from local lords allowing residents to govern themselves outside the feudal structure. Thus if a runaway serf went to a town and escaped capture for a year and a day, he or she was free. In general, then, town charters gave the burgers (townspeople) many freedoms. However, the charters did not determine how the various groups within the town were to organize themselves, and during the Middle Ages townspeople began to organize themselves into "guilds."

Guilds came to be organized among people engaged in the same enterprise. There were merchant guilds and guilds for craftsmen. And these became so popular, that by the thirteenth century there was a guild for every conceivable occupation. For example, just within the cloth industry there were guilds of spinners, weavers, fullers, and dyers. In some cities, there were even guilds of prostitutes. Generally, the members of a guild lived together on the same street, which gave an organization to the urban space itself. There were streets of goldsmiths, bakers, cobblers, and so on.

The basic functions of the guild were to care for its members and regulate the trade of the guildsmen. Guilds first decided who would be allowed to enter the craft. Although most members of a guild were men, women could enter a craft during most of the Middle Ages. Only at the end of the period were women slowly excluded from guild membership. An artisan started a career by becoming an apprentice and serving under a craftsman until he or she learned the trade. The number of apprentices and their length of service were decided by the guild. Guilds might also regulate the treatment of apprentices, requiring them to be properly housed, fed, and not overworked.

After an apprentice had served his time in training—often about 5 years, but it varied considerably—he was required to produce a piece of work to be judged by the guild. This was called his "masterpiece" to see if it demonstrated enough skill to warrant the apprentice's promotion to "master." Sometimes apprentices were required to serve a further number of years as "journeymen," a paid craftsman, before being allowed to open their own shop. Guilds would often forbid journeymen to become masters if they believed there would be too much competition within their town. Guilds could also forbid anyone who was not a member to sell in their town, so foreign merchants could not come in and offer competition.

Guilds also controlled prices and wages within their guild and guaranteed quality of the product. But the guilds would not have been so popular if they did not provide many benefits for their members. If a merchant lost his stock in a fire, the guild would help him start again. When a member died, the other members would provide burial and care for his widow and children, even providing schooling for them.

In larger towns, guilds were so prosperous that they often acted as religious fraternities to sponsor festivals and aid the local church. Some of the stained-glass windows in the great cathedrals of Europe were paid for by craft guilds.

The guilds provided a large measure of security for townspeople who wanted to enter the commercial world. The very success of medieval towns and the vibrant commercial life they developed can be attributed to these entities that organized the new economic centers. *See also* Document 17.

Further Reading

Reynolds, Susan. *An Introduction to the History of English Medieval Towns*. Oxford, UK: Clarendon Press, 1977.
Singman, Jeffrey L. *Daily Life in Medieval Europe*. Westport, CT: Greenwood Press, 1999.

Heresies

In the early fourth century, the Roman Emperor Constantine threw his support to the Christian Church, which then became a church of the powerful as well as the poor. Leaders of this newly constituted "Roman Catholic Church" began to search for a unity of belief that had been lacking in the more informally organized years of the early, persecuted church. Beginning in the eastern part of the Empire (that would come to be called the "Byzantine Empire"), rulers beginning with Constantine himself involved themselves in religious disputes, presiding over church conferences, and giving political support to various positions. This drive for a unity of belief led to one of the hallmarks of medieval society—those who disagreed with the established church's opinion (called the "orthodox" position) came to be called "heretics," and they were persecuted for their beliefs, called "heresies." Many heresies grew through the Middle Ages, and here I have clustered them under general characteristics they shared.

Gnosticism

From the earliest centuries after the crucifixion of Jesus, believers differed on their understanding of Jesus's message. Some, whom we have come to call generally "Gnostics" believed that Jesus had imparted secret knowledge to his followers (*gnostic* comes from the Greek word for "knowledge" and means "one who knows"). This knowledge urged them to "not so much to *believe* in Jesus, . . . as to seek to know *God* through one's own, divinely given capacity since all are created in the image of God" (Pagels, *Beyond Belief*, 54). Many Gnostic texts, like the *Gospel of Thomas* and the *Gospel of Judas* offer believers a guide to exploring this self-searching. Gnostic texts were kept out of what came to be the accepted Bible, and many subsequent heresies adopted elements of Gnosticism. Even today, in the twenty-first century, there are many people who believe in a Gnostic form of Christianity.

Christological Controversies

In the fourth century, most of the religious disputes had to do with the nature of Christ. The first question had to do with whether Christ had always existed—even before the world had been created—or did God the Father bring him forth at a particular time. In about 320, Arius, bishop of Alexandria, raised a furor when he argued that Jesus had been created by God. The bishop had many followers called "Arians"—including Germanic tribes who had been converted by Arian bishops. In 325, Emperor Constantine called a church council at Nicaea, which formulated the Nicene Creed, which stated that Christ had always existed. Many churches today continue to chant the Nicene Creed as their statement of faith.

Even Christians who accepted this formulation began to wonder about how Christ's humanity and divinity were united with Jesus. Some argued that His divinity was so powerful that his humanity was obliterated. These heretics were called "monophysites," which means "believe in one nature"—His divine one. Others argued that for the miracle of his resurrection to matter to humans, his human nature had to predominate. These heretics were called "Nestorians," named after Nestorus, one of their leaders. The church condemned both these positions arguing that Jesus was miraculously all human and all divine. However, advocates of both heresies moved away from the centers of Christian power to continue to practice their own brand of Christianity. When Christians traveled as far as China in the thirteenth century, they found long-standing Nestorian congregations living there.

Dualism

One of the questions that has long troubled many Christians is "With a God of love, where does evil come from?" Several groups of heretics came up with one answer: There are two Gods, the loving God of Christ and another evil God, and this world represents a struggle between these two forces. These heretics are generally called "dualists" from the word *two*, and they believe that humans are composed of two parts: a spiritual bit of the good deity trapped in flesh that was created by the evil god. The goal of humans was to cultivate their spiritual side and thus escape a cycle of rebirth that would entrap them in this world of pain created by the evil principle.

The earliest dualists who were condemned by the Christian Church were the Manichaeans, whose intellectual brand of dualism even drew the famous Saint Augustine in his youth. Augustine's later writings against the Manichaeans represent our fullest information about this sect.

In the ninth and tenth centuries, the Byzantines discovered a strong strand of dualism among Bulgars, a Slavic tribe newly converted to Christianity. These dualists were called "Bogomils." In the twelfth and thirteenth centuries, there was a strong resurgence of dualism in southern France and Italy. These were called "Cathari" or "Albigensians." This group was so popular, that in the thirteenth century, popes called a crusade against these heretics, and the resulting Albigensian Crusade brutally suppressed the heresy and allowed northern France to break the power of the southerners.

Historians have disputed the degree to which each of these dualist heresies influenced the others, and there has been no consensus. Some historians even suggest that this wasn't even Christianity, because any religion that posits two gods cannot be part of the monotheistic tradition. Regardless of modern historical discussions, medieval practitioners believed they were following a pure form of Christianity.

Heresies of the Apostolic Life

A more serious threat to the established church were movements that struck at the heart of the church rejecting its sacraments, hierarchy, and wealth and arguing that Christians should live as the Bible described the life of the early apostles. For these heretics, true Christians should be poor—giving up all their worldly wealth—and wander about preaching God's word. The most famous of these movements were the Waldensians, which began in the twelfth century. Its originator was Valdes of Lyons, a wealthy merchant who gave up all he owned to follow Christ. (Subsequent sources named him Peter Waldo, probably in imitation of Saint Peter.) A few years after his conversion, Valdes and his followers began preaching against clerical vice and wealth and were declared heretical for their critique.

There were many other groups condemned for criticizing churchmen for not following the apostolic life of poverty, preaching, and Bible reading. Some were called the "Humiliati" and the "Poor of Lyon." Many were persecuted and killed for their beliefs.

Toward the Reformation

By the late fourteenth and early fifteenth centuries, the swell of criticism of the established church began to rise. Two popular theologians dominated the critique: John Wycliffe from Oxford and John Hus from Prague were both intellectuals attached to universities. They were able to marshal arguments that supported popular anticlerical movements. Both called for a simpler religion, grounded in scripture rather than in the authority of the Church. Wycliffe had many followers, called "Lollards." John Hus was executed for his beliefs.

The arguments of Wycliffe and Hus would be adopted again in the early sixteenth century, when Martin Luther launched the Reformation of the Church that split the medieval church. After that, there was no more universal doctrine of beliefs, and instead of becoming heretics, people chose denominations that were more conducive to their beliefs. But that would happen only after the end of the Middle Ages. *See also* Document 28.

Further Reading

BeDuhn, Jason David. *The Manichaean Body in Discpline and Ritual*. Baltimore: Johns Hopkins University Press, 2000.

Evans, Austin P. *Heresies of the High Middle Ages*. New York: Columbia University Press, 1991.

Pagels, Elaine. *Beyond Belief: The Secret Gospel of Thomas*. New York: Vintage Books, 2003.

Hildegard of Bingen (1098–1179)

The twelfth century was an age that saw wonderful innovations in learning, medicine, and music. Many of these developments took place at the growing universities, but women were not allowed into these schools (*see* **Education**). Yet in monasteries that drew women, many were educated and were able to enjoy the intellectual arts. The greatest of these was Hildegard of Bingen, a German Benedictine abbess who founded two monasteries for women. She became well respected in her age for her accomplishments in theology, medicine, and music and was considered a visionary of God.

Hildegard was born in 1098 in the village of Bermershein in the Rhineland. She was the tenth child of noble parents. From a young age, she suffered from visions that often included seeing dazzling lights. Some historians have suggested that these debilitating experiences were some form of migraines, but Hildegard saw them as messages from God. Her parents sent her to a monastery in her childhood where she must have received a good education, though little is known of her experience during these early years.

In 1136, the abbess died and Hildegard was elected abbess. Five years later, she received a prophetic calling to publicize her visions. With the help of two nuns, she wrote her most famous work of visionary theology, the *Scivias* (short for *Scito vias Domini*, or *Know the Ways of the Lord*). This work took about 10 years to complete and was illustrated with stunning visual portrayals of her visions.

During the next decade, her life was dominated by her desire to found a new monastery. She was involved in construction, fund-raising, music, and caring for the growing number of nuns who joined her. She composed music for the new house, including a music-drama, called *Ordo virtutum* (*Play of Virtues*) which is often considered one of the first morality plays.

Her scientific and medical writings reveal the breadth of her knowledge available in the twelfth-century monastic libraries. Her comprehensive encyclopedia of natural history is called the *Nine Books on the Subtleties of Different Kinds of Creatures*. This collection includes a bestiary, a lapidary (on the properties of rocks and gems), and an herbal and summarizes the state of twelfth-century science. A more original work is her medical volume, *Causae et Curae* (*Causes and Cures*). In this, Hildegard builds on traditional Galenic **medicine**. However, Hildegard goes beyond Galen in considering the different impact of various humors on gender, including reflecting on male and female sexuality. Hildegard also includes practical folklore remedies probably drawn from her own care of her nuns.

Hildegard's reputation spread all over Europe. She was revered as a prophet and engaged in correspondence with the greatest figures of the age, including Emperor Frederick Barbarossa (c. 1122–1190), several popes, and the influential monk, **Bernard of Clairvaux**. Hildegard even undertook several preaching tours delivering sermons not only at monasteries, but more surprising in the cathedrals of several German towns.

Her final work of her old age was the *Book of Divine Works* in which she synthesized much of her wide-ranging knowledge, from science to theology. She died in 1179, and modern scholars have repopularized this astonishing medieval woman. *See also* Document 18.

Angel overcoming the Devil, from 11th–12th century Latin codex Visions of Saint Hildegard of Bingen, *Book of the Works of God*. The Art Archive/Biblioteca Civica Lucca/Gianni Dagli Orti.

Further Reading

King-Lenzmeier, Ann. *Hildegard of Bingen: An Integrated Vision*. Collegeville, MN: Liturgical Press, 2001.

Newman, Barbara. *Sister of Wisdom: St. Hildegard's Theology of the Feminine*. Berkeley: University of California Press, 1997.

Hundred Years War

In 1337, England and France entered into a century-long conflict that became the final straw that brought the Middle Ages to an end. The war began as a feudal struggle between a lord and his vassal and ended as a nationalistic struggle between nations whose armies were made up largely of commoners armed with longbows and guns. The world indeed changed in this century of devastation.

The issue that triggered the conflict was the succession to the throne of France. When the French King Charles IV died in 1328 without a son, the closest heir was Edward III of England (r. 1327–1377) because his grandmother had been the daughter of the French king. Edward was at first in no position to complain when the French gave the crown to Philip VI of Valois (r. 1328–1350), a first cousin of the previous ruler. However, soon another issue arose between the two kings. Philip VI tried to interfere in the lucrative wool trade between England and Flanders, and the Flemish asked Edward to assert his claim to the French crown so the rich trade could continue unimpeded. Because Edward did not like being the vassal of the French king for his lands in France, he declared war on Philip, whom he called the "so-called king of France."

The long struggle began with some stunning English victories. The English first secured their communications across the Channel with a naval victory at Sluys in 1340; they then could turn to a land invasion of France. The French outnumbered the English, but the English took advantage of the longbow and pike, weapons that allowed foot soldiers to gain a solid advantage over mounted knights (*see* **Warfare**). Edward won a stunning victory at the Battle of Crecy in 1346, and an eyewitness described a sky blackened by English arrows as the flower of French knighthood fell crushed. By this victory, the English secured Flanders and the important port of Calais. The strategy was repeated at Poitiers in 1356, and the exhausted French were forced to sue for peace (the Peace of Bretigny) in 1360. By the terms of this peace, King Edward renounced his claim to the French throne in exchange for Calais and enlarged holdings in Aquitaine. (*See* **Eleanor of Aquitaine** for background on English holdings in France.)

The French were not willing to allow so much of their land to remain in English hands, so the war was reopened in 1369 under the French king Charles V (r. 1364–1380). He introduced a wise strategy of avoiding major military confrontation and instead wearing down the English forces on the continent. During this phase of the war, soldiers on both sides devastated the countryside, making civilian misery part of the cost of this long war.

The cautious tactics of Charles V led to French victories. By 1380, the English had almost been pushed out of France—they held only Calais and a small strip of land between Bordeaux and Bayonne. But once again the English rallied, and the last stage of the war (from 1415 to 1453) was marked by rapidly changing fortunes between the two sides. Early in the fifteenth century, France itself seemed to be disintegrating, for the Duke of Burgundy allied with the English to try to dismantle France.

The warfare of feudalism itself came further under attack as new weapons were developed that eventually made heavily armored knights obsolete. In the 1420s, a new kind of gunpowder was developed that was not only stable, but also exploded virtually instantly. Eventually, mounted knights simply grew too expensive and ineffective for the new warfare; the future lay with the infantry armed with longbows, pikes, and guns.

With their Burgundian allies, the English gained ground rapidly. The English king Henry V (r. 1413–1422) reasserted his claims to the French throne, invaded, and had a brilliant victory at the Battle of Agincourt in 1415. This battle was a replay of Crecy, and the French cavalry was defeated again. The French king was forced to sue for peace and declare his heir (called the "Dauphin") illegitimate. For all practical purposes, France was defeated. In 1428, the English laid siege to Orleans, and its fall would have ensured the English control of all the lands north of the Loire River. It seemed it would take a miracle to restore the French monarchy, and remarkably, many people believed they got one in the person of Joan of Arc.

During these darkest days of France, a young peasant girl—Joan of Arc (c. 1412–1431)—believed she saw visions in which angels urged her to put on men's clothing and lead the French troops to victory. The Dauphin, who was desperate, gave her command of an army. Miraculously, Joan stirred the determination of the French armies and lifted the siege at Orleans. After this victory, she escorted the Dauphin to Reims—the city where French kings were traditionally crowned—where he received the crown of France, thus renouncing the previous treaty. The French rallied around their king and by 1453, the English only held Calais.

Joan did not live to see the victory. She had been captured in 1431 by the Burgundians, who turned her over to their English allies. They put her on trial for witchcraft and heresy. She was condemned to be burned at the stake.

As a result of the Hundred Years' War, the English were expelled from French soil. The French king emerged more powerful than all his vassals, and the slow consolidation of royal rule was effectively complete. The monarchy had a permanent army, and a great deal of prestige among people who were coming to see themselves as "French." Nationalism—one of the hallmarks of the modern age—was born, and the feudal ties of the Middle Ages were fading. *See also* Document 27.

Further Reading

Allmand, Christopher. *The Hundred Years' War: England and France at War, ca. 1300–ca. 1450*. Cambridge, UK: Cambridge University Press, 1988.

Curry, Anne. *The Hundred Years' War*. New York: St. Martin's Press, 1993.

Wagner, John A. *Encyclopedia of the Hundred Years War*. Westport, CT: Greenwood Press, 2006.

Iconoclasm

In the eighth century a religious controversy arose that served to create a decisive split between the Byzantine Empire and the western kingdoms that were loyal to the pope in Rome. This controversy was about whether or not people should venerate "icons"—images of saints and the Virgin Mary that were displayed prominently in the churches, East and West. The controversy was over "iconoclasm," which means "image breaking."

From the earliest times, Christians used images, paintings, mosaics, and sculptures of Christ and the saints in their churches. These were to supply concrete inspiration to worship, but some believed it looked like people were worshiping the images instead of the saints they represented. This was particularly true in places where people had recently converted from paganism, where the habits of worshiping images remained strong. Beginning in the late seventh century, there was an additional reason to question the presence of images in churches: The Prophet Muhammad had claimed Christians had fallen into idolatry, and that Islam adhered to a purer form of monotheism.

These criticisms came to a head in Byzantium in the reign of Leo III (717–741), who came from Asiatic provinces where there was a strong feeling that perhaps Muhammad had a point. Leo was very devout and brought this sensibility to his reign. Leo also had a practical reason for attacking idols: Wealthy monasteries had a monopoly on the creating of idols, and Leo wanted to break some of their power.

In 726, Leo brought the issue to a head by banning icons, and this decree led to revolts in Greece and Italy that were suppressed but only after considerable struggle. The theological issue that generated such passion was based in the idea of whether the material world was good or evil. Supporters of icons believed that portraying Christ supported the incarnation by allowing that the material representation of Christ reflected his material body. Iconoclasm seemed to downplay this central mystery of Christianity.

A more significant political result of the struggle with iconoclasm came when Pope Gregory II (r. 715–731) refused to obey Leo's iconoclastic decree. In fact, the pope said that he would ally with Western barbarians rather than tear down the image of St. Peter at Rome. This split confirmed that East and West had parted, and popes allied with the Franks as their secular arm (*see* **Charlemagne**).

The iconoclastic dispute continued in Byzantium for more than a century, with different emperors taking different sides. Not until 843, when an empress finally restored the images, did the iconoclastic controversy come to an end. Perhaps ironically, it was in the East, in the Byzantine Empire where the veneration of icons continued with the greatest force. The Eastern Orthodox Church continues this tradition today.

Further Reading
Hussey, J. *The Orthodox Church in the Byzantine Empire.* Oxford, UK: Oxford University Press, 1986.

Inquisition

Medieval society was founded on a solid legal tradition. Lawyers and judges used a rich body of **law**s to bring order and justice to the land. However, in the thirteenth century, the prevalence of **heresies** caused church authorities to establish a new kind of court. This court—called "the Inquisition"—differed from other courts in one particular way: Regular courts were established to determine the guilt of someone after a crime had been committed. Now the church was worried about finding people who might jeopardize others by their wrong beliefs instead of their criminal actions.

In 1233, Pope Gregory IX (r. 1227–1241) established a permanent organization to combat heretics. He wanted people who were educated to go all over Europe to inquire about the beliefs of parishioners. Most of these inquisitors were Dominican Friars who had been trained at universities and who were skilled in the nuances of religious thought. The purpose of the Inquisition was twofold: to save the soul of a heretic and prevent him or her from corrupting others. The danger of heresy seemed so pervasive that the Inquisition could use methods that were not allowed in criminal courts. For example, good Catholics were urged to denounce heretics, but the accused was not allowed to confront his accuser, nor even know what the charge exactly was.

Once people came to the attention of the Inquisition, they were questioned to determine their beliefs. Of course, if they were heretics, they would lie to the inquisitors, so the judges were left with a dilemma: how to ascertain a person's real thoughts? Handbooks for inquisitors recommended various kinds of trickery to trap the accused into revealing a heretical opinion. Sometimes the accused were imprisoned and even starved into making a confession.

If a man or woman seemed guilty to the inquisitors, yet persisted in denying the charges, he or she could be tortured. According to church law, there were rules surrounding the application of torture. The accused could only be tortured once, and the confession was supposed to be voluntary. However, inquisitors regularly broke these rules, saying they were "continuing" the first torture, not adding a second. Many innocent people confessed under these circumstances.

Once a confession of guilt was obtained, the inquisitors assigned a penance. This might consist of a pilgrimage, public flogging, imprisonment, or other public humiliation. The property of a confessed heretic was also taken and divided up between the king and the church. These "penances" were so onerous, it was difficult for anyone who had been condemned to reenter society.

The Inquisition did not kill people — that was against church law. However, it did work with secular authorities to rid society of those it deemed dangerous. If someone resisted torture and questioning and refused to confess and accept penance, and if the inquisitors believed this individual was indeed a heretic, they turned the accused over to the government. The government then would execute — usually burn — the unrepentant heretic. Anyone who con-

Burning heretical books, from Santo Domingo y los albigenses (Saint Dominic or Domingo Guzman of Castile), 1170–1221. The Art Archive/Museo del Prado Madrid/ Gianni Dagli Orti.

fessed did penance, and then relapse into heresy was immediately turned over to the secular authority for punishment.

Joan of Arc (c. 1412–1431), the famous saint who helped the French drive the English out of France during the **Hundred Years' War**, fell into this second category. Under much pressure, she had confessed to the Inquisition and promised to wear women's clothing again. When, her "voices" told her to once again wear men's clothing, she was declared unrepentant and burned at the stake.

The Inquisition is a dark part of the history of Christianity. Although there were many good men who deeply believed that heresy could harm society, the result was horrifying. When people can be persecuted for their ideas, it is hard for any idea to be safe. *See also* Document 28.

Further Reading

Peters, Edward. *Inquisition.* Berkeley: University of California Press, 1989.

Investiture Controversy

Medieval political thinkers, religious and secular, believed that society on earth should be ordered in accordance with God's wishes, indeed should mirror a heavenly order. This desire for a well-ordered world led to a controversy that began in the late eleventh century. At the heart of the question was who should be on top of a well-ordered hierarchy, pope or kings? The struggle called the "Investiture Controversy" slowly led to a papal monarchy which by the thirteen century placed the popes as leaders of a Christian Europe.

The controversy began over control of the papal office itself. In 1059, a council at Rome decreed that only the cardinals should elect future popes, and their deliberations should be free from interference by aristocratic factions and the imperial government. This system, with procedural modifications, has remained in place ever since. The real controversy lay in a related decree issued by this council, claiming that no priest should receive any church from a layman. At first, this portion of the decree was not implemented, but it remained a principle that future popes might enforce.

In 1073, Gregory VII was elected pope. He was a passionate reformer, who believed it was his duty to break royal control of ecclesiastical appointments. He brought the issue to a head with the Holy Roman Emperor Henry IV (r. 1056–1106). Gregory claimed that Henry could not "invest" bishops with their ring and staff, the symbols of episcopal power. This meant that the pope could choose bishops in all the lands of Europe, and because bishops were important politically as well as religiously, papal appointments could effectively undercut the powers of the kings.

Through the struggle, the two sides liberally wielded their weapons: Henry sent his armies marching into Italy; Gregory excommunicated the emperor, claiming that this action could free the ever-rebellious vassals from their feudal obligations (see **Law, Feudal**). The battle waged on indecisively. Gregory died in exile in 1085, but Henry was unable to secure a decisive victory before his own death. The strengthened claims of papal power allowed popes to call the first **crusade** in 1096, demonstrating their ability to field armies of Christendom.

In 1122, the new emperor, Henry V, negotiated a compromise to the investiture controversy, called the "Concordat of Worms." In this compromise, the popes would invest the bishops with their symbols of office, but the elections of bishops would take place in the presence, and under the influence of kings. Tensions between papal and royal power did not end with the Concordat of Worms, however, and sporadic struggles broke out in various regions of Europe.

Perhaps the most famous incident to the royal/papal tensions took place in England. King Henry II (r. 1154–1189) was exerting royal authority through centralizing the law courts in his land. In doing so, he came into conflict with his archbishop and once-best-friend, Thomas Becket. Becket wanted to preserve the church's right to be exempt from Henry's legal authority. One day, a small group of knights seeking to please their king surprised Becket in his church at Canterbury and split his head with their swords. Becket died on the altar he had served so well. Beckett quickly became a martyr in the battle for church autonomy, and Henry was forced to compromise with the pope to gain forgiveness for his archbishop's murder. The power of the popes grew.

As church power grew, the papacy developed structures that increasingly resembled the powerful medieval monarchies. The pope created an administrative unit to handle financial matters, and a legal branch to handle appeals covered by the growing body of canon law (see **Law, Roman and Canon**). By the beginning of the thirteenth century, popes could with some accuracy claim that they presided over a universal Christendom, and the most powerful pope was Innocent III (r. 1198–1216).

Innocent was able to exert leadership over princes of Europe, reprimanding them and requiring their obedience. He called the important Fourth Lateran Council in 1215 that pronounced on many issues that came to define the Roman Catholic Church: It identified exactly seven sacraments and reaffirmed their essential role for salvation; it established qualifications for the priesthood, and the monastic life. In effect, the medieval church had become an empire that superseded all other empires. *See also* Document 13.

Further Reading

Morris, Colin. *The Papal Monarchy: The Western Church from 1050–1250.* New York: Oxford University Press, 1991.

Sayers, Jane. *Innocent III: Leader of Europe, 1198–1216.* New York: Longman, 1994.

Jews

Since the time of the Roman Empire, many towns had a significant population of Jews. For centuries, Jews had played a vital role in town life as merchants, artisans, and members of many other professions. By the eleventh and twelfth centuries when commerce became more prevalent, Christian merchants and craftspeople began to view the Jewish community as competition. Slowly, they excluded Jews from guilds and, in some places, kept them from owning land.

The Wandering Jew (character in medieval myth, who supposedly offended Christ on way to crucifixion and cursed to walk the earth eternally). Print from Orléans, France, c. 1785. The Art Archive/Private Collection/ Marc Charmet.

Even as they were restricted from some enterprises, Jews were allowed—indeed encouraged—to enter into money lending, which is essential to commercial enterprises. The Christian religion forbade its followers to collect interest on loans, for they believed it was unseemly to make money from time, which belonged to God. To explain this, a Franciscan in the fourteenth century said that merchants could not charge interest because "in doing so he would be selling time and would be committing usury by selling what does not belong to him" (Le Goff, 29). Muslims, like Jews, also had no religious strictures against lending money, so Muslims and Jews prospered on the important banking trade of the Middle Ages.

Their work in money lending placed Jews in an increasingly precarious position. They were at the mercy of local lords who protected them and helped them collect their debts, but Jews had no rights against a lord who wanted to avoid repaying them. Jews in England were there by the king's permission and were under his protection. Whenever a Jew made a loan, it was registered with royal officials, and the king collected 10 percent from each loan. By the thirteenth century, Christian merchants had begun to practice money lending on a large scale. This made Jews less necessary, and they were expelled from England in the thirteenth century.

In addition to economic pressures, there were other reasons that Jews faced increasing persecution during the Middle Ages. Some Crusaders, who traveled long distances to fight the "infidel" in the Holy Land, believed that Jews, too, were worthy targets of crusading zeal. Even the saintly crusader king Louis IX believed persecuting Jews to be a religious duty. Periodically crusading armies conducted pogroms (persecutions) on Jewish communities along their way.

In the fourteenth century when plague devastated Europe, Christians wondered at the cause of such suffering. In their quest for scapegoats, they often turned to Jews, the perennial targets of Christian anger in the Middle Ages. There were hideous massacres of Jews in German cities when the plague spread there in 1348. Pope Clement VI opposed these pogroms, logically pointing out that Jews, too, were victims of the plague. But this did not stop more massacres in 1349.

Anti-Jewish sentiment increased through the fourteenth century and reached a culmination at the end of the Middle Ages. In the fifteenth century there were large-scale expulsions of Jewish communities from many cities and countries. Vienna began expelling Jews in 1421, and many other German cities followed. King Ferdinand and Queen Isabella forced all of Spain's Jews to leave in 1492, causing one of the largest movements of peoples in the era. Portugal did the same in 1497. Many Jews from Spain and Portugal fled to the Muslim lands in North Africa, and some Muslims today still trace their ancestry back to this exodus. German Jews moved eastward into Poland and Russia, and the center of Judaism shifted from western Europe to the East. As a result of this intolerance, western Europe lost the talents of the many Jews who had inhabited these lands for centuries. *See also* Document 8.

Further Reading
Johnson, Paul. *A History of the Jews.* London: Weidenfeld & Nicholson, 2001.
LeGoff, Jacques. *Time, Work, and Culture in the Middle Ages.* Translated by Arthur Goldhammer. Chicago: University of Chicago Press, 1980.

Justinian (c. 483–565)

The sixth century was a formative time for the eastern part of the old Roman Empire. This was the pivotal period of transition from Roman to the Byzantine Empire, and it was shaped by the Emperor Justinian and his remarkable wife, Theodora.

Justinian was born about 483 in the Balkans. His parents had been Macedonian peasants, and little is known of his early life. When Justinian was 20 years old, he was brought to Constantinople by his uncle, Justin I, who had risen through the ranks and become an important military officer. Justin had no children, so he brought several of his nephews to the capital where they were given a good education and trained for the military. Justinian proved so promising, he was adopted by his uncle.

Justin was able to have himself proclaimed emperor in 518, and Justinian played an important role in his administration. When Justin died in 527, Justinian was proclaimed emperor. Shortly before he was acclaimed emperor,

Justinian married his great love, Theodora. She, too, was of humble origins, but a great beauty and highly intelligent. She apparently had been an exotic dancer when she captured Justinian's eye, but once she was empress, she used her talents and love of power to share rule with Justinian.

The great crisis of Justinian's reign was the Nika Riot of 532. This began as a dispute between rival chariot racing teams but ended as a riot against the emperor. Justinian was ready to flee the violence, but Theodora urged him to stand firm and crush the rioters. He prevailed and was able to impose an autocratic rule that marked future Byzantine Emperors. The Nika Riots also destroyed much of the city, so Justinian had the opportunity to rebuild the city in significant ways. He built forts, bridges, aqueducts, and many public buildings like baths. The greatest church was the magnificent Hagia Sophia, a complex building featuring a great central dome with semidomes on each side of the central nave (*see* **Architecture**). It was breathtaking at its time and remains one of the world's architectural masterpieces.

Justinian's building program extended beyond Constantinople into Jerusalem and Ravenna, Italy, the old capital of the western empire. In Ravenna, particularly notable is the Church of San Vitale, which features magnificent mosaics of Justinian and Theodora.

Even more influential than his building program was the emperor's legal reforms (*see* **Law, Canon**). Shortly after becoming emperor, Justinian called together a commission of legal scholars to update the compilations of the old Roman laws. The resulting work, the *Codex Justinianus*, the *Digest*, and the *Institutes* together are called the *Corpus Juris Civilis*, or the *Body of Civil Law*. This was intended to serve all the legal needs of the empire, as well as be the official manual for law students. It was in this form that Roman law was passed on to the future in the West. The legal reform stands as Justinian's greatest achievement.

The least successful enterprise of this emperor was his attempt to reunite the two parts of the empire. He was able to take North Africa from the Vandals and Italy from the Ostrogoths. However, these reconquests proved short sighted. Justinian raised the taxes in the reconquered territories, causing dissatisfaction. Furthermore, to hold these lands, Justinian had to rely on German mercenaries, and this strategy paved the way for the Lombards—a less tolerant tribe of Germans than the Ostrogoths—to conquer Italy in 568. Justinian could not maintain a firm grip on the western provinces, and the constant battling drained the eastern empire of needed resources. Justinians attempt to reunify the old Roman Empire would be the last—from his reign on, the Byzantine Empire would go its own way, divorced from the West.

Theodora died of cancer in 548, and her death marked the end of the productive part of Justinian's reign. By the time Justinian died in 565, at the age of eighty-two, his people cheered his death. They hoped that the era of expansion and autocratic taxation would end, but their hopes were misplaced. Justinian and Theodora had no children, and Justinian made his nephew Justin his heir, and years of difficult, autocratic rule continued. *See also* Document 4.

Further Reading

Barker, John W. *Justinian and the Later Roman Empire*. Madison: University of Wisconsin Press, 1966.

Moorhead, John. *Justinian*. London: Longman, 1994.

Law, Feudal

People throughout medieval society were joined to each other in a system of mutual obligations. These relationships grew stronger in the violence of the ninth and tenth centuries and turned into a complex system in which people contracted with each other to fulfill certain tasks. Thus, the feudal ties that linked people together developed into sophisticated interpretations of contract law.

The early contracts of feudal ties illustrate the central components of these new contracts. One formula read as follows:

> Since I had not wherewith to feed and clothe myself, I wish to commend myself to you and to put myself under your protection. I have done so . . . and as long as I live I shall never have the right to withdraw from your power and protection. (Cheney, 3)

With these words, eighth-century noblemen placed themselves in a mutually binding, lifelong contract with their superior. What was the nature of this contract?

After signing this contract, a "vassal"—that is, a nobleman who entered into this contract—placed his hands between those of his lord and swore to be faithful to him. In return, the vassal received from the lord a "fief," which offered the vassal his means of livelihood. A fief was usually a large piece of land complete with villagers to work it to provide for all the vassal's needs, but later in the Middle Ages a fief could also mean a town or other job that provided income.

As appropriate to a contract, each party owed the other specific things. Lords owed their vassals "maintenance"—usually their fiefs—and protection. The lord was also to act as his vassal's advocate in public court. Lords were also to treat the vassal with "good faith," doing no harm to him and his family.

On their part, vassals owed lords "aid and counsel." The primary "aid" took the form of military service, specifically periods of fighting time. These varied, but an average length of service might be 40 days a year. Vassals owed certain specified monetary "aid" as well: They had to contribute when their lords incurred extra expenses, such as a daughter's wedding or a son's knighting. Vassals also owed lords "counsel," or advice when the lord required it. This seemingly simple requirement proved very important in the development of **Parliament** as vassals gathered to discuss the business of the land. Vassals also owed their lords "good faith."

Over time, vassals took on other titles, like baron or duke, that showed their position relative to other greater or lesser vassals, but the word *vassal* remained a general term that applied to all noblemen bound in contract and loyalty to a lord. Theoretically, a vassal only held his fief as long as he was able to fight for his lord, but in fact, by the ninth century, vassals expected to be able to pass their fiefs on to their sons. A son was expected to place his hands between those of his lord and renew his father's vows before he took full possession of the fief.

Because this was a legal system of mutual obligation, if either party breached the contract, the arrangement could be rendered null. For instance, if a vassal failed to fight or give counsel, the lord could declare his land forfeit and give it to someone else. Of course, enforcement became complicated when armies of me were involved, but the system did establish the idea of the primacy of contract law that bound people together in an ordered system.

Disputes about feudal obligations led to one of the most important documents in the history of American legal developments: the Magna Carta, or "Great Charter." In the thirteenth century, King John of England (r. 1199–1216) ran afoul of his vassals as he cut corners in the traditional feudal contract to raise money and increase his power. His vassals revolted, and at a battle at Runnymeade outside London, John was forced to sign the Great Charter promising to adhere to old feudal agreements. This document, signed in 1215, demonstrated that the king was not above the law and recorded principles that formed the core of many American liberties, like no "taxation without representation."

One of the ironies of the Middle Ages is that the system of feudal law that bound individuals together to field armies of mounted knights has been long obsolete. Yet the legal contracts that formed the basis of these relationships have formed the basis for modern democracies that place freely made contracts above the whims of the powerful. *See also* Document 6.

Further Reading

Cheyney, Edward P., ed. "Documents Illustrative of Feudalism," in *Translations and Reprints from the Original Sources of European History*, vol. IV, no. 3. Edited by the Department of History of the University of Pennsylvania. Philadelphia: University of Pennsylvania Press, 1898.

Holt, J.C. *Magna Carta*. Cambridge, UK: Cambridge University Press, 1965.

Law, Germanic

Long before the Germanic tribes had any contact with the Roman Empire and its strong legal tradition, they had their own ways of trying to ensure that their clans and tribes were not ruptured by violence and injustice. Through centuries, principles of law were not written down or even legislated by leaders; instead laws were thought of as customs of past, remembered by elders and discussed in community.

When disputes arose, leaders gathered in assembly to assess the matters at hand. The key to their deliberations was not necessarily any consideration of abstract right and wrong or theoretical justice. They preferred to consider the value of the tribal members. For, if a crime had been committed, whether it was theft, assault, murder, or anything else, the main issue was not the injury to an individual, but the injury or loss experienced by the clan or community. Therefore, leaders in deliberation might consider the character of an accused, or his or her value to the community. In a practice called "compurgation," twelve honorable men would testify to the character of the accused, even if they had no knowledge of the facts of the matter under discussion. The most important fact in ancient tribal society was the value of the accused, so a decision would likely go in favor of the most valuable member of the community, regardless of any facts in evidence.

If compurgation could not resolve a dispute, the assembly might call for a trial by "ordeal." If the disputing parties were fighting men, they might engage in a trial by combat, in which case the stronger was considered right—demonstrating that the strongest was the most valuable to a community that depended on strength and fighting ability for its survival.

Other kinds of ordeals appealed to the supernatural, allowing God to reveal guilt or innocence. There were several kinds of ordeals: Sometimes an accused had to grasp a red-hot poker and carry it a certain way, or plunge his or her hand in boiling water. Some days later, the wound would be examined, and a festering wound demonstrated guilt. Some trials by ordeal might leave people out of it altogether. For example, when priests in Spain were arguing about what was the correct form of liturgy to use, they brought two fighting bulls out. They named one "Toledo" and one "Rome" after the two varying types of liturgy and set them to fight. Toledo won, winning churches the right to use that form of prayer service.

Once the Germanic tribes established themselves in the old Roman Empire at the beginning of the Middle Ages, they brought this strong legal tradition with them. From the Romans, however, they learned the value of a written law code that was intended to last longer, and stand beyond, any living memory. When the tribes began to record their laws from the fifth century on, they brought with them all the elements that had shaped their oral traditions of justice, and these became part of the Western legal tradition.

In addition to recording accounts of ordeals and compurgation, the written law codes kept the value and integrity of the community as the overriding principle of justice. At the center of all the codes is the concept of "wergeld," which means "man-gold," literally the price or value of a man (or woman) to the community. In this system, the value of an individual, an animal, or a piece of property was set by law. When this value was violated (or diminished), then the offending party could make up for the violence by paying the price of the violated. This system was intended to restore the damaged community and to preclude family members from taking vengeance and perpetuating a cycle of violence that would further disrupt the community. The law codes used the techniques of ordeal and compurgation to determine who should pay the wergeld.

Early medieval law codes list a bewildering range of wergeld assessments. The Lombard laws (from Italy), for example, give a price for cutting off noses, ears, arms, hands, and fingers, and for knocking out teeth (Drew, 62–63). Laws also indicate the price of injury to women, children, animals, and trees in the forest. They even offered a price for such things as insults or watching a woman urinate behind a bush.

Despite all these law codes that preserve for us ideals of proper behavior, there was little mechanism for enforcement in an age when might made right. Throughout the eighth and ninth centuries, most of western Europe remained violent and lawless. The growth of feudal law would serve to offer the next step in bringing Europeans under the rule of law. *See also* Documents 2 and 3.

Further Reading

Drew, K.F. *The Lombard Laws*. Philadelphia: University of Pennsylvania Press, 1973.

Musson, A. *Medieval Law in Context*. Manchester, UK: Manchester University Press, 2001.

Law, Roman and Canon

The Romans made a significant contribution to medieval culture through its tradition of law, which was different from the Germanic legal customs.

Romans had developed abstract notions of justice, a respect for written laws, and a tradition of interpreting laws by lawyers and jurors. However, this long tradition of accumulated laws, commentaries (that is, explanations), and legal decisions left a body of work that was full of obscurities and internal contradictions. To be fully useful for medieval jurists (legal scholars), this legal heritage needed to be synthesized. This was accomplished in Byzantium in the early sixth century.

In 528, the Byzantine Emperor **Justinian** assigned his jurists to begin to codify the old and new laws of the Roman Empire. This formidable task was completed a few years later and included the *Codex Justinianus* and the *Digest*, fifty books of law. Justinian's jurists completed the work by publishing the *Institutes*, a summary of the main principles of Roman law that was intended for use as a textbook. Justinian's compilation was the highly influential text that preserved Roman legal principles for the future (up to today).

Justinian's codification was rediscovered in western Europe at the end of the eleventh century, where it exerted a profound influence on the growing body of religious law, or "canon law." Even in the early Middle Ages, church courts claimed jurisdiction over wills as part of their care for widows and orphans, but after the **Investiture Controversy** popes began to claim jurisdiction over many more areas of life, so church law became more developed. Justinian's *Digest* and *Institutes* offered church lawyers a ready body of laws to shape their own work.

In about 1140, the church lawyer Gratian issued his "Decretum," a collection of canon law that showed that church canons formed as complete a body of law as secular law. Gratian's collection with commentaries became accepted as church law. Consistent with the growing power of the popes through the twelfth century, canon lawyers began to argue that the pope was the supreme judge and legislator for all of "Christendom," and that he had jurisdiction over any religious matter. Interpreted broadly, "religious matter" encompasses every part of life: Marriage, a sacrament, was under papal jurisdiction. So was criminal law, since crimes were moral issues. Most controversial for medieval kings and nobles, canon lawyers claimed that contracts—including the all-important feudal ties—were under papal jurisdiction. Thus, the growing body of canon law placed religious leaders at the top of the social order.

Lawyers were trained at the University of Bologna, which was Europe's premier law school, and as lawyers worked, they further developed the body of Roman law they inherited and made it increasingly relevant to the medieval church that was claiming more and more jurisdiction over everyday life. Late in the twelfth and early thirteenth centuries, groups of canon lawyers, called the "Decretalists," reconciled old texts with new legislation and continued the growth of canon law.

Perhaps not surprisingly, toward the end of the Middle Ages there was a reaction against allowing the church to be the main arbiter of laws. Kings increasingly began to reclaim legal jurisdiction over church courts. Through this process, much of canon law became incorporated into secular law codes, which brought an unintended consequence: Much legislation of morality—such as prohibitions of some sexual activity—became part of secular law for the first time.

Our legal heritage from the Middle Ages is significant and complicated. Medieval lawyers and judges reconciled Roman, canon, Germanic, and feudal laws in a dynamic way, and this legal heritage became the basis for modern western democracies.

Further Reading
Mango, C. *Byzantium: The Empire of New Rome*. New York: Macmillan, 1980.
Musson, A. *Medieval Law in Context*. Manchester, UK: Manchester University Press, 2001.

Marco Polo (c. 1254–1324)

There were many travelers who went from Europe to Asia (and the reverse) during the Middle Ages. Most were anonymous traders who brought significant technical innovations to Europe from India and China; others were religious travelers trying to spread Christian ideas. The most famous traveler, however, was the Venetian Marco Polo, who with his father and uncle spent many years in China at the court of Kublai Khan. Marco's enduring influence came because of his book of memoirs that captured the imagination of Europeans for centuries. Christopher Columbus carried a well-marked copy of Marco's book with him as he crossed the Atlantic.

Marco Polo was born about 1254 in Venice to a leading merchant family. Venice was at the height of its influence, with its traders dominating the eastern part of the Mediterranean and merchants growing rich bringing in goods from the furthest reaches of Asia. At the same time, China was opening up for trade. The Mongol Empire ruled by Kublai Khan stretched from China to Russia, and the Great Khan happily received foreigners in his court because he was suspicious of Chinese who did not want to be ruled by a Mongol dynasty.

With this favorable trade atmosphere, a number of merchants ventured into the Mongol lands, including members of the Polo family. Around 1260, Marco's father, Niccolo and his uncle Maffeo traveled all the way to China to the court of Kublai Khan. The Great Khan gave them a warm welcome, appointed them emissaries to the pope, and ensured their safe travel back to Europe. They were told to return to China with one-hundred learned men who could instruct the Mongols in Christian religion and western science. It was quite possible that the Khan was influenced in this by his favorite wife, who was a Nestorian Christian (*see* **Heresies**).

The Polos arrived back in Venice in 1269. Niccolo found that his wife had died during his absence, and their son, Marco, who was about 15 years old, was running free in the streets of Venice. Marco was eager to join his father in future adventures, and Niccolo believed his son needed the steadying hand of his father.

In about 1271, the Polos were ready to return to China. The pope did not send one hundred scholars, only two Dominican friars, who turned back at the first sign of difficulty in travel. The journey took 3½ years by horseback through some of the world's most rugged terrain, such as the Gobi desert. If Marco's account is to be believed, the Polos became great favorites of the khan, and Marco became one of his trusted ambassadors. The Polos stayed in Khanbalik (Beijing) for 17 years. The elder Polos engaged in trading while Marco worked for the Khan, but after 17 years the family looked for ways to return to Venice without alienating the aging Kublai.

Finally an opportunity to leave presented itself when Kublai needed trusted emissaries to accompany a Mongol princess to Persia where she was to marry the local khan. The Polos sailed from China with a fleet of fourteen ships and a wedding party of six hundred people. The journey took 2 years, and most of the wedding party died along the way. Fortunately, the Polos and the princess survived, and she was duly delivered to Persia. From there the Polos went to Venice, arriving home in 1295 with rich goods.

Marco was not ready to settle down, and in his early forties he became involved in naval warfare between the Venetians and their trading rivals, the Genoese. He was captured and in 1298 found himself in prison in Genoa. While imprisoned, Marco met a man named Rustichello from Pisa, who was a writer of romances. To pass the time, Marco dictated an account of his travels in Asia and his many observations of strange lands. Marco and Rustichello were released from prison in 1299, and the book became an instant success.

After his prison experience, Marco was content to lead a quiet life in Venice. He married Donata Badoes, a member of the Venetian aristocracy, and they had three daughters, all of whom grew up to marry nobles. Marco died in 1324 at about 70 years of age. In his will, he left most of his wealth to his daughters, but more interestingly he set free a Chinese slave, named Peter, who had remained with him since his return from the court of the Great Khan.

The impact of Marco Polo was his book, translated into English as *The Travels of Marco Polo*. For centuries it was the main source of Western information about Asia, and it drew subsequent travelers. By 1300, there was a community of Italians living permanently in China. His life is a perfect example of the global interactions that shaped the Middle Ages. *See also* Documents 24 and 25.

Further Reading
Polo, Marco. *The Travels of Marco Polo*. Translated by Ronald Latham. Harmondsworth, UK: Penguin Books, 1958.

Marriage

Long before the coming of Christianity, marriage was an essential element in society. Through marriage, families were aligned and the future assured through children. In medieval Europe, however, there was a significant change in the philosophy of marriage; it became joined to religion as a sacrament (a rite containing grace for salvation), and its nature changed in ways that continued to shape marriages into the modern world.

Throughout the Middle Ages, marriages were arranged, recognizing the importance of this alliance to the families and the economic units that were being joined. At the beginning of the Middle Ages, Germanic tribes practiced polygyny—the taking of multiple wives and concubines. This practice ensured that many families might be united to the powerful war leaders and chiefs, contributing to the cohesiveness of the society. Emperor **Charlemagne**, for example, married four wives and took six concubines. The difference between wives and concubines was small, and all the resulting children were legitimate.

As early as the fourth century, the **Fathers of the Church** had begun to offer a different view of marriage that differed from the practical alliances that had formed the basis for older forms of marriage. Some church authorities wrote that marriage is an earthly reflection of Christ's union with the Church, and others argued that husbands and wives should love each other. Even nuns committed to lives of chastity began to phrase their vows in marital terms—they were Brides of Christ through a mystical marriage based on love. By the ninth

century, church leaders were able to impose monogamy on the previous po-
lygynist rulers, and the first significant change in marriage had begun: It came
under the province of religious authorities.

Church authorities also declared marriages to be indissoluble, changing previous fluid practices in which marriages were undone as easily as they had
been performed. The Church also regulated who could marry, eventually de-
claring that a couple may not marry if they were related by four degrees. That
meant that a couple who shared a great-great-grandparent could not marry. In
practice, many aristocrats married within this level of consanguinity, and this
formed the basis for dissolution of various marriages.

A turning point in Christian marital ideology came in the twelfth century
with the development of canon law (*see* **Law, Roman and Canon**). Two authors, Gratian and Peter Lombard, addressed the theory and practice of marriage and established the rules that governed it. Both affirmed that marriage
was monogamous and indissoluble, but both added that consent—even more
than sexual consummation—was required for a marriage to be valid. This was
a significant movement in the theory of marriage, because in theory it gave
individuals some autonomy from pressure from family and feudal lords, and
began a trend toward individualist nature of marriage that exists today. Ecclesiastical domination of the marriage rite was completed in the thirteenth century, when marriage was declared a sacrament.

Throughout the Middle Ages, marriage rituals consisted of two main parts:
the betrothal and the marriage ceremony itself. The betrothal included the exchange of gift giving between the prospective families, and the fixing of the
amount of the dowry—the money to be paid to the husband by the bride's
family. Theoretically, the dowry remained the property of the wife to be used
for her and any children in the event of her husband's death. However, because the dowry went into the control of the husband, this was not a certain
source of income for a woman. Nuns, too, had to bring a dowry into a convent
when they became brides of Christ, and this requirement often kept poor
women from following a religious vocation.

The ceremony itself was celebrated at the door of the church, with a priest
conducting the ceremony and the community serving as witness. At the ceremony, the couple gave their consent and the union was announced. After the
ceremony, the couple entered the church for a nuptial mass.

After the wedding, the families celebrated the unions as lavishly as they
could. Banquets were held often followed by dancing and other celebrations.
In some regions, the couple was escorted to the marital bed with bawdy laughter.
The consummation of the marriage, in which brides were proven to be virgin
was considered as essential completion of the marital union.

Marriage was a sacrament controlled by the church therefore there was to
be no divorce. In reality, wealthy people could appeal to the church for annul-
ments of marriages, which means that the marriage had not been valid in the
first place, so it didn't exist. There were several reasons possible for annulment.
Most commonly, partners claimed to have discovered an illegal consanguinity
that would render the marriage invalid. This was often hypocritical, because
usually partners knew in advance of the close ties between their families.
Eleanor of Aquitaine, for example, had her first marriage annulled due to
consanguinity, then married Henry II, to whom she was also related within
the forbidden degrees.

Another reason to dissolve marriage was if one partner claimed coercion, or that he or she had not consented to the union. This was harder to prove because the marriage ceremony required a stated consent. The final reason for annulment—and hardest to prove—was that the husband was unable to consummate the marriage. This claim sometimes led to odd trials in which midwives were to try to stimulate the husband to see if he could be aroused sexually.

The difficulty of dissolving a marriage made it a serious central component of medieval life. Men and women were married for life even if they separated and lived apart. Families had to consider very carefully what ties they wanted to negotiate. Only after the Reformation in the modern era would marriage again move to the civil arena creating the marriage patterns we have in the modern United States. *See also* Documents 8 and 18.

Further Reading

Brooke, Christopher N.L. *The Medieval Idea of Marriage*. Oxford, UK: Oxford University Press, 1989.

Duby, Georges. *Love and Marriage in the Middle Ages*. Translated by Jane Dunnett. Chicago: University of Chicago Press, 1994.

Murray, Jacqueline, ed. *Love, Marriage, and Family in the Middle Ages*. Ontario, Canada: Broadview Press, 2001.

Medicine

Medieval medicine in Europe was a mixture of several traditions: Germanic folk wisdom and classical understandings of medicine that had come from the Greco/Roman world. In addition, the advances made by Muslim physicians slowly made their way into Christendom. For all this study, however, diseases were rampant and health elusive.

Germanic women had traditionally been responsible for medical care, and this continued through the early medieval period. Medicines consisted primarily of herbs, as shown by the manuscripts form this era that preserve information about medicinal herbs and long-treasured medical recipes. Nasturtium, for example, was recommended for indigestion, wormwood for sleep disorders, and frankincense and oil for sore hands and fingers. Germanic women depended upon those with experience in treating illnesses to offer much-needed wisdom. For example, when someone was ill in the hill towns of northwestern Spain during the Visigothic era, he or she was placed outside by the pathways so that passersby might offer suggestions for a cure.

The most important source of information about classical medicine was Isidore of Seville, who was born around 560. He produced a prodigious amount of writing, including one of the most influential works in the Middle Ages, *The Etymologies*, which provided

Applying wound dressings, scarification with cupping glasses, from *Tractatabus de Pestilentia* (Treatise on Plague), 15th century manuscript by M. Albik. The Art Archive/University Library Prague/Gianni Dagli Orti.

medieval people with much information from the classical world. Most significantly, Isidore transmitted the beliefs of Galen (131–201), whose understandings of the human body continued into the modern period.

Galen embraced the notion of balance and therefore saw disease as the result of an imbalance within the body. Galen believed that good health resulted from a balance among the four "humors," or bodily fluids: blood, bile, urine, and phlegm. He argued that each of these humors had its own properties—warm, cold, dry, and moist—and when a person was out of balance—that is, when one humor dominated—the cure was to restore an appropriate equilibrium. For example, if a person were feverish and flushed, he or she was considered to have an excess of blood. An application of blood-sucking leeches or the initiation of bleeding would reduce the blood and restore the balance. These ideas may not have improved people's health, but they made sense to people and dominated the medical field for millennia.

Isidore of Seville transmitted Galen's ideas, but he also included more practical knowledge in his encyclopedia. He described treatment of amputation and cauterization to stop bleeding. He discussed the use of bandages, compresses, and other medicines. Indeed his work provides a fine description of the practical medicine available to medieval physicians.

Even food was considered medicinal if prepared properly, and women were in charge of designing a healthful diet. Just as our notion of a "balanced" diet changes with the latest research, early medieval ideas about nutritious eating relied on contemporary understandings of health. Consistent with Galen's views of health, people applied his idea of balance to menus that would be medicinal. If bodies were supposed to be a balance of wet, dry, cold, and hot humors, diets should be also. A proper diet must be "tempered"—that is, feature a balance of foods in each category of humor. For example, beans were considered "cold," so they were supplemented by "hot" spices to balance them.

Medicine in the West improved in the twelfth century when the writings of the Muslim scientist Avicenna (also known as Ibn Sina) (980–1037) became accessible. Avicenna became a court physician to a sultan when he was only 18 and began his prolific writing career then. His famous work, *Canon of Medicine*, served as the main medical text for more than six centuries and was copied throughout the Mediterranean world. In the West, the *Canon* was probably second only to the Christian Bible in the number of times it was reproduced. Although the Muslim physician argued for experimentation and observation, nevertheless, the West remained wedded to Galen's theoretical analysis of disease.

Women's health largely suffered under medieval understandings. Most physicians were men, and their theoretical studies were informed often by imperfect understandings of female anatomy. They drew from Aristotle in viewing women as imperfect males, whose bodies in the womb were too "cool" to be "cooked" into men. Two female medical writers form exceptions: **Hildegard of Bingen** wrote a tract that integrated Galen's understandings with her own observations of women. Trotula of Salerno wrote on medical matters in general and women's health in particular.

Many anonymous women worked as healers in some capacity. We have already seen that women were expected to have knowledge of herbs and cooking to bring health, but there were also women who practiced as surgeons. By the twelfth century, surgeons were expected to be licensed to practice medicine, and at least twenty-seven women have been documented as licensed in Naples and more elsewhere. As we might expect, most women participated in medicine as midwives who helped other women in childbirth.

By the thirteenth century, universities — particularly the University of Salerno — began to gain the exclusive right to train physicians. In doing so, they prevented many charlatans from practicing medicine, but they were also slowly moving women out of healing occupations because they were not allowed to attend universities.

The great visitations of **bubonic plague** of the fourteenth century showed the inadequacy of medieval medicine. Doctors, leeches, diets, and prayers could not stop the deaths that swept through Europe killing many and helping bring about the end of the Middle Ages.

Further Reading

Cadden, Joan. *Meanings of Sex Difference in the Middle Ages: Medicine, Science, and Culture.* Cambridge, UK: Cambridge University Press, 1993.

Siraisi, Nancy. *Medieval and Early Renaissance Medicine: An Introduction to Knowledge and Practice.* Chicago: University of Chicago Press, 1990.

Military Orders

The **Crusades** generated the need for a new kind of monk, one whose function was not simply to pray, but to protect pilgrims on their way to the visit the holy spaces of Jerusalem and its surroundings. In the twelfth century, then, new religious orders were established, called "Military Orders," which created armies of skilled knights who took vows of poverty, chastity, and obedience as they fought.

The Military Orders began in the early twelfth century, when a French knight, Hugh de Payen, and eight companions took religious vows and served as escorts for pilgrims. Soon they were given a house near the Temple of Solomon and became known as the Knights of the Temple. In 1128, the pope formally established the Knights of the Temple as a religious order whose chief purpose was to fight Muslims. They were also known as the Knights Templars, and were the most famous of the Military Orders.

Other Military Orders were established along the model of the Templars. For example in Spain, the pope established three Military Orders to fight against the Muslims in the Iberian Peninsula and to protect pilgrims going to Santiago de Compostella, the famous pilgrimage site in northwest Spain that purportedly held the bones of Saint James the Elder. The Teutonic Knights were founded in Germany along the same model. In the thirteenth century, the Teutonic Knights were used to convert the pagan Slavs beyond the borders of Germany. Thanks in large part to the force of their arms, Prussia became predominantly German and Christian in the thirteenth century.

In Jerusalem, men who had been serving in the Hospital of St. John to help sick pilgrims took the same vows as the Templars and became a fighting order of monks. They continued to serve in the hospital, but fighting became their main occupation, and they were called the "Hospitalers."

The western crusader kings of Jerusalem depended heavily on the Military Orders to protect their lands. Consequently, they gave the orders vast tracts of land along the edges of the crusader kingdoms, where the Templars and

Hospitalers built fortified castles to guard the borders. The most famous of these fortifications was the Crac des Chevaliers, a castle whose walls rose high over the border with the Turks.

At their height, the Hospitalers could supply five hundred knights, and the Templars three hundred. They served as the backbone of the garrison guarding the Holy Land, and even the Muslims greatly respected their military strength.

The Military Orders soon began to serve another vital function for pilgrims: banking. The Templars and Hospitalers held larger properties all over western Europe and had the military might to protect possessions in their charge. Therefore, they accepted money in one country and paid it out in another. A pilgrim leaving from France could deposit his funds there and withdraw it in Jerusalem. This banking function helped make the Military Orders very rich.

When Acre fell to the Muslims in 1291, most of the Templars who bravely guarded the walls until the end were killed. The remaining Templars retired to live on their extensive estates in Europe. However, the wealth they had accumulated brought them to the attention of the French king, Philip IV (r. 1285–1314). Philip arranged to charge the Templars with terrible, secret vices: sodomy and devil worship. Some Templars confessed under torture, and some fifty Templars were burned as heretics. The order was dissolved, and its property confiscated. The other orders remained in a weakened state to fight Muslims in the Mediterranean, or on the borders of Germany. This significant feature of medieval military culture would die out at the end of this era. *See also* Documents 15 and 23.

Further Reading
Martin, Sean. *The Knights Templar: The History and Myths of the Legendary Military Order.* New York: Avalon, 2004.
Nicolle, David. *Teutonic Knight: 1190–1561.* Oxford, UK: Osprey Publishing, 2007.

Money

The Roman Empire had established a long tradition of using coins made of precious metals: silver for a *denarius*, bronze for a *sestertius* or smaller *as*, and more rarely, gold for an *aureus*. Over the long duration of the Empire, money changed in value, for example, becoming mixed with lesser metals as coins became scarce. Such mixing resulted in devaluation of the coins and inflation. Emperors carefully regulated the ability to mint gold coins; these mints were only permitted in the capitals, by the late empire this meant Constantinople in the east and Ravenna in the West. During the late empire in many regions money was so scarce that many people retreated to the barter system — trading goods and labor without using coins as intermediary currency.

As Germanic tribes settled on the borders of the Roman Empire, they began to see the value of coins and learned to trade for them. However, the traditional barter system remained strong within the tribes, and many people treated coins like jewelry — to wear rather than spend. This pattern reemerged with the Vikings in the tenth century, and archeologists have unearthed gold coins with holes drilled into them so they could be strung on necklaces for decoration. Coins are only useful when there are things to purchase; otherwise they were more useful as high-status jewelry.

In spite of the continuation of the barter system in pockets of society, by the late ninth century, coins were well established in Europe as the medium for trade. Precious metal was so rare that coins were silver until the thirteenth century, when gold coins were reintroduced. However, gold coins remained rare throughout the Middle Ages. Even silver was so precious that a single ounce of the precious metal was worth a week's wages for even a skilled worker.

The advantage of using coins was that minted coins retained their value more than other things, such as agriculture produce or manufactured goods. However, unlike modern coins, medieval coins were less standardized. Modern money is almost always issued by national governments, but during the Middle Ages only the Byzantine emperor managed to maintain a monopoly on issuing coins, and by the thirteenth century, the English monarchy was also able to exert control over minting coins. In most of Europe, there were many local mints producing coins of varying amounts of silver, and thus of various values.

The main system of money of the Middle Ages was that of pounds, shillings (also called *solidi*), and pence, although the actual names of the coins varied by the language. The pound in France was called the *livre*, for example. Theoretically, it was worth a pound of silver coins, and the English monarchy was so proud of its ability to maintain the integrity of its pound that it was called a "pound sterling." A pound was equivalent to 20 shillings (in French, *sou*), and the shilling was equal to 12 pennies (in French, *denier*). The pound was purely a theoretical amount, because it would be worth so much that no coin would actually be used for such a great value. In practice, the penny was the main form of coin. The English penny was the most stable coin in Middle Ages, weighing generally about 1.4 grams (about .05 oz) with a purity of silver of about 92 percent (Singman, 59).

As people began to use coins for even small, local transactions, the penny was too valuable. In about 1280, England issued a half-penny and even a quarter penny, called a "farthing." These denominations are evidence of the spread of the use of coins throughout society.

At the macroeconomic level, as long-distance trade in luxury goods increased, there was a demand for larger coins. In the middle of the thirteenth century, Florence and Genoa began issuing medieval Europe's first gold coins, and France soon followed. Extremely valuable gold coins allowed merchants to travel long distances with relatively small treasure chests filled with coins.

When Marco **Polo** and his relatives journeyed to China in the mid-thirteenth century, they witnessed what to them was a shocking innovation in currency—paper money circulated and was given the same value as coins made of precious metal. The Europeans brought back tales of this currency that was so light and convenient to move, but few believed them. Centuries would pass before the West was ready to take on this new kind of currency.

Instead of moving to paper money, western travelers looked to other innovations in banking and credit to facilitate the movement of goods and people over long distances. Credit had long been used by villagers and townsfolk, and in the thirteenth century, credit entered the world of long-distance trade. The Italians established networks of financial houses across Europe, so that a merchant with a letter of credit from a financier in one place might redeem it at another (Singman, 61). In this way, merchants could move safely without transporting valuable coins. The Military Order of Knights Templars performed this service for pilgrims going to the Holy Land. A deposit made to the Templars in France could be redeemed safely in Jerusalem.

These banking innovations of the thirteenth century point the way to a new financial order that marked the early modern period beginning in the Renaissance. The early Middle Ages marked a retreat from the kind of global economy that had made the Roman Empire so prosperous. For centuries, people trading locally could use the coins in their pockets to satisfy their needs. However, at the end of the Middle Ages global trade and expansion required new forms of monetary transactions to fuel a growing prosperity. *See also* Document 9.

Further Reading

Pick, F., and R. Sedillot. *All the Monies of the World – A Chronicle of Currency Values.* New York: Pick Publishing Co., 1971.

Singman, Jeffrey L. *Daily Life in Medieval Europe.* Westport, CT: Greenwood Press, 1999.

Mysticism

Mysticism is a technical term that refers to the feeling of becoming one with—or joined to—God while still alive. This feeling is often described as being a loss of self, while accompanied with an awareness of God that is incredibly sweet and joyful. Mystics usually experience this union while in a trance, so the experience is temporary but may be experienced again many times. The possibility of a mystic union with God (or Christ) was available from the beginning centuries of Christianity and offered one path to the Deity. Throughout history, mystics sometimes were considered to be heretics because their individual longings seemed at odds with the established church's program for salvation. Nevertheless, we can trace a steady continuity of mysticism throughout the Middle Ages.

Many of the early Church Fathers embraced mystic experiences as part of their religious lives, arguing that God became man in the person of Jesus to show that humans can become godlike through union with the Holy Spirit. However, the most important early theologian to make explicit how this mystic union might happen was an author that is known as Pseudo-Dionysius, who was probably an anonymous Syrian monk writing sometime around 500. The most famous Pseudo-Dionysian texts are *On the Divine Names* and *Mystical Theology*, which describe the ascent of the soul and its ecstatic experience of union with God.

These writings established a threefold process that became almost universal in later Christian mysticism: Aspiring mystics had to experience purification, illumination, and finally perfection through union. Implicit in the search for divine union is an anti-intellectualism that argues that God must be "felt," not "understood." In this way, mysticism became a path to God that was alternative to **scholasticism** that argued that God could be known through study and logic. This tension may be seen in the struggle between the scholastic Peter Abelard and the great mystic **Bernard of Clairveaux**.

The thirteenth century saw a further flowering of mystic impulses that found its fullest expression in the life of **Francis of Assisi** (c. 1182–1226). Francis believed all animals and inanimate objects were imbued with God's essence. Late in his life he was reputed to have had an intense mystic experience in which he received the stigmata—wounds like those of Christ's on his hands, feet, and side. The Franciscan movement was an order that spread widely and was influential in the church. Franciscans popularized a variety of devotions that were designed to help believers experience a mystical connection with God. For example, they advocated repetitious prayers and popularized the "stations of the cross," a meditation on fourteen events in the passion of Christ ending with his burial. These devotions showed that slowly the ideal of mystical connection was being popularized rather than left to religious specialists. The great Franciscan Bonaventure (c. 1217–1274) wrote *The Journey of the Mind to God*, which was a masterpiece of mystical theology that showed that the mind is drawn to God by divine love, and it can be reached through prayer and meditation.

The Eastern Orthodox Church had also always embraced mystical connections. The popularity of icons in the Orthodox Church was in part a desire to achieve a connection with the divinity (*see* **Iconoclasm**). In the eleventh century, Eastern mysticism was further developed with the emergence of Hesychasm, a form of mystical prayer and contemplation that came to be associated primarily with the monks of Mt. Athos in northern Greece. These monks practiced a form of meditation that included controlled breathing, placing the chin on the chest, and reciting the "Jesus Prayer"—"Lord Jesus Christ, Son of God, have mercy on me." The hesychasts claimed to experience a divine light in the course of this meditation. By the thirteenth century, the Orthodox Church had embraced the hesychast experience sufficiently that they counted the divine light as God's energies that are God, yet that are available to mystics in this life.

By the fourteenth century, there were more and more mystics who came to the fore. This rise of mysticism suggests a reaction against the institutional nature of the medieval Church and an increasing desire for a deeper and more personal religious experience than that which was afforded by formal worship in the Mass. The German mystic, Meister Eckhart (c. 1260–1327) described how everyone could cultivate an interior life and transform his or her soul. Although Eckhart had to defend himself against charges of heresy, his writings remained popular and led to many following his lead.

Women, excluded from institutional service in the Church, were drawn to mystical experiences and exerted an influence on Christianity through this venue. Women like Catherine of Siena, Julian of Norwich, and Margery Kempe left writings that continue to be read. Women's mystic writings received great legitimacy in the early modern period when Catherine of Genoa and Teresa of Avila were declared "Doctors of the Church," whose writings about their mystic experience were deemed worthy of study by all the faithful.

In the Netherlands, the practice of individual mysticism led to important movements. Communities were founded based on the ideas of combining mysticism with service to others, and this practice came to be known as the *devotio moderna* ("Modern Devotion"), and it emphasized a deep personal relationship with God and constant meditation on the life of Christ. The Modern Devotion spread quickly, and its most famous representative was Thomas a Kempis (1380–1471), who wrote *The Imitation of Christ*, which is the most widely read devotional book in the history of Christianity. The longing for a personal relationship with Christ that is implicit in the mystic journey would ultimately help lead to the Reformation of the early sixteenth century. *See also* Documents 21 and 29.

Further Reading
Egan, Harvey. *Christian Mysticism.* Collegeville, MN: Liturgical Press, 1992.
Underhill, Evelyn. *Mysticism.* New York: E.P. Dutton, 1911.

Parliament

The most important political institution in the modern world—representative governments—appeared in the Middle Ages. By the thirteenth century, representative assemblies were developing in many parts of Europe, Spain, Sicily, and Hungary for example gathered nobles and churchmen together in political assemblies. The French Estates General met for the first time in 1302, and the "Model Parliament" met in England during the reign of Edward I (r. 1272–1307). Even church councils, such as the Fourth Lateran Council of 1215 were conceived of as representative bodies.

Because these representative councils are uniquely European, scholars have spent a great deal of time speculating on the origins of representative governments. Some argue that the tradition of tribal participation in the Germanic tribes led to an expectation of representation among the nobles. Others suggest that the requirement of "giving advice" within feudal law (*see* **Law, Feudal**) led to nobles gathering to their king. Still others see the origins of parliament in the gathering of nobles to render legal judgment. Whatever the origins, it is clear that by the thirteenth century it was an idea that was established.

The word *parliament* was first used in the thirteenth century, and at first it referred not to a particular institution, but any discussion ("parley") among people. In the 1240s, the word began to refer to meetings of the English Great Council when the King and his advisers met with the nobles of the land.

The tradition of legal representation received a great boost in England in the reign of John I (r. 1199–1216). When John had money problems, he high-handedly departed from feudal custom and tread on the traditional rights of his vassals. In the spring of 1215, John's barons staged a rebellion and forced the king to sign the Magna Carta (Great Charter). This document asserted that the king was not above the law and that he would preserve traditional feudal rights. However the charter also included principles that shaped the future of English (and North American) law: The king would impose no new taxes without the consent of the governed and would not violate the due process of law. This document warned future kings not to try to rule without consulting with his people.

In 1265, two knights from every shire and two burgesses (townsmen) from every borough were invited to meet with the barons and churchmen. This was the first time that elected representatives attended an English Parliament. Edward I made a practice of holding Parliaments regularly and of summoning representatives to them occasionally. In 1295, Edward held a particularly full assembly, which is usually called the "Model Parliament." As this body gathered, the knights and the lower nobility sat with the burgesses and began to act together for their mutual benefit, while the clergy sat with the upper nobility. In time, the nobles would become the House of Lords, and the burgesses with the lower nobility the House of Commons. At first, the House of Commons did little more than approve the rulings of the Lords, but in time this institution came to rule England.

The rise of Parliament in France took a different path (in part due to the greater power of French kings over their barons). In 1302, King Philip IV "the

Fair" (r. 1285–1314) needed the support of the realm in his struggles against the pope as he tried to raise money from church lands. In response, he summoned representatives from church, nobility, and towns to the first meeting of the Estates General. As these men gathered to advise their king, they sat according to the medieval order: those who prayed, fought, and worked (including townsmen) deliberated separately. This triple arrangement, so different from the two houses of Parliament that grew up in England, helped diffuse each group's power, allowing kings to maintain tight control. This had dramatic consequences for the future of France.

Further Reading

Blythe, J.M. *Ideal Government and the Mixed Constitution in the Middle Ages.* Princeton, NJ: Princeton University Press, 1992.

Holt, J.C. *Magna Carta.* 2nd ed. Cambridge, UK: Cambridge University Press, 1992.

Peasant Revolts

In the fourteenth century, Europe was devastated by the **bubonic plague**, which reduced the population by between one-third and one-half. As an immediate result of the plague, the European countryside suffered a disabling shortage of labor. Lords desperate to get their work done tried to increase the amount of work serfs owed them by custom. Because serfs' obligations were already excessive, that generated some anger. Free laborers seeing a chance to make more money began to demand higher wages, prompting some lords to pass laws freezing earnings. This policy enraged peasants across Europe. Determined to resist, they roamed the countryside, burning manor houses and slaughtering the occupants.

The first uprising came in France, where peasants faced the additional hardships of the **Hundred Years' War** in which knights from England devastated the countryside. The French *Jacquerie*, as the peasant revolt was called, broke out in 1358, and it was a savage outburst. Peasants revolted against their lords, and there were even reports of cannibalism of the poor against the wealthy who had kept them hungry for so long.

The peasant revolt that broke out in England 1381 was a more organized affair. Not only did many well-armed and disciplined soldiers support the peasants in their revolt offering needed military leadership, but also popular preachers added a religious dimension to the revolt. The two most famous preachers in England were Wat Tyler and John Ball. They cast the revolt in apocalyptic terms, arguing that the many disasters of the fourteenth century presaged Christ's Second Coming, and that revolting against wealthy landowners was their way of helping God redress the ills in the world. Peasants who believed God was on their side rallied vigorously to their cause. The English peasants burned houses of aristocrats, lawyers, and government officials, at times burning the records that they believed contributed to their oppression. Other peasant revolts broke out in Spain in 1395, and sporadic risings occurred in Germany and other regions of Europe. The final large-scale peasant revolt in Germany took place in 1524.

For all the popular violence, the peasants in all regions could not hold out for long against the aristocracy and its superior arms. Eventually, all the revolts were suppressed with many peasants and leaders massacred. Yet the violence, the labor shortages, and the prevailing belief that things were changing had begun to erode the old medieval manorial system. Over time, peasants who owed only rent gradually replaced serfs who had owed labor as well as rents. For these new peasants, their labor was now their own, giving them more freedom and opportunities to work for their own profit.

Although the condition of many peasants improved, the trend was not uniform throughout Europe. The situation of the peasants in western Europe improved more quickly than of those in eastern Europe, where peasant revolts would continue into the twentieth century. Nevertheless, in western Europe the medieval order in the countryside was brought down in part by peasants who had had enough of the old ways. *See also* Document 27.

Further Reading

Hilton, Rodney. *Bond Men Made Free*. New York: Methuen, 1973.
Rösener, Werner. *Peasants in the Middle Ages*. Chicago: University of Illinois Press, 1992.

Scholasticism

Scholasticism is the term that is used to refer to medieval philosophy, and its main goal was to reconcile faith with reason—that is, to understand with one's mind what one believed in one's heart. The medieval thinkers applied a particular form of logic, called "dialectic," to try to get at metaphysical truths. Dialectic involves using logic to explore various sides of an issue, so the scholastic writings often take the form of questioning. This kind of exploration may be contrasted with the scientific method, which involves testing hypotheses by experimentation and observations; the scholastics—also called "schoolmen"—did not observe, they thought about things. That was why they believed they could understand faith, which defies observation.

The earliest medieval philosopher to explore the religious applications of dialectic was Anselm of Canterbury (1033–1109). Anselm's famous "proof" of God's existence was that by definition, God was a being that is the greatest that can be thought of. And, for Anselm, something that exists is greater than something that does not exist, therefore God must exist. The flaws in this argument were quickly demonstrated, but there remain many who are still drawn to Anselm's logic.

The application of dialectic was continued at the University of Paris by the brilliant scholar, Peter Abelard (*see* **Education**). Abelard is best known for his love affair with Heloise, a talented 17-year-old girl he was hired to tutor. Teacher and student were soon lovers, and Heloise became pregnant. Her infuriated uncle had Abelard castrated in revenge. Ultimately, Heloise left her child (named Astrolabe) to be raised by relatives, and Abelard and Heloise took religious vows and lived their lives in monasteries, where they each continued brilliant careers of learning and influence.

Abelard established a method of applying critical reason to even sacred texts. His most famous work, *Yes and No* (*Sic et Non*), assembled a variety of authoritative sources, from the Bible to the **Fathers of the Church**, which seemed to contradict each other. From these, the scholar compiled 150 theological questions and the passages relevant to each question, which allowed scholars to consider the full range of the questions. Although his book has such provocative chapters as "Is God the Author of Evil, or No?" Abelard had no desire to undermine faith; on the contrary he believed that this kind of inquiry would strengthen faith through the discovery of truth.

The progress of scholastic philosophy increased rapidly in the twelfth century, when Christian universities acquired advanced texts of Aristotle's logic that had been preserved and commented on by Muslim and Jewish scholars from centers as far apart as Baghdad in the East and Toledo in Spain. The Muslim scholar Averroes (1126–1198) and the Jewish scholar Maimonides (1135–1204) left extensive commentaries on Aristotle's sophisticated ideas, and these commentaries along with the advanced logic of Aristotle generated much intellectual excitement in the university communities of western Europe.

Scholasticism reached its height in the thirteenth century with the works of Thomas Aquinas (1225–1274), an Italian churchman whom many regard as the greatest scholar of the Middle Ages. Aquinas wrote many works, from commentaries on biblical books and Aristotelian texts to essays on philosophical problems. However, his most important work was the *Summa Theologiae* (*Summary of Theology*), which was intended to offer a comprehensive summary of all knowledge available at the time.

Aquinas taught that faith and reason were compatible paths to a single truth, but that the mind by itself could grasp on the truth of the physical world. Faith, however, could help reason grasp spiritual truths such as the Trinity. This central understanding—that faith and nature cannot contradict each other, and that each can inform the other—has remained one of Aquinas' most important contributions. The most famous examples of his use of nature to yield divine truth were his "proofs" of God's existence in which, like Anselm, he wanted to use logic from the physical world to "understand" the mysteries of God.

Throughout the Middle Ages, there were always those who objected to the very enterprise of understanding faith through reason. These critics, who might be broadly called "mystics" (*see* **Mysticism**) claimed that the only way to reach God was through shutting down the mind and reaching with the heart through love. For example, the famous cleric **Bernard of Clairveaux** condemned Abelard for corrupting the mind of the young by false teaching and had him accused of heresy. So there was always a parallel path to God. Thomas Aquinas believed he had incorporated the concerns of the mystics in his *Summa*, but the final criticism of scholasticism would come from those who believed they could prove the shortcomings of logic by logic itself.

Scholasticism was generally based on the idea that philosophers could extract general truths (called "universals") from individual cases. Franciscan thinkers, particularly in England, challenged this approach. They were called "nominalists" or "new nominalists," because they said we cannot know anything about universals—things are only what we name them. (The term *nominalism* comes from "name.") The greatest of the new nominalists was William of Ockham (c. 1300–c. 1349).

New Nominalists believed that it was impossible to know God or prove his existence through reason—because God was all-powerful, he did not have to act logically, so the scholastic enterprise at its core limited the understanding of God by eliminating anything illogical (like miracles). Ockham also founded a fundamental principle that has remained the basis of scientific analysis. Called "Ockham's razor," this principle says that between alternative explanations for the same phenomenon, the simpler is always to be preferred. Nominalists became popular in universities, and Ockhamite philosophy became known as the *via moderna* (modern way).

By freeing scholars from the enterprise of studying God, the nominalists, perhaps in an unintended fashion, encouraged the great minds of the age to focus on studying what was logical—the natural world. This fostered the growth of science that in the modern world separated the West from the Age of Faith that characterized the Middle Ages. *See also* Document 21.

Further Reading
Evans, G.R. *Philosophy and Theology in the Middle Ages*. New York: Routledge, 1993.
Leff, Gordon. *William of Ockham*. Manchester, UK: Manchester University Press, 1975.

Warfare

One way to define medieval culture is through warfare. At the beginning of the Middle Ages, mounted horsemen dominated the fields of battle, and much warfare was defensive in which armies worked to prevent attackers from taking their castles and other walled fortifications. The Middle Ages ended in the fifteenth century when gunpowder brought down castle walls and foot soldiers defeated knights in shining armor.

During the Roman Empire, armies had increasingly made use of mounted cavalry to provide a rapid deployment force. These mounted men were armed with bows and arrows and throwing spears and relied on supporting heavily armed foot soldiers who were the backbone of the fighting force. In about the eighth century, a technological innovation changed this fighting style. The armies of the Germanic Franks creatively figured out how to use a stirrup—an innovation that had spread from the East—perhaps China or India. By using a stirrup, riders were able to brace themselves on the back of the horse so they could directly engage an enemy instead of just riding by him. Now the rider could put the force of a horse behind the thrust of a lance or the strike of a sword. Shock troops of mounted cavalry, known as "men-at-arms" were born.

These mounted soldiers, who came to be called "knights," were expensive to train and maintain. They needed heavy armor that might cost a laborer's salary of one full year; they also needed expensive horses who were bred to be large enough to carry a heavily armored knight. (Modern draft horses like Percherons are the descendants of these medieval warhorses.) In addition, it took a long time to train these specialized soldiers. Boys were sent to train for years with skilled warriors until they could move from the ranks of squire to knight. In fact, estimates suggest it took about ten peasant families to support one mounted knight. It is easy to see how knights were at the top of the medieval military hierarchy.

The knight's main body armor consisted on a long tunic of chain mail, called a "hauberk." This chain mail consisted of rings of metal riveted together. This mail was expensive to make and during battle, winners were careful to strip the mail off losers as part of their booty. Chain mail offered a good deal of protection against the cut of a blade, but the flexible links did not protect from bruising or bones breaking from impact. To address this danger, knights wore padded cloth tunics, called "aketons," under the mail to absorb the shock of a blow. On their legs, knights wore long stockings of mail, which by the thirteenth century were covered with metal plate armor to further protect him from foot soldiers. During most of the Middle Ages, knights carried large metal shields as further protection.

The most vulnerable part of the knight's body was his head. Therefore, in addition to padding and chain mail, a knight wore a steel helmet. Throughout the Middle Ages, the helmet grew more and more elaborate until it covered his face.

Although armies of well-armored knights remained the heart of medieval battle, they nevertheless were supported by other fighting men. The highest paid were the archers. Until the fourteenth century, archers used crossbows. They could not fire very quickly, but a clean shot from these bows could pierce armor, so these men were valuable for fighting from fixed positions or defending castle walls. Crossbows were so effective that the Second Lateran Church Council in 1139 banned their use in warfare in hopes of keeping warfare more humane, requiring men to kill each other without resorting to long-distance carnage (Marcus, 302). Of course, like many attempts to regulate warfare, this ban did not last, and crossbows remained part of medieval arsenals until they were displaced by more lethal weapons.

In the fourteenth century, the long **Hundred Years' War** between England and France saw the development of new weapons and warfare techniques that would render the mounted knight obsolete. The English fought on French soil where their knights were outnumbered. They could, therefore, not rely on traditional fighting techniques in which large groups of knights charged into each other. Instead, the English brought with them archers armed with longbows, originally used by the Welsh. Longbows had a longer range than crossbows, and archers could fire many more arrows a minute, darkening the sky with their lethal projectiles. An experienced archer could pull a bow with 80 to 150 pounds of draw, giving a range of about 400 yards. English archers brought down crossbowmen and horses long before either was in range to cause the English damage.

The effectiveness of foot soldiers increased as fourteenth century as leaders saw new possibilities for using different weapons. Swiss pike men lined up with long lethal spears that effectively kept charging horses at bay. The real military innovation that ultimately ended the medieval age of knighthood was gunpowder. Gunpowder—a mixture of sulfur, charcoal, and saltpeter—spread from China and began to be used in warfare in the West in the mid-thirteenth century. Early attempts to use gunpowder in weapons were crude, but they were most successful in siege engines. Early cannons made short work of the thickest stonewalls—the great city of Constantinople fell to the Turks in 1453 when they used their cannons to breach the walls.

Early handguns were less reliable. Each consisted of a tube probably shorter than 10 inches long attached to a wooden stock (because the metal tubes grew too hot to touch). These early guns were loaded through their muzzles and ignited by a smoldering cloth used to ignite the gunpowder and fire the projectile. These early guns were inaccurate and posed dangers to the gunman himself. By 1500, however, Europeans had developed the arquebus, a reliable weapon. With weapons like guns, warfare was no longer limited to well-trained mounted knights; anyone could kill effectively from a distance, and early critics lamented the change in warfare: One wrote, "Often and frequently . . . a virile brave hero is killed by some forsaken knave with a gun." Another wrote, "Would to God that this unhappy weapon had never been invented" (Marcus, 299).

Medieval armorers tried to adapt to new lethal weapons by strengthening the armor that marked the knights. Plate armor was perfected and rounded to try to have bullets bounce off. For all their efforts, knights in shining armor were rendered obsolete. Warfare until the twenty-first century (when improved body armor of kevlar and new lightweight materials again enters the battlefields) was a matter of reach, not defensive armor. Guns that could kill, by keeping the soldier out of range, became the goal of modern armies, and the age of medieval armies of mounted knights was over. *See also* Document 23.

Further Reading

Contamine, Philippe. *War in the Middle Ages*. Translated by Michael Jones. Oxford, UK: Basil Blackwell Ltd., 1990.

Marcus, Alan I. *Building Western Civilization*. New York: Harcourt Brace, 1998.

Norman, A.V.B. *The Medieval Soldier*. New York: Barnes & Noble, 1993.

Women

Medieval women, like men, thought of themselves as placed within a particular social order. In this social organization, some people fought, some prayed, and the rest worked. Therefore, most women found solidarity and comfort with others in their social order rather than identifying themselves with women as a whole. To consider the roles of women in medieval Europe, it is necessary to separate the various orders.

Aristocratic women—members of the ruling order of "those who fight"—experienced the most restrictive lives. Their primary function was to provide heirs—new fighting men—and to ensure the children's legitimacy; most

Eleanor of Aquitaine led into captivity by Eleanor's husband, Henry II, in 1173 after their rebellion, 12th–13th century fresco, Chapelle de Sainte Radegonde, Chinon, France. The Art Archive/Gianni Dagli Orti.

aristocratic women led lives that kept them close to home. They gathered with their ladies-in-waiting and spent a good deal of time spinning, weaving, and doing intricate needlework. Although this was the role of most aristocratic women, we can nevertheless find examples of extraordinary women who left their mark on the pages of even medieval chroniclers who were more interested in the deeds of men. Rulers like **Eleanor of Aquitaine** changed the political face of Europe, and other women like Marie de France transformed the literary landscape. Inevitably even anonymous aristocratic women had to take charge in their husbands' absence—a frequent occurrence for those of the fighting order.

Women who entered a religious life made a significant impact on medieval society. Because women were not allowed to become priests, those who felt a call for a religious life entered convents, or after the thirteenth century joined one of the female orders associated with the mendicants like the Franciscans and Dominicans. Women had various motivations for becoming nuns. Women who were interested in intellectual pursuits and the arts could find an outlet for their interests in the cloister; families who had too many daughters to provide dowries sent some to the convents, and some women found the spiritual life deeply rewarding.

Religious women, famous and anonymous, transformed medieval culture. Early Christians like Radegund were influential in helping the Germanic peoples convert to Christianity and preserving learning during the violent years of invasions. The writings of mystics such as **Hildegard of Bingen** changed people's view of God and the universe. Convents of women throughout Europe gained respect by their work caring for the hungry and sick, educating the young, and living pious lives. Although women from all walks of life could theoretically enter the monastic life, the very poor were usually excluded because they could not bring dowries to the monastic house.

Most women (like men) belonged to the broad order of "those who work." These included everyone from wealthy merchants living in the burgeoning towns to poor peasants struggling to earn a living from small holdings. Regardless of the income or status, all women of these groups worked hard inside and outside the home.

Peasant women had to work as hard as their men (and children). In addition to maintaining the home—preparing food, spinning and making cloth—women also had to contribute to the household economy. They raised poultry, handled the dairy tasks, and tended the garden. In all these activities, a peasant woman tried to produce more than the family needed so she could sell or barter the remainder. Perhaps the most lucrative sources of income for a peasant woman were her skills in brewing beer or spinning wool to weave.

A peasant women could become a landholder, holding joint tenancy with her husband, or inheriting in her own right. In most regions of Europe, a daughter inherited land only if there were no surviving sons, but peasant households generally only had two or three children, so it was likely for only a girl to not survive until adulthood.

Some peasant women, again like some men, held no land, so they had to work as day laborers. They were hired in dairies, field work, sheep shearing, road repair, and even plowing, which was traditional thought of as man's work. One thirteenth-century estate management document recommended that women be hired even as dairy managers because they could be paid a lower wage than men.

City women were also active participants in the town's economic life. Like peasant women, urban women were responsible for running the household. However, they also earned money through a trade. For example, guilds allowed wives of journeymen to practice their husband's craft. Some trades allowed women to be guild members in their own right, and some trades were practiced principally by women. For example, spinners and ribbon-makers were predominately women. City women could inherit shops from their fathers or husbands, and records indicate testify to some prosperous women.

A particularly poignant incident that shows how women were central to urban economies took place in the town of Douai in medieval Flanders (now in France). In the early fourteenth century, the town felt a shortage of food, and rumors spread that rich merchants were hoarding grain. Cloth workers took to the streets in protest and eighteen workers, including two women, were arrested. The women were charged with being especially vocal, and in punishment they had their tongues cut off before they were banished from the city for life. The women's excessive penalty shows the prevailing misogyny that lay beneath medieval attitudes toward women.

Patristic writers had long argued that women had caused the fall of humankind. From the first temptation of Eve to every man's seduction, writers argued that women tempted men to lust. In fact, the woman held up as the perfect model was the Blessed Virgin Mary who was what no other woman could be—mother and virgin at the same time. By the fourteenth century, the disconnect between perceptions of women and the actions of actual women had worked its way into the literary tradition.

The most famous advocate for women was Christine of Pizan, a famous woman writer of the late fourteenth century. Christine was a young widow who ended up supporting her family by her writing and has thus been often called the first professional writer in Europe. One of Christine's most famous works is *The Book of the City of Ladies*, which she claims to have written to vindicate women to demonstrate that women were as virtuous and hard-working as men. The same kind of work was written in the fifteenth century by the Frenchman, Martin Le Franc whose long work, *Le Champion des Dames* (*Champion of Women*) also intends to rehabilitate views of women. The fourth book *The Trial of Womankind* is in the form of a dialogue with two lawyers arguing the merits and flaws of women. Here at the end of the Middle Ages theorists raise the question of women's value, finally expressing the obvious, that the magnificent culture of the medieval world was built by men and women together. *See also* Documents 8, 18, and 29.

Further Reading

Bennet, Judith M. *Ale, Beer, and Brewsters in England: Women's Work in a Changing World*. Oxford, UK: Oxford University Press, 1999.

Christine de Pizan. *The Book of the City of Ladies*. Translated by E.J. Richards. New York: Persea Books, 1982.

Herlihy, David. *Opera Muliebria: Women and Work in Medieval Europe*. New York: McGraw-Hill, 1990.

Le Franc, Martin. *The Trial of Womankind*. Translated by Steven Millen Taylor. Jefferson, NC: McFarland & Co., Inc., 2005.

Wilson, Katharina M., and Nadia Margolis, eds. *Women in the Middle Ages: An Encyclopedia*. 2 vols. Westport, CT: Greenwood Press, 2004.

Primary Documents

1. Augustine Writes of Childhood Sinning, 397

In 397, the Church Father, Augustine of Hippo, in North Africa, wrote his *Confessions*, in which he described his life and conversion to Christianity. Augustine had been born in 354, so his account came after much reflection. The *Confessions* were one of the most widely read books in the Middle Ages (and beyond) and served to establish the principle of "original sin," that is, that we are all born sinners. Notice how his account of infant sinning reinforces this idea.

Who can recall to me the sins I committed as a baby? For in your sight no man is free from sin, not even a child who has lived only one day on earth. Who can show me what my sins were? Some small baby in whom I can see all that I do not remember about myself? What sins, then, did I commit when I was a baby myself? Was it a sin to cry when I wanted to feed at the breast? I am too old now to fee on mother's milk, but if I were to cry for the kind of food suited to my age, others would rightly laugh me to scorn and remonstrate with me. So then too I deserved a scolding for what I did; but since I could not have understood the scolding, it would have been unreasonable, and most unusual, to rebuke me. We root out these faults and discard them as we grow up, and this is proof enough that they are faults, because I have never seen a man purposely throw out the good when he clears away the bad. It can hardly be right for a child, even at that age, to cry for everything, including things which would harm him; to work himself into a tantrum against people older than himself and not required to obey him; and to try his best to strike and hurt others who know better than he does, including his own parents, when they do not give in to him and refuse to pander to whims which would only do him harm. This shows that, if babies are innocent, it is not for lack of will to do harm, but for lack of strength.

I have myself seen jealousy in a baby and know what it means. He was not old enough to talk, but whenever he saw his foster-brother at the breast, he would grow pale with envy. This much is common knowledge. Mothers and nurses say that they can work such things out of the system by one means or another, but surely it cannot be called innocence, when the milk flows in such abundance from its source, to object to a rival desperately in need and depending for his life on this one form of nourishment? Such faults are not small or unimportant, but we are tender-hearted and bear with them because we know that the child will grow out of them. It is clear that they are not mere peccadilloes, because the same faults are intolerable in older persons. . . . But if I was born in sin and guilt was with me already when my mother conceived me, where, I ask you Lord, where or when was I, your servant ever innocent?

Source: Augustine. *Saint Augustine Confessions.* Translated by R.S. Pine-Coffin. Harmondsworth, UK: Penguin, 1961, pp. 27–28.

2. Ordeals under the Law

Under Germanic law, one of the ways to determine the guilt or innocence of an accused was to appeal to God's judgment. The following rules for ordeals are drawn from German sources of the tenth century and show how tightly united faith were influenced laws for medieval jurists. Notice also how much discretion is given the person interpreting the results of the ordeals. Notice in the third case, how simple the ordeal is!

1. Ordeal by Hot Water.
    a. When men are to be tried by the ordeal of hot water, they shall first be made to come to church in all humility, and prostrate themselves, while the priest says these prayers: . . .
    b. The man who is to undergo the ordeal shall say the Lord's prayer and make the sign of the cross; then the caldron shall be taken from the fire, and the judge shall suspend a stone in the water at the prescribed depth in the regular manner, and the man shall take the stone out of the water in the name of the Lord. Then his hand shall be immediately bound up and sealed with the seal of the judge, and shall remain wrapped up for three days, when it shall be unbound and examined by suitable persons.
2. Ordeal by Hot Iron.
    a. First the priest says the prescribed mass; then he has the fire lighted and blesses the water and sprinkles it over the fire, over the spectators, and over the place where the ordeal is to be held; then he says this prayer: . . .
    b. Then the priest approaches the fire and blesses the pieces of iron, saying: O God, the just judge, who art the author of peace and judgest with equity, we humbly beseech thee so to bless this iron; which is to be used for the trial of this case, that if this man is innocent of the charge he may take the iron in his hand, or walk upon it, without receiving harm or injury; and if he is guilty this may be made manifest upon him by thy righteous power; that iniquity may not prevail over justice, nor falsehood over truth. . . .
    c. Then he who is about to be tried shall say: In this ordeal which I am about to undergo, I put my trust rather in the power of God the omnipotent Father to show his justice and truth in this trial, than in the power of the devil or of witchcraft to circumvent the justice and the truth of God.
    d. Then the man who is accused takes the sacrament and carries the [hot] iron to the designated place. After that the deacon shall bind up his hand and place the seal upon it. And until the hand is unwrapped [at the

end of three days] the man should put salt and holy water in all his food and drink.

3. Ordeal by Bread and Cheese.

a. [The Priest prays] ... O God, I beseech thee, hear the words of my prayer, that this bread and cheese may not pass the jaws and the throat of him who has committed the theft. . . .

b. Then bread and cheese to the weight of nine denarii shall be given to each man. The bread shall be of barley and unleavened; the cheese shall be made in the month of May of the milk of ewes. While the mass is being said, those who are accused of the theft shall be in front of the altar, and one or more persons shall be appointed to watch them that they do not contrive any trick. When the communion is reached the priest shall first take the communion of the body of Christ, and then shall bless the bread and cheese, which has been carefully weighed out as above, and shall immediately give it to the men. The priest and the inspectors shall watch them carefully and see that they all swallow it. After they have swallowed it, the corners of the mouth of each shall be pressed to see that none of the bread and cheese has been kept inj the mount. Then the rest of the mass shall be said.

Source: Thatcher, Oliver, ed. *A Source Book for Mediaeval* History. New York: Charles Scribner's Sons, 1905, pp. 401–406, 410.

3. King Clovis Kills His Kinsmen (fifth and sixth centuries)

Clovis was the first to unite the Germanic tribes of the Franks and establish the dynasty of the Merovingians. Gregory, bishop of Tours, wrote a chronicle called *The History of the Franks* that recounts Clovis's achievement. Notice the violence that introduced the medieval period and formed the background for the subsequent establishment of laws to try to restrain the carnage.

When King Clovis was dwelling at Paris he sent secretly to the son of Sigibert saying: "Behold your father has become an old man and limps in his weak foot. If he should die," said he, "of due right his kingdom would be yours together with our friendship." Led on by greed the son plotted to kill his father. And when his father went out from the city of Cologne and crossed the Rhine and was intending to journey through the wood Buchaw, as he slept at midday in his tent his son sent assassins in against him, and killed him there, in the idea that he would get his kingdom. But by God's judgment he walked into the pit that he had cruelly dug for this father. He sent messengers to king Clovis to tell about his father's death, and to say: . . . "Send men to me, and I shall gladly transmit to you from his treasures whatever pleases you." And Clovis replied: "I thank you for your good will, and I ask that you show the treasures to my men who come, and after that you shall possess all yourself." When they came, he showed his father's treasures. And when they were looking at the different things he said: "It was in this little chest that my father used to put his gold coins." "Thrust in your hand," said they, "to the bottom, and uncover the whole." When he did so, and was much bent over, one of the lifted his hand and dashed his battle-ax against his head, and so in a shameful manner he incurred the death which he had brought on his father. Clovis heard that Sigibert and his son had been slain, and came to the place and summoned all the people, saying: "Hear what has happened, [father and son are dead] . . . Now I know nothing at all of these matters. For I cannot shed the blood of my own kinsmen, which it is a crime to do. But since this has happened, I give you my advice. . . . ; turn to me that you may be under my protection." They listened to this, and giving applause with both shields and voices, they raised him on a shield, and made him king over them.

And having killed many other kings and his nearest relatives, of whom he was jealous lest they take the kingdom from him, he extended his rule over all the Gauls. However he gathered his people together at one time, it is said, and spoke of the kinsmen whom he had himself destroyed. "Woe to me, who have remained as a stranger among foreigners, and have none of my kinsmen to give me aid if adversity comes." But he said this not because of grief at their death but by way of a ruse, if perchance he should be able to find some one still to kill.

Source: Gregory, Bishop of Tours. *History of the Franks.* Translated by Ernest Brehaut. New York: W. W. Norton & Co., Inc., 1969, pp. 47–48, 49.

4. A Historian Slanders Empress Theodora (sixth century)

In 550, Procopius (c. 500–c. 565), a historian of the reign of Justinian, wrote a "Secret History" that attacked the Empress Theodora. Historians assume Procopius did not intend this to be published until after the emperor's death. We do not know if this is true or simply a way to slander a powerful woman. Notice what charges he uses to shock the audience. Notice also how this text gives information about entertainment in Byzantium.

But as soon as she arrived at the age of youth, and was now ready for the world, her mother put her on the stage. Forthwith, she became a courtesan, and such as the ancient Greeks used to call a common one, at that: for she was not a flute or harp player, nor was she even trained to dance, but only gave her youth to anyone she met, in utter abandonment. Her general favors included, of course, the actors in the theater; and in their productions she took part in the low comedy scenes. For she was very funny and a good mimic, and immediately became popular in this art. There was no shame in the girl, and no one ever saw her dismayed: no role was too scandalous for her to, accept without a blush.

She was the kind of comedienne who delights the audience by letting herself be cuffed and slapped on the cheeks, and makes them guffaw by raising her skirts to reveal to the spectators those feminine secrets here and there which custom veils from the eyes of the opposite sex. With pretended laziness she mocked her lovers, and coquettishly adopting ever new ways of embracing, was able to keep in a constant turmoil the hearts of the sophisticated. And she did not wait to be asked by anyone she met, but on the contrary, with inviting jests and a comic flaunting of her skirts herself tempted all men who passed by, especially those who were adolescent.

On the field of pleasure she was never defeated. Often she would go pic-nicking with ten young men or more, in the flower of their strength and viril-ity, and dallied with them all, the whole night through. When they wearied of the sport, she would approach their servants, perhaps thirty in number, and fight a duel with each of these; and even thus found no allayment of her crav-ing. Once, visiting the house of an illustrious gentleman, they say she mounted the projecting corner of her dining couch, pulled up the front of her dress, without a blush, and thus carelessly showed her wantonness. And though she flung wide three gates to the ambassadors of Cupid, she lamented that nature had not similarly unlocked the straits of her bosom, that she might there have contrived a further welcome to his emissaries.

But when she came back to Constantinople, Justinian fell violently in love with her. At first he kept her only as a mistress, though he raised her to patri-cian rank. Through him Theodora was able immediately to acquire an unholy power and exceedingly great riches. She seemed to him the sweetest thing in the world, and like all lovers, he desired to please his charmer with every pos-sible favor and requite her with all his wealth. The extravagance added fuel to the flames of passion. With her now to help spend his money he plundered the people more than ever, not only in the capital, but throughout the Roman Empire.

Source: Procopius, "Secret History," Book 9 in http://www.procopius.net/procopiuschapter9 .html. Retrieved August 8, 2007.

5. Bede Describes the Conversion of the English (sixth and seventh centuries)

In 596, Pope Gregory I sent a group of monks led by Augustine (not the Church Father) to convert the British. This important incident was de-scribed by Bede the Venerable in his *Ecclesiastical History*. Notice that the Queen was already a Christian, yet Bede gives the credit for the con-version to Augustine's virtues.

Then St. Gregory sent a letter to them [Augustine], and advised them in that letter: that they should humbly go into the work of God's word, and trust in God's help; and that they should not fear the toil of the journey, nor dread the tongues of evil-speaking men; but that, with all earnestness, and with the love of God, they should perform the good things which they by God's help had begun to do; and that they should know that the great toil would be followed by the greater glory of everlasting life; and he prayed Almighty God that he would shield them by his grace; and that he would grant to himself that he might see the fruit of their labor in the heavenly kingdom's glory, because he was ready to be in the same labor with them, if leave had been given him.

Then Augustine was strengthened by the exhortation of the blessed father Gregory, and with Christ's servants who were with him returned to the work of God's word, and came into Britain. Then was at that time Ethelbert king in Kent, and a mighty one. . . . [The mission landed on an island off the coast and sent word to Ethelbert.]

When the King heard these words, then ordered he them to abide in the isle on which they had come up; and their necessaries to be there given them until he should see what he would do to them. Likewise before that a report of the Christian religion had come to him, for he had a Christian wife, who was given to him from the royal kin of the Franks—Bertha was her name; which woman he received from her parents on condition that she should have his leave that she might hold the manner of the Christian belief, and of her religion, unspotted, with the bishop whom they gave her for the help of that faith; whose name was Luidhard.

Then [it] was after many days that the King came to the isle, and ordered to make a seat for him out of doors, and ordered Augustine with his fellows to come to his speech [conference]. He guarded himself lest they should go into any magic whereby they should overcome and deceive him. But they cam endowed—not with devil-craft, but with divine might. They bore Christ's rood-token—a silver cross of Christ and a likeness of the Lord Jesus colored and delineated on a board; and were crying the names of holy men; and singing prayers together, made supplication to the Lord for the everlasting health of themselves and of those to whom they come. [Augustine then preached to him.] . . .

Then answered the King, and thus said: Fair words and promises are these which ye have brought and say to us; but because they are new and unknown, we cannot yet agree that we should forsake the things which we for a long time, with all the English nation, have held.

But because ye have come hither as pilgrims from afar, and since it seems and is evident to me that ye wished to communicate to us also the things which ye believed true and best, we will not therefore be heavy to you, but will kindly receive you in hospitality, and give you a livelihood, and supply your needs. Nor will we hinder you from joining and adding to the religion of your belief all whom you can through your lore. Then the King gave them a dwelling and a place in Canterbury, which was the chief city of all his kingdom. . . .

Then came it about through the grace of God that the King likewise among others began to delight in the cleanest life of holy men and their sweetest promises, and they also gave confirmation that those were true by the showing of many wonders; and he then, being glad, was baptized.

Source: Bede. "Augustine's Missionary Work in England, A.D. 597," in *The Great Events by Famous Historians.* Vol. 4. Edited by Rossiter Johnson. n.p. The National Alumni, 1905, pp. 183–186.

6. Documents of Feudal Law (seventh and eighth centuries)

These documents are taken from books of documents that serve as examples for drawing up contracts. They are taken from the collection of Germanic Laws, *Monumenta Germaniae, volume v.* In the first form, a vassal turns himself over to a lord, and in the second the lord promises his protection. Notice the mutual nature of the contract.

Form for Commendation. Middle of Eighth Century

To my great lord, (name), I, (name). Since, as was well known, I had not wherewith to feed and clothe myself, I came to you and told you my wish, to commend myself to you and to put myself under your protection. I have now done so, on the condition that you shall supply me with food and clothing as far as I shall merit by my services, and that as long as I live I shall perform such services for you as are becoming to a freeman, and shall never have the right to withdraw from your power and protection, but shall remain under them all the days of my life. It is agreed that if either of us shall try to break this compact he shall pay ___ solidi, and the compact shall still hold. It is also agreed that two copies of this letter shall be made and signed by us, which also has been done.

Form for the creation of a vassal by the king, seventh century

It is right that those who have promised us unbroken faith should be rewarded by our aid and protection. Now since our faithful subject (name) with the will of God has come to our palace with his arms and has there sworn in our hands to keep his trust and fidelity to us, therefore we decree and command by the present writing that henceforth the said (name) is to be numbered among our *antrustiones* (vassals). If anyone shall presume to slay him, let him know that he shall have to pay 600 solidi as a wergild for him.

Source: Thatcher, Oliver, ed. *A Source Book for Mediaeval* History. New York: Charles Scribner's Sons, 1905, pp. 342–344.

7. Charlemagne Promotes Education (eighth and ninth centuries)

Charlemagne enacted educational reforms as part of reform of churches in his realm. In the following letter that Charlemagne wrote to the clergy of his lands, we can see how he valued texts and scholars. In his letter, the emperor refers to himself as "Karl."

Karl, by the aid of God king of the Franks and Lombards and patricius of the Romans, to the clergy of his realm. . . . Now since we are very desirous that the condition of our churches should constantly improve, we are endeavoring by diligent study to restore the knowledge of letters which has been almost lost through the negligence of our ancestors, and by our example we are encouraging those who are able to do so to engage in the study of the liberal arts. In this undertaking we have already, with the aid of God, corrected all the books of the Old and New Testament, whose texts had been corrupted through the ignorance of copyists. Moreover, inspired by the example of our father, Pippin, of blessed memory, who introduced the Roman chants into the churches of his realm, we are now trying to supply the churches with good reading lessons. Finally, since we have found that many of the lessons to be read in the nightly service have been badly compiled and that the texts of these readings are full of mistakes, and the names of their authors omitted, and since we could not bear to listen to such gross errors in the sacred lessons, we have diligently studied how the character of these readings might be improved. Accordingly, we have commanded Paul the Deacon, our beloved subject, to undertake this work; that is, to go through the writings of the fathers carefully, and to make selections of the most helpful things from them and put them together into a book, as one gathers occasional flowers from a broad meadow to make a bouquet. And he, wishing to obey us, had read through the treatises and sermons of the various catholic fathers and has picked out the best things. These selections he has copied clearly without mistakes and has arranged in two volumes, providing readings suitable for every feast day throughout the whole year. We have tested the texts of all these readings by our own knowledge, and now authorize these volumes and commend them to all of you to be read in the churches of Christ.

Source: Thatcher, Oliver, ed. *A Source Book for Mediaeval History.* New York: Charles Scribner's Sons, 1905, pp. 56–57.

8. A Jewish Merchant Writes to His Wife

Many Jewish merchants traveled long distances to engage in global trade, leading to long separations from their family. A journey from Europe to India could take 2 years or more. This excerpt of a letter from a Jewish merchant in India to his wife in Egypt indicates the stress such separations placed on family life. Notice that Jews, unlike Christians, could obtain divorces, and he was willing to let his wife make the decision.

Would I try to describe the extent of my feelings of longing and yearning for you all the time, my letter would become too long and the words too many. But he who knows the secrets of the heart has the might to bring about relief for each of us by uniting us in joy. . . .

In your letters you alternately rebuke and offend me or put me to shame and use harsh words all the time. I have not deserved any of this. I swear by God, I do not believe that the heart of anyone traveling away from his wife has remained like mine, all the time and during all the years—from the moment of our separation to the very hour of writing this letter—so constantly thinking of you and yearning after you and regretting to be unable to provide you with what I so much desire: your legal rights [for intercourse] on every Sabbath and holiday, and to fulfill all your wishes, great and small, with regard to dresses or food or anything else. . . .

Now, if this [divorce] is your wish, I cannot blame you. For the waiting has been long. And I do not know whether the Creator will grant relief immediately so that I can come home, or whether matters will take time, for I cannot come home with nothing. Therefore I resolved to issue a writ which sets you free. Now the matter is in your hand. If you wish separation from me, action the bill of repudiation and you are free. But if this is not your decision and not your desire, do not lose these long years of waiting: perhaps relief is at hand and you will regret at a time when regret will be of no avail.

And please do not blame me, for I never neglected you from the time when those things happened and made an effort to save you and me from people talking and impairing my honor.

Source: Goiten, S.D., trans. *Letters of Medieval Jewish Traders.* Princeton, NJ: Princeton University Press, 1973, pp. 221, and 116.

9. Lords Create Markets (ninth and tenth centuries)

The Champagne Fairs were the largest of the medieval fairs, but other lords saw the profit in establishing markets. No one had the right to set up a market without the king's permission, and the following documents are examples of royal permissions to establish markets. Notice the necessities that come with markets—mints and safety.

Lothar II (855–869) Grants a Market to the Monastery of Prum, 861

Therefore, let all our faithful subjects, both present and future, know that Ansbald, abbot of the monastery of Prum, has told us that that place suffers great disadvantage because it is so far distant from a market and mint. On this account, he begged us to grant his monastery our permission for the establishment of a market and mint in a place which is called Romarivilla, which is not far from his monastery. Out of reverence for the Lord Jesus Christ, and for the salvation of our soul, we gladly grant his petition, and have ordered this document to be written, by which we decree and command that hereafter that monastery may have an ordinary market in the above-named place and a mint for coining denarii of the proper weight and quality. And no public official shall levy a tax of any sort on the monastery for this market and mint, but they shall be wholly for the profit of the monastery and its inmates. And that this concession may never be violated, we have ordered it to be sealed with our ring and we have signed it with our own hand.

Otto I Grants a Market to and Archbishop, 965

In the name of the undivided Trinity. Otto by the favor of God emperor, Augustus. If we grant the requests of clergymen and liberally endow the places which are dedicated to the worship of God, we believe that it will undoubtedly assist in securing for us the eternal reward. Therefore, let all know that for the love of God we have granted the petition of Adaldagus, the reverend archbishop of Hamburg, and have given him permission to establish a market in the place called Bremen. In connection with the market we grant him jurisdiction, tolls, a mint, and all other things connected therewith to which our royal treasury would have a right. We also take under our special protection all the merchants who live in that place, and grant them the same protection and rights as those merchants have who live in other royal cities. And no one shall have any jurisdiction there except the aforesaid archbishop and those to whom he may delegate it. Signed with our hand and sealed with our ring.

Source: Thatcher, Oliver, ed. *A Source Book for Mediaeval History.* New York: Charles Scribner's Sons, 1905, pp. 579–580.

10. Asser's Life of Alfred the Great, King of Wessex (tenth century)

A biography of King Alfred was written by his bishop Asser, who was his companion through many of his achievements. After the king's death, Asser purportedly wrote this biography to preserve the account of his deeds. Asser died in 910. Scholars have disputed whether the biography was actually written by Asser, but the text remains an important source for early England. This excerpt describes his childhood and his love of learning that marked his reign.

Now, he was loved by his father and mother, and indeed by everybody, with a united and immense love, more than all his brothers, and was always brought up in the royal court, and as he passed through his childhood and boyhood he appeared fairer in form than all his brothers, and more pleasing in his looks, his words and his ways. And from his cradle a longing for wisdom before all things and among all the pursuits of this present life, combined with his noble birth, filled the noble temper of his mind; but alas, by the unworthy carelessness of his parents and tutors, he remained ignorant of letters until his twelfth year, or even longer. But he listened attentively to Saxon poems day and night, and hearing them often recited by others committed them to his retentive memory. A keen huntsman, he toiled unceasingly in every branch of hunting, and not in vain; for he was without equal in his skill and good fortune in that art, as also in all other gifts of God, as we have ourselves often seen.

When, therefore, his mother one day was showing him and his brothers a certain book of Saxon poetry which she held in her hand, she said: "I will give this book to whichever of you can learn it most quickly." And moved by these words, or rather by divine inspiration, and attracted by the beauty of the initial letter of the book, Alfred said in reply to his mother, forestalling his brothers, his elders in years though not in grace: "Will you really give this book to one of us, to the one who can soonest understand and repeat it to you?" And, smiling and rejoicing, she confirmed it, saying: "To him will I give it." Then taking the book from her hand he immediately went to his master, who read it. And when it was read, he went back to his mother and repeated it.

Source: "Life of King Alfred," in *Readings in Medieval History.* Edited by Patrick J. Geary. Lewiston, NY: Broadview Press, 1989, pp. 120.

11. Serfs Struggle for Freedom (tenth and thirteenth centuries)

Serfs, who owed their labor and other dues to their lord, had two main ways they could become free: Their lord might free them, and they might run away to a city and hide for a year and a day. These documents show these two possibilities. The first is a form by which Henry I of Germany freed a serf in 926. The second document comes from 1224 and claims that the King will give protection to those nobles who searched in a city for their runaway serfs. Both documents reveal the tensions in the medieval social structure.

Henry I frees a serf, 926

In the name of the holy and undivided Trinity. Henry, by the divine clemency king. Let all our faithful subjects, both present and future, know that at the request of Arnulf, our faithful and beloved duke, and also to increase our eternal reward, we have freed a certain priest, named Baldmunt, who is our serf, born on the land of the monastery of Campido. We freed him by striking a penny out of his hand in the presence of witnesses, according to the Salic law, and we have thereby released him entirely from the yoke of servitude. And by this writing we have given a sure proof of his freedom and we desire that he shall remain free forever. We ordain that the said Baldmunt, the reverend priest, shall enjoy such freedom and have such rights as all those have who up to this time have been set free in this way by the kings or emperors of the franks.

The Recovery of Fugitive Serfs, 1224

When a quarrel arose between our cities of Elsass and the nobles and ministerials of the same province in regard to the serfs who had run away and gone to the cities, or might hereafter do so, . . . it was settled by the following decision: If a serf belonging to a noble or ministerial runs away and goes to one of our cities and stays there, his lord may recover him if he can bring seven persons who are of the family of the serf's mother, who will swear that he is a serf, and belongs to the said lord. If the lord cannot secure seven such witnesses, he may bring two suitable witnesses from among his neighbors, who will swear that before the serf ran away the said lord had been in peaceable possession of him, . . . and he may then recover his serf. We also decree and command that all nobles and ministerials who wish to recover their serfs may enter a city for this purpose with our permission and protection, and no one shall dare injure them. At their request a safe conduct shall be furnished them by the . . . council of the city.

Source: Thatcher, Oliver, ed. *A Source Book for Mediaeval History.* New York: Charles Scribner's Sons, 1905, pp. 546–548.

12. Vikings Trade with Natives in North America (eleventh century)

The Viking explorer, Leif Erikson, discovered North America in the early eleventh century, and there were several subsequent Viking expeditions to this bountiful land that they called "Vinland." Inevitably, they encountered Natives, whom they called by the insulting name, *Skraelings.* At times they traded, at other times they fought, and it is likely that the presence of hostile natives prevented the Vikings from settling North America. This account from the *Greenland Saga* recounts the explorations and describes the trade goods that interested the natives. Notice that women took part in these explorations.

That same summer a ship arrived in Greenland from Norway. Her captain was a man called Thorfinn Karlsefni. He was a man of considerable wealth. He spent the winter with Leif Eiriksson at Brattahlid. . . . There was still the same talk about Vinland voyages as before, and everyone, . . . kept urging Karlsefni to make the voyage. In the end he decided to sil and gathered a company of sixty men and five women. He made an agreement with his crew that everyone should share equally in whatever profits the expedition might yield. They took livestock of all kinds, for they intended to make a permanent settlement there if possible. . . . [They successfully make the crossing.]

The first winter passed into summer, and then they had their first encounter with Skraelings, when a great number of them came out of the wood one day. The cattle were grazing near by and the bull began to bellow and roar with great vehemence. This terrified the Skraelings and they fled, carrying their packs which contained furs and sables and pelts of all kinds. They made for Karlsefni's houses and tried to get inside, but Karlsefni had the doors barred against them. Neither side could understand the other's language.

Then the Skraelings put down their packs and opened them up and offered their contents, preferably in exchange for weapons; but Karlsefni forbade his men to sell arms. Then he hit on the idea of telling the women to carry milk out to the Skraelings, and when the Skraelings saw the milk they wanted to buy nothing else. And so the outcome of their trading expedition was that the Skraelings carried their purchases away in their bellies, and left their packs and furs with Karlsefni and his men.

[At a later trading exchange, a Skraeling was killed when he tried to steal a weapon, so the Vikings prepared for further attacks.]

[After a few more skirmishes] Karlsefni and his men spent the whole winter there, but in the spring he announced that he had no wish to stay there any longer and wanted to return to Greenland. They made ready for the voyage and took with them much valuable produce, vines and grapes and pelts. They put to sea and reached Eiriksfjord safely and spent the winter there.

Source: "Graenlendinga Saga," in *The Vinland Sagas: The Norse Discovery of America.* Translated by Magnus Magnusson and Hermann Palsson. Harmondsworth, UK: Penguin, 1965, pp. 64–65, 67.

13. The Pope Claims Supremacy in the Investiture Controversy (eleventh century)

During the Investiture Controversy of the late eleventh century, Pope Gregory VII claimed rule over Christendom. In this famous document, called the *Dictatus Papae* (Dictate of the pope), he, or his officers, laid out astonishing claims of supremacy. Notice how these claims would take away lords' authority (paragraph 27) and make the popes emperors on earth (paragraph 8), and that they claim the authority comes from God. Notice also in paragraph 22, that this is the first claim of papal infallibility. This text was written about 1090.

That the Roman church was established by God alone.
That the Roman pontiff is rightly called universal
That he alone has the power to depose and reinstate bishops.
That his legate [representative], even if he be of lower ecclesiastical rank, presides over bishops in council, and has the power to give sentence of deposition against them.
That the pope has the power to depose those who are absent [i.e, without giving them a hearing.
That, among other things, we ought not to remain in the same house with those whom he has excommunicated.
That he alone has the right, according to the necessity of the occasion, to make new laws, to create new bishoprics, to make a monastery of a chapter of canons, and vice versa, and either to divide a rich bishopric or to unit several poor ones.
That he alone may use the imperial insignia.
That all princes shall kiss the foot of the pope alone.
That his name alone is to be recited in the churches.
That the name applied to him belongs to him alone.
That he has the power to depose emperors.
That he has the right to transfer bishops from one see to another when it becomes necessary.

That he has the right to ordain as a cleric anyone from any part of the church whatsoever.

That anyone ordained by him may rule [as bishop] over another church, but cannot serve [as priest] in it, and that such a cleric may not receive a higher rank from any other bishop.

That no general synod may be called without his order.

That no action of a synod and not book shall be regarded as canonical without his authority.

That his decree can be annulled by no one, and that he can annul the decrees of anyone.

That he can be judged by no one.

That no one shall dare to condemn a person who has appealed to the apostolic seat [pope].

That the important cases of any church whatsoever shall be referred to the Roman church [pope].

That the Roman church has never erred and will never err to all eternity, according to the testimony of holy scriptures.

That the Roman pontiff who has been canonically ordained is made holy by the merits of St. Peter, according to the testimony of St. Ennodius, bishop of Pavia, which is confirmed by many of the holy fathers, as is shown by the decrees of the blessed pope Symmachus.

That by his command or permission subjects may accuse their rulers.

That he can depose and reinstate bishops without the calling of a synod.

That no one can be regarded as catholic who does not agree with the Roman church.

That he ahs the power to absolve subjects from their oath of fidelity to wicked rulers.

Source: "Dictatus Papae," in Thatcher, Oliver, ed. *A Source Book for Mediaeval History.* New York: Charles Scribner's Sons, 1905, pp. 136–138.

14. Anna Comnena Describes the First Crusade (twelfth century)

The Emperor Alexius Comnenus' daughter Anna (1083–1153) was an historian who offers a valuable description of the first crusade in the eleventh century. She is the first to describe the growing suspicion between East and West that you can see in this account that describes the emperor's irritation at Crusaders like Tancred and Bohemund who seized land he thought was his own. Notice the arguments made by both sides.

Soon the Emperor learnt of the seizure of Laodicea by Tancred, and therefore sent a letter to Bohemund which ran as follows: "You know the oaths and promises which not only you but all the Counts took to the Roman Empire. Now you were the first to break them, by retaining possession of Antioch, and then taking more fortresses and even Laodicea itself. Therefore withdraw from Antioch and all the other cities and do what is just and right, and do not provoke more wars and troubles for yourself." Now Bohemund after reading the Emperor's letter could not reply by a falsehood, as he usually did, for the facts openly declared the truth, so outwardly he assented to it, but put the blame for all the wrong he had done upon the Emperor and wrote to him thus, "It is not I, but you, who are the cause of all this. For you promised you would follow us with a large army, but you never thought of making good your promise by deeds. When we reached Antioch we fought for three months under great difficulty both against the enemy and against famine, which was more severe than had ever been experienced before, with the result that most of us ate of the very foods which are forbidden by law. We endured for a long time and while we were in this danger even Taticius, your Majesty's most loyal servant, whom you had appointed to help us, went away and left us to our danger. Yet we captured Antioch unexpectedly and utterly routed the troops which had come from Chorosan to succour Antioch. In what way would it be just for us to deprive ourselves willingly of what we gained by our own sweat and toil? " When the envoys returned from him the Emperor recognized from the reading of his letter that he was still the same Bohemund and in no wise changed for the better, and therefore decided that he must protect the boundaries of the Roman Empire, and as far as possible, check his impetuous advance.

Source: Anna Comnena. *The Alexiad.* Edited and translated by E.R.A. Sewter. Harmondsworth, UK: Penguin, 1969, pp. 290–291.

15. The Founding and Decline of the Knights Templars (twelfth century)

The twelfth-century chronicler, William of Tyre, describes the founding of the Knights Templars who were so essential during the Crusades. He also describes how their success began to corrupt their ideals, which foreshadows their destruction in the fourteenth century.

In the same year [1118–1119] certain nobles of knightly rank, devout, religious, and God-fearing, devoting themselves to the service of Christ, made their vows to the patriarch [of Jerusalem] and declared that they wished to live forever in chastity, obedience, and poverty, according to the rule of regular canons. . . . Since they had neither a church nor a house, the king of Jerusalem gave them a temporary residence in the palace which stands on the west side of the temple. The canons of the temple granted the, on certain conditions, the open space around the aforesaid palace for the erection of their necessary buildings, and the king, the nobles, the patriarch, and the bishops, each from his own possessions, gave them lands for their support. The patriarch and bishops ordered that for the forgiveness of their sins their first vow should be to protect the roads and especially the pilgrims against robbers and marauders. . . . Up to their ninth year they had only nine members, but then their number began to increase and their possessions to multiply. Afterward, in the time of Eugene III, that their appearance might be more striking, they all, knights as well as the other members of a lower grade, who were called serving men, began to sew crosses of red cloth on their robes. Their order grew with great rapidity, and now [about 1180] they have 300 knights in their house, clothed in white mantles, besides the serving men, whose number is almost infinite. They are said to have immense possessions both here [in Palestine] and beyond the sea [in Europe]. There is not a province in the whole Christian world which has not given property to this order, so that they may be said to have possessions equal to those of kings. . . .

For a long time they were steadfast in their purpose and were true to their vows, but then they forgot their humility, which is the guardian of all virtues, and rebelled against the patriarch of Jerusalem who had assisted in the establishment of their order and had given them their first lands, and refused him the obedience which their predecessors had shown him. They also made themselves very obnoxious to the churches by seizing their tithes and first-fruits and plundering their possessions.

Source: Thatcher, Oliver, ed. *A Source Book for Mediaeval History.* New York: Charles Scribner's Sons, 1905, pp. 493–494.

16. The Great Pilgrimage Church of Saint James in Spain (twelfth century)

Throughout the Middle Ages, pilgrimage remained at the heart of popular worship. Travelers went to the great shrines that held relics of saints, and the most famous pilgrimage site throughout the period (even today) is Santiago de Compostella in northwest Spain. According to the faithful, this shrine holds the bones of James the Elder, and once they were discovered in the ninth century, Santiago lured people from all over Europe. A magnificent Romanesque cathedral was built to hold the relics. This source describes the church and is an excerpt from a medieval work designed to guide pilgrims to Santiago and relate the wonders they would see. Notice its information on building the cathedral as well as its emphasis on hospitality for pilgrims.

The master stonecutters that first undertook the construction of the basilica of the Blessed James were called Master Bernard the elder—a marvelously gifted craftsman—and Robert, as well as other stonecutters, about fifty in number, who worked assiduously under the most faithful administration of Don Wicart, the head of the chapter . . . during the reign of Alphonso king of Spain during the bishopric of Don Diego I, a valiant soldier and a generous man.

The church was begun in the year 1116 of the era. From the year it was started until the death of Alphonso, valiant and famous king of Aragon, there are fifty-nine years, . . . And from the year that the first stone of the foundations was laid down until such a time that the last one was put in place, forty-four years have elapsed.

This church, furthermore, from the moment it was started until today, has shined by the refulgence of the miracles of the Blessed James: in fact, the sick have been restored to health in it, the blind have been rendered their eyesight, the tongue of the dumb has been untied, the ear of the deaf unplugged, movement has been restored to the lame, the possessed has been delivered and, what is more, the prayers of the faithful have been fulfilled, their wishes granted, the afflicted have been given consolation, and the foreign people of all parts of the world have rushed in in large masses bringing in laudation their gifts to the lord. . . .

Pilgrims, whether poor or rich, who return from or proceed to Santiago, must be received charitably and respectfully by all. For he who welcomes them and provides them diligently with lodging will have as his guest not merely the Blessed James, but the Lord himself, who in His Gospels said: "He who welcomes you, welcomes me." Many are those who in the past brought upon themselves the wrath of God because they refused to receive the pilgrims of Saint James or the indigent. . . .

Two valiant Frenchmen, returning one day from Santiago destitute of all, kept asking for lodging, by the love of God and Saint James, all about the city of Poitiers . . . and they could find none. And having finally been put up by some poor man in the last house of that street . . . by divine vengeance, an violent fire burned to the ground that very night the entire street, starting from the house where they first asked for lodging and up to the one which had welcomed them. And these were about one thousand houses in all But the one in which the servants of God had been put up remained, by divine grace, untouched.

This is the reason why it should be known that the pilgrims of Saint James, whether poor or rich, have the right to hospitality and to diligent respect.

Source: The Pilgrims Guide to Santiago de Compostela. Translated by William Melczer. New York: Italica Press, 1993, pp. 130–133.

17. The Life of Godric, Merchant Saint (twelfth century)

The "Life of Saint Godric," written by a friend and monk, describes the life of a merchant who lived during the twelfth century. Godrick became a prosperous merchant who ended his life by going on pilgrimage to Jerusalem and giving his wealth to the church. It is a rare source of information on the life of merchants.

He chose not to follow the life of a husbandman, but rather to study, learn and exercise the rudiments of more subtle conceptions. For this reason, aspiring to the merchant's trade, he began to follow the chapman's [trader's] way of life, first learning how to gain in small bargains and things of insignificant price; and thence, while yet a youth, his mind advanced little by little to buy and sell and gain from things of greater expense. For, in his beginnings, he was wont to wander with small wares around the villages and farmsteads of his own neighborhood; but, in process of time, he gradually associated himself by compact with city merchants. Hence, within a brief space of time, the youth who had trudged for many weary hours from village to village, from farm to farm, did so profit by his increase of age and wisdom as to travel with associates of his own age through towns and boroughs, fortresses and cities to fairs and to all the various booths of the marketplace, in pursuit of his public chaffer [trading]. . . . At first, he lived as a chapman for four years in Lincolnshire, going on foot and carrying the smallest wares; then he traveled abroad, first to St. Andrews in Scotland and then for the first time to Rome. On his return, having formed a familiar friendship with certain other young men who were eager for merchandise, he began to launch upon bolder courses, and to coast frequently by sea to the foreign lands that lay around him. Thus, sailing often to and fro between Scotland and Britain, he traded in many diverse wares and, amid these occupations, learned much worldly wisdom. . . . For he labored not only as a merchant but also as a shipman . . . to Denmark and Flanders and Scotland; in all which lands he found certain rare, and therefore more precious, wares, which he carried to other parts wherein he know them to be least familiar, and coveted by the inhabitants beyond the price of gold itself; wherefore he exchanged these wares for others coveted by men of other lands; and thus he chaffered most freely and assiduously. Hence he made great profit in all his bargains, and gathered much wealth in the sweat of his brow; for he sold dear in one place the wares which he had bought elsewhere at a small price.

Source: Coulton, G.G. *Social Life in Britain from the Conquest to the Reformation.* Cambridge, UK: Cambridge University Press, 1918, pp. 415–419.

18. Hildegard of Bingen Discusses Marriage (twelfth century)

Hildegard of Bingen (1098–1179) was a remarkable visionary who wrote on many subjects of everyday interest. This excerpt from her visions describes marriage. Notice how she keeps a standard Biblical interpretation while offering a woman's perspective that insists marriage is a mutual relationship.

Because a mature woman was given not to a little boy but to a mature man, namely Adam, so now a mature woman must be married to a man when he has reached the full age of fertility, just as due cultivation is given to a tree when it begins to put forth flowers. For Eve was formed from a rib by Adam's ingrafted heat and vigor, and therefore now it is by the strength and heat of a man that a woman receives the semen to bring a child into the world. For the man is the sower, but the woman is the recipient of the seed. Wherefore a wife is under the power of her husband because the strength of the man is to the susceptibility of the woman as the hardness of stone is to the softness of earth.

But the first woman's being formed from man means the joining of wife to husband. And thus it is to be understood: this union must not be vain or done in forgetfulness of God, because he who brought forth the woman from the man instituted this union honorably and virtuously, forming flesh from flesh. Wherefore, as Adam and Eve were one flesh, so now also a man and woman become one flesh in a union of holy love for the multiplication of the human race. And therefore there should be perfect love in these two as there was in those first two. For Adam could have blamed his wife because by her advice she brought him death, but nonetheless he did not dismiss her as long as he lived in this world, because he knew she had been given to him by divine power. Therefore, because of perfect love, let a man not leave his wife except for the reason the faithful church allows. . . .

But if either husband or wife breaks the law by fornication, and it is made public either by themselves or by their priests, they shall undergo the just censure of the spiritual magisterium. For the husband shall complain of the wife, or the wife of the husband, about the sin against their union . . . , but not so that the husband or wife can seek another marriage; either they shall stay together in righteous union, or shall both abstain from such unions, as the discipline of church practice shows. And they shall not tear each other to pieces by viperous rending, but they shall love with pure love, since both man and woman could not exist without having been conceived in such a bond.

Source: Hildegard of Bingen. *Scivias.* Translated by Columba Hart and Jane Bishop. New York: Paulist Press, 1990, pp. 77–78.

19. Guibert of Nogent Studies at Home (twelfth century)

In the early twelfth century, Guibert, abbot of Nogent in France, wrote an autobiography that gives rare insight into child-rearing and educational practices. In this text we can see how difficult it was to get suitable tutors to teach children. Notice how it was customary to beat students. Guibert's parents had promised at his birth that he would grow up to be a monk, so his education pointed him in this direction.

There was a little before that time, and in a measure there is still in my time, such a scarcity of grammarians that in the towns hardly anyone, and in the cities very few, could be found, and those who by good hap could be discovered, had but slight knowledge and could not be compared with the itinerant clerks of these days. . . .

Placed under him [his tutor] I was taught with such purity and checked with such honesty in the excesses which are wont to spring up in my youth, that I was kept well-guarded from the common wolves and never allowed to leave his company, or to eat anywhere without his leave; in everything I had to show self-control in word, look or act, so that he seemed to require of me the conduct of a monk rather than a clerk. For whereas others of my age wandered everywhere at will and were unchecked in the indulgence of such inclinations to their age, I [was] hedged in with constant restraints. . . .

Although, therefore, he crushed me by such severity, yet in other ways he made it quite plain that he loved me as well as he did himself. . . . As for me, considering the dull sensibility of my age and my littleness, great was the love I conceived for him in response, in spite of the many weals [marks] with which he marked my tender skin so that not through fear, as is common in those of my age, but through a sort of love deeply implanted in my heart, I obeyed him in utter forgetfulness of his severity.

Source: Guibert de Nogent. *The Autobiography of Guibert, Abbot of Nogent-Sous-Coucy.* Translated by C.C. Swinton Bland. London: George Routledge & Sons, Ltd., 1926, p. 32.

20. The Legendary King Arthur Is Born (twelfth century)

In the twelfth century, the English historian Geoffrey of Monmouth, who was influenced by the new movements of courtly love and romance, elaborated on the story of an early English king named Arthur. Geoffrey's account served as the basis for future tales of the romantic King Arthur. In this section, Geoffrey describes the conception of Arthur, surrounded by magic and passionate love. Notice also the description of the impregnable castle that was typical of those that had begun to dominate the twelfth-century landscape.

Finally, after a week had gone by, the King's [Uther Pendragon] passion for Ygerna became more than he could bear. He called to him Ulfin of Ridcaradoch, one of his soldiers and a familiar friend, and told him what was on his mind. "I am desperately in love with Ygerna," said Uther, "and if I cannot have her I am convinced that I shall suffer a physical breakdown. You must tell me how I can satisfy my desire for her, for otherwise I shall die of the passion which is consuming me." "Who can possibly give you useful advice," answered Ulfin, "when no power on earth can enable us to come to her where she is inside the fortress of Tintagel? The castle is built high above the sea, which surrounds it on all sides, and there is no other way in except that offered by a narrow isthmus of rock. Three armed soldiers could hold it against you, even if you stood there with the whole kingdom of Britain at your side. If only the prophet Merlin would give his mind to the problem, then with his help I think you might be able to obtain what you want." The King believed Ulfin and ordered Merlin to be sent for, for he, too, had come to the siege.

Merlin was summoned immediately. When he appeared in the King's presence, he was ordered to suggest how the King could have his way with Ygerna. When Merlin saw the torment which the King was suffering because of this woman, he was amazed at the strength of his passion. "If you are to have your wish," he said, "you must make use of methods which are quite new and until now unheard-of in your day. By my drugs I know how to give you the precise appearance of Gorlois, [Ygrain's husband], so that you will resemble him in every respect. . . . In this way you will be able to go safely to Ygerna in her castle and be admitted."

The King agreed. . . . The King spent that night with Ygerna and satisfied his desire by making love with her. He had deceived her by the disguise which he had taken. He had deceived her, too, by the lying things that he said to her, things which he planned with great skill. . . . She naturally believed all that he said and refused him nothing that he asked. That night she conceived Arthur, the most famous of men, who subsequently won great renown by his outstanding bravery.

Source: Geoffrey of Monmouth. *The History of the Kings of Britain.* Translated by Lewis Thorpe. Harmondsworth, UK: Penguin, 1966, pp. 206–207.

21. Bernard of Clairvaux Condemns Abelard and Scholasticism, 1140

Bernard of Clairvaux was horrified when Peter Abelard presumed to use reason to understand faith. For Bernard, a great mystic, the path to God was through faith only. In this letter that Bernard wrote to Pope Innocent II in 1140, he attacks Abelard and medieval philosophy in general, praising faith over reason.

We have in France an old teacher turned into a new theologian, who in his early days amused himself with dialectics [logic], and now gives utterance to wild imaginations upon the Holy Scriptures. He is endeavoring again to quicken false opinions, long ago condemned and put to rest, not only his own, but those of others; and is adding fresh ones as well. I know not what there is in heaven above and in the earth beneath which he deigns to confess ignorance of: He raises his eyes to Heaven, and searches the deep things of God, and then returning to us, he brings back unspeakable words which it is not lawful for a man to utter, while he is presumptuously prepared to give a reason for everything, even of those things which are above reason; he presumes against reason and against faith. For what is more against reason than by reason to attempt to transcend reason? And what is more against faith than to be unwilling to believe what reason cannot attain? For instance, wishing to explain that saying of the wise man: "He who is hasty to believe is light in mind (Eccles., xix, 4), he says that a hasty faith is one that believes before reason; when Solomon says this not of faith towards God, but of mutual belief amongst ourselves. For the blessed Pope Gregory denies plainly that faith towards God has any merit whatever if human reason furnishes it with proof. But he praises the Apostles, because they followed their Savior when called but once. He knows doubtless that this word was spoken as praise: "At the hearing of the ear he obeyed me" (Ps., xviii, 44), that the Apostles were directly rebuked because they had been slow in believing (Mark, xvi, 14). Again Mary is praised because she anticipated reason by faith, and Zacharias punished because he tempted faith by reason (Luke, I, 20, 45), and Abraham is commended in that "against hope he believed in hope" (Romans, iv, 18).

But on the other hand our theologian says: "What is the use of speaking of doctrine unless what we wish to teach can be explained so as to be intelligible?" An so he promises understanding to his hearers. Even on those most sublime and sacred truths which are hidden in the very bosom of our holy faith.

Source: Eales, Samuel J., trans. *The Life and Works of St. Bernard.* London: J. Hodges, 1889, pp. 565–566.

22. An Agricultural Instruction Manual (thirteenth century)

The prosperity of the late Middle Ages stemmed from agricultural innovations. Nevertheless, agriculture remained a difficult, skill-intensive task. This source is from a thirteenth-century agricultural manual written by Walter of Henley to help landowners make a profit from the land, and it offers a valuable glimpse into medieval farm life.

At the beginning of fallowing and second fallowing and of sowing let the bailiff, and the messer, or the provost, be all the time with the ploughmen, to see that they do their work well and thoroughly, and at the end of the day see how much they have done, and for so much shall they answer each day after unless they can show a sure hindrance. And because customary servants neglect their work it is necessary to guard against their fraud; further, it is necessary that they are overseen often; and besides the bailiff must oversee all, that they all work well, and if they do not well let them be reproved.

With a team of oxen with two horses you draw quicker than wit a team all horses if the ground is not so stony that oxen cannot help themselves with their feet. Why? I will tell you: the horse costs more than the ox. Besides a plough of oxen will go as far in the year as a plough of horses, because the malice of ploughmen will not allow the plough [of horses] to go beyond their pace, no more than the plough of oxen. Further, in very hard ground, where the plough of horses will stop, the plough of oxen will pass. And will you see how the horse costs more than the ox? I will tell you. It is usual and right that plough beasts should be in the stall between the feast of St. Luke and the feast of the Holy Cross in May, five-and-twenty weeks, and if the horse is to be in a condition to do his daily work, it is necessary that he should have every night at the least the sixth prt of a bushel of oats, price one halfpenny, and at the least twelve pennyworth of grass in summer. And each week more or less a penny in shoeing, if he must be shod on all four feet. The sum is twelve shillings and fivepence in the year, without fodder and chaff.

Source: Walter of Henley. *Walter of Henley's Husbandry.* Translated by Elizabeth Lamond. London: Longmans, Green and Co., 1890, pp. 11–13.

23. Crusaders Besiege a Tower during the Fifth Crusade (thirteenth century)

In the Fifth Crusade, 1217–1222, Europeans attacked Egypt in hopes of approaching the Holy Land from the south. This crusade failed, but the detailed accounts of the battles offer vivid details about warfare and the challenges of taking fortified positions. Notice the important role played by the Military Orders who supported the crusaders.

A tower located in the middle of the river [Nile] had to be captured before crossing. The Frisians, however, who were impatient of delay, crossed the Nile and carried off the animals of the Saracens [Muslims]. Wishing to pitch camp on the farther shore, they held their ground, fighting against the Saracens who came out of their city to oppose them. They were recalled through obedience because it did not seem wise to our leaders that a tower filled with pagans should be left behind the Christians. Meanwhile the Duke of Austria and the Hospitallers of Saint John prepared two ladders on two ships, and the Teutons and Frisians fortified a third ship with bulwarks, setting up a small fortress on the top of the mast without hanging a ladder. . . . The ladder of the Hospitallers was shattered and crashed with the mast, hurling its warriors headlong; the ladder of the Duke, being broken in like manner at almost the same time, sent up to heaven soldiers who were vigorous and well armed, wounded in body to the advantage of their souls, crowned with a glorious martyrdom. The overjoyed Egyptians, mocking us violently, raised their voices, beating drums and sounding sackbuts [a kind of trumpet]; gloom and sadness invaded the Christians. . . .

Thus our men, with renewed vigor, manfully fought with the defenders of the tower by means of swords, pikes, club, and other weapons. A certain young knight of the diocese of Liege was the first to ascend the tower; a certain young Frisian, holding a flail by which grain is usually threshed, but which was prepared for fighting by an interweaving with chains, lashed out bravely to the right and to the left, knocked down a certain man holding the saffron standard of the Sultan and took the banner away from him. One came after another, vanquishing the enemy, who were known to be hard and cruel in their resistance. . . . [The Crusaders develop new ships for besieging the tower while fighting against the flooding of the Nile. Finally they make another attack.]

Meanwhile the Saracens, who had withdrawn to the inner part of the tower, having put fire under the top part of the tower, burned it; our men, though victorious, retreated over the ladder, not being able to stand the heat. But the bridge, which had been prepared in the lower part of the fortification, was let down to the narrow foot of the tower, with deep waters surging about on all sides. With iron hammers the victors attacked the door while the Saracens who were within defended it. Both fortifications remained impregnable; the rungs of the ladder, in part, and the circuit of the work which was held together by very strong ropes were pierced by blows of the machines. . . . Finally, being enclosed in the tower, the Saracens sought a conference, and, under a guarantee that their lives would be spared, they surrendered to the Duke of Austria.

Source: Oliver of Paderborn. "The Capture of Damietta," in *Christian Society and the Crusades, 1198–1229.* Edited by Edward Peters. Philadelphia: University of Pennsylvania Press, 1971, pp. 63–65.

24. Marco Polo Describes Religious Toleration in the Mongol Empire, 1271

Marco Polo's account remains one of our main sources for information about the Yuan Empire of the Great Khan. In this account, Marco describes the uprising of one of Kublai's relatives, named Nayan, who had been defeated. Nayan fought under the banner of Christianity, and this account shows the religious toleration that marked the Mongol empire.

At length, however, Nayan, perceiving that he was nearly surrounded, attempted to save himself by flight, but was presently made prisoner, and conducted to the presence of Kublai, who gave orders for his being put to death. This was carried into execution by enclosing him between two carpets, which were violently shaken until the spirit had departed from the body; the motive for this peculiar sentence being that the sun and the air should not witness the shedding of the blood of one who belonged to the imperial family. Those of his troops which survived the battle came to make their submission and swear allegiance to Kublai.

Nayan, who had privately undergone the ceremony of baptism, but never made open profession of Christianity, thought proper, on this occasion, to bear the sign of the cross in his banners, and he had in his army a vast number of Christians, who were among the slain. When the Jews and the Saracens [Muslims] perceived that the banner of the cross was overthrown, they taunted the Christian inhabitants with it, saying: "Behold the state to which your vaunted banners, and those who followed them, are reduced!" On account of these derisions the Christians were compelled to lay their complaints before the Grand Khan, who ordered the former to appear before him, and sharply rebuked them. "If the cross of Christ," he said, "has not proved advantageous to the party of Nayan, the effect has been consistent with reason and justice, inasmuch as he was a rebel and a traitor to his lord, and to such wretches it could afford its protection. Let none therefore presume to charge with injustice the God of the Christians, who is himself the perfection of goodness and of justice."

The Grand Khan, having obtained this signal victory, returned with great pomp and triumph to the capital city of Kanbalu. This took place in the month of November, and he continued to reside there during the months of February and March, in which latter was our festival of Easter. Being aware that this was one of our principal solemnities, he commanded all the Christians to attend him, and to bring with them their book, which contains the four gospels of the evangelists. After causing it to be repeatedly perfumed with incense, in a ceremonious manner, he devoutly kissed it, and directed that the same should be done by all his nobles who were present. This was his usual practice upon each of the principal Christian festivals, such as Easter and Christmas; and he observed the same at the festivals of the Saracens, Jew, and idolaters. Upon being asked his motive for this conduct, he said: "There are four great prophets who are reverenced and worshipped by the different classes of mankind. The Christians regard Jesus Christ as their divinity; the Saracens, Mahomet [Muhammad]; the Jews, Moses; and the idolaters, Sogomombar-khan [Buddha], the most eminent of their idols. I do honor and show respect to all the four, and invoke to my aid whichever among them is in truth supreme in heaven."

Source: Polo, Marco. "Height of the Mongol Power in China, A.D. 1271," in *The Great Events by Famous Historians.* Vol. 5. Edited by Rossiter Johnson. n.p. The National Alumni, 1905, pp. 291–293.

25. Marco Polo Describes the Mongol Capital, 1271

Marco Polo gave a detailed description of Khanbaliq ("Khan's City") near modern Beijing. The city was laid out in a grid pattern (unlike the cities of Western Europe, which were unplanned) and dominated by his great palace, which served as the prototype for the Forbidden City of subsequent dynasties. During the Renaissance, Italians began city planning on a grid plan; some historians suggest that this might have been in imitation of China.

The Grand Khan usually resides during three months of the year—December, January, and February—in the great city of Kanbalu, situated toward the northeastern extremity of Cathay; and here, on the southern side of the new city, is the site of his vast palace, in a square enclosed with a wall and deep ditch; each side of the square being eight miles in length, and having at an equal distance from each extremity an entrance gate. Within this enclosure there is, on the four sides, an open space one mile in breadth, where the troops are stationed, and this is bounded by a second wall, enclosing a square of six miles. The palace contains a number of separate chambers, all highly beautiful, and so admirably disposed that is seems impossible to suggest any improvement to the system of their arrangement. The exterior of the roof is adorned with a variety of colors—red, green, azure, and violet—and the sort of covering is so strong as to last for many years.

The glazing of the windows is so well wrought and so delicate as to have the transparency of crystal. In the rear of the body of the palace there are large buildings containing several apartments, where is deposited the private property of the monarch, or his treasure in gold and silver bullion, precious stones, and pearls, and also his vessels of god and silver plate. Here are likewise the apartments of his wives and concubines; and in this retired situation he dispatches business with convenience, being free from every kind of interruption. [He describes how the Khan also built a new city across the river from the palace.]. . . .

This new city is of a form perfectly square, and twenty-four miles in extent, each of its sides being neither more nor less than six miles. It is enclosed with walls of earth that at the base are about ten paces thick, but gradually diminish to the top, where the thickness is not more than three paces. In all parts the battlements are white. The whole plan of the city was regularly laid out by line, and the streets in general are consequently so straight that when a person ascends the wall over one of the gates, and looks right forward, he can see the gate opposite to him on the other side of the city. In the public streets there are on each side, booths and shops of every description. All the allotments of ground upon which the habitations throughout the city were constructed are square and exactly on a line with each other; each allotment being sufficiently spacious for handsome buildings, with corresponding courts and gardens. One of these was assigned to each head of a family; that is to say, such a person of such a tribe had one square allotted to him, and so of the rest. Afterward the property passed from hand to hand. In this manner the whole interior of the city is disposed in squares, so as to resemble a chess-board, and planned out with a degree of precision and beauty impossible to describe.

Source: Polo, Marco. "Height of the Mongol Power in China, A.D. 1271," in *The Great Events by Famous Historians.* Vol. 5. Edited by Rossiter Johnson. n.p. The National Alumni, 1905, pp. 295–297.

26. Giovanni Boccaccio Describes the Plague, 1350

In 1348, the bubonic plague (also known as the Black Death) swept through Europe devastating the population. Boccaccio, who was born in 1313 in Florence, Italy, was a witness to the scourge. When he wrote his famous (and funny) collection of stories, *The Decameron* in about 1350, he described the plague, and his description is one of our best first-hand accounts, and it reveals the fear that accompanied this epidemic. Here is only a short excerpt of his long, detailed account.

But what made this pestilence even more severe was that whenever those suffering from it mixed with people who were still unaffected, it would rush upon these with the speed of a fire racing through dry or oily substances that happened to be placed within its reach. Nor was this the full extent of its evil, for not only did it infect healthy persons who conversed or had any dealings with the sick, making them ill or visiting an equally horrible death upon them, but it also seemed to transfer the sickness to anyone touching the clothes or other objects which had been handled or used by its victims. . . .

The plague I have been describing was of so contagious a nature that very often it visibly did more than simply pass form one person to another. In other words, whenever an animal other than a human being touched anything belonging to a person who had been stricken or exterminated by the disease, it not only caught the sickness, but died from it almost at once. To all of this, as I have just said, my own eyes bore witness on more than one occasion. One day, for instance, the rags of a pauper who had died from the disease were thrown into the street, where they attracted the attention of two pigs. In their wonted fashion, the pigs first of all gave the rags a thorough mauling with their snouts after which they took them between their teeth and shook them against their cheeks. An within a short time they began to write as though they had been poisoned, and they both dropped dead to the ground, spreadeagled upon the rags that had brought about their undoing.

These things, and many others of a similar or even worse nature, caused various fears and fantasies to take root in the minds of those who were still alive and well. And almost without exception, they took a single and very inhuman precaution, namely to avoid or run away from the sick and their belongings, by which means they all thought that their own health would be preserved. . . .

It was not merely a question of one citizen avoiding another, and of people almost invariably neglecting their neighbors and rarely or never visiting their relatives, addressing them only from a distance; this scourge had implanted so great a terror in the hearts of men and women that brothers abandoned brothers, uncles their nephews, sisters their brothers, and in many cases wives deserted their husbands. But even worse, and almost incredible, was the fact that fathers and mothers refused to nurse and assist their own children, as though they did not belong to them.

Source: Boccaccio, Giovanni. *The Decameron.* Translated by G.H. McWilliam. Harmondsworth, UK: Penguin, 1972, pp. 51–54.

27. Jean Froissart Describes a Peasant Revolt, the *Jacquerie* in France (fourteenth century)

In 1358, French peasants revolted in an uprising called the *Jacquerie*, named for the nickname of peasants—Jacques. The chronicler Froissart described the violent revolt. Notice how his description would have been particularly frightening to his noble audience. Notice also how the nobles and peasants alike saw this as a movement that would engulf all Europe, not just France.

They [peasants] had no leaders and at first they numbered scarcely a hundred. One of them got up and said that the nobility of France, knights and squires, were disgracing and betraying the realm, and that it would be a good thing if they were all destroyed. At this they all shouted: "He's right! He's right! Shame on any man who saves the gentry from being wiped out!"

They banded together and went off, without further deliberation and unarmed except for pikes and knives, to the house of a knight who lived near by. They broke in and killed the knight, with his lady and his children, big and small, and set fire to the house. . . .

They did similar things in a number of castles and big houses, and their ranks swelled until there were a good six thousand of them. Wherever they went their numbers grew, for all the men of the same sort joined them. The knights and their squires fled before them with their families. They took their wives and daughters many miles away to put them in safety, leaving their houses open with their possessions inside. And those evil men, who had come together without leaders or arms, pillaged and burned everything and violated and killed all the ladies and girls without mercy, like mad dogs. Their barbarous acts were worse than anything that ever took place between Christians and Saracens [Muslims]. Never did men commit such vile deeds. They were such that no living creature ought to see, or even imagine or think of, and the men who committed the most were admired and had the highest places among them. I could never bring myself to write down the horrible and shameful things which they did to the ladies. But among other brutal excesses, they killed a knight, put him on a spit and turned him at the fire and roasted him before the lady and the children. . . . They tried to force her and the children to eat the knight's flesh before putting them cruelly to death.

They had chosen a king from among them who came, at it was said, from Clermont in Beauvaisis; and they elected the worst of the bad. This king was called Jack Goodman. Those evil men burned more than sixty big houses and castles in the Beauvais region. . . . [After much devastation, the noblemen rally.]

The foreign noblemen joined forces with those of the country who guided and led them, and they began to kill those evil men and to cut them to pieces without mercy. Sometimes they hanged them on the trees under which they found them. . . . When they were asked why they did these things, they replied that they did not know; it was because they saw others doing them and they copied them. They thought that by such means they could destroy all the nobles and gentry in the world.

Source: Froissart, Jean. *Chronicles*. Translated by Geoffrey Brereton. Harmondsworth, UK: Penguin, 1968, pp. 151–152.

28. John Hus Is Burnt for Heresy, 1415

In 1415, the Czech priest John Hus was brought to the attention of the Council of Constance because of his writings that supported John Wycliffe. These writings challenged the authority of the church and were quickly condemned by the Council. Hus was sentenced to death by burning, and the eyewitness account of his death is given below. Hus's death launched a fierce uprising in Bohemia. Notice how Hus appeals to the authority of Scripture, foreshadowing the Reformation that will come with the ending of the Middle Ages.

When therefore all the articles offered against him were completed and read, a certain old and bald auditor, a prelate of the Italian nation commissioned thereto, read the definitive sentence upon Master John Hus. And he, Master John responded, replying to certain points in the sentence, although they forbade it. And particularly when he was declared to be obstinate in his error and heresy, he replied in a loud voice: "I have never been obstinate, and I am not now. But I have ever desired, and to this day I desire, more relevant instruction from the scriptures. . . "

And having come to the place of execution, bending his knees and stretching his hands and turning his eyes toward heaven, he most devoutly sang psalms, and particularly, "Have mercy on me, God," . . . His own friends who stood about then heard him praying joyfully and with a glad countenance. . . .

When the executioners at once lit the fire, the Master immediately began to sing in a loud voice, at first "Christ, Thou son of the living God, have mercy upon us," and secondly, "Thou Who are born of Mary the Virgin." And when he began to sing the third time, the wind blew the flame into his face. And thus praying within himself and moving his lips and the head, he expired in the Lord. While he was silent, he seemed to move before he actually died for about the time one can quickly recite "Our Father" two or at most three times.

When the wood of those bundles and the ropes were consumed, but the remains of the body still stood in those chains, hanging by the neck, the executioners pulled the charred body, along with the stake, down to the ground and burned them further by adding wood from the third wagon to the fire. And walking, they broke the bones with clubs so that they would be incinerated more quickly. . . .

Thus I have described briefly but very clearly the sequence of the death and agony of the celebrated Master John Hus, the eminent preacher of the evangelical truth, so that in the course of time his memory might be vividly recollected.

Source: Peter of Mldonovice. "The Examination and Execution of Hus," in *Heresy and Authority in Medieval Europe*. Edited by Edward Peters. Philadelphia: University of Pennsylvania Press, 1980, pp. 295–296.

29. Margery Kempe Has a Vision of Jesus, 1436

Margery Kempe was an English mystic who wrote the first autobiography to be written in English in 1436. In this *Book of Margery Kempe*, she detailed how she received visions of Christ and how her religious expressions often took the form of ecstatic shouting and crying in church. This remarkable autobiography reveals much about late medieval religious sensibilities, mysticism, and the experience of women. In this excerpt, Margery has her first vision that sets her onto her religious path.

When this creature [Margery] was twenty years old or somewhat more, she was married to an honorable townsman and she conceived a child after a short time, as these things happen. And, after she conceived, she was troubled by severe illness until the child was born, and then, on account of the trouble she had in childbirth and the illness before, she despaired of her life, thinking she might not live. . . .

And day and night during this time she thought she saw devils with open mouths all a-flame with burning waves of fire as though they would swallow her, sometimes raging at her, sometimes threatening her, sometimes pulling her and grabbing her. And the devils also cried out dire threats and demanded that she forsake her Christianity and her faith, and deny her God, his Mother, all the saints in Heaven, her good works and all the virtues, her father, her mother and all her friends. And so she did. She slandered her husband, her friends and her own self; she spoke many hard and scolding words; she knew no virtue or goodness; she desired all wickedness. Exactly what the spirits tempted her to say and do, she said and did. She would have destroyed herself many times and been damned with them in Hell, and to show that, she bit her own hand so hard that the mark could be seen for the rest of her life. And she tore the skin over her heart spitefully with her nails because she had nothing else. And she would have done worse but she was bound and restrained both night and day so she could not have her way. . . .

[Then Jesus Christ appeared to her.] In the likeness of a man, the most hand-some and beautiful and amiable that might ever be seen, wearing a purple cloak, sitting on her bedside, looking upon her with such a blessed expression that she felt strengthened in her spirits, he said these words to her: "Daughter, why have you forsaken me and I never forsook you?" And as soon as he said these words, she actually saw the sky open like a flash of lightning; and he climbed up into the air, not too quickly or hastily, but gracefully and easily, so that she could see him in the sky until it closed again.

And immediately this creature was as sound in her wits and her reason as she had ever been before.

Source: Kempe, Margery. "From the *Book of Margery Kempe*," in *Medieval Women's Visionary Literature*. Edited by Elizabeth Alvilda Petroff. Translated by Susan Dickman. New York: Oxford University Press, 1986, pp. 314–315.

Appendix: Dynasties of Medieval Europe

England

Anglo-Saxon Kings
Egbert (802–839)
Ethelwulf (839–857)
Ethelbald (857–860)
Ethelbert (860–866)
Ethelred I (866–871)
Alfred the Great (871–899)
Edward I the Elder (899–924)
Ethelstan (924–940)
Edmund I (940–946)
Edred (946–955)
Edgar I (959–975)
Edward II the Martyr (975–978)
Ethelred II (978–1016)
Edmund II Ironsides (1016)

Danish Kings
Canute (1016–1035)
Harald Harefoot (1035–1040)
Harthacanute (1040–1042)

Anglo-Saxon Kings
Edward III the Confessor (1042–1066)
Harold (1066)

Norman Dynasty
William I (1066–1087)
William II (Rufus) (1087–1100)
Henry I (1100–1135)
Stephen (1135–1154)

Plantagenet Dynasty
Henry II (1154–1189)
Richard I (1189–1199)
John (1199–1216)
Henry III (1216–1272)
Edward I (1272–1307)
Edward II (1307–1327)
Edward III (1327–1377)
Richard II (1377–1399)

France

Merovingian Dynasty
Clovis I (481–511)
Lothair (511–561)
Chilperic I (561–584)
Lothair II (584–629)
Dagobert I (629–639)
Clovis II (639–657)
Lothair III (656–660)
Childeric (662–675)
Theodoric III (675–691)
Clovis III (691–695)
Childebert III (695–711)
Dagobert III (711–716)
Chilperic II (719–720)
Theodoric IV (721–737)
Chilperic III (743–752)

Carolingian Dynasty
Pepin III the Short (747–768)
Charlemagne (768–814)
Louis the Pious (814–840)
Lothair I (840–855)
Louis II the Stammerer (855–875)
Charles the Bald (875–877)
Arnulf (887–899)
Guido (891–894)
Labert (892–898)
Charles III the Simple (898–922)
Louis III (901–905)
Berenger (915–924)
Rudolph (923–936)
Louis IV from Overseas (936–954)
Lothair (954–986)
Louis V the Fat (986–987)

Capetian Dynasty
Hugh Capet (987–996)
Robert II the Pious (996–1031)
Henry I (1031–1060)

Philip I (1060–1108)
Louis VI the Fat (1108–1137)
Louis VII (1137–1180)
Philip II Augustus (1180–1223)
Louis VIII (1223–1226)
Louis IX (1226–1270)
Philip III (1270–1285)
Philip IV the Fair (1285–1314)
Louis X (1314–1316)
John I (1316)
Philip V (1316–1322)
Charles IV (1322–1328)

Valois Dynasty
Philip VI (1328–1350)
John II (1350–1364)
Charles V (1364–1380)
Charles VI (1380–1422)
Charles VII (1422–1461)

Holy Roman Emperors of Germany
Ottonian (Saxon) Dynasty
Otto I the Great (962–973)
Otto II (973–983)
Otto III (996–1002)
Henry II the Saint (1014–1024)

Salian (Frankish) Dynasty
Conrad II (1027–1039)
Henry III (1046–1056)
Henry IV (1084–1105)
Henry V (1111–1125)

Supplinburger Dynasty
Lothair III (1133–1137)

Hohenstaufen Dynasty
Frederick I Barbarossa (1155–1190)
Henry VI (1191–1197)

Welf Dynasty
Otto IV of Brunswick (1209–1215) (d. 1218)

Hohenstaufen Dynasty
Frederick II (1211–1250)

Luxembourg Dynasty
Henry VII (1312–1313)

Wittelsbach Dynasty
Louis IV the Bavarian (1328–1347)

Luxembourg Dynasty
Charles IV (1355–1378)

THE AMERICAS

James L. Fitzsimmons

Chronology

c. 30,000 B.C.E.	First humans cross the Bering land bridge from Asia into the Americas
6000–1500 B.C.E.	Archaic Age in Mesoamérica: domestication of agricultural plants, such as corn and beans, occurs in Central Mexico
1500–400 B.C.E.	Olmec and Oaxacan civilizations flourish in Central Mexico
1500–250 B.C.E.	Early May civilization flourishes
900–200 B.C.E	Early Horizon Period in Peru: Chavín artistic style popular
c. 700 B.C.E.	Writing develops in Mesoamérica
c. 400 B.C.E.	The earliest known solar calendars carved in stone come into use among the Maya
400–200 B.C.E.	Earliest carved monuments appear among the Maya
c. 300 B.C.E.	Maya adopt the idea of a hierarchical society ruled by nobles and kings
200 B.C.E.–400 C.E.	Hopewell culture flourishes in northeastern and midwestern North America
c. 150 B.C.E.	City of Teotihuacán is founded in Central Mexico and for centuries is the cultural, religious, and trading center of Mesoamérica
c. 100 C.E.	Decline of the Gulf Coast Olmec civilization
150–1350	Mogollon culture flourishes in the American Southwest
200–600	Early Intermediate Period in Peru: Moche and Nasca cultures flourish
200–900	Classic Period in Mesoamérica; characterized by the development of great urban civilizations and progress in art, astronomy, mathematics, medicine, and the development of writing systems
250–900	Middle Maya civilization: population increases and the cities of Tikal and Calakmul are prominent
c. 400	Maya highlands fall under the domination of Teotihuacán, and the disintegration of Maya culture and language begins in some parts of the highlands
c. 450	Teotihuacán begins to decline
c. 500	Tikal becomes the first great Maya city, as immigrants from Teotihuacán introduce new ideas involving weaponry, captives, ritual practices, and human sacrifice
583–604	Maya queen Lady Kanal Ikal rules Palenque

c. 600	An unknown event destroys the civilization at Teotihuacán, along with the empire it supported; Tikal becomes the largest city-state in Mesoamérica
600–1000	Middle Horizon Period in Peru: Tiahuanaco and Huari civilizations flourish
650–1350	Cahokia flourishes along the Mississippi in what is today southwestern Illinois
683	Pakal, ruler of the Mayan state of Palenque dies at the age of 80 and is buried in the Temple of the Inscriptions at Palenque
700–1300	Classic period of Anasazi culture in the American Southwest
c. 750	Long-standing Maya alliances begin to break down; trade between Maya city-states declines, and interstate conflict increases
800–1500	Mississippian culture flourishes in midwestern and southeastern North America
869	Construction ceases in Tikal, marking the beginning of the city's decline
899	Tikal is abandoned
c. 900	Classic Period of Maya history ends, with the collapse of the southern lowland cities; Maya cities in the northern Yucatán continue to thrive
900–1524	Late Maya civilization: Rise of Mayapán and eventual fragmentation of Mayan polities into various warring groups
950–1150	Toltec civilization flourishes in Central Mexico
c. 1000	Viking Leif Erikson travels to North America
c. 1050	Mound building begins at Cahokia under the influence of Mississippian culture
1150–1450	Classic Period of the Hohokam culture in the American Southwest
c. 1200	Northern Maya cities begin to be abandoned; manufacture of earliest surviving Inca artifacts in Peru
1224	City of Chichén Itzá in the Yucatán is abandoned by the Toltecs; Itzá people settle in the deserted area
1244	Itzá abandons Chichén Itzá for unknown reasons
1263	Itzá begin building the city of Mayapán
1283	Mayapán becomes the capital of Yucatán and the League of Mayapán rules the country
c. 1300	Mexico (Aztec) groups migrate from the north into the Valley of Mexico
1325	Tenochtitlán, the future Aztec capital is founded on an island in the Valley of Mexico
1375–1396	Acamapichtli reigns as first *tlatoani* (ruler) of the Aztecs
1428–1440	Reign of Itzcoatl, *tlatoani* of the Aztecs, who brings the Aztecs to political prominence in the Valley of Mexico by sacking the previously dominant Tepanec city of Azcapotzalco
1438	Chanca tribe attacks Inca at Cuzco; King Inca Urcon flees, but Inca Yupanqui saves city, claims Inca kingship, and takes name Pachacuti

1438–1463	King Pachacuti leads expansion of Inca Empire, taking Lake Titicaca and Lake Junin
1440–1469	Reign of Moctezuma Ilhuicamina, which sees the beginning of Aztec military expansion
1441	Rebellion within Mayapán leads to abandonment of the city by 1461
c. 1460–1500	Political union is lost in Yucatán; various rival groups strive for power
1463	Topa Inca, son of Pachacuti, extends Inca Empire to include northern and central Peru and western Ecuador
1471	Topa Inca brings most of Chile, Bolivia, and northwestern Argentine into the Inca Empire
1486–1502	Reign of the Aztec *tlatoani* Ahuitzotl, who rebuilt the great temple in Tenochtitlán and dedicated it by sacrificing over twenty-thousand victims
1493	Huayna Capa become Inca ruler and brings empire to its greatest extent
1500	First Maya contact with Spaniards
1502–1520	Moctezume Xocooyotzin rules as ninth *tlatoani* of the Aztecs; thinking Cortés might be the god Quetzelcoatl returned, Moctezuma allows him to come to Tenochtitlán, where the Spanish take the Aztec ruler prisoner
1517	Spanish first arrive on the shores of Yucatán under Hernández de Córdoba, who later dies of wounds received in battle against the Maya; arrival of the Spanish ushers in Old World diseases unknown among the Maya, including smallpox, influenza, and measles, which eventually kill off a large percentage of the Mayan population
1519	Hernan Cortés arrives in Mexico
1521	Spanish under Cortés conquer Tenochtitlán, the Aztec capital
1524–1527	Pedro de Alvarado conquers the Southern Maya
1527	Inca ruler Huayna Capac dies; civil war erupts between two rivals for the Incan throne: Huascar and Atahuallpa
1527–1547	Spanish conquest of the northern Maya
1531	Virgin of Guadalupe appears to Juan Diego, a Mexican Indian
1532	Atahuallpa defeats Huascar to become Inca ruler; Spaniards arrive in Peru, kill Atahuallpa, and install a puppet ruler as Inca king
1537	Manco Inca leads a revolt against the Spanish, but his defeat marks the end of large-scale resistance to Spanish rule in Peru

South and Mesoamérica, c. 900 C.E.

temple mound builders

hunter gatherers

Maize farmers

c a r i b f a r m e r s

TOLTEC EMPIRE

MAYA CITY STATES

Maya Chiefdoms

City states and chiefdoms

Tropic of Cancer

CHIMU EMPIRE

HUARI EMPIRE

TIAHUANACO EMPIRE

Tropic of Capricorn

hunter gatherers

Amazonian Chiefdoms

manioc farmers

sauanna and Highland farmers

hunter gatherers

N

South and Mesoamerica c.900 CE

States or empires

Chiefdoms-farming societies

farmers-with some hunter gatherers

hunter gatherers

The Rise of the Aztec Empire A.D. 1200 to 1500

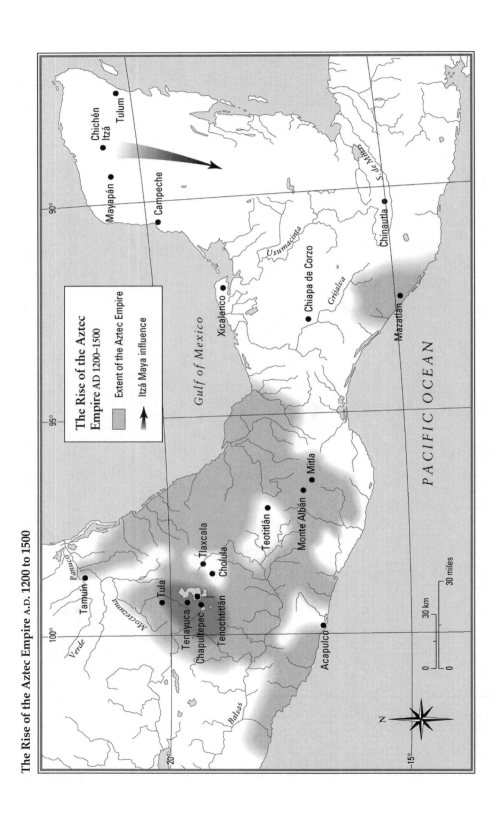

The Rise of the Aztec
Empire AD 1200–1500

Extent of the Aztec Empire

Itzá Maya influence

Mayan Sates, 300 B.C.–A.D. 1500

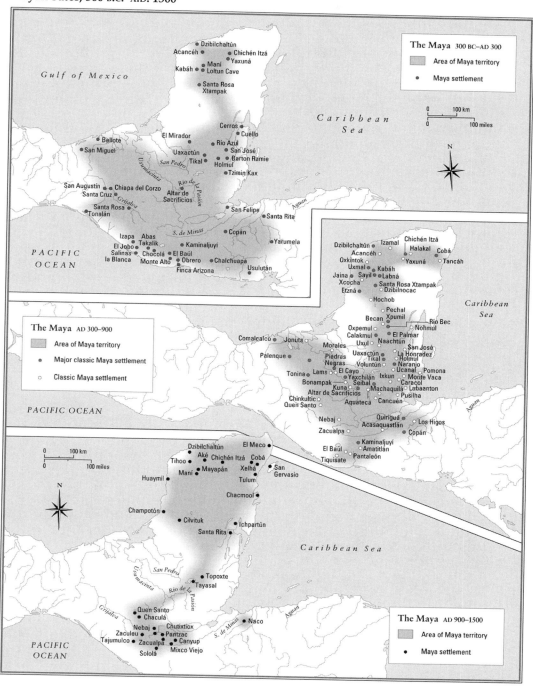

The Maya 300 BC–AD 300
  Area of Maya territory
  • Maya settlement

Gulf of Mexico

Dzibilchaltún
Acancéh •
Chichén Itzá •
Maní • Yaxuná
Kabáh • Loltun Cave
Santa Rosa Xtampak •

Caribbean Sea

0   100 km
0   100 miles

N

Cerros • Cuello •
El Mirador •
Bellote •
San Miguel •
Río Azul •
Uaxactún • San José •
San Pedro • Tikal • Barton Ramie
Holmul •
• Tzimin Kax

San Augustín • Chiapa del Corzo •
Santa Cruz • Altar de Sacrificios
Santa Rosa • Grijalva
Tonalán •

San Felipe •
Santa Rita •

S. de Minas • Copán
Aguan

PACIFIC OCEAN

Izapa Abas
El Jobo • Takalik • Kaminaljuyú
Salinas la Blanca • Chocolá • El Baúl
Monte Alto • Obrero • Chalchuapa
Finca Arizona
Usulután •
Yarumela •

The Maya AD 300–900
  Area of Maya territory
  • Major classic Maya settlement
  ○ Classic Maya settlement

PACIFIC OCEAN

Dzibilchaltún • Izamal
Acancéh ○ Chichén Itzá • Halakal Cobá
Oxkintok ○ Yaxuná • Tancáh
Uxmal ○ Kabáh
Jaina • Sayil • Labná
Xcocha ○ Santa Rosa Xtampak
Etzná ● Dzibilnocac
Hochob ○

Caribbean Sea

Pechal •
Becan • Xpumil
Oxpemul ○ Río Bec
Comalcalco • Jonuta ○ Calakmul • El Palmar
Palenque ● Uxul ○ Naachtún
Morales ○ San José •
Piedras Negras • Uaxactún ○ La Honradez
Tonina ● Lams ○ Voluntún • Tikal • Holmul
Bonampak ○ El Cayo Naranjo ○
Kuna • Yaxchilán • Ikxun • Ucanal • Pomona
Altar de Sacrificios ○ Seibal Monte Vaca
Chinkultic ○ Machaquilá ○ Caracol
Quen Santo ○ Aguateca • Lubaanton
Cancuén • Pusilha

Nebaj ○ Quiriguá ○ Los Higos
Zacualpa ○ Acasaquastlán Copán •

El Baúl • Kaminaljuyú
Tiquisate Amatitlán
Pantaleón

The Maya AD 900–1500
  Area of Maya territory
  • Maya settlement

0   100 km
0   100 miles

N

Dzibilchaltún • El Meco •
Tihoo • Aké • Chichén Itzá Cobá •
Maní • Mayapán Xelhá • San Gervasio
Huaymil • Tulum •
Chacmool •

Champotón •
Cilvituk •
Santa Rita • Ichpartún •

Caribbean Sea

San Pedro
Quen Santo • Topoxte •
Tayasal •
Grijalva • Chaculá
Nebaj • Chutixtiox • Naco •
Zaculeu • Pantzac
Tajumulco • Zacualpa • Canyup
Sololá • Mixco Viejo
S. de Minas
Aguan

PACIFIC OCEAN

187

The Inca Empire, 1438–1525 C.E.

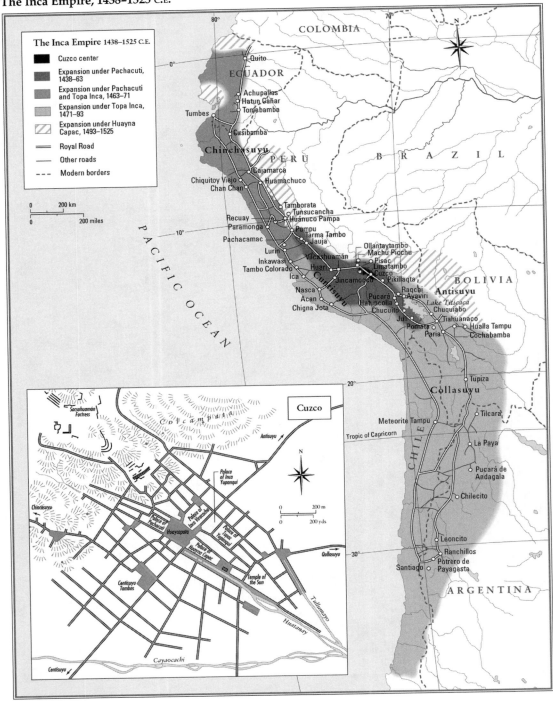

The Inca Empire 1438–1525 C.E.

- ■ Cuzco center
- Expansion under Pachacuti, 1438–63
- Expansion under Pachacuti and Topa Inca, 1463–71
- Expansion under Topa Inca, 1471–93
- Expansion under Huayna Capac, 1493–1525
- ═══ Royal Road
- ─── Other roads
- ─ ─ Modern borders

0   200 km
0   200 miles

COLOMBIA

ECUADOR

Quito

Achupallas
Hatun Cañar
Tomebamba

Tumbes

Cusibamba

Chinchasuyu

PERU

BRAZIL

Chiquitoy Viejo
Chan Chan

Cajamarca
Huamachuco

Tamborata
Tunsucancha
Recuay   Huánuco Pampa
Paramonga   Pumpu
Pachacamac   Tarma Tambo
                Jauja

Lurin   Ollantaytambo
Inkawasi   Machu Picchu
Tambo Colorado Vilcashuamán Pisac
                Huari   Limatambo
                Ica   Cuzco
                        Jincamocco Pikillaqta
Nasca   Cuntisuyu
Acan   Pucará   Raqchi
Chigna Jota   Hatuncolla Ayaviri   Antisuyu
                Chucuito   Lake Titicaca
                          Chuquiabo
                     Juli   Tiahuanaco
                    Pomata Hualla Tampu
                       Paria   Cochabamba

BOLIVIA

PACIFIC OCEAN

Tupiza

Collasuyu

Meteorite Tampu
Tropic of Capricorn

Tilcara

La Paya

Pucará de
Andagala

CHILE

Chilecito

Leoncito

Ranchillos
Santiago   Potrero de
           Payagasta

ARGENTINA

Cuzco

Sacsahuamán
Fortress

Colcam...

Antisuyu

Chincasuyu

Palace of
Inca Yupanqui

Palace of
Pachacuti   Palace of
Huaycapa   Inca Viracocha   Palace of
                Palace of   Lupac
                Huayna Capac   Yupanqui

N

0   200 m
0   200 yds

Qollasuyu

Cuntisuyu
Tambos   Temple of
                 the Sun

Tullumayu

Cuntisuyu

Huatanay

Cayaocachi

188

Overview and Topical Essays

1. HISTORICAL OVERVIEW

In the Americas, the centuries between 400 and 1400 were characterized by a proliferation of complex, urban societies whose rise and fall are documented by the archaeological record and—in the case of Mesoamérica—indigenous written sources. Between the two, we can gain insight into the lives of the original inhabitants of the Americas and appreciate the ways in which they addressed (and continue to address) the problems all societies share. Although this volume is largely concerned with the events prior to 1400, there are many societies which flourished before and after this arbitrary date; this situation is perhaps best exemplified by the Aztec or the Inca Empires, both of which had their origins in the centuries leading up to 400 but generally flourished after that date. As a result, such societies have been included here and can be seen as inheritors of broad, sweeping and ancient cultural traditions in the Americas.

Scholars geographically divide the Americas into different culture areas, or regions in which the societies therein are more like one another than they are with those of a different region. To draw such lines across the Americas is by no means a perfect endeavor, but overall it allows us to view and understand social, political, artistic, religious, and economic regional trends. As such, the essays in this volume are divided into several regions: (1) Eastern Woodlands and the Great Plains; (2) American Southwest and the Great Basin; (3) Arctic and Subarctic; (4) Mesoamérica; (5) Lower Central America and the Andes; and (6) Amazonia and the Caribbean. Some of these regions are further subdivided into different cultures, such as the Teotihuacános of Mesoamérica or the Mississippians of the Eastern Woodlands. These are but a sample of the numerous civilizations flourishing in the Americas between 400 and 1400 and are chosen to represent some of the largest—geographically, politically, or both—and most complex societies in the Americas. Where possible, the perspectives and situations of other cultures, such as the Zapotecs of Mesoamérica or the Taino of the Caribbean, are also included and stand testament to the great diversity of the Americas before the period of European contact.

In addition to defining distinct culture areas of the Americas, scholars typically divide each of the culture areas into different time periods. These time periods are usually bounded by major events, such as the rise and fall of a given society, a major technological development, or an artistic style. Unfortunately, each culture area often has its own set of time periods, or chronology, and scholars like to use the same terms for different cultures areas (e.g., the use of

"Classic" to describe time periods in Mesoamérica and South America). This situation can be confusing, especially to individuals trying to compare the different civilizations with one another.

Moreover, there is sometimes more than one chronology for a given culture area, such as with the Hohokam and Ancestral Puebloan societies of the Southwest. This reflects modern scholarship among these societies as well as the recognition of significant differences between them. In other cases, the chronological time periods are so vast as to entirely encompass the years between 400 and 1400 or are restricted to smaller areas within the broad geographic regions discussed for this work (e.g., within Lower Central America, the Gulf of Chiriquí, Panama, has its own chronology). In such situations, the 400 to 1400 range has been employed in this volume for ease of understanding.

Keeping all of these limitations and nuances in mind, however, one can find the production of such time periods and categories useful. Chronology is the framework against which each of the civilizations described can ultimately be set, allowing us to make comparisons between groups and even different culture areas. Thinking about time periods in this way allows us to look at what is happening in a place like the American Southwest around 1000 and see the larger picture. One must remember that for most of the Americas, the vast majority of geographically removed, major cultural events are unrelated (save, perhaps, some environmental effects). But no part of the Americas was ever in complete isolation.

Eastern Woodlands and the Great Plains

In the Eastern Woodlands and the Great Plains, the year 400 conveniently falls at the end of one time period traditionally used by archaeologists: the Middle Woodland (200 B.C.E.–400 C.E.). The subsequent phase, known as the Late Woodland (400–1000), was dominated by societies who had abandoned the tradition of mound-building. Mounds, as centers of social and political activities as well as burial sites, seem to have largely fallen out of fashion in the Late Woodland. Likewise, long-distance trade had all but ceased, and although individual villages were increasing in population (and, in the case of the Great Plains, people were becoming more sedentary), warfare was escalating. A few settlements in the latter half of the Late Woodland, most notably **Toltec**, Arkansas, seem to have become powerful and anticipate a trend which was to last for the next 500 years. This trend, represented by the subsequent Mississippian phase (1000–1500), saw the birth of urbanism in the Eastern Woodlands, with the largest towns like **Cahokia** and **Moundville** becoming the paramount economic, religious, and possibly political powers in Eastern Woodlands. Their gradual collapse between the years 1300 and 1500 was largely the result of societal woes as well as climatic deterioration: A long period of global cooling, termed the "Little Ice Age," seems to have affected these and other parts of the Americas in a negative way, resulting in problems that some societies simply could not deal with adequately. Despite these internal and external problems, however, there were some populous Mississippian centers in the Eastern Woodlands as well as villages on the Great Plains at the time of European contact.

American Southwest and the Great Basin

In the Great Basin, the major culture explored in this volume is the so-called Fremont Culture, a collection of societies from 400 to 1300 that exhibit many similarities as well as regional differences; the idea of **Fremont** Culture stems from the fact that it was during this period that peoples of the Great Basin became more sedentary and, in some ways, much like the American Southwest. The agricultural way of life in the Great Basin was, archaeologically, a brief phenomenon, however, by 1300 most of the peoples collectively termed "Fremont Culture" had abandoned intensive agriculture in favor of hunting and gathering. This was perhaps due to the effects of the Little Ice Age, as mentioned earlier.

The American Southwest is dominated by two culture areas and thereby two major chronologies. The first of these involve the Hohokam of the Sonoran Desert, and consists of Preclassic (700–1150) and Classic (1150–1450) Hohokam. The Preclassic Hohokam Period was largely characterized by numerous settlements, indirect connections with Mesoamérica in terms of materials and culture, and a preference for cremation as the main form of burial. The Classic Hohokam Period saw the intensification of settlements in a few areas and the abandonment of others; likewise, architecture as well as burial practices changed (from cremation to inhumation) and connections with Mesoamérica became less pronounced.

The second chronology for the American Southwest involves a series of periods known as Pueblo I (750–950), Pueblo II (900–1150), Pueblo III (1150–1300), and Pueblo IV (1300–1500). The people who occupied the Colorado Plateau and correspond to these time periods are known as the Ancestral Puebloans and are colloquially known as the Anasazi. Pueblo I saw the development of towns and villages on the plateau as well as the emergence of "great **kivas**," or multipurpose structures used for such things as religious rituals or political events. Pueblo II is characterized by the development of major urban centers in and around **Chaco Canyon**, which seems to have become a place of religious pilgrimage during that time; for whatever reason, Chaco was abandoned around 1150, as people moved north and into the fabled "cliff dwellings" of the Southwest. This Pueblo III phenomenon was most pronounced at the site of **Mesa Verde**, Colorado, where the dwellings could have as many as two-hundred rooms, all built in shallow caves and rock shelters on the sides of steep cliffs. Drought, combined with the influx of hunting and gathering groups from the Great Plains and the Great Basin, seems to have lead to the near-complete abandonment of the Colorado Plateau between 1450 and 1500.

Pacific Coast

The historical trajectory for the Pacific Coast is much like that of other parts of North America: People living in sedentary or semisedentary conditions eventually conglomerated into larger and larger social groupings. Chiefdoms emerged along the coast between 1000 and 1300, with people continuing to rely on combinations of agriculture, hunting and gathering, and fishing to survive. Chronologically, the periods that scholars use are quite broad, and for the years 400 to 1400 there is only one generally accepted time period, the Late Pacific (c. 400–1600).

Arctic and Subarctic

Like the Pacific Coast, the chronological sequence of the Arctic and Subarctic is quite broad for the period between 400 and 1400 and consists of two phases corresponding to periods when either the **Dorset** or their successors, the Thule, were dominant in the region. The first of these, Dorset (500 B.C.E.–1000 C.E.), saw the spread the Dorset culture throughout most of the Arctic and Subarctic. These peoples were hunter-gatherer-fishers who created some of the finest art in bone and ivory ever made in the Americas. Unfortunately, they began to be replaced around 1000 by the **Thule**, a people from the western Arctic who had a few major technological advances: Using bows, specialized spears, and seaworthy craft, they were able to outperform the Dorset in nearly every environment. Able to hunt whales and other sea mammals on a regular basis, the Thule gradually replaced the Dorset until the latter were all but extinct in the Arctic. The ultimate fate of the Dorset remains unknown.

Mesoamérica

The Mesoamérican chronology is relatively streamlined to include three major phases associated with agricultural societies: Preclassic (2400 B.C.E.–250 C.E.), Classic (250–909), and Postclassic (909–1519). Each of these major time periods, however, is further divided into subphases; this is largely because of the enormous time depth as well as a result of the growing body of knowledge about Mesoamérican societies. Although the Preclassic is divided into three phases—Early (2400–1200 B.C.E.), Middle (1200–400 B.C.E.) and Late (400 B.C.E.–250 C.E.)—for the purposes of this volume the final part of the Preclassic is the most important. The Late Preclassic saw the beginnings of most of the societies that were to dominate the period between 400 and 1400.

The Classic Period in Mesoamérica is so defined because it is associated with the florescence of two great civilizations in Mesoamérica: the Teotihuacános and the Classic Maya. The former dominated Mesoamérica from the latter half of the Late Preclassic to the middle of the Classic Period, or around 600. These peoples, based in Central Mexico, created what was at one time the sixth largest city in the world: **Teotihuacán**. From this city, the Teotihuacános appear to have wielded great political influence over Mesoamérica, successfully invading some areas—including the Classic Maya lowlands—and establishing trading centers in others. The great metropolis of Teotihuacán collapsed around 600, and although the precise nature of this collapse is not clear, what is certain is that it was violent: Parts of the city were burned.

The reign of Teotihuacán in Mesoamérica during this time defines what is known as the Early Classic (250–600 C.E.). Although the Maya created vast cities and kingdoms during that time, it was during what is known as the Late Classic (600–909) that they truly flourished: Art, architecture, social complexity, and population levels reached their peak at this time. Great kings of this era such as **K'inich Janaab' Pakal** of **Palenque** or **Jasaw Chan K'awiil I** of **Tikal** wielded enormous political influence, commissioning many of the great masterpieces of sculpture and architecture for which the Maya are famous. Maya civilization collapsed between 760 and 909, however, with the kingdoms of the southern lowlands—comprising southern Mexico, northern Guatemala, western Honduras, and parts of El Salvador and Belize—abandoned to the jungle. Scholars continue to debate the reasons for the **Maya collapse**, which were many and probably all related. The final inscription on a monument in the lowlands was carved in 909, marking the end of the Classic Period.

The Postclassic Period in Mesoamérica is defined by great societal disruption as well as, somewhat paradoxically, the forging of ties to societies internal and external to Mesoamérica. In Yucatán and along the Caribbean coast, new Maya kingdoms—albeit far less absolute than those of the past—arose; members of one of these would be the first peoples of the mainland that Christopher Columbus encountered on his fourth voyage to the Americas between 1502 and 1503. Stronger Maya kings bent on empire-building arose in the Maya highlands of contemporary Guatemala, most notably those belonging to the kingdom of the K'ichee; the K'ichee managed to unify much of highlands under their rule—either through conquest or alliance—until the early sixteenth century, when the Aztecs, internal divisions, and finally the Spanish brought an end to their state.

Likewise, the Postclassic Period saw the resurgence of Central Mexico as the most powerful region of Mesoamérica, with first the Toltecs (950–1170) and then the Aztecs (1345–1521) dominating the Basin of Mexico—then a vast lacustrine region—and beyond. The Aztecs created a conquest-oriented, tribute-based empire stretching from Central Mexico to coastal Chiapas, incorporating many different civilizations into a larger sociopolitical and economic system. The other major development of the Postclassic was the introduction of metallurgical technologies into Mesoamérica from Lower Central America and South America; gold, silver, copper, and even alloys like bronze were being worked at the time of European contact. Most scholars place the end of the Postclassic either at 1519, when Hernan Cortés and his conquistadores first encountered the Aztecs, or in 1521, when the Aztec Empire became the first major urban civilization in the Americas to fall to the Spanish.

Lower Central America and the Andes

The chiefdoms of Lower Central America between 400 and 1400 were heavily engaged in trade with their neighbors. Although no states or large urban centers arose in this region at that time, the peoples of Lower Central America—sometimes called the "Intermediate Area"—were well versed in metalworking at a time when the societies of Mesoamérica were not, having probably imported this technology from their neighbors to the south. One of the most famous ceremonial centers of this region was the site of Rivas, Costa Rica, where peoples from surrounding villages would migrate to feast and engage in sociopolitical maneuvering. The peoples of Lower Central America became even more integrated into the larger world of the Americas after 1000 and appear to have had sporadic contact with peoples as far as West Mexico by that time. The chronology used in this volume for Lower Central America is the arbitrary 400 to 1400 sequence.

In the Andes (including the desert Pacific Coast), the chronological sequence is quite complex, stretching as far back as 5000 B.C.E. with numerous phases and subphases. For the purposes of this volume, however, there are five major time periods in Andean prehistory: (1) Initial Period (1800–400 B.C.E.), (2) Early Intermediate Period (400 B.C.E.–650 C.E.), (3) Middle Horizon (650–1000), (4)

Late Intermediate Period (1000–1476), and (5) Late Horizon (1476–1533). During what is known as the Initial Period, the intensive agriculture, weaving, pottery, and animal husbandry (camelids like llamas, for example) became common for the first time. Large monuments and temple pyramids were also built on a much broader geographic scale than ever before, and sites such as Chavín—which were to become extremely important at the beginning of the Early Intermediate—were settled.

The Early Intermediate Period (sometimes stretched to 1000) saw the growth and spread of religious traditions like those employing the **Staff God**, a deity derived from the site of Chavín de Huantar in the Andes. On the desert coast of Peru, moreover, two major civilizations developed that have since captured the popular imagination: **Moche** and Nazca. The Moche, erecting their grand mud-brick pyramids as well as creating some of the most detailed and ornate pottery in the Americas, are most famous for their massive tombs: The discovery of the gold-laden tombs at Sipán, for example, ranked as one of the greatest archaeological finds of the twentieth century. The Nazca, for their part, are most famous for creating the **Nazca lines**: These were enigmatic designs created on the desert floor of the south coast of Peru. Both civilizations appear to have suffered greatly from climatic disasters, including droughts, flooding, or both, and had largely vanished by 650. New civilizations, such as the city-states of the Lambayeque Region (the largest of which was **Batán Grande**), followed in the region before its conquest by the empire of **Chimor** in the fourteenth century.

During the Middle Horizon, two empires rose and fell in the Andes. They were **Tiwanaku** and **Wari**. Tiwanaku, originally based around Lake Titicaca in Bolivia, appears to have adopted many of the traditions of prior civilizations of the Andes: The Staff God, born of Chavín, may have been one such tradition. Building temples, sunken plazas, and other monumental architecture from stone, Tiwanaku appears to have been the leader of a loose confederation of states in the southern Andes. Although much less is known about Wari, it too created an empire in the Andes, but one that appears to have been more centralized and hierarchical. Like some of their forebears in the Americas, Tiwanaku and Wari suffered greatly from climatic problems, including a long drought beginning around 1050. Neither appears to have been able to mitigate these problems successfully, and both began a decline that resulted in sociopolitical fragmentation.

One of these fragments appears to have been the Inca, who were to become dominant during the Late Horizon. Before this happened, however, South America saw an empire rise on the desert coast: Chimor. During the Late Intermediate Period, the Chimor conquered and consolidated the region once occupied by the Moche, eventually expanding to become the second largest empire ever created in South America. At their capital of Chan Chan, they built massive mud-brick and adobe palace compounds. Their religious traditions appear to have been precursors to those of the Inca, who would conquer them in 1476. The Inca, in turn, created an empire stretching along the Pacific Coast and the Andes, from Ecuador to Chile; building almost twenty-five thousand miles of roads, palaces, temples, and mountain retreats, the Inca Empire was an impressive sight. Disease, warfare, and trickery—the latter on the part of Francisco Pizarro and his small band of conquistadores—brought this last empire of the Americas to ruin in 1533.

Amazonia and the Caribbean

The time between 400 and 1400 in the Caribbean, as the period used in this volume, was one that saw settlements of Arawak-speaking peoples from coastal South America becoming more complex and exhibiting connections with other parts of the Americas. For example, the dominant Taino peoples appear to have had some ties—at the very least, indirect ones—with Mesoamérica: Ball courts ultimately derived from that region appear at Taino sites. Around 1400, the Taino became threatened by newcomers to the Caribbean from Venezuela, the Carib, who were successfully overrunning Taino sites at the time Christopher Columbus encountered the Caribbean peoples in 1492.

As with some other parts of the Americas, the Amazonian chronological sequence is more defined by the individual cultures within it than a broad regional chronology. Thus far, sequences such as Formative (1000 B.C.E.–500 C.E.), Developmental (1–1000 C.E.), and Classic (1000–1533) have been used in different parts of Amazonia, but for the purposes of this volume they have been disregarded in favor of time periods associated with individual sites. The overall trajectory for the Amazon involves widespread population diasporas of Arawak- and Tupiguarani-speaking peoples, between 1000 B.C.E. and 500 C.E., from northeast and southwest Amazonia, respectively. These peoples came to dominate what had probably been sparsely occupied regions of Amazonia by 500 C.E. The Arawak speakers were dominant, however, for the entire period covered by this volume; Tupiguarani speakers began a second diaspora around 1500, replacing Arawak speakers in many areas.

Between 400 and 1400, several parts of the Amazon saw the development of towns and villages. Although they are not nearly as well understood as those of North America, Mesoamérica, or the Andes, they do appear to have been based on agriculture. The largest of these were located in the Lower and Central Amazon, at places like Marajó Island and **Acutuba**. There is considerable disagreement among scholars as to the nature of Amazonian urbanism, however, and much more exploration of this region will be necessary to determine how similar Amazonia was to some of the other densely populated regions of the Americas before European contact—and colonization—in the seventeenth and eighteenth centuries.

Further Reading

Arnold, J. "Complex Hunter-Gatherer-Fishers of Prehistoric California: Chiefs, Specialists, and Maritime Adaptations of the Channel Islands. *American Antiquity* 57 (1992): 60–84.

Bayman, J. "The Hohokam of Southwest North America." *Journal of World Prehistory* 15 (2001): 257–311.

Carmack, Robert M., and Gary Gossen. *The Legacy of Mesoamerica: History and Culture of a Native American Civilization.* 2nd ed. Upper Saddle River, NJ: Prentice Hall, 2006.

Evans, Susan. *Ancient Mexico and Central America: Archaeology and Culture History.* London: Thames and Hudson, Ltd., 2004.

Fagan, Brian. *Ancient North America.* London: Thames and Hudson, 1991.

Heckenberger, Michael. "Rethinking the Arawakan Diaspora: Hierarchy, Regionality, and the Amazonian Formative." In J. Hill and F. Santos-Granero, eds. *Comparative Arawakan Histories: Rethinking Culture Area and Language Group in Amazoniay*. Urbana: University of Illinois Press, 2002, pp. 99–121.

Hosler, Dorothy. *The Sounds and Colors of Power: The Sacred Metallurgical Technology of Ancient West Mexico.* Cambridge, MA: MIT Press, 1994.

Martin, Simon, and Nikolai Grube. *Chronicle of the Maya Kings and Queens*. London: Thames and Hudson, Ltd., 2000.

Milner, G.R. *The Cahokia Chiefdom: The Archaeology of a Mississippian Society*. Washington, DC: Smithsonian Institution Press, 1998.

Moseley, Michael E. *The Incas and their Ancestors: the Archaeology of Peru*. 2nd ed. London: Thames and Hudson, Ltd., 2001.

Roosevelt, Anne. *Moundbuilders of the Amazon: Geophysical Archaeology on Marajo Island, Brazil*. New York: Academic Press, 1991.

Scarre, Chris, ed. *The Human Past: World Prehistory and the Development of Human Societies*. London: Thames and Hudson, Ltd., 2005.

Sharer, Robert J., and Loa P. Traxler. *The Ancient Maya*. 6th ed. Stanford, CA: Stanford University Press, 2005.

Smith, Michael E. *The Aztecs*. Oxford, UK: Wiley-Blackwell, 2003.

Vivian, R. *The Chacoan Prehistory of the San Juan Basin*. San Diego, CA: Academic Press, 1990.

2. RELIGION

Religious expression in the Americas between 400 and 1400 took near innumerable forms, from the strong, centralized "state" religions of Mesoamérica and Andean South America to the generalized belief systems embodied by such loose religious traditions as the Southern Cult, in the Eastern Woodlands. Despite this variability, a number of general themes in Pre-Columbian religions and religious expression emerge: (1) a focus on the creation of earthen mounds, masonry temples, or similar architecture for mortuary purposes and for public ceremony; (2) a set of deities or ritual behaviors tied to agricultural fertility; (3) the practice of ancestor veneration in a variety of forms, such as the use of mummies in ritual or the creation of shrines to prominent antecedents; and (4) a belief in sacred locations (natural or built), many of which were places of pilgrimage and centers where groups would congregate for sociopolitical or religious functions. These themes were by no means common to all religions of the Americas, however.

One final common theme in the religions of the Americas involves change: As with most things, religion and expressions of it change over time. Thus indigenous deities of Mesoamérica or the Andes, like **Quetzalcoatl** and the **Staff God**, respectively, saw many different incarnations over the period between 400 and 1400. They witnessed the births and deaths of states as well as empires and were adopted and adapted by different peoples to suit their needs and the conditions of their day.

Eastern Woodlands and the Great Plains

The beginning of the Late Woodland Period in the Eastern Woodlands around 400 saw the demise of long-distance relationships between settlements. Prior to this era, elaborate burial mounds and associated ceremonies—including the ritual destruction or burial of precious materials—were common at sites such as Hopewell, Fort Ancient, and other centers in the Midwest and Southeast. After 400 the construction of these burial mounds had all but ceased, and mound-building as a social and religious phenomenon would only reemerge around 1000 with the development of large chiefdoms and towns at places like **Toltec**, Arkansas, and Lake George, Mississippi. These towns became not only the centers of redistributive networks—places where food and other economically important items were collected and then distributed to surrounding peoples— but also places for ceremony and pilgrimage.

This trend ushered in the beginning of the Mississippian Period (1000–1600), a time defined by distinctive trends in artifacts, architecture, and dense settlement. Flat-topped, earthen mounds were a part of this: Modified gradually over time, they often housed the remains of elites and were a constant, visible reminder of elite ancestry to the occupants of the Mississippian chiefdoms. Although most centers had only a few mounds, some of the largest—including **Cahokia**, Illinois— had over one hundred such buildings. Human sacrifice seems to have been occasionally practiced as part of these burials; a particularly important individual might be interred with one or more decapitated or otherwise dispatched individuals. Precious items, inscribed or otherwise decorated with symbols that are collectively known as the **Southern Cult** or the Southeastern Ceremonial Complex, were a more common feature of elite burials in Mississippian mounds.

Designs decorating objects of shell, copper, polished stone, wood and ceramic vessels include forked or weeping eyes, sunbursts, winged humans, eyes set within the palms of open hands, and other supernatural phenomena. In general the Southern Cult seems to have focused on ancestors, the power of elites, warfare, cardinal directions, and death. Some have suggested a vague Mesoamérican connection on the basis of some religious similarities, but these motifs are general enough to make any commonalities coincidental. Overall, the Southern Cult appears to have been a loosely homogenous set of symbols and ideas that reinforced the power of elites at Mississippian centers. It seems to have peaked between 1200 and 1300. Although many of the major Mississippian centers were in decline by 1400, the basic ideas and practices represented by the Southern Cult continued well into the era of European contact.

To the west, over the Great Plains, there is some evidence that elements of the symbolic systems of the Eastern Woodlands were popular, particularly in the period before 400. Though smaller than those of the Eastern Woodlands, mounds from Oklahoma to the Dakotas occasionally bear evidence of these ties: Shells, cut bones, and other objects are occasionally found that show traces of religious influence. Overall, however, this region of small settlements and villages probably saw a combination of local and nonlocal religious expression both before and after 400. There does not seem to be much evidence for artifacts emphasizing the power of elites or the great quantities of prestigious funerary offerings so characteristic of Mississippian societies, for example. Moreover, the wealth of evidence for long-distance contact and trade with the Pacific Coast, Southwest, and Eastern Woodlands suggests that the peoples of the Great Plains were in touch with a variety of religious ideas. As this region was not densely settled and instead characterized by small, sedentary agricultural communities as well as hunter-gatherers, there was likely no one overarching religion similar to the Southern Cult in this region.

American Southwest and the Great Basin

It is difficult to generalize the religious practices of the Great Basin, as the groups here appear to have been influenced by nearly all their neighbors with much regional variation. The one major sedentary society from the Great Basin, the **Fremont** Culture, likewise appears to have had regional varieties with influences from all over the Southwest and the Great Plains; rock paintings by these peoples may have had a religious component, however. For the peoples of the Southwest, however, there are a number of discernable religious practices.

The Hohokam (700–1450)

Isolated pockets of farmers had been present in the Southwest since at least 1300 B.C.E., but it was not until the eighth century C.E. that these individuals coalesced into communities sharing readily identifiable common cultures. For the Hohokam, some of the most easily identified cultural traits are religious: During the Preclassic (700–1150) and Classic Periods (1150–1450), marine shells etched with naturalistic designs and clay figurines were more or less standardized by design. They seem to have been used by religious leaders in ritual activities, although the precise nature of these activities is unclear. Like the shells, which were imported from the Pacific Coast and then worked locally, the preferred materials for Hohokam religious rituals were rare or imported from great distances. Copper bells and tropical feathers from West Mexico, occasionally found at Hohokam sites, may have served just this function.

Further insight into the religious practices of the Hohokam comes from ball courts, dated to the Preclassic, and a switch from inhumation to cremation as the dominant form of burial in the Classic Period. Ultimately derived from Mesoamérica, Hohokam ball courts almost certainly had a ritual component to them; what is not clear is whether that component was, like the form, carried from Mesoamérica into the Southwest (*see* **Ballgame**). Social and political changes likely led to the abandonment of ball courts as the dominant public architectural feature; similar factors may have been involved in the shift to cremation at the beginning of the Classic Period.

Ancestral Pueblo (750–1450)

Like the situation described for the Hohokam, identifiably common cultural patterns emerged on the Colorado Plateau in the eighth century C.E. Perhaps the most striking facet of religious life to emerge during the period known as Pueblo I (750–900) was the architectural development of the "great **kiva**": a centrally located, often circular, multipurpose public room in a settlement used for political and religious purposes. One of the earliest of these is found at Grass Mesa Pueblo, Colorado, and appears to have been used by several settlements as a focal point for political and religious activities. Kivas continue to play a major role within indigenous societies of the Southwest today and are employed in rites involving natural phenomena as well as ancestors. Their early development in the eighth century was a major event and perhaps signifies the beginning of these modern practices.

A second major religious development was the growth and collapse of **Chaco Canyon** during Pueblo II (900–1150). From 900 to 1140 the population of this settlement swelled into the thousands, and enormous house compounds composed of hundreds of rooms and up to four stories were constructed. Some of these houses had multiple kivas inside them and may even have served as temples; the houses themselves were linked throughout the canyon by roads. Although models for the agricultural productivity of the area surrounding Chaco are constantly in flux, archaeologists generally agree that one of the reasons why Chaco became the focal point for population density in this part of the Southwest involves religion: The canyon appears to have become a major pilgrimage center, with buried caches of precious objects (including turquoise) and remains of other ritual activities suggestive of a religious component to the sudden growth of the site. Although Chaco Canyon itself appears to have been abandoned in the twelfth century, collapsing by 1150, elements derivative of Chaco would continue on the Colorado Plateau until the thirteenth century.

The third major religious development in this part of the Southwest was the development of what is called the "Southwest Cult," a shared set of symbols on pottery emphasizing agricultural productivity, the control of water, and fertility. Following a period of sustained population growth on the Colorado Plateau in Pueblo III (1150–1300), the end of the thirteenth century saw droughts and incursions by foreign groups into the region. By the beginning of Pueblo IV (1300–1542), the Colorado Plateau had been abandoned by the Ancestral Puebloans. Immigrating to the Rio Grande and Little Colorado rivers, they merged with local populations and created the largest towns yet seen in the Southwest. The Southwest Cult seems to have been the result of these population upheavals and migrations. Although its origins can be traced to approximately 1275, it gained widespread popularity by 1400 and was used by many different ethnic groups. Designs reminiscent of the Southwest Cult continue to proliferate on traditional ceramics from this region.

Pacific Coast

Societies along the Pacific Coast, like their contemporaries elsewhere in North America, lived between 400 and 1400 in permanent and seasonal villages. Along the coast of California, chiefdoms had arisen by 1300; with them came social distinctions represented in mortuary customs, such as an increase in prestige items—most notably objects made from shell—buried with elites. Chiefdoms seem to have emerged at about 1000 in the Pacific Northwest, with similar variability in mortuary practices emerging at that time. What makes any generalization about the religious practices in these areas difficult is that the media of choice for ritual expression may have been wood. Given what we know about historic populations of these regions and sites like Ozette—a fifteenth-century village in Washington where wooden ritual and utilitarian goods were preserved through historical accident—such a scenario seems likely. Some of the most visible and ritually significant remains of this region, such as totem poles or other elaborately carved objects, may simply not have survived the test of time.

Arctic and Subarctic

The religious practices of the **Dorset** and **Thule**, who dominated the Arctic and Sub-Arctic regions of the Americas between 400 and 1400, are similarly obscure. Certainly carved images of animals—and even Norse—appear in the archaeological record, but in large part there is not enough material culture to create an adequate picture of religious life for this period. Like the Pacific Coast, a more complete image emerges at the beginning of the historic era. However, it is likely that many of the ideas and ceremonial practices encountered in recent times have antecedents in the distant past.

Mesoamérica

One can trace the development of Mesoamérican belief systems to the Early Preclassic Period (2500–1000 B.C.E.), with some of the earliest characteristics represented among civilizations like the Olmec. By 400, Mesoamérican societies shared a number of religious traits derived from these earlier periods, including practices like autosacrifice, human sacrifice, public ritual display atop massive temple pyramids, astronomical observances, and the conjuring of gods and ancestors. All continued well past the year 1400. Likewise, most Mesoamérican religious traditions were characterized by themes of and ideas about agricultural fertility, world renewal, death and the afterlife, ancestor veneration, quasi-historical metropolises, oppositional forces, semidivine rulers, and anthropomorphic conceptions of the earth. There are two important things to remember about Mesoamérican gods, moreover: (1) most were believed to have more than one aspect or "personality" and, at the very least, could appear as male or female (or both) depending upon the situation; and (2) most Mesoamérican gods could overlap in their dominant associations (e.g., sun, wind, moon, etc.) with other gods, to the extent that they were identified more by their host of attributes than their individual names. As an example of these two considerations, one could theoretically have the Aztec god Quetzalcoatl (traditionally male and associated with knowledge and wisdom) appearing as the wind god, Ehecatl, in a predominantly feminine context wearing imagery borrowed from even more Aztec gods. Although he would still be understood as Quetzalcoatl, with a host of traits identifying the "base" as such, he would be employing the powers of other entities. These ideas took different forms over time but were some of the common threads by which Mesoamérica as a culture area was woven. Some elements of Pre-Columbian ideas (as well as indigenous ideas postdating the Spanish Conquest) can be found in contemporary, Christian contexts within Mesoamérica.

The Teotihuacános (100 B.C.E. to 600 C.E.)

Like all Mesoamérican civilizations, the Teotihuacános practiced many of the behaviors outlined above: Themes of agricultural fertility, death and the afterlife, and other shared concepts were key facets of the art and activities of the Teotihuacános in 400.

In addition to this, however, Teotihuacános appear to have been responsible for the spread—and possibly the origin—of two deities that were to echo all the way through Mesoamérican prehistory to the Aztecs. Not all deities popular at **Teotihuacán** were enjoying such distribution: The Teotihuacán fertility goddess seems to have had a limited impact in Mesoamérica, for example. On the other hand, the deity that the Aztecs would later call Tlaloc saw a distribution stretching all the way to the Maya lowlands. This god was associated with rain, water and agricultural fertility. In Mesoamérican art, **Tlaloc** appears with characteristic "goggle" eyes and a missing lower jaw.

Quetzalcoatl, called "the Feathered Serpent" by the Aztecs, was perhaps even more important. Although the Aztecs saw Quetzalcoatl as a wise figure, opposed to human sacrifice and supremely knowledgeable, this was almost certainly not the way in which Quetzalcoatl operated among the Teotihuacános. On a pyramid at Teotihuacán known to archaeologists as the Temple of the Feathered Serpent, repetitive images of this deity appear alongside those of Tlaloc. Beneath the pyramid, a massive, partially looted tomb housed the remains of a lord interred with approximately forty sacrificial victims. Surprisingly, these victims do not appear to have been captives but rather warriors drawn from the Teotihuacán military. This military, as noted in other essays, was extremely effective and spread Teotihuacáno political influence in many directions. It was probably through martial interactions with Teotihuacán that the Classic Maya came into contact with Tlaloc and Quetzalcoatl; although the name of the Maya version of Tlaloc is unknown, Quetzalcoatl came to be known in the Maya area as Kukulkan "the Feathered Serpent."

The Maya (Classic [250–909] and Postclassic [909–1697] Periods)

The Classic Maya pantheon consisted of a host of gods, many of whom embodied forces of the natural world. Some of the most popular were the Sun God (K'inich Ajaw, or "Sun-Faced Lord"), the Maize God and the Storm God (Chaak), with the god Tlaloc—also a god of storms, rain, and agriculture—being the most popular deity imported from Teotihuacán in Central Mexico. Other gods or god-like entities of note included Itzamnaaj, a creator deity associated with knowledge, and K'awiil, a god-like individual who was the embodiment of royal power and an intermediary between rulers and the supernatural world.

Likewise, there were a whole host of gods and creatures associated with the Underworld, a place where the dead were believed to go for trials. Although its full nature is not understood, there seems to have been a general belief—among the Maya elites, at the very least—that passing those trials allowed individuals to be reborn as ancestors, who would then play a significant role in the fortunes of the living. Much like with Mesoamérican conceptions of gods, prominent royal ancestors (but even then, probably not all of them) could overlap in aspect and ability with deities of the Maya pantheon. As an example, K'inich Yax K'uk' Mo', one of the most famous rulers of Copan, was portrayed after death not only as a guiding ancestor but also as an aspect of the Sun God. These ancestors were central to the authority of Maya kings in the Classic and the Postclassic Periods; ancestor veneration was then, as now, a major component of Maya religious life.

As mentioned earlier, during the later Postclassic Period, a version of the Central Mexican deity Quetzalcoatl became popular in the Maya area, most notably at the site of **Chichén Itzá**. Called Kukulkan "the Feathered Serpent," his growth in popularity coincided with the decline of some other gods of the Maya pantheon (K'awiil was perhaps the most noteworthy example of this, following the **Maya collapse**). Most of the mentioned gods of the Maya area, however, persisted until the era of European contact.

The Toltecs (950–1170) and the Aztecs (1345–1521)

The Toltecs and the Aztecs continued many of the prominent religious traditions and practices of Teotihuacán, although at least one of the gods—Quetzalcoatl—appears to have undergone a radical transformation. Appearing as one of the central gods of Teotihuacan engaged in human sacrifice, Quetzalcoatl was now associated with knowledge, wisdom, and opposition to that practice. Such opposition was significant in light of the fact that the Aztecs were particularly engaged in human sacrifice, on a scale seemingly unsurpassed in the Americas. In fact, human sacrifice was, for the Aztecs, a central part of public religious expression; it was designed not only as entertainment or ritual but also as dramatic, state-sanctioned theater where victories of the state could be demonstrated and the powers of the ruling class exalted. The chief deity of the Aztecs, a war god named Huitzilopochtli, was a new introduction to the Mesoamérican pantheon and his worship demanded human sacrifice.

Individuals to be sacrificed at the Aztec capital of **Tenochtitlán**, for example, were usually war captives who were prepared for death up to a year in advance. Death by sacrifice was considered a "good death" by the Aztecs, who believed that the manner of one's death determined where they would live in the afterlife: Individuals who died a warrior's death, including death on the battlefield, sacrifice, or death in childbirth (women died providing warriors for the state), would ascend to an exalted paradise. The worst way to die, in the Aztec mind-set, was to expire as a result of natural causes like disease or infirmity; such individuals would be sent to an afterlife that was far from ideal.

Lower Central America (Intermediate Area) and the Andes

Ceremonial centers built for the communal feasts, rituals, and other activities of surrounding villages, such as the one at **Rivas**, Costa Rica, were one of the hallmarks of religious expression in Lower Central America. Although this area never saw the growth of state religions or the construction of massive temple architecture, it was characterized by many centers involved in the production of metal items—particularly gold—for ultimate interment with the burials of high-ranking individuals. Large cemeteries, sometimes divided or separated geographically by social rank or lineage, were common in this region. Unfortunately, given the quantities of gold interred in such cemeteries, most have been heavily damaged by looting activities.

On the Pacific Coast and in the Andes, the material remains of religious expression are dominated by ruling elites (*curacas*), who built temples and similar structures either of mud-brick, as on the coast, or of the readily available stone in the Andes. Most took the form of colossal platform mounds with attached plazas, with some mirroring or augmenting natural features in the landscape. Solar and agricultural themes predominated in religious pantheons of these regions, with mythological creature also playing a major role in sacred imagery. Perhaps the most ubiquitous feature of coastal and Andean religious ideology, however, was the concept of a **huaca**: These were sacred places, from mountains to temples, which served as locations for pilgrimage and even (occasionally) human sacrifice. The centrality of huacas to religious expression in these regions continues today.

Moche (200–600) and Nazca (200 B.C.E.–650 C.E.)

Moche society revolved largely around the worship of solar, feline, and other types of deities derived from the natural world, as evidenced by stucco portraits and other images of gods on Moche temples. Most of what we know about Moche religion does not derive from temple contexts, however, but from elite ceramics: As depicted on bottles, vases, and bowls, the Moche nobility appear to have had a rich mythology involving anthropomorphic animals, warring gods, and ritual sacrifice. One of the most popular of the mythological themes appears to have been the Presentation Theme, where war captives were sacrificed for the good of the gods and of society. Their blood was apparently consumed by Moche elites in elaborate ceremonies. Such elites have been recovered at Moche sites such as **Sipán**, where individuals from high-status burials were dressed like specific characters from Moche ceramics.

Some parallels between Moche and Nazca religions exist, particularly with regard to the types of deities worshipped: emphases on anthropomorphic beings and a warrior ideology are in evidence on Nazca ceramics. Unlike the Moche, the Nazca appear to have had a ceremonial center, Cuachi, where individuals from nearby villages would gather for sociopolitical and religious functions. It is not clear if the **Nazca lines**, for which that civilization is most famous, served a religious purpose; in general, the reasons for the geometric, animal, vegetative, and other designs in the desert are not clear.

Tiwanaku (650–1000), Chimor (1000–1476), and the Birth of the Inca Empire (c. 1000–1532)

Like many of the other societies of the Andes, **Tiwanaku** civilization was characterized by masonry buildings, stelae, and megalithic archways, with platform mounds and other forms of monumental architecture designed to convey the power of the nobility and the dominant religious ideology. As in some other parts of the Americas, the architecture was built to make an impression upon visitors to Tiwanaku sites and to stir the public in ceremonies involving elite ritual display. At Tiwanaku, the dominant deity appears to have been a late version of a deity whose origins stretched back to Chavín (1200–400 B.C.E.) times, the Staff God. A composite of human, animal, and solar attributes, the Tiwanaku Staff God appears to have been associated with natural phenomena, particularly with regard to agricultural fertility.

Religious behavior at Chimor appears to have been a continuation of the traditions of previous peoples of the north coast of Peru, including the Moche, as well as an anticipation of Inca customs. In addition to practicing human sacrifice and bearing a mythology dominated by anthropomorphic creatures and natural phenomena, particularly with regard to marine creatures and the sea, there seems to have been an emphasis on ancestor veneration in Moche society. Mummified nobles occupied privileged positions in royal ceremonial behavior and may have been viewed as actively participating in the affairs of state. By the birth of the Inca Empire in the early fifteenth century, mummies were paramount players in political affairs, the mummies of emperors continuing to "own" land and property; they were also brought forth to participate in important state rituals. In part, their prominence was due to the general belief that Inca emperors were direct, lineal descendents of the paramount Inca deity, the sun god Inti. As gods themselves, the Inca emperors thus retained their divine nature even after death! Like their antecedents in coastal and Andean South America, the Inca believed in sacred nature of mountains and ritually significant places (huacas) and would provide these places with offerings in the forms of material goods or humans specially chosen to be sacrificed.

Amazonia and the Caribbean

The Arawak-speaking peoples who spread from the northern parts of South America to the Caribbean between 500 B.C.E and 500 C.E. were characterized by theocratic chiefdoms; chiefs in these societies built monuments to their power and created earthen and stone ceremonial buildings. Ball courts similar to those found in Mesoamérica and the Southwest were erected in the Caribbean, as were large circular plazas designed for political and religious use. Like their contemporaries elsewhere, peoples of the Caribbean held certain areas of their islands to be sacred and continued in all of these practices and beliefs well past 1400.

The Arawak- and Tupiguarani-speaking peoples of Amazonia, by comparison, followed a different political trajectory: Strongly hierarchical chiefdoms emerged much later, as at Santarem in the sixteenth century, or not at all. At the same time, however, religious expression took similar forms. At Marajó Island, on the Amazonian estuary, the **Marajóara** people erected large earthen mounds housing burial urns; the largest of the mounds seem to have been reserved for the burials of elites and were focal points for political and religious activities between 400 and 1400. **Acutuba**, in the Central Amazon, saw the construction of a large amphitheater thought to have served similar political and religious purposes during this time period. As more research is done in this area we may find that, like their contemporaries in the Eastern Woodlands, the Amazonians engaged in the building of mounds and other public architecture as a social and religious activity.

Further Reading

Alva, W., and C.B. Donnan. *Royal Tombs of Sipan*. Los Angeles: University of California Press, 1993.

Bell, R.E. *Prehistory of Oklahoma*. Orlando, FL: Academic Press, 1984.

Carrasco, Davíd. *Religions of Mesoamerica*. Long Grove, IL: Waveland Press, 1998.

Crown, Patricia. *Ceramics and Ideology: Salado Polychrome Pottery*. Albuquerque: University of New Mexico Press, 1994.

Fagan, Brian. *Ancient North America*. London: Thames and Hudson, 1991.

Knight, V.J., Jr., J.A. Brown, and G.E. Lankford. "On the Subject Matter of Southeastern Ceremonial Complex Art." *Southeastern Archaeology* 20 (2001): 129–141.

Miller, Mary Ellen, and Simon Martin, eds. *Courtly Art of the Ancient Maya*. London: Thames and Hudson, Ltd., 2004.

Miller, Mary Ellen, and Karl Taube. *An Illustrated Dictionary of the Gods and Symbols of Ancient Mexico and the Maya*. London: Thames and Hudson, Ltd., 1997.

Moseley, Michael E. *The Incas and their Ancestors: the Archaeology of Peru*. 2nd ed. London: Thames and Hudson, Ltd., 2001.

Petersen, James, E.G. Neves, and M. Heckenberger. "Gift from the Past: Terra Preta and Prehistoric Amerindian Occupations in Amazonia," in C. McEwan, C. Barreto, and E.G. Neves, eds. *The Unknown Amazon: Culture in Nature in Ancient Brazil*. London: British Museum Press, 2001, pp. 86–105.

Roosevelt, Anne. *Moundbuilders of the Amazon: Geophysical Archaeology on Marajo Island, Brazil*. New York: Academic Press, 1991.

Scarre, Chris, ed. *The Human Past: World Prehistory and the Development of Human Societies*. London: Thames and Hudson, Ltd., 2005.

Sharer, Robert J., and Loa P. Traxler. *The Ancient Maya*. 6th ed. Stanford, CA: Stanford University Press, 2005.

Smith, Michael E. *The Aztecs*. Oxford, UK: Wiley-Blackwell, 2003.

Taube, Karl. *Aztec and Maya Myths*. Austin: University of Texas Press, 1993.

3. ECONOMY

The various economies of the Americas were largely based on agriculture or, in the case of hunter-gatherers, highly specialized food-procurement technologies.

Although nearly all societies of the Americas refrained from using metal or the wheel for tools, implements, or modes of transportation (see **Pacific Coast, Arctic, and Subarctic**), their economies were able to involve goods from far-flung locations. Some of these were traded across continents through local exchanges, whereas others were directly imported from great distances. Elites in the societies of the Americas particularly relied on such long-distance trade, as imports of prestige items were vital to maintaining status distinctions. They were likewise valuable to elites because of their varied functions in ritual: broad regional religious ideologies, such as the **Southern Cult** of the Eastern Woodlands or the system of **divine kingship** employed by the Classic Maya, required certain objects and materials for religious efficacy (and the politics that went with such rituals).

Eastern Woodlands and the Great Plains

The Eastern Woodlands and the Great Plains were, in 400 C.E., undergoing a decline in regional trade. Between the Early and Middle Woodland Periods (800 B.C.E.–400 C.E.), sites such as Fort Ancient and Hopewell, Ohio, had seen the vigorous trading of copper, chert, shell, and obsidian artifacts as well as raw materials; they were part of an economic network stretching from Wyoming to the Atlantic to the Gulf Coast of Louisiana. By 400, such activities had largely ceased: Although village populations continued to increase in nearly all areas, economies became far more localized. Warfare—in part a cause as well as a result of this economic decline—among the members of these local economies was a major facet of life between 400 and 1000 C.E. Likewise, the sudden adoption of maize as the staple crop and its replacement of most native cultigens was a key development in the latter years of the first millennium C.E.

The economic and social instability of these times, coupled with increasing reliance on maize as well as booming populations, led around 1000 to the birth of Mississippian chiefdoms (1000–1500) over much of the Eastern Woodlands and the Great Plains. How did this happen? In these turbulent times, enterprising, ambitious individuals and their supporters appear to have taken permanent control of favorable locations at places such as **Cahokia**, Illinois, and **Moundville**, Alabama, lending stability at the cost of permanent, hierarchically arranged as well as hereditary leadership. Economically, long-distance trade as well as the exploitation of wild food sources appears to have resumed, although the primary mode of subsistence in most areas continued to be maize agriculture and supporting crops like squash or beans. Although the Mississippian chiefdoms would begin their long decline around 1400, in many areas related to the colder temperatures of the Little Ice Age (1400–1850), they were not extinct at the time of European colonization. New social and economic systems would emerge to deal with problems such as increased warfare, mass population movements, and other issues leading to social unrest, although around 1400 the situation in the Eastern Woodlands and the Great Plains certainly seemed dire.

American Southwest and the Great Basin

The economies of the American Southwest and the Great Basin were somewhat linked together through the exchange of goods and ideas. The Great Basin was a crossroads for peoples from the American Southwest and the Great Plains (and, from there, the Eastern Woodlands), as best evidenced by the **Fremont** Culture (400–1300 C.E.). The American Southwest, by comparison, had intermittent economic ties not only with the Great Plains but also with the Pacific Coast as well as Mesoamérica. Most notably, turquoise from the Southwest is occasionally found in Mesoamérican contexts. The specifics of such trade—and whether it was direct or simply local exchange moving such items gradually north or south—are unknown, but sites like **Casas Grandes**, Mexico, may hold the key: Casas Grandes appears to have been an intermediary between these regions, most notably during the era of the Toltecs in Central Mexico.

The Hohokam (750–1450)

Although the foundations of the Hohokam economy certainly predate 750— irrigation, for example, had been practiced in the American Southwest since 1000 B.C.E.—the Hohokam were the first cohesive cultural group in the area to engage in the long-distance export and import of ideas as well as materials. From what has been reconstructed archaeologically, the Preclassic Period (700–1150) was characterized by intensive irrigation, village organization, and population increase as well as exchange with northern Mexico (and perhaps Mesoamérica). Such long-distance ties are evidenced by Mexican-style ball courts at Preclassic sites such as **Snaketown**. As mentioned in the Arts section, the subsequent Classic Period (1150–1450) was characterized by further long-distance trade from areas throughout the continent, although the majority of the foreign objects found in Classic sites appear to have been procured for ritual purposes rather than economic display. The entire economic system appears to have been agrarian, with vast canals being dug to support a burgeoning population. Drier conditions as well as environmental degradation seem to have taken a major toll on this economy by the end of the fifteenth century, such that most Hohokam settlements were abandoned by the time of Spanish colonization.

Ancestral Pueblo (750–1450)

The Ancestral Puebloan societies between 750 and 1450 went through several phases in which different parts of the Colorado Plateau and surrounding regions gained political, religious, or economic ascendancy. Throughout these periods the agrarian economy was largely based upon staples ultimately derived from Central Mexico—such as maize, beans, and squash—as well as local cultigens and wild resources. During Pueblo I (750–900), the first true villages appeared on the Plateau; likewise, the first "great **kivas**" (or large, multipurpose rooms used for political and religious functions) were built at this time. The economy centered on the production capacities of these villages as well as remote communities on the Colorado Plateau. Pueblo II (900–1150) saw increasing numbers of centralized villages and towns, including massive constructions at **Chaco Canyon**, a pilgrimage center for many of the peoples in the region; economically, it may have also been an agriculturally favorable oasis in arid times, drawing people not only for religious but also subsistence purposes. Pueblo III (1150–1300) and Pueblo IV (1300–1450) saw massive population movements, first to cliff dwellings in New Mexico and Colorado followed by the abandonment of the Colorado Plateau entirely. By the early phase of Pueblo IV, Ancestral Puebloan societies had rebounded from massive drought and social upheaval, immigrating to the Rio Grande Valley. Villages reached their socioeconomic heights, with densely packed populations engaged in intensive agriculture along the Rio Grande and Little Colorado rivers. Unfortunately, by 1400 the negative consequences of such urbanism were also taking their toll. Increased warfare, endemic diseases, and malnutrition in the region contributed to broad population decline and even the collapse of several major centers of Ancestral Puebloan society. Nevertheless, many communities did manage to weather the troubles of the fifteenth century and survive Spanish colonization.

Pacific Coast, Arctic, and Subarctic

The subsistence economies of the Pacific Coast and the Arctic were shaped by the ocean. Peoples on the Pacific, from Alaska to California, largely relied upon marine resources such as seals, whales, fish, shellfish, and birds. Although these communities were not all directly connected through coastal trade, there is plenty of evidence for indirect long-distance exchange in precious or utilitarian items such as obsidian, copper, and shell. The **Dorset** and **Thule** peoples of the Arctic, meanwhile, depended upon seals, walruses, and—particularly with regard to the Thule—whales in addition to fish. In terms of access to resources, the Thule eventually gained an economic and numerical advantage over the Dorset in their ability to exploit deep-water resources: They were skillful whale hunters and eventually overran the Dorset to extinction. The Dorset were, however, around to encounter the Vikings in their brief exploration of the Americas; some remains of their presence, in the form of carvings and other small items (as well as a settlement, **L'Anse aux Meadows**, in Newfoundland), may have been traded with these Arctic peoples. Likewise, the Thule were engaged in the long-distance trade and distribution of a limited number of copper and even iron objects (meteoric and terrestrial); they produced tools from these objects or, in the case of terrestrial iron, largely traded with the Norse for them.

Mesoamérica

Our picture of Mesoamérican economies between 400 and 1400, although more detailed than some other parts of the Americas, is far from clear. Although we can pinpoint the types of goods traded; differences between royal, elite, and commoner consumption; local and regional trade networks, mines, or quarries; and the various modes of subsistence (e.g., slash-and-burn agriculture, terracing, raised-field agriculture, and the other forms of irrigation that supported a maize-based agrarian lifestyle) that formed the economic backbones of societies like the Teotihuacános or the Classic Maya, it is difficult to identify the methods of exchange within individual sites. That is to say, although there is much detail provided by the archaeological record on Mesoamérican economies, it is difficult to say how much control Mesoamérican rulers and their subordinates actually had over trade. Some scholars have suggested strong, centralized market exchange as the predominant mode of economic activity in ancient Mesoamérica, particularly within large cities such as **Teotihuacán** or **Tenochtitlán**. Others promote a looser model of exchange, with gift giving and redistributive networks managed among locals—in such a model, the ruler might manage prestige goods while basic subsistence items were managed by elites and even commoners in different situations. There is probably no one model that fits a given civilization or situation, with combinations of centralized and decentralized economic activities likely being the norm in ancient Mesoamérica.

Furthermore, there is no one model for currency in Mesoamérica between 400–1400: **Cacao** (chocolate) beans and thin, copper axes were clearly used as currency by the Postclassic Period, depending upon their availability. Other goods, ranging from jaguar pelts to textile bundles to jade boulders, were bartered, gifted, sent as tribute, or otherwise combined with these currencies. By the tenth century, even gold and silver were being traded or otherwise exchanged—but not specifically as "currency."

The Teotihuacános (100 B.C.E. to 600 C.E.)

Teotihuacán, being a vast, meticulously planned city, was the hub of economic activity in Central Mexico between 100 B.C.E and 600 C.E. In addition to the tremendous, daily flow of agricultural products into the city from the Valley of Mexico, Teotihuacán obtained clay for ceramics as well as salt from nearby Lake Texcoco. Somewhat further afield, to the north and east at Pachuca and Otumba, respectively, Teotihuacán imported obsidian for tool making. Teotihuacán also maintained political and economic ties with several civilizations to the south, east, west, and southeast, importing materials such as chocolate, cinnabar, cotton, feathers, incense, jade, onyx, feathers, and shell from the Maya area, for example. Such items were brought by merchants who may have lived in the eastern part of the site, an area dubbed the "Merchant's Barrio" by archaeologists.

Teotihuacán was also home to hundreds of craft workshops, where goods were made for local consumption as well as export. Although many of the artisans who worked in these shops were local, it is clear that some were from various parts of the Mesoamérican world. Ethnic enclaves of peoples from West Mexico, the Gulf Coast, the Valley of Oaxaca, and possibly the Maya area have been identified at the site, providing evidence that Teotihuacán was a cosmopolitan place in its heyday.

Unfortunately, we do not know as much as we would like about the government at Teotihuacán, largely because there are few surviving written records. Nevertheless, it is clear that Teotihuacán was governed by kings living in palaces, and given the level of organization which would have been needed to design and maintain a city of this size (about one hundred twenty-five thousand people), it seems likely that rulers and their subordinates played more than just a minor role in administering the economy at Teotihuacán. At least one ruler, Spearthrower Owl, appears to have been involved in the conquest of several cities in the Maya area, installing rulers friendly to Central Mexico. In part, the motivations for this were almost certainly economic.

The Maya (Classic [250 to 909] and Postclassic [909–1697] Periods)

The many cities of the Maya Lowlands during the Classic and Postclassic Periods were never politically unified. Likewise, each of the cities was variable in its degree of centralized authority, making a universal image of the ancient Maya economy almost impossible to create. Like Teotihuacán, the major goods being traded at Maya centers can be divided into two categories: prestige and utilitarian. Chocolate (cacao beans), feathers, jade, shell, sumptuous textiles, and other prestige goods were near-ubiquitous features of royal and/or elite consumption at Classic Maya centers, whereas utilitarian goods such as chert, cotton, foodstuffs, obsidian, salt, stone, and plainer textiles had a much wider distribution among the masses. In addition to trade, some of these goods were obtained through threat of force or force itself: Maya monuments show defeated or subordinate rulers bringing tribute, in the form of cacao beans or other items, to their new (and likely temporary) masters. Although the political situation for the Maya changed during the Postclassic, there is good evidence that all of these goods—and more—were imported and exported in large numbers.

Although certain goods, such as foodstuffs, were often obtained locally via intensive agriculture or hunting-gathering, many of these items—prestige and utilitarian—were traded at great distances. For example, the obsidian used at lowland Classic Maya sites came from several locations in highland Guatemala (El Chayal or Ixtepeque, for example) or even Central Mexico (Pachuca). Likewise, the major source of jade in all of Mesoamérica was the Motagua River Valley, on the present-day Guatemalan–Honduran border. As the material most prized by Mesoamérican rulers and elites, jade was one item that required extensive trade networks: Traded over land, sea, and rivers, jade was even exported out of the Maya area as far south as Lower Central America. During the Late Classic and especially the Postclassic, long-distance trade with this and other regions flourished, to the extent that gold and other nonlocal items filtered into the Maya economy. Perhaps the greatest Maya city of the Postclassic, **Chichén Itzá**, owed its florescence between about 750 and 1250 in part due to such long-distance trade: As the largest Maya city of its time, it was a major center for pilgrimage as well as a hub for the salt trade in Yucatán.

One of the great questions in Maya archaeology is, as mentioned above, whether site economies were highly centralized. One way to answer this question would be to further explore the degree of craft specialization at Classic and Postclassic sites. Workshops have not been encountered in great numbers at Maya sites, as they have been at Teotihuacán, in large part because archaeologists are only beginning to look at the mechanics of ancient Maya economies. This is a big gap in our knowledge of this civilization. Nevertheless, workshops have been occasionally found: Shops dedicated to the working of shell bone, jade, and obsidian are evident at the major Classic Maya city of **Copan**, for example. What such activity areas reveal is that the Maya, like the Teotihuacános, were engaged in the production and consumption of goods for local consumption as well as export. Time will tell if this activity was heavily centralized, as is suspected for Teotihuacán, or decentralized, with Maya kings engaged primarily with the prestige economy and paying far less attention to the day-to-day trade of utilitarian items.

The Toltecs (950–1170) and the Aztecs (1345–1521)

Although the Toltecs were never as politically or economically powerful as their Teotihuacáno predecessors, their capital—**Tula**—can be compared with Teotihuacán. Like that site, Tula had many workshops dedicated to the working of obsidian and stone as well as to the production of ceramics. Likewise, the Toltecs established long-distance trading relationships with other parts of Mesoamérica, including the Gulf Coast and Yucatán: The political and economic fortunes of the Postclassic Maya site of Chichén Itzá, for example, seem to have been tied to events at Tula. In one economic respect, the Toltecs even surpassed the Teotihuacános: They appear to have traded with peoples well outside of Mesoamérica, from Lower Central America in the south to northern Mexico.

So great was their influence upon the material culture of Central Mexico at this time that their successors, the Aztecs, believed the Toltecs to have been superior craftsmen. The Aztecs often invoked the Toltecs when describing skilled workmanship; they believed the Toltecs were wealthy, wise traders and artisans; they attributed nearly all major scientific and technological discoveries to these ancient peoples. The reality is that the Toltecs created a small, likely tribute-based, empire comprising cities in the Basin of Mexico as well as several centers to the north. In 1400, the Toltecs were the civilization that many ethnic groups in the Basin, including the Mexica, aspired to be. The Aztecs would soon create an even larger, tribute-based empire. Nearly every item of value in Mesoamérica, whether bought, sold, or brought as spoils of war, would find its way to the Aztec marketplace.

Lower Central America and the Andes

By 400, the peoples of Lower Central America had long been trading metals with peoples to the south; groups from Ecuador and Peru had independently invented metallurgy in the Americas, and such metals as gold or silver had become common in exchanges between the elites of these areas. Jade and other Mesoamérican goods likewise filtered into the chiefdoms of Lower Central America, who economically became intermediaries for coastal trade between the dense urban populations of that region and the Andes. Peoples from Lower Central America were at least in part (if not totally) responsible for the dissemination of metallurgy to Mesoamérica, for example, with the first gold reaching the Maya area around 600. By 1400, several places in Lower Central America, including villages in present-day Costa Rica and Panama, had become vital ports in a burgeoning, vast network of trade along the Pacific Coast. Cotton, tropical feathers, root crops, marine shell, medicinal plants, and other goods flowed in and out of these ports linking Mesoamérica, the Andes, and Amazonia in turn. Although direct contact between these distant regions was sporadic at its very best, Lower Central America was in many ways an economic hub through which indirect contact was possible.

The Andes, home to several urban civilizations between 400 and 1400, had previously seen the growth and development of an agrarian economy as well as an established elite class: the *curaca*. Economically, the *curaca* nobles fostered the development of several industries dedicated to the production of prestige goods, ranging from ceramics and textiles to gold, silver, and alloyed ornaments. Depending upon time and location, these intensive, agrarian economies were based on maize cultivation (similar to Mesoamérica), root crops such as potatoes, or a combination of both. All the societies discussed were characterized by compounds of artisans; workshops for the production of ceramics, for example, have been encountered at many Andean sites.

Moche (200–600 c.e.) and Nazca (200 b.c.e.–650 c.e.)

The **Moche** culture, often regarded as the first true state of South America, produced some of the most ornate, detailed pottery and metalworking in the

Americas. Whole mud-brick compounds at Moche sites, sometimes housing large, extended families, were dedicated to the production of high-quality ceramics: For example, stirrup-spouted drinking vessels, decorated with historical and mythological events, were produced using moulds and presented to curaca nobles on a massive scale. Other compounds were home to master goldsmiths: **Metallurgy** was well developed in the Moche world, and metallurgists cast objects and produced alloys of gold, copper, and silver using a variety of techniques. Somewhat less-prestigious workshops were dedicated to the production of mud-bricks, used in the construction of temples and other buildings on the north coast of Peru. Some archaeologists believe that these bricks were produced as part of a labor tax exacted by the curaca nobles.

The nature of the Moche political system, as it related to the economy and economic control, is unclear. However, the Moche were certainly players in a vast trade network stretching from Chile to Ecuador: Lapis lazuli from Chile and spiny oyster shells from Ecuador have been recovered at Moche sites. The natural disasters of the sixth century temporarily disrupted these trade networks, although some remnants of Moche society—and these networks—continued to exist until the eighth century.

Unfortunately, the Nazca economy is somewhat difficult to describe. As a cluster of dispersed farming communities, the Nazca seem to have been ceremonially unified around the pilgrimage center of Cahuachi; the economic role of Cahuachi in Nazca life is not well understood. The Nazca did have a developed craft industry, however: Nazca textiles and ceramics were among the most colorful and iconographically abstract goods produced on the Pacific Coast of South America. In the seventh century, Nazca society may have coalesced into a larger political unit; certainly this would have brought with it no small measure of economic change. Unfortunately, the region was invaded by another rising civilization, **Wari**, and Nazca civilization ceased to exist as an independent entity (*see* **Nazca Lines**).

Tiwanaku (650–1000), Chimor (1000–1476), and the Birth of the Inca (1300–1532)

Tiwanaku and its rival, Wari, mark the beginning of empire in the Andes. In many ways, Chimor represents its refinement before the eventual conquest of all of these regions by the Inca in the late fifteenth century. Unfortunately, the absence of written records for all three, and the degree to which the Inca purposefully destroyed **Chimor**, has made understanding the political nature of these empires difficult. Archaeologists are divided as to the degree of control exerted by the rulers of Tiwanaku, Wari, and Chimor. Some see Tiwanaku, for example, as a loose confederation of curaca families, ethnic groups, and lineages; others see a distinct hierarchy, with a strong central government at Tiwanaku. Of course, such differences have major implications for the ways in which Andean economies worked during these periods. Each had colonies and client-cities, networks of roads linking cities politically and economically, and llama caravans to facilitate exchange. Tiwanaku and Chimor are the best understood of the three Andean empires prior to the Inca.

One of the reasons why Tiwanaku remained powerful for so long is that it was able to control many of the Andean grazing lands for llamas and alpacas. Llamas were the only domesticated animal in the Americas able to carry heavy loads, whereas alpacas provided fibers for textile production. Control over land able to support these populations enabled the Tiwanaku curaca to economically dominate other peoples. Another factor contributing to the power of Tiwanaku was its multivariate approach to empire. Some regions were incorporated directly into the empire, with territories annexed, villages conquered, people resettled, and tribute exacted, whereas others were allowed to remain semiautonomous, so long as they supported the state with economic resources or fulfilled other obligations as needed. Likewise, the Tiwanaku state actively supported the colonization of areas with important economic resources. Unfortunately, climate change—a prolonged dry period—seems to have severely affected their agricultural resources and they, in addition to Wari, started to collapse around 1000.

Chimor, from its capital Chan Chan in the Moche Valley, was an even larger state, extending more than 600 miles along the northern coast of Peru. The city center of Chan Chan alone was over 2 square miles, with skilled weavers, metalworkers, woodcarvers, potters, and other craftsmen living in apartment compounds. At almost thirty-thousand people, the city was the political and economic hub of a vast empire surpassed only by the Inca, who conquered it in 1470. The rural and the urban inhabitants of Chimor were economically specialized: Workshops have been found in both settings, and it is clear that the empire was able to muster resources from the Pacific Coast and the Andes. By comparison, the Inca of 1400 were provincial; they had just renovated their capital of **Cuzco**, from which they would soon launch a military conquest of the Andean world.

Amazonia and the Caribbean

By 400, one diaspora of Arawak-speaking peoples had occupied a stretch of territory ranging from modern-day Venezuela to the Caribbean islands. These peoples were agriculturalists living in densely populated villages ruled by chiefs; these chiefdoms had existed for quite some time, perhaps as early as 1000 B.C.E. The social and economic networks that these chiefdoms participated in stretched across northern South America and, after 500 B.C.E., into the Greater Antilles. Those who lived on islands in the Caribbean seem to have had some contact with the Maya: Mesoamérican-style ball courts appear in a great range over the Caribbean, with one as far north as Puerto Rico (*see* **Ballgame**). Although it is not known what else may have been traded between these areas, there was almost certainly some economic exchange.

As for Amazonia, large, densely populated villages were in the process of being established in 400 c.e.; antecedents to these did exist, most notably in Ecuador and Bolivia, but settlements in vast numbers only began to emerge between 400 and 1000. The founding of these settlements seems to have been accompanied by the growth of long-distance trade networks: There is some evidence for metals, ceramics, precious stones (amethyst), gold, ceremonial axe heads, and other items moving between areas as distant as the Amazon estuary and the Peruvian border during this era. Some of the best evidence supporting regular contact between regions of Amazonia comes from a wide distribution of many ceramic traits: The tradition known as Amazonian Polychrome, for example, stretches over much of this region. Some of the earliest evidence for this style comes from the precocious site of Marajó Island (400–1300).

Unfortunately, it is quite possible that much of what was traded between these regions between 400 and 1400 did not survive. Accounts from the early colonial period, for example, point to economic activity centered on goods such as tropical feathers, salt, animal pelts, and medicinal plants, all of which would be almost impossible to recover from the archaeological record. Their absence, combined with poor conditions for preservation and lack of archaeological data, makes reconstructing what was traded and how it moved about the landscape difficult. However, growing interest in sites like Marajó Island, where mounds were built and used between 600 and 1300, is starting to change our image of Amazonian prehistory, and with it the political systems present in the region. As these sites gain more attention, the economic picture will slowly come into focus.

Further Reading

Arnold, J. "Complex Hunter-Gatherer-Fishers of Prehistoric California: Chiefs, Specialists, and Maritime Adaptations of the Channel Islands. *American Antiquity* 57 (1992): 60–84.

Bayman, J. The Hohokam of Southwest North America." *Journal of World Prehistory* 15 (2001): 257–311.

Carmack, Robert M., and Gary Gossen. *The Legacy of Mesoamerica: History and Culture of a Native American Civilization*. 2nd ed. Upper Saddle River, NJ: Prentice Hall, 2006.

Crown, Patricia. *Ceramics and Ideology: Salado Polychrome Pottery*. Albuquerque: University of New Mexico Press, 1994.

Demarest, Arthur. *The Ancient Maya. The Rise and Fall of a Rainforest Civilization*. Cambridge, UK: Cambridge University Press, 2004.

Fagan, Brian. *Ancient North America*. London: Thames and Hudson, 1991.

Heckenberger, Michael. "Rethinking the Arawakan Diaspora: Hierarchy, Regionality, and the Amazonian Formative." In J. Hill and F. Santos-Granero, eds. *Comparative Arawakan Histories: Rethinking Culture Area and Language Group in Amazoniay*. Urbana: University of Illinois Press, 2002, pp. 99–121.

Hosler, Dorothy. *The Sounds and Colors of Power: The Sacred Metallurgical Technology of Ancient West Mexico*. Cambridge, MA: MIT Press, 1994.

Knight, V.J., Jr., J.A. Brown, and G.E. Lankford. "On the Subject Matter of Southeastern Ceremonial Complex Art." *Southeastern Archaeology* 20 (2001): 129–141.

McGee, R. "Contact between Native North Americans and the Medieval Norse: A Review of Evidence." *American Antiquity* 49 (1984): 4–26.

Moseley, Michael E. *The Incas and their Ancestors: the Archaeology of Peru*. 2nd ed. London: Thames and Hudson, Ltd., 2001.

Pillsbury, Joanne. *Moche Art and Archaeology in Ancient Peru*. London: NGW Studies in the History of Art, 2006.

Roosevelt, Anne. *Moundbuilders of the Amazon: Geophysical Archaeology on Marajo Island, Brazil*. New York: Academic Press, 1991.

Scarre, Chris, ed. *The Human Past: World Prehistory and the Development of Human Societies*. London: Thames and Hudson, Ltd., 2005.

Silverman, H. *Cahuachi in the Ancient Nasca World*. Iowa City: University of Iowa Press, 1991.

Smith, Michael E. *The Aztecs*. Oxford, UK: Wiley-Blackwell, 2003.

Vivian, R. *The Chacoan Prehistory of the San Juan Basin*. San Diego, CA: Academic Press, 1990.

4. THE ARTS

The millennium preceding the Spanish Conquest and the first permanent European settlements in the Americas (c. 1492–1600) saw the rise and fall of several major civilizations. Artistic achievements, in the forms of stone sculpture, painting, and several other media, too reached new heights in this period. The cultures that existed between 400 and 1400 inherited a rich legacy of earlier civilizations, such as the Adena-Hopewell of the American Southeast, the Olmec of southern Mexico (1200–300 B.C.E.), or the Chavín culture of Andean South America (1200–200 B.C.E.). As societies in the Americas became more complex, with chiefdoms, city-states, and even empires forming in different regions, the demand for large public monuments, mural paintings, or other great works of art grew. Likewise, this complexity allowed for the production of portable goods, the raw materials of which were often transported over great distances. These works were often used to convey and to support elite claims to supernatural authority, royal lineage, and even divinity. Likewise, many of the portable objects that one might consider art had sacred or political associations to the groups who produced them; in many cases, such objects would not have been separated according to these categories. To understand the arts of this era, we will look at the works of the dominant civilizations of this period and at the various media used by the peoples of the Americas before Columbus, collectively known as the Pre-Columbian era.

Eastern Woodlands and the Great Plains

In the years prior to 400 C.E., the Mississippi and Ohio Valleys had been home to the Adena and Hopewell cultures, societies whose burial mounds, rich ceremonial life, and production of visually stunning artifacts—typically crafted of materials from exotic origins—had become a fixture in eastern North America. The decline of these activities around 400 C.E. was accompanied by an increase in warfare and the formation of ever-increasingly more complex political groups, until by 1000 powerful chiefdoms had emerged at places like **Cahokia**, Illinois, and **Moundville**, Alabama. Archaeologists deem the era between 1000 and the fifteenth century the Mississippian Period an era of unprecedented urban construction in a region stretching from Oklahoma to portions of the Atlantic Coast. Towns literally erupted from the landscape, with massive burial earthworks and a resurgence of aesthetically pleasing portable objects—largely produced from nonlocal materials—serving as testament to the power of the new chiefdoms, collectively called the "Mississippians." The largest of the mounds were enormous earthen pyramids, with Monk's Mound at Cahokia being the best example: About 100 feet high, it alone covered 13.8 acres and was one of the largest structures in the Pre-Columbian world.

The most precious of the portable objects were usually interred with deceased elites, including objects from rare or high-status materials such as seashell and copper. Stylistically, such items were often decorated with a common set of motifs, termed the **Southern Cult** or Southeastern Ceremonial complex: Weeping eyes, birds, warriors, crossed objects, and cosmic imagery are the primary characteristics of this widespread art style. Carved artifacts of stone or, more commonly, wood have also been found in burial contexts and usually deal with ancestors and warriors as their primary subject matter. Overall, the idea seems to have been to reinforce the position of elites within Mississippian society, and although such items occur throughout the era, they are most common in the thirteenth and fourteenth centuries, after which time the region went into decline. Further resurgences were to occur within the Southeast in the years before European colonization.

As in the Southeast, the years between 400 and 1000 in the Great Plains saw the emergence of villages alongside—and sometimes in combination with—traditional nomadic society. Mounds and other earthworks were also produced in this region; prestigious portable art took the form of carved marine shells, obsidian artifacts, and pottery designs that—like the earthworks—demonstrated an exchange of ideas with the societies of the Southeast. A shift toward larger-scale architecture took place after 1000, when large lodges, walls, and ditches became characteristic of large agricultural settlements, which flourished into the fifteenth century.

American Southwest

The Hohokam (750–1450)

Although the roots of urbanism in the Southwest date back to about 1000 B.C.E. and agriculture far earlier—the Hohokam culture provides one of the most famous, and best-defined examples of Southwest art and architecture for the 1,000-year period between 400 and 1400. From the earliest settlements around 700 to the general abandonment of their sites by 1450, the Hohokam imported a variety of goods from outside the Southwest, including copper bells from Mesoamérica and shell from the Pacific Coast. They were skilled at working this exotic shell, as well as local clay, into a variety of figurines and etched ornaments with human and animal motifs. Unlike the Southeast, however, exotic artifacts do not appear to have been restricted to elites and were generally ceremonially used. The contacts that the Hohokam had with other areas of the Pre-Columbian world resulted in some surprising architecture: In addition to the characteristic settlement pattern of adobe platforms and mounds surrounding central plazas, the Hohokam appear to have imported the **ballgame**—and, correspondingly, ball courts—from Mesoamérica. Round, semisubterranean ball courts are hallmarks of early Hohokam culture, from about 700 to 1150, with the last falling into disuse about 100 years later. From this point, Hohokam society becomes somewhat more hierarchical, a factor that translates into larger and more centralized architecture until the demise of the Hohokam settlements around 1450.

Ancestral Pueblo (750–1450)

The peoples collectively termed "Ancestral Puebloan" comprise several distinct cultures and eras on the Colorado Plateau, although the majority are linked by, among other characteristics, a distinctive style of art and architecture. By 400 C.E., pottery and small settlements had become widespread in this portion of the Southwest; this led to the development of the first major villages here by 750 and the birth of what is called the "Pueblo I" (750–950) period. One of the hallmarks of this period is the spread of a now-familiar art style on pottery consisting of white- and black-painted geometric designs. Swirls and stepped designs were also common, as were regional variations in style. Pueblo II (950–1150) saw further cultural change in the region, most notably the rise and fall of what is called the "Chaco Phenomenon": This was the sudden development of masonry architecture and huge settlements in **Chaco Canyon**, including four-story buildings containing several hundred rooms at sites like

Pueblo Bonito. Portable art in this era took the form of turquoise beads and pendants, ceramic vessels, and wooden objects. By 1150, the production of these objects in Chaco Canyon had all but ceased, and the center of Ancestral Puebloan society had moved northwards; Pueblo III (1150–1300) saw the continuation of Southwest ceramic styles and the development of the cliff-dwelling architecture for which this region is so famous today.

By Pueblo IV (1300–1500), settlements had once again moved to the areas around the Rio Grande and Little Colorado rivers. Architecturally, they were much larger than earlier settlements, with individual pueblos ranging from several hundred to over a thousand rooms. Artistically, the Pueblo IV peoples used more sophisticated pottery techniques than their ancestors, with lead glaze and polychrome vessel technology becoming ever more important. Black-and-white pottery gave way to multicolored geometric designs with religious and agricultural associations, the descendents of which can be seen today in pottery from the Southwest. Although Pueblo IV was a golden era for ceramic art, this period saw a gradual decline in population and the migration of Plains and other groups into the area. Thus this art style, called "Salado polychrome," may have masked greater social problems for the Ancestral Puebloan peoples that would have clearly been evident in 1400.

Pacific Coast and Arctic

Societies of the Pacific Coast are often associated with a specific art style including painted totem poles and other large, carved wooden objects. However, it is today unclear whether this specific style predates 1700, when metal tools were first introduced into the region. What is clear is that peoples of the Pacific Northwest between 400 and 1400 had a rich tradition of woodcarving and wooden architecture, particularly in the form of plank houses set in rows upon the shorelines. Stone lip and cheek plugs appear to have been common body decorations throughout this period of history, as well as small portable objects of copper, obsidian, jade, shell, and even iron. The discovery of the famous site of Ozette (dating to c. 1400–1500), Washington, with its well-preserved wooden tools, bowls, boxes, and clubs, as well as basketry, indicates the degree to which poor preservation has played a role in history of art in this region.

Much of the art of the Arctic is characteristically functional as well as aesthetically pleasing. Stretching in a band from Alaska to Greenland, the Arctic and sub-Arctic peoples of the Americas are unsurprisingly varied in art styles, and were subject to a variety of influences from their southern neighbors. Two of the dominant cultures of the Arctic between 400 and 1000 were the **Dorset** and **Thule**. The Dorset, who were dominant in the Arctic between 500 B.C.E. and 1000 C.E., created beautiful harpoons, needles, and figurines of walrus ivory, antler, and bone; their houses were of snow blocks, stone, or bone depending upon the region. The Thule, who became dominant after 1000, were proficient whale hunters. This had a corresponding effect on their art and architecture, which included whale bone as an artistic medium and a household building block. By way of Greenland, both cultures came into contact with the Norse in their brief foray into the Americas around 1000; art from this period includes carvings of Norse as well as Norse artifacts of wood and iron at Dorset and Thule sites. The Norse had no lasting effect on either of these peoples, however; life would change dramatically, however, with the advent of European exploration in the sixteenth century.

Mesoamérica

The area known as Mesoamérica, as defined in the Historical Overview, comprises a cultural and geographic region extending from what is today southern Mexico (roughly the state of Jalisco, Mexico) to northwestern Honduras. In addition to several social and political traits common to this region in Pre-Columbian times, Mesoamérica was characterized by similarities in architecture and art. Nearly all of the most powerful civilizations—including but not limited to Teotihuacáno, Classic Maya, Toltec, and Aztec—produced stepped pyramids decorated in painted plaster (traditionally red or a combination of colors), had the corbelled vault or false arch, erected large stone monuments bearing the portraits and deeds of rulers. Most created specialized buildings such as palaces, sweat baths, and ball courts as well (*see* "Society" section).

Portable art often took the forms of clay figurines and decorated ceramic vessels as well as objects composed of shell, feathers, bone, wood, and stone. Perhaps the most valuable portable object in Mesoamérica, one that could be found only around the Motagua River Valley in Honduras, was jade. Prized greater than any other substance, jade was the material most associated with high political or religious office in all Mesoamérican societies; it was so prized that similar greenstones, such as serpentine or other imitations, were often used as substitutes when jade was unavailable or unattainable. Carved into figurines, ear-flares (a type of plug earring), pendants, plaques, beads, flowers, and even animals, jade was first among several highly prized portable goods used in Mesoamérican art and ritual. Others included feathers from prized birds like the quetzal and macaw, Spondylus (spiny oyster) shells from the coast, and obsidian (volcanic glass) from the mountainous highlands of Mesoamérica.

The Teotihuacános (100 B.C.E. to 600 C.E.)

Having prized feathers, jade, and obsidian in abundance, it is no wonder that the indigenous peoples of Guatemala had drawn the attention of outsiders. The most powerful state at the beginning of the fifth century was, and had been since the first century C.E., **Teotihuacán** (the people who settled in this city are known to archaeologists as Teotihuacános). This single megalopolis in Central Mexico had a great impact on Mesoamérican civilization as well as art. Through a program of invasion and aggressive cultural domination, it had spread its influence to the tropical and highland regions of Guatemala (*see* "Society" section) by 400 C.E.; the influence was not only social and political but also artistic. A militaristic art style born of this domination, characterized by pictorial representations of gods, uniforms, and even weapons, would be felt well after its collapse around 600. In fact, we find elements of this Teotihuacán style in Mesoamérica stretching all the way to 1400.

What was this art style like? The site of Teotihuacán had a rich artistic tradition as represented by mural painting and portable stonework, particularly with regard to life-sized stone burial masks. Like several Mesoamérican peoples, the Teotihuacános constructed a city filled not only with low-lying domestic buildings but also magnificent temples, stepped pyramids, and murals dedicated to their deities (including an enigmatic "Goddess" figure). Painted in a variety of colors and adorned with sculptures of deities, these pyramids are some of the most spectacular examples of Pre-Columbian architecture; their form is called the "talud-tablero" style, where a succession of slanting walls are interrupted by flat platforms. The most noteworthy example of this architectural style, the Pyramid of the Sun, was constructed in tiers of adobe, soil, and rubble faced with smooth stone. At 70 meters in height and containing approximately 1,000,000 cubic meters of rubble fill, it was—until late in the Industrial Revolution—the largest structure in the New World. The **talud-tablero** architectural style was frequently replicated at sites that Teotihuacán conquered or came into contact with; it was also occasionally imitated by peoples who held the Teotihuacános and their civilization in awe.

The Maya (Classic [250–909] and Postclassic [909–1697] Periods)

However, much "Teotihuacán style" art comes to us not from Teotihuacán itself, but from the places and peoples it conquered or came into contact with. As mentioned in the "Historical Overview," above, in 378 C.E. the Teotihuacános had swept into the tropical lowlands of Guatemala and established new dynasties at sites originally dominated by the Lowland or Classic Maya (250–909), a people with local roots stretching far back into what is today called the "Preclassic Period" (2000 B.C.E. to 250 C.E.). Although ethnically, we know that these Maya quickly absorbed their would-be conquerors through intermarriage, culturally the impact of Teotihuacán remained quite strong. In their art, Classic Maya rulers within their numerous city-states sought to emulate the dress and overwhelmingly militaristic appearance of the Teotihuacános, to the point where "Teotihuacán style" art became synonymous with the art of a strong, powerful, legitimate Maya ruler. As a result, talud-tablero architecture was popular in the fifth century C.E., alongside more traditional stepped forms of construction.

Despite a rich artistic tradition in nearly all media, from carved bone and jade to ceramics bearing historical as well as mythological tales and images, the best-known feature of Maya art is perhaps its monumental sculpture. Usually taking the form of square or circular altars paired with large stone monoliths called "stelae," the Maya sculptural tradition has been lauded as one of the great cultural achievements of Pre-Columbian Latin America (*see* **Stela**). Although not the first civilization to produce similar monuments in Mesoamérica (the earliest stelae date from the Preclassic period), the Classic Maya took depictions of the human form as well as three-dimensional sculpture to their height between 250 and 850.

Apart from visual depictions of rulers, daily life in the royal court, religious ceremonies, and warfare, Classic Maya monuments often bear hieroglyphic inscriptions. Although the Maya probably did not invent written language on their own, borrowing concepts, style, and imagery from earlier peoples such as the Olmecs or geographic neighbors such as the Zapotecs of the Valley of Oaxaca (500 B.C.E. to 700 C.E.), they did create the most elaborate and sophisticated writing system the Pre-Columbian world would ever see. The writing system, designed as means of conveying information as well as an art form, was well-developed by the time the Teotihuacános "arrived" in Mesoamérica. So too was the general format of the stela and the altar, which usually display a central figure—a semidivine ruler or *k'uhul ajaw* "holy lord"—as well as subordinates or war captives. Any texts would either surround these figures or be placed on stelae sides and backs.

Tikal Stela 31, recording the victory of Teotihuacános over the native Maya king, is an example of the fusion of Teotihuacáno and Maya elements. Framing the Maya hieroglyphic inscriptions are warriors dressed in the typical style of Teotihuacán warriors from Central Mexico: They wear scaled, feathered helmets, carry spear-throwers (otherwise known as **atlatls**) and use square shields bearing the image of a god with "goggle-eyes" known to us as **Tlaloc**, a rain-fertility deity worshipped in many parts of Mesoamérica. We find this basic dress, carved into stone monuments or painted on ceramics and other media, persisting on monuments throughout the Maya lowlands well into the eighth century C.E. despite the collapse of Teotihuacán itself in 600.

As mentioned in the Historical Overview, Classic Maya civilization not only survived the Teotihuacán invasion but also thrived for over 600 years. During this time, stelae and other stone monuments were erected to coincide with significant astronomical, calendrical, or historical dates. Due to the efforts of countless scholars, approximately 80 percent of all of the Maya hieroglyphics, or glyphs, can now be read. Accessions, deaths, anniversaries of conquests, and even birthdays were recorded and set within a visual program on Classic Maya monuments. Several different calendars set to the solar year, lunar year, or other astronomical cycles were also kept. Among these was a Long Count or tally of the days elapsed since the creation of the Maya, believed to have occurred in the year 3114 B.C.E. (*see* **Mesoamérican Calendar**). We now know that these dates framed a text fully capable of recording names, actions, places, and other events. Each glyph was composed of several parts, some more pictorial than others but standing for words and sounds in the Maya language. One has only to look at the Maya inscriptions to see the artistry and technical skill required to produce them in stone. They were meant to be artistically complex, for they were created by and for a small elite population at each site. Rulers wanted their monuments—and the writing on them—to impress potential rivals and neighbors visiting from other sites. At the same, they wanted to restrict the knowledge and information conveyed by their political artwork to a small elite class within their cities. Mass literacy was not a priority, a condition similar to that existing in medieval Europe in the first millennium C.E.

The subject matter found on Maya monuments was not, of course, restricted to stelae or altars. Decorated ceramic vessels, such as drinking bowls (for chocolate) or serving dishes, could—in addition to patterns—bear hieroglyphics or even scenes from Classic Maya mythology and history. The most elaborate of these, termed "**codex**-style" vessels, bore creatures and figures that would, over the next 1,000 years, continue to be found in Maya creation stories and historical narratives. In addition to ceramics, nearly every possible form of media was used for artistic expression among the Classic Maya. One of the most popular forms, particularly in the final century before the Maya collapse in the ninth and tenth centuries C.E., was that of mural painting: The scenes of battle, torture, and human sacrifice on the murals of Bonampak are among the most famous paintings in the Pre-Columbian world. Thematically, most of the Late Classic (600–909) murals deal with war as a central theme, a condition paralleled by similar grisly scenes on stelae from this time period. In spite of the increased warfare and elite competition characteristic of the Late Classic, however, it is clear that many of the finest examples of Maya art come from this darker era of lowland history.

Not surprisingly, several of these works — including the Bonampak murals — were never finished. As the Classic Maya sites were abandoned and left to the forest, other Postclassic (909–1697) Maya centers grew and changed in what is today highland Guatemala and northern Yucatán, Mexico; they demonstrate increased social, political, religious, and artistic interaction with other parts of Mesoamérica, particularly with Central Mexico. Sites like **Chichén Itzá**, Yucatán (1000–1200), with its stepped pyramids, ball courts, and *chacmools* (reclining figures designed for ritual offerings), continued the trajectory of Maya art and civilization, albeit in a more cosmopolitan way. But the focus on the semidivine *k'uhul ajaw* was broken, and no more stelae were to be erected. Powerful civilizations and correspondingly foreign art styles were to make their way into the Maya area from other locations: The Toltecs, and subsequently the Aztecs, were to leave an indelible mark on Mesoamérica over the next 500 years.

The Toltecs (950–1170) and the Aztecs (1345–1521)

The two major civilizations that followed in the highlands of Central Mexico, the Toltecs (950–1170) and the Aztecs (1345–1521), were among the most powerful and centrally organized states Latin America had ever seen. Both descended from northwest Mexico upon the peoples of southern Mesoamérica and embarked upon waves of conquest, and both blended elements of their own culture with those of subject peoples; in particular, native gods such as Tlaloc and **Quetzalcoatl** joined a pantheon of "foreign" deities in Toltec and Aztec art. The Toltecs, for their part, appear to have taken the preexisting practice of human sacrifice in Mesoamérica to new extremes as well as played a role in the hybridization of Mexican and Maya culture in northern Yucatán, particularly at the site of Chichén Itzá. Art from this period thus reflects these changes, with low-relief carvings and stylized representations of gods, captives, and warriors — arranged in columns — the dominant attributes at the Toltec capitol of **Tula** and the Toltec-Maya city of Chichén Itzá. From the founding of Tula in 950 to its destruction by *Chichimecs* (a Nahuatl word for "barbarians") in 1170, however, the era of Toltec dominance was relatively short-lived. The "idea" of Toltec art, however, survived until the Conquest.

The major reason why Toltec art was and continues to be well known in Mesoamérica is because the Aztecs, one of several Chichimec populations that moved into Central Mexico around 1345, popularized — and likely overrepresented — their accomplishments. According to the Aztecs, the Toltecs had been proficient feather workers, lapidaries, and metal smiths. They had perfected mining, painting, agriculture, and textile production and had even invented medicine. For the Aztecs, "the true artist works like a true Toltec" and "the good painter is a Toltec, he creates with red and black ink." Being foreigners surrounded by preexisting, well-established subject peoples, the Aztecs felt the need to identify themselves with the "glorious" Toltec past: They saw themselves as continuing an ancient, well-established (yet ultimately foreign) tradition in southern Mesoamérica. All good art was "Toltec" art.

In reality, the various peoples who made up the Aztec empire, particularly the Mixtecs of Oaxaca, surpassed the artistic accomplishments of the Toltecs, much as the Aztecs themselves exceeded the Toltecs in social, political, and economic complexity.

In terms of monumental art and architecture, Aztec artists excelled in the construction of massive, stepped pyramids and the carving of statues dedicated to gods such as Huitzilopochtli, Tlaloc, and Quetzalcoatl. Large "public" art designed around a militaristic state ideology, particularly with respect to the taking and sacrifice of captives on a scale unequalled in the Americas, was reflected in stucco, paint, and stone throughout the empire. Its tribute-based economy saw a constant flow of gold, cotton, turquoise, and feathers—as well as finished goods—into its primary cities. Some of the most famous, portable Aztec art was actually designed as tribute: The Mixtecs of Oaxaca, for example, produced polychrome pottery and were experts in the production of textiles, gold jewelry, and objects of jade, onyx, shell, and stone. When the Spanish brought the Aztec empire to an abrupt end in 1521, production of these goods largely ceased, and new art forms—born of a blend of Spanish and Pre-Hispanic cultures—made their way into the Mesoamérican world.

Lower Central America and the Andes

Between 400 and 1400, art in Lower Central America, also called the "Intermediate Area," took the form of portable objects designed for display, trade, and grave offerings. Although the peoples of this region did not, for the most part, engage in the production of stone sculpture or massive architecture as compared to their northern and southern neighbors, metalworking—a limited practice in Mesoamérica until 900—was a major art form. Elaborate status objects, particularly gold figurines and plaques, were a major component of burials at sites such as **Rivas** (900–1300), a Chiriquí site on the Pacific Coast of Costa Rica. Unfortunately, the use of gold and other precious metals within Pre-Columbian chiefdoms in Nicaragua, Costa Rica, Panama, and Colombia had a direct impact not only on the excesses of Spanish colonization, but also on the integrity of local archaeological sites as well: Much of the art of this region can now be found only on the black market and in private collections.

The technology used to produce these gold objects was, by 400, quite ancient and of Andean origin. The working of gold, silver, and copper—and the combination of these into dazzling alloys—had begun during a period known as the Early Horizon (400–200 B.C.E.); prefabricated sheets of gold and other alloys were being shaped into three-dimensional art in places such as Chavín de Huantar long before the birth of the first empires of the Americas. From 400 to 1400, the Andes witnessed the rise and/or fall of several major civilizations—including the **Moche**, Nasca, **Tiwanaku**, and **Chimor**—as well as the foundation of the capital of that most famous Andean civilization, the Inca, in 1300. Architecturally, all of these civilizations produced massive temple-pyramids, palaces, or other public works. Artistically, each was influenced by preceding civilizations and took several common forms: polychrome painted ceramics, multicolored textiles, and a dazzling array of metal goods. Smiths mastered the techniques of gilding and making alloys and were even able to cast gold using molds as well as a technique called the "lost-wax" method. Perhaps the most famous alloy in use within the Andes was known as *tumbaga* and was an alloy of gold and copper.

Moche (200–600 C.E.) and Nazca (200 B.C.E.–650 C.E.)

The Moche culture of northern Peru produced one of the most well known art styles in the Pre-Columbian world. Like the Classic Maya and several other peoples of Mesoamérica, art in the Moche world was in the hands of the elite;

by 400 this style was well developed and had taken form in the painted ceramics and stuccoed temple-pyramids of sites such as Moche and Sipán along the north coast of Peru. Supernatural beings, human-supernatural composites, warriors, rulers, and captives feature prominently on spouted, globular bottles.

Thematically, the scenes on these ceramics deal with the taking of war captives, their nude humiliation, and their ritual sacrifice. Moche ceramics are famous for their graphic depiction of this latter practice, including scenes of throat cutting, blood collecting, and ritualized dismemberment in a motif commonly known as the "Presentation Theme." This blood sacrifice was, despite its humiliating aspects, considered to be an honorable death and commemorated as such in Moche art.

The graphic aspects of this art style played out on Moche temple-pyramids, which were designed as spaces for similar public rituals. Large earthen temples such as the *Huaca del Sol* (Temple of the Sun) and *Huaca de la Luna* (Temple of the Moon) at the site of Moche were, on one level, mortuary complexes where the Moche elites buried their dead; on the other, they were vibrantly stuccoed and painted buildings that were the scenes of elite display as well as human sacrifice. Mural paintings and stucco friezes from the Moche area display spider-like supernatural creatures, parades of war captives, and images of the Moche rulers.

Unlike the realistic portrayals of humans and graphic depictions of violence, the art of the Nazca, a people who existed on the south Coast of Peru at approximately the same time as the Moche, is relatively abstract. For the most part, Nazca architecture was modest by comparison, consisting mainly of plazas and low-lying platforms punctuated by small mounds; the one exception occurs at the site of Cuachi, where a temple-pyramid analogous to others found in the Andes has recently come to light. Portable art in the Nazca area takes the form of painted ceramic vessels and rich textiles preserved by the hot, dry climate; images of plants, animals, people, and supernatural creatures are commonplace on these media but are rarely shown in any kind of scene or narrative like those featured in Moche art. Perhaps the most famous Nazca art, however, is not portable: The so-called **Nazca lines** or geoglyphs are lines and figures created in the desert plains by removing darker surface rocks to expose a lighter layer of rock beneath. There are over 600 miles of lines and upwards of three-hundred figures of animals, plants, humans, and geometric designs. Why these were initially created, other than for aesthetic purposes, remains a mystery.

Tiwanaku (650–1000), Chimor (1000–1476), and the Birth of the Inca (1300–1532)

Tiwanaku was one of the first great empires of the Andes and based along the Bolivian shores of Lake Titicaca. One of its distinguishing features, particularly with regard to its northern rival, **Wari**, was its lavish use of monumental stone architecture, well-cut masonry, and large stelae and lintels bearing the portraits of rulers or deities. Its capital of the same name bears the largest platform mound in the southern Andes, with a sunken ceremonial court, stone gates, and stelae reminiscent of similar arrangements in Classic (250–850) and Postclassic (850–1500) Mesoamérica. The most lavish gateway at Tiwanaku is known as the Gateway of the Sun and bears a portrait of a ray-headed deity holding two ceremonial scepters. This deity, known as the **Staff God**, appears at Chavín de Huantar by the third century B.C.E., indicating a very old—if not unchanged—religious tradition in the Andes.

These ties with the past are represented in the art and architecture of the last great civilizations of the Andes, Chimor, and Inca. Arising from the ashes of Moche civilization around 900, Chimor civilization was based at the metropolis of Chan Chan in the Moche Valley, Peru; by 1450 Chimor controlled over 600 miles of the Pacific coast and ranged from southern Ecuador to the middle of Peru. Although known primarily for their political exploits as well as their defeat by and subsequent incorporation into the Inca empire in 1476, the Chimor were also skilled weavers, architects, and metal smiths, creating mud-brick cities with royal palaces, temples, warehouses, and storehouses. Textiles, ceramics, and even wood carvings depict these centers and other aspects of elite life in the years preceding the Incan conquest. Some of the best-preserved art by the Chimor is found in the walls of elite house compounds: One adobe frieze shows fish, aquatic birds, mythical creatures, and other watery elements indicating a local emphasis on the resources of the sea. Such was the prelude to the growth and development of the largest empire of the Americas, the Inca Empire, whose art and architecture would incorporate the themes and motifs of these earlier civilizations. But in 1400, the Inca were simply one of many groups vying for power in what is today Peru, and their art was largely indistinguishable from that of Chimor.

Amazonia and the Caribbean

As related in the Historical Context, Amazonia has long been relegated to the backwaters of archaeology; as a result, its societies and the art they produced are only beginning to be recognized and analyzed in a systematic way. Although it is a vast region, ceramic art from Amazonia is remarkably uniform, with only a few basic ceramic styles dominating the entire region; this is testament to the contacts and ties different groups had with one another. Other art from this vast area is more regionalized and includes objects of shell, semi-precious stones, and metal.

By 400, densely populated settlements had begun to appear along many of the chief rivers in Amazonia. Marajó Island, in the Amazon estuary, is perhaps the best-known of these, with the earliest expression of the Amazonian Poly-chrome Tradition, a pottery style associated with burial urns and characterized by painted and/or modeled anthropomorphic and geometric designs. Another pottery style, Konduri, was popular between 400 and 1400, and associated with animal forms and modeled designs; it was largely associated with peoples between the Orinoco and Amazon rivers. Architecturally, the Amazonian settlements between 400 and 1400 were associated with earthen mounds (and some stone works), platforms, and plazas; the largest sites, such as Santarem, on the Tapajós River, appear to have been organized as urban centers in some ways similar to Cahokia or Chimor.

Likewise, some similarities can be seen between the art and architecture of the Caribbean, with whom peoples of coastal Amazonia share common ancestry, and other societies of the Americas. Between 400 and 1400, the Caribbean was home to—among other groups—various Arawak-speaking peoples. Arawak (Taino) sites such as Caguana and En bas Saline have yielded evidence of plazas, public architecture, and even ball courts, suggesting that the world before 1400—including the artistic one—was interconnected as part of a greater world system.

Further Reading

Ames, K., and H. Maschner. *Peoples of the Northwest Coast: Their Archaeology and Prehistory.* London: Thames and Hudson, Ltd., 1999.

Bayman, J. "The Hohokam of Southwest North America." *Journal of World Prehistory* 15 (2001): 257–311.

Carmack, Robert M., and Gary Gossen. *The Legacy of Mesoamerica: History and Culture of a Native American Civilization.* 2nd ed. Upper Saddle River, NJ: Prentice Hall, 2006.

Crown, Patricia. *Ceramics and Ideology: Salado Polychrome Pottery.* Albuquerque: University of New Mexico Press, 1994.

Demarest, Arthur. *The Ancient Maya. The Rise and Fall of a Rainforest Civilization.* Cambridge, UK: Cambridge University Press, 2004.

Fagan, Brian. *Ancient North America.* London: Thames and Hudson, 1991.

Heckenberger, Michael. "Rethinking the Arawakan Diaspora: Hierarchy, Regionality, and the Amazonian Formative." In J. Hill and F. Santos-Granero, eds. *Comparative Arawakan Histories: Rethinking Culture Area and Language Group in Amazonia.* Urbana: University of Illinois Press, 2002, pp. 99–121.

Hosler, Dorothy. *The Sounds and Colors of Power: The Sacred Metallurgical Technology of Ancient West Mexico.* Cambridge, MA: MIT Press, 1994.

Knight, V.J., Jr., J.A. Brown, and G.E. Lankford. "On the Subject Matter of Southeastern Ceremonial Complex Art." *Southeastern Archaeology* 20 (2001): 129–141.

Martin, Simon, and Nikolai Grube. *Chronicle of the Maya Kings and Queens.* London: Thames and Hudson, Ltd., 2000.

Moseley, Michael E. *The Incas and Their Ancestors: the Archaeology of Peru.* 2nd ed. London: Thames and Hudson, Ltd., 2001.

Roosevelt, Anne. *Moundbuilders of the Amazon: Geophysical Archaeology on Marajo Island, Brazil.* New York: Academic Press, 1991.

Scarre, Chris, ed. *The Human Past: World Prehistory and the Development of Human Societies.* London: Thames and Hudson, Ltd., 2005.

Silverman, H. *Cahuachi in the Ancient Nasca World.* Iowa City: University of Iowa Press, 1991.

Smith, Michael E. *The Aztecs.* Oxford, UK: Wiley-Blackwell, 2003.

Vivian, R. *The Chacoan Prehistory of the San Juan Basin.* San Diego, CA: Academic Press, 1990.

Wilcox, David. "The Mesoamerican Ballgame in the American Southwest." In V. Scarborough and D. Wilcox, eds. *The Mesoamerican Ballgame.* Tucson: University of Arizona Press, 1991, pp. 101–128.

5. SOCIETY

One cannot draw a general picture for the different societies of the Americas between 400 and 1400. The sheer variety of societal types is staggering: North America and South America were characterized by hunter-gatherers, societies ruled by chiefs (chiefdoms), city-states, and even empires during this time period. All regions of the Americas had had two or more of these types at once, with the lone exception being societies of the far north such as the **Dorset** or the **Thule**. Some parts of the Americas were clearly more urban than others, however, with the densest populations before the period of European contact being in Mesoamérica and the Andes. In these regions, hunter-gatherers had all but disappeared by 1400. Both had been dominated by succession of empires and city-states, with those of the Aztecs and the Incas being the last and the most famous.

Eastern Woodlands and the Great Plains

Prior to 400, the Eastern Woodlands and Great Plains had been home to an array of groups living in seasonal as well as semipermanent—though isolated and dispersed—camps and settlements. Engaging in mound-building and trading with far-flung peoples in places such as the Gulf Coast or the Great Lakes, groups in this region were relying more and more upon farmed cultigens as their populations increased. The Late Woodland Period (400–1000) saw the growth of permanent villages and, particularly toward its end, the development of chiefdoms and densely populated centers. As related in other sections, however, these transitions were accompanied by the growth of communal tensions that often became violent conflicts. Warfare throughout this region was accompanied, not surprisingly, by a decline in mound-building and long-distance trade by 400 that would last until the end of the first millennium.

Early Late Woodland settlements were characterized by several houses circling centralized open areas; these shared spaces, oftentimes filled with posts or large buildings, are similar to the plaza arrangements common in later societies of the Americas, including the Mississippians and most Mesoamérican civilizations. These were not permanent villages, however: Most farms were occupied for about 8 to 10 years by twenty to thirty individuals. Exceptions to this general rule—as well as the resurgence of mound-building—become more and more common between 800 and 1000, however. The precocious village of **Toltec**, Arkansas, consisting of over 100 acres of mounds, plazas, and ditches, was a noteworthy example and one of the first chiefdoms in the Eastern Woodlands. Dominant kin groups, clearly defined leaders, and buildings serving community/governmental needs were hallmarks of this (or any) chiefdom.

By the Mississippian Period (1000–1500), the Eastern Woodlands and Great Plains were dominated by such chiefdoms. The dominant ones were at the center of a tiered settlement hierarchy, for example, they were socioeconomically orbited by several subordinate villages and isolated semipermanent settlements (*see* "Economy" section). Most powerful polities, centered at villages such as **Moundville**, Alabama, were characterized by (1) scores of earthen mounds topped by wooden buildings; (2) the elite desire for locally and non-locally made precious or manufactured goods, such as marine shell or copper items; (3) evidence of a trade network stretching from the Rocky Mountains and Great Lakes to the Gulf Coast of Mexico; (4) ancestral veneration in the form of elite interments within earthen mounds; (5) evidence of participation in a series of religious practices collectively known as the **Southern Cult** or Southeastern Ceremonial Complex (*see* "The Arts" and "Religion" sections); (6) intensive maize cultivation, accompanied by squash, beans, or other crops; and (7) populations numbering from a few to several thousand people. Most commoners lived in plaza-centered building arrangements and were heavily dependent on maize and the other crops listed above; they also relied on domesticated animals such as turkeys as well as wild plant and animal resources.

Common residences were situated on the outskirts of mounds, which supported wooden houses for chiefs and close kin, community buildings, or charnel houses. The prominence and elevation of these mounds, in addition to the labor needed to produce them, was a constant reminder of elite power in these chiefdoms. Some have argued that the largest Mississippian center, at **Cahokia**, Illinois, was so politically and economically centralized and distinct from its contemporaries as to constitute a state society; others have suggested that Cahokia, like the other Mississippian towns, was an usually powerful chiefdom.

In any event, the Mississippian polities in the Eastern Woodlands and the Great Plains were never politically unified and are, for scholarly purposes, divided into several different cultural spheres of interaction including but not limited to Oneota, Middle Mississippian, Fort Ancient, Caddoan Mississippian, Lower Mississippian, and South Appalachian Mississippian. Between the tenth and fifteenth centuries, dozens of powerful chiefdoms in these regions rose and fell. Political collapse, warfare, environmental degradation (natural and man-made), or a combination of the three are often blamed for the collapse of major centers—Cahokia, for example, was abandoned by 1400—although new ones usually took their place. Unfortunately, these three factors would be exacerbated by the beginning of the Little Ice Age (*see* "Historical Overview" and "Science and Technology" sections) in 1400, the rise of new forms of social organization (e.g., the rise of the **Iroquois** Confederacy) and waves of European diseases—followed by Europeans and, consequently, the collapse of Mississippian civilization—in the 1500s.

American Southwest and the Great Basin

Overall, the societal traditions in the Great Basin are those associated with egalitarian hunter-gatherers, although the short florescence of maize-based agricultural villages within the **Fremont** Culture (400–1300) may have seen greater social stratification. The collapse of Fremont around 1300 saw a return to hunting and gathering and the traditional lifestyle of the Great Basin. In comparison, the Southwest had seen agriculture for quite some time before 400—as early as 1000 B.C.E.—and small villages had been developing there well before 750 C.E. It was only after that time, however, that larger sociopolitical units began to develop in the Southwest, in part due to favorable climatic conditions and the creation of larger and more efficient irrigation networks. Such advances, however, did not lead to states as in some other parts of the Americas and do not appear to have led to marked social stratification.

The Hohokam (750–1450)

Much like their distant contemporaries in the Great Plains, the Preclassic (700–1150) and Classic (1150–1450) Hohokam were characterized by (1) trade in exotic materials, with evidence of a network stretching from the Pacific to Mesoamérica; (2) the creation of public, monumental architecture; (3) houses arranged around plazas and courtyards; (4) intensive cultivation of maize, beans, and squash, in addition to wild and domesticated plant/animal resources such as chenopodium or turkey; and (4) a shared religious tradition. Unlike the Mississippians, however, the Hohokam practiced cremation, created structures that were predominantly of wattle-and-daub or adobe, cultivated agave cactus, and consumed a significant array of native wild plants such as mesquite or amaranth.

Although irrigation had been practiced for over a millennium in Arizona (*see* "Science and Technology" section), the Preclassic Period was the first era to see the development of the first permanent villages in the Sonoran Desert. These villages depended upon seasonal flooding and ready access to easily diverted waters such as the Gila River. Houses at settlements like Snaketown, Arizona, surrounded plazas and communal spaces. These thatched, wattle-and-daub buildings in plazas were themselves arranged around even larger courtyards housing oval, semisubterranean structures. These were courts for a sport played—with significant variations—from Arizona to southern Mesoamérica known as the **ballgame**. As the Mesoamérican ballgame is of great antiquity, it is clear that contact between this region and the American Southwest is at the heart of the Hohokam ballgame; what is not clear is how much similarity there was—in terms of rules or ritual associations, for example—between the two ballgames.

The beginning of the Classic Period was a time of troubles. Major flooding and water-management issues seem to have led to the abandonment of isolated communities and the clustering of populations along the Gila and Salt rivers. This era also saw the decline of the ball courts and the rise of large, adobe platform mound compounds, many of which were associated with specific irrigation systems at Hohokam sites. Likewise, inhumation largely replaced cremation as the predominant form of mortuary behavior. Some scholars have argued that all of these changes represented the growth of chiefdoms among the Hohokam, in some ways similar to the burgeoning chiefdoms in the Southeast in the tenth and eleventh centuries. The evidence is far from clear, however. Certainly, some increased level of sociopolitical organization was necessary to deal with the environmental pressures of this era. Such organization was successful in allowing the Hohokam to thrive in this hostile environment until 1450, when agricultural problems, changes in climate, and/or human factors led to the widespread abandonment of the Hohokam settlements.

Ancestral Pueblo (750–1450)

Between 400 and 750 C.E., the Colorado Plateau saw an intensification of agriculture and the growth of small, dispersed farming settlements. The following era, termed "Pueblo I" (750–900), was characterized by the growth of permanent villages housing approximately one hundred to two hundred people apiece. Buildings in these villages were of wattle-and-daub manufacture and were occasionally plastered. They were often accompanied by pit houses and arranged around what is called a "great **kiva**," a communal circular structure that could be used for religious, political, or other aspects of public life. Life in these villages appears to have been relatively egalitarian, with little-to-no evidence of status differences in the archaeological record. From Pueblo I to Pueblo III, the primary means of subsistence for these groups was maize agriculture, supplemented by traditional domesticated staples such beans, squash, turkey, as well as a variety of wild resources.

The growth and collapse of villages was a relatively commonplace phenomenon during Pueblo I, possibly owing to fluctuations in climate as well as human factors. Such behavior continued during Pueblo II (900–1150), although the hallmark of this era was a bit of a departure: Populations moved from small settlements around **Chaco Canyon** to larger villages centered about "Great Houses," communal masonry buildings characterized by hundreds of rooms and multiple stories. Buildings up to four stories in height were supported by thousands of beams; the wood for Pueblo Bonito, the largest great house at over six hundred rooms, was imported from over 50 miles away in a colossal cooperative endeavor. This not only suggests a high degree of social organization but also begs an explanation, given the apparently sudden shift in the Puebloan way of life. Although the reasons for why the "Chaco phenomenon" occurred are in some dispute, most scholars believe that Chaco was the product of a religious movement. This view holds that Chaco became a pilgrimage center on the Colorado Plateau, with ritual activity focused in the kivas of the Great Houses. The movement of populations to Chaco may also have had a practical component: What once may have been a natural lake as well as arable land may have contributed to the clustering of people within the canyon.

Ancestral Puebloan society went through yet another dramatic shift during Pueblo III (1150–1300). For reasons that remain unclear, by the mid-twelfth century Chaco had largely been abandoned. New strategies for survival on the plateau were on the rise, as skirmishes between rival villages and population movements caused the settlement of new communities with different traditions. People not only moved to new Great Houses and Chaco-like settlements in New Mexico and Colorado but also to defensible areas guarding water sources, with agricultural settlements centered in the unlikeliest of areas: Several major defensive settlements were astride cliffs and noticeably lacked large kivas (these were replaced by small, household ones) or other public buildings characteristic of the "Chaco phenomenon." The most famous of the cliff dwellings, **Mesa Verde**, was a village consisting of over two-hundred rooms with multistoried buildings. Like others of its kind, it appears to have been created with conflict in mind: The small-scale skirmishes of the eleventh century had given way to endemic warfare by the twelfth century, necessitating the construction of villages that could withstand the attacks of their rivals.

A severe drought in the last decades of the thirteenth century, combined with the movement of foreign hunter-gatherers into the Colorado Plateau, seems to have led to the complete abandonment of the plateau village sites by 1300. Some of the people from these sites seem to have moved further south to preexisting communities along the Rio Grande and Little Colorado rivers, resulting not only in a population influx but major socioeconomic change. The villages that emerged from this troubled period were even larger than had previously existed, with the largest pueblos bearing between eight-hundred and eleven-hundred rooms. Chaco-like kivas and major public architecture reemerged during this era, known as Pueblo IV (1300–1542); another characteristic perhaps similar to Chaco was the presence of a unifying religious ideology, termed the "Southwest Cult" (*see* "Religion" section). Farming by means of dams, reservoirs and terraces—as opposed to irrigation—became the primary activity associated with agriculture, a situation that continued until the colonial period. Some have suggested that the labor needed to create such earthworks required, in turn, a chiefdom or similar institution, although the evidence for such social organization is far from clear.

In spite of the above considerations, Pueblo IV was not an idyllic time for the Ancestral Puebloans. Although the villages themselves were increasing in size and becoming ever more complex, the overall population in the Southwest was on the decline. Malnutrition and disease were on the rise, as were incursions by hunter-gatherers into agricultural lands. Initially, native hunter-gatherers had moved to occupy the areas vacated by the Ancestral Puebloans on the Colorado Plateau. By 1400, these groups were pressuring the margins of the Pueblo IV settlements; they were subsequently joined by immigrant hunter-gatherers from coastal Canada, the Great Basin, and the Great Plains. This human mosaic of agriculturalists and hunter-gatherers was to be a feature of life in the Southwest from the beginning of Pueblo IV to the colonial period.

Pacific Coast

Permanent villages and ranked societies all along the Pacific Coast of North America are of great antiquity; clear evidence of social inequality in coastal British Columbia, for example, dates to approximately 1800 B.C.E. Two regions were home to chiefdoms at the time of European contact: southern California and the Pacific Northwest. Unlike the maize agriculturalists of much of North America, the peoples of the Pacific Coast relied primarily on hunting, gathering, and fishing for subsistence; they are good examples of how complex societies can arise without intensive agriculture. Both employed seaworthy canoes and other fishing technologies to gain access to a wide variety of marine resources between 400 and 1400. In southern California, chiefdoms appear to have emerged by 1200 and seem to have followed on the heels of widespread intercommunity violence as well as food shortages. In the Pacific Northwest, by comparison, chiefdoms originated around 500 and were accompanied by endemic warfare. In fact, many of the cultural institutions encountered by Europeans in the eighteenth century were in place by this time, including plank houses on posts, long-distance exchange and consumption networks, cranial deformation, lip/cheek jewelry, and slavery. As in the American Southwest, population levels on the Pacific Coast were on the decline by 1400, although European contact and colonization was largely responsible for the demographic collapse of coastal societies between 1500 and 1900.

Artic and Subarctic

As noted in the "Science and Technology" section, below, Arctic peoples such as the Dorset and the Thule were largely reliant on hunting and fishing, with a heavy reliance on sea mammals such as seal, walruses and — in the case of the Thule — whales. The Dorset, who were predominant in the Arctic until 1100 or 1200, lived in small clusters of seasonal, snow-block houses. The Thule, who migrated eastwards from Alaska across much of Arctic Canada, had pushed the Dorset societies to extinction by 1200 largely because of technological advantages like the bow and arrow (*see* "Science and Technology" section); they created a variety of house types depending upon the construction materials available, with whale bones and sod among the most common building materials. The Thule were largely dependent upon whale hunting and the exploitation of other sea mammals but were so well-adapted to life in a variety of Arctic conditions that they witnessed the growth as well as subsequent collapse of European (Norse) settlements in Greenland between 1000 and 1400. Their descendents encountered the second wave of European exploration in the Arctic world around 1700.

Mesoamérica

As a culture area rather than a geographic region, the term *Mesoamérica* encompasses a set of beliefs, institutions, and practices common to most—if not all—Mesoamérican societies of the Pre-Columbian era. These include shamanism, awareness/use of writing, the use of a 260- and/or 365-day calendar, human sacrifice, esteem for jade and other green stones, monumental stone architecture, the Mesoamérican ballgame, and cranial deformation or other bodily modification. Other shared religious beliefs included the idea that the world had been created several times, the use of five cardinal directions associated with particular colors, beliefs in multiple or divisible souls, ideas about oppositional/complementary duality in the supernatural world, and reverence for a multiplicity of deities in particular associated with maize, death, and the sun.

Likewise, Mesoamérican societies were characterized by populous urban centers; in fact, almost no hunter-gatherers were present in Mesoamérica at the time of European contact. The origins of settled village life in Mesoamérica date back to approximately 1600 B.C.E., with the first major chiefdoms developing around 1200 B.C.E. with the rise of Olmec civilization. Between 400 and 1400 A.D., the four major areas of Mesoamérica (Central Mexico, Valley of Oaxaca, Gulf Coast, Maya Region) were occupied by several major civilizations, including Teotihuacános, Maya, Toltecs, and Aztecs. These were by no means the only complex societies in Mesoamérica: Rivals to the Aztecs, for example, included the Tarascan Empire of western Mexico and the long-lived Zapotec/Mixtec city-states of the Valley of Oaxaca, Mexico. Nevertheless, the impact of the societies mentioned below—in terms of their overall influence and the geographic extent of their political control—cannot be understated.

The Teotihuacános (100 B.C.E. to 600 C.E.)

Although its origins stretched back to approximately 100 B.C.E., by the year 400 C.E. the city-state of **Teotihuacán** had become the major player in the geopolitics of Mesoamérica. At its height, between 400 and 600 C.E., it was the sixth largest city in the world, with approximately one-hundred twenty-five thousand people. In size this city dwarfed anything that had previously existed in the hemisphere, with an urban population stretching over 8.5 square miles in dense, apartment-like compounds; much of the city was laid out according to a grid plan enviable even today. Prior to the fourth century, the Teotihuacán city-state had control over what is today the Basin of Mexico; shortly thereafter, its power expanded outwards to include over 9,500 square miles of territory in Central Mexico. In 378 C.E., moreover, Teotihuacán had invaded portions of the Maya lowlands, asserting its influence—either indirectly through client-kings or directly through conquest—in major Maya cities such as **Tikal**, Guatemala, and **Copan**, Honduras. By 400 C.E., Teotihuacán enclaves and satellite communities could be found at sites throughout central and southern Mesoamérica, from Kaminaljuyú (highland Guatemala) and Matacapan (Gulf Coast) to **Monte Albán** (Valley of Oaxaca), and Chunchucmil (northern Yucatán). Teotihuacán's cultural influence, from architecture and ideology to material goods, spread further still. In fact, few places in all of Mesoamérica would have not had some contact — however indirect — with the Central Mexican metropolis.

Teotihuacán society was industrious, mercantile, and above all else, cosmopolitan. In addition to the numerous apartment compounds housing peoples native to the Valley of Mexico, the city was characterized by several foreign enclaves: Different ethnic groups from the Valley of Oaxaca, the Gulf Coast, West Mexico, and even the Maya area appear to have been living in this precocious metropolis. Workshops of almost every kind were centered within these apartment compounds, where people manufactured tools, jewelry, ritual goods, and other items from ceramic, stone, obsidian, shell, wood, feathers, and other materials for local consumption as well as export.

Although a royal palace at Teotihuacán has yet to be clearly identified, it is clear that its governance was strongly centralized; like other Mesoamérican polities, Teotihuacán was likely graced by a set of administrative buildings as well as palatial accommodations for its rulership. Such considerations will likely become clearer with further excavations as well as developments in the interpretation of the Teotihuacáno writing system. Although this society was once believed to lack the written word, recent discoveries of painted murals and floors point to a system similar to that of later civilizations in the area, such as the Mixtecs or the Aztecs.

Nevertheless, archaeologists do have some information about the Teotihuacáno rulers and their behavior: A successful invasion by Teotihuacán forces into the southern Maya lowlands was recorded by the Classic Maya at several locations, including the major sites of Tikal and El Peru. A lord from Teotihuacán named Siyaj K'ahk' ("Fire is Born") appears to have captured the largest Maya site, Tikal, in 378 C.E. and installed his son Yax Nuun Ayiin I as king; further puppet or sympathetic rulers appear to have been installed at several other Maya sites. Additional rulers claiming to have been involved with or related to the Teotihuacán invaders subsequently made their appearance throughout the Maya lowlands, from Piedras Negras, Guatemala, in the west to Copan, Honduras, in the east. Some of these relationships were clearly fictive, but from the fifth century onwards — even past the fall of Teotihuacán in the seventh century — claims of special relationships with the Central Mexican metropolis were commonplace, attesting to the cultural influence of Teotihuacán on Maya society. In spite of this influence, however, Teotihuacá does not seem to have created a land empire in the traditional sense. Rather, it would seem as if the Teotihuacános engaged in colonialism, setting up colonies and client kingdoms in far-flung areas to create favorable economic relationships. How many of these relationships were *directly* controlled by the state of Teotihuacá itself is another matter; opportunistic or — equally likely — disenfranchised nobles and their followers cannot be ruled out from most situations in which "Teotihuacá" makes an appearance, including the aforementioned events at Tikal and El Peru.

The Maya (Classic [250–909] and Postclassic [909–1697] Periods)

In 400, the Maya area was culturally divided into three major regions: the Highlands, the Southern Lowlands, and the Northern Lowlands. None of these areas ever experienced political unification: City-states, chiefdoms, and loose confederations of cities were the rule in all three areas until the colonial period. The highland peoples, having experienced their major florescence from the first to the third centuries, had had a system of centralized, dynastic kingship that made use of the Long Count calendar (*see* "Science and Technology," section), carved hieroglyphic inscriptions, and historical portraits of rulers in urban, mountainous settings. By the third century, however, this centralized system had declined; the lords of the highland towns in 400 were but political shadows of their ancestors. Likewise, the "kings" of the Northern Maya Lowlands—and to a lesser extent, parts of modern-day Belize—do not appear to have been strong, centralizing figures in 400; the history of this region prior to the fifth century was dominated by chiefdoms and loosely organized kingdoms.

By comparison, the Southern Lowlands were characterized by numerous centralized dynasties during the Classic Period (250–909). Although the origins of these Maya kingdoms stretch back to the first century C.E., with urbanism beginning in the Maya area as early as 500 B.C.E., the third century C.E. is considered the starting point for "Classic Maya civilization." It was during the Classic Period that local Pre-Columbian populations reached their height, with extensive architectural projects and a widespread elaboration of a series of traits that were uniquely Maya and associated with Maya elites. These traits included sophisticated calendrical, mathematical, and astronomical systems, a hieroglyphic writing system, and a series of architectural innovations including the corbeled vault or "false arch." Networks of roads, temple complexes, hierarchical settlement patterns, sweat baths, and other innovations are also hallmarks of the period. Although Maya sites in the Highlands and northern Lowlands shared many of features discussed below with their neighbors, the Southern Lowlands saw the greatest elaboration of these traits and combined them with a hierarchical, clearly defined social system within city-states governed by kings who gradually assumed divine powers.

By 400, the Southern Lowlands had weathered the arrival of interlopers from the central Mexican metropolis of Teotihuacá, and although the effects of this "arrival" were to have repercussions for centuries, the basic model of society in the Southern Lowlands remained relatively unchanged. From approximately 250 to 600, Maya sociopolitical organization was dominated by an *ajaw* ("lord") whose duties ranged from the practicalities of governing a city-state to religious rites ensuring agricultural fertility as well as divine favor. The *ajaw* was likewise the ultimate authority in economic and diplomatic affairs, oftentimes forging (and breaking) alliances with other city-states in an ever-changing political landscape. Over time, kings seem to have gained even greater authority, relegating the mere title of *ajaw* to subordinate members of the royal family and taking on further names, such as *k'uhul ajaw* ("holy lord") or *k'inich* ("sun-faced") (an allusion to the Maya sun god). By the seventh century, a multiplicity of titles were firmly entrenched in the royal court, with the ruler clearly having become a divinity in his (or occasionally, her) own right, responsible for the maintaining the unique relationship between the city and its patron gods; it is about this time that we also see the greatest elaboration of ancestor "cults" within the royal line (*see* **Ancestor Veneration**). Together with the king and the royal family, other elites—including artisans and probably merchants—formed a complex web of social and political relationships that extended inside and between different Maya polities.

Such relationships were expressed in the production and distribution of several items restricted to elites, including worked objects of jade, feathers, ceramic, bone, shell, and paper. Literacy, which was restricted to Classic Maya nobles, was expressed through the production of large stone portraits and accompanying texts on monoliths, or stelae, as well as altars or other forms (*see* **Stela**). Other aspects of Maya society that were restricted to nobles included a host of royal dances, public rituals, and other pageantry. Two facets of life that spanned the royal and common spheres were sweat baths and the ritual ballgame. **Sweat baths** were stone buildings or, in the case of commoners, more modest structures similar to saunas; their use was probably tied to medicinal purposes (sweating out infirmities, for example), although in the royal context they also involved various drugs (hallucinogenic or otherwise) as well as sexual activity.

As for the ballgame, this was a sport played by two teams with a large rubber ball on a court (ball court); the rules and play of this game seem to have varied in time and space—indeed, most Mesoamérican cultures had versions of this game—but the Maya ballgame was much like a cross between modern-day basketball and volleyball, with body armor and padding reminiscent of American football. Attached to this game were cosmological themes, ritual conflicts, and perhaps economic activity in the form of betting. Royal ball courts were usually of stone, with clearly defined alleyways, while commoner ball courts were minimal affairs.

Commoners, not surprisingly, were in the majority in Maya polities and formed the backbone of an agricultural system supporting the ways of life listed above. Taxes in the form of tribute, labor, or military service appear to have been levied on this population. As a result, we might view many of the aspects of Classic Maya society we are familiar with—including soaring temples and vast public works—as a product of commoner labor. Common society was organized around spatially defined lineages: Platforms fronting a central plaza area formed a basic social unit that was replicated hundredfold in the hinterlands surrounding urban centers.

Although the number of subjects governed within a given Maya city-state could be quite large, between fifty thousand and one hundred thousand people, most Maya centers and their associated territories had populations of approximately ten thousand to twenty thousand people. During the Late Classic Period (600–909), following the fall of Teotihuacá, Maya society experienced its greatest political, artistic and social florescence: Some of the largest Maya centers, such as Tikal or **Calakmul**, headed networks of loosely confederated cities in feudal arrangements. Nevertheless, even Late Classic Maya societies were never strictly politically unified and relationships could—and did—change within the feudal structure.

As a result of this instability, warfare within Maya society was almost constant and involved war not only for territory but also for tribute, glory, and revenge. As a result, conflicts could be large and protracted, as in the well-documented wars between Calakmul, Tikal, and their associated allies, or more limited engagements; such skirmishes occasionally involved the targeted capture of prominent nobles. One of the ubiquitous aspects of Maya warfare involved the taking and humiliation of captives, oftentimes destined for sacrifice to one of the many gods in the Classic Maya pantheon. Elites—even the king—was not exempt from this fate, as attested in Classic Maya sources.

Maya society in the Southern Lowlands was beset by a number of stresses that seem to have increased over time. Endemic warfare, peasant revolts, environmental degradation, droughts, or other natural disasters, population increase, and growing numbers of petty elites within cities each strained the abilities of city-states to maintain the status quo. By the late eighth century, the institution of divine kingship started to fail. Several key sites, such as **Palenque**, Yaxchilan, and Piedras Negras, collapsed early and were largely abandoned between 800 and 850. Others, like Copan and Tikal, began a long process of decline. By the tenth century, the institution of divine kingship in the lowlands was no more, with the last carved hieroglyphic monument erected at the site of Tonina in 909. Elites and commoners, however, continued to thrive in places for a few hundred years more, although they too gradually dwindled in population until the majority of the Southern Lowlands was reclaimed by the forest. Although some shadows of Classic civilization survived here up to the Conquest, particularly around Lake Peten, Guatemala, the momentum of Maya society would shift decisively to the northern Lowlands and subsequently, after 1400, to the Maya Highlands, where a series of expansionist, highly organized states like the K'iche and K'ak'chiquel would make a final stand against the Spanish in the sixteenth and seventeenth centuries. Although the Classic Maya collapse in did involve population movements to the northern and southern regions, the dramatic social upheaval of the eighth to the tenth centuries—and all of the ills associated with it—did result in massive destruction and death for the once-urban civilization occupying the Southern Lowlands.

This political transition, having started in the eighth century, was firmly in place by the mid-late ninth century at places such as Uxmal, Kabah, Labna, and Sayil in the Puuc region of northwest Yucatán. Many of these polities seem to have actually benefited from the Classic Maya collapse. These polities and their successors in Yucatán retained many of the institutions and innovations of Classic society—including writing, monumental stone architecture, sweat baths, and ballgames—although in most cases the government seems to have revolved around weaker kings and elite councils rather than strong authoritarian rule. These small states seem to have briefly coalesced around Uxmal around 900, although by 1000 the Puuc centers met the same general fate as their Classic Period counterparts to the south. These Puuc collapses, in turn, benefited centers even further to the north: The years between 1000 and 1400 were dominated, in succession, by the city-states of **Chichén Itzá** and Mayapán.

Chichén Itzá, one of the largest cities in the Americas, dominated northern Yucatán between 900 and 1200; it was one of the primary economic centers in Mesoamérica at this time and may have been influenced by—if not politically dominated—the Toltecs, a rival civilization based in Central Mexico. In any event, it was also a major center for religious pilgrimage during and after its collapse in 1200: The name *Chichén Itzá* refers to the "well of the Itzá (a Maya group)," a huge water-filled sinkhole into which precious goods—and even human sacrifices—were ritually and habitually thrown. Mayapán , prominent from 1200 to 1440, likewise engaged many of the trappings of Classic Maya society without the institution of divine kingship, although in many ways it was a diminutive, lesser copy of Chichén Itzá. The ends at Chichén Itzá and Mayapán appear to have been violent, although a multiplicity of explanations abounds for precisely why and how their collapses occurred. Ultimately, Maya political organization and society would regroup into a series of competing, petty kingdoms—a situation that was still in place at the time of Spanish colonization.

The Toltecs (950–1170) and the Aztecs (1345–1521)

Much of what we know about Toltec society comes from later sources, particularly from the Aztecs: They believed that the Toltecs were a powerful expansionist empire whose people were not only skilled craftsmen but also the inventors of most of the technologies and practices of Mesoamérica. Quasi-historical figures, deities in the Aztec traditions, were said to have lived during the time of the Toltecs, including **Quetzalcoatl** and Tezcatlipoca (gods associated, among other things, with human creation and magic, respectively). The truth is somewhat more modest: Although the Toltecs did not invent Mesoamérica, they certainly had a small empire with far-flung trade relationships extending to northern Mexico and as far south as Central America. Based at **Tula** in Central Mexico, they dominated much of the Basin of Mexico and, much like the earlier Teotihuacános, were characterized by a cosmopolitan society that fused Central Mexican architectural characteristics with those from the Maya area and the Gulf Coast of Mexico. Tula alone may have housed a population of about sixty-thousand people, most of whom resided in adobe apartment compounds. Also like Teotihuacá, Tula employed a network of artisans and craftsmen manufacturing goods for local as well as foreign consumption; like most Mesoamérican cities, it was surrounded by an agrarian commoner class supporting the urban center.

Suffering a violent collapse at about the same time as Chichén Itzá, the Toltecs were supplanted by a network of competing city-states in Central Mexico. Many of the city-states that formed were actually founded by Nahuatl-speaking invaders from northwest Mexico. One of these invading groups, the Tepanecs of Atzcapotzalco, had just begun to forge an empire here in the 1300s when another set of Nahuatl speakers arrived in the Basin of Mexico: the Mexica. In 1325, the Tepanecs allowed the Mexica, a wandering, hunter-gatherer group, to settle on a swampy island in their territory. The city founded there, **Tenochtitlán**, was to become the basis for a Mexica-led empire—otherwise known as the Aztec empire—that overthrew the Tepanecs and eventually subjugated most of northern Mesoamérica. This rebellion was to begin in 1428, such that by the time of the Spanish arrival in Mesoamérica c. 1519, the Aztec empire would be the largest empire Mesoamérica had ever seen. But in the 1300s, Mexica society was undergoing an agrarian transformation, its people serving primarily as mercenaries for other, more powerful city-states. Much of what Aztec society would become famous for—large urban centers, mass human sacrifices, emperors, courts, laws, and philosophy—was only in its infancy at this time.

Lower Central America and the Andes

Moche (200–600 C.E.) and Nazca (200 B.C.E.–650 C.E.)

The **Moche** are credited with having produced the first state society in South America. Although the Moche were culturally unified behind a shared religious, artistic and sociopolitical system, they were territorially organized as city-states and thus somewhat comparable to the Maya. Sites such as Pampa Grande, **Sipán**, and Moche were ruled by sovereigns living on high atop palatial mud-brick pyramids. Other elites, as well as servants, often lived in lower tiers of these structures, although the bulk of the commoner Moche population lived in adobe compounds outside the city centers, oftentimes arranged to accommodate different family groups.

Although the majority of the population was agrarian, artisans and craft specialists played a major role in the supply of elite ceramics, fine arts, and utilitarian goods to various segments of the population. Extensive pottery workshops, as well as metalworking centers (copper, gold, silver) and textile "factories" found at Moche sites are testament not only to the specialization but also to the class differences in Moche society. The largest sites, moreover, seem to have made use of secondary administrative or ceremonial centers, indicating a rather large bureaucracy headed by individual Moche rulers.

Lacking a written language, the Moche nevertheless produced elite ceramics with elaborate pictographic designs that shed light on everyday life. Some of the most common themes are maritial and/or religious in nature; surprisingly, several events and even characters demonstrably tied to real occasions have been identified by archaeologists. For example, blood sacrifice, particularly those involving foreign prisoners of war or even dishonored Moche, is a common theme in Moche art that has been corroborated archaeologically: Archaeologists have found the remains of people dressed as sacrificial priests, victims bearing telltale wounds, and even objects traditionally associated with sacrifice in Moche burials. From the analysis of many painted Moche ceramics, it seems that blood sacrifice—particularly for the benefit of the gods and Moche society—was a necessary facet of life on the north coast of Peru.

Unlike the Moche, the Nazca of the south coast of Peru were not organized along state lines. The decentralized farming communities dotting this region were, however, situated around a pivotal ceremonial center, Cahuachi, which may have served as a place of pilgrimage for these agriculturalists. Declining in the seventh century, in part due to disastrous floods, droughts, and other consequences of El Niño weather patterns, the Moche and the Nazca orders would be replaced by other city-states until the empire building activities of Chimor and, subsequently, the Inca.

Tiwanaku (650–1000), Chimor (1000–1476), and the Birth of the Inca (1300–1532)

Tiwanaku and **Chimor**, Andean and coastal civilizations respectively, can be seen as antecedents of the Inca, who ultimately united the various peoples in parts of Ecuador, Peru, Chile, Bolivia, and Argentina under one political banner. Although environmentally and temporally separated, the two empires were remarkably similar in overall sociopolitical organization. Both societies employed tribute labor to produce vast cities and associated monuments; the capitals of both empires may have held between thirty thousand to forty thousand people each. Tiwanaku, ruling from its high-altitude (over 10,000 feet above sea level) capital of the same name near Lake Titicaca, was characterized by an elite dedicated to the construction of religious monuments and austere stone temple mounds and courts. The Tiwanaku elites were supported by a large outlying agrarian and pastoral population as well as far-flung colonies and client polities, which provided much-desired crops and goods unobtainable in the capital region. Chimor, a Pacific coastal empire, was characterized by similarly grandiose—but adobe—compounds, pyramids, and walls in its capital, Chan Chan: Buildings were typically arranged according to a grid plan, with the urban majority consisting of craft specialists as well as the ruling elite. The agrarian commoner communities, as in other parts of the Americas, lived well outside the city center. Tiwanaku and Chimor controlled some territory outside their capitals, although towns and villages in such territories were not nearly as hierarchically or architecturally complex.

Although the Inca can be said to have originated about 1000 as a distinct ethnic group within the Andes, their emergence as an expansionist state—as well as their conquest of much of Pacific coastal South America—took place in the 100 years before the Conquest. In 1400, the Inca were one of several groups of petty kingdoms competing for dominance in southern Peru; based at the city-state of Cuzco, they would begin the process of expansion in 1438—a process largely cut short by the arrival of the Spanish and European-derived diseases.

Amazonia and the Caribbean

In the year 400, the Caribbean was occupied by different Arawak, Tupiguarani, and Carib-speaking peoples. Ultimately these populations derived from coastal and interior Amazonia and had taken with them social systems and practices similar to those on the mainland. This diaspora, particularly in the case of the Arawak (Taino), had resulted in the transplantation of chiefdoms onto many of the Caribbean islands; these chiefdoms were characterized by large villages, roads, plazas, and ceremonial buildings such as ball courts (the latter ultimately derived through contact with Mesoamérica).

Amazonia proper was characterized by different types of societies between 400 and 1400. Small hereditary chiefdoms had probably emerged well before this time, during what is called the "Amazonian Formative Period" (1000 B.C.E.–500 C.E.), but it was after 500 that large, densely populated regional centers began to dot the Amazonian landscape. The island of Marajó in the Amazon estuary is a case in point. From 400 to 1400 the **Marajóara** people created large earthen mounds here; some were used for burial and ceremonial purposes, whereas others appear to have been the bases for impermanent buildings. People at Marajó and other large villages in the Amazon appear to have been trading for gold, ceramics, feathers, precious stones, and other goods at vast distances; socially, these settlements seem to have had clear divisions between classes, with elites receiving special funerary treatments as well as greater numbers of precious goods. Hunter-gatherers, agricultural chiefdoms, and perhaps even more complex societies made up a complex web of interactions in the Amazon; likewise, many of these groups would not have been completely economically or culturally isolated from their Andean neighbors. Although none of the Amazonian societies left behind written records, archaeology points to an image vastly different from that usually provided for Amazonia: As more research is undertaken in this understudied area, Amazonian societies of the Pre-Columbian world are becoming more and more urban as well as complex.

Further Reading

Arnold, J. "Complex Hunter-Gatherer-Fishers of Prehistoric California: Chiefs, Specialists, and Maritime Adaptations of the Channel Islands." *American Antiquity* 57 (1992): 60–84.

Bayman, J. "The Hohokam of Southwest North America." *Journal of World Prehistory* 15 (2001): 257–311.

Carmack, Robert M., and Gary Gossen. *The Legacy of Mesoamerica: History and Culture of a Native American Civilization.* 2nd ed. Upper Saddle River, NJ: Prentice Hall, 2006.

Crown, Patricia. *Ceramics and Ideology: Salado Polychrome Pottery.* Albuquerque: University of New Mexico Press, 1994.

Demarest, Arthur. *The Ancient Maya. The Rise and Fall of a Rainforest Civilization.* Cambridge, UK: Cambridge University Press, 2004.

Fagan, Brian. *Ancient North America.* London: Thames and Hudson, 1991.

Heckenberger, Michael. "Rethinking the Arawakan Diaspora: Hierarchy, Regionality, and the Amazonian Formative." In J. Hill and F. Santos-Granero, eds. *Comparative Arawakan Histories: Rethinking Culture Area and Language Group in Amazonia.* Urbana: University of Illinois Press, 2002, pp. 99–121.

Hosler, Dorothy. *The Sounds and Colors of Power: The Sacred Metallurgical Technology of Ancient West Mexico.* Cambridge, MA: MIT Press, 1994.

Knight, V.J., Jr., J.A. Brown, and G.E. Lankford. "On the Subject Matter of Southeastern Ceremonial Complex Art." *Southeastern Archaeology* 20 (2001): 129–141.

Martin, Simon, and Nikolai Grube. *Chronicle of the Maya Kings and Queens.* London: Thames and Hudson, Ltd., 2000.

Moseley, Michael E. *The Incas and their Ancestors: the Archaeology of Peru.* 2nd ed. London: Thames and Hudson, Ltd., 2001.

Rolingson, M. *Toltec Mounds and Plum Bayou Culture: Mound D Excavations.* Research Series 54. Fayetteville: Arkansas Archaeological Survey, 1998.

Roosevelt, Anne. *Moundbuilders of the Amazon: Geophysical Archaeology on Marajo Island, Brazil.* New York: Academic Press, 1991.

Scarre, Chris, ed. *The Human Past: World Prehistory and the Development of Human Societies.* London: Thames and Hudson, Ltd., 2005.

Silverman, H. *Cahuachi in the Ancient Nasca World.* Iowa City: University of Iowa Press, 1991.

Smith, Michael E. *The Aztecs.* Oxford, UK: Wiley-Blackwell, 2003.

Vivian, R. *The Chacoan Prehistory of the San Juan Basin.* San Diego, CA: Academic Press, 1990.

Wilcox, David. "The Mesoamerican Ballgame in the American Southwest." In V. Scarborough and D. Wilcox, eds. *The Mesoamerican Ballgame.* Tucson: University of Arizona Press, 1991, pp. 101–128.

6. SCIENCE AND TECHNOLOGY

In the Americas, drastic cultural and social changes were not necessarily the product of technological change, an assumption that runs counter to many of the experiences of civilizations in the Old World. In fact, much of the basic technology employed by Pre-Columbian civilizations in 1400 had been around—nevertheless, with some significant changes—well before 400. Science and technology common to all of the regions described below before 400 included advancements in pottery, stone tool manufacture (including weapons like the bow and arrow, spears, and the atlatl or spear-thrower—*see* individual entries), domesticated plants and/or animals (*see* "Society" section), masonry and construction (in stone, earthworks or both), and irrigation; most native groups employed medicinal plants and kept track of astronomical events, particularly the equinoxes and groups of stars such as the **Pleiades**. Nearly all public works and trade, save in Andean South America, were based upon human labor and the capacity to mobilize large groups of people for construction. The major difference between 400 and 1400, in terms of science and technology, was the scale to which labor and technological advances were employed: Huge cities and even empires were developing out of smaller-scale chiefdoms.

Having already witnessed the birth of urbanism and several technologies key to the development of chiefdoms, states, and empires, the Americas in 400 saw the apex of several major civilizations, particularly within highland Mesoamérica and Andean South America. Yet the spread of scientific advancements and technological change throughout the Americas was oftentimes limited and sporadic in the best of circumstances. Advancements such as metallurgy, the sail, and writing are good examples of this. Complex metallurgy, for example, was largely confined to Lower Central America and Andean South America from 800 B.C.E to 800 C.E. until its spread to western Mesoamérica. By comparison, the sail as a technology seems not have been used by Mesoamérican peoples, although it is likely that sailing vessels from places such as Ecuador and Colombia brought metallurgy to Mesoamérica around 800. Writing—a key feature of most states and empires—was invented in the Americas about 900 B.C.E. but was largely confined to central and eastern Mesoamérica; the literate civilizations in these areas traded (and even fought) with their contemporaries in a variety of settings, yet the written word seems never to have become a predominant feature in North or South America prior to the 1500s. Other developments, such as mathematics and the calendar, were perhaps independently invented at several times and places, although the complexity of these systems varied.

Oft-cited, interrelated explanations for such limited technological transfers are (1) the near complete absence of large, domesticated animals such as horses or oxen (the one exception is the llama of Andean South America); (2) the lack of several key supporting technologies that would have facilitated transport or movement of goods, ideas, and people, including wheeled vehicles, pulleys, or other complex machines; and (3) the almost universal persistence of stone and wood tools, even among expansion-oriented states and empires with access to copper and bronze technology. Although the basic facts behind these explanations are correct (civilizations like the Maya or Inca, who created vast cities within jungle or mountainous landscapes, indeed lacked wheeled vehicles), we must be careful in assuming that people will always adopt "better" technology—or adopt the most utilitarian stance toward it—whenever new technology is available. If anything, history has shown that people do not always behave in this way: For example, objects of copper, silver, gold, and bronze were typically appreciated for their rarity, color, and musical properties in ancient Mesoamérica and were rarely fashioned into weapons or large tools. Stone tools were the medium of choice for all of the civilizations discussed below, with the emphasis being on choice: As with any society past or present, culture—not necessarily utility—determined how science was used in Pre-Columbian America.

Eastern Woodlands and the Great Plains

The Eastern Woodlands and the Great Plains saw varying degrees of architectural change between 400 and 1400, with the greatest extent of sophistication in architectural engineering coinciding with the growth of widespread urbanism around 1000. Although the construction of mounds, walls, canals, ditches and other earthworks had been commonplace in the Mississippi and Ohio River Valleys prior to 400, the years between 1000 and 1400 saw the unprecedented growth of villages and towns here and in the Great Plains. The greatest of these was the Mississippian town of **Cahokia**, which—as mentioned elsewhere—contained mounds of a scale to rival those in Mesoamérica and South America. Towns like these continued earlier traditions of metalworking, in the form of copper artifacts, as well as pottery, shell- and woodworking, and stone tool manufacture, but most of these areas—like engineering—were augmented during the Mississippian Period (1000–1500). Of particular note were changes in ceramic manufacture, where the introduction of shell temper allowed not only new forms but also thin-walled pottery in some ways comparable to porcelain.

Technologically, the greatest change affecting the Eastern Woodlands and Great Plains between 400 and 1400 was the introduction of intensive maize agriculture. Cultivation of native plants such as chenopodium, sunflower, and marsh elder had already been grown en masse in the eras known as the Early and Middle Woodland Period (800 B.C.E.–400 C.E.), in many ways contributing to the transition from hunting and gathering to sedentary life. The growth of villages, chiefdoms and—unfortunately—warfare in the Late Woodland (400–1000) was coupled with the mass adoption of a new crop, maize, in different parts of the Eastern Woodlands between 800 and 1100. Having originally been domesticated in Central Mexico around 4300 B.C.E. and spread to the Eastern Woodlands by 1 C.E., maize does not originally appear to have had much of an impact on the peoples of this region. Archaeologists believe that the social changes of the Late Woodland period, coupled with a population boom, suddenly made the adoption of this productive crop desirable. Such adoption made further chiefdoms and social complexity possible over a vast area and led to the large towns of the Mississippian Period; other Mexican crops such as beans and squash were to follow, creating a complex of crops that continues to be associated with native agriculture in this region to the present day. Improvements to existing technology were the general rule during the Mississippian Period, and the several thousand people living in major centers such as Cahokia, Illinois, and **Moundville**, Arkansas, used technology that would have largely been familiar to their ancestors, but for its scale: Villages in 400 would have been occupied by only a few dozen people. Ultimately sociopolitical and natural events, including a period of low temperatures termed the "Little Ice Age" (1300–1850), contributed to the decline of the Mississippian chiefdoms, to the extent that new societies were on the ascent at the time of European contact.

American Southwest and the Great Basin

In some ways, the American Southwest and the Great Basin could not be more different in terms of overall technological trajectories between 400 and 1400.

In others, they follow a similar pattern. In the Great Basin, the long-term tradition of hunting and gathering was just beginning to be complemented by maize-based agriculture as well as pottery among groups of desert peoples known as the **Fremont** Culture. By comparison, pottery and limited agriculture in the Southwest were of great antiquity: As with the Eastern Woodlands and the Great Plains, maize, beans and squash from Central Mexico had been introduced into the Southwest far before the growth of major towns there, with maize agriculture dating as early as 1000 B.C.E.

Yet both regions shared similar problems in terms of agriculture after 1300. The collapse of Fremont Culture in the Great Basin around that time led not only to large-scale abandonment of the region but also the return—for stragglers—of hunting and gathering as the primary means of subsistence. In the American Southwest, maize-based agriculture was not abandoned per se between 1300 and 1500, but the overall number of people engaged in farming certainly decreased precipitously. Hunting and gathering, correspondingly, became more important in the Southwest as well. Most likely, these two areas suffered from related problems, with some blaming an influx of hunter-gatherers from the Great Basin itself (and other areas) as the reason for why the Southwest declined in this way.

The Hohokam (750–1450)

As mentioned above, maize agriculture and small villages are of great antiquity in the Southwest and had been complemented—as early as the first millennium B.C.E.—by limited irrigations systems allowing water from distant areas to serve these as well as native crops such as mesquite and prickly pear cactus. Around 700, perennial floods and a narrow channel made the Gila River an ideal place for the growth of even larger irrigation systems; settlement here during the Preclassic Hohokam (700–1150) was paired with a series of engineering projects at sites such as **Snaketown** and Casa Grande. These and other water-management projects in the American Southwest—though, in principle, not new technology—were of a scale so vast and so well built that the first European settlers were using them up to 1,000 years later.

The Classic Hohokam Period (1150–1450) saw the growth of major villages and a shift from wattle-and-daub, thatched roof architecture to adobe, a technological change that continues to resonate today. Likewise, increased populations and changes to sociopolitical systems may have seen the growth of chiefdoms as well as a near-total dependence on irrigation agriculture. Such technological dependence had its drawbacks: Climate change is one of the leading reasons for why Hohokam civilization declined, its settlements abandoned by 1450.

Ancestral Pueblo (750–1450)

Technological innovations on the Colorado Plateau for the Ancestral Puebloans largely mirrored that of the Hohokam, with many of the primary developments involving vast engineering projects, terracing, and other techniques designed to maximize the use of water for agriculture in a relatively dry, hostile environment. Other than the aforementioned canals, the most significant technological advancements stemming from this era involve pottery. As mentioned in the "Arts" essay, above, lead and other glazes were invented around the thirteenth century, allowing for what is now a familiar sight in contemporary pottery of the Southwest: geometric, polychrome designs in red, black, and white.

Pacific Coast and Arctic

As noted in the introduction, the Pacific Coast and Arctic are home to an array of maritime societies that historically have relied on hunting, gathering, and fishing for subsistence. Seaworthy canoes allowing deepwater fishing as well as nets, harpoons, and fish weirs were the primary food-gathering implements between 400 and 1400. Houses on the Pacific Coast during this time were, as in the contact era, constructed primarily of wooden planks; sites such as Ozette have revealed archaeological remains from this era, including evidence of long-distance trade in objects of copper, obsidian, and shell. In the Arctic, technologies were adapted to tundra life and the hunting of land as well as sea mammals including whales, walruses, and seals; specialized harpoons and skin-covered boats for whale hunting were developed after 1000 by the Thule culture of Arctic Canada. The **Thule** spread eastwards across Canada, to the lasting detriment of the native **Dorset** peoples, largely as a result of this technology. It should be noted that sporadic encounters between native peoples of the Arctic and European explorers (Vikings) in Greenland, confined to the years 1000 to 1500, had no lasting technological effect on either group; ultimately, the Thule proved technologically better adapted to life in the Arctic, and by the fifteenth century no Europeans remained in Greenland.

Mesoamérica

Between 400 and 1400, Mesoamérica was one of the major centers of scientific and technological achievement in the Americas. Although the cultures themselves were ethnically and linguistically diverse, in terms of science and technology they were remarkably uniform. Unlike the regions of North America or South America, there were almost no hunter-gatherer societies in Mesoamérica between 400 and 1400; Mesoamérican society during this millennium was primarily agricultural and urban in nature, with trading ties as far north as the American Southwest and as far south as the Pacific Coast of Columbia and Panama. Many Mesoamérican societies were literate and versed in astronomy and mathematics, and—given the limitations outlined earlier—were accomplished masters of architectural and agricultural engineering. All had a complex calendar, predating the Classic Maya but ultimately perfected by them. Most were builders of pyramids, royal palaces, and other large structures in addition to residential structures; the stepped buildings for which Mesoamérican civilizations are famous would have required the capacity—as outlined above—to use large numbers of people to build retaining walls as well as transport, cut, and/or carve stone blocks of sizes ranging from miniscule to enormous! Most of the towns and cities of Mesoamérica in this era were well planned and often aligned to accommodate astronomical phenomena and/or natural features in the landscape. The Central Mexican metropolises of **Teotihuacá** (100 B.C.E.–600 C.E.) and **Tenochtitlán** (1325–1521) were easily two of the most impressive planned cities in the hemisphere, with populations exceeding well over one hundred thousand people apiece; both were laid out according to a grid plan, a feature of world cities that only became commonplace in the modern era. Despite the similarities, however, there were technological differences between Mesoamérican civilizations; some the most noteworthy advances in science and technology are mentioned below.

The Teotihuacános (100 B.C.E. to 600 C.E.)

Until recently, it was believed that the Teotihuacá, the sixth largest city in the world at its apex (about one-hundred twenty-five thousand people), lacked a writing system; discoveries in the last several years have not only proved this false but also suggested that its writing system—consisting of painted hieroglyphs with pictographic characteristics—was ancestral to the Aztec and other Central Mexican writing systems. Although most glyphs cannot currently be read, archaeologists have begun to decipher names of people, places and other signs suggesting that the Teotihuacános had a calendar (and possibly a mathematical system) similar to their contemporaries the Classic Maya.

In addition to a building a massive network of roads, the Teotihuacános were architecturally famous for creating stepped pyramids built in a style known as talud-tablero: Rectangular and sloping elements were set atop one another in regular fashion, providing for an aesthetically pleasing and stable pyramid structure. Teotihuacá is also noteworthy for its apartment compounds, where different ethnic enclaves as well as native Teotihuacános manufactured obsidian tools, ceramic vessels, jewelry, and other goods for local consumption as well as foreign export. That so many people moved to and lived in Teotihuacá at this early time was testament to the technological sophistication of this city: Feeding this many people at once would have required highly productive agricultural system and a network of institutions to bring this food to the masses.

The Maya (Classic [250–909] and Postclassic [909–1697] Periods)

Compared to other Mesoamérican civilizations, the Classic Maya are perhaps the best known for their achievements in science and technology. Their cities in the jungle continue to fascinate scholars and laymen alike. Like Teotihuacá, most Maya city centers were built primarily of stone, requiring a heavy investment in labor and architectural planning; Maya cities were plastered, lavishly painted, and well drained to accommodate the rainy, tropical climate. One technological innovation used in Maya buildings as well as tombs was the corbelled vault or false arch. Also used in Mycenean Greece, this technique involved stacking courses of stone at the springline of each wall successively, such that they projected toward the center; the top of the arch was then capped by flat stones, creating a stand-alone doorway much like an arch. Much like the Teotihuacán talud-tablero, the corbelled vault was a readily identifiable characteristic of Classic Maya architecture.

The Classic Maya were particularly accomplished in the interrelated fields of mathematics, calendrics, and astronomy. Mathematically, they had the concepts of zero and place, which allowed them to algebraically employ large numbers and afforded complex calculations. Although the use of an actual sign for zero (or the concept of zero, for that matter) is today regarded as commonsense, it was not a feature of mathematics worldwide until the first century B.C.E. In the Americas, the first documented use of a sign for zero occurs with the Classic Maya, as part of what is called the "Long Count" of the **Mesoamérican calendar**. The Long Count is much older than the Classic Maya, however, and would have required the use of a zero or a placeholder: It dates to at least 36 B.C. and is associated with Epi-Olmec civilization at the site of Chiapa de Corzo, Chiapas, Mexico. Other Mesoamérican calendars which served as antecedents to the Long Count date back as early as the sixth century B.C.E. As a result, Mesoamérican civilizations may have invented a sign for zero around the same time—or even before—their contemporaries in the Old World! In any event, the Classic Maya certainly perfected the use of zero and place in Mesoamérica, taking computations to a level never seen before (and perhaps after).

These computations were largely calendrical in nature; they were designed to (1) track the movement of celestial bodies such as the sun, moon, and other planets; (2) predict astronomical events such as solar eclipses; and (3) keep track of historical or other events of celebratory and divinatory importance. Unlike many of the other mathematical systems in use between 400 and 1400, Mesoamérican math was based upon a vigesimal (base-20) instead of decimal (base-10) system, with dots and bars signifying increments of ones and fives, respectively (there were also more pictographic glyphs that could be used to signify numbers as well, particularly in the Maya system). For example, the number 14 would have been represented by four dots and two bars.

There were three basic calendars employed in Mesoamérica. Although the Classic Maya were not the first to use all three of these together, by 400 they were the only civilization to do so. The first of these was the 260-day calendar, or Sacred Almanac, where each day was given a number ranging from 1 to 13 as well as one of twenty names (hence, 13 x 20 = 260). The second was a rough 365-day calendar designed to approximate the solar year. It consisted of a number ranging from 1 to 20 as well as one of eighteen-month names plus five extra days (hence, 20 x 18 + 5 = 365). Although there were exceptions, the 260- and 365-day calendars were often combined to produce what is called the "Calendar Round," which provided each day with a set of four signs (2 numbers and 2 names). The Classic Maya did this, with an example being the day 4 Ajaw 8 Kumk'u (day number + day name + month number + month name). The same combination of numbers and days would occur only once every 52 years.

In the short term, this was not a problem. In fact, many civilizations that postdated the Classic Maya used only the first two. But for long-term dates, a third calendar was required: the aforementioned Long Count. This calendar was, like Western calendars, fixed and began on a specific date. Scholars have reconstructed this day as August 11, 3114 B.C.E., allowing us to know precisely when any Long Count date—recorded in Classic Maya—was written. The Long Count itself was divided into units called k'in (day), winal (20 days), tuun (360 days), k'atun (7,200 days), and b'aktun (144,000); although several larger units were habitually used, these five units were the most common. As the beginning date of the calendar was fixed to a Calendar Round (4 Ajaw 8 K'umk'u), the entire Long Count could be attached to the other two calendars. The result is that the beginning date in our own script would be written (Long Count + Calendar Round) as: 0.0.0.0.0 4 Ajaw 8 K'umk'u, or August 11, 3114 B.C.E. A sample date within the actual florescence of Classic Maya civilization would be 9.15.0.0.0 4 Ajaw 13 Yax, or August 20, 731 C.E. Needless to say, the calculations required to keep track of all three calendars are complex by any standard and are testament to the mathematical prowess of the Classic Maya. Today, archaeologists make such calculations via computer programs.

Astronomically, the Classic Maya kept track of lunar and planetary movements, creating further calendars by which to know precisely where and when each body would appear in the sky; some buildings were even designed to accommodate such phenomena. The sun, moon, and **Venus** were of particular interest, although some constellations as well as Mercury, Mars, Jupiter, and Saturn were appreciated by the Maya. The Classic Maya were primarily concerned with solstices, equinoxes, and other dramatic celestial events. Given these concerns, it is probable that the Classic Maya were aware of inaccuracies in their solar calendar of 365 days. Nevertheless, no corrections (such as leap years) appear to have been made.

The other major technological achievement of the Classic Maya was their writing system, elements of which were in place among the Postclassic Maya until the Spanish Conquest of the sixteenth century. Although the earliest writing in Mesoamérica dates to approximately 900 B.C.E., the Classic Maya are credited with creating the most complex and complete writing system ever created in Mesoamérica. Like all other writing systems of this region, the Maya system was hieroglyphic in nature. Unlike others, however, the Maya system excelled in the ability to express person, tense, and other elements of complex grammar and syntax, to the extent that one could write poetry, prose, and even humorous phrases; the majority of inscriptions, however, are formulaic but riveting records of dynastic succession, divine kingship, warfare, sacrifice, ancestral/deity veneration, marriages, and political/trade relationships. The inscriptions consisted of two basic types of glyphs: logographs (signs equivalent to words) and syllables (signs equivalent to sounds). These were usually arranged top-to-bottom and left-to-right in columns. Dates were usually followed by a verb-object-subject (VOS) order, such that a sample phrase in Classic Maya might translate as: "(on) 4 Ajaw 13 Yax, (he) arrived at 7-Bone-Place, K'inich Yax K'uk' Mo'." Maya hieroglyphs were written on almost every medium available, although the materials remaining to archaeologists are primarily of stone and ceramic; large monoliths or stelae, for example, were quarried and moved for great distances before being carved with images of kings and stories of their deeds. Weighing several tons, they would have required considerable effort in their movement (without the wheel) through hills and jungle terrain. Unfortunately, no Classic Maya books, or codices, have survived to the present day; decayed fragments of Classic Maya codices and a few Postclassic books that survived the Conquest are all that remain. The scientific and technological innovations mentioned in this section persisted long after the collapse of Classic Maya civilization in the tenth century. The Postclassic Maya, from the tenth to the fifteenth centuries, employed tools and techniques that would have been recognizable to the Classic Maya people, although the days of the divine kings were long gone by the time of the Spanish Conquest.

The Toltecs (950–1170) and the Aztecs (1345–152)

The abandonment of the southern Classic Maya cities in the tenth century (and new beginnings for the Postclassic Maya at northern Yucatecan sites such as Chichén Itzá and Mayapán) was accompanied by the political resurgence of expansionist states and empires in Central Mexico. As outlined in the introduction to this section, Postclassic Mesoamérica was characterized by increasing trade relationships with distant areas. One major technological consequence of long-distance trade was the influx of metallurgical techniques into Mesoamérica from places such as Ecuador, Colombia, and Lower Central America. Although the first gold in Mesoamérica dates to around 600, it appears to have been a foreign import, with the first clear case of local metallurgy occurring in West Mexico around 800. Initially, metallurgy in West Mexico concentrated on working copper, although gold and silver were also employed; between 1200 and 1300 West Mexican metallurgists—perhaps through further long-distance contacts with Lower Central America and coastal South America—started creating alloys and using a wider variety of metals, including a type of bronze. As mentioned earlier, the materials produced from metals were often ritual objects or small utilitarian goods such as tweezers, needles, and axes; they were almost never fashioned into weapons or functional protective gear. Metal was primarily appreciated for its color, rarity, and ability to be fashioned into beautiful (even musical) objects, much like gold or silver is today. As a result, large civilizations to the east like the Toltecs or the later Aztecs, to whom this technology eventually spread, continued to use stone as the primary medium for weapons of war, farming implements, and the like.

As mentioned in the introduction to this section, many aspects of science and technology present in the 1400s would have been familiar to an individual from 400. What oftentimes changed was the ability of this technology to be altered and adapted for increasingly larger and more complex societies and political institutions. The Aztecs, in particular, are a good example of this. Population estimates for the entire Aztec empire, as mentioned in the Society section, range from 3.5 to 6.5 million people. Such a populous empire had never before been seen in Mesoamérica and would have required an enormous amount of resources. Although technologies such as terracing, irrigation, and swamp reclamation had all been known well before 400, the Aztecs of 1345 adapted the basics of these techniques to great advantage. Terrace walls built by the Aztecs, for example, have proved durable enough to the point where they continue to be used in farming within Mexico. Nearly all sources of fresh water throughout the Valley of Mexico were employed for irrigation—and frequently transported through aqueducts, an Aztec innovation—at the time of the Conquest.

However, the most readily identifiable agricultural technology associated with the Aztec empire were chinampas, or raised fields. These were a series of large, straightened ditches used to drain away the excess water from swamps. Between the ditches were artificial islands, which were augmented by soil from the swamp bottom. The islands were stabilized by trees and wooden stakes; they become home to a variety of cultivated plants originally germinated on floating reed rafts in the ditches. What made this technology so astonishing is that three to four crops could be grown each year in the chinampas, making them the most productive farming areas of the Aztec empire. Although the initial creation of chinampas is labor intensive, such production levels are, even with modern agribusiness, unprecedented.

Like the Maya, the Aztecs also employed a writing system, although it was far more pictorial in character. A given text could have not only logographs and syllables but also pictographs (narrative images "read" as text), and the subject matter was far more limited than the Classic Maya script. Most of the texts remaining to archaeologists are from codices of deerskin, cloth, or bark paper; they primarily deal with divination, agricultural cycles, and trade/tribute from different provinces of the Aztec empire. The calendar employed by the Aztecs was the Calendar Round, although the names for days and months were different and largely associated with animals, plants, and other natural phenomena. As mentioned earlier, the sole use of the Calendar Round meant that the same combination of numbers, days, and months would occur every 52 years. This "reset" in the Aztec calendar was considered to be a dangerous time and required a number of appropriate sacrifices and rituals, collectively called the "New Fire Ceremony" (*see* "Religion" section).

Also like other Mesoamérican civilizations, the Aztecs were avid astronomers. They kept track of solar, lunar, and other planetary movements, seeking to predict their movements throughout the year. They also associated specific gods and traits to planets and constellations. For example, the planet Venus (when it was seen in the morning) was known as Tlahuizpantecuhtli and thought to be an enemy of the sun, throwing darts at it to prevent its rise. Moreover, although what is known about Aztec constellations is severely limited, the Aztecs seem to have paid attention to stars in the constellations Orion, Gemini, the Big Dipper, and Scorpio. Particular attention was also paid to comets and other transitory celestial phenomena: Several accounts of the Conquest cite the appearance of an unpredicted comet as an omen (possibly apocryphal) foretelling the coming of the Spanish in 1519.

Lower Central America and the Andes

Although large, literate urban societies were not characteristic of the societies stretching from Lower Central America to Colombia between 400 and 1400, the peoples of this region did engage with many of the practices and technologies associated with their immediate neighbors to the north and south, including monumental architecture in the form of earthworks and limited stone constructions as well as metallurgy. In fact, this region was home to an advanced, ancient metallurgical tradition centering on gold and dating to approximately 500 B.C.E. By 400, peoples of this region had long been using gold or gold and copper alloys for objects such as masks, figurines, and personal adornments; they were familiar with several casting methods, including the "lost-wax" technique (*see* "The Arts" section). In fact, it seems likely that the oldest gold in Mesoamérica, dated to 600, originally came from this region of the Americas.

The Andean region, consisting of mountainous terrain as well as coastal deserts, was one of the cradles of empire in the Americas and the source of many scientific and technological achievements. Between 400 and 1400, it was home to a series of states and empires that competed with one another for political and economic domination; by 400 most Andean civilizations had had a long history of urbanism and the technologies associated with it; for example, public monumental architecture, in the form of pyramidal buildings, may date back early as 3000 B.C.E. Masonry walls, terraces, and buildings, as well as decorative lapidary work had also begun by this period. Furthermore, technologies such as mining and **metallurgy** were well-established before 400, with early metallurgy in the Andes dating to 800 B.C.E.; techniques such as soldering, welding, casting, and alloying were about 1,000 years old by 400 C.E. Unlike some other parts of the Americas, however, none of the Andean civilizations to be discussed employed a writing system in the traditional sense; the one exception may be the Inca.

Moche (200–600 c.e.) and Nazca (200 b.c.e.–650 c.e.)

In 400, the Andean region was dominated by two cultures based in desert coastal Peru: **Moche** and Nazca. In terms of science and technology, the Moche were accomplished architectural engineers on the north coast, creating some of the largest pyramids ever erected in South America; millions of adobe bricks and painted friezes were employed in the creation of pyramids housing sacrificial victims and richly attired rulers of the Moche state. Architecturally, Nazca pyramids on the south coast of Peru were somewhat more modest, although the famous "**Nazca lines**" are perhaps the most enduring images associated with this civilization. They consisted of hundreds of enormous images of animals, plants, and geometric figures and would have been relatively easy to create in terms of labor: Dark stones were removed from the desert to expose lighter ones beneath. However, the size and form of these images (some are up to 12 miles in length) would have required considerable planning and coordination, particularly in cases where they appear on flat, featureless terrain. Exactly how some of these were made — and why — remains open to speculation, ever-fueling proposals of varying credulity. Although neither the Moche nor the Nazca had a writing system, elite forms of communication similar to writing may have existed, particularly with regard to the Moche (*see* "The Arts" section).

Tiwanaku (650–1000), Chimor (1000–1476), and the Birth of the Inca (1300–1532)

Among the several states antecedent to the Inca, **Tiwanaku** and **Chimor** are perhaps the most famous. In terms of science and technology, Tiwanaku is perhaps most noteworthy for its architectural style, set dramatically among the mountains and plains of Peru, Bolivia, and northern Chile; although this style has antecedents, it was perfected by the Tiwanaku and adopted by later civilizations. The largest cut stones at the capital (also known as Tiwanaku, on the coast of Lake Titicaca), weighing between 100 and 200 tons apiece, are remarkable not only for having been moved up to 40 kilometers without wheels but also for having been set within buildings so tightly fit together that mortar was not required; each stone was cut to match its neighbor (and thus not of a standard size). Like later Inca buildings, Tiwanaku structures were fairly resistant to earthquakes or other disturbances and were complemented by drains and tunnels for water.

Chimor civilization was also noteworthy for its architecture. Inheriting the north coast of Peru from the Moche and eventually controlling approximately 620 miles of Pacific coast, Chimor in many ways anticipated what the Inca Empire was to become. Architectural engineering within this desert coast civilization was truly remarkable, with multistoried adobe compounds and a civic center at the capital, Chan Chan, stretching 2.3 square miles. Gridded cities with geometrically designed complexes of settlement were the result of meticulous urban planning, a characteristic that would be equaled — if not surpassed — by the Inca during their rise to power.

Although the origins of the Inca stretch back to 1000, the Incas were but one of many ethnic groups until 1438, when Sapa Inca Pachacuti began his conquest

Machu Picchu, Sacred City of the Incas, built 1438–1471 by Inca leader Pachacuti, Cuzco, Peru, seen from burial site. Courtesy of photos.com.

of the Andes and coastal South America. In fact, readily definable "Inca" art, style, or other traits only emerge around 1375. As a result, it is difficult to isolate specific hallmarks of Inca science or technology for the period between 400 and 1400. Nevertheless, one might say that the Inca technologically approximated Tiwanaku civilization in architectural style, but on a much grander level: Using millions of workers at its height in the late fifteenth century, the Inca Empire was able to create vast cities such as Cuzco and Machu Picchu and over twenty thousand miles of roads stretching from Ecuador to Southern Chile. By 1400, the Inca had started along this path architecturally and employed the mortarless style pioneered by Tiwanaku. Inca architecture ranks as a marvel of engineering in the preindustrial world.

The Inca were likewise noteworthy, in terms of science and technology, for their achievements in medicine and astronomy. The Inca were known to have practiced trephination (cutting holes in the skull to relieve swelling from head injuries) as well as herbal medicine; coca leaves were used, as today, to lessen hunger, relieve pain, and provide energy. Astronomically, the Inca are known to have kept a calendar as well as records of stars, constellations, solstices, and equinoxes much like their counterparts in Mesoamérica; they set up stone towers around the capital, **Cuzco**, to mark the passage of celestial phenomena. Records of astronomical events, as well as mathematics and trade/tribute lists, were kept on **quipu.** These devices of knotted strings were once thought to have been mnemonic devices for the Inca, used to recall specific events. Recent discoveries, however, suggest that the quipu may have recorded more complex information, much like a writing system. As the quipu are deciphered it is likely that more on the science and technology of the Inca will come to light.

Amazonia and the Caribbean

The years prior to 400 had, in Amazonia and the Caribbean, seen large-scale population movements in which nearly every corner of this vast area had been colonized, with agricultural chiefdoms living in large, settled villages dominating the landscape. By 400 this process had largely wound down, and the incipient chiefdoms in Amazonia embarked upon a process of mound-building and huge earthworks. The Caribbean societies, spreading outwards from Amazonia in seaworthy canoes, had likewise settled down and begun to create large plaza-centered settlements. In terms of science and technology, one major development between 400 and 1400 was the creation, in Amazonia, of so-called black earth (*terra preta*) sites: sedentary villages in the Lower Amazon that bear evidence of managed forest gardens and manufactured agricultural landscapes. Contrary to the popular model of the Amazon as relatively infertile and inhospitable to large-scale agriculture, it would seem as if populations living at sites such as Santarem purposefully created agricultural land through a long-term process of fertilizing the earth—literally creating "black earth" for agriculture that continues to be fertile today. The discovery of such sites is a relatively recent development archaeologically; future studies may reveal further evidence of social complexity and the mechanisms behind this distinctively Amazonian technology of the Pre-Columbian Americas.

Further Reading

Ames, K., and H. Maschner. *Peoples of the Northwest Coast: Their Archaeology and Prehistory*. London: Thames and Hudson, Ltd., 1999.

Arnold, J. "Complex Hunter-Gatherer-Fishers of Prehistoric California: Chiefs, Specialists, and Maritime Adaptations of the Channel Islands. *American Antiquity* 57 (1992): 60–84.

Bayman, J. "The Hohokam of Southwest North America." *Journal of World Prehistory* 15 (2001): 257–311.

Carmack, Robert M., and Gary Gossen. *The Legacy of Mesoamerica: History and Culture of a Native American Civilization*. 2nd ed. Upper Saddle River, NJ: Prentice Hall, 2006.

Crown, Patricia. *Ceramics and Ideology: Salado Polychrome Pottery*. Albuquerque: University of New Mexico Press, 1994.

Demarest, Arthur. *The Ancient Maya. The Rise and Fall of a Rainforest Civilization*. Cambridge, UK: Cambridge University Press, 2004.

Fagan, Brian. *Ancient North America*. London: Thames and Hudson, 1991.

Hosler, Dorothy. *The Sounds and Colors of Power: The Sacred Metallurgical Technology of Ancient West Mexico*. Cambridge, MA: MIT Press, 1994.

Kolata, A. *The Tiwanaku: Portrait of an Andean Civilization*. Oxford, UK: Blackwell, 1993.

Kolata, A. *Tiwanaku and Its Hinterland: Archaeology and Paleoecology of an Andean Civilization*. Washington, DC: Smithsonian Institution Press, 1996.

Martin, Simon, and Nikolai Grube. *Chronicle of the Maya Kings and Queens*. London: Thames and Hudson, Ltd., 2000.

Moseley, Michael E. *The Incas and Their Ancestors: The Archaeology of Peru*. 2nd ed. London: Thames and Hudson, Ltd., 2001.

Petersen, James, E.G. Neves, and M. Heckenberger. "Gift from the Past: Terra Preta and Prehistoric Amerindian Occupations in Amazonia." In C. McEwan, C. Barreto, and E.G. Neves, eds. *The Unknown Amazon: Culture in Nature in Ancient Brazil*. London: British Museum Press, 2001, pp. 86–105.

Roosevelt, Anne. *Moundbuilders of the Amazon: Geophysical Archaeology on Marajo Island, Brazil*. New York: Academic Press, 1991.

Scarre, Chris, ed. *The Human Past: World Prehistory and the Development of Human Societies*. London: Thames and Hudson, Ltd., 2005.

Smith, Michael E. *The Aztecs*. Oxford, UK: Wiley-Blackwell, 2003.

Vivian, R. *The Chacoan Prehistory of the San Juan Basin*. San Diego, CA: Academic Press, 1990.

7. GLOBAL TIES

As noted in the Economy section, peoples of the Americas were often able to procure goods originating from distant places. Visitors from the Europe of the fifth century would likely be surprised, as many of the things that they would have taken for granted did not exist. Moreover, some objects and materials that were readily recognizable were not used in the same way. In terms of tools, the Americas were largely dominated by works of stone; although metals such as gold, copper, silver, and platinum were readily available in some places, they were usually employed for ornamentation and not typically used to fashion utilitarian implements or weapons. As noted in the "Science and Technology" essay, above, all potential beasts of burden in the Americas, save the camelids (e.g., llamas, alpacas, etc.) of the Andes, had been extinct since around 11,000 to 10,000 B.C.E. As a potential consequence of this major absence, the wheel was not adopted. Although the wheel was, in fact, known to some peoples of the Americas, it was (as far as we know) never employed for labor and, consequently, complex machines were unknown. Moreover, the sail was only in use in a few areas and absent among some key urban peoples, most notably those of Mesoamérica. All these factors limited the global ties of the peoples of the Americas. Yet there are many cases—in the prehistory of all regions—where long-distance trade not only occurred but also flourished. Such is a testament to the ingenuity of the peoples of the Americas.

Eastern Woodlands and the Great Plains

As mentioned in the "Economy" section, the year 400 C.E. was a poor time for ties between societies of the Eastern Woodlands and the Great Plains. Prior to this point, much of the eastern half of North America was linked through a series of trade networks; although the most distant networks were, presumably, never characterized by direct exchange (e.g., Wyoming was not directly engaged in trade with Florida), there had been a flow—if intermittent—of goods and ideas between the Rockies and the Atlantic. By the beginning of the Late Woodland Period (400–1000), this gradual exchange of cultural and material traditions had ended in the Eastern Woodlands. It had been replaced with a far more provincial system. War, social instability, and economic insularity were the rules of the day, and towns and villages withdrew into local networks.

Although the Great Plains did see a reduction in ties with the Eastern Woodlands during this era, it nevertheless seems to have had sporadic exchanges with places as distant as the Pacific Coast and the American Southwest, as evidenced by pottery styles and even exotic imports such as shell; such exchanges would continue well after the period of European contact.

The recovery of a wider system of exchange in the eastern half of North America came in the eleventh century with the birth of the Mississippian tradition.

Although certainly distinct in terms of levels of urbanization and degree of intensive agriculture, the Eastern Woodlands and the Great Plains saw connections once more. Artifacts—notably pottery—diagnostic of the Mississippian centers have been found at a wide variety of archaeological sites in the Great Plains, particularly during the height of such centers as **Cahokia** and **Moundville**. In fact, the period of greatest social and economic exchange between the two areas seems to have occurred between 1000 and 1200. By 1300, however, any major global ties had faded, and the Eastern Woodlands was becoming even more defined regionally than it had been. The decline of the Mississippian tradition between 1400 and 1500 would see new beginnings in other areas, notably in the northeast with such peoples as the **Iroquois**, but overall eastern North America became less global in its cultural and economic ties.

American Southwest and the Great Basin

Like the Great Plains, the Great Basin was a crossroads of cultures and ideas between 400 and 1400. As noted in other sections, the **Fremont** Culture (400–1300) of the Great Basin appears to have been a collection of regional societies bound together by a new, increasingly widespread agricultural tradition; these societies appear to have been in direct contact with and influenced by their surrounding neighbors, such that one can see traditions imported from the Great Plains or the American Southwest in Fremont artifacts.

The American Southwest, for its part, appears to have had closest economic and cultural ties—not surprisingly—with the peoples of the Great Basin, the Pacific Coast and Mesoamérica. Trade goods from these regions appear at archaeological sites in the Southwest (and vice versa). Between 1300 and 1500, however, the American Southwest appears to have been integrated into larger events taking place in North America: The region seems to have been invaded by waves of immigration from the Pacific Northwest, the Great Basin, and the Great Plains. New farmers as well as hunter-gatherers made the Southwest their homes, forever altering the local population ethnically and culturally. Explanations for this demographic upheaval have largely centered on climatic shifts associated with a cold period (the Little Ice Age) around 1400.

The Hohokam (750–1450)

The period of greatest global interaction for these peoples was perhaps the Preclassic Hohokam (700–1150). During this era, the Mesoamérican ballgame appears to have made its way into the American Southwest, perhaps via sites such as Casas Grandes, in northern Mexico, or similar sites in the Mexican state of Chihuahua to the west. Likewise, Mesoamérican imports such as parrots and copper bells also made their way to Hohokam sites. The latter were likely brought to the region, if directly, from the workshops of West Mexico, where Mesoamérican metallurgy was at its most advanced. From the Preclassic to the Classic (1150–1450), the Hohokam also appear to have maintained ties with the Pacific Coast: Shells from California were imported into the Gila River area and etched with the images of local animals. Agricultural collapse and climate change were the likely culprits of the end of the Hohokam tradition around 1450, when the population collapsed. Few remained in the area at the time of European contact.

Ancestral Pueblo (750–1450)

Sporadic movements into and out of the Colorado Plateau region during the Pueblo I and Pueblo II Periods (750–1150) was probably a major factor in the exchange of culture into and out of this area of the American Southwest. Connections between the Colorado Plateau and the Great Basin likely intensified during the Pueblo III period (1150–1300), when peoples from the latter region seem to have been making territorial incursions into the former. What followed was wholesale societal disruption, as the Colorado Plateau was abandoned and populations moved into the Rio Grande Valley. Despite these problems, however, the thirteenth century did see the invention of a pottery tradition that was to become widespread over the American Southwest: Salado Polychrome, often cited as a direct marker for a phenomenon known as the Southwest Cult. Somewhat analogous to the Southeast Cult or Southeastern Ceremonial Complex of the Eastern Woodlands, the Southwest Cult was a set of shared symbols on pottery indicating a general religious tradition involving agricultural fertility and water management (*see* **Southern Cult**). Thus one might say that the time between the thirteenth and fifteenth centuries, when portions of the Southwest experienced a demographic collapse, was a period when the area was unified by a (more or less) single religious tradition.

Pacific Coast, Artic, and Subarctic

Between 400 and 1400, the peoples of the Pacific Coast were in intermittent contact with those of the Great Basin and the American Southwest, trading in shell and other local goods. These and other exchange networks were also responsible for exotic items found in coastal contexts, particularly within the Pacific Northwest, where obsidian, copper, shell, and even iron (likely traded from Asia into the Bering area) appear at coastal archaeological sites.

In terms of sheer geographic area, the Arctic and Subarctic worlds were among the largest areas in which long-distance trade occurred in the Americas. The **Dorset** and the **Thule** were present to encounter the Norse in their brief foray into the Americas around 1000; the Norse called the peoples they met "skraelings" in their saga of the discovery of Vinland, which, until the site of **L'anse aux Meadows** in Newfoundland was found, was thought to have been embellished at best. In terms of global ties, the Thule were probably the only peoples of the Americas to remain in long-term contact with the Old World: In addition to obtaining, through trade, items of copper from the interior of North America, they seem to have been trading limited quantities of iron from Asia as well as—in the brief case of the Norse—Europe. As a result the Thule were, for a brief period, the only tenuous link between the Pacific and Atlantic worlds.

Mesoamérica

The Mesoamérican world was, at times, what Robert Carmack and others have called a "world system," for example, a region that was—to a certain extent—economically, culturally, and politically linked, where the fortunes of one affected those of the others. The Aztec world at the time of European contact in 1519, for example, fits this description. In addition to being the masters of a multiethnic state encompassing a vast portion of Mesoamérica, the Aztecs were engaged with most of the peoples of Mesoamérica directly or indirectly through fighting, trading, or both. They fought regularly, for example, with the only other multiethnic empire in Mesoamérica, the Tarascans of West Mexico, and at times could count portions of the Valley of Oaxaca, another great culture area of Mesoamérica to the south, among their economic and political vassals. The Aztecs were likewise engaged with the Maya area, trading with the coastal centers of Yucatán (and thereby indirectly with the remaining Maya kingdoms of the interior) and fighting with the K'ichee Maya of the highlands for supremacy on the Pacific coasts of Chiapas, Mexico, and Suchitepequez, Guatemala; in the sixteenth century they managed to carve out a province there and had made the K'ichee their vassals. They had even subjugated parts of the Gulf Coast of Mexico and established enclaves in the trading centers of the Caribbean as well as in more distant locations, with the furthest of these possibly in Panama. As a result, the global impact of Late Postclassic peoples like the Aztecs was considerable: By this time, a significant portion of the Americas was cosmopolitan and interdependent. The roots of this interdependency, however, stretch back several hundred years.

The Teotihuacános (100 B.C.E. to 600 C.E.)

Other than the Olmecs of the Middle Preclassic (1200–400 B.C.E.), no civilization before the year 400 had so much impact in Mesoamérica as **Teotihuacá**. As mentioned in other essays, Teotihuacá was the dominant political, economic, and cultural force in Mesoamérica from approximately 100 B.C.E. to 600 C.E. Teotihuacános, either at the behest of their rulers or as independent fortune seekers, had set up puppet dynasties in the Maya lowlands by 400 C.E. and were in the process of increasing their influence among the highland Maya, the Zapotecs of the Valley of Oaxaca, the Gulf Coast of Mexico, and even far into northwest Mexico. Many of the places they came into contact with had, in short order, Teotihuacán-style art and architecture as well as an assemblage of Central Mexican artifacts (including ceramics and obsidian from near the great metropolis).

Furthermore, even following the demise of Teotihuacá around 600 C.E., many places in Mesoamérica were employing Teotihuacán-style imagery and symbolism for status reasons: Materials derived—or thought to derive—from Teotihuacá were viewed as prestigious well into the ninth and tenth centuries.

The Maya (Classic [250–909] and Postclassic [909–1697] Periods)

The Classic Maya kingdoms, by virtue of their individual independence, were relatively insular in terms of broader impact within Mesoamérica. However, the collective actions of the Maya kingdoms, often uncoordinated, had far-reaching implications for many Mesoamérican societies. This can be seen in the trade of jade within and outside the Maya area: As the only source for this most valuable of substances, the Motagua River Valley (on the present Guatemala–Honduras border) was mined for jade that was exported as far as Lower Central America (Intermediate Area). Salt, feathers, cacao, obsidian, and other local materials also made their way into northern Mesoamérica during the Classic Maya era, albeit in much smaller quantities than during the Postclassic.

It was, in fact, during the period following the collapse in the lowlands that the Maya area became a hub of economic activity and a major player in long-distance exchange. Instead of many different centers in the southern area of the Yucatán, there were now a few major centers near reliable water sources in the north, many of which had concentrated populations; such centers required robust markets and more complicated networks of exchange. The result of this was the birth of a more global, market economy focused on external trade in goods such as honey, cotton, and chert in addition to more traditional exports. Although the individual kingdoms on the coast were, in terms of royal authority, relatively weak by Classic Maya standards, the economies were more robust and engaged with the wider world.

The Toltecs (950–1170) and the Aztecs (1345–1521)

The time between the rise of the Toltecs and the fall of the Aztec Empire was the most cosmopolitan era in Mesoamérican prehistory. The exchange of ideas and overall culture between the Maya area and Central Mexico had reached a new level following the collapse of Classic (250–909) civilization in the Maya lowlands, for example, with clear evidence for increased ties between the two regions occurring at Maya sites such as Seibal, Guatemala, and **Chichén Itzá**, Mexico. This cultural exchange was not one way, however, and there is good evidence to suggest that the Toltecs were influenced by the Maya as much as, if not more than, the reverse. Moreover, regions that had always been in major contact but still culturally and politically independent were being drawn together: The Gulf Coast of Mexico, the Valley of Oaxaca, and even parts of West Mexico were all being bound—as a result of increased trade, conquest, or both—more closely. This was particularly the case during the florescence of Aztec civilization.

Connections between Mesoamérica and other parts of the Americas, moreover, were becoming stronger by the last centuries of the first millennium C.E. To the north, the Mesoamérican ballgame appears to have spread up into the American Southwest as far as the Hohokam cultural sphere; resources from Mesoamérica, such as parrots and copper bells, likewise were moving northwards to places such as Casas Grandes. To the immediate south, ties were being forged between Mesoamérica and Lower Central America (the Intermediate Area). Although ceramics and ceramic styles, for example, had always moved between eastern Mesoamérica and Lower Central America, now such items were moving to great distances beyond their places of origin: Ceramics from Lower Central America began to make appearances in Central Mexico, indicating a greater level of contact between these regions. Such extra-Mesoamérican contacts mostly intensified during the Aztec hegemony in Central Mexico, largely due to the size and organization of the Aztec Empire but also a consequence of Aztec origins: The Aztecs themselves, who appear to have invaded Central Mexico in waves of migrations between the twelfth and thirteenth centuries, appear to have originally come from the northern fringes of Mesoamérica and certainly brought with them ideas and practices not native to the region.

Perhaps the most noteworthy global ties between Mesoamérica and the outside world at this time, however, were the connections forged between West Mexico and Andean South America: Sometime around the late ninth or early tenth century, metallurgical technology spread from places such as Peru, Ecuador, and Colombia to the region of West Mexico. From there, it then spread to most of Mesoamérica. By the time of the Aztecs, the most accomplished metalworking cultures were located in West Mexico (the Tarascans) and the Valley of Oaxaca (the Mixtecs). Although objects of metal had been traded northwards from Lower Central America and the Andes prior to the ninth century, it was only in the Toltec era that the technology to produce them was transmitted to Mesoamérica. This indicates a more sustained contact between parts of the Americas than had ever existed before.

Lower Central America and the Andes

Most global ties within Lower Central America (the Intermediate Area) were, not surprisingly, between Mesoamérica, Amazonia, and the Andean world between 400 and 1400. Jade and other Mesoamérican objects have been found deep into Central America, whereas long-term cultural exchange is indicated by ceramics mutually traded between the two areas throughout this period. Lower Central America was traditionally, however, more integrated with the areas to the south than it was to Mesoamérica. Indeed, until the tenth century, one could draw a border between Mesoamérica and the Intermediate Area in terms of metallurgical technology. After the tenth century, exchange between all of these regions seems to have intensified, with enclaves of foreign peoples established along the Atlantic and Pacific Coasts. The most noteworthy of these were the Aztec merchant enclaves, which ranged as far south as Panama. The Andes and Amazonia, however, present a very different picture in terms of global ties.

Moche (200–600 C.E.) and Nazca (200 B.C.E.–650 C.E.)

Much like the Classic Maya (250–909 C.E.) of Mesoamérica, the **Moche** and the Nazca peoples were far more insular politically and culturally than their successors on the coast of Peru. These cultures were certainly influenced by prior developments on the desert coast as well as the Andes during the Andean Preceramic (3000–1800 B.C.E.), Initial Period (1800–400 B.C.E.), and the Early Horizon (400–200 B.C.E.), particularly in terms of architecture. In terms of global ties, however, contacts between Moche or Nazca and other regions of the Americas were likely sporadic.

Tiwanaku (650–1000), Chimor (1000–1476), and the Birth of the Inca (1300–1532)

During the period of the first empires in South America, comprising **Tiwanaku** and **Wari** (650–1000), ties with other regions do appear to have become more pronounced. Prior long-term contact between the Andes and Amazonia seems resulted in the development of some hierarchically organized societies on the Amazonian side of the Andes, and presumably such interactions continued on—at the very least—a limited scale. Perhaps more importantly in terms of global ties, metallurgy from the Andes was introduced into Mesoamérica around the time of the first expansionist empires (this was probably not a coincidence) in South America.

By the time of **Chimor** and the Inca, empire-building in South America had reached its largest expression. The major empires had long since come into direct contact and conflict with individuals from Lower Central America and, at the time of European contact, the Inca were engaged in a seemingly inexorable push northwards. Ties with the western Amazon were also pronounced.

That being said, cultural exchange outside this immediate zone was, even at the height of the Inca Empire, sporadic at best.

Perhaps the most surprising contacts that the desert coast and the Andes had with the outside world were not with the North or East, but with the West: There are signs of ephemeral, but surprisingly influential, contact with eastern Polynesia after 700 and certainly by 1000. Certain agricultural crops native to the Andes—that is, sweet potatoes and bottle gourds—were clearly brought to eastern Polynesia, as they can be found in the archaeological record there (the sweet potato was a food staple in Polynesia from then on). Moreover, it is possible that the first sailing rafts in South America were brought to coastal Ecuador during this period; they, in turn, became a staple of the coastal peoples of South America. Despite these potential exchanges, however, there is no evidence for settlement of peoples in either direction, nor are there any other long-term shared cultural or technological traits in these regions. As this would be expected from consistent contact, it seems likely that any ties between the two were rare and very short lived.

Amazonia and the Caribbean

Prior to 500 C.E., Amazonia had seen massive diasporas of Arawak- and Tupiguarani-speaking groups. These had spread outwards from the western and southern Amazon, respectively, to colonize not only the rest of Amazonia but also the entire Caribbean world. Cultural groups like the Arawak-speaking Taino of **Los Buchillones**, Cuba, were thus the result of far-reaching population movements and cultural spread. Given that ball courts can be found at archaeological sites in the Caribbean, it seems clear that at points between 500 and 1400, Caribbean peoples had established ties with Mesoamérica and their exploits probably allowed for some limited cultural exchange with many of the peoples of the Gulf Coast of Mexico. Amazonian peoples were likewise in contact with peoples of the Intermediate Area. As a result, the cultural impact of Arawak- and Tupiguarani-speaking societies was geographically very significant indeed.

Some scholars believe, moreover, that there was limited, long-term contact between some of the earliest Andean societies or small Andean states and the peoples of Amazonia. There is some evidence, for example, of hierarchically organized societies on the Amazonian side of the Andes that bear similarities to civilizations further to the west. Further research in the Amazon will be needed to further tease out the relationship between this vast geographical zone and other societies of the Americas.

Further Reading
Bellwood, P. *The Polynesians.* 2nd ed. London: Thames and Hudson, 1987.
Carmack, Robert M., and Gary Gossen. *The Legacy of Mesoamerica: History and Culture of a Native American Civilization.* 2nd ed. Upper Saddle River, NJ: Prentice Hall, 2006.
Crown, Patricia. *Ceramics and Ideology: Salado Polychrome Pottery.* Albuquerque: University of New Mexico Press, 1994.
Demarest, Arthur. *The Ancient Maya. The Rise and Fall of a Rainforest Civilization.* Cambridge, UK: Cambridge University Press, 2004.
Fagan, Brian. *Ancient North America.* London: Thames and Hudson, 1991.
Heckenberger, Michael. "Rethinking the Arawakan Diaspora: Hierarchy, Regionality, and the Amazonian Formative." In J. Hill and F. Santos-Granero, eds. *Comparative*

Arawakan Histories: Rethinking Culture Area and Language Group in Amazonia. Urbana: University of Illinois Press, 2002, pp. 99–121.

Hosler, Dorothy. *The Sounds and Colors of Power: The Sacred Metallurgical Technology of Ancient West Mexico.* Cambridge, MA: MIT Press, 1994.

Knight, V.J., Jr., J.A. Brown, and G.E. Lankford. "On the Subject Matter of Southeastern Ceremonial Complex Art." *Southeastern Archaeology* 20 (2001): 129–141.

Moseley, Michael E. *The Incas and their Ancestors: the Archaeology of Peru.* 2nd ed. London: Thames and Hudson, Ltd., 2001.

Scarre, Chris, ed. *The Human Past: World Prehistory and the Development of Human Societies.* London: Thames and Hudson, Ltd., 2005.

Skjolsvold, A. *Archaeological Investigations at Anakena, Easter Island.* Oslo, Norway: Kon-Tiki Museum Occasional Papers 3, 1994.

Smith, Michael E. *The Aztecs.* Oxford, UK: Wiley-Blackwell, 2003.

Wilcox, David. "The Mesoamerican Ballgame in the American Southwest." In V. Scarborough and D. Wilcox, eds. *The Mesoamerican Ballgame.* Tucson: University of Arizona Press, 1991, pp. 101–128.

Short Entries: People, Ideas, Events, and Terms

Acutuba

The Amazonian site of Acutuba, located near present-day Manaus, Brazil, is one of the longest-occupied villages in South America. With people living here almost continuously from 500 B.C.E. to the colonial period, Acutuba provides us with a barometer for the major social and technological changes in the Central Amazon. Possibly first inhabited by Arawak speakers, the culture that first dominated Acutuba and the surrounding region is known as Barrancoid. It was they who first determined the overall plan of Acutuba, which was a classic architectural arrangement for the central Amazon: Houses were arranged around a large, centralized plaza of approximately 10 acres. The Barrancoid people who lived here used a diagnostic, modeled-incised type of pottery (named after this culture), one that was common in the region, between 500 B.C.E. and 900 C.E. Later phases of occupation at Acutuba show a blending of the Barrancoid style with a more widespread ceramic tradition known as Amazonian Polychrome; the result was a regional variant called "Guarita," which lasted until the colonial period.

Acutuba, like some other sites in the Amazon, is also noteworthy for having constructed earthen mounds and employing **terra preta** "black earth," a fertile soil—created and managed by Amazonian peoples over time—used for agricultural purposes which stands in marked contrast to the relatively poor natural soils of Amazonia. For these reasons, some scholars have suggested that Acutuba was a populous urban center by 1000. There are even some archaeological indications that Acutuba was a major center for Amazonian trade. At the moment, however, the nature of Amazonian urbanism is ill defined, so it is difficult to say how sociopolitically complex Acutuba was. What is certain is that Acutuba, in addition to the site of Santarem in the Lower Amazon, is one of the best candidates for a densely populated, complex settlement in this region of the Pre-Columbian Americas.

Further Reading

Heckenberger, Michael, James Petersen, and Eduardo Goes Neves. "Village Size and Permanence in Amazonia: Two Archaeological Examples from Brazil." *Latin American Antiquity* 10(4) (1999): 353–376.

Petersen, James, E.G. Neves, and M. Heckenberger. "Gift from the Past: Terra Preta and Prehistoric Amerindian Occupations in Amazonia," in C. McEwan, C. Barreto, and E.G. Neves, eds. *The Unknown Amazon: Culture in Nature in Ancient Brazil.* London: British Museum Press, 2001, pp. 86–105.

Woods, W., and J. McCann. "The Anthropogenic Origin and Persistence of Amazonian Dark Earths. *Yearbook: Conference of Latin American Geographers* 25 (1999): 7–14.

Ancestor Veneration

Ancestor veneration played a major role in most culture areas of the Pre-Columbian Americas. In general, it took the form of a belief system whereby deceased kin were interested by — and, more important, could play a role in — the affairs of the living. In most instances, ancestors needed to be fed, clothed, prayed to, or otherwise satisfied so as to ensure their continued assistance and to prevent them from becoming so angry that they took out their displeasure on the living. Sometimes, as was common in the early historic period in the American Southwest, the venerated dead were considered more as a group, for example, as a pool of ancestors largely undifferentiated in terms of identity. In other cases, specific individuals from a society might be singled out for veneration by a state; in these examples, not everyone would be considered an "ancestor" for the purposes of state ritual or prayer. However, the boundaries between these two types of ancestors were, even in societies that were more focused on one or the other, somewhat vague. In trying to understand how ancestor veneration works in the Pre-Columbian context, one of the key points involves remembrance: As memories fade, only undifferentiated dead or particularly well-known ancestors remain, such that who or what is venerated can change over time.

In most societies where it occurred, ancestor veneration was an important part of reinforcing and maintaining social, political, and ritual well-being. In the case of elites, ancestors were often used to justify the wealth and power of their descendents. This was particularly the case in the chiefdoms and kingdoms of the Americas, most notably those of Mesoamérica. There the community of the dead quite literally organized the community of the living: In the Maya lowlands of the Classic Period (250–909), for example, kings based their right to rule on lineage ties to deified ancestors. Sacred shrines were often at the heart of Maya sites, and attention to them by the king was a matter of correct ritual behavior and of political necessity.

Some of the most venerated of Classic Maya ancestors, for example, were K'inich Yax K'uk' Mo' of **Copan** and **K'inich Janaab' Pakal** of **Palenque**. For the former, much of the city of Copan seems to have been built around his tomb, with shrines and images of him built by subsequent kings and persisting for the entire history of the site. His most famous shrine, a building dubbed Rosalila by archaeologists, was so venerated that it was carefully buried with earth before a new temple was erected on top of it. Typically, the Maya would damage and at least partially destroy temples before they built new ones in their place; such reverence is unheard of not only at Copan but also at most sites in the Maya lowlands. In the case of K'inich Janaab' Pakal, almost all of the subsequent rulers of Palenque continued to dedicate monuments bearing his portrait or name for the next 100 years. Mortuary shrines for both of these kings were visited for several generations after their deaths, with even their tombs visited and offerings placed by the Classic Maya nobility. Such behavior continues, albeit in modified form, to the present era in the Maya area and in other parts of the Americas.

Further Reading

Fitzsimmons, James. *Death and the Classic Maya Kings*. Austin: University of Texas Press, 2009.

Hays-Gilpin, Kelley, and Jane H. Hill. "The Flower World in Material Culture: An Iconographic Complex in the Southwest and Mesoamerica." *Journal of Anthropological Research*, 55(1) (Spring, 1999): 1–37.

Martin, Simon, and Nikolai Grube. *Chronicle of the Maya Kings and Queens*. London: Thames and Hudson, Ltd., 2000.

Atlatl

Invented over 30,000 years ago, the atlatl or spear thrower is a notched, wooden hunting device used to extend the normal range and overall throwing power of a dart or spear. Essentially, the atlatl consists of a wooden shaft with a handle on one side and a cupped or notched protrusion on the other end, into which the base of the spear is fitted. In an action similar to that of a baseball pitch, the spear is thrown from the atlatl in an overhand motion and—if done correctly—can fly over 100 meters. Accuracy is affected not only by this motion but also by such factors as spear length, wind, projectile point size, and atlatl design. What makes the atlatl so interesting is that it has been used by peoples throughout the world at different points in history (indeed, there are places where it continues to be employed) and was used in some parts of the Americas regularly until the sixteenth century. As such, the atlatl is one of the most widely utilized and long-lived hunting devices in human history.

By 400, the atlatl had largely been abandoned as a hunting tool by most peoples of the Americas in favor of the bow and arrow, a process that had begun by the beginning of the millennium and one that was almost certainly finished by 500. However, the atlatl did remain in common use in a few regions, most notably as a hunting/fishing device in the Arctic. Perhaps the most noteworthy wielders of the atlatl between 400 and 1400, however, were the peoples of Mesoamérica. In this portion of the Americas, the atlatl was most closely associated with the inhabitants of Central Mexico and was employed not only as a hunting/fishing device but also as a weapon of war. The Teotihuacános and the later Aztecs used atlatls to extend the range of their war darts. In the places that they conquered or influenced, the atlatl took on a symbolic quality: The Classic Maya (250–850), for example, always associated the atlatl with the great metropolis of **Teotihuacá** and used images of atlatl-wielding warriors in their sculpture when they wanted to illustrate powerful conquerors. Among the Maya, in fact, the atlatl as a symbol of power far outlived the actual metropolis of Teotihuacá, which collapsed by the early seventh century. Classic Maya kings of the eighth century were still showing themselves with atlatls in their sculpture, portraying themselves as descendents of a powerful warrior tradition. When the Aztecs met the Spaniards on the fields of battle in the sixteenth century, they were using atlatls along with bows and arrows to hurl projectiles at their enemies. The Spanish borrowed the Aztec term for this fishing tool and weapon of war: atlatl.

Further Reading

Fagan, Brian. *Ancient North America*. London: Thames and Hudson, Ltd., 1991.

Muller, John. *Archaeology of the Lower Mississippi Ohio River Valley*. New York: Academic Press, 1986.

Sharer, Robert J., and Loa P. Traxler. *The Ancient Maya.* 6th ed. Stanford, CA: Stanford University Press, 2005.
Smith, Michael E. *The Aztecs.* 2nd ed. Oxford: Wiley-Blackwell, 2003.

Avonlea

Like its more famous "contemporary" from Alberta, Canada, Head-Smashed-In (5400 B.C.E. to 1600 C.E.), Avonlea was a place used specifically for killing—and then processing—bison. Located in southern Saskatchewan, Avonlea was one of a host of such places on the Great Plains, including sites such as Glenrock, Muddy Creek, Ruby, Wardell, and Vore. Instead of being a bison jump, as at Head-Smashed-In (here, bison were herded over a cliff), it was simply a "corral." From 500 all the way to the sixteenth century, bison would be driven to this place by large, cooperative hunting parties, who would perform shamanic rituals before trying to move the bison in the direction they wanted. It was a testament to the hunters' skill that they could track and (sometimes) actually get the bison to move in the direction that they wanted: Lacking horses until the sixteenth century, all of this was done on foot and thereby depended upon local knowledge of where the bison would be and what they would do.

Avonlea is also important because it is one of the earliest sites in which the bow and arrow makes an appearance on the Great Plains, having been introduced there around 500. In fact, Avonlea is the type name for one of the earliest side-notched projectile points yet found on the Great Plains. In addition to allowing for smaller (and more easily made) projectile points than those needed for an **atlatl** (a spear thrower), the bow and arrow revolutionized bison hunting on the Plains. It enabled hunters to kill more prey and even gain a surplus of meat or hides, with which Plains peoples could trade. In particular, they could exchange such valuables for items not normally found on the Great Plains, such as pottery from the Southwest or the Great Basin. This, in turn, facilitated contact between areas that would not usually interact. Hence, places like Avonlea were representative of new changes sweeping across the Great Plains, including the greater facilitation of cultural and technological exchange.

Further Reading
Fagan, Brian. *Ancient North America.* London: Thames and Hudson, Ltd., 1991.
Frison, G.C. "The Wardell Buffalo Trap 48 SU 301: Communal Procurement in Post-Altithermal Populations in the Northwestern Plains." *University of Michigan Anthropological Papers* 46: 11–20.

Ayllu

In some ways comparable to the Aztec calpolli system, an ayllu was the basic unit of religious and sociopolitical life within Andean societies by the Late Horizon (1476–1533), with antecedents dating back at least several hundred years. Typically ruled by two (or more) **curaca** nobles, one for each moiety or descent group, ayllus were familial groups of real and fictive kin organized so as to be economically self-sustaining. An ayllu would usually have its own huaca or sacred location, which would be ritually fed with offerings. Likewise, ayllus would educate their members in agricultural and domestic skills, with descent groups sharing the burden of work for the ayllu and regularly supplying labor—as tax—for public works projects of the Inca Empire. In return, an ayllu could be assured of protection from military and socioeconomic disaster, such as famines or flooding, by gaining access to imperial storehouses in times of need. They are perhaps best understood as a mutual, extended familial support network with ritual undertones: Nearly all aspects of land tenure, from inheritance to pastoral management, were governed by the ayllu. Far from being communal in all aspects, however, the ayllu was characterized by a civil and a religious hierarchy, in which some members—ultimately the nobles—claimed closer descent to the founding ancestors of individual ayllus.

As noted earlier, this form of social organization certainly predates the Late Horizon and the Inca Empire, with clear archaeological evidence of similar social groupings in the Late Intermediate Period (1000–1476); they probably functioned similarly for the prior states of the Andes like **Tiwanaku** or **Wari**. However, in the absence of written records it is difficult to determine their precise nature. Most of what we know about ayllus comes from Spanish ethnohistorical accounts of Inca organization as well as anthropological research within ayllu communities of the Andes today.

Further Reading

Godoy, R. "The Fiscal Role of the Andean Ayllu." *Man* 21(4) (1986): 723–741.
Moseley, Michael E. *The Incas and Their Ancestors: The Archaeology of Peru.* 2nd ed. London: Thames and Hudson, Ltd., 2001.

Aztlan

The word *Aztlan,* or "Place of the White Heron," refers to the legendary homeland of the Chichimecs, a series of Nahua-speaking desert peoples who migrated into the Valley of Mexico from the northern frontiers of Mesoamérica sometime between 1150 and 1250. According to later Nahua legends, the Chichimecs emerged from a series of seven caves beneath a sacred mountain within the homeland of Aztlan. Collectively known as Chicomoztoc, the "Seven Caves" corresponded to the birthplaces of seven different Nahua-speaking groups: the Acolhua, Chalcas, Mexica, Tepaneca, Tlahuica, Tlaxcalan, and Xochimilca. Divinely inspired to leave Aztlan for places further south, the Chichimecs abandoned their homeland for Central Mexico and, under the tutelage of deities such as Mixcoatl and Huitzilopochtli, conquered the preexisting inhabitants of the region.

Archaeologically, there is plenty of evidence for population upheavals and migrations during this era. Although the location of Aztlan is currently unknown, these Nahua-speaking peoples who moved into Central Mexico did come to dominate the previous inhabitants, although it is clear that they borrowed many of their cultural traditions. The resultant blend of Chichimec and local traditions resulted in a common, widespread culture that we know today as "Aztec." One of the Chichimec groups from Aztlan, the Mexica, would come to dominate the others between 1428 and 1519, with the resultant state known as the Aztec Empire. Thus Aztlan can be counted as the mythical homeland of the Aztecs. In point of fact, the word *Aztec* was never used by these peoples: It is a word derived from Aztlan and was created as well as popularized by Europeans in the nineteenth century. Since that time many theories, some purely speculative or even fantastical, have been suggested for the actual location of Aztlan, ranging from Utah to Wisconsin to northern Mexico.

Further Reading

Durán, Diego. *The History of the Indies of New Spain (1579)*. Translated and edited by D. Heiden and F. Horcasitas. Norman: University of Oklahoma Press, 1971.

Miller, Mary Ellen, and Karl Taube. *An Illustrated Dictionary of the Gods and Symbols of Ancient Mexico and the Maya*. London: Thames and Hudson, Ltd., 1997.

Smith, Michael E. *The Aztecs.* 2nd ed. Oxford, UK: Wiley-Blackwell, 2003.

Ballgame

The ballgame, sometimes called the "Mesoamérican ballgame," was an athletic sport as well as a ritual invented sometime around 1400 B.C.E. by the Olmecs on the Gulf Coast of Mexico. That being said, it was widely adopted by all major Mesoamérican societies such that it could be found from northern Mexico all the way to western Honduras in a near continuum by the time of European contact. It was played sporadically, if not continuously, throughout the colonial period and into the modern era, and is currently enjoying a revival in some parts of Mesoamérica.

The play, rules, and even equipment of the Mesoamérican ballgame varied with time and space, but the basic idea of this team exercise seems to have been to strike a rubber ball such that it went into the opponents "end zone" or even a stone ring, usually set up on the side walls of the court. The playing alley was usually shaped like an "I" or similar, sunken somewhat below the normal ground surface with walls of earth or masonry (other courts, most notably in northwest Mexico, were round). Players would wear body armor to protect themselves from the ball, which, as it was of solid rubber and sometimes of great size, was capable of seriously injuring them; likewise, they would wear gear in places where the ball was allowed to strike them.

Symbolically, the game was set in a space that connected the living surface world with the Mesoamérican realm of death, the Underworld. The dead—and even the sun, on a daily basis—were believed to journey here and, as a result, the game could take on supernatural as well as cosmological significance. Human sacrifice, moreover, was sometimes part of the ritual associated with the ballgame. There is much popular literature on the association between human sacrifice and the ballgame, but the specifics of who actually died and when they were killed are not uniform for Mesoamérica. Suffice to say, the individuals killed before, during, or after ballgames are almost always depicted as war captives.

In places where we have visual depictions or descriptions of the ballgame, such as in the Maya lowlands or West Mexico, ballgames seem to have been played for a variety of reasons under different circumstances.

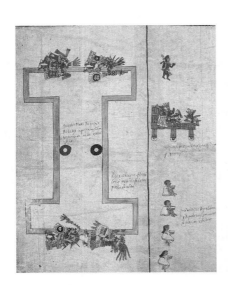

Ullamalitzli ball game, Codex *Borbonicus*, 16th century Aztec postconquest manuscript; The "I" shape of the ball court itself was called "tlachtli." The Art Archive/Bibliothèque de l'Assemblée Nationale Paris/Gianni Dagli Orti.

Sometimes they appear to have taken place just for fun: Some ball courts were simple affairs, the playing alleys built well outside city centers and clearly not designed for mass elite spectacle. In other cases, most notably among the Classic Maya (250–850) and the Aztecs (1325–1521), ballgames were occasionally mechanisms for diplomacy, with rulers—or surrogates for them—playing one another. Likewise, ballgames were, as with some sports today, occasions for serious gambling: The Aztecs, for example, are known to have bet themselves into (temporary) slavery over the outcomes of such contests.

The ballgame as a concept seems to have been exported out of Mesoamérica to the American Southwest for time. Between 700 and 1250, ball courts were built and used by the Hohokam of Arizona. Their courts were round rather than rectangular and appear to have the most similarities with those employed by peoples on the fringes of northern Mesoamérica, who themselves had adopted and adapted the Mesoamérican ballgame from places further south. The Hohokam abandoned the ballgame in the thirteenth century, and it is not known whether they, like the Mesoaméricans, attached supernatural or cosmological significance to it. Most archaeologists, however, believe that the Hohokam Ballgame, like its ancestor, did combine ritual with sport.

Further Reading

Sharer, Robert J., and Loa P. Traxler. *The Ancient Maya.* 6th ed. Stanford, CA: Stanford University Press, 2005.

Smith, Michael E. *The Aztecs.* 2nd ed. Oxford, UK: Wiley-Blackwell, 2003.

Wilcox, David. "The Mesoamerican Ballgame in the American Southwest," in V. Scarborough and D. Wilcox, eds. *The Mesoamerican Ballgame* Tucson: University of Arizona Press, 1991, pp. 101–128.

Batán Grande

This archaeological site in the Lambayeque region of the north coast of Peru was the largest and most powerful city in the area between 800 and 1100. Following a series of massive natural disasters that weakened and ultimately precipitated the decline of Moche civilization between 700 and 800, the political scene on the north coast came to be dominated by two powers: the empire of Chimor and the Lambayeque city-states (also known as Sican Culture), a loose confederation of polities dominated by Batán Grande. According to native accounts, Batán Grande was founded by a grandson of the quasi-historical culture hero **Naymlap**; it was, according to the story, one of twelve such federated and related settlements in the Lambayeque region.

Archaeologically, we know that between 800 and 1000, Batán Grande grew into a major city with an urban core of approximately 1.5 square miles. It appears to have become a favored locale for burial as well, with thousands of elite interments having been discovered thus far. Unfortunately, the majority of the known interments at Batán Grande have been looted for their gold. From the looted objects, however, it is clear that Lambayeque continues some of the traditions found in **Moche** civilization; moreover, there is a clear continuum from Lambayeque to succeeding cultural traditions in the area.

Like Moche, moreover, Batán Grande was hit hard by natural disasters: An especially strong El Niño event in 1100 appears to have flooded the site and precipitated its abandonment. Interestingly enough, the native accounts also mention such a disaster in connection with Lambayeque: A later descendent of Naymlap angers the gods and precipitates its collapse. Although the Lambayeque region did recover, it was eventually conquered by the empire of **Chimor** in the fourteenth century.

Further Reading

Moseley, Michael E. *The Incas and their Ancestors: The Archaeology of Peru.* 2nd ed. London: Thames and Hudson, Ltd.

Moseley, Michael E., and A. Cordy-Collins, eds. *The Northern Dynasties: Kingship and Statecraft in Chimor.* Washington, DC: Dumbarton Oaks, 1990.

Pillsbury, Joanne. *Historiographic Guide to Andean Sources in Art History and Archaeology.* Oklahoma: University of Oklahoma Press, 2001.

Cacao

Although the wild variety of the cacao tree—whose fruits hang from its trunk rather than its branches—appears to be native to the Amazon and Orinoco river basins of South America, cacao does not appear to have been of great importance to this region. Rather, it was the peoples of Mesoamérica who held cacao in great regard, using its beans to make the first chocolate in the world. Like all peoples who encountered chocolate before 1591, from the Americas to Europe, Mesoamérican civilizations drank their chocolate: There was no such thing as solid chocolate until that time. In the Pre-Columbian world, chocolate was a drink reserved for elites and was a mark of high status. It was the only major stimulant drink in the Americas until tea and coffee were imported by the Europeans. In Europe, it was to become the most popular stimulant drink until the mid-seventeenth century. And although solid chocolate appears to have been invented early in the colonial period—in present-day Guatemala—the chocolate bar, as we know it, was not invented until the early nineteenth century.

We do not know how cacao was imported to Mesoamérica. Some scholars have even suggested that the original range of the cacao tree extended as far north as Chiapas, Mexico, so it may not have been imported at all. What is clear is that Mesoamérican peoples domesticated this plant and that the most likely individuals (but not the only candidates) to have done so were the Maya, sometime during the Preclassic Period (1200 B.C.E.–250 C.E.). It is actually from the ancient Maya word *kakaw*, that we get the word for these beans: Most of the peoples of Mesoamérica borrowed this word and modified it in their languages, including the Aztecs, who used the word *cacaoatl* ("chocolate water") to refer to the final product. Cacaoatl may be the original source of the English word for chocolate, although there are other possibilities.

Chocolate as a drink was made by gathering and fermenting the fruits of the cacao tree. Their seeds were then taken out, dried, and peeled before they were finely ground. The grounds were then mixed with water as well as a host of ingredients that varied according to region, time period, and taste: Ground chili peppers, maize dough, fruits, vanilla, and possibly honey were the main additives. One of the reasons why this drink was so prestigious in Mesoamérica was because cacao could only be grown within portions of that region: The Maya area was ideal for growing this tropical fruit, whereas Central Mexico was not. As a result, peoples such as the Aztecs had to import chocolate—either peaceably or as tribute—to enjoy it. The ultimate consequence of the value of chocolate was that it came to be used as money, with the cacao beans being the smallest, lowest form of currency in some parts of Mesoamérica.

Further Reading

Coe, Sophie, and Michael Coe. *The True History of Chocolate*. London: Thames and Hudson, Ltd., 2000.

Miller, Mary Ellen, and Simon Martin, eds. *Courtly Art of the Ancient Maya*. London: Thames and Hudson, Ltd., 2004.

Miller, Mary Ellen, and Karl Taube. *An Illustrated Dictionary of the Gods and Symbols of Ancient Mexico and the Maya*. London: Thames and Hudson, Ltd., 1997.

Cahokia

As the most famous of all of the mound-building settlements of the Mississippian era (1000–1500), Cahokia was the most populous center in the present-day United States between 1050 and 1250. With population estimates widely varying from as little as four thousand to as much as forty thousand, it is difficult to say how densely settled this site was, but it was certainly built on a grand scale: For example, the largest mound, popularly known as Monk's Mound, is over 100 feet tall and covers 16 acres alone. Close to modern St. Louis, Missouri, the site is characterized by over one hundred earthen mounds of various shapes and sizes, erected in stages so as to give the appearance of several steps or courses. It is also noteworthy for its large, open plaza, as well as a wooden palisade protecting the center of the site. In its heyday, Cahokia was at the top of a local hierarchy of over fifty sites and appears to have been an important locus of sociopolitical and religious activity, particularly with regard to the **Southern Cult** or Southeastern Ceremonial Complex. It declined by the fourteenth century and was long abandoned by the time of European contact.

One of the reasons why Cahokia is so important to the prehistory of the Americas is that it, together with **Moundville**, Alabama, provides us with the best case for an indigenous state north of Mexico. Some archaeologists have characterized Cahokia as a huge, populous urban center, with public works, craft specialization, and a politically centralized elite dominating the Midwest in the eleventh and twelfth centuries; in this model the dominant groups were vastly different, in terms of personal wealth and power, from the average inhabitant of the site. Others see Cahokia as an unusually complex chiefdom, where the chief did not live a vastly different life from the rest of the population and craft specialization extended only to a select few elite objects. In that model, a modest population built up the site as well as its mounds over generations, participating in a cultural exchange of ideas with other Mississippian centers.

Clearly there is much disagreement on the size and nature of Cahokia: There is no consensus as to whether Cahokia (or Moundville) represented a sharp break with local social and political traditions. Certainly, settlements such as Cahokia were more complex than had previously existed, but whether or not they represented something new—versus an elaboration of the old—is not something that is going to be resolved soon. One argument that is somewhat in favor of the "state" hypothesis is that like peoples from other archaic state-level societies, the inhabitants of Cahokia practiced human sacrifice in elite mortuary ritual. The interment within Mound 72 at Cahokia, perhaps the most famous burial in the Southeast, included an elite man who was accompanied by twenty-thousand shell beads, eight-hundred arrowheads, sheets of copper and mica, and a host of other objects. Also included as part of his burial were three high-status men and women as well as four decapitated men missing their hands. In a nearby (and related) pit, archaeologists found the remains of over fifty young women, at least some of whom appear to have been strangled.

Further Reading
Fowler, M.L., J. Rose, B. Vander Leest, and S.R. Ahler. *The Mound 72 Area: Dedicated and Sacred Space in Early Cahokia*. Springfield: Illinois State Museum, 1999.
Milner, G.R. *The Cahokia Chiefdom: The Archaeology of a Mississippian Society*. Washington, DC: Smithsonian Institution Press, 1998.
O'Brien, P.J. "Early State Economics: Cahokia, Capital of the Ramey State," in H. Claessen and P. van de Velde, eds. *Early State Economics*. London: Transaction, 1991, pp. 143–175.

Calakmul

This archaeological site in Yucatán, Mexico, was one of the preeminent cities of the Lowland Maya. Certainly settled by the Late Preclassic (300 B.C.E.–250 C.E.), Calakmul steadily grew in population and political influence for hundreds of years thereafter. It eventually became the largest of the Classic Maya (250–850) cities and a bitter rival of **Tikal**. Although the majority of its hieroglyphic monuments have not weathered the centuries well, archaeologists are continuing to learn more about the past at this major Maya center. Known to the ancient Maya as *Kaan* (kingdom of *Kaanal*), Calakmul embarked upon a series of political and military maneuvers in the sixth century to threaten and isolate its rival: It conquered, subjugated, or allied itself with many of the major players of the Classic era, including Caracol, Dos Pilas, El Peru, Naranjo, and Piedras Negras. These maneuvers ultimately resulted in the utter defeat of Tikal, to the extent that no new monuments were erected there for most of the sixth and seventh centuries. The capture of the ruler of Tikal, Wak Chan K'awiil, in 562 by the king of Calakmul—as well as a series of victories over **Palenque** shortly thereafter—marked a turning point in the political fortunes of the *Kaan* kingdom.

Calakmul was at the apex of its power in the seventh century, and its epicenter may have been home to over fifty-thousand people. Under kings such as Yuknoom Ch'een II (r. 636–686) or his son, Yuknoom Yich'aak K'ahk' (r. 686–695), Calakmul built some of the largest temple-pyramids in the Maya Lowlands (Structure 2, for example, was the largest temple-pyramid of the Classic era) and extended its influence over much of the Central Petén. Its vassals were many and geographically widespread, and although they often squabbled among themselves their individual allegiance to Calakmul generally held. Some of the most successful attacks on Tikal, for example, were made by allies such as Dos Pilas or Caracol seemingly at the behest of Calakmul. For whatever reason, however, the kings of Calakmul were unable to fully subjugate or destroy Tikal and its allies. Their gradual resurgence under seminal leaders such as **K'inich Janaab' Pakal** (r. 615–683) of Palenque and **Jasaw Chan K'awiil I** (r. 682–734) of Tikal eroded the power base of the loose Calakmul confederation. For whatever reason, the great center was largely unable to protect its vassals during this time. Disaster for Calakmul finally came in 732 with the capture and public killing of its king, Yuknoom Took' K'awiil, by Jasaw Chan K'awiil I in the central plaza at Tikal. Although future kings of Calakmul were to follow, the site experienced a precipitous decline in the latter half of the eighth century from which it was unable to recover. By the tenth century Calakmul, like most of its contemporaries, had been abandoned to the ravages of the jungle, its royal dynasty long since destroyed.

Further Reading

Folan, William, ed. *Campeche Maya Colonial*. Colección Arqueología 3. Campeche, Mexico: Universidad Autónoma de Campeche, 1994.

Martin, Simon, and Nikolai Grube. *Chronicle of the Classic Maya Kings and Queens*. London: Thames and Hudson, Ltd., 2000.

Martin, Simon, and Nikolai Grube. "Maya Superstates." *Archaeology* 48(6) (1985): 41–46.

Calmecac

Between 1325 and 1519, the Aztec Empire was the most powerful military and political force in Mesoamérica. Although it is most commonly associated with warfare and militaristic expansionism, the Aztec Empire was remarkable for its time and place in its social institutions. One of the most basic characteristics of the empire was its emphasis on education: All boys and girls were required to attend a school at some point between 10 and 20 years of age, with separate schools for males and females. Aztec schools were divided into two types, known as the telpochcalli and the calmecac. The telpochcalli was a school largely for commoners and could be found in nearly every Aztec town. Males there were primarily trained in the basics of agriculture as well as warfare, whereas females learned domestic skills as well as the basics of textile production. The latter was a skill essential to the functioning of the empire, as textiles were often provided as tribute to the Aztec capital at **Tenochtitlán**. A calmecac was a school for nobles and select individuals being trained for governmental and administrative positions, the priesthood, or leadership in battle. Literacy and "correct speech" were of paramount importance to elite education. Men and women were trained in all manner of courtly skills and behavior and, in a sense, taught how to perform as a member of the nobility or upper class. It should be mentioned, however, that in the calmecac and the telpochcalli, all students learned how to sing, dance, and play musical instruments. Although the primary function of school was to prepare for the daily activities—and hazards—of Aztec life, particularly with respect to warfare, the arts were considered an essential part of Aztec education.

Further Reading

Evans, Susan. *Ancient Mexico and Central America: Archaeology and Culture History*. London: Thames and Hudson, Ltd., 2004.

Smith, Michael E. *The Aztecs*. 2nd ed. Oxford, UK: Wiley-Blackwell, 2003.

Townsend, Richard. *Aztecs*. New York: Thames and Hudson, Ltd., 1992.

Calpolli

In the towns and cities of the Aztecs (1325–1521), a calpolli was a residential ward or block of land serving as a basic unit of settlement within the empire, oftentimes factoring into administrative needs and decisions, such as the calculation of annual tribute payments. Given the size of the Aztec Empire and the many peoples within it, the relative importance of the calpolli varied from region to region. In some places, people from the same calpolli shared a common occupation, with the land maintained and managed by a calpolli council; land here was communal in that it could not be bought, sold, or otherwise dispatched but as a group. These calpollis, in turn, were under the jurisdiction of a noble, with the nobles themselves living there but having their own lands apart from the calpolli where peasants were not allowed. The well-excavated towns of Cuexcomate and Capilco, for example, may have been examples of this system. With over one hundred houses, the calpolli town of Cuexcomate had its own palace for a noble and his family as well as a temple and perhaps a telpochcalli school; there, peasant children aged 10 to 20 would be expected to learn the arts as well as martial, agricultural, and domestic skills (*see* **Calmecac**).

In other portions of the Aztec Empire, calpollis were of minimal importance or even absent. Nobles might, for example, directly own lands upon which peasants were attached by daily service and annual tribute. Ever-increasing tribute payments as well as worsening environmental conditions in the late years of the Aztec Empire increased the gap between nobles and commoners drastically, such that for many the calpolli—with its council—was probably a welcome buffer institution.

Further Reading

Evans, Susan. *Ancient Mexico and Central America: Archaeology and Culture History*. London: Thames and Hudson, Ltd., 2004.

Smith, Michael E. *The Aztecs*. 2nd ed. Oxford: Wiley-Blackwell, 2003.

Townsend, Richard. *Aztecs*. New York: Thames and Hudson, Ltd., 1992.

Casas Grandes

Located in the northwest part of Chihuahua, Mexico, near the Mexico-U.S. border, the Pre-Columbian settlement of Casas Grandes (1130–1500) was an important stop on the Postclassic (909–1519) trade route between Mesoamérica and the American Southwest. Like peoples from the Southwest, the inhabitants of Casas Grandes—and surrounding settlements—created residential, storied apartment compounds of adobe and had elaborate water-management systems. Similarities to Mesoamérican culture included the presence of an I-shaped ball court (*see* **Ballgame**), stone-faced architecture, and craft centers producing copper bells similar to those being manufactured in West Mexican, Mesoamérican communities of that time. Effigy mounds, a local innovation, as well as craft production involving marine shell, were also hallmarks of this site, which at its height housed perhaps twenty-five hundred people. Moreover, these inhabitants appear to have been importing and raising scarlet macaws, native to Mesoamérica. Casas Grandes, also known as Paquimé, began to decline in the final decades of the fifteenth century, when public architecture fell into ruin. Residential abandonment followed soon after, and by 1500 the site was deserted.

Casas Grandes and related local communities are also known archaeologically for their pottery, which is usually white or red and decorated in brilliant colors or earth tones. Ceramics in the overall forms of animals or humans are also common, and so distinctive is the Casas Grandes ceramic type that it has been identified in archaeological contexts all over the American Southwest. Given that regions to the north and west show clear evidence of Mesoamérican influence during this time, it is likely that this area of Chihuahua played a role in the spread of cultural ideas—and goods—between the Southwest, northern Mexico, and Mesoamérica. The period of greatest exchange seems to have been in the early Postclassic, when Central Mexican powers such as the Toltecs (700–1200) and Southwest societies such as the Preclassic Hohokam (700–1150) were at their height. The Toltecs actually appear to have been trading with Casas Grandes, although the extent of this trade is not fully understood. Casas Grandes, then, is an important site for its apparent connections to two major worlds as well as the indigenous developments in northern Mexico. However intermittent, it stands as a testament to contact between cultural areas in the Americas.

Further Reading

Braniff Cornejo, Beatríz, ed. *Papeles Norteños*. Mexico City: Instituto Nacional de Antropología e Historia, 1997.

Johnson, Grace, ed. *From Paquimé to Mata Ortíz: The Legacy of Ancient Casas Grandes.* San Diego, CA: San Diego Museum of Man, 2001.

Schaafsma, Curtis F., and Carroll L. Riley, eds. *The Casas Grandes World.* Salt Lake City: University of Utah Press, 1999.

Chaco Canyon

Although signs of sporadic occupation in Chaco Canyon, New Mexico, located in the Four Corners region of the American Southwest, date back thousands of years, it was not until the founding of **Shabik'eschee** in the late fifth century that the area saw permanent settlement. Small farming settlements spread here and into the San Juan basin of the Colorado Plateau thereafter, but population levels remained low for the next 300 to 400 years. Between 800 and 900, these farming communities began to get larger, with subterranean kivas (communal sociopolitical and religious spaces) and the beginnings of masonry architecture for either residential or ritual functions. Between 950 and 1050, however, this trend intensified greatly. Communal masonry buildings with hundreds of rooms—called "great houses"—exploded over the landscape of the San Juan basin. This building activity intensified over the next 100 years and was particularly concentrated within Chaco Canyon. Dubbed the "Chaco phenomenon," these events abruptly took a turn for the worse by the mid-twelfth century. By 1200, most of Chaco Canyon was abandoned, and new population centers had sprung up to the north.

Archaeologists have fiercely debated the events surrounding the Chaco phenomenon: Why it was settled so rapidly has been a topic laden with environmental and religious explanations. Most environmental explanations center on the idea that Chaco became an agriculturally desirable place to live in the early eleventh century (or even earlier); conflicting environmental data has portrayed Chaco Canyon as a forested oasis, a lacustrine paradise, or an inhospitable desert. Religious explanations usually portray Chaco Canyon as a pilgrimage center, with turquoise and other precious objects ritually deposited by pilgrims—themselves from disparate geographic origins—at this sacred center in the Southwest. At the moment, there is enough archaeological evidence to support both of these explanations, with ideology and favorable climate not being mutually exclusive. Nevertheless, archaeological consensus does not look to be in the immediate future, and explanations for the abandonment of Chaco Canyon—almost as rapid as its settlement—are equally elusive.

Further Reading

Fagan, Brian. *Ancient North America*. London: Thames and Hudson, Ltd., 1991.

Mills, Barbara. "Recent Research on Chaco: Changing Views on Economy, Ritual, and Society." *Journal of Archaeological Research* 10 (2002): 45–117.

Vivian, R. *The Chacoan Prehistory of the San Juan Basin*. San Diego, CA: Academic Press, 1990.

Chichén Itzá

The ancient Maya site of Chichén Itzá was one of the most powerful cities of the early part of the Postclassic (909–1519) and, for part of that time, was the largest settlement in the northern lowlands. Up until recently, Chichén Itzá was believed to have been a city-state dominated by the Toltecs, a major civilization of Central Mexico. According to native accounts from the early colonial period as well as prior archaeological research, the site had risen to local prominence in the Yucatán by the Late Classic (600–909). Native accounts held that around 987, a Toltec lord from the site of **Tula** named Ce Acatl Topiltzin **Quetzalcoatl** and his followers migrated to Chichén Itzá and came to power, displacing the local Itzá Maya elite. Founding a dynasty that was to last until the site's violent destruction between 1200 and 1250, this figure brought Toltec influence to the Maya area and transformed Chichén Itzá into the principal economic and political force in southern Mesoamérica.

Castillo or Great Pyramid and Palace of 1000 Columns. Mayan and Toltec city of Chichen Itza, Mexico. Courtesy of photos.com

Recent scholarship, however, has demonstrated that at least part of this story is wrong. It is now known that Chichén Itzá, as a major power, predates the rise of the Toltecs in Central Mexico: Its period of greatest florescence and power was between 750 and 1050. To be sure, the art and architecture of Chichén Itzá (and those cities in the Maya area with which it had prolonged contact) show styles long associated with the Toltecs. As the Toltecs of Tula did not become a major power in Central Mexico until 900, however, there is a distinct possibility that Chichén Itzá influenced Tula—and not the other way around.

The revised dates also set Chichén Itzá as a direct beneficiary of the Maya collapse: All of the sites of the southern lowlands, from **Tikal** and **Palenque** to **Calakmul** and **Copan**, were being abandoned as Chichén Itzá grew in strength. Other sites in the northern lowlands seem to have benefited from the collapse as well, including the major centers of Uxmal and Coba, and now appear to have been in direct competition with the northern metropolis. Chichén Itzá seems to have won this protracted engagement, however, conquering parts of the Coba kingdom and gaining control over lucrative maritime and inland trade routes, where salt, textiles, and **cacao** (chocolate) were imported and exported to many parts of Mesoamérica on a massive scale.

Such trade enabled Chichén Itzá to become a new version of the Classic Maya kingdoms of Tikal or Calakmul for a time. Chichén Itzá became a major center for pilgrimage, in part due to its newfound power and as a result of its proximity to a gigantic cenote, or water-filled sinkhole, into which precious items—including sacrificed individuals—would be thrown (the name *Chichén Itzá* means "Well of the Itzá"). Building a massive ball court (*see* **Ballgame**), the Monjas Palace, and the iconic Castillo Pyramid, the rulers of Chichén Itzá could boast of being the natural successors to the splendor of the Classic Period (250–909).

Yet Chichén Itzá was different from these earlier centers in many respects. Divisions between different types of elites, notably merchants, priests, and warriors, were more pronounced than they ever had been. Elite factions, oftentimes centered on competing lineages, were now more the rule than the exception; the kings of Chichén Itzá did not hold absolute power and had entered into power-sharing arrangements with groups of nobles in councils. Economically, people at Chichén Itzá concentrated more on producing goods for trade than their ancestors had ever been, and Mesoamérica was seeing the birth of a market economy. As a result, Chichén Itzá can be thought of as a transition between the sociopolitical and economic organization of the Classic Period (250–909) and the new order of the Postclassic (909–1519). It does seem to have suffered a violent destruction around 1050, perhaps—as in native accounts—by an internal, factional conflict. Some of its peoples are believed to have migrated further south, to Lake Petén Itzá in present-day Guatemala (*see* **Tayasal**).

Further Reading

Demarest, Arthur. *Ancient Maya*. Cambridge, UK: Cambridge University Press, 2005.

Martin, Simon, and Nikolai Grube. *Chronicle of the Maya Kings and Queens*. London: Thames and Hudson, Ltd., 2000.

Sharer, Robert J., and Loa P. Traxler. *The Ancient Maya*. 6th ed. Stanford, CA: Stanford University Press, 2005.

Chimor

The empire of Chimor, founded by its quasi-mythical ancestor Taycanamu at Chan Chan, on the north coast of Peru, was the second-largest empire ever to reign in South America. Together with the Lambayeque city-states (*see* **Batán Grande**), Chimor was one of the two states, which followed after the disintegration of **Moche** civilization. Chimor, by far, was the dominant player and had come to dominate the Moche Valley around 900. Shortly thereafter, it sought to expand its sociopolitical domains and had begun a campaign of conquest along the coast that was, by 1450, to stretch over 600 miles. From southern Ecuador to southern Peru, Chimor could boast that it had conquered all of the land held by the previous, powerful coastal states of South America. In the late fourteenth century, however, Chimor would see its holdings and empire challenged—and destroyed—by an upstart Andean culture: the Inca.

The Chimor capital of Chan Chan was the largest city of its day on the north coast, housing approximately twenty-nine thousand people. Like other settlements in this area, the capital was built of mud-bricks and adobe and consisted of a political center bearing vast residential and royal compounds known as ciudadelas. Occasionally the ciudadelas also housed mortuary mounds, where the mummies of the Chimor nobility would be kept for the purposes of ancestor veneration. The ciudadelas themselves were sometimes surrounded by towering, thick walls and were exclusive to the nobility: The entire effect would have been a vast political center in which a disproportionate few actually lived. By comparison, the vast majority of people at Chan Chan lived outside the ciudadelas in meager households of wattle-and-daub, working as farmers, laborers, and skilled craftsmen. These individuals produced some of the finest goods in the hemisphere, particularly with regard to metallurgy. Although pottery and textile manufacture were highly developed in Chimor, it was in the realm of metalworking that the craftsmen of the north coast were particularly skilled, especially with regard to gold. The empire of Chimor was thus an economic as well as a political prize to the Inca when they started to expand in the late fourteenth century.

Further Reading

Moore, Jerry. *Architecture and Power in the Ancient Andes: The Archaeology of Public Buildings.* Cambridge, UK: Cambridge University Press, 1996.

Moseley, Michael E. *The Incas and Their Ancestors: the Archaeology of Peru.* 2nd ed. London: Thames and Hudson, Ltd., 2001.

Moseley, Michael E., and A. Cordy-Collins, eds. *The Northern Dynasties: Kingship and Statecraft in Chimor.* Washington, DC: Dumbarton Oaks, 1990.

Chinampas

Swamp reclamation and the use of canals for agricultural purposes are of great antiquity in Mesoamérica, dating back to the Preclassic (2500 B.C.E.–250 C.E.). The fabled chinampas of Central Mexico were the latest of these agricultural methods and were common in the Basin of Mexico prior to the arrival of the Aztecs there in the twelfth and thirteenth centuries. These newcomers employed chinampas to great effect, particularly during the creation and expansion of the Aztec Empire between 1325 and 1521. As a series of artificial islands and fields built within swamps and lakes, chinampas were one of the keys to the success of the Aztec Empire. Aztec engineers in their capital of Tenochtitlán, for example, created thousands of hectares (one hectare equals 10,000 square meters) of chinampas in and around their city. Such well-watered—and drained—agricultural fields produced an enormous amount of food, which could be transported through canals easily and efficiently throughout the city via boat. The population boom that ensued was one of the major factors in the Aztec rise. Chinampas transformed Tenochtitlán from a minor village in a swamp to the capital of Mesoamérica's largest empire within a little over 100 years! In fact, as the Aztec Empire expanded, its rulers paid particular attention to the conquest of areas of Central Mexico already using chinampas. These areas became breadbaskets for the state, most notably in and around the cities of Xochimilco and Chalco, in the southern Basin.

Also known as "floating gardens," chinampas were built by taking sediment from the lake or swamp bottom and building it up in fenced-off or similarly secured areas. Arranged in long rows facing the water, these fields had the advantage of being raised high enough to prevent watery inundation but low enough to ensure that all crops had a continual supply of water as needed. Canals built between theses artificial islands ensured rapid transportation of goods and workers throughout the chinampas. Houses for caretakers were sometimes built on the chinampas as well, which grew the majority of the food consumed by the Aztec Empire. Those around Tenochtitlán were used to grow food for its two-hundred-thousand inhabitants (chinampas alone accounted for over half of food consumption in the city) as well as specialty items like flowers for sale and export. Chinampas largely fell out of use after the Spanish conquest of the Aztecs in 1521, primarily because much of Lake Texcoco was filled in, although there are pockets of Mexico today where they continue to function.

Further Reading

Evans, Susan. *Ancient Mexico and Central America: Archaeology and Culture History*. London: Thames and Hudson, Ltd., 2004.

Smith, Michael. *The Aztecs*. London: Thames and Hudson, Ltd., 2003.

Townsend, Richard. *Aztecs*. New York: Thames and Hudson, Ltd., 1992.

Codex

Pre-Columbian codices (sing. codex) were books painted by different civilizations of Mesoamérica to record mythology, history, astronomical observations, and agricultural information. Although produced by all literate civilizations of Mesoamérica, the most prolific producers of codices were the Classic (250–909) and Postclassic (909–1519) kingdoms of the Maya and the Mixtec, as well as the scribes of the Aztec Empire in the late Postclassic. Although the writing systems of these three distinct linguistic and ethnic groups were vastly different, the basic construction and purpose of a codex remained the same.

Codices were usually constructed of paper made from bark or other plant fibers, although occasionally deerskin would be used. The bark or plant fiber was boiled and then pounded with stone to produce a rough, long stretch of thin paper. A layer of white plaster was then applied to create a smooth surface for painting. The paper was then folded, screenlike, so as to produce a book. The pages would be painted on both sides by professional scribes, who existed as a class of artisans in Mesoamérica from the birth of writing in the Preclassic (c. 900 B.C.E.) to the early colonial period.

At the very least, thousands of codices were likely produced by Mesoamérican civilizations, from the Olmec in the first millennium B.C.E. to the Aztecs of the fifteenth and sixteenth centuries. Almost none survive today. Archaeologists have certainly found the remains of Pre-Columbian codices at archaeological sites such as Uaxactun, Guatemala, or **Copan**, Honduras, but they are illegible and largely destroyed. The only known codices that have survived to the present were produced just before, or shortly after, the Spanish Conquests of the sixteenth and seventeenth centuries. Unfortunately, the vast majority of the extant codices were destroyed by the Spanish as heretical works. At present there are four existing Maya codices (Madrid, Dresden, Paris, and Grolier), approximately five-hundred Aztec codices, and eight Mixtec codices (the most famous of these is the Codex Nuttall). Of the numerous Aztec codices, the vast majority were created in a hybrid Aztec-Spanish style after the Conquest, so the actual number of purely indigenous codices is quite small, perhaps numbering around 20.

Further Reading

Boone, Elizabeth. *Stories in Red and Black: The Pictorial Histories of the Aztec and Mixtec.* Austin: University of Texas Press, 2000.

Martin, Simon, and Nikolai Grube. *Chronicle of the Maya Kings and Queens.* London: Thames and Hudson, Ltd., 2000.

Sharer, Robert J., and Loa P. Traxler. *The Ancient Maya.* 6th ed. Stanford, CA: Stanford University Press, 2005.

Troike, Nancy P., ed. *Codex Zouche-Nuttall.* London: British Museum, 1987.

Copan

The ancient Maya site of Copan, located in present-day western Honduras, is one of the most well known and excavated of all Classic Maya (250–850) cities. During its heyday it was the capital of a kingdom (*Xukpi*), which held sway over the sites of the Motagua River valley, a border region between present-day Guatemala and Honduras. This region was important because it was the only source of one of the most precious items in Classic Maya trade: jade. Copan today is justifiably famous for the unique, 3-dimensional sculptural style of its royal monuments and for the Hieroglyphic Stairway, the longest written Pre-Columbian text in the Americas. Settled in the Late Preclassic (300 B.C.E.–250 C.E.), Copan rose to political importance in 426, when an individual named K'inich Yax K'uk' Mo' is said to have "arrived" there and founded a new royal dynasty. What makes this arrival interesting is that he is clearly described on hieroglyphic monuments as having associations with the Central Mexican metropolis of **Teotihuacá**. Although K'inich Yax K'uk' Mo' was probably not from Central Mexico, the manner of his ascension is similar to that of other central Mexican-related dynasties in the Maya area (*see* **Tikal**). Some have suggested that Copan, like its contemporaries to the northwest, was strongly influenced—if not directly, then certainly indirectly—by Teotihuacá during the fourth to sixth centuries.

Perhaps the most famous ruler of Copan, however, lived well past the era of Teotihuacá influence: Waxaklajuun Ub'aah K'awiil, popularly known as "18

Mayan Temple in Copan. Courtesy of photos.com.

Rabbit." Following his accession in 695, this king transformed the site with three-dimensional self-portraits, an early version of the Hieroglyphic Stairway, a new ball court, and other monumental works. Art during his reign flourished, with scribes and sculptors breaking many Classic Maya conventions. As an example, **Stela** J—his first commission—was sculpted such that its text was visually "woven" (and read) like a mat; unlike any other Maya stela, moreover, it was provided with a roof and thus transformed into a symbolic house. Many consider his reign to have been the apex of a "golden age" at Copan.

Unfortunately, this time came to an abrupt end in 738. After some initial military successes early in his reign, Waxaklajuun Ub'aaj K'awiil was killed by an unlikely foe: His vassal, the king of Quirigua. Quirigua had been a subject state to Copan since the time of K'inich Yax K'uk' Mo', but in the early eighth century its new king, K'ak' Tiliw Chan Yoaat, seems to have had his eyes on independence. In 738, he took Waxaklajuun Ub'aah K'awiil hostage and had him beheaded, taking control of at least part of the lucrative Motagua trade in jade. Copan never fully recovered from the ascendance of its new competitor, although it did experience a major period of revitalization in the mid- to late-eighth century, when the Hieroglyphic Stairway was finally finished. Unfortunately for eighth-century Copan, archaeologists have found signs that the state was coming under increasing stress from two sources: the nobility and the larger population. Nobles appear to have gained in power, at the expense of kings, steadily during the late eighth century, while the population continued to grow at environmentally unsustainable rates. By 822, the royal dynasty at Copan was collapsing, with the site abandoned and reoccupied sporadically— and sparsely—over the next 200 years.

Further Reading

Braswell, Geoffrey, ed. *The Maya and Teotihuacá*. Austin: University of Texas Press, 2004.

Fash, William L. *Scribes, Warriors and Kings*. 2nd ed. London: Thames and Hudson, Ltd., 2001.

Martin, Simon, and Nikolai Grube. *Chronicle of the Maya Kings and Queens*. London: Thames and Hudson, Ltd., 2000.

Corvée Labor

This system of labor tax or tribute is one where people in authority have the right to compel subjects to perform menial labor for a specified, usually cyclical period. Although it is usually associated with such ancient civilizations as Egypt or Rome, or the feudal conditions of medieval and early modern European nations, corvée labor was practiced throughout the Americas. The most noteworthy culture to employ corvée in the building of public works and monuments was the Inca.

Sometime around 1375, the Inca city-state of **Cuzco** began to transform from a provincial center—virtually indistinguishable from other city-states of the time—to a growing metropolis on the verge of conquering its neighbors. Architecture became grandiose in style and massive in size, with enormous stone blocks cut to fit one another in walls devoid of mortar. Corvée labor was almost certainly a factor in this construction and appears to have been borrowed as a concept from earlier civilizations in the Andes, most likely the **Wari** or **Tiwanaku** (1000–1476). Called *mit'a* in Quechua, it was the dominant form of tribute—as public service—required by the Inca of their subjects, who became more and more numerous as the Inca expanded out from their homeland. This process accelerated during the reign of Pachacuti (1438–1471), who conquered other nations to become the first Inca emperor and founder of the Inca Empire. In the process of empire-building, the mit'a labor draft became a dominant force in the lives of commoners, with a significant percentage of a given year devoted to corvée projects.

Further Reading

Moore, Jerry. *Architecture and Power in the Ancient Andes: The Archaeology of Public Buildings*. Cambridge, UK: Cambridge University Press, 1996.

Moseley, Michael E. *The Incas and their Ancestors: The Archaeology of Peru*. 2nd ed. London: Thames and Hudson, Ltd., 2001.

Cotzumalhuapa

The Cotzumalhuapa archaeological zone, stretching over 75 miles along the Pacific Coast of present-day Guatemala, is home to a series of ancient—but problematic—archaeological sites, including El Baúl, Bilbao, and El Castillo. The Cotzumalhuapan sites bear some of the earliest inscriptions in this portion of the Mesoamérica area, including the earliest legible Long Count date in Guatemala: 37 C.E., at the site of El Baúl. The area is problematic, however, because it may not have been settled by Maya at all: at the time of the Conquest, in the sixteenth century, the area was occupied by the Pipil, a Nahua-speaking people with ethnic and linguistic ties to Central Mexico. Closer attention to

Cotzumalhuapan art and architecture, much of it dating to the Late Preclassic (400 B.C.E.–250 C.E.) and the Classic Periods (250–909) reveals influences from the lowland Maya, the Gulf Coast, and even the Central Mexican metropolis of **Teotihuacá**. As a result, it is difficult to say which ethnic group was responsible for the florescence of this zone early on in its history.

The Cotzumalhuapa sites are characterized by a distinctive style, often involving ballplayers (*see* **Ballgame**); realistically rendered images of men, women, and animals; scenes of sacrifice, and vegetative imagery. Cotzumalhuapan artifacts bearing this style have been found along the coast from Chiapas to Nicaragua; they have likewise been recovered deep into highland Guatemala, as far as the present-day city of Antigua. As a result, these sites would appear to have been important to the trade between Mesoamérica and Lower Central America. Cosmopolitan and culturally heterogenous, the Cotzumalhuapan sites are a testament to the far-reaching economic activities of early Mesoamérica societies.

Further Reading

Carrasco, Davíd, ed. *The Oxford Encyclopedia of Mesoamerican Cultures*. Oxford, UK: Oxford University Press, 2001.

Evans, Susan. *Ancient Mexico and Central America: Archaeology and Culture History*. London: Thames and Hudson, Ltd., 2004.

Crow Creek

This archaeological site on the Missouri River, South Dakota, was one of the largest agricultural settlements on the Great Plains. Populated by one of a host of peoples collectively called "Plains Village," Crow Creek dates to approximately 1350 and appears to have been a seasonally occupied and farmed settlement. Despite its seasonal nature, approximately five-hundred people may have lived there. Like some other large settlements of its time, it consisted of tightly packed houses surrounded by a moat and a wooden palisade. The latter of these defenses was eventually removed as the settlement grew larger. Unfortunately, such defenses appear to have been sorely needed in the fourteenth century: Endemic, small-scale conflicts were common on the Great Plains at this time, and at Crow Creek resulted in the decimation of its inhabitants.

Crow Creek is perhaps most famous as an archaeological site for this bloody occasion. At least 486 people, of all ages and sexes, appear to have died in a surprisingly deadly—but common, in the prehistory of the Great Plains—raid on the site. Of the 486 people, most appear to have been killed with arrows or clubs. Decapitated, scalped, and dismembered, their bodies were left in the open for scavengers to devour. At a later date, some bones were eventually gathered up and placed in the defensive ditch, but numerous others remained elsewhere at the site or scattered about. Crow Creek and its buildings were burned shortly after the mass grave was produced, ending a devastating chapter in the prehistory of this region.

Further Reading

Willey, P., and Thomas E. Emerson. "The Osteology of the Crow Creek Massacre." *Plains Anthropologist* 38(145) (1993): 227–269.

Zimmerman, Larry J. *Peoples of Prehistoric South Dakota*. Lincoln: University of Nebraska Press, 1985.

Zimmerman, Larry J., and Lawrence E. Bradley. "The Crow Creek Massacre: Initial Coalescent Warfare and Speculations about the Genesis of Extended Coalescent." *Plains Anthropologist* 38(145) (1993): 215–226.

Curaca

The curaca were Andean and Pacific Coastal elites whose authority was based upon prestigious ancestors. The word *curaca* (sometimes spelled "kuraka") was actually coined by the Spanish, who used it as a blanket term to refer to South American elite classes. In the Pre-Columbian world, many different societies had versions of curaca nobles, who served as intermediaries between the living and the ancestors. They maintained social and political distance from commoners through the commission and production of specialty items, ranging from distinct pottery and textiles to metalwork, and through differential mortuary treatment. Oftentimes, such individuals would be buried with vast quantities of gold and other finery or were mummified and housed in sacred locations; occasionally, the mummies would be brought from these locations to attend public ceremonies as ancestral authorities.

The curaca as a class were firmly established by the Early Intermediate Period (200 B.C.E.–650 C.E.) of Andean prehistory and appear as portrait vessels or characters on ceramics of the **Moche** and Nazca civilizations. The most noteworthy examples of curaca are on Moche vessels with narrative scenes. On these, curaca nobles are shown fighting with one another and even as victims of human sacrifice: Prestigious Moche nobles engaged in warfare with enemy sites would depict nobles ritually killing prestigious captives and drinking their blood, as in the Presentation Theme (*see* **Sipán**). On these vessels and in Moche and Nazca contexts, curaca nobles are given supernatural qualities, occasionally hybridized with jaguars or other feline creatures.

Over time, particularly as empires in the Andes became more authoritarian, different gradations of curacas appeared, such that by the time of the Inca ascendancy in the late fifteenth century, there was a hierarchy of curacas ranging from local leaders, leaders of several communities, rulers of territories, and the ultimate curaca himself, the Tupa Inca, or emperor. Most curaca nobles were male, although there were female curacas, and on the local level there were usually two in charge of a given settlement or extended family grouping (*see* **Ayllu**). Beyond this, to carry the status of Inca within the Inca Empire carried with it its own set of privileges. Members of the royal lineage, in turn, were superior to the traditional curaca nobles, who came from annexed and conquered provinces. In 1400, however, much of the Andes and Pacific Coast was divided into territories ruled by curaca nobles.

Further Reading
Donnan, Christopher. *Moche Art of Peru*. Los Angeles: University of California, 1978.
Moseley, Michael E. *The Incas and Their Ancestors: The Archaeology of Peru*. 2nd ed. London: Thames and Hudson, Ltd., 2001.
Ramirez, Susan. *The World Upside Down*. Stanford, CA: Stanford University Press, 1996.

Cuzco

The city of Cuzco, in modern-day Lima, Peru, is best known as the capital of the Inca Empire, or Tawantinsuyu. However, settlement here seems to predate the Inca: Recent excavations here have proven that an earlier culture, known as Killke, lived here between 900 and 1200. They appear to have built a temple, roads, and irrigation systems here in the 1100s. Their most famous contribution was the fortress of Sacsayhuamán, which was occupied and elaborated upon by the Inca, who seem to have supplanted Killke by 1200 and founded their own capital here.

In the thirteenth century, Cusco was one of many towns struggling for dominance in the region: Encircled in a radius of approximately 60 miles by different groups, it was not at all clear that Cusco would become the capital of a vast empire until the fifteenth century. The nobles of Cusco spent most of their energy in these early years making allies and fighting their neighbors. Their most dangerous enemies at this time were the Mohina, a people who had inherited part of the **Wari** Empire, which had disintegrated around 1050. Founding their capital, Chokepukio, at the old, abandoned Wari center of Pikillacta, the Mohina came close to preventing the formation of the largest land empire in the Americas. Unfortunately for them, Cusco and its allies prevailed in subjugating the Mohina and others by 1400 and began a campaign of conquest outside the region shortly thereafter.

The years surrounding 1400 saw the architectural transformation of Cuzco from a minor center to a regional capital, at which time it began to take on the form in which the Inca capital stands today. Nevertheless, it would not be until the reign of Pachacuti Inca (1438–1471) that the city was formally divided into four parts to accommodate the four quarters of the burgeoning Inca Empire (**Tawantinsuyu** or "Land of the Four Quarters"). Cuzco ultimately fell to the Spanish in 1534, although the ruling Inca lineages continued to wield some measure of power for the next few decades.

Further Reading

Moore, Jerry. *Architecture and Power in the Ancient Andes: The Archaeology of Public Buildings*. Cambridge, UK: Cambridge University Press, 1996.

Moseley, Michael E. *The Incas and Their Ancestors: the Archaeology of Peru*. 2nd ed. London: Thames and Hudson, Ltd., 2001.

Ramirez, Susan. *The World Upside Down*. Stanford, CA: Stanford University Press, 1996.

Cyclical Time

The concept of cyclical time is one that was common in Mesoamérica civilizations throughout the Pre-Columbian era. It refers to the general belief that life has no end but rather constantly changes forms. This applies to all living beings and even abstract concepts such as time and space, which die or are destroyed periodically only to be reborn into new and ephemeral forms. Most Mesoamérican civilizations believed, for example, that the world they knew had been destroyed several times. When they died, people would be reborn into new roles, which, theoretically, would also be temporary.

Aztec mythology provides a very literal example of cyclical time. According to the Aztecs, the people of the known world were living in what was known as Nahui Ollin, "the Fifth Sun," or fifth epoch of creation. It was also known as Four Earthquake, so titled because it was believed to have begun on the day in the Aztec calendar bearing that name; Four Earthquake was dominated by a solar deity named Tonatiuh. The previous worlds had similar names based on the calendar: Four Ocelot, Four Wind, Four Rain, and Four Water. They were each dominated and eventually destroyed by the gods who represented them, with people killed by a variety of natural and supernatural disasters including people being devoured by jaguars, killed by hurricanes, annihilated by a rain of fire, and drowned in a massive flood. After each destruction, people were re-created by the gods, with the fifth creation believed to have occurred at the Central Mexican metropolis of **Teotihuacá**. According to Aztec mythology, the present world would be destroyed by earthquakes. *See also* **Mesoamérica Calendar**.

Further Reading

Carrasco, Davíd. *Religions of Mesoamerica*. Prospect Heights, IL: Waveland Press, 1998.
Miller, Mary Ellen, and Karl Taube. *An Illustrated Dictionary of the Gods and Symbols of Ancient Mexico and the Maya*. London: Thames and Hudson, Ltd., 1997.
Taube, Karl. *Aztec and Maya Myths*. Austin: University of Texas Press, 1993.

Divine Kingship

The two areas of the Americas for which the institution of divine kingship can be securely attested are Mesoamérica and the Andes. In each region, there were a number of states where rulers were believed to wield divine powers and who—as clearly attested for societies such as the Inca—were explicitly descended from major gods of their respective religious pantheons. The supernatural powers of a divine king might include such abilities as the capacity to perform rituals ensuring good harvests, rain, or similar essentials as well as the sole ability to communicate with and receive favors from royal ancestors or gods. Most such kings had, by virtue of their divinity, the authority to wage war and the control of vital, strategic natural resources. In some but not all cases, such rulers had some measure of control over foreign trade.

Two examples of divine kingship in the Americas come from the Classic Maya (250–850) and the Inca Empire (1438–1533). A Maya king was known as a k'uhul ajaw (divine/holy lord) and was believed to have all of the supernatural and most of the secular abilities listed above; the one sole exception may have involved royal economic control, which is hotly debated among scholars. During the Late Classic Period (600–750), each divine king was the supreme member of a royal lineage claiming descent from a founding, deified ancestor; in the city of **Palenque**, moreover, kings explicitly claimed lineal descent from creator deities and traced their heritage well back into mythical time. The final collapse of Classic civilization in the tenth century saw the end of this tradition, and although there would be kings elsewhere in the Maya highlands and lowlands, none would be strong enough to claim divine status.

In comparison, a divine king in the Inca Empire was known simply as a Sapa Inca, or "the Only Inca," or Apu, "Divinity." The term *Inca*, in fact, only applied to members of the ruling ethnic group or individuals who were provided with that status and made "Inca by privilege." The Sapa Inca was the supreme one among them and was believed to be descended from Inti, the god of the sun. Inti was responsible for the protection and growth of all agricultural crops; by extension, the Sapa Inca could—by virtue of his descent—claim a special relationship with the sun and agricultural fertility. As a god, the Sapa Inca theoretically owned all lands, people, and property of the empire. When he died, he was mummified and his mummy continued to participate in the affairs of state, albeit in the hands of priests and his successor. More important, each Sapa Inca retained the right to his lands and property after death, such that a new emperor theoretically needed to conquer more land and obtain more property for personal use. This pattern continued until the dissolution of the Inca Empire in 1533.

Further Reading

D'Altroy, Terence N. *The Incas.* Oxford, UK: Wiley-Blackwell, 2003.

Martin, Simon, and Nikolai Grube. *Chronicle of the Maya Kings and Queens.* London: Thames and Hudson, Ltd., 2000.

Moseley, Michael E. *The Incas and Their Ancestors: The Archaeology of Peru.* 2nd ed. London: Thames and Hudson, Ltd., 2001.

Sharer, Robert J., and Loa P. Traxler. *The Ancient Maya.* 6th ed. Stanford, CA: Stanford University Press, 2005.

Dorset

In the year 400, the Dorset were the dominant peoples of the eastern Arctic. Living in small groups of thirty to forty, they occupied seasonal settlements and were beginning to recolonize the northern extremes of the Arctic after a prolonged period of abandonment. Taking advantage of warmer temperatures, which began after 500, they steadily occupied islands and stretches of coastline into the far north. By 1000, they had occupied nearly all of the eastern Arctic and reached the apex of their population. Lacking dogsleds or the ability to extensively hunt at sea, they were unable to hunt whales effectively or travel long distances after game.

Yet the Dorset were able to forage for plants, fish, hunt seals, and even manage to kill an occasional whale or other large mammal. Likewise, their art was second-to-none in the Arctic world: Dorset peoples produced some of the most finely carved objects in the Americas of bone and ivory, many of which seem to have been created for religious (shamanic) purposes. They were likely the first native peoples to encounter the Norse, who had recently "discovered" the Americas and begun to hunt (and eventually settle) in Greenland. Yet by 1200 the Dorset had all but disappeared from the Arctic, replaced by the **Thule**. Superior hunting technologies and techniques, coupled with possible diseases inadvertently introduced by the Thule, seem to have hastened the Dorset demise. Some archaeologists believe, however, that some Dorset groups were able to survive past 1400 in isolated pockets of the Arctic. The ultimate fate of the Dorset is currently unknown.

Further Reading

Fagan, Brian. *Ancient North America.* London: Thames and Hudson, Ltd., 1991.

McGhee, Robert. "Contact between Native North Americans and the Medieval Norse: A Review of Evidence." *American Antiquity* 49 (1984): 4–26.

Morrison, D., and J. Pilon. *Threads of Arctic Prehistory: Papers in Honor of William E. Taylor, Jr.* Quebec: Canadian Museum of Civilization, 1994.

Eight Deer Jaguar Claw (1063–1115)

Eight Deer Jaguar Claw was the most famous and powerful king of the Mixtecs, a major Mesoamérica civilization, which was based in the present-day

King Eight Deer Jaguar Claw of Tilantongo Captures Four-Wind. Illumination from a Mexican painted book, *Late Post Classic Period* (vellum). Additional Info Codex *Zouche Nuttall*. British Museum, London, UK, Ancient Art and Architecture Collection Ltd./The Bridgeman Art Library International.

Mexican state of Oaxaca as well as portions of the states of Puebla and Guerrero. He was the only ruler to unite most of the independent kingdoms of the Mixtec under one banner—his—and was an ally of the nearby city-state of Cholula, an ancient political and religious center that was one of the dominant forces in Central Mexico at that time.

Most of what we know about this figure comes from Mixtec codices (*see* **Codex**), painted books with texts describing the history and mythology of their civilization. According to native accounts, Eight Deer Jaguar Claw was the son of the high priest at the city of Tilatango, which at that time was ruled from afar by the lords of an as yet undiscovered site named Red-and-White-Bundle. One of the chief nobles of Tilatango, he was nevertheless not in line for the throne there and spent the majority of his life making and breaking marriages to different Mixtec royal lines in an attempt to gain political power. One of his other great political victories was gaining the support of the ruler of Cholula, who was of Toltec (and therefore prestigious) ancestry: That king provided him with symbols of Toltec royal authority, which he displayed on his monuments.

Eight Deer Jaguar Claw's other pursuits were military. A consummate general, he is listed as having conquered ninety-four Mixtec cities during his life. He finally conquered Red-and-White-Bundle between 1099 and 1101, taking the throne of Tilatango and making it the capital of a large state based in Oaxaca. Having killed many of his in-laws to do so, Eight Deer Jaguar Claw was not without enemies, and ultimately this was to prove his undoing: One of his nephews, 4 Wind, was able to convince some of the Mixtec kingdoms to ally against the conqueror in 1115. Eight Deer Jaguar Claw was captured by his nephew and eventually sacrificed. With his death, the Mixtec kingdoms once again devolved into competing factions. Although the Aztecs gained a loose hegemony over this region in the fifteenth century, the Mixtec area—despite its factionalization—was never fully subdued until the Spanish conquest.

Further Reading

Boone, Elizabeth. *Sories in Red and Black: The Pictorial Histories of the Aztec and Mixtec.* Austin: University of Texas Press, 2000.

Evans, Susan. *Ancient Mexico and Central America: Archaeology and Culture History.* London: Thames and Hudson, Ltd., 2004.

Evans, Susan, and David Webster, eds. *Archaeology of Ancient Mexico: An Encyclopedia.* New York: Garland, 2001.

Pohl, John. *The Legend of Lord Eight Deer: An Epic of Ancient Mexico.* Oxford, UK: Oxford University Press, 2002.

Spores, Ronald. *The Mixtec Kings and Their People.* Norman: University of Oklahoma Press, 1967.

"Flowery Wars"

Perhaps the most widely cited battles in Aztec warfare, "flowery wars" were engagements that the Aztecs described as being primarily for prestigious captives. Highly stylized, they were almost like training battles and—from the Aztec point of view—mutually agreed upon as such. The Aztec enemy states most often cited as participating in such wars were Tlaxcala, Huexotzinco, and Cholula. Although the latter two were eventually conquered formally, Tlaxcala—a mountainous city-state close to the Aztec capital—was never subjugated and seems to have participated in "flowery wars" on a regular basis.

Some scholars believe that the concept of these engagements, as related by the Aztec nobility in their accounts, was a pleasant fiction designed to mask the fact that the Aztecs were either unable or unwilling to subjugate certain enemy states. For Tlaxcala, "flowery wars" may have been a combination of both: Set in mountainous terrain, of lesser agricultural or economic value than other regions of Mexico, the cost of conquering this state may have been deemed too high. Another, alternate interpretation of "flowery war," sees these exercises as minor acts of aggression by the Aztecs, designed to wear the enemy down for eventual conquest.

The weapons used in such battles were the same that the Aztecs used to conquer other nations and consisted of warriors wielding bows and arrows, **atlatls**, slings, lances, war clubs, and a wooden club or "sword" studded with volcanic glass (obsidian). Known as the macuahuitl or "hand stick," it had been used by many peoples of the Americas prior to the Aztecs. Warriors of higher rank wielded better weapons and wore quilted cotton armor as well as wooden or cane shields. Those of the highest rank belonged to warrior societies, like the Cuachicqueh "shorn ones" or the Eagle Warriors, and had specific costumes they wore into battle. In "flowery wars," such specialized warriors might challenge one another on the battlefield, each attempting to subdue the other to bring them back to their city for eventual sacrifice.

Further Reading

Evans, Susan. *Ancient Mexico and Central America: Archaeology and Culture History*. London: Thames and Hudson, Ltd., 2004.

Evans, Susan, and David Webster, eds. *Archaeology of Ancient Mexico: An Encyclopedia*. New York: Garland, 2001.

Smith, Michael. *The Aztecs*. London: Thames and Hudson, Ltd., 2003.

Fremont

Between 400 and 900, the Great Basin area of the present-day United States saw changes in subsistence and settlement patterns consistent with the emergence of a new culture. The peoples of this culture were semisedentary horticulturalists collectively known to archaeologists as "Fremont Culture." Although there are demonstrably strong cultural continuities between Fremont and earlier peoples in the area, who were hunter-gatherers, Fremont represented a marked change in local lifestyle. People began to grow maize, live in pit houses, employ stone in their architecture, and use pottery. All of these provide indications that the peoples of this area were in contact with the American Southwest, if not facing migration from the Southwest itself. Given the wide range of dates with which these changes are associated, some archaeologists have suggested that Fremont actually represents different ethnic groups receiving these traits at different times. In any event, Fremont was a sea change with respect to local subsistence.

Fremont art and artifacts show, as would be expected, strong ties to the Southwest and the Great Plains. Likewise, there are regional variations over much of present-day Utah, eastern Nevada, western Colorado, and southern Idaho, with some communities far more sedentary than others. Yet many seem to have suffered the same fate: By 1400, all but the most northern Fremont sites appear to have been abandoned. This was due, in part to the Little Ice Age and concomitant droughts that began at about that time. Some of the peoples that survived in these newer, drier conditions gave up maize horticulture and became full-time hunter-gatherers once more, whereas others grew maize — but in much more limited contexts.

Further Reading

Fagan, Brian. *Ancient North America*. London: Thames and Hudson, Ltd., 1991.

Fawsett, William B. *Transitions between Farming, Hunting, and Gathering along the Fremont/Puebloan Frontier*. Contributions to Anthropology No. 26. Logan: Utah State University, 1999.

Madsen, David B. *Exploring the Fremont*. Salt Lake City: University of Utah Press, 1989.

Huaca

A huaca represents, in ancient as well as contemporary Andean ritual, a sacred object or location. Often associated with natural features or imitations of them — such as temple-pyramids or similar monuments — huacas were of paramount importance to Andean and Pacific coastal societies at the time of European contact in the sixteenth century. In Andean religions, much of the natural world is animate, with prominent locations and features being of sacred significance. Such natural features might be located on the tops of mountains, the depths of watery springs, or even be noteworthy rock formations. Features of the built environment might be burial places (particularly those associated with mummies) as well as temples or other structures belonging to early civilizations.

The idea of a huaca is probably of great antiquity, dating at least to the time of the first settlements in the Andes and on the Pacific Coast (c. 3000–1800 B.C.E.). As with all major religious phenomena, however, what constituted a huaca likely changed over time and space.

As there are no written records for the Andes, much of what we know about ancient huacas comes from fifteenth- and sixteenth-century Spanish or indigenous accounts of the Inca Empire. At that time, many of the centers of civilizations that the Inca had conquered or come into contact with were considered to have huacas, in the forms of temples, palaces, and significant natural features. The Inca consciously cultivated the images and functions of certain huacas, which served as focal points or pilgrimage centers for many of the disparate ethnic groups living within the empire. Today, the ruins of such civilizations as **Moche**, Nazca, **Wari**, **Tiwanaku**, and **Chimor**—in addition to those of the Inca—are considered to have huacas. Some of these were huacas during the Pre-Columbian period, whereas others became huacas after the coming of the Spanish.

Further Reading

Bauer, Brian S. *The Sacred Landscape of the Inca: the Cusco Ceque System.* Austin: University of Texas Press, 1998.

Moore, Jerry. *Architecture and Power in the Ancient Andes: The Archaeology of Public Buildings.* Cambridge, UK: Cambridge University Press, 1996.

Moseley, Michael E. *The Incas and Their Ancestors: The Archaeology of Peru.* 2nd ed. London: Thames and Hudson, Ltd., 2001.

Iroquois

Although the League of the Iroquois, perhaps the most famous indigenous alliance in North America, was formed around the era of European contact (c. 1500–1600), the ancestors of the tribes collectively known as Iroquois are believed to have settled in what is today the northeast United States by the beginning of the second millennium C.E. Preceded by Algonquin-speaking peoples and then sharing an uneasy coexistence, the ancestors of the Iroquois seem to have established themselves in the northeast—particularly within New York—through a series of migrations from the Midwest. Between 800 and 1000, different elements of these migrants' cultures combined to create a distinct, Iroquois archaeological assemblage.

Living in seasonal camps and combining hunting and gathering with maize horticulture, the early Iroquois groups lived much like their Algonquin contemporaries in small villages of between one-hundred and four-hundred people. Between 1000 and 1300, these villages not only grew in size but also became fortified centers, with wooden palisades protecting a population that was becoming ever more dependent upon maize as its dietary staple. By 1300, the Iroquois were clearly relying on maize as a major food crop: The largest Iroquois villages may have held up to fifteen-hundred people. Such population densities had implications for political life in the Northeast, with chiefs becoming paramount authorities in war, ritual, and diplomacy. By the year

1400, worsening climactic conditions—a result of a period of low temperatures in North America called the "Little Ice Age"—as well as competition for resources among the largest villages had precipitated two major events: (1) greater numbers of conflicts in the Northeast, as represented by an increased emphasis on defense in Iroquois villages and signs of major violence in Iroquois burials and (2) the birth of distinct tribes, which likely coalesced as a result of said violence. The League of the Iroquois, which was to follow soon after, was a successful attempt by some groups to deal with this troubled time. Likewise, the League was able to make collective decisions about non-Iroquois rivals, whether diplomatic or martial. It persisted well into the contact era.

Further Reading

Fagan, Brian. *Ancient North America*. London: Thames and Hudson, Ltd., 1991.

Haviland, William, and Marjory Powers. *The Original Vermonters*. Hanover, NH: University Press of New England, 1994.

Ritchie, William. *Archaeology of New York State*. Garden City, NY: Natural History Press, 1981.

Ritchie, William, and R.E. Funk. *Aboriginal Settlement Patterns in the Northeast*. Albany: New York State Museum and Science Service Memoir 20, 1973.

Itzcoatl (d. 1440)

Born at the beginning of the fifteenth century, Itzcoatl was one of the most significant figures in Mesoamérica prehistory and was an Aztec emperor second only to Motecuhzoma II (Montezuma) in contemporary fame. He was the first ruler of the Mexica city of **Tenochtitlán** to rebel against the Tepanec Empire, which had employed the Mexica as warriors, vassals, and aides to their expansionist designs in the Basin of Mexico since 1325. Deteriorating relations with the Tepanecs began during the reign of his father, who was assassinated by the Tepanec emperor Maxtla in 1426. Apparently, Maxtla believed that the Mexica were becoming a threat and as such wanted to formally conquer them. He laid siege to Tenochtitlán, under its new king Itzcoatl, in 1428.

Knowing that others in the Basin of Mexico were disaffected with Maxtla, he called for assistance to repel the siege. In 1428, he was joined by the Acolhua ruler of Texcoco and the rebellious Tepanec king at Tacuba, close to Atzcapotzalco, and successfully defeated the empire. The result was the beginning of the **Triple Alliance**. This fourth **tlatoani**, or king, of the Mexica had become the first emperor of the conquest state we know as the Aztec Empire.

Itzcoatl as well as his immediate successors proceeded to transform the new empire politically and ideologically, inventing many of the

Coronation of Montezuma, last king of the Aztecs, folio 152V of the *Historia de los Indios* by Diego Duran, 1579. The Art Archive/Biblioteca Nacional Madrid/Gianni Dagli Orti.

traditions, which were to be fundamental parts of Aztec life. These included systems of taxation and tribute for provinces as they were conquered. Perhaps their most significant invention, however, was their "official" history of the Mexica: Trying to erase years of vassalage as well as the image of the people of Tenochtitlán as Chichimecs, or "barbarians" (*see* **Aztlan**), Itzcoatl had all available historical books, or codices (*see* **Codex**), burned. A new history was written, one that saw the Mexica and their paramount deity, Huitzilopochtli, as natural descendents of the Toltecs—the most powerful civilization in the Central Mexico of recent memory—and their traditions. Huitzilopochtli, the Mexica god of war and of the sun, was elevated to become the chief deity of the empire. In time, this new history became fact. Nevertheless, alternate versions of the Aztec past did survive and provide a counterpoint to the new order in the Basin of Mexico. Itzcoatl died in 1440, starting a political and military juggernaut that was to endure until the reign of Motecuhzoma II (1466–1520), whose failure to effectively deal with Hernan Cortés as well as his Spanish and native allies would spell disaster for the Triple Alliance.

Further Reading

Evans, Susan. *Ancient Mexico and Central America: Archaeology and Culture History*. London: Thames and Hudson, Ltd., 2004.

Evans, Susan, and David Webster, eds. *Archaeology of Ancient Mexico: An Encyclopedia*. New York: Garland, 2001.

Smith, Michael E. *The Aztecs*. 2nd ed. Oxford: Wiley-Blackwell, 2003.

Ixiptla

The concept of an ixiptla, or "god impersonator," was central to the practice of human sacrifice among the Aztecs (1325–1521) and was usually associated with the very public ritual of heart sacrifice. Heart sacrifice would typically involve a war captive who, held over an altar atop a temple, would be cut open with a knife by a priest. Extracting the heart, the priest and others would then throw the body off the steps of the temple; at some point they would remove the head of the captive for display on a rack, composed of rotting skulls, near the pyramid.

An individual sacrificed in this way, however, was experiencing the end point of a process that could, at times, take up to a year of preparation. For an ixiptla was considered a living incarnation of a very particular god, usually one that was considered a good "match" for the god's attributes. Children, warriors, women, and even individuals with specific qualities were all selected to fit a given god. For example, the Central Mexican storm god **Tlaloc** required children, whereas Tezcatlipoca—a god associated with a host of concepts including the night, sorcery, and warfare—needed a male ixiptla who was cultured and exceedingly handsome.

These individuals, prior to the day of their sacrifice, literally became avatars of their chosen gods and were worshipped as such. An ixiptla would be bathed, treated to rich feasts, and clothed in finery; such individuals might even expect to be provided with wives and sexual favors. Likewise, they were expected to sing, dance, parade around the city, and otherwise perform in ceremonies dedicated to their specific god. Finally, they would be taken to the place of sacrifice, stripped of their finery, and be killed.

Aztec human sacrifice, offering blood to the gods, from Mexican codex
Magliabechiano. Courtesy of photos.com.

The death of an ixiptla was considered a "good death," honorable and certainly preferable to dying of old age or illness: Believing in multiple realms of the afterlife, the Aztecs felt that what we consider to be a natural death resulted in a miserable eternity filled with work and even torture. Death by sacrifice, however, resulted in the ixiptla going to the paradise of his or her chosen god. As a result, captives who became ixiptla—however miserable—knew that they would die with honor.

Further Reading

Austin, Alfredo López. *The Human Body and Ideology: Concepts of the Ancient Nahuas*. Salt Lake City: University of Utah Press, 1988.

Evans, Susan, and David Webster, eds. *Archaeology of Ancient Mexico: An Encyclopedia*. New York: Garland, 2001.

Smith, Michael E. *The Aztecs*. 2nd ed. Oxford, UK: Wiley-Blackwell, 2003.

Taube, Karl. *Aztec and Maya Myths*. Austin: University of Texas Press, 1993.

Jasaw Chan K'awiil I (d. 734)

Jasaw Chan K'awiil I (r. 682–734), the *k'uhul ajaw* (holy lord) of the ancient Maya site of **Tikal**, was largely responsible for the resurgence of his kingdom in the late seventh century after a long period of decline. A distant descendent of Yax Nuun Ayiin I, Jasaw Chan K'awiil I grew up during one of the darkest periods in Tikal's history. A series of wars between Tikal and **Calakmul** (and its many allies) in the sixth and seventh centuries had resulted in severe dynastic turmoil and even exile for at least some members of the royal family. Jasaw Chan K'awiil came to power at the end of this 130-year period, known to archaeologists as the Hiatus. Memories of the last major defeat of Tikal in 679 were certainly fresh when he came to power in 682.

By some means, however, Jasaw Chan K'awiil I was able to reverse the fortunes of his embattled kingdom, defeating the king of Calakmul, Yuknoom Yich'aak K'ahk', in 695. Further victories against Calakmul and its allies were to follow, with one king of that site, Yuknoom Took' K'awiil, captured and killed in the central plaza at Tikal in 732. Calakmul was never to fully recover from this event: Its vassals were to either assert their own independence, go into precipitous decline, or themselves become vassal states to Tikal as a result. The resurgence was coupled with a flurry of building activity over the succeeding decades, with many of the major buildings visible at Tikal today having been augmented or built during this time. As a result, Jasaw Chan K'awiil I can be counted among the greatest of the kings of the ancient Maya during the Late Classic (600–850). At his death, he was placed within the now-famous Temple I at Tikal, which was started by Jasaw but completed by his son and successor, Yik'in Chan K'awiil. It continues to be the most iconic of the Classic Maya temple-pyramids.

Further Reading

Harrison, Peter. *The Lords of Tikal*. London: Thames and Hudson, Ltd., 1999.

Martin, Simon, and Nikolai Grube. *Chronicle of the Maya Kings and Queens*. London: Thames and Hudson, Ltd., 2000.

Sharer, Robert J., and Loa P. Traxler. *The Ancient Maya*. 6th ed. Stanford, CA: Stanford University Press, 2005.

K'inich Janaab' Pakal (d. 683)

This long-lived king (r. 615–683), or *k'uhul ajaw* (holy lord), of the ancient Maya site of **Palenque** is perhaps the most famous of the Classic Maya (250–850) rulers. Like his far younger contemporary Jasaw Chan K'awiil I of **Tikal**, K'inich Janaab' Pakal grew up during the hegemony of **Calakmul** and its allies in the Maya area. Palenque had been sacked twice in recent memory by Calakmul, first in 599 and again in 611. Abnormal dynastic successions, most notably the reign of his mother Lady Sak K'uk' amidst a generally patriarchal society, were likewise hallmarks of this troubled period. When Pakal came to power in 615 at the age of 12 there was no reason to think that such problems were at an end. In fact, the early portion of his reign was not particularly noteworthy: the inscriptions from this era are notably silent, and there are indications that Palenque continued to struggle politically and militarily against its enemies.

In the mid-seventh century, however, K'inich Janaab' Pakal oversaw a series of major constructions, with most of the palaces and temples of Palenque remodeled or built during that time. Politically and militarily, he sought to check the advances of Calakmul and its vassals on all fronts, allying himself with the royal dynasties at Tikal and Yaxchilan. He fought the Calakmul alliance for much of the mid-seventh century and even provided a temporary safe haven for the exiled ruler of Tikal, Nuun Ujol Chaak, when he was driven from that site in 657. Although he was never able to confront Calakmul in its own territory, he was successful in defeating one of its allies on the Usumacinta River, Pomona, making it a tribute-paying subject state for the remainder of the Classic Period. In a time when Calakmul was still a major force to be reckoned with, this was no mean feat.

K'inich Janaab' Pakal is perhaps best known, however, for his tomb in the Temple of the Inscriptions at Palenque. Completed by his son, K'inich Kan B'alam II (r. 684–702), this tomb was started by Pakal in 675 and is perhaps the most elaborate and famous Maya tomb of all time. Discovered by Alberto Ruz Lhuillier in 1948 and excavated over a period of 4 years, the tomb consists of a winding, vaulted stairway descending into the heart of the temple, terminating in a decorated burial chamber and stone sarcophagus. Carved with images of the deceased king being reborn from the Maya Underworld, the Sarcophagus Lid is one of the iconic monuments of the ancient Maya. Aged 80 years at the time of his death, K'inich Janaab' Pakal was revered by every successive king of Palenque (indeed, he overshadowed them) and continues to fascinate visitors to the site today. As a testament to his fame and abilities, many scholars refer to K'inich Janaab' Pakal simply as Pakal the Great.

Further Reading

Evans, Susan, and David Webster, eds. *Archaeology of Ancient Mexico: An Encyclopedia.* New York: Garland, 2001.

Martin, Simon, and Nikolai Grube. *Chronicle of the Maya Kings and Queens.* London: Thames and Hudson, Ltd., 2000.

Schele, Linda, and Peter Mathews. *The Code of Kings: the Language of Seven Sacred Maya Temples and Tombs.* New York: Scribner, 1999.

Kiva

Modern kivas of the American Southwest are used in Pueblo villages for sociopolitical and religious functions; they normally consist of a circular room of masonry or adobe, with the word *kiva* being Hopi for "ceremonial room." Most pueblos have at least one of these, and archaeologists have been able to trace such rooms architecturally back to around 500. During the Pueblo I Period (750–900) of the Colorado Plateau, pit houses—which had been the major form of household in this part of the Southwest up to that time—gave way to aboveground structures, with the pits themselves being converted into kivas. Larger versions, dubbed "Great Kivas," first emerged at places like Grass Mesa Pueblo, Colorado, in the eighth century. By the tenth century, during Pueblo II (900–1150) drastic population increases and emerging sociocomplexity in **Chaco Canyon** had lead to the creation of several interlinked settlements characterized by the construction of massive masonry buildings up to four stories in size. These buildings, or "great houses," were themselves complemented by Great Kivas.

One of the best known of these is at Casa Rinconada, the Great Kiva consists of a circular, subterranean room approximately 63 feet in diameter. Graced with numerous wall niches for offerings, antechambers, a central entrance ladder, benches, and a hearth, this Great Kiva can be thought of as an archetype for all of the major kivas of Chacoan Pueblo II. Other contemporary—and later—societies not within the Chaco sphere, such as those based at **Mesa Verde** (500–1300), employed slightly different architectural conventions, including keyhole-shaped kivas, but the general idea of these as multipurpose ceremonial, political, and social rooms was similar.

Further Reading

Fagan, Brian. *Ancient North America*. London: Thames and Hudson, Ltd., 1991.
Mills, Barbara. "Recent Research on Chaco: Changing Views on Economy, Ritual, and Society." *Journal of Archaeological Research* 10 (2002): 45–117.
Scarre, Christopher, ed. *The Human Past*. London: Thames and Hudson, Ltd., 2005.
Vivian, R. *The Chacoan Prehistory of the San Juan Basin*. San Diego, CA: Academic Press, 1990.

L'Anse aux Meadows

This short-lived village, founded by the Vikings in 1000, is located in Newfoundland, Canada. Discovered in 1960, L'Anse aux Meadows does not appear to have lasted as a settlement for more than a generation. Nevertheless, it remains an important site because it marks the southernmost settlement of Vikings in the hemisphere and an important point of interaction between Europeans and Native Americans 500 years before Columbus. The eight longhouses that have been excavated may have held a population of over seventy men and women—probably from Greenland—and were built of sod as well as wood with thatched roofs. Workshops, notably those used to smelt iron and repair Viking longships, were also in evidence at L'Anse aux Meadows.

Unlike the Viking diaspora settlements in Greenland and Iceland, however, L'Anse aux Meadows was so short lived as to have left no lasting cultural impact on native peoples of the region. Certainly the Vikings ventured farther south: Plants not native to the region have been recovered from the site. But there seem to have been too few Vikings to make lasting settlement or significant cultural exchange remotely possible. In the end, L'Anse aux Meadows was left in a way similar to that of the disappearance of the Norse colonies in Greenland a few centuries later: L'anse aux Meadows was left with only scant remains of the peoples who had inhabited it.

Further Reading

Fagan, Brian. *Ancient North America*. London: Thames and Hudson, Ltd., 1991.
Ingstad, Helge, and Anne Stine Ingstad. *The Viking Discovery of America: The Excavation of a Norse Settlement in L'Anse Aux Meadows, Newfoundland*. New York: Checkmark, 2001.
Nydal, Reidar. "A Critical Review of Radiocarbon Dating of a Norse Settlement at L'Anse aux Meadows, Newfoundland, Canada." *Radiocarbon* 31 (1989): 976–985.

Lineage Organization

In most Pre-Columbian cultures of the Americas, a lineage was one of the primary social units of familial, economic, religious, and political life. Defined as a descent group tracing common heritage from a known ancestor, a lineage can be matrilineal (tracing descent from the female line), patrilineal (tracing descent from the male line), or bilateral (tracing descent from both lines). The ways in which ancestry was traced could—and still can—determine who inherited property, marriage rules (e.g., who can marry whom), membership in a given social or political group, methods of ancestor veneration (*see* **Ancestor Venera-tion**) and a host of other factors crucial in daily life. Indigenous cultures of the Americas today are either matrilineal or, more commonly, patrilineal: Most matri-lineal descent groups are currently found in native North America, whereas patrilineal societies can be found in a wide band through both continents of the hemisphere. Given that most of the Pre-Columbian societies of the Americas did not use writing systems, it is oftentimes difficult to prove patterns of descent, but spatial distributions of cemeteries, individual burials, artifact distributions, and even settlement patterns—in addition to writing systems, where applica-ble—have all been used by scholars to argue for or against patrilineal and matri-lineal kin organization in specific societies. In any event, it is clear that lineage organization was paramount in the lives of most peoples of the Americas.

Lineages, as some of the smallest units of sociopolitical organization, can be combined to form even larger social groupings, such as clans, phratries, or moi-eties. These terms are common in anthropology, and the organizations they rep-resent can be found worldwide as well as in many Pre-Columbian societies. Clans typically involve multiple lineages, all of whom lay claim to a common—usually fictive—forebear, whereas phratries are groups of clans tracing descent through a supposed common ancestor. Moieties, by comparison, occur in societ-ies divided into two dominant lineages (each is called a "moiety"), such as the Chiriquí of Costa Rica (*see* **Rivas**). As a general rule, hierarchies within these forms of lineage organization serve as the primary means of determining politi-cal organization in most hunting and gathering societies of the Americas. Within agricultural chiefdoms, such as those found among the **Iroquois** of northeast North America, chiefs would derive from only the most powerful of lineages and pass their titles to fellow lineage members.

Such organization can be found in even more hierarchically organized soci-eties, as in the kingdoms of Mesoamérica and the Andes. However, in some contexts the lineage mode of sociopolitical organization came into direct ideo-logical conflict with the tools of state. Strong, centralized forms of kingship, such as those found among the Classic Maya (250–909) or the Inca (1438–1533), often encouraged state worship of divine kings or similar individuals (*see* **Di-vine Kingship**). Although the ruling body was ultimately derived from a dominant lineage in these states, their worship—as supreme ancestors ulti-mately disconnected from inferior lineages—undermined the religious, social, and political authorities of lineages not connected to royal families. These were major tensions in the states of the Pre-Columbian Americas.

Further Reading
McAnany, Patricia. *Living with the Ancestors*. Austin: University of Texas Press, 1992.
Nanda, Serena, and Richard L. Warms. *Cultural Anthropology*. 9th ed. Boston: Wads-worth Publishing, 2006.
Quilter, Jeffrey. *Cobble Circles and Standing Stones: Archaeology at the Rivas Site, Costa Rica*. Iowa City: University of Iowa Press, 2004.
Ramirez, Susan. *The World Upside Down*. Stanford, CA: Stanford University Press, 1996.

Los Buchillones

Occupied from 1220 to 1620, the archaeological site of Los Buchillones, Cuba, was one of the largest settlements of the Taino culture. Prevalent in the Caribbean islands from 500 until the fifteenth century, when it came under increasing stress from the Caribs, who were emigrating from coastal South America to take over much of what had formerly been Taino territory. Los Buchillones is prominent as a location for the quality and preservation of its artifacts as well as architecture, which have survived to the present day largely because the site is located underwater. Underwater archaeologists have discovered, among other materials, the remains of a near-perfectly preserved, wooden Taino house (the only one of its kind in the Americas).

Los Buchillones was, like other Taino villages, built with houses surrounding an open plaza known as a batey and ruled by chiefs. As the Taino were Arawak-speaking agriculturalists who had contact with not only Atlantic South America but also portions of Mesoamérica, it seems likely that the inhabitants of Los Buchillones—one of the largest Taino villages discovered thus far—were participants in the long-distance exchange of ideas and objects in the Atlantic world. Under constant stress from the Caribs and slowly being pushed northeastwards, the Taino on Cuba were ultimately decimated by the Spanish in the sixteenth century.

Further Reading

Graham, Elizabeth, David M. Pendergast, Jorge Calvera, and Juan Jardines. "Excavations at Los Buchillones, Cuba." *Antiquity* 74(284) (2000): 263–264.

Pendergast, David. "Up to Your Knees (not Headfirst, Luckily) in the Fango: el Sitio Arqueológico Los Buchillones, prov. de Ciego de Avila, Cuba." *Archaeological Newsletter, Royal Ontario Museum, Toronto* 55 (1994): 1–4.

Valcárcel Rojas, R., J. Cooper, J. Calvera Rosés, O. Brito, and M. Labrada. "Postes en el mar: Excavación de una Estructura Constructive Aborigen en Los Buchillones." *El Caribe Arqueologico* 9 (2006): 76–88.

Marajóara

The settlement of Marajó Island in the Lower Amazon was the principal center of the Marajóara culture between 400 and 1400. Characterized by large earthen mounds used for residences, burials, and sociopolitical activity, Marajó Island is the earliest place where archaeologists have encountered a widespread ceramic style known as the Polychrome Tradition: This style, consisting of large ceramic vessels painted and incised with images of animals and plants, was to become dominant in a large part of the Amazon until the period of European contact.

Other Marajóara settlements range from northern Brazil to French Guyana and collectively provide some of the earliest evidence for complex societies in the Amazon. The wide variety of mounds at Marajóara settlements, in terms of size, spatial organization, architecture, and artifact assemblage, has prompted some scholars to suggest sociopolitical hierarchies within settlements. In this scheme, the largest and most centralized mounds would have been used for politics and public ritual, whereas smaller, peripheral mounds served as the foundations for residences. Marajóara settlements with few or no mounds have also been recovered in outlying areas. These, together with the evidence from Marajó Island, may reflect degrees of Amazonian urbanism that until recently were believed to be limited in South America to Andean societies.

Further Reading

Bradshaw, G., and P. Marquet, eds. *How Landscapes Change*. Berlin, Germany: Springer-Verlag, 2003.

Heckenberger, M., J. Petersen, and E. Neves. "Of Lost Civilizations and Primitive Tribes, Amazonia: Reply to Meggers. *Latin American Antiquity* 12(3) (2001): 328–333.

McEwan, C., C. Barreto, and Eduardo Gomes Neves, eds. *The Unknown Amazon: Culture and Nature in Ancient Brazil*. London: British Museum Press, 2001.

Roosevelt, Anne. *Moundbuilders of the Amazon: Geophysical Archaeology on Marajó Island*. San Diego, CA: Academic Press, 1992.

Maya Collapse

The collapse of Classic Period (250–909) civilization in the southern Maya lowlands stands as one of the most dramatic events of Mesoamérica prehistory. What makes the collapse so interesting, archaeologically, is that the Maya were—up until that point—at the apex of their sociopolitical, technological, artistic, and architectural complexity. Equally profound is the rapidity with which it happened. The royal dynasties of the southern Maya kingdoms fell apart beginning around 760 and accelerating by 800 in the western Maya area. The rest of the southern lowlands followed suit shortly thereafter, and the royal dynasties of the Maya were all but extinct by the beginning of the tenth century. Archaeologically, this decline and collapse can be seen in the cessation of monumental inscriptions as well as large-scale architectural construction. Following the demise of these royal dynasties, most Maya cities— great and small—were abandoned by the end of the tenth century. Left to squatters and scattered periods of reoccupation, most had been swallowed up by the jungle within 200 years. A few portions of the southern lowlands, most notably around Lake Petén Itzá, would see new beginnings in the ninth century. Other areas, most notably the northern lowlands of Yucatán and the Maya highlands to the south, would actually benefit. Much of the heartland of Classic Maya civilization, however, would remain unoccupied until the modern era.

Many reasons for the Classic Maya collapse have been proposed, but they generally center around three ideas: (1) systemic ecological collapse, as a result of overexploitation of agricultural land; (2) economic or political collapse brought on by warfare, competing elite factions, disruption of key trade routes, or loss of faith in the Maya leadership; and (3) droughts brought on by climate change. Applying one of these as the cause is, unfortunately, problematic: No one theory explains why the collapse happened. Rather, there is incredible diversity in the ways in which individual sites fell apart, particularly in the eighth and early ninth centuries. What we see is a "domino-effect" thereafter. Following the collapse, new Maya kingdoms would arise and flourish elsewhere, but the time of the divine king (*see* **Divine Kingship** and **Popol Nah**) was over.

Further Reading

Demarest, Arthur. *Ancient Maya*. Cambridge, UK: Cambridge University Press, 2005.

Evans, Susan. *Ancient Mexico and Central America: Archaeology and Culture History*. London: Thames and Hudson, Ltd., 2004.

Martin, Simon, and Nikolai Grube. *Chronicle of the Maya Kings and Queens*. London: Thames and Hudson, Ltd., 2000.

Sharer, Robert J., and Loa P. Traxler. *The Ancient Maya*. 6th ed. Stanford, CA: Stanford University Press, 2005.

Webster, David. *The Fall of the Ancient Maya*. London: Thames and Hudson, Ltd., 2002.

Mesa Verde

The area surrounding Mesa Verde, Colorado, was sparsely settled as early as 600. It was not until the Pueblo III Period (1150–1300), however, that southwestern Colorado experienced population growth and warfare significant enough to see dense population aggregations in highly defensible locations. At Mesa Verde itself, such aggregations took the form of a host of related settlements set within the sides of cliffs. Each settlement or village was built inside caves and rock shelters along the walls of the canyon and consisted of multistoried, adobe apartment compounds with **kiva**s. The influx of populations into this region, and the growing importance of settlements in southwestern Colorado, was likely the result of the collapse of Chaco civilization to the south (*see* **Chaco Canyon**). Although there is some continuity with Chaco in terms of artifacts, much of Mesa Verde—and cliff-dwelling sites like it—represents a break with the past.

The largest of the cliff dwellings at Mesa Verde is known as Cliff Palace and contains around two-hundred rooms and over twenty kivas. Other dwellings include Mug House, Spruce Tree House, and Square Tower House. Some of these dwellings originally had structures with up to four stories. Most appear to have been augmented as needed over time, with new buildings and features seemingly constructed without regard for an overall site plan. Unfortunately, the majority of the cliff dwellings at Mesa Verde and elsewhere were occupied for little more than a century. Severe droughts, migrations of new peoples into the area, escalating warfare, or some combination of the three may have caused the people here to abandon their homes around 1300.

Further Reading

Duff, A., and R. Wilshusen. "Prehistoric Population Dynamics in the Northern San Juan Region, A.D. 950–1300. *Kiva* 65 (2000): 167–190.

Fagan, Brian. *Ancient North America*. London: Thames and Hudson, Ltd., 1991.

Noble, David Grant, ed. *The Mesa Verde World*. Santa Fe, NM: School of American Research Press, 2006.

Mesoamérican Calendar

The various systems by which Mesoamérican peoples kept track of time, commonly called the "Mesoamérican calendar," were some of the most accurate in the world before the use of contemporary technological advances. They are important because they can be correlated with modern calendars, providing archaeologists with fixed dates for many events of the Pre-Columbian world. Most peoples used at least two cycles, consisting of 260 and 365 days apiece. The former, though it does not appear to have been based on astronomical observations, may have corresponded to the rough period of human gestation; another idea as to its origins suggests that it was a multiplication of the numbers 20 and 13, both significant in Mesoamérican mathematics and religious expression. In fact, the individual units of the 260-day calendar were written with a coefficient ranging from 1 to 13 as well as one of 20 day names; the exact same day in the calendar would repeat itself every 260 days (13 x 20).

The 365-day calendar, by comparison, was designed to approximate the solar year. Like the 260-day calendar, it was also written with a coefficient, but this time ranging from 1 to 20 (or 0–19). That coefficient was then followed by one of 18 day names. Given that this works out to only 360 days (20 x 18), Mesoaméricans added a period of 5 days to come closer to the true solar cycle. This second calendar would then be added to the 260-day calendar to create a larger set of cycles known as the Calendar Round. An example of this is the date, here in the Classic Maya calendar, of 4 Ahau 8 Cumcu; here "4 Ahau" refers to the 260-day calendar, whereas "8 Cumcu" provides the coefficient and day name of the 360-day calendar.

The exact same date (e.g., the same combination of numbers and names) in the Calendar Round occurs every 52 years. Some societies, though they kept track of these 52-year periods and saw them as significant ritually, did not use a more complicated method of reckoning time. Most noteworthy among these were the Aztecs, who would perform a complicated ritual of human sacrifice on these 52-year, liminal periods of their calendar. Other societies, however, employed a third system of reckoning to deal with these vagaries, called the "Long Count." Invented sometime during the Preclassic (2500 B.C.E.–250 C.E.), it gradually fell out of favor with all Mesoamérican societies save the Maya, who adopted and perfected it in the Late Preclassic (400 B.C.E.–250 C.E.) and the Early Classic (250–600).

Given that the Maya, like most Mesoamérican peoples, believed that time was cyclical (*see* **Cyclical Time**), the Long Count is technically a cycle like the others. However, the origins of the present cycle—and its projected end point—were so greatly separated in time that it functioned, for all intensive purposes, as a calendar with a fixed starting date: 3114 B.C.E., corresponding to the day in which the present world was created. It consisted of a series of

Templo Mayor, Mexico City, Sun Stone Aztec Calendar stone, National Anthropological Museum Mexico City. © Tomasz Otap/Shutterstock.

small cycles arranged in ascending, notational forms. Although there were many cycles corresponding to vast units of time, most were not used in day-to-day recording (if ever). As such, we might conceive of the Long Count having five different cycles: k'in (day), winal (20 days), tuun (360 days), k'atun (7,200 days), and b'aktun (144,000 days). A sample Long Count date is written, in Roman notation, as 9.12.0.0.0, meaning that nine b'aktun and twelve k'atun have passed since the world was created. Many Maya monuments use the Long Count in combination with the 260-day and 360-day calendars; some even use further calendrical systems, such as the cycles of the moon or those of various planets. This calendar persisted well into the colonial period, and elements of the 260-day and 360-day calendars can still be found in use by indigenous communities throughout Mesoamérica.

Further Reading

Demarest, Arthur. *Ancient Maya*. Cambridge, UK: Cambridge University Press, 2005.

Evans, Susan. *Ancient Mexico and Central America: Archaeology and Culture History*. London: Thames and Hudson, Ltd., 2004.

Martin, Simon, and Nikolai Grube. *Chronicle of the Maya Kings and Queens*. London: Thames and Hudson, Ltd., 2000.

Sharer, Robert J., and Loa P. Traxler. *The Ancient Maya*. 6th ed. Stanford, CA: Stanford University Press, 2005.

Metallurgy

The earliest use of metals in the Americas dates to 4000 B.C.E. and is associated with a culture known simply as the Old Copper Culture (4000–2000 B.C.E.). Living around the Great Lakes, which bear high-quality, natural copper, they made utilitarian items from copper such as spears, knives, axes, and fishhooks as well as decorative items in more limited quantities. Stone tools were the norm in North America, however, and by the Woodland Period (800 B.C.E.–1000 C.E.) copper was being used sporadically as a prestige item, typically for decorative and ritual objects. By the Mississippian era (1000–1500), copper artifacts of upper North America were firmly in the realm of religion; they were hammered and decorated objects bearing images of supernatural imagery (*see* **Southern Cult** or Southeastern Ceremonial Complex). Notably, the regions of North America that departed from this general pattern for copper were the sub-Arctic and Arctic, where peoples like the Thule used copper, in addition to stone, for tools from the twelfth century to the modern era. Even more surprisingly, they appear to have been the only peoples of the Americas to use iron—when available—for tool use: Limited quantities of meteoritic iron, as well as terrestrial iron traded from the Norse, were regularly features of the economic landscape of the north.

The first complex metallurgy in the Americas, however, comes from the southern hemisphere. It slightly predates what is known as the Initial Period (1800–400 B.C.E.) in the Andes, when agriculture, pottery, weaving, and other technological innovations became commonplace. The first examples come from Peru, although metalworking technologies appear to have spread rapidly to places such as Ecuador and Colombia thereafter. The types of metals used in these early years included gold, silver, copper, tin, and platinum. Of these, gold was considered to be the most important: Andean as well as later

Mesoamérican peoples associated it with the sun and mystical solar properties. It was first used from river deposits and then subsequently mined by many of the earliest Andean peoples.

By the Andean Early Horizon (400–200 B.C.E.), many of the major metallurgical techniques appear to have been invented, including welding, soldering, and the ability to alloy gold with such metals as copper or silver. The major innovator at this time was the Chavín civilization (1200–200 B.C.E.) of present-day Peru, which appears to have invented tumbaga, a catch-all category of alloyed gold objects (*see* **Tumbaga**). By 500 C.E., this and other metallurgical technologies—including hammering, casting, gilding, lost wax, and raised relief—had spread all the way to the Intermediate Area, with gold being a major facet of ritual life among the polities of what is today Panama and Costa Rica. Alloys of gold and platinum, moreover, were being made in Ecuador 500 years before they were fashioned in Europe.

From coastal South America and the Intermediate Area, metal ornaments spread into Mesoamérica between 500 and 900, although the actual technologies (save soldering) for making such items was only introduced to West Mexico between 800 and 900. From there, the technologies spread into Central Mexico, such that by the time of European contact, metallurgy was common in much of the tropical Americas. In fact, some of the gold-working techniques established by these peoples, such as the Mixtecs of the Valley of Oaxaca, Mexico, have never been surpassed.

Metal usage for tools and other practical, large-scale implements was not common, however. For all intensive purposes stone remained the medium of choice for tools and weapons until European contact. Metals were primarily employed for personal ornamentation, from masks and rings to bells and headdresses. There was, however, the limited production of a type of bronze in some areas—most notably, among the Tarascans of West Mexico—and it seems possible that had the Europeans arrived a few centuries later they would have encountered a very different world than the one that they did.

Further Reading

Benson, Elizabeth. *Pre-Columbian Metallurgy of South America*. Washington, DC: Dumbarton Oaks, 1979.

Bray, Warwick. *Metallurgy in Ancient Mexico*. Greeley: University of Northern Colorado, 1982.

Fagan, Brian. *Ancient North America*. London: Thames and Hudson, Ltd., 1991.

Hosler, Dorothy. *The Sounds and Colors of Power: The Sacred Metallurgical Technology of Ancient West Mexico*. Cambridge, MA: MIT Press, 1994.

Mitla

Archaeological remains at the site of Mitla, located in Oaxaca, Mexico, date back to the Middle Preclassic (1000–400 B.C.E.), but it was only around 200 C.E. that the site became one of the major settlements of Zapotec civilization (*see* **Monte Albán**). It is noteworthy for having some of the best-preserved architecture in Oaxaca and for having passed under the political control of a few different Mesoamérican civilizations: Although it was more or less continuously occupied by the Zapotecs, it came to be dominated by the Mixtecs (c. 1000–1200) and then the Aztecs (1494–1521), who conquered and sacked the city in 1494. As a result, its architecture and artifact assemblage shows a blending of three of the great civilizations of Mesoamérica.

Visually, the architecture at Mitla is most noteworthy for its decorated stonewalls and door frames, which are decorated with geometric patterns called "grecas." Composed of thousands of cut and polished stones, these patterns consist of swirls, stepped elements, and rectangular designs. The patterns date to the Postclassic, during the period of Mixtec dominance, and show a strong influence from that civilization. Tombs of the Oaxacan elites were built beneath many of these palatial buildings and are cruciform in design. The visible ruins of Mitla today consist of a palace and related structures: When the Spanish conquered the area in the early sixteenth century, they dismantled much of the original settlement for building materials, erecting a church atop one of the original temples.

Further Reading

Evans, Susan, and David Webster, eds. *Archaeology of Ancient Mexico: An Encyclopedia.* New York: Garland, 2001.

Boone, Elizabeth. *Stories in Red and Black: The Pictorial Histories of the Aztec and Mixtec.* Austin: University of Texas Press, 2000.

Feinman, Gary, and Linda Nicholas. "Hilltop Sites of Oaxaca, Mexico." *Fieldiana* 37 (2004): 1–240.

Flannery, Kent, and Joyce Marcus. *Zapotec Civilization.* London: Thames and Hudson, Ltd., 1996.

Pohl, John. "Lintel Paintings of Mitla." *Arqueología Mexicana* 10(55) (2002): 97–98.

Moche

The Moche of the north coast of Peru were one of the major civilizations of South America, forming a series of independent city-states by 200 C.E. The civilization is named after the archaeological site of Moche, which is located in the Moche Valley of Peru and seems to have governed a region spanning the Chicama and Nepeña rivers. It and its contemporaries may have been the first states, as opposed to chiefdoms, in that continent. The warring elites who governed these city-states commissioned some of the largest structures and most famous pottery in the hemisphere, the latter bearing portraits as well as pictorial, historical narratives of life in the Moche world. Although independent, the city-states had a common material culture, architectural style, and religion, elements of which persisted for centuries following the complete collapse of Moche civilization between 750 and 800.

Moche architecture, like that of succeeding civilizations on the desert coast, consisted of mud-brick temples, platforms, and walled residential compounds faced with adobe and painted plaster. The bricks themselves are often labeled with the names of the workshops in which they were made; millions of them were used in temples that the Moche commissioned, likely through corveé labor (*see* **Corveé Labor**). The largest such temples or huacas (*see* **Huacas**) occur at Moche itself and include the Huaca del Sol and the Huaca de la Luna. One of the most famous Moche settlements, however, is the archaeological site of **Sipán**. Intact royal tombs there and at the site of San Jose de Moro, rare for not having been looted, have revealed individuals in roles (e.g., priests, warriors, etc.) recognizable on Moche ceramics.

It is Moche pottery, in addition to ornately decorated works of gold, shell, and other precious items, that reveals the most about their sociopolitical organization and daily life. Moche ceramic vessels are often what are called "portrait vessels": These are ceramic portraits on vases of the nobility, lifelike, and intended to represent specific individuals. Others are formed in the likenesses of deities or animals. But the most famous Moche vessels are those painted with mythological scenes, activities in daily life, the lives or deaths of rulers, and most famously, images of war and human sacrifice. One recurring set of images, known as the Presentation Theme, involves nobles killing captives and drinking their blood; one such noble, wearing accoutrements recognizable from such pictorial ceramics, was discovered in a tomb at Sipán.

In the final decades of the sixth century C.E., the Moche area was hit hard by an El Niño flood as well as a severe drought. The site of Moche, as well as several other centers, appears to have collapsed at that time, although survivors lasted well into the eighth century C.E. The weakened Moche states collapsed and gave way to the Lambayeque city-states or Sican culture (*see* **Batán Grande**; **Naymlap**) by 800.

Further Reading

Alva, W., and C. Donnan. *Royal Tombs of Sipan*. Los Angeles: Fowler Museum of Culture History, University of California, 1993.

Donnan, Christopher. *Moche Art of Peru*. Los Angeles: University of California, 1978.

Moseley, Michael E. *The Incas and Their Ancestors: the Archaeology of Peru*. 2nd ed. London: Thames and Hudson, Ltd., 2001.

Monte Albán

As one of the oldest major cities in Mesoamérica, Monte Albán was founded around 500 B.C.E. by the Zapotecs, a major cultural and ethnic group flourishing in the Valley of Oaxaca from the Preclassic (2500 B.C.E.–250 C.E.) to the present day. With its civic center located atop a flat hill near the center of the Valley, it was the predominant player in a loose confederation of settlements that conquered (or otherwise unified) much of the Oaxacan highlands starting around 200 B.C.E. In fact, Monte Albán appears to have entered the path to statehood via war: Prominent images of captives and other signs of an aggressive, expansionist state are the hallmarks of its architectural and artistic style. Archaeologists estimate that these wars of conquest were costly, with the population of the entire Valley declining by 20 percent during this period of Zapotec unification. Establishing administrative centers throughout the Valley of Oaxaca by 100 C.E., Monte Albán may have ruled over forty-thousand people in the Valley alone and seems to have conquered other areas of Mesoamérica as well. The specifics of this, however, are not clear.

Its greatest period was over by the beginning of the Early Classic (250–600), with some centers inside the Valley successfully asserting their independence. There are indications, moreover, of growing influence from the Central Mexican metropolis of Teotihuacá: This was a much larger and even more aggressive expansionist state that dominated Mesoamérica culturally—and in some places, perhaps politically—during the Early Classic. Monte Albán was still, however, the preeminent Zapotec city, and its time was far from over. Construction at the site continued, with an increased emphasis on defensibility (in the form of city walls) and agricultural intensification: The population here, as elsewhere in the Early Classic, was increasing and becoming more densely settled in the Valley. By the beginning of the Late Classic (600–909), the population of Monte Albán had reached twenty-five thousand people, who lived around an urban core of pyramids, elite residences, victoriously carved monuments, and even a ball court (*see* **Ballgame**).

Local assertions of independence within the Valley and the decline of Monte Albán as a geopolitical force abroad, however, seem to have precipitated a crises around 700. The site was not to recover and experienced a sharp drop in building and ceremonial activity. By 900, the population in and around Monte Albán had dwindled to the thousands, and other Zapotec centers had become more important. Never fully abandoned, however, Monte Albán continued to have a small local population until the Spanish Conquest.

Further Reading

Blanton, Richard. *Monte Alban: Settlement Patterns at the Ancient Zapotec Capital*. Clinton Corners, NY: Percheron Press, 2004.

Blomster, Jeffrey, ed. *After Monte Alban: Transformation and Negotiation in Oaxaca, Mexico*. Boulder: University Press of Colorado, 2008.

Evans, Susan, and David Webster, eds. *Archaeology of Ancient Mexico: An Encyclopedia*. New York: Garland, 2001.

Flannery, Kent, and Joyce Marcus. *Zapotec Civilization*. London: Thames and Hudson, Ltd., 1996.

Moundville

This archaeological site on the Black Warrior River in Alabama was one of the largest centers of the Mississippian culture (1000–1500), second only to **Cahokia** in Illinois in terms of size. With a population of about one thousand in its core and a regional population of approximately ten thousand, Moundville appears to have been a socially and politically complex chiefdom. Like the inhabitants of most Mississippian chiefdoms, the people of Moundville practiced intensive, maize-based agriculture to support their population and engaged in religious activities that were part of what is known as the **Southern Cult** or Southeastern Ceremonial Complex. Built atop a natural bluff overlooking the river, the heart of Moundville was surrounded on three sides by a wooden palisade, within which were twenty-six earthen mounds. The majority of these were arranged around a central plaza, with Mound B being perhaps the most imposing structure at the site: This steep pyramid, rising 58 feet high and accessed by ramps, overshadows most other structures at the site. Mound A, located in the center of the plaza, was equally imposing and ringed by smaller mounds. At the time of its occupation, most of these earthen mounds would have had perishable structures built atop them, housing elites or serving as focal points for large-scale ceremonies. The earthen mounds themselves often doubled as mortuary structures, with those of the highest rank being buried in structures like Mound A or B.

The elites at Moundville appear to have had these mounds built by exacting tribute—in the form of labor—from the local population. The arrangement of the residential mounds suggests a hierarchical social order: Some scholars have proposed that they were organized according to lineage groups of greater and lesser prestige. Like those at other Mississippian centers, these elites imported luxury goods through long-distance trade, to further distinguish themselves from commoners: Archaeologists have found worked artifacts of high-status materials, such as copper, mica, and shell, in burials at the site.

Around 1350, the site seems to have been in the throes of dramatic sociopolitical change. Moundville was abandoned as a residential zone but held onto its political and ceremonial importance. Presumably, elements of the regional population became more important during this time. Whatever the social experiment, however, it did not last for long: The onset of colder climactic conditions in North America around 1400, known as the Little Ice Age, coupled with deteriorating social relations between the Mississippian centers, led to collapse of Moundville and its environs. The area was almost abandoned by the early 1500s, although pockets of settlement were still in evidence at the time of European contact in the mid-sixteenth century.

Further Reading

Fagan, Brian. *Ancient North America*. London: Thames and Hudson, Ltd., 1991.
Walthall, John A. *Moundville: An Introduction to the Archaeology of a Mississippian Chiefdom.* 2nd ed. Tuscaloosa: Alabama Museum of Natural History, 1994.
Wilson, Gregory. *The Archaeology of Everyday Life at Early Moundville*. Tuscaloosa: University of Alabama Press, 2007.

Naymlap

This culture hero of the north coast of Peru was believed to have founded a dynasty that ruled over the loosely federated Lambayeque city-states (also known as Sican Culture). Although written records of Naymlap date to the late sixteenth century and thus the period of European colonization, this culture hero appears to have been a major part of oral tradition on the north coast, with images of him dating back as early as the ninth century.

According to legend, he arrived at the north coast of Peru with a retinue of warriors, wives, and concubines, having sailed there from the west. Bearing a green stone representation of himself, called "Yampellec," he established a dynasty at a city called "Chot." As he died, he is said to have grown wings and flown away, leaving Chot to his son. That individual was believed to have had twelve sons, each one of which became ruler of a city-state on the north coast. Their descendents ruled for ten generations, until such time as one ruler of Chotona — Fempellec — invoked the wrath of the gods by moving Yampellec. The gods then brought floods, famine, and pestilence to the region, precipitating a peoples' revolt and the end of the Naymlap dynasties.

The archaeological remains of Chotona, corresponding to Chot, and **Batán Grande** are two of the largest of the states mentioned in the history. They do appear to have suffered massive flooding around 1100, followed by abandonment. Yet some centers in the Lambayeque region do seem to have survived these events. All, however, were conquered by the empire of **Chimor** around 1370 and remained its subjects until the conquest of the entire area by the Inca Empire in the fifteenth century.

Further Reading

Fagan, Brian. *The Great Warming: Climate Change and the Rise and Fall of Civilizations*. London: Bloomsbury Press, 2008.

Moseley, Michael E. *The Incas and Their Ancestors: The Archaeology of Peru.* 2nd ed. London: Thames and Hudson, Ltd., 2001.

Moseley, Michael E., and A. Cordy-Collins, eds. *The Northern Dynasties: Kingship and Statecraft in Chimor.* Washington, DC: Dumbarton Oaks, 1990.

Rostworowski de Diez Canseco, Maria. *History of the Inca Realm.* Cambridge, UK: Cambridge University Press, 1998.

Nazca Lines

The Nazca civilization of the south coast of Peru, flourishing between 200 B.C.E. and 650 C.E., was at least partially contemporary with the city-states of the **Moche** to the north (*see* **Sipán**). With a ceremonial center at the site of Cahuachi, where they built mounds, plazas, and platforms for periodic gatherings, feasts, and rituals, the everyday Nazca lived in small and dispersed agricultural communities. Culturally, they shared some similarities with the Moche and other peoples of the desert coast, in terms of the ideas and images portrayed on ceramics (e.g., **curaca** elites, warfare, and feline imagery). But overall, their society was not nearly as politically complex as the Moche or later Lambayeque culture (*see* **Batán Grande**). They are most famous for having produced the Nazca lines, which were hundreds of outlines of animals, geometric shapes, plants, and abstractions created in the desert and surrounding hills. They were made fairly quickly and easily by removing dark-colored rocks and soils to expose lighter soils beneath.

Featuring in popular culture, particularly in movies and in fictional literature, the Nazca lines have been the source of many a far-fetched theory. There is no consensus on their purpose—indeed, they may have served different purposes to different groups over time—and they show no apparent organization in terms of where and when they occur. And although they are best seen through aerial photography (and hence, the fantastic theories), some were clearly meant to be seen from the ground and others from the surrounding hills. Many appear to have been forgotten or have fallen into disfavor: New lines and shapes often cross older ones without regard for orientation, shape, or any other discernable characteristic. They remain today as silent testaments to an enigmatic culture.

Further Reading

Moseley, Michael E. *The Incas and their Ancestors: the Archaeology of Peru.* 2nd ed. London: Thames and Hudson, Ltd., 2001.

Silverman, Helaine, and Donald Proulx. *The Nasca.* Oxford, UK: Wiley-Blackwell, 2002.

Nezahualcoyotl (1402–1472)

The king of the Acolhua known as Nezahualcoyotl, ruler of the city-state of Texcoco, spent most of his early life in fear of the Tepanec Empire. His father, Ixlilxochitl I (r. 1409–1418), had spent the latter years of his reign fighting a losing battle with them and was eventually executed. As further punishment, Texcoco was given to the Mexica at Tenochtitlán (future masters of the Aztec Empire) as a vassal. Nezahualcoyotl, for his part, spent years in intermittent exile: He was forced to move between his native city and others, as the fury of the Tepanecs with him—as heir to Texcoco—waxed and waned.

Relations between the Mexica and the Tepanecs eventually soured in 1428, resulting in the assassination of the Mexica king by Maxtla, ruler of the Tepanec Empire. The new Mexica king, **Itzcoatl**, called for an attack on the empire and requested assistance. Nezahualcoyotl (who was technically his vassal) answered that call and rallied a number of cities to the cause, including the disaffected Tepanec city of Tacuba. After a series of military engagements between the two forces, the allies prevailed and this new force—known as the **Triple Alliance**, or Aztec Empire—began a series of conquests that would bring much of Mesoamérica under its rule. Nezahualcoyotl was finally crowned tlatoani, or king, of Texcoco in 1431. He had waited 18 years to accede.

Despite being one of the original architects of the Triple Alliance, Nezahualcoyotl is best remembered for being a patron of knowledge and the arts and, above all, the greatest poet in Mesoamérican prehistory. During his reign he appears to have transformed Texcoco into what was arguably the preeminent intellectual center in Mesoamérica, with scholars from many fields—including music, sculpture, philosophy, law, and engineering—living and working in the royal court. It became the "Athens" of the Americas: He is said to have established an extensive library, a zoological garden, and even a self-governing academy of scholars and poets (none of these survived the Spanish Conquest). Poems attributed to Nezahualcoyotl are the among the best surviving examples of Pre-Columbian philosophy, and deal with the ephemeral nature of life, peace, love, friendship, and his own relationship to the gods. The traditions he is believed to have started were continued by his descendents, the future kings Nezahualpilli (r. 1472–1494) and Cacamatzin (r. 1494–1520).

Recently, the view of Nezahualcoyotl as a scholar king, and even a poet, has been challenged in the academic literature. It has been argued that there are some vagaries as to the authorship of his poems and that much of the favorable traits associated with Nezahualcoyotl were the products of his descendents recasting their ancestor in a favorable light following the Conquest. As a result, there is some dissension on some of the exploits of this character, but regardless he remains one of the most well known figures in Pre-Columbian history.

Further Reading

Evans, Susan, and David Webster, eds. *Archaeology of Ancient Mexico: An Encyclopedia.* New York: Garland, 2001.

Gillmor, Frances. *Flute of the Smoking Mirror.* Salt Lake City: University of Utah Press, 1983.

Lee, Jongsoo. "A Reinterpretation of Nahuatl Poetics: Rejecting the Image of Nezahualcoyotl as a Peaceful Poet." *Colonial Latin American Review* 12(2) (2003): 233–249.

Lee, Jongsoo. *The Allure of Nezahualcoyotl: Pre-Hispanic History, Religion, and Nahua Poetics.* Albuquerque: University of New Mexico Press, 2008.

Overking

The term *overking* is one that was coined by scholars Simon Martin and Nikolai Grube to describe the nature of Classic Maya (250–909) political relationships. The southern Maya area was, at that time, home to scores of competing city-states, each one vying for local or regional supremacy. Traditional scholarly models of sociopolitical organization had focused on the physical territories of the Maya kingdoms, with the southern lowlands carved into small or large political units with loosely defined geographic boundaries. These models, however, failed to account for an emerging pattern found in Maya hieroglyphic inscriptions: Certain rulers were being described in feudal terms, with masters and their vassal lords explicitly mentioned on many Maya monuments. Moreover, these master–vassal relationships appeared and disappeared over time, such that sites appeared to be arrayed in a complex web of ever-changing diplomatic relationships. Some sites, however, were consistently "masters," whoever their vassals might be.

The overking model sees some political centers as dominant, with others deriving prestige—as well as possible protection, enhanced diplomatic relations, and favorable economic relationships—from alliances with powerful kingdoms. Geographic proximity, though certainly a determining factor in such relationships, is not necessarily required. Rather it is prestige, combined with real or token support from the overking, that seems to have been the motivating factor for these relationships. The most powerful overkings in the Maya area were based at the sites of **Tikal** and **Calakmul**. As these were implacable enemies and the most powerful of the Maya kingdoms, alliances with them—against others—were often made and broken in what appear to be moments of political desperation or opportunism. Thus though the Classic Maya area never saw unification or an empire, there were moments when political units larger than an individual city-state were formed. Sometimes these were real, and sometimes they were little more than fictive, but they were usually temporary.

Further Reading

Evans, Susan, and David Webster, eds. *Archaeology of Ancient Mexico: An Encyclopedia.* New York: Garland, 2001.

Martin, Simon, and Nikolai Grube. "Maya Superstates." *Archaeology* 48(6) (1995): 41–46.

Martin, Simon, and Nikolai Grube. *Chronicle of the Classic Maya Kings and Queens.* London: Thames and Hudson, Ltd., 2000.

Pachacamac

During the Early Intermediate Period (200 B.C.E.–650 C.E.), the town of Pachacamac, in the Lurín Valley near Lima, Peru, was but one of several competing coastal centers. The growth of the Wari Empire, and its corresponding expansion into this region during the Middle Horizon (650–1000), may have resulted in the transformation of this small town into a city. Surviving the collapse of **Wari**, Pachacamac appears to have become a local power, perhaps serving as the heart of a small state after 1000. By the Late Intermediate Period (1000–1476), Pachacamac had also become the locus of worship for a creator god of the same name (Pachacamac), serving as a religious shrine and pilgrimage center.

The majority of what we currently know about the religious and political history of Pachacamac dates to the mid-fifteenth century, when the Inca conquered the region and made Pachacamac an administrative center. They left its oracle and priests largely to themselves, allowing the city to retain its status as a major pilgrimage center. The god Pachacamac was incorporated into the Andean pantheon and—though transformed into a fire god and now subordinate to the Inca god of creation, Viracocha—maintained a substantial following.

The city of Pachacamac remained one of the holiest cities in the Inca Empire until the Spanish Conquest.

Further Reading

MacCormack, Sabine. *Religion in the Andes: Vision and Imagination in Early Colonial Peru.* Princeton, NJ: Princeton University Press, 1991.

Moseley, Michael E. *The Incas and Their Ancestors: the Archaeology of Peru.* 2nd ed. London: Thames and Hudson, Ltd., 2001.

Shimada, Izumi. *Pachacamac Archaeology: Retrospect and Prospect.* Philadelphia: University Museum Press, University of Pennsylvania, 1985.

Palenque

This ancient Maya archaeological site near the Usumacinta River in Chiapas, Mexico, was at the peak of its power during the middle part of the Late Classic Period (600–850), when it was the capital of a kingdom (*B'aakal*) that could count its one-time enemy, Pomona, as its vassal and the major site of **Tikal** as its ally. Historically, it was engaged in long-term hostilities with some of the major powers of the Classic Maya Period (250–850), including **Calakmul**, Piedras Negras, Pomona, and Tonina.

Like some other major centers of the Classic Period, Palenque may have witnessed the incursion of Teotihuacános into the Maya area (*see* **Copan**) in the late fourth century; some scholars have suggested a connection between that incursion and the founding of the Classic dynasty at Palenque in 431. From this point until the sixth century, Palenque was one of many struggling centers on the Usumacinta River, in direct competition with sites such as Pomona, Piedras Negras, Yaxchilan, and others. Its growing power on that river seems to have drawn the attention of distant Calakmul, capital of one of the most

Mayan ruins at Palenque, Chiapas, Mexico. Elisa Locci/Shutterstock.

influential and militarily powerful of the Maya kingdoms, which launched repeated, successful attacks on Palenque in 599 and 611. Years of sociopolitical disarray ensued, but the royal dynasty eventually righted itself under **K'inich Janaab' Pakal** or "Pakal the Great" (r. 615–683), who took the throne in 615 and would rule for the next 68 years until his death at age 80. Although the early years of his reign were marked by wars and possibly setbacks, by the mid-600s K'inich Janaab' Pakal had stabilized the situation enough to go on the offensive, attacking and subjugating Pomona. Palenque was enough of a powerhouse during his reign to be able to offer safe haven for a ruler of Tikal, who had fled the site as it was overrun by forces from Calakmul.

After the death of the long-lived Pakal, who was housed in the now-famous Temple of the Inscriptions, Palenque passed into the hands of K'inich Kan B'alam II (r. 684–702) and then K'inich K'an Joy Chitam II (r. 702–711), both of whom were sons of the late Pakal. During this time Palenque expanded its political influence south and west, engaging in often-successful but occasionally disastrous wars with its neighbors. Following the unfortunate capture of K'inich K'an Joy Chitam II by Tonina in 711, Palenque suffered a dynastic disruption. Nevertheless, the site managed to right itself eventually and enjoyed some measure of stability under succeeding rulers. By the beginning of the eighth century, however, the story changed: Palenque underwent a precipitous decline, with the population dropping to a fraction of its former level as carved inscriptions and buildings ceased to be produced. Although we do not know what precise circumstances arose at Palenque to cause this, it is clear that its abandonment in the early eighth century was part of the wider phenomenon of the **Maya collapse**.

Further Reading

Evans, Susan, and David Webster, eds. *Archaeology of Ancient Mexico: An Encyclopedia*. New York: Garland, 2001.

Martin, Simon, and Nikolai Grube. *Chronicle of the Maya Kings and Queens*. London: Thames and Hudson, Ltd., 2000.

Schele, Linda, and Peter Mathews. *The Code of Kings: the Language of Seven Sacred Maya Temples and Tombs*. New York: Scribner, 1999.

Patolli

Patolli is the Nahuatl term for a board game popular in Pre-Columbian Mesoamérica. Although its origins are unknown, it was widely played in central and southern Mesoamérica by such civilizations as the Classic Maya (250–909) and the Aztecs (1325–1521), from whom the current name of the game derives. Much like the Mesoamérican ballgame, patolli—as a game of chance as well as skill—was associated with betting activity. In the Aztec Empire patolli was a winner-take-all game, with individuals betting nearly anything and occasionally risking significant financial losses.

The patolli game board was shaped like an *X* and marked with 52 spaces through which several tokens would move. Colored beans, thrown by each player, would determine how many spaces those tokens could pass along the board. The overall object was to move all of one's tokens from their starting positions to finishing ones, much like the unrelated contemporary game of Parcheesi, thereby winning the bet and whatever objects were involved.

Needless to say, patolli involved a great deal of luck—much of which was provided by the god of patolli (as well as music, dance, and other gambling endeavors), Macuilxochitl.

Further Reading

Evans, Susan. *Ancient Mexico and Central America: Archaeology and Culture History*. London: Thames and Hudson, Ltd., 2004.

Evans, Susan, and David Webster, eds. *Archaeology of Ancient Mexico: An Encyclopedia*. New York: Garland, 2001.

Holmer, Rick. *The Aztec Book of Destiny*. North Charleston, SC: BookSurge Publishing, 2005.

Miller, Mary Ellen, and Karl Taube. *An Illustrated Dictionary of the Gods and Symbols of Ancient Mexico and the Maya*. London: Thames and Hudson, Ltd., 1997.

Smith, Michael E. *The Aztecs*. Oxford, UK: Wiley-Blackwell, 2003.

Pleiades

The Pleiades appear to have been one of the most important celestial bodies of the night sky observed by Pre-Columbian peoples. Peoples of northeast North America, for example, appear to have kept watch of the Pleiades in the spring and in the fall to calculate frost-free dates (e.g., when it was safe to plant and to harvest). The ancient Maya used the rising of the Pleiades, at dawn in late May, to know when it was safe to plant as well—but in their case it was tied to the beginning of the rainy season in Mesoamérica. The use of the Pleiades as a barometer for maximum agricultural productivity does not appear to have been limited to this region or to have died out with European contact: Similar ideas appear in the ethnohistoric and ethnographic records of many peoples of the Americas.

Likewise, the Pleiades—though usually connected to agriculture—had other meanings and associations. Among the Aztecs, for example, a specific position of the Pleiades in the night sky—overhead at midnight—was linked to one of their chief rites of renewal. We know that the Pleiades were important to the Aztecs specifically, moreover, because they are one of the few identifiable celestial bodies featured in the "Cronica Mexicayotl," a document written by Fernando Alvarado Tezozomoc, a grandson of Motecuhzoma II (1466–1520), around 1598.

Further Reading

Aveni, Anthony. *Skywatchers of Ancient Mexico*. 2nd ed. Austin: University of Texas Press, 2001.

Ceci, Lynn. "Watchers of the Pleiades: Ethnoastronomy among Native Cultivators in Northeastern North America." *Ethnohistory*, 25(4) (1978): 301–317.

Popol Nah

A popol nah, or "council house" (literally, mat house), was an institution developed in the Maya area of Mesoamérica toward the end of the Late Classic (600–909). These were meeting places for nobles and thus centers of government, of paramount importance at sites where kings no longer held sole authority. The most famous Classic Maya popol nah occurs at the site of **Copan**, Honduras. Identified as Structure 22A, it was decorated with carved stone versions of reed mats, one of the symbols of ruling authority in the Maya area. The building of Structure 22A, and thereby the institution of the popol nah, appears to have coincided with the death of its most famous king, Wax-aklajuun U'baah K'awiil, who was captured and killed in 738. Archaeologists believe that the ensuing dynastic crisis required the new king to enter into a power-sharing arrangement with local nobles.

The popol nah was thus a sign that kings at Copan no longer had sole au-thority, a disturbing prospect from the perspective of ruling dynasties in the Maya area. After the collapse of Classic Maya civilization in the southern low-lands (*see* **Maya Collapse**) in the ninth to tenth centuries, council houses be-came a common facet of political life in the northern lowlands and the Maya highlands. Postclassic (909–1519) cities such as **Chichén Itzá** or Uxmal, in north-ern Yucatán, as well as many of the fifteenth- and sixteenth-century Maya high-land cities had buildings like these for dispersed leadership. They were clearly a facet of life for the K'ichee Maya, who wrote about them in the most famous extant Maya religious text, the **Popol Vuh**.

Further Reading

Eggebrecht, Eva, Wilfried Seipel, Nikolai Grube, and Estella Krejci (translated by Ines Paola de Castro). *Maya Amaq': Mundo Maya*. Guatemala City: Cholsamaj Fundacion, 2001.

Evans, Susan, and David Webster, eds. *Archaeology of Ancient Mexico: An Encyclopedia*. New York: Garland, 2001.

Fash, William. *Scribes, Warriors and Kings*. 2nd ed. London: Thames and Hudson, 2001.

Popol Vuh

Known as the "Book of Council" and written by the K'ichee Maya in the mid-sixteenth century, the Popol Vuh is one of the most important religious texts from the Americas. Although it was written after the Spanish Conquest, it was based on Pre-Columbian Maya versions that date back—at the very latest—to the Late Preclassic (400 B.C.E.–250 C.E.). It details the creation myths of the K'ichee Maya, from the creation of the world to the birth of the K'ichee Maya as a people. It thus incorporates mythological and historical elements into its narrative. Given the antiquity of some of the stories of the Popol Vuh, it is the single most important surviving text—outside of Maya hieroglyphic inscriptions—for understanding ancient Maya religion.

The book can largely be divided into four parts, consisting of (1) multiple creations and destructions of the world, where missteps in the fabrication of human beings by the gods result in catastrophic events; (2) exploits by the mythological culture heroes Hunahpu and Xbalanque, the "Hero Twins." who—as gods before the dawn of the present world—are born to set in motion the current world order and eventually die to become the sun and moon; (3) the creation of humanity and the K'ichee, who become differentiated from other tribes and travel under the guidance of their tutelary deity, Tohil; and (4) the events leading up to and immediately following the founding of Gumar-caaj (*see* **Utatlán**) around 1400. Stories imparting the ideals, ideas, and overall culture of the Maya can be found in all four parts. Archaeologists have been able to identify echoes of these stories in the distant past, as at the sites of Izapa, Guatemala, and **Copan**, Honduras, and combine the ideas of the Popol

Vuh with independent interpretations of Maya artifacts. The result has been a greater understanding of what the ancient Maya believed in—and of what links they share with present-day peoples.

Further Reading

Christenson, Allen J., trans. *Popol Vuh: the Sacred Book of the Maya.* Norman: University of Oklahoma Press, 2003.

Tedlock, Dennis, trans. *Popol Vuh: The Definitive Edition of the Mayan Book of the Dawn of Life and the Glories of Gods and Kings.* New York: Simon and Schuster, 1985.

Pulque

Pulque was one of the primary alcoholic drinks of Pre-Columbian Mesoamérica. Made from the fermented juice of the agave, pulque was of particular importance in Central Mexico. Although the origins of pulque are not clear, it played a major role in Mixtec as well as Aztec ceremonial life in the second millennium C.E. It was a main staple of feasts and festivals in Central Mexico, where consumption of pulque was a norm, but public drunkenness was not: Peoples such as the Aztecs had strong cultural prohibitions against such behavior, which was permitted in only a few select circumstances. This was due to cultural ideas about appropriate behavior as well to the ritual and religious associations of pulque. For example, it was a common substitute for human blood in sacrificial rites and may have been associated with such bodily fluids as semen or breast milk.

Pulque was even the source of specific origin myths involving famous Central Mexican gods such as **Quetzalcoatl**. The most widespread myth comes from the Aztecs, who believed that it was created by the gods Quetzcoatl and Mayahuel. According to legend, the peoples of earth had been created and provided with food but had nothing that provided them directly with joy. Noticing this, Quetzalcoatl persuades a young sky goddess named Mayahuel—the goddess of the maguey plant—to come with him to the surface of the earth. Her grandmother, one of the fearsome tzitzimime or "star demons" believed to attack the sun daily at dawn and dusk, rouses the other tzitzimime to pursue the two errant gods, who transform themselves into the branches of a tree when the tzitzimime give chase from the heavens. Unfortunately, the branches suddenly break and the grandmother recognizes Mayahuel, who is killed and torn to pieces as punishment for leaving the sky. Quetzalcoatl escapes this fate and buries her bones in the earth, where they become the first maguey plant and thus the source of all pulque.

Further Reading

Evans, Susan. *Ancient Mexico and Central America: Archaeology and Culture History.* London: Thames and Hudson, Ltd., 2004.

Monaghan, John. "Sacrifice, Death, and the Origins of Agriculture in the Codex Vienna." *American Antiquity* 55(3) (1990): 559–569.

Taube, Karl. *Aztec and Maya Myths.* Austin: University of Texas Press, 1993.

Quetzalcoatl

One of the premier deities of the Aztec (1325–1521) pantheon, Quetzalcoatl or "the Feathered Serpent" is of great antiquity in Mesoamérica. His associations change over time and space, and we do not know what various peoples before the Post-classic (909–1519) actually called him (*Quetzal-coatl* is his Aztec name). Like **Tlaloc**, the Central Mexican rain god, Quetzalcoatl appears early on in the archaeological record of Mesoamérica at the Central Mexican metropolis of **Teotihuacá** (300 B.C.E.–600 C.E.). The most noteworthy ex-ample of this god can be found on the aptly named Temple of the Feathered Serpent, where repetitive images of Quetzalcoatl appear along-side those of Tlaloc. A tomb discovered below this temple housed the remains of approxi-mately forty sacrificial victims; most of these victims were young men and were probably not war captives. They appear to have been killed in a ritual involving martial prowess or military display, as most were dressed as pow-erful warriors.

Feathered serpent (symbol of Quetzalcoatl) emerg-ing from a flower (stone). From Temple of Quetzal-coatl, Teotihuacan civilization, c. 100 AD, Mexico. The Art Archive/Archaeological Museum Teoti-huacan Mexico/Gianni Dagli Orti.

Quetzalcoatl survived the collapse of Teoti-huacá in the late sixth or early seventh century to become a major figure at some Late Classic sites, including Xochicalco in Central Mexico. Further flores-cence of Quetzalcoatl as a god would come with the rise of the Toltecs at **Tula**, also in Central Mexico, and with the preeminence of Chichén Itzá in Yucatán. In both places, Quetzalcoatl the god became conflated mythologically with a quasi-historical figure named Ce Acatl Topiltzin Quetzalcoatl. According to native chronicles from the era of European contact, he was a ruler of the Toltecs who was opposed to human sacrifice and advocated, in its place, the sacrifice of butterflies. Although he was a wise and knowledgeable figure, he managed to be tricked and humiliated by his rivals and, so shamed, departed across the sea to the east. As the native chroniclers relate, he came to rule the city of **Chi-chén Itzá** and was known in Maya languages as K'uk'ulkan (a translation of Quetzalcoatl).

Although archaeologically there are chronological problems with this myth, having implications for the process of cultural transmission between the two centers (*see* **Chichén Itzá** and **Tula**), the changes to Quetzalcoatl's persona — from a god involved with human sacrifice to one associated with "butterfly sacrifice," knowledge, and wisdom — between the Early Classic (250–600) and the early Postclassic (909–1519) were real. By the time of the Aztecs, moreover, Quetzalcoatl was associated with the planet **Venus** as well as many aspects of creation mythology. He was credited with the destruction of one of the previ-ous mythological epochs (*see* **Cyclical Time**), the creation of human beings, and the invention of books as well as the **Mesoamérican calendar**. He was also credited with having provided humanity with maize and was a symbol of death and rebirth. With all of these attributes, the Quetzalcoatl of the late Post-classic was truly one of the most important deities in Mesoamérica.

Further Reading

Evans, Susan. *Ancient Mexico and Central America: Archaeology and Culture History*. Lon-don: Thames and Hudson, Ltd., 2004.

Miller, Mary Ellen, and Karl Taube. *An Illustrated Dictionary of the Gods and Symbols of Ancient Mexico and the Maya*. London: Thames and Hudson, Ltd., 1997.

Taube, Karl. *Aztec and Maya Myths*. Austin: University of Texas Press, 1993.

Quipu

A quipu (also spelled "khipu") is a single strand of wool from which a series of knotted threads hang; the number of hanging threads can vary considerably, as can the knots, weave of threads, and even colors. In the time of the Inca Empire (1428–1533), quipus were used to record—among other things—tribute payments and other basic economic information vital to the functioning of the Inca state. Although not a writing system per se, quipus were used by accountants in much the same way: They were record-keeping devices that could be linked together to tell a larger economic story and passed on through time.

Recently, research by Gary Urton and others at Harvard University has suggested that the ties between the quipu method of recording and traditional forms of writing are closer than previously thought. The researchers have found that there are patterns in the types of fibers used to make the quipu and in all of the other variables of quipu construction, down to such factors as the spin direction of quipu threads and their colors. These patterns may have served to encode more than simple mathematical and economic calculations, and although the quipus are far from deciphered, the idea that they functioned beyond the Inca economy is an exciting one. Just as exciting has been the recent discovery of a quipu at the site of Caral, on the Pacific desert coast: This site is one of the earliest in the Americas and dates to the Andean Preceramic (3000–1800 B.C.E.). This proves that quipus were of great antiquity in South America and that they existed as a form of communication from that early time all the way to the colonial period!

Further Reading

Mann, Charles C. "Unraveling Khipu's Secrets." *Science* 309(5737) (2005): 1008–1009.

Moseley, Michael E. *The Incas and their Ancestors: the Archaeology of Peru*. 2nd ed. London: Thames and Hudson, Ltd., 2001.

Urton, Gary. *Signs of the Inka Khipu*. Austin: University of Texas Press, 2003.

Urton, Gary, and Carrie Brezine. "Khipu Accounting in Ancient Peru." *Science* 309(5737) (2005): 1065–1067.

Rivas

This settlement, located near San Isidro, Costa Rica, on the Chirripó Pacifico River, was home to the Chiriquí culture of southwest Costa Rica between the tenth and fifteenth centuries. It is situated below the burial grounds of the Panteón de la Reina, an elite cemetery located atop a long ridge. One of the two major, excavated Chiriquí centers in Costa Rica, Rivas has provided archaeologists with a glimpse of life in the Intermediate Area, the area between the populous urban societies of Mesoamérica and the Andes. Characterized by petroglyphs, rings of stone cobbles, and standing stones, Rivas—like most sites of the region—was not characterized by monumental stone architecture. In fact, it seems to have started like many centers in the Intermediate Area, as a populous farming village ruled by chiefs and competing lineages. Between 1250 and 1400, however, it was transformed architecturally into a regional economic, political, and ceremonial center.

Three separate cemeteries at the site, coupled with the elite cemetery above, appear to have made Rivas a locus of mortuary activity. Based upon the locations of these cemeteries as well as differences in house construction, archaeologists believe that there were at least four different social groups at Rivas, with only one of them having access to the Panteón de La Reina and high-prestige items such as gold. These high-status individuals appear to have been engaged in long-distance trade with societies of the Pacific Coast of Costa Rica.

As a ceremonial center, however, Rivas does not appear to have been occupied by a regular village population during this time. Rather it seems to have been a place where people came together in rites of feasting and ritual display. Such behaviors may have been designed to emphasize lineage ties or to reinforce social bonds between different gathered groups. Such behaviors seem to have ceased by the end of the fifteenth century, however, when Rivas was finally abandoned.

Further Reading

Quilter, Jeffrey. *Cobble Circles and Standing Stones: Archaeology at the Rivas Site, Costa Rica*. Iowa City: University of Iowa Press, 2004.

Quilter, Jeffrey, and Aida Blanco Vargas. "Monumental Architecture and Social Organization at the Rivas Site, Costa Rica." *Journal of Field Archaeology* 22(2) (1995): 203–221.

Shabik'eschee

This archaeological site in the American Southwest was one of the first sedentary, agricultural villages on the Colorado Plateau. The years between 100 and 400 had seen the widespread adoption of pottery in this region as well as the development of local strains of maize. By 400, agricultural production in the area had intensified—in large part due to changes in the ability to store food and an increase in rainfall—and the first year-round villages had developed. The founding of Shabik'eschee in the late fifth century, on the south side of **Chaco Canyon**, New Mexico, was part of this new trend. Houses here consisted of pits with earthen walls, roofed either with wood or wattle-and-daub. Storage facilities, located behind these houses, held crops such as maize, beans, and squash. In the years to come, these storage facilities would become less and less public, eventually being moved inside houses as the population increased and as distinctive, familial residential areas emerged. Shabik'eschee was thus one of the first in a long line of village settlements on the Colorado Plateau that eventually gave way, after 900, to densely populated communities centered about communal buildings or "great houses." Sometime after 700, the pithouses of Shabik'eschee and other settlements were abandoned in favor of above-ground settlements, forerunners of the pueblos that were common in the region in the years before Spanish contact.

Further Reading

Akins, Nancy J., Linda S. Cordell, Jeffrey S. Dean, and Stephen H. Lekson. *Archaeology of Chaco Canyon*. Santa Fe, NM: School of American Research Press, 2006.

Roberts, Frank, Jr. *Shabik'eschee Village, a Late Basket Maker Site in the Chaco Canyon, New Mexico*. Washington, DC: Bureau of American Ethnology, 1929.

Sebastian, Lynne. *The Chaco Anasazi*. Cambridge, UK: Cambridge University Press, 1996.

Sipán

During its heyday, Sipán was one of the primary settlements of the **Moche** civilization, on the north coast of Peru. It is most famous for the archaeological discovery of El Señor de Sipán, the "Lord of Sipán," a noble dressed in ceremonial garb. The tomb is noteworthy for two reasons. First, the majority of Moche tombs are looted, and finding one that was undisturbed was an extremely rare occurrence: Since the collapse of Moche civilization around 800, the tombs have been periodically stripped of their gold and other precious items by grave robbers. Second, the tomb belonged to an individual of the highest status within Moche society—a ruling noble, if not a ruler himself. What makes the second point so remarkable is that from his clothing, gold headgear, and chalice, it is clear that this individual was playing the role of a familiar figure painted on Moche ceramics. Known as the "warrior-priest," this role is part of an overall motif on those ceramics called the "Presentation Theme."

As one of the chief narratives of Moche ceremony, the Presentation Theme usually shows the aftermath of a battle, in which captives have been taken and stripped of their clothing. Brought before the ruling nobility, their throats are cut and the blood caught in a chalice. As the other nobles stand around, the chief figure—the "warrior-priest"—drinks the blood, dressed in gold finery and accompanied by a spotted dog.

Until the discovery of the Lord of Sipán, this scene was thought to have been mythical, but the excavations at Sipán (and, subsequently, other Moche sites) suggest that ruling nobles participated in these activities regularly. As if to add further confirmation, the Lord of Sipán was buried with a host of other individuals (presumably participants) as well as a small dog.

Further Reading

Alva, W., and C. Donnan. *Royal Tombs of Sipan*. Los Angeles: Fowler Museum of Culture History, University of California, 1993.

Donnan, Christopher. *Moche Art of Peru*. Los Angeles: University of California, 1978.

Moseley, Michael E. *The Incas and Their Ancestors: The Archaeology of Peru*. 2nd ed. London: Thames and Hudson, Ltd., 2001.

Snaketown

This site on the Gila River, Arizona, was the largest settlement of the Hohokam people during the Preclassic and Classic Periods (700–1150 and 1150–1450, respectively) and is today one of the principal archaeological sites of the American Southwest. Also known as Skoaquik, "place of snakes," this settlement was characterized by hundreds of thatched, wattle-and-daub houses arranged in small groups around plazas. At its height, Snaketown was at the center of a series of hierarchically arranged settlements with trading ties as far as Mexico. Its population of approximately two-thousand people—in the present-day Sonoran Desert—was managed agriculturally through an elaborate irrigation system.

Snaketown and the other Hohokam settlements appear to have had strong ties, in terms of trade and exchange, with peoples on the fringes of Mesoamérica during the Preclassic (700–1150). Perhaps the most striking evidence for this contact at Snaketown is its ballcourt, seemingly patterned after the earthen ballcourts of northern Mexico. The court at Snaketown consists of soil piled up along the edges of an oval playing field; it is only one of approximately two hundred ballcourts at Hohokam sites in Arizona.

The **ballgame** was invented very early in Mesoamérican prehistory and, interestingly enough, only appears in the American Southwest during the Hohokam florescence. Combined with the fact that the peoples of Snaketown appear to have obtained macaw feathers, copper bells, and other exotics from Mexico, the connection between the Hohokam and northern Mesoamérica appears to have been prolonged and rather strong. Nevertheless, it is not clear that the ballgame—or the exotic items traded in from Mexico—carried the same meaning in Arizona as it did in Mesoamérica. Thus far, the consensus interpretation among archaeologists is that the Snaketown ball court, like others in the area, represents public architecture with a ritual component.

The connections between Mesoamérica and Snaketown appear to have declined during the Classic Period (1150–1450), when the ballgame fell out of favor. Greater numbers of platform mounds (which replaced the ball court as the preferred style of public architecture) and adobe house compounds were the hallmarks of this era, and Snaketown became a focal point for migration from the smaller, surrounding towns. Unfortunately, the site began to decline in the fifteenth century due to environmental changes as well as agricultural problems and was abandoned to the desert by 1450.

Further Reading

Bayman, J. "The Hohokam of Southwest North America." *Journal of World Prehistory* 15 (2001): 257–311.

Fagan, Brian. *Ancient North America.* London: Thames and Hudson, Ltd., 1991.

Haury, Emil W. *The Hohokam, Desert Farmers and Craftsmen: Excavations at Snaketown, 1964-1965.* Tucson: University of Arizona Press, 1976.

Wilcox, David. *Snaketown Revisited.* Tucson: Arizona State Museum, 1981.

Southern Cult

The *Southern Cult* or *Southeastern Ceremonial Complex* refers to a series of symbols as well as a general artistic style found in elite burials from archaeological sites of the American Midwest and Southeast during the Mississippian Period (1000–1500). The style appears to be indicative of a general belief system in which ancestors, agricultural fertility, warfare, and shamanism played a central role. Southern Cult artifacts were often made from rare or precious materials such as copper and marine shell, as well as from more mundane materials such as wood. Symbols included weeping eyes, woodpeckers, crosses within circles, birds-of-prey, warriors or weapons, skulls, striped poles, hands, and serpents. Because these symbols were found in a broad band ranging from the outer Midwest to the Gulf and Atlantic coasts, scholars initially believed that these areas were connected and integrated within a single cultural network. More recently, the recognition of significant regional variations, as well as a greater understanding of the individual Mississippian centers, has prompted many scholars to question the existence of the Southern Cult as a "unified" or "standardized" religious tradition.

In all likelihood, there was never one religion that tied the Mississippian sites together. Rather, the Southern Cult may be viewed as a set of symbols and styles, often—but not always—regionally distinct over a broad geographic area. Elements of the Southern Cult appear to have been used by local elites or chiefs, at places such as **Cahokia** or **Spiro**, to highlight their authority vis-à-vis the general population. Oftentimes, Southern Cult objects tie leaders with supernatural beings, prominent ancestors, and even martial prowess. Some of the themes of the Southern Cult were originally thought to bear evidence of influence from Mesoamérica: Imagery involving long-nosed or solar deities, human sacrifice, and the elements was initially thought to have been derived from Central Mexico. Most scholars no longer believe this, however: the earliest incarnations of the Southern Cult seem to derive from local artistic and religious traditions first developed during the Early Woodland Period (800 B.C.E.–400 C.E.). Any connections with Mesoamérica were probably sporadic and indirect at best.

Further Reading

Brown, J. *The Spiro Ceremonial Center*. Ann Arbor: Museum of Anthropology, University of Michigan, 1996.

Fagan, Brian. *Ancient North America*. London: Thames and Hudson, Ltd., 1991.

Knight, Jr., V., J. Brown, and G. Lankford. "On the Subject Matter of Southeastern Ceremonial Complex Art." *Southeastern Archaeology* 20 (2001): 129–141.

Spiro

Spiro, in present-day Oklahoma, is one of the most famous of all of the Mississippian (1000–1500) sites. Falling within the Caddoan cultural subdivision of Mississippian civilization, Spiro was the largest and most complex settlement in the region, comparable in some ways to the great centers at **Moundville**, Alabama, or Etowah, Georgia. Spiro is most noteworthy for its large pyramidal mound, dubbed Craig Mound. The site rose to fame in the 1930s, when looters tunneled into the mound and partially destroyed one of the most elaborate burial deposits in North America. Luckily, the looters were caught before finishing their work, and archaeologists were able to find and document the materials located therein.

Known as the Great Mortuary, the burial deposit within Craig Mound housed many burials outfitted with wooden litters, masks, marine items, and even woven materials. The artifacts from the Great Mortuary are noteworthy for their high degree of preservation as well as what they tell us about religious life among the Mississippians. After the individuals of the Great Mortuary were interred, wooden poles were used to mark the spot even as Craig Mound was modified and enlarged, suggesting a long-term reverence for these dead. Likewise, there is ample evidence that shamanism was a regular facet of religious life at Spiro, with the designs and imagery of many of the artifacts in the Great Mortuary similar to those found in religious or ritual contexts at other Mississippian sites.

Archaeologists believe that this shared symbolism is indicative of a widespread set of ideas or beliefs among the Mississippians, often dubbed the **Southern Cult** or Southeastern Ceremonial Complex. Politically, these ideas may have been central to the power of the Mississippian chiefs at Spiro and elsewhere: As in some other parts of the Americas, public ritual at Spiro may have been one way in which the political elite expressed its authority. By the fourteenth century, this authority was gone, and Spiro—like other Mississippian centers in the Midwest—was largely abandoned.

Further Reading

Brown, James. *The Spiro Ceremonial Center*. Ann Arbor: Museum of Anthropology, University of Michigan, 1996.

Fagan, Brian. *Ancient North America*. London: Thames and Hudson, Ltd., 1991.

Phillips, Phillip, and James Brown. *Pre-Columbian Shell Engravings from the Craig Mound at Spiro, Oklahoma*. Cambridge, MA: Peabody Museum Press, 1984.

Staff God

This deity, originally appearing at the Early Horizon site of Chavín de Huantar, Peru, was the primary god of Chavín civilization (400–200 B.C.E.). A composite of Amazonian animals, the Staff God is often depicted as a humanoid with a feline face, sporting serpents for eyebrows as well as hair, with claws on his hands and feet. Typically the Staff God, in his original form, was carved on Chavín stone monoliths or stelae holding staves. The Staff God functioned as a kind of oracle to local priests, and because of the relative power and influence of Chavín as a ceremonial center, his imagery spread during the Early Horizon to most of central and northern Peru.

The Staff God appears to have survived the rise and fall of several societies in Peru, as his next appearance as a major religious icon occurs with **Tiwanaku**. During the Middle Horizon (650–1000), his serpentine and feline characteristics merged with avian qualities: Felines and solar rays sometimes emerge from his head, as he wields two serpentine–avian scepters. These were the three basic types of animals common in religious imagery of that time. With one of his renditions standing in a key position at Tiwanaku, the Gateway of the Sun, the Tiwanaku Staff God seems to have been the most important, recognizable deity there. Moreover, he appears to have been exported to and adopted by the other major Andean civilization of that time, **Wari**. There his staves terminate in maize cobs, suggesting his role as a god (at least in part) of agricultural fertility. The decline of Wari around 1050, however, saw the Staff God decline in importance, as new gods—and ancestors—took a more prominent role in the Andean pantheon.

Further Reading

Fiedel, Stuart J. *Prehistory of the Americas*. Cambridge, UK: Cambridge University Press, 1992.

Moseley, Michael E. *The Incas and Their Ancestors: The Archaeology of Peru*. 2nd ed. London: Thames and Hudson, Ltd., 2001.

Quilter, Jeffrey. *Treasures of the Andes*. London: Duncan Baird, 2006.

Stela

Broadly defined in the Americas as a stone, rectangular monolith erected for commemorative purposes, a stela was a common form of sculpture in Mesoamérica and, to a lesser extent, in Andean South America. In South America, the earliest stelae occur during the Initial Period (1800–400 B.C.E.) and the Early Horizon (400–200 B.C.E.) at sites like Cerro Sechín, on the north coast of Peru, and Chavín de Huantar in the Andes. Images on these monuments range from warriors and dismembered victims (Cerro Sechín) to a humanoid, oracle deity known as the **Staff God**. Depictions of the latter individual persisted well into the first millennium C.E. (*see* **Wari**). The raising of stelae in the Andes continued well after the demise of Chavín, with stelae decorating the open plazas and other monumental architectural forms built by the **Tiwanaku** (650–1000) and Inca (1438–1533) civilizations. Some of these appear to have been decorated with royal portraits.

In Mesoamérica, the stela dates back to the time of the Olmec (1200–400). There these monoliths were not only carved with images of rulers but also inscriptions. By the Late Preclassic (400 B.C.E.–250 C.E.), the format for a Mesoamérican stela had been more or less standardized. Portraits of rulers were now complemented by dates, historical information, sociopolitical relations with other rulers, personal names, as well as a host of titles. Stelae were considered to be not only portraits of rulers but also—in a sense—sacred images or embodiments of the rulers themselves. Nearly every Mesoamérican civilization erected stelae in accordance with significant historical, astronomical, or calendrical events. Of all of these, the stelae of the Maya were the most elaborate, bearing three-dimensional portraits of kings and an elaborately decorated hieroglyphic writing system that was designed not only to convey information but also to be aesthetically pleasing.

It was, in fact, the Maya pattern of erecting such elaborate stelae that prompted scholars to define the Classic Period for Mesoamérica in the first place: The Classic Period (250–909) was initially bounded by the times in which the first and last stelae were erected in the southern Maya lowlands. This scheme quickly fell apart in light of new monumental discoveries, although the latest final date encountered—that of 909 at the site of Tonina, Mexico—has endured in the literature for a long time. That being said, stelae were being erected in other parts of Mesoamérica well into the sixteenth century, serving similar purposes.

Further Reading

Demarest, Arthur. *Ancient Maya*. Cambridge, UK: Cambridge University Press, 2005.

Evans, Susan. *Ancient Mexico and Central America: Archaeology and Culture History*. London: Thames and Hudson, Ltd., 2004.

Sharer, Robert J., and Loa P. Traxler. *The Ancient Maya*. 6th ed. Stanford, CA: Stanford University Press, 2005.

Sweat Bath or Sweat Lodge

Many societies of the Pre-Columbian Americas employed heated saunas in rituals, social activities, and medicine. They typically consisted of an enclosure wherein heated rocks would be placed; water would then be poured over or otherwise distributed on the rocks, perhaps in addition to medicinal herbs or similar substances, causing the enclosure to fill with steam. Individuals or groups of individuals would then enter the room to sweat, with the purpose being to cleanse the body, mind, and/or spirit.

That being said, the architectural, ritual and medicinal specifics of such places—as well as the types of behaviors allowed inside—varied widely. Sweat lodges at the time of European contact ranged over the entire breadth of North America, from such culturally diverse places as the Pacific Coast, the Great Plains, and the Northeast. Variability was thus likely more the rule than the exception, with evidence of different songs, prayers, complete silence, clothes (or lack of them), gender roles, and even offerings presented by European accounts and common to contemporary peoples. The origin of these traditions is unclear, although some of the earliest sweat lodges appear in the archaeological record of the Middle Woodland Period (200 B.C.E.–400 C.E.) in the American Southeast. There, they are associated with the Adena–Hopewell culture.

By comparison, there is much indigenous as well as contact-era literature on sweat baths, as they are known in Mesoamérica. Here the sweat bath was but one masonry structure in a larger bathing complex, complete with benches for sleeping as well outer and inner zones. Although sweat baths were not confined to royalty, scenes showing kings and other nobles engaged in rather bizarre activities—as well as texts describing these activities—provide us with some of the most detailed information on "bathing" in Mesoamérican cultures. Among the ancient Maya, for example, nobles might receive enemas containing tobacco, alcohol, or other inebriants as part of their sweat bath experience. Such activities could be coupled with binge eating and drinking as well as purging (e.g., vomiting). The Maya sweat baths of nobles were boisterous affairs, with the playing of music and sexual liaisons part of the overall activity. Although such behavior stands in marked contrast to that believed for Pre-Columbian North America, the overall idea was similar: The excesses of this lewd, drunken behavior were ultimately countered by the cleansing effects of the actual sweat bath. In a sense, the idea was to completely throw the body off balance so that the balance itself could be restored via the sweat bath.

Further Reading

Evans, Susan. *Ancient Mexico and Central America: Archaeology and Culture History.* London: Thames and Hudson, Ltd., 2004.

Evans, Susan, and David Webster, eds. *Archaeology of Ancient Mexico: An Encyclopedia.* New York: Garland, 2001.

Fagan, Brian. *Ancient North America.* London: Thames and Hudson, Ltd., 1991.

Talud-Tablero

This architectural term refers to a building style popularized in Pre-Columbian Central Mexico and most closely associated with the metropolis of **Teotihuacán**. Prior to the use of talud-tablero architecture, Mesoamérican temple-pyramids were typically stepped, for example, with successive courses of stone arranged in pyramidal fashion. In the Late Preclassic (400 B.C.E.–250 C.E.), architects at Teotihuacán adopted a modified pattern in which they added, between each successive course of stone, a sloping wall (talud). Combined with the flat, rectangular and stepped course (tablero), the overall effect of talud-tablero is to create a broadly based pyramid with sloping and stepped walls. Oftentimes, portions of the tablero section were inset slightly, creating a panel on which to paint murals or affix plaster sculpture.

Talud-tablero is one of the primary diagnostic traits of Teotihuacán architecture and was oftentimes adopted by those civilizations, which wanted to emulate or to demonstrate ties to the great metropolis (real or fictive). Likewise, it appears at sites that are believed to have been conquered or dominated by Teotihuacános: Talud-tablero architecture in the Maya area, for example, is particularly evident there around 400.

However exported, talud-tablero architecture was popular in many parts of Mesoamérica, from northwest Mexico all the way to western Honduras, and is testament to the power—military and cultural—of Teotihuacán. It was so popular, in fact, that this architectural style lasted long after the collapse of Teotihuacán: Talud-tablero, and echoes of it, carries well into Postclassic Period (850–1500) Mesoamérica.

Further Reading

Braswell, Geoffrey, ed. *The Maya and Teotihuacán*. Austin: University of Texas Press, 2004.

Evans, Susan. *Ancient Mexico and Central America: Archaeology and Culture History*. London: Thames and Hudson, Ltd., 2004.

Evans, Susan, and David Webster, eds. *Archaeology of Ancient Mexico: An Encyclopedia*. New York: Garland, 2001.

Tawantinsuyu

The Quechua word *Tawantinsuyu*, or "Land of the Four Quarters," was the name given by a Sapa Inca, Pachacuti (1438–1471), to his new empire in the Andes. Commonly known as the Inca Empire, Tawantinsuyu was created in the late fifteenth century as the Inca conquered territory after territory in the Andes and on the Pacific Coast. The story of Tawantinsuyu, however, begins around 1200, when the kingdom of Cuzco was founded by a quasi-mythical ancestor named Manco Capac. Archaeological evidence points to the emergence of an identifiable Inca culture somewhat earlier, around 1000, placing it around the same time as the states of Lambayeque and Chimor were forming. Apparently, the Inca were but one of the many groups to emerge out of the waning power of the Tiwanaku and Wari Empires (650–1000) of the Andes. In any event, it is clear that the royal origins of the Inca were humble indeed: The "kingdom" of Cuzco started simply as a precocious town, which gradually drew in allies and followers who—as the Inca became stronger—were made "Inca by privilege."

The architecture of Tawantinsuyu is justifiably famous: With almost 25,000 miles of roads leading out of Cuzco and through the Andes in all four directions, massive stone blocks individually carved to fit into one another in walls, mountaintop shrines and noble estates, and almost vertical terracing, the architecture of the Inca Empire is staggering to behold. Although, to be sure, there were antecedents in the Andes, the distinctive "imperial" Inca style was almost new in 1400. In fact, the first examples of it around Cuzco appear in 1375, when the Inca were still struggling with their immediate neighbors, the Chanca people. Fewer than 100 years later, they would control—under one of their greatest leaders, Huayna Capac—a territory encompassing portions of modern-day Ecuador, Peru, Bolivia, Chile, and Argentina. It was the largest ever of the empires of the Americas before the coming of the Spanish in 1533.

Like the **Triple Alliance** (Aztec Empire) of Central Mexico some 12 years earlier, Tawantinsuyu was felled by disease, disorganization, and treachery: The last strong ruler of the Inca, Huayna Capac (1493–1527), was killed by smallpox, initiating a struggle for dynastic succession that had just been successfully resolved by Atalhuapa (1532–1533) when the Spanish arrived. In fact, Atalhuapa was returning from the last battle of that civil war—with tens of thousands of warriors—to formally claim his throne when the Spanish arrived in the Andes. Following a couple of months of diplomacy, subterfuge, and cultural ignorance on both sides, Atalhuapa agreed to meet the Spanish at the walled Inca city of Cajamarca. Led by Francisco Pizarro, the band of fewer than two-hundred Spanish waited as up to eighty-thousand warriors surrounded the city. Believing himself invulnerable and behaving according to established rules of diplomacy, Atalhuapa decided to leave the majority of his warriors outside the city walls and enter, largely unarmed, with a small contingent of commanders and others in the royal retinue. Of divine heritage and descended from the Inca sun god, Inti, Atalhuapa was ill prepared for what became a Spanish ambush. Most were killed, and the emperor himself was taken hostage. Given the perceived divinity of Atalhuapa and the loss of military leadership in the ambush, no counterattack came. Rather, attempted ransoms and forced decrees by Atalhuapa ensued, including measures designed to execute political rivals and exacerbate the already-deep wounds of civil war. Pizarro finally had the emperor executed, installing two succeeding puppet emperors before formally taking control of the empire for himself. Tawantinsuyu, however, effectively died with Atalhuapa in 1533.

Further Reading

Moore, Jerry. *Architecture and Power in the Ancient Andes: The Archaeology of Public Buildings*. Cambridge, UK: Cambridge University Press, 1996.

Moseley, Michael E. *The Incas and Their Ancestors: The Archaeology of Peru*. 2nd ed. London: Thames and Hudson, Ltd., 2001.

Ramirez, Susan. *The World Upside Down*. Stanford, CA: Stanford University Press, 1996.

Tayasal

The Postclassic (850–1500) Maya site of Tayasal, known as Noj Petén "Great Peten," was located on the banks of Lake Petén Itzá. According to native accounts, it was founded by refugees from the famous site of Chichén Itzá, which was destroyed through treachery by the Cocom, one of the lineages of the Itzá Maya. Archaeology places the destruction of Chichén Itzá around 1050, with migrations into the Petén region occurring shortly thereafter. Tayasal appears to have been settled by these and other stragglers from the last throes of the **Maya collapse**. It was, however, the last in a long series of settlements on and around Lake Petén, which had been densely settled since the Late Preclassic (400 B.C.E.–250 C.E.). The new kingdom of Tayasal, forged from the islands and peninsulas of the lake, would preserve many of the traditions of the Classic Period (250–850) and those of Postclassic **Chichén Itzá** for hundreds of years. It was a natural draw for the inhabitants of waning societies throughout the Maya area and was the most densely populated center in the southern Lowlands during the Postclassic. Tayasal also has the dubious distinction of being one of the last Maya strongholds to fall to colonial Spanish aggression. It was taken by force in 1697.

Further Reading

Clendinnen, Inga. *Ambivalent Conquests: Maya and Spaniard in Yucatan, 1517–1570*. Cambridge, UK: Cambridge University Press, 2003.

Evans, Susan, and David Webster, eds. *Archaeology of Ancient Mexico: An Encyclopedia*. New York: Garland, 2001.

Freidel, David, and Linda Schele. *A Forest of Kings*. London: Harper Perennial, 1992.

Tenochtitlán

Founded in 1325 by the Mexica, Tenochtitlán was the capital city of the Aztec Empire. In 1325, however, it was a swampy island in Lake Texcoco: The Mexica, loyal subjects of the Tepanec Empire, had been given permission by its ruler to settle there in one of the most inhospitable locations in the Basin of Mexico. Shortly thereafter, they began to drain the swamp and build up the terrain to produce an urban space that would eventually hold two-hundred thousand people. Several roads connecting the island to different parts of the mainland were built, and by 1400 the city—by virtue of this remarkable transformation—was a thriving place rivaling many of the older centers in the Basin of Mexico. In 1428, the Mexica of Tenochtitlán would combine with the Acolhua at Texcoco and disaffected Tepanecs at Tacuba to form the **Triple Alliance**. This Alliance, otherwise known as the Aztec Empire, would overthrow the Tepanecs and expand its influence over much of Mesoamérica. During this time Tenochtitlán, under the guidance of the Mexica, would emerge as the most powerful of the three cities.

Organized into eighty different neighborhoods, Tenochtitlán was densely settled according to a grid plan, at the heart of which was a massive ceremonial precinct. Temples, schools, ball courts, houses for warrior societies, and living quarters for priests were all housed within this precinct. But perhaps the most architecturally significant building in this center was the Templo Mayor or Great Temple, which consisted of twin stairways leading to two different temples: one was for the Aztec tutelary deity, Huitzilopochtli, who in Aztec mythology had guided the Mexica to Tenochtitlán, and the other was for **Tlaloc**, the Central Mexican storm god.

In addition to the central precinct and its myriad neighborhoods, Tenochtitlán was home to vast markets, in which greater and greater varieties of goods were flowing from 1325 onwards. The Spanish, when they arrived at Tenochtitlán in 1519, saw its markets and numerous canals and instantly compared it with some of the most cosmopolitan cities in Europe. Tenochitlán was also a place of palaces, gardens, storage facilities, and even a zoo. The imperial palace, as well as several palaces belonging to the nobility, was characterized by living quarters as well as libraries, meeting rooms, craft workshops, kitchens, and armories. Tribute in vast quantities flowed to these places, even more so after the beginning the Aztec Empire in 1428. Tenochtitlán would remain the preeminent city in Mexico until its fall in 1521.

Further Reading

Calnek, E. "The Internal Structure of Tenochtitlán." In E. Wolf, ed. *The Valley of Mexico*. Santa Fe, NM: School of American Research Press, 1972, pp. 287–303.

Evans, Susan, and David Webster, eds. *Archaeology of Ancient Mexico: An Encyclopedia*. New York: Garland, 2001.

Smith, Michael. *The Aztecs*. London: Thames and Hudson, Ltd., 2003.

Teotihuacán

The great metropolis of Teotihuacán, in present-day Central Mexico, was the sixth largest city in the world in the sixth century C.E. With a peak population of approximately one-hundred twenty-five thousand people, Teotihuacán had humble origins: In the third century B.C.E., it had been one of a host of newly founded centers competing for dominance in the Basin of Mexico. By the first century C.E., it had undergone a rapid rise to become the preeminent city in Mesoamérica and was to remain so until the seventh century. We do not know the ethnic or linguistic identity of the people who occupied Teotihuacán, in large part because what remains of their written language has not yet been deciphered. In fact, word *Teotihuacán* is derived from a later culture, the Aztecs, who saw the ruins of the great city and called it "place where the gods live" in their native tongue, Nahuatl.

By the year 400, Teotihuacán had expanded its cultural and political influence far beyond the boundaries of the Basin of Mexico. The city had been a home to immigrants from different parts of Mesoamérica—including Maya, Zapotecs, and various peoples from western Mexico and the Gulf Coast—for hundreds of years, each in their own ethnic enclaves much as in some cities today. Nobles, too, from different parts of Mesoamérica visited and may have even lived inside this cosmopolitan city. Outside the city, Teotihuacán appears to have had political control of the Basin of Mexico and probably a vast amount of territory in the neighboring highlands. Although the degree of political control maintained by Teotihuacán outside this immediate area is in some dispute, the Teotihuacán presence in Mesoamérica—in terms of artifacts, imagery, architecture, and even religious expression—during the Early Classic Period (250–600) is near ubiquitous.

Between 300 and 600, individuals from Teotihuacán appear in the records and archaeology of many key sites in Mesoamérica. Sometimes, they appear as conquerors: In 378, a Teotihuacáno lord known as Siyaj K'ak' appears to have dethroned the Maya king of **Tikal** and installed a Central Mexican ruler

Pyramid of the Moon, Teotihuacan, Mexico. Ian D Walker/Shutterstock.

there, whose dynasty was to flourish for hundreds of years. In other cases, the connections are vaguer and suggest conquest, outright imitation by locals, political influence, or some combination of these. Not surprisingly, the sites that show the most connections with Teotihuacán are those that were of political or economic importance to the great city: The shadow of Teotihuacán looms large, for example, over key Maya sites such **Copan** and Kaminaljuyu as well as the Zapotec capital of **Monte Albán**. As a result, Central Mexican gods such as **Tlaloc** and **Quetzcoatl**, as well as Teotihuacán-style pottery and dress, can be found all over Mesoamérica during this period.

By 400, most of the major constructions at Teotihuacán had been completed. The city had recently been renovated, perhaps a result of its expanding influence, wealth, and prestige. Characterized by a grid plan and thousands of apartment compounds, the city was cut by numerous causeways, of which the Street of the Dead is the most famous. It also had numerous palaces and temples, including the Pyramid of the Moon, the Pyramid of the Feathered Serpent, and the Pyramid of the Sun. The latter, on the east side of the Street of the Dead, is as large at its base as the Great Pyramid of Khufu in Egypt.

The collapse of Teotihuacán as a major force in Mesoamérica occurred sometime around 600. Parts of the site were violently burned, with the population plummeting to perhaps thirty thousand to forty thousand people in the span of 100 years. Although we do not know precisely why Teotihuacán collapsed, most of the archaeological evidence suggests an internal conflict. Whatever happened, the demise of Teotihuacán had serious repercussions in the fates of many Mesoamérican civilizations: Periods of turmoil as well as political and economic reorganization were common at this point. Teotihuacán retained a fragment of its former influence, however, as most Mesoamérican societies—even after its collapse—continued to equate Central Mexico with martial and cultural prestige. By 1400, Teotihuacán was the capital of a small city-state about to come under the influence of the Aztecs, who saw themselves as successors to this once-great polity.

Further Reading

Berrin, K., and Esther Pasztory, eds. *Teotihuacán: Art from the City of the Gods*. London: Thames and Hudson, Ltd., 1993.

Braswell, Geoffrey, ed. *The Maya and Teotihuacán*. Austin: University of Texas Press, 2004.

Evans, Susan, and David Webster, eds. *Archaeology of Ancient Mexico: An Encyclopedia*. New York: Garland, 2001.

Terra Preta

This type of soil, literally "dark earth" in Portuguese, was created by Amazonian peoples over a vast period of time, ranging from 5000 B.C.E. to the colonial period. Uncharacteristically fertile for the Amazon, in which poor soil for cultivation is the norm, terra preta was one of the ways in which Pre-Columbian peoples of the region were able to farm and achieve high population densities. It appears to have been made through intentional, intensive deposition of charcoal, pottery shards, and organic matter (plant and animal); in some places this compost-heavy soil is over 2 meters deep, in marked contrast to surrounding soils which are extremely nutrient poor.

Terra preta sites occur all over the Amazon and are a good benchmark for determining whether the area was settled by agriculturalists. Noteworthy centers include Acutuba and Santarem, in the Central and Lower Amazon, respectively. Some estimates of the original scope of terra preta in Amazonia are quite large. Its cultivation raises questions as to how much of the present tropical forest was in place in Pre-Columbian times (and how much of it was managed by Amazonian peoples).

Further Reading

Heckenberger, Michael, James Petersen, and Eduardo Goes Neves. "Village Size and Permanence in Amazonia: Two Archaeological Examples from Brazil." *Latin American Antiquity* 10(4) (1999): 353–376.

Petersen, James, E.G. Neves, and M. Heckenberger. "Gift from the Past: Terra Preta and Prehistoric Amerindian Occupations in Amazonia." In C. McEwan, C. Barreto, and E.G. Neves, eds. *The Unknown Amazon: Culture in Nature in Ancient Brazil.* London: British Museum Press, 2001, pp. 86–105.

Woods, W., and J. McCann. "The Anthropogenic Origin and Persistence of Amazonian Dark Earths." *Yearbook: Conference of Latin American Geographers* 25 (1999): 7–14.

Thule

With its origins around 700 B.C.E. in the Bering Strait, the Thule culture of the Arctic was a well-developed, marine mammal–hunting society by 400 with influences from both sides of the Strait. Marine kayaks as well as bone-, ivory- or antler-tipped harpoons enabled the Thule people to hunt whales and other sea mammals previously unavailable to peoples in the Arctic. Harpoons were decorated with distinctive, carved art styles such as Okvik (c. 500 B.C.E.), Old Bering Sea (200 B.C.E.–800 C.E.), Punuk (c. 500), and Birnik (c. 600). By Punuk times, Thule settlements were becoming larger and more elaborate: People started living in semisubterranean, wooden buildings with sod roofs, a lifestyle that would continue well into the nineteenth century.

Between 900 and 1100, Thule technology—in the form of the aforementioned marine kayaks, hunting tools and methods, and house designs as well as dogsleds and large boats—enabled Thule culture to spread far beyond the boundaries of the Bering Strait. Whether simply a cultural spread or a more direct spread of population, Thule culture largely merged with and/or replaced the other cultures of coastal Alaska, ranging as far south as the Aleutian Islands and as far west as the Siberian coastline. Around 1000, populations of Inupiat speakers—themselves part of the Thule tradition—began migrating eastwards from present-day Alaska. Far-ranging hunting techniques and technological adaptations enabled the Thule speakers to migrate quickly and expand in population rather rapidly at the expense of the other major ethnic group in the Arctic, the Dorset, and facilitated their encounter with the first Europeans to venture into the Americas, the Norse. Within a few hundred years, Thule peoples had largely replaced the **Dorset** and the Norse colonies had collapsed. The Dorset may have survived the Thule incursion in pockets of the Arctic well past 1400, but by this time the Thule had long-dominated a region stretching from Alaska to Greenland. Their descendants continue to populate this area.

Further Reading

Fagan, Brian. *Ancient North America*. London: Thames and Hudson, Ltd., 1991.

McGhee, Robert. "Contact between Native North Americans and the Medieval Norse: A Review of Evidence." *American Antiquity* 49 (1984): 4–26.

Morrison, D., and J. Pilon. *Threads of Arctic Prehistory: Papers in Honor of William E. Taylor, Jr.* Quebec: Canadian Museum of Civilization, 1994.

Tikal

This archaeological site in the Petén region of Guatemala, one of the preeminent cities of the Lowland Maya, was settled in the Late Preclassic (300 B.C.E.–250 C.E.) and flourished during the Classic Period. Perhaps the best known and most studied of all Maya sites, Tikal was known to the ancient Maya as *Yax Mutal* (the larger kingdom was simply known as *Mutal*) and was the leader of a loose, often changing, confederation of polities that often came into conflict with those led by its primary rival to the north, Calakmul. In 378 C.E., a lord from the Central Mexican metropolis of **Teotihuacán**, known to the Maya as Siyaj K'ahk', or "Born of Fire," successfully invaded Tikal and installed a new dynasty there headed by king Yax Nuun Ayiin I (r. 379–410). This dynasty was to remain unchallenged, leading the most powerful and vast kingdom in the Lowlands, for the next 200 years. At its apex, the epicenter of Tikal was populated by at least fifty-thousand people.

Although there is little evidence that Teotihuacán directly controlled affairs at Tikal, the fortunes of the two sites were probably linked. The sudden demise of Teotihuacán in the sixth century was coupled with troubled times at the Lowland metropolis. Protracted wars with sites like **Calakmul** and Caracol

Temple I or Great Jaguar Temple as seen from the terrace of northern acropolis, Mayan city of Tikal, Guatemala. RJ Lerich/Shutterstock.

led to great political and social instability at Tikal: Lords fled into exile and alternated between victory as well as defeat in quick succession. Sites claiming to have been founded by members of the Tikal dynasty proliferated; some of these, like Dos Pilas or Aguateca, became major centers in their own right. Ultimately, the great Tikal was sacked by Calakmul and its allies in the sixth and seventh centuries, with many of its monuments destroyed in the process. It did not recover until the reign of its great king **Jasaw Chan K'awiil I** (682–734), who defeated Tikal's enemies and restored it to "superpower" status in the Lowlands. Yet Tikal would never fully regain its preeminent status and had to contend with many other cities and their rulers. By 800, Tikal had, like many major Classic Maya centers, begun to decline in population and political influence. Unlike many of its contemporaries, however, this decline was gradual and took place over the next 150 years. By the mid-ninth century, Tikal had been swallowed by the jungle, its royal dynasty long gone. Some of the region over which Tikal held sway, however, was never fully abandoned: Some settlements around Lake Petén Itzá, for example, were not only settled but also thriving at the time of Spanish contact.

Further Reading

Braswell, Geoffrey, ed. *The Maya and Teotihuacán*. Austin: University of Texas Press, 2004.

Evans, Susan, and David Webster, eds. *Archaeology of Ancient Mexico: An Encyclopedia*. New York: Garland, 2001.

Harrison, Peter. *The Lords of Tikal*. London: Thames and Hudson, Ltd., 1999.

Martin, Simon, and Nikolai Grube. *Chronicle of the Maya Kings and Queens*. London: Thames and Hudson, Ltd., 2000.

Tiwanaku

The name *Tiwanaku* (or Tihuanaco) refers to a major Andean empire and its capital city, located just south of Lake Titicaca in modern-day Bolivia. Tiwanaku civilization flourished during an archaeological time period known as the Middle Horizon, or 650 to 1000, and was one of two major empires in the Andes during that time. At its height, the Tiwanaku Empire held sway over Bolivia, northern Chile, and southern Peru; the somewhat larger empire to the north, **Wari**, was its neighbor and its competitor for dominance in the Andes. Unlike Wari, Tiwanaku did not incorporate many long-lived urban centers within its sphere of influence, and it is not clear how much direct control the capital had over its subject cities. In fact, some have suggested that Tiwanaku and its subjects were more a loose confederation of cities than a centralized state. What is clear, however, is that the peoples of the Tiwanaku Empire had the resources and access to labor to be able to build enormous temples, platforms, and courtyards at the capital and in its subject centers.

The religious traditions of Tiwanaku, as expressed throughout these buildings, largely stemmed from previous civilizations: Tiwanaku appears to have inherited or adopted wholesale—albeit in modified form—a pantheon of avian and feline deities represented as early as Chavín (400–200 B.C.E.) times. Such religious imagery was carved upon massive, imported stone blocks, which were either freestanding or inset within masonry structures. Some have suggested that this religious continuum, continuing at Tiwanaku, eventually made its way from the Bolivian capital to Wari. Certainly the two shared a border.

Unfortunately, they also shared the same fate: 1000 marked the beginning of a prolonged dry spell (about 200 years), during which time social and political stresses became too much for the two empires to bear. They collapsed soon thereafter, and Tiwanaku was replaced by a number of smaller, localized powers. Eventually, all would come under the dominion of the Inca during their expansion in the fifteenth century.

Further Reading

Moore, Jerry. *Architecture and Power in the Ancient Andes: The Archaeology of Public Buildings*. Cambridge, UK: Cambridge University Press, 1996.

Moseley, Michael E. *The Incas and Their Ancestors: The Archaeology of Peru*. 2nd ed. London: Thames and Hudson, Ltd., 2001.

Salomon, Frank, and Stuart B. Schwartz, eds. *Cambridge History of the Native Peoples of the Americas: Volume III, South America, Part I*. Cambridge, UK: Cambridge University Press, 2000.

Tlaloc

This Central Mexican deity was revered in Pre-Columbian Mesoamérica by several peoples, with ceramics from the site of Tlapacoya (c. 100 B.C.E. at the earliest) perhaps being his earliest pictorial appearance. As a god of lightning and rain, Tlaloc is usually depicted in scenes or contexts involving agricultural fertility. Although his appearance varies widely between cultures on ceramics, buildings, and monuments, Tlaloc is usually depicted with large circles or "goggles" over his eyes, jaguar teeth, and a missing (oftentimes bleeding) lower jaw. By the time of the Aztecs (1325–1519), Tlaloc was a deity associated with one of the thirteen Aztec heavens (the fourth), known as Tlalocan: This was a watery place, an agricultural paradise, where the souls of the drowned resided. He had likewise become associated, at some point in the Postclassic, with caves, a consort (Chalchiutlicue), and a series of helping spirits, the Tlaloque, who lived inside of mountains and assisted Tlaloc with the production and distribution of rain.

At least some of this mythology may have developed at **Teotihuacán** (100 B.C.E.–600 C.E.), where he seems to have enjoyed no small measure of popularity. The most striking example of Tlaloc imagery occurs on the facade of the Temple of the Feathered Serpent, where he appears alongside an early version of **Quetzalcoatl** amid shells and watery layers. The Teotihuacános may have introduced this Central Mexican deity to the Maya after 378 C.E., when Teotihuacáno warriors entered the Petén region of Guatemala and installed a series of friendly Maya or even ethnically Teotihuacáno rulers. Bearing square shields emblazoned with this god, they had a lasting impact at such notable centers as **Tikal** and **Copan**. The Maya already revered their own storm god, Chaak, however, and as a consequence Tlaloc—although widely popular— was often invoked by Maya rulers on monuments when they wanted to link themselves to the great Central Mexican metropolis or talk about the past.

Tlaloc handily survived the upheavals of the Teotihuacáno (c. 600) and Maya (c. 850) collapses and seems to have been well-entrenched in Central Mexican religion during the Chichimec invasions (*see* **Aztlan**) of 1150 to 1200. He was so influential a deity that the Aztecs (1325–1519) adopted Tlaloc and co-opted him within their pantheon, headed by the Aztec tutelary deity Huitzilopochtli.

Tlaloc was so influential in the Aztec Empire that he, and he alone, shared a place of worship with Huitzilopochtli atop the largest building at the Aztec capital of Tenochtitlán: the Great Temple. Excavations beneath the Tlaloc side of the Great Temple by archaeologists have revealed a grave where numerous adolescents sacrificed to Tlaloc were buried. With these were incense burners and other artifacts bearing images of Tlaloc himself.

Further Reading

Braswell, Geoffrey, ed. *The Maya and Teotihuacán*. Austin: University of Texas Press, 2004.

Evans, Susan. *Ancient Mexico and Central America: Archaeology and Culture History*. London: Thames and Hudson, Ltd., 2004.

Miller, Mary Ellen, and Karl Taube. *An Illustrated Dictionary of the Gods and Symbols of Ancient Mexico and the Maya*. London: Thames and Hudson, Ltd., 1997.

Taube, Karl. *Aztec and Maya Myths*. Austin: University of Texas Press, 1993.

Tlatoani

In the latter part of Postclassic (909–1519) Central Mexico, each of the city-states around the Basin of Mexico—what was to become the core of the Aztec Empire—was ruled by a king known in the Nahuatl language as a tlatoani, or "speaker." These rulers were the pinnacles of sociopolitical and religious power at their respective sites. They were also expected to exemplify a refined model of courtly behavior, which included, as alluded to by the term, great proficiency in public speech and performance.

The term *tlatoani* likely gained its first widespread political usage during the late twelfth and early thirteenth centuries, when Nahuatl-speaking peoples were moving into the Basin of Mexico and founding—or often conquering—cities to form new kingdoms. One such city, **Tenochtitlán**, was founded by a member of the Mexica tribe known as Acamapichtli (r. 1376–1395). As the first tlatoani there, his power was limited: He was actually a vassal of the Tepanec Empire, the most powerful state in the Basin of Mexico. By 1400, though, Tenochtitlán had seen a smooth transition to its second tlatoani, Huitzilihuitl, and the reduction of its tribute to the Tepanecs to a pittance. Huitzilihuitl and his immediate successors would support the Tepanecs in various wars, gaining in power and influence. A successful war with the Tepanecs in 1428, as part of the **Triple Alliance**, would see the tlatoani of Tenochtitlán—a figure named **Itzcoatl**—become the most powerful ruler in Mesoamérica. At this time, the title of tlatoani no longer sufficed. Itzcoatl became the first Hueh Tlatoani, "Great Speaker" or "emperor" of the Aztec Empire.

Further Reading

Evans, Susan. *Ancient Mexico and Central America: Archaeology and Culture History*. London: Thames and Hudson, Ltd., 2004.

Evans, Susan, and David Webster, eds. *Archaeology of Ancient Mexico: An Encyclopedia*. New York: Garland, 2001.

Smith, Michael. *The Aztecs*. London: Thames and Hudson, Ltd., 2003.

Toltec

The archaeological site of Toltec, Arkansas, was one of the most important settlements in the American Southeast prior to the rise of Mississippian civilization around 1000. Believed in the nineteenth century to have been built by the Toltecs, an ancient civilization from Central Mexico (and hence, its name), the site of Toltec was built by local peoples and flourished from 600 to 1050.

What is unusual about Toltec is that it was created in a time of sociopolitical flux. The dominant culture in the American Southeast, known as Hopewell–Adena, had collapsed around 400 and long-distance trade within the eastern portion of the present-day United States had almost ceased. Intensive, maize-based agriculture would not be adopted until 800. Moreover, populations in the Southeast were steadily increasing, but so was warfare: This era, known as the Late Woodlands (400–1000), was one of devastating conflicts between increasingly fortified centers. Ultimately, these events would lead to complex societies in the Mississippi Valley based at cities such as **Cahokia**, Illinois, but not for a few centuries.

Toltec seems to have anticipated all of these developments, was outside the Mississippi Valley, and was one of the first chiefdoms in the American Southeast. With eighteen mounds, plazas, and other signs of public works projects, Toltec was a bit of an anomaly in 600. Although it was abandoned around 1050, the site was eventually reoccupied around 1400. Sporadic occupation continued in the area until the sixteenth century.

Further Reading

Rolingson, Martha. *Prehistoric Arkansans at Toltec Indian Mounds State Park*. Fayetteville: Arkansas Archaeological Survey, 1977.

Rolingson, Martha. *Toltec Mounds and Plum Bayou Culture: Mound D Excavations*. Research Series 54. Fayetteville: Arkansas Archaeological Survey, 1998.

Van Dyke, Ruth, and Susan E. Alcock, eds. *Archaeologies of Memory*. Oxford, UK: Wiley-Blackwell, 2003.

Triple Alliance

The Triple Alliance, more commonly known as the Aztec Empire, was the most powerful Pre-Columbian empire in Mesoamérica between 1428 and 1519. The Spaniards, when they saw the capital city of **Tenochtitlán** in 1519, were exposed to a sophisticated city of over two-hundred-thousand people with vast markets bearing goods from all over Mesoamérica and beyond. Yet this was a recent vision. In fact, the Triple Alliance was not even a thought—much less an imperial entity—until the early fifteenth century. Its key members, however, were already cities by 1400: Tacuba (or Tlacopan), Texcoco, and, of course, Tenochtitlán. In 1428 they allied themselves against the major power of the day, the Tepanec Empire centered at the city of Atzcapotzalco. They succeeded—one by one—in conquering or exacting pledges of vassalage from most of the major centers in a region of Mexico stretching from Michoacan in the west to Chiapas in the east. From its base on the banks of Lake Texcoco, within the city limits of present-day Mexico City, the Triple Alliance governed an empire of perhaps 6.5 million people. Late in its history, the Triple Alliance even managed to conquer a swath of the Pacific coast from Chiapas to western Guatemala, exacting tribute from the Maya highlands. Trade entrepots were set up by the Alliance as far south as Panama, making it a truly far-reaching native state.

In terms of the Alliance members, Tacuba was by far the least powerful: It only received one-fifth of all tribute flowing into the empire. More a puppet than true partner, Tacuba was a Tepanec city—originally subject to Atzcapot-zalco—which threw off servitude to enter into a junior partnership with Teno-chtitlán and Texcoco in 1428. It may have been founded in the late tenth century, but like other centers around Lake Texcoco, it was probably infil-trated and eventually taken over by Chichimec migrants (*see* **Aztlan**) in the twelfth and thirteenth centuries. Texcoco, in comparison to Tacuba, was a major player in the Alliance and received two-fifths of all tribute. Founded in the twelfth century on the eastern bank of Lake Texcoco, it became the capital of the Acolhua people in 1337 and was one of the most populous cities in the Basin of Mexico. At its height, it may have housed approximately twenty-five thousand people.

Like Tacuba, Texcoco had come to be dominated by the Tepanec Empire. Unlike Tacuba, however, it grew in power and influence—so much so, that by 1400 it was clear that Texcoco would soon be a threat to its master. During the reign of the Texcoco king Ixtlilxochitl (r. 1409–1418), this indeed came to pass: Texcoco led an initially successful but ultimately disastrous rebellion against the Tepanecs. According to native accounts, Ixtlilxochitl was killed in front of his son and successor, **Nezahualcoyotl** (c. 1402–1472), who was finally able to exact revenge upon the Tepanecs by convincing his neighbors to answer a call to arms by the Mexica at Tenochtitlán. Cobbling together a massive military force comprised of a host of smaller centers, he joined the rulers of Tenochtit-lán and Tacuba to defeat his hated enemy.

Although Texcoco was a major player in the Alliance, Tenochtitlán was by far the most powerful of the three. Founded in 1325, Tenochtitlán was the capi-tal of the Mexica people. According to native accounts, the Mexica were among the last of the Chichimecs to arrive in the Basin of Mexico and served in the armies of various peoples of the Basin before entering into the service of the Tepanecs, who gave them permission to settled on the swampy island that was to become the Aztec capital. They were loyal to the Tepanecs for the next 50 years, even refusing to help Ixtlilxochitl of Texcoco in his rebellion. As a re-ward, the Mexica were given Texcoco as a vassal state. The growing power of the Mexica after 1400, however, coincided with deteriorating relations between Atzcapotzalco and Tenochtitlán, with the end result being the assassination of the Mexica king in 1426 by Maxtla, ruler of the Tepanec Empire. Maxtla at-tempted to conquer Tenochtitlán formally in 1428, prompting the new ruler of the Mexica, **Itzcoatl**, to ask for help from his neighbors. The result was the Tri-ple Alliance, a power that would dominate Mesoamérica for almost a century.

Despite its strengths, the Triple Alliance failed to deal effectively with the Spanish upon their arrival in the Basin of Mexico in 1519. In part, this was due to its very nature: As a tribute-oriented empire whose rule, in many places, was maintained by threat of force, the Triple Alliance suffered throughout its existence from resistance and rebellion. When Hernan Cortés (Cortez) and his small group of Spanish conquistadores (about four-hundred men) marched into Aztec territories in August of 1519, they did so with thousands of indigenous peoples disaffected with Aztec oppression. Likewise, the Aztec leadership also committed a series of political and strategic blunders: The ruler of the Triple Alliance at that time, Motecuhzoma II (1466–1520), trying to determine the in-tentions of the Spanish and believing himself safe in his capital, invited Cortés and his men to his palace. Not following the rules of Aztec diplomacy and tak-ing advantage of this hospitality, the Spanish eventually took the bewildered emperor hostage in his own palace. The death of Motecuhzoma II—either at the hands of the Spanish or the rioting populace of Tenochtitlán—was followed by a near-impossible escape by Cortés from the palace. Returning with reinforcements in 1521, Cortés found Tenochtitlán—and subsequently, much of the Basin of Mexico—decimated by disease. Unintentionally carried by Europeans to the Americas, diseases such as smallpox and typhus destroyed with equal success the flower of Aztec nobility and the general populace. Although the Alliance was to have two more emperors after Motecuhzoma II, consisting of Cuitlahuac (1520) and Cuahtemoc (1520–1521), they were killed in short order by smallpox and Cortés, respectively. What resistance there was to the Spanish was quickly overcome, and the Triple Alliance was no more.

Further Reading

Berdan, F., Richard Blanton, Elizabeth Boone, E. Hodge, Michael Smith, and E. Umberger. *Aztec Imperial Strategies*. Washington, DC: Dumbarton Oaks, 1996.
Evans, Susan. *Ancient Mexico and Central America: Archaeology and Culture History*. London: Thames and Hudson, Ltd., 2004.
Smith, Michael. *The Aztecs*. London: Thames and Hudson, Ltd., 2003.

Tula

The archaeological site of Tula, located to the north of the Basin of Mexico, was settled during the Classic Period (250–850) but rose to prominence during the first few centuries of the Postclassic Period (850–1500). Its first settlers appear to have been peoples with strong ties to the then Central Mexican metropolis of Teotihuacán, but as time passed these settlers appear to have been eclipsed in population and culture by waves of migrants from northwestern Mesoamérica collectively known as the Tolteca-Chichimeca. At least some of this may have been in response to the collapse of Teotihuacán between 550 and 600, and by 700 a firm community of Tolteca-Chichimeca had been established within the site core. By 900, the Tolteca-Chichimeca were dominant, and Tula matured into a robust metropolis in its own right: housing approximately sixty-thousand people, Tula became a cosmopolitan political center demonstrating a fusion of Tolteca-Chichimeca and other regional cultures. As with most other Mesoamérican centers, Tula was characterized by large, stepped temple-pyramids, ball courts, and monumental art including written texts. At its height, Tula dominated much of the Basin of Mexico and may have been the center of a small, tribute-based empire, with several subject cities to its north. Its trading connections with other parts of the Mesoamérica world were, however, much more grandiose than anything that had come before in the Basin: The rulers at Tula enjoyed ties with the Pacific and Atlantic coasts, northwestern Mexico, the Maya area (most notably, between 900 and 1050, with the northern Postclassic metropolis of **Chichén Itzá**), Lower Central America, and perhaps the American Southwest. Between 1150 and 1200 Tula abruptly and violently collapsed, with many of its buildings burnt to the ground.

Meager settlement continued here well into the 1500s, however, and local peoples quickly became subjects of the Aztec Empire during its florescence. What is interesting about this facet of Tula's history is that for the Aztecs, Tula was their legendary city of Tollan. Like its predecessor Teotihuacán, Tula was viewed as ancestral to the Aztec capital of Tenochtitlán. Practically speaking, this was an attempt by the Aztecs to legitimize their place in Mesoamérica, which had largely been achieved through conquest. Nevertheless, as the Aztecs borrowed much from the peoples they conquered they did have some claim to this heritage and called the civilization that produced Tula by a name well known to people today: the Toltecs. The Aztecs believed that the Toltecs had invented almost everything, were wise in all arts and sciences, and were the most skilled of all craftsmen. The downfall of Tula, in Aztec legend, was the result of a dishonorable episode involving their last king, Ce Acatl Topiltzin Quetzalcoatl and an individual named Tezcatlipoca. How much this quasi-historical episode applies to the actual collapse of Tula is unknown.

Further Reading

Evans, Susan. *Ancient Mexico and Central America: Archaeology and Culture History*. London: Thames and Hudson, Ltd., 2004.

Evans, Susan, and David Webster, eds. *Archaeology of Ancient Mexico: An Encyclopedia*. New York: Garland, 2001.

Miller, Mary Ellen, and Karl Taube. *An Illustrated Dictionary of the Gods and Symbols of Ancient Mexico and the Maya*. London: Thames and Hudson, Ltd., 1997.

Tumbaga

This alloy of copper and gold appears to have been invented during the Early Horizon (400–200 B.C.E.) of Andean prehistory. Although scholars have proposed several inventors of this substance, including peoples from Lower Central America and Colombia, the Chavín civilization (1200–200 B.C.E.) of Andean Peru appears to have been the first to alloy gold with other metals, including copper and silver. With proportions ranging around 80 percent gold to 20 percent copper, tumbaga is harder and thus more difficult to work than pure gold—it is almost akin to bronze—and has a lower melting point than gold or copper alone. Likewise, tumbaga can be burned or treated with corrosives to remove copper from the surface, with the result being a golden object with a harder base of gold–copper alloy inside. Pre-Columbian peoples prized tumbaga not only for these technical qualities but also for its reddish color, associated with the morning or evening sun, and its symbolic associations: Some peoples believed it to represent the fusing of male (gold) and female (copper) properties as well as the mixing of divinity (gold) with mortality (copper). This gold–copper alloy was occasionally mixed with proportions of silver as well, so as to change its color.

Tumbaga spread throughout the Andes and Lower Central America shortly thereafter, where in all cases it was used in ritual and for ornamentation. Between 500 and 900, tumbaga objects from these areas were traded northwards into Mesoamérica, with one of the first examples recovered from the Classic Maya city of Altun Ha, Belize.

After 900, however, the technique of manufacturing tumbaga was, along with other metallurgical techniques, permanently introduced into West Mexico (*see* **Metallurgy**). Mesoamérican metallurgists there remained dominant technologically, although the basic technique was passed to most societies of this region. By 1400, the manufacture of tumbaga in all of its shades and hues, from red to yellow, was a major part of metallurgy in a band stretching from northwest Mexico to the Andes.

Further Reading

Bruhns, Karen Olsen. *Ancient South America*. Cambridge, UK: Cambridge University Press, 1994.

Moseley, Michael E. *The Incas and Their Ancestors: The Archaeology of Peru*. 2nd ed. London: Thames and Hudson, Ltd., 2001.

Salomon, Frank, and Stuart B. Schwartz, eds. *Cambridge History of the Native Peoples of the Americas: Volume III, South America, Part I*. Cambridge, UK: Cambridge University Press, 2000.

Tzintzuntzan

This capital city of the Tarascan Empire (c. 1300–1530) in Mesoamérica was located on the shores of Lake Pátzcuaro in present-day Michoacán, Mexico. Founded around 1300 by the first king, Taríacuri, of the P'urhépecha ethnic group, Tzintzuntzan was one of a few major centers controlled by the P'urhépecha and only later came to be the dominant center. Historically, this region was somewhat independent of the cultural traditions of other Mesoamérican regions — and was the only part of Mesoamérica where bronze working had been developed to the extent that it was used alongside stone for some agricultural implements and tools — although there is good evidence for some Teotihuacán influence in the region during the Early Classic Period (250–600). Like other Mesoamérican centers, Tzintzuntzan was characterized by ball courts and some rectangular-shaped, stepped temple-pyramids. However, oval and T-shaped buildings — characteristic of Tarascan architecture — set Tzintzuntzan apart from most Mesoamérican capitals.

Between 1300 and 1400, local P'urépecha lords were able to consolidate their power around Lake Pátzcuaro and conquer other regions and peoples, to the extent that by 1400 they held sway over several groups of Otomi, Nahua, and Mazatlinca and had become a true empire. This Tarascan Empire expanded and contracted several times as it came into conflict with the larger Aztec Empire to the southeast, but unlike most peoples who fought against that expanding empire, the Tarascans managed to hold back the Aztec tide until the Spanish arrived in the 1500s. The city was largely destroyed during the Conquest but in 1400 was the grand center of an empire competing with the Aztecs for geopolitical dominance in Mesoamérica. Its population in 1400 was perhaps twenty-five thousand people, however, a far cry from the over two-hundred thousand Aztecs living in their capital of **Tenochtitlán**.

Further Reading

Evans, Susan. *Ancient Mexico and Central America: Archaeology and Culture History*. London: Thames and Hudson, Ltd., 2004.

Evans, Susan, and David Webster, eds. *Archaeology of Ancient Mexico: An Encyclopedia*. New York: Garland, 2001.

Smith, Michael. *The Aztecs*. London: Thames and Hudson, 2005.

Upper Xingu

Arawak-speaking peoples of the southern Amazon, including the Bauré, Parece, and Xinguano, are known to have had occupied the Upper Xingu region of present-day Brazil by 500. Yet archaeological research on the settlements of this area has not been as extensive as in other parts of the Americas. In the Upper Xingu region, Arawak speakers lived—like their relatives elsewhere in the Amazon—in hierarchically arranged villages and towns with circular plazas. Some of the towns and their dependencies were heavily settled, with population estimates for the major communities ranging from twenty-five thousand to five thousand people. Likewise, some of the towns were characterized by outwardly radiating roads, linking one with another and facilitating socioeconomic activity. Moreover, what appear to be moats, bridges, managed forests, and even agricultural fields have also been encountered in the Upper Xingu, suggesting not only long-term occupation but also extensive remodeling of the landscape. Most of the modification in the Upper Xingu, including population increases and evidence for urbanism, appears to have taken place after 1200.

Ongoing archaeological reconnaissance in this region, as in other parts of the Amazon, is thereby revealing aspects of cultural development that have long been ignored. Although the precise nature of Amazonian urbanism in the Upper Xingu region is not clear at the time of writing, the area is promising: There is clear cultural continuity between the modern inhabitants of the region and the archaeological remains of the settled communities. Time will tell if the Upper Xingu—with its towns and villages—was as socially complex a landscape as that found in other parts of the Americas.

Further Reading

Heckenberger, Michael. "War and Peace in the Shadow of Empire: Sociopolitical Change in the Upper Xingu of Southeastern Amazonia, ca. AD 1400–2000." Ph.D. dissertation, University of Pittsburgh. Ann Arbor, MI: University Microfilms, 1996.

Heckenberger, Michael. *The Ecology of Power: Culture, Place, and Personhood in the Southern Amazon, AD 1000–2000.* New York: Routledge, 2004.

Steward, J., and L. Faron. *Native Peoples of South America.* New York: McGraw Hill, 1959.

Utatlán

Otherwise known as Kumarcaaj, "the place of rotted reed houses," this fortified mountain city was the capital of the K'iche Maya Empire in 1400. Having moved their political center here from an older city to the northeast, the K'iche Maya ruled a vast portion of what is today highland Guatemala. In the year 1400 they could count among their allies the Kaqchikel Maya to their west and could boast of an annual tribute from peoples on the Pacific Coasts of Chiapas, Mexico, and Guatemala. In many ways, then, the founding of Kumarcaaj represented a high point of K'iche dominance in the Maya area, for they had succeeded in doing what the Classic Maya (250–850) of the Lowlands and other successor states of the Highlands had not: establish a large territory, ruled from one location, which incorporated other ethnic groups within a single political entity. They had created an empire and could boast that they had largely united the highlands through alliances as well as a system of direct and indirect control.

Unfortunately for the K'iche at Utatlán, this was not to last. In 1470, internal rebellions within the K'iche state—largely precipitated by lineages who felt that they were not getting enough out of the empire—caused it to fragment. Perhaps the most devastating blow, also occurring in 1470, came from the

Kaqchikel: They broke with the K'iche and founded their own new capital, coming into military conflict with their former allies. To make matters worse, the K'iche came into quasi-military conflict with the Aztecs and eventually became their vassals in 1510. In fact, the very name *Utatlán* (place of reeds) is the more commonly used, Aztec term for Kumarcaaj! It has been passed down to the current era by way of the Aztecs and then the Spanish, who conquered and then set fire to the city in 1524.

Further Reading

Carmack, Robert M. *The Quiche Mayas of Utatlan.* Norman: University of Oklahoma Press, 1981.

Demarest, Arthur. *Ancient Maya.* Cambridge, UK: Cambridge University Press, 2005.

Sharer, Robert J., and Loa P. Traxler. *The Ancient Maya.* 6th ed. Stanford, CA: Stanford University Press, 2005.

Venus

The planet Venus was a particularly important celestial body for peoples of the Americas, in large part because it is one of the brightest objects appearing in the night sky. Likewise, it seems to rise in the night sky at different points depending upon the time of the year: It can appear in morning, rising just before dawn, or at dusk. Sometimes it does not appear at all. Native astronomers were quick to observe this phenomenon and determine that it was cyclical (the entire cycle takes 583.92 days). With the most complicated and precise calendars in the hemisphere, many of the peoples of Mesoamérica calculated that Venus went through five cycles almost precisely every eight solar years. What this means is that one can observe Venus exhibiting almost exactly the same behavior every eight years, on or near the exact date. Both the ancient Maya and the Aztecs were particularly concerned with this behavior, with the former keeping Venus calculation tables from at least the Classic (250–850) to the Postclassic (850–1500).

Goddess of the Waters (planet Venus, responsible for rain cycle), Teotihuacan civilization. The Art Archive/Archaeological Museum Teotihuacan Mexico/ Gianni Dagli Orti.

The Maya called Venus Noj Ek' (Great Star) and, during the Postclassic Period, linked Venus with the god Kukulkán (known as Quetzalcoatl in Central Mexico). They saw Venus as the companion of the sun: The morning Venus led the Sun God out from a place of death (the Maya Underworld) into the sky, while the evening Venus followed the Sun God into the realm of death. The Classic Maya occasionally appear to have timed wars with the position of Venus in the sky. Informally called "star wars," these battles were particularly bloody and seem to have taken place more often toward the end of the Classic Period. During the Postclassic, buildings were erected with Venus imagery (as at Uxmal) and were occasionally aligned to track the appearance and disappearance of this celestial body.

Venus became an even more malevolent force among the Aztecs (1325–1521). Although they sometimes associated aspects of **Quetzalcoatl** with the morning and evening versions of Venus, one of the entities most commonly associated with Venus was Tlahuizcalpantecuhtli. This was a god specifically tied to Venus as a morning "star," and one of the most feared gods of the Central Mexican pantheon. In native accounts, this god is constantly trying to kill Tonatiuh, the Aztec solar deity. He (always) misses, but his early morning rays were considered extremely dangerous and personified as cosmic, fiery atlatl darts. In fact, Mexica priests undertaking rituals when Tlahuizpantecuhtli was in evidence would wear stylized turquoise masks for protection—donned because of their association with the god of fire, Xiuhtecuhtli! In any event, the idea that a celestial body was attempting to kill the sun was a frightening prospect, and one that the Aztecs took seriously.

Further Reading

Aveni, Anthony. *Skywatchers of Ancient Mexico.* 2nd ed. Austin: University of Texas Press, 2001.

Miller, Mary Ellen, and Karl Taube. *An Illustrated Dictionary of the Gods and Symbols of Ancient Mexico and the Maya.* London: Thames and Hudson, Ltd., 1997.

Taube, Karl. *Aztec and Maya Myths.* Austin: University of Texas Press, 1993.

Wari

The name *Wari* (or Huari) refers to a major Andean empire and its capital city, located west of modern-day Cuzco, Peru. Wari civilization flourished during what is known as the Middle Horizon, or 650 to 1000. At its height, the Wari Empire dominated most of the old centers of Andean and coastal South American civilization north of Lake Titicaca, including the territories of such notable cultures as Chavín (400–200 B.C.E.), **Moche** (200–800), and Nazca (200 B.C.E.–650 C.E.). Although it is unclear as to how much direct control Wari had over its subject cities, Wari does appear to have at least dominated most of what is today western Peru politically, culturally, and architecturally. Subject centers replicated the style and conventions of the capital city, from the massive terracing systems on the sides of mountains to the building compounds, which served residential and administrative functions. Networks of roads to and from the Wari capital foreshadowed those of the Inca centuries later.

Wari is perhaps the only major civilization centered in the Andes that did not regularly erect buildings of cut stone. Such structures were relatively scarce and were far outnumbered by the aforementioned compounds, which consisted of one or two stories of plastered, rough stone held together with mortar. The compounds would usually be arranged around a central patio and were occasionally augmented by small, D-shaped temples. In this way, Wari sites were architecturally distinct from what came before and what was to come afterwards, although some parallels can be drawn with prior civilizations on the Pacific Coast.

Although Wari society is generally characterized as relatively secular when compared with its contemporaries in South America, it did share a pantheon of deities with its neighbor, **Tiwanaku**. Ultimately, this pantheon derived from Chavín (400–200 B.C.E.) and consisted of avian and feline deities as well as a ubiquitous Andean god of agricultural fertility known to archaeologists as the **Staff God**. Like Tiwanaku, moreover, Wari appears to have collapsed shortly after 1000 due to prolonged dry conditions (about 200 years) and sociopolitical woes. Ultimately, the successors to Wari in the region were a host of formerly subject states, who successfully carved out pieces of the Wari Empire in the years prior to the coming of the Inca.

Further Reading

Moore, Jerry. *Architecture and Power in the Ancient Andes: The Archaeology of Public Buildings*. Cambridge, UK: Cambridge University Press, 1996.

Moseley, Michael E. *The Incas and Their Ancestors: The Archaeology of Peru*. 2nd ed. London: Thames and Hudson, Ltd., 2001.

Salomon, Frank, and Stuart B. Schwartz, eds. *Cambridge History of the Native Peoples of the Americas: Volume III, South America, Part I*. Cambridge, UK: Cambridge University Press, 2000.

Primary Documents

1. Leif Erikson's Exploration of North America: Coming to Vinland (c. c.e. 1003)

The Viking explorations of the Americas in the early eleventh century had little, if any, lasting impact on the indigenous peoples occupying what is today northeast Canada. That being said, the voyages of the Vikings along the eastern coast of North America represented a turning point in the history of the Atlantic world: For the first time, far-ranging Arctic cultures such as the Thule would gaze upon peoples who had never crossed Beringia into the Americas and who had had a very different historical trajectory. Motivated by a search for timber and other goods valuable to the Norse colonies in Iceland and Greenland, the Vikings would soon find that they were not alone in the new lands they had "discovered," which they called Vinland in their sagas.

They sailed to the land, anchored, put out the boat, and went ashore. No grass grew there, and great glaciers were seen inland, while the coast between the glaciers and the sea looked like one large, flat stone, and this land did not seem to them to have any value. Then Leif said: "Now it has gone better with us than with Bjarni, who came here and did not go ashore; now I will give this land a name and call it Helluland."

After that they went on board the ship, sailed out on the sea, and found another land. They sailed again to the land, anchored, put out the boat, and went ashore. This land was flat and covered with woods, and there were extensive white sands, wherever they went, and the beach was not steep. Then Leif said: "This land shall be named according to its nature and it shall be called Markland [Forestland]." After that they went as soon as possible to the ship and sailed out on the open sea with a northeast wind and were on the sea two days before they saw land. They went ashore on an island to the north of the land. It was fine weather. They looked around and noticed that there was a dew on the grass. This dew was found to have a very sweet taste. After that they went on board the ship and sailed into the sound between the island and a cape which stretched northward from the coast, and steered westward past the cape. The water was so shallow there that the ship ran aground and stood dry at ebb tide; the sea was then visible only at a great distance. But Leif and his men were so anxious to get ashore that they did not care to wait till the water rose again under their ship, and they ran ashore at once to where a river flowed out from a lake. At next high tide they took the boat, pulled to the ship, and took it up through the river into the lake, anchored, and carried their leather bags ashore. They first built wooden hits (sheds), but later they decided to prepare to remain there during the winter, and they built then large houses.

Salmon, larger than they had seen before, were plentiful in the river and lake. The land seemed to them so good that there would be no need of storing fodder for the cattle for the winter; there came no frost in the winters and the grass withered but little. Day and night were there more nearly of equal length than is the case in Greenland and Iceland.

Source: Hovgaard, William. *The Voyages of the Norsemen to America.* New York: The American-Scandinavian Foundation, 1914, pp. 85–86.

2. Leif Erikson's Exploration of North America: The Naming of Vinland (c. c.e. 1003)

> Until the 1960s, the Viking sagas referring to a place called "Vinland," or "land of grapes," were largely believed to have been a product of medieval Norse fantasy. Greenland was thought to have been the westernmost edge of the Viking world. This all changed with the discovery of the archaeological site of L'anse aux Meadows in 1960 by Helge Ingstad and Anne Stine Ingstad. Located in Newfoundland, Canada, the site consists of typical Norse longhouses like those described in the sagas. Perhaps just as important, the site lies within the typical range of wild grapes, also mentioned in the account below. This attempt at permanent settlement by the Norse was ultimately unsuccessful, with the experiment at life in Newfoundland lasting perhaps a generation before being abandoned.

But when they had completed their house building, then Leif said to his men: "Now we shall divide our company in two parts and explore the vicinity. Half of the men shall remain here and the other half shall explore the country, going no further than they can return by nightfall, and they must not separate." And this they did for some time, Leif sometimes going with the explorers and sometimes staying at home. Leif was big and strong and the most noble-looking of men. He was intelligent and in all respects a most capable commander.

One evening it was found that a man was missing. It was Tyrk, the southerner. Leif was much distressed to learn this as Tyrk had long been with him and his father and had been very fond of Leif as a child. Leif therefore severely reprimanded the man and made ready to go look for him with twelve men. But they had gone only a short distance when they met Tyrk. . . . Leif saw at once that Tyrk was in high spirits. He was a small insignificant man but a good craftsman. . . .

The Leif said: "Why are you so late in coming home, foster-father, and why did you separate from the others?"

Tyrk for a long time spoke in German, rolled his eyes, and made many grimaces, but they could not understand him. Then he spoke in Norse and said: "I did not go much farther than you, but I found something new to report. I found grapes and grapevines!"

"Can that be possible, foster-father?" exclaimed Leif.

"It is certainly true," answered Tyrk, "for I was born where there was no scarcity of grapevines or grapes."

They now went to bed for the night, but in the morning Leif spoke to his men: "We shall now get busy with two occupations and we shall take alternate days for each. [One shall be] to pick grapes or cut vines and [the other] to cut logs for our cargo when we return home." This plan was followed, and it is said that their stern boat was filled with grapes. They also cut the logs.

And when spring came they made ready to sail and sailed away with a favorable wind. And Leif named the land after its special product and called it "Vinland."

Source: Holand, Hjalmar R. *Westward from Vinland: An Account of Norse Discoveries and Explorations in America 982–1362.* New York: Duell, Sloan and Pearce, 1940, pp. 27–28.

3. Thorfinn Karlsefni's Exploration of North America: An Encounter with the Natives (c. c.e. 1005)

The Vikings traveling around Vinland (Newfoundland) very soon realized that they were not alone. Thorfinn Karlsefni's encounter with the inhabitants of Vinland, possibly the Thule or the Dorset, was fairly typical of the earliest interactions between Europeans and native peoples of the Americas: Neither side really understood or grasped the larger significance of what they were seeing, each viewing the other through its own particular cultural lens. The Norse came to fearfully believe, for example, that the first peoples they had seen were skraelings, or "trolls." Although the ideas of the Dorset and the Thule about the Norse in the eleventh century were not recorded, they may have been somewhat similar: It was fairly commonplace in the Americas, for example, for indigenous peoples to question whether the people they were seeing for the first time were, in fact, human or something entirely different.

Now it is to be told that Karlsefni cruised southward off the coast with Snorri and Bjarni and their people.

They journeyed a long time until they came at last to a river which flowed down from the land into a lake and thence into the sea. There were such great sandbars at the mouth of the estuary that it could only be entered at the height of flood tide. Karlsefni and his people sailed into the estuary and called it there, Hop.

They found wild wheat fields on the low-lying land, and wherever there was woodland they found [grape] vines. Every brook was full of fish. They dug trenches on the tidal flats, and when the tide fell there were flatfish in the trenches. There were a great number of wild animals of all kinds in the woods.

They remained there two weeks enjoying themselves and not keeping any watch. They had their livestock with them.

Now one morning when they looked about they saw nine skin-boats, and staves were being brandished from these boats, and they were being whirled in the same direction that the sun moves, and they made a noise like flails.

Then Karlsefni asked: "What can this mean?"

Snorri Thorbandsson answered him: "It may be that this is a peace signal, so let us display a white shield."

This they did whenever the strangers rowed toward them and came ashore and [the Norse] marveled at them. They were swarthy people and queer looking, and the hair of their heads was ugly. They had remarkable eyes and broad cheeks. They stayed for some time, staring curiously at the people they saw before them, then they rowed away to the southward around the point.

Karlsefni and his men had pitched their booths above the lake, some of their houses being at the lake, and some farther away near the main part of the land. They remained there all winter. No snow came, and their livestock found their own food for grazing.

Source: Mowat, Farley. *Westviking: The Ancient Norse in Greenland and North America.* Boston: Little, Brown and Company, 1965, pp. 233–234.

4. Christopher Columbus Remarks on the Generosity of the Taino People of Hispaniola (December 1492)

The early encounters between Europeans and native peoples of the Americas were filled with cultural misconceptions. Neither side understood the motives or intentions of the other. This is clear even from the account by Christopher Columbus, where the Taino chief is literally begging the European newcomer to take whatever he wants—particularly gold, which is said to be present in vast quantities—in any amount. In hindsight, we know that Hispaniola did not have gold in any amount even close to the scale that the Europeans would have desired. We also know that gold was not viewed with nearly the same sense of value by the peoples of the Americas as it was by the Europeans and that the Taino of the fifteenth century were in the midst of a losing, long-term struggle with another island people, the Carib. Therefore, though the chief in this example may indeed have been simply being generous, it is plausible that he also saw Columbus as a potential ally against the Caribs or, at the very least, a problem that might go away if he gave him what he wanted.

The Chief of this country [Guacanagari], who lives near here, sent a large canoe full of people, among whom was one of his principal advisors. He begged me to go with the ships to his country and said that he would give me anything he had. He sent me a belt which had hanging from it, in place of a purse, a mask with two large ears, a tongue, and a nose of hammered gold. These people are so generous; they give whatever is asked of them, willingly, and it seems that you are doing them a favor to request something from them. . . . Later they returned to the ships with a Chief, and with news that in this Isla Española there is a great quantity of gold and that people from other places come here to buy it. They said that there is as much gold as we desire. Others came who confirmed that there is much gold on the island, and they showed me the manner of obtaining it. I understood all this with great difficulty, but I felt certain that there was a very large amount of gold and that if I found the source I could get it very cheaply, or even for nothing. In the three days that I have been in this harbor I have received good pieces of gold, and I cannot believe that it is brought from another country.

Source: Columbus, Christopher. *The Log of Christopher Columbus.* Translated by Robert H. Fuson. Camden, ME: International Marine Publishing Company, p. 147.

5. Columbus Dines with the Local Taino Chieftain Guacanagari (December 1492)

The Taino, like most indigenous peoples of the fifteenth and sixteenth centuries, incorporated utilitarian and decorative goods as well as ideas imported from afar into their culture. Materials that were difficult to obtain were then, as now, often seen as prestigious; it is therefore not surprising that Guacanagari wears the gloves given to him by Columbus, particularly in what appears to have been a diplomatic context. Geographically widespread over the Caribbean and engaged in long-distance trade, the Taino were a cosmopolitan society drawing upon foreign cultural influences, including those from Mesoamérica, at the time they encountered Columbus and his party.

The King dined with me on the Niña and afterwards went ashore with me, where he paid me great honor. Later we had a meal with two or three kinds of ajes [sweet potatoes], served with shrimp, game, and other foods they have, including bread; which they call cazabe. Then the King took me to see some groves of trees near the houses, and fully 1,000 people, all naked, went with us. The King was already wearing a shirt and a pair of gloves which I had given him, and he was more excited about the gloves than anything else that had been given him. By his manner of eating, his decent behavior, and his exceptional cleanliness, he showed himself to be of good birth.

After the meal we remained at the table for some time, and we were brought some herbs with which to rub our hands—I believe they use these to soften the skin. We were also given water for our hands.

Source: Columbus, Christopher. *The Log of Christopher Columbus.* Translated by Robert H. Fuson. Camden, ME: International Marine Publishing Company, p. 154.

6. The Marketplace of Tenochtitlán, the Aztec Capital (1519)

Markets were a central part of urban life in ancient Mesoamérica. They were hubs of economic life for most Mesoamerican civilizations, where local and exotic goods ranging from foodstuffs to slaves to textiles were bought, sold, or traded. The best-documented markets are those from Central Mexico at the time of the Aztecs. Tenochtitlán was an enormous city by Spanish standards, and certainly beyond anything the conquistadores had experienced in the Caribbean. This, as well as the fact that most of the agricultural products in Aztec markets were alien to Europeans, was largely the reason why Bernal Díaz del Castillo described them in such detail: He was in awe of the range of goods available to the population of Tenochtitlán.

Cortés at the head of his cavalry, and the principal part of our soldiers under arms, marched to the grand square, attended by many noblemen of the court.

When we arrived there, we were astonished at the crowds of people, and the regularity which prevailed, as well as at the vast quantities of merchandise, which those who attended us were assiduous in pointing out. Each kind had its particular place, which was distinguished by a sign. The articles consisted of gold, silver, jewels, feathers, mantles, chocolate, skins dressed and undressed, sandals, and other manufactures of the roots and fibers of nequen, and great numbers of male and female slaves, some of whom were fastened by the neck, in collars, to long poles. The meat market was stocked with fowls, game, and dogs. Vegetables, fruits, articles of food ready dressed, salt, bread, honey, and sweet pastry made in various ways were also sold here. Other places in the square were appointed to the sale of earthen ware, wooden household furniture such as tables and benches, firewood, paper, sweet canes filled with tobacco mixed with liquid amber, copper axes and working tools, and wooden vessels highly painted. Numbers of women sold fish, and little loaves made of a certain mud which they find in the lake, and which resembles cheese. The makers of stone blades were busily employed shaping them out of the rough material, and the merchants who dealt in gold, had the metal in grains as it came from the mines, in transparent tubes, so that they could be reckoned, and the gold was valued at so many mantles, or so many xiquipils of cocoa, according to the size of the quills. The entire square was enclosed in piazzas, under which great quantities of grain were stored, and where were also shops for various kinds of goods. I must apologize for adding, that boat loads of human ordure were on the borders of the adjoining canals, for the purpose of tanning leather, which they said could not be done without it. Some may laugh at this but I assert the fact is as I have stated it, and moreover, upon all the public roads, places for passengers to resort to, were built of canes, and thatch with straw or grass, in order to collect this material. The courts of justice, where three judges sat, occupied a part of the square, their under-officers going in the market, inspecting the merchandise.

Source: Díaz del Castillo, Bernal. *The True History of the Conquest of Mexico.* London: Harrap, 1927, pp. 177–178.

7. The View from the Great Temple of Tenochtitlán, the Aztec Capital (1519)

Despite the fact that Bernal Díaz, like many conquistadores with Cortés, was repulsed by Aztec religious traditions, there is ever a sense of wonder and admiration in his account for the capital of the Aztec empire. Tenochtitlán was a bustling city of perhaps 200,000 people and one of the largest cities of the world in 1519. Having been built atop an artificial island and characterized by numerous canals, aqueducts, and waterways, Tenochtitlán was by all standards a marvel of human engineering and political will. As the foremost city in the Empire, it was the center of social, political, and economic life in the Basin of Mexico. From the top of the Great Temple, Montezuma (Motecuhzoma II) and Cortés would have been able to see many of the major local towns and the organizational capacity needed to communicate, trade with, and control them. Unfortunately, the awe that Díaz and others had for the capital city of the Aztecs did not prevent them from razing most of the major buildings of Tenochtitlán after its conquest in 1521, including the Great Temple.

They went to take his arms to help him climb the 114 steps, as they did for their lord Montezuma, thinking that Cortés would tire, but he would not allow them to come near. When we climbed to the top of the great *cu* there was a kind of platform, with huge stones where they put the poor Indians to be sacrificed, and an image like a dragon and other evil figures, with a great deal of blood that had been shed that day.

Montezuma, accompanied by two priests, came out from an oratory dedicated to the worship of his cursed idols at the top of the *cu*, and said with great deference toward all of us, "You must be tired, Señor Malinche, after climbing up this great temple of ours."

Through our interpreters, who went with us, Cortés replied that neither he nor the rest of us ever got tired of anything. Then Montezuma took him by the hand and bade him look at his great city and at all the other cities rising from the water, and the many towns around the lake; and if he had not seen the marketplace well, he said, he could see it from here much better.

Then we stood looking, for that large and evil temple was so high that it towered over everything. From there we could see all three of the causeways that led to Mexico: the road from Iztapalapa, by which we had entered four days earlier; the Tacuba road, by which we fled the night of our great rout; and the road from Tepeaquilla.

We saw the fresh water that came from Chapultepec, which supplied the city, and the bridges on the three causeways, built at certain intervals so the water could go from one part of the lake to another, and a multitude of canoes, some arriving with provisions and others leaving with merchandise. We saw that every house in this great city and in the others built on the water could be reached only by wooden drawbridges or by canoe. We saw temples built like towers and fortresses in these cities, all whitewashed; it was a sight to see. We could look down on the flat-roofed houses and other little towers and temples like fortresses along the causeways.

After taking a good look and considering all that we had seen, we looked again at the great square and the throngs of people, some buying and others selling. The buzzing of their voices could be heard more than a league away. There were soldiers among us who had been in many parts of the world, in Constantinople and Rome and all over Italy, who said that they had never before seen a marketplace so large and so well laid out, and so filled with people.

Source: Díaz del Castillo, Bernal. *The Bernal Díaz Chronicles: The True Story of the Conquest of Mexico.* Translated and edited by Albert Idell. Garden City, NY: Doubleday and Company, 1956, pp. 158–159.

8. A Description of Xibalba, the Mayan Underworld from the *Popol Vuh* (early sixteenth century)

Although the Popol Vuh or "Book of Council," one of the paramount indigenous religious texts of the Americas, was written by the K'ichee Maya in the sixteenth century, its themes and many of its stories date back to the Late Preclassic Period (400 B.C.E.-250 C.E.). One of its major tales involves the victory of two mythological Hero Twins—identified with the Sun and the Moon—over the Lords of Death and disease. The Twins, descending into the Underworld (Xibalba, or literally "the place of fright"), are forced to endure many trials before emerging victoriously from the darkness. This part of the Popol Vuh is a story of rebirth and the triumph of life over death, with which many K'ichee identified: Elites, in fact, believed that they might go through a similar journey after death.

The Popol Vuh is also a classic tale of revenge. What is represented in the excerpt below is the prelude to the victory of the Hero Twins, where their father and uncle try to make a similar journey to the Underworld and fail. The Hero Twins succeed where others cannot, eventually tricking and defeating the Lords of Xibalba as their ancestors were defeated.

Immediately they [the brothers Hun-Hunahpú and Vucub-Hunahpú] arrived at the House of Gloom. There was only darkness within the house. Meanwhile, the Lords of Xibalba [Hun-Camé and Vucub-Camé] discussed what they should do.

"Let us sacrifice them tomorrow, let them die quickly, quickly, so that we can have their playing gear [for the ballgame] to use in play," said the Lords of Xibalba to each other. . . .

There were many punishments in Xibalba; the punishments were of many kinds.

The first was the House of Gloom, Quequma-ha, in which there was only darkness.

The second was Xuxulim-ha, the house where everybody shivered, in which it was very cold. A cold, unbearable wind blew within.

The third was the House of Jaguars, Balami-ha, it was called, in which there were nothing but jaguars, which stalked about, jumped around, roared, and made fun. The jaguars were shut up in the house.

Zotzi-há, the House of Bats, the fourth place of punishment was called. Within this house there were nothing but bats which squeaked and cried and flew around and around. The bats were shut in and could not get out.

The fifth was called Chayim-há, the House of Knives, in which there were only sharp, pointed knives, silent or grating against each other in the house.

There were many places of torture in Xibalba, but Hun-Hunahpú and Vucub-Hunahpú did not enter them. We only mention the names of these houses of punishment.

Hun-Hunahpú and Vucub-Hunahpú came before Hun-Camé and Vucub-Camé, [the latter] said: "Where are my fine cigars? Where are my sticks of fat pine which I gave you last night?"

"They are all gone, Sir."

"Well. Today shall be the end of your days. Now you shall die. You shall be destroyed, we will break you into pieces and here your faces will stay hidden. You shall be sacrificed," said Hun-Camé and Vucub-Camé.

They sacrificed them immediately and buried them in the Pucbal-Chah, as it was called. Before burying them, they cut off the head of Hun-Hunahpú and buried the older brother together with the younger brother.

"Take the head and put it in that tree which is planted by the road," said Hun-Camé and Vucub-Camé. And having put the head in the tree, instantly the tree, which had never borne fruit before the head of Hun-Hunahpú was placed among its branches, was covered with fruit. And this calabash tree, it is said, is the one which we now call the head of Hun-Hunahpú.

Source: Goetz, Delia, and Sylvanus G. Morley, eds. and trans. *Popol Vuh: The Sacred Book of the Ancient Quiché Maya.* Norman: University of Oklahoma Press, 1991, ii, pp. 116–118.

9. Francisco Pizarro's First Encounter with the Inca Ruler Atahualpa (November 1532)

The first encounter between Atahualpa (Atalhuapa) and Pizarro followed years of civil war within the Inca Empire (Tawantinsuyu). The preceding Inca ruler, Huayna Capac, had died from smallpox (caught through indirect contact with the Spanish) in 1527 and had left a mighty empire without a sole heir. The war for succession that ensued had just been resolved by Atahualpa when the Spanish arrived; Pizarro actually entered the Andes as the new emperor was returning to his capital at Cuzco—with tens of thousands of warriors—to formally claim his throne. He and his subjects believed that he was descended from the Inca sun god, Inti, and that the emperor was invulnerable (understandably) to the party of less than 200 Spaniards awaiting him. Unfortunately, he chose to behave by the well-established rules of diplomacy in the Andes and did not see the Spanish as capable of causing him any harm. He finally chose to meet Pizarro in person and approached the small group of Europeans unarmed while his army waited from afar. Atahualpa was taken hostage by the desperate Spanish after a brief struggle and kept as such until the Spanish had no need of him. He was eventually executed.

While Atahualpa was speaking, thousands of them [Inca soldiers] put on breast plates of knotted palm fronds so strong that the lance and the sword find them hard, and they wore a woolen shirt to conceal their weapons. And others, thus disguised, carried slings and bags of stones, others metal clubs with long and sharp points, others ayllus [weapon with balls attached to three cords], and all wore their clothes so artfully that no one who would see them would realize that they were armed. There were also other squadrons behind these who were to enter first into battle, furnished with other arms. The lord's litter was open and uncovered and opulently and beautifully adorned, and ahead of it went those designated to clean the road so that not a piece of grass or stone could be seen. The orejones [Spanish term for Inca leaders] and natives of Cuzco went next to the litter, dressed in livery as the king's attendants. The guard went between them, and the litter had to be carried by the chiefs, men who came from the highest lineages or were lords of many vassals. Twelve thousand armed men went in their squadrons, as has been said, ahead of everybody as the center; then went another five thousand Indians with ayllus, instructed to capture the horses with them. The rest of the people—which they say would have been a total of seventy thousand warriors with more than thirty thousand service [Indians], not counting the women—all went, placing themselves in the order that was commanded.

The Christians saw the movement. They knew that soon they would be surrounded by those who were advancing against them. Pizarro encouraged them once again, dispelling their fear of the multitude that was with Atahualpa, to whom he sent one of the Indians who was there to tell him that he begged him to come quickly because he was expecting him to dine. Atahualpa asked this messenger about the state of the Christians. He assured him that they were fearful, news that made him more presumptuous. And, in keeping with his design and aims, he sent one chieftain to tell Pizarro that he would have already come to see him, but he could not convince his people because they had such great fear of the horses and dogs, and this fear became deeper seeing them at closer range. Therefore, he begged him—if he wished to meet him—to order that the horses and dogs be firmly tied and that the Christians should all hide, some in place and others in another, so that none would appear while they conversed together.

Source: Cieza de León, Pedro de. *The Discovery and Conquest of Peru: Chronicles of the New World Encounter.* Translated and edited by Alexandra Parma Cook and Noble David Cook. Durham, NC: Duke University Press, 1998, pp. 206–207.

10. Diego de Landa's Description of the Clothing and Food of the Maya of Yucatan (written c. 1566)

As part of his defense against accusations of cruelty in his treatment of the Maya, the Spanish friar Diego de Landa—later Bishop of Yucatan, Mexico—produced an account of the peoples and customs of Yucatan that cast his actions there in a more scholarly, favorable light. Much of the account is descriptive and portrays the Maya shortly after Christianization efforts had begun. Although Landa was responsible for destroying much of what we could have known about the Maya of the colonial period, including scores of their painted books (codices), his account of Yucatan is one of the most valuable scholarly sources on the Maya from this era. In fact, portions of this account were vital to deciphering the hieroglyphic writing system produced by the Maya—but at what cost?

They had the custom of painting their faces and bodies red, and, although it was very unbecoming to them, yet they thought it very pleasing.

Their clothing was a band of the width of the hand, which served them for drawers and breeches. They wound it several times round the waist, so that one end fell in front and one end behind, and these ends the women made with a great deal of care and with feather-work. And they wore large square *mantas* and they tied them over their shoulders. They wore sandals of hemp or of the dry untanned skin of the deer, and they wore no other garments.

Their principal subsistence is maize of which they make various foods and drinks, and even drinking it as they do, it serves them both as food and drink. The Indian women put the maize to soak one night before in lime and water, and in the morning it is soft and half-cooked, and thus the husk and the stalk are separated from it; and they grind it upon stones, and they give to the workmen and traveler and sailors large balls and loads of the half-ground maize, and this lasts for several months merely becoming sour. And of that they take a lump which they mix in a vase made of the shell of the fruit, which grows on a tree by which God provided them with vessels. And they drink this nutriment and eat the rest, and it is a savory food and of great sustaining power. From the maize which is the finest ground they extract a milk and they thicken it on the fire, and make a sort of porridge for the morning. And they drink it hot and over that which remains from the morning's meal they throw water so as to drink it during the day; for they are not accustomed to drink water alone. They also parch the maize and grind and mix it with water, thus making a very refreshing drink, throwing in it a little Indian pepper of cacao.

Source: Landa, Diego de. *Landa's Relación de las Cosas de Yucatan.* Translated and edited by Alfred M. Tozzer. Cambridge, MA: Peabody Museum, 1941, pp. 89–90.

11. Garcilaso de la Vega, "El Inca," on Inca Irrigation and Agriculture (published 1609)

Although the Inca did not invent the engineering and irrigation techniques they used in agriculture, borrowing much from prior civilizations of the Andes and the desert coast such as Tiwanaku and Chimor, they did implement such technologies on a much greater scale. The Sapa Inca, or emperor, had access to millions of workers: He owned not only all labor but also all land and claimed a special relationship with the sun and agricultural fertility by way of his descent from Inti, the sun god. The emperor was powerful enough to demand rights to periodic labor from his subjects, who built the cities, roads, and public works projects integral to the Inca Empire. Some of the terraces built on the slopes of the Andes during this time were so well made that they continue to survive and to be used in agriculture today.

When the Inca had conquered a new province he immediately sent engineers there, who were specialized in building canals for irrigation, in order to increase the corn acreage, which otherwise could not flourish in these torrid lands. In the same way, he irrigated the prairie lands, as may be seen today from the evidences of canals that still subsist all over Peru. On the mountain sides, on the peaks and on all the rocky surfaces, they built terraces, sustained by stone walls, which they filled with light soil brought from elsewhere. These terraces grew wider from the top to the bottom of the slope, where they occasionally attained to as much as to hundred and forty acres in size. These were arduous undertakings, but they made it possible to give the maximum development to the tiniest plots of barren land. Indeed it often happened that they would build canalizations fifteenth to twenty leagues long, to irrigate only a few acres of land.

Community records of landholdings were carefully kept up to date in all the provinces and villages, and the arable land was divided into three parts: that belonging to the Sun, that of the Inca, and that of his vassals. The latter part was calculated to permit each village to provide for its own needs and, in case there was an increase in population, the Inca reduced the surface of his own holdings. Thus it may be said that he kept for himself only that part that, without him, would have remained uncultivated. The major part of the terrace crops belonged to the king and to the Sun, which was only normal, inasmuch as it was the Inca who had the terraces built. Other cereals and vegetables were raised, such as potatoes, *oca*, and *anius*, on other land which, not being irrigated and fertilized the way the corn lands were, did not yield an annual crop. *Quinoa*, which is a sort of rice, was also cultivated in the cold climates.

Source: El Inca Garcilaso de la Vega. *The Incas: The Royal Commentaries of the Inca.* Translated by Maria Jolas. New York: Orion Press, 1961, pp. 115–16.

12. Garcilaso de la Vega, "El Inca," on Inca Music
(published 1609)

> The following passage shows the beginning of cultural syncretism be-
> tween the musical styles and practices of indigenous Andean peoples
> and the Spanish. The musical traditions of the Andes, largely based on
> flutes like pan-pipes as well as drums and other percussives, are meet-
> ing those of the Spanish. Here, as elsewhere in the Americas shortly
> after the Conquest, native instruments were quickly supplemented by
> stringed ones such as guitars and violins. The Spanish also introduced
> Western-style meter to music here as well; unfortunately, not much is
> known of Pre-Columbian musical style in the Andes and no composi-
> tions have yet been identified. It is notable that the author, Garcilaso de
> la Vega, is interpreting the actions of the Incas here in medieval terms
> (almost like troubadours).

In music they had acquired a knowledge of some tunes, which the Indians
of the Collas district played on instruments made of hollow reeds, four or five
being tied in a row, each one having the point higher than its neighbour, like
an organ. These canes were fastened in fours, different one from another. One
of them ran in high notes and the others each higher in the scale; so that the
four natural voices, treble, tenor, contralto, and counter-bass were represented
by the four sets of reeds. When an Indian played on one of these pipes, another answered on a fifth or any other note; then another played on another
note, sometimes rising to the high notes, and at others going down, but always
in tune. They did not understand accompaniments on different keys, but always played in one compass. The players were Indians instructed for the
amusement of the king, and for the lords his vassals, and although their music
was so simple, it was not generally practiced, but was learnt and attained to
by study. They had *la* flutes with four or five notes, like those of shepherds;
but they were not made on a scale, each one being of only one note. Their
songs were composed in measured verses, and were for the most part written
to celebrate amorous passions expressive now of joy now of sorrow, now of
the kindness now of the cruelty of the fair.

Each song had its appropriate tune, and they could not put two different
songs to the same tune. Thus the enamoured swain, playing his flute at night,
with the tune that belonged to it, apprised the lady and the whole world of the
state of his feelings, arising from the smiles or frowns of the object of his love.
But if two tunes were used for the same song, it could not be known what sentiment the lover wished to express; for it may be said that he talked with his flute.
One night a Spaniard met an Indian girl of his acquaintance, and asked her to go
with him to his lodging. The girl said, "Sir! let me go whither I desire; for know
you not that that flute is calling me with much love and tenderness, so that it
obliges me to go towards it. Leave me, then. I cannot help going, for love drags
me to where the flute-player will be my husband, and I his wife."

They did not play the songs composed to celebrate their warlike deeds, because they were not fit to play before ladies, nor to express on their flutes. But
they were sung at the principal festivals, in memory of their victories. When I
departed from Peru in the year 1560, I left five Indians in Cuzco who played
the flute very well, from any music book for the organ that was placed before

them. They belonged to Juan Rodriguez de Villalobos, formerly a citizen of that town. At present, being the year 1602, they tell me that there are so many Indians expert in playing on instruments, that they may be met with in all directions. In my time the Indians did not use their voices, because, no doubt, they were not sufficiently good, and because they did not understand singing; but, on the other hand, many mestizos had very good voices.

Source: El Inca Garcilaso de la Vega. *First Part of the Royal Commentaries of the Yncas.* Translated by Clements R. Markham. Vol. 1. London: Hakluyt Society, 1869, pp. 191–193.